The Phratries of Attica

Michigan Monographs in Classical Antiquity

The Play of Fictions: Studies in Ovid's *Metamorphoses* Book 2
  A.M. Keith

Homeric Misdirection: False Predictions in the *Iliad*
  James V. Morrison

The Triumviral Narratives of Appian and Cassius Dio
  Alain M. Gowing

The Stranger's Welcome: Oral Theory and the Aesthetics of the
Homeric Hospitality Scene
  Steve Reece

The Phratries of Attica
  S.D. Lambert

The Phratries of Attica

S.D. Lambert

Ann Arbor

THE UNIVERSITY OF MICHIGAN PRESS

Copyright © by the University of Michigan 1993
All rights reserved
Published in the United States of America by
The University of Michigan Press
Manufactured in the United States of America

1996   1995   1994   1993   4   3   2   1

Library of Congress Cataloging-in-Publication Data

Lambert, S. D., 1960–
     The phratries of Attica / S.D. Lambert.
          p.   cm. — (Michigan monographs in classical antiquity)
     Includes bibliographical references and index.
     ISBN 0-472-10388-1
     1. Athens (Greece)—Social life and customs. 2. Athens (Greece)—
Religious life and customs. 3. Citizenship—Greece—Athens.
4. Kinship—Greece—Athens. 5. Clans—Greece—Athens.   I. Title.
II. Series.
DF275.L36   1993
306.2′0938′5—dc20   92-41140
                                                                              CIP

*A CIP catalogue record for this book is available
from the British Library.*

Preface

Though much useful work has been done on the Attic phratry over the last century or so, no comprehensive study dedicated to the institution has been published. Guarducci's *L'istituzione della fratria nella Grecia antica e nelle colonie greche di Italia,* published in 1937–38, contained a useful collection of the epigraphical material then available and a serviceable summary description of the institution in Attica and elsewhere. Since then, the number of Attic inscriptions known to be relevant, if not the total volume of epigraphical text, has increased by more than half, and much relevant scholarship has been produced. In recent years, with the publication of works in related areas such as Roussel's *Tribu et Cité* (1976), Bourriot's *Récherches sur la nature du genos* (1976), and Whitehead's *Demes of Attica* (1986), the gap in the literature has become increasingly marked. This book is intended to fill that gap and, it is hoped, to move our understanding forward, both in matters of detail and on the more general questions of the nature of the institution and its role in Athenian society and life.

The seeds of this book were sown in 1982–83, during occasional visits to the Seminar für alte Geschichte of the University of Tübingen. Most of the work was done in Oxford from 1983 to 1986 and in various places, including most productively the Seminar für alte Geschichte of the University of Marburg, in 1990. Some of the material in this book appeared in different guise in my 1986 Oxford D.Phil. thesis, *The Ionian Phyle and Phratry in Archaic and Classical Athens.*

For academic help, criticism, or encouragement I should like to express gratitude in particular to the late Professor A. Andrewes and the late Sir R. Syme; to Professor D.M. Lewis; to Drs. P.S. Derow and D. Whitehead; and most especially to my former supervisor, Professor W.G. Forrest.

I am pleased to have this opportunity to acknowledge the contribution made to this subject over the last decade, particularly in the epigraphical field, by Dr. C.W. Hedrick. I am particularly grateful to him for permission to use, in T 5 and T 21 in appendix 1, unpublished epigraphical material from his 1984 dissertation, *The Attic Phratry*.

For financial support from 1983 to 1986 I am grateful to Wolfson College, Oxford, to the Department of Education and Science, and to the British Academy; for financial support during 1990 I am grateful to the Leverhulme Trust.

For their generous hospitality at the University of Tübingen in 1982–83 I am grateful to the late Professor K.F. Stroheker and to Professor J. Schlumberger; for similar hospitality at the University of Marburg in 1990 to Professor R.M. Errington.

I would also mention with gratitude my first Oxford college, Keble; Dr. D. Shotter, Dr. J.B. Salmon, and other colleagues at the former Department of Classics at the University of Lancaster in 1985–86; and the Ministry of Agriculture, Fisheries and Food for allowing me special leave without pay in 1990.

I thank my father for his generous help at various times with tasks such as word processing and copying.

I acknowledge with gratitude the permission of J.S. Traill to use the map of Attica in his *Demos and Trittys* (1986) as a basis for that in this book, and the permission of *Hesperia* to use illustrations from volume 7 of that journal.

Finally I should like to express my gratitude and admiration for the work of Ms. E. Bauerle and her colleagues at the University of Michigan Press, not least for undertaking the thankless task of adapting my English to American usage.

Contents

Abbreviations

Standard abbreviations have been used for ancient texts and modern periodicals; see, e.g., the lists in *LSJ* and *L'Année Philologique*. For ancient authors beginning with A, abbreviations for which can sometimes cause confusion, my practice has been:

Aesch.: Aeschylus
Aeschin.: Aeschines
Andoc.: Andocides
Ar.: Aristophanes
Arist.: Aristotle
Aristid.: Aristides
Athen.: Athenaeus

I am not among those who believe in the exclusive Aristotelian authorship of the fourth-century work known as the *Athenaion Politeia* and I follow common convention in referring to it as the *Ath. Pol.* I have not, however, differentiated in references to works in the Demosthenic corpus between acknowledged works of Demosthenes and those which modern scholars would attribute to contemporaries.

I have not adhered to a consistent convention in spelling Greek names, though it will be found that Latinized or Anglicized forms are generally used for major figures.

In citing modern authors I give in the text and footnotes the name and the date of the work, differentiated 1960a, 1960b, etc., where more than one work by an author referred to appeared in a single year. Full details can be found in the bibliography.

The following epigraphical conventions are used:

[   ] enclose letters believed to have stood in the text, but that are now lost.

(   ) enclose letters that complete words abbreviated on the inscription.

⟨   ⟩ enclose letters believed to have been accidentally omitted on the inscription, or that should stand in place of letters believed to have been wrongly inscribed.

{   } enclose letters believed to have been wrongly inscribed.

《   》 for an inscription now lost, and for the text of which we rely on a modern transcription, enclose letters that should stand in place of letters believed to have been wrongly transcribed by a modern scholar.

⟦   ⟧ enclose space that appears to have been erased in antiquity, or letters inscribed in such space.

⟦⟦   ⟧⟧ enclose space that appears to have been erased twice in antiquity, or letters inscribed in such space.

α̣ A dot under a letter indicates traces on the inscription compatible with the letter printed, but that would not, in isolation, dictate the reading of that letter.

[. . .] indicates lost or illegible text for which no restoration is suggested, the number of letters missing being equivalent to the number of dots shown, or the number of spaces indicated.

v, vacat, or *vacant* indicate vacant space on the inscription.

h represents an aspirate sign and ⦂ or : punctuation in the original text. Otherwise modern conventions of orthography, accentuation, and word division are followed.

Other abbreviations used are:

Agora   The Athenian Agora: results of excavations conducted by the American School of Classical Studies at Athens 1953–

CIG   *Corpus Inscriptionum Graecarum,* 4 vols. 1828–77

E.M.   Epigraphic Museum, Athens (in nonepigraphical contexts this abbreviation refers to the Etymologicum Magnum)

FGH   F. Jacoby, *Die Fragmente der griechischen Historiker,* Berlin and Leyden, 1923–58

IG   Inscriptiones Graecae, Berlin 1873–

LSJ   Liddel and Scott's *Greek Dictionary,* with revisions by Jones

ML   ed. R. Meiggs and D.M. Lewis, *A Selection of Greek Historical Inscriptions,* Oxford 1969, etc.

OCT   Oxford Classical Text

PA	J. Kirchner, *Prosopographia Attica,* Berlin, 1901–3
POxy	The Oxyrhyneus Papyri
RE	Pauly-Wissowa. Pauly A. *Real-encyclopädie der classischen Altertumswissenschaft,* ed. G. Wissowa, Stuttgart, 1893–
SEG	*Supplementum Epigraphicum Graecum*
SIG	Dittenberger, *Sylloge Inscriptionum Graecarum* Leipzig, 3d edition 1915–24

The Phratries of Attica

Introduction

In 508,[1] Cleisthenes, regarded by later generations of Athenians as the founder of their democracy,[2] introduced to the Assembly of the Athenian People the radical package of reforms that was to make his reputation. The major element in that package was a new system of organization of the Athenian citizen body. The intentions of the reformer and the motives of the Athenians in accepting his proposals are a matter for debate no less today than in antiquity. In Herodotus' opinion two generations later, Cleisthenes, like his maternal grandfather Cleisthenes of Sicyon, was motivated by racial considerations: distaste for institutions which Athens had in common with other "Ionian" states regarded as sharing a common ancestry.[3] In the fourth century in Aristotle's *Politics* and in the work of his School on the Athenian constitution, the *Athenaion Politeia,* a somewhat more sophisticated view is proposed, though it shows traces both of anti-Cleisthenic political bias and Aristotelian political theorizing: in establishing new institutions for the organization of the citizens that cut across the old, Cleisthenes wanted to "mix up the people," and to provide a cover under which new citizens could be surreptitiously enfranchised.[4]

Today it is generally agreed that the new arrangements were designed to give more say to more people, both locally and centrally, in the running of Athens' affairs, though it remains unsettled precisely how this was intended to be done. Most agree that the internal organization of the

---

1. All dates are B.C. unless specified otherwise.

2. See, e.g., *Ath. Pol.* 29.3, with Rhodes 1981 ad loc. and Herodotus' famous comment that Cleisthenes "took the People into his faction" in his power struggle with Isagoras, p. 26, n. 4.

3. Hdt. 5.67–69.

4. See p. 262.

system must in some way have been more democratic than before. Some take up the Aristotelian concept of mixing up the people and would ascribe to Cleisthenes a policy of destroying old aristocratic power structures, seen as having stood in the way both of Athenian unity and of the exercise of effective power by the ordinary Athenian.[5] Others would see the reforms as in the first place a military exercise, devised to exploit the Attic road system for maximum military efficiency in a crisis; greater power for the ordinary Athenian was the price paid for their crucial support and participation in the new military arrangements.[6]

While there is room for difference on the interpretation of the reforms, at least some of the basic facts are clear.[7] The Athenian people were organized afresh into 139 or 140 demes, village-like units in the countryside or sectors within the city of Athens itself.[8] The demes were responsible for running their own affairs as local communities and formed the basic units for the organization of the state as a whole. Each deme, for example, sent a fixed quota of members every year to sit on the *Boule* (Council) of five hundred that was responsible for preparing the business of the sovereign Assembly and for carrying out many of the executive functions of government. Official nomenclature for a citizen after Cleisthenes' time included the demotic, a reference to the deme to which the citizen belonged. The demes were combined, generally with others in the same area, to form trittyes, of which there were thirty in all. A trittys from, broadly, the coastal region of Attica was combined with one from the city and one from the inland region to form a phyle—ten phylai altogether. These two higher tiers of the system seem to have been too large and too artificial to play much of a role in their own right. In effect, they functioned as aggregates of the demes for purposes where larger sub-groups of the population were needed—in the military organ-

---

5. See, e.g., Lewis 1963; Forrest 1966, 197–200.

6. Siewert 1982. For a recent general discussion of Cleisthenes' work see Manville 1990, ch. 7.

7. For further detail see most conveniently *Ath. Pol.* 21 with Rhodes 1981 ad loc. On the demes in general see Whitehead 1986a; on the details of the organization of demes and trittyes, Traill 1986, Siewert 1982, and the map on p. 344.

8. While the number of Cleisthenic phylai and trittyes is certain, that of the demes is not reliably attested in any ancient source and must be inferred from known demotics, Bouleutic quotas, and so on. In the current state of scholarship, the total may be 140 (see Traill 1986, 123) or 139 (e.g., Whitehead 1986a, 17–21) depending on whether one accepts Traill's theory that the very large deme Acharnai was split into two separate demes for administrative purposes.

ization for example,[9] and in the Boule, where the five hundred members were subdivided into phyle and trittys units.[10] The presidency of the Boule and other duties rotated among these units each year under a new system that divided the year into ten periods called prytanies.

Cleisthenes' system of organization was not new in every respect. As already mentioned, Herodotus thought it was distaste for a previously existing system that had motivated Cleisthenes' reforms. There had been four old phylai and, as Herodotus makes clear, they were understood to belong to Athens' Ionian heritage. Each phyle had been divided into three trittyes and in addition into twelve groups called naukraries. The old phylai and trittyes were effectively made obsolete by Cleisthenes' reforms, though they retained some formal religious functions. The naukraries continued in modified form until abolished, probably by Themistocles. I shall have more to say on the nature and function of this older phyle system in chapter 8.[11]

Both before and after Cleisthenes, however, Athenian citizens also belonged to another set of groups, the phratries.[12] It is these groups that are the subject of this book. We do not know of any individual Athenian phratries that had counterparts in other Ionian states, but the institution was viewed, like the old phylai, as part of the shared Ionian heritage.[13] Herodotus identifies the phratry festival Apatouria as a touchstone of Ionian identity,[14] and the foundation of the phratries, along with the phylai, was attributed by the *Ath. Pol.* to the mythical figure of Ion, the personification of Ionian identity.[15] Phratries also existed in some non-Ionian Greek states;[16] as far as we know, in all dialects of Greek before the Roman period the word *phrater,* cognates of which in other Indo-European languages mean "brother," was used exclusively to refer to a member of a phratry.[17]

9. For trittyes as well as phylai in the military organization, see p. 256, with n. 54.

10. It was previously thought that the trittyes into which the Bouleutic prytanies (phyle groups) are known to have been divided at a later period did not correspond to Cleisthenes' trittyes. It is now coming to be recognized, however, that they did; see, e.g., Traill 1978, 109, and Siewert 1982. Contrast Rhodes 1983, 203–4, and 1985, 305.

11. See pp. 252–59.

12. For the question whether all citizens belonged to phratries in the classical period, see chapter 1; for the various phratry subgroups, see below pp. 19–21.

13. Cf. p. 144 and p. 268, n. 105.

14. See p. 144.

15. See p. 268.

16. See Jones 1987, 388 (not a complete list), and Roussel 1976; also n. 57 below.

17. Cf. pp. 268–69.

Much has been written about the origins and early role of the phratry in Greek society. In particular it is disputed whether the institution did indeed have its roots in a time when all Ionians, or indeed all Greeks, were a single people speaking a single form of Greek, or whether it was a product of the circumstances prevailing between the fall of the Mycenaean kingdoms at the end of the second millennium and the re-emergence of the historical record in the eighth and seventh centuries. I shall touch on issues relevant to these questions later in this Introduction and in the next seven chapters, and address some of them directly, if briefly, in chapter 8. The focus of this work, however, lies in a description and analysis of the phratry in the city in which we have by far the largest quantity of evidence for it, Athens, in the period to which nearly all that evidence relates, ca. 450–250.

That evidence falls into a number of categories. First, there is the epigraphical material. We now have around thirty inscriptions, all of them cut in the period 450–250, nine or ten of them phratry decrees, that attest the activities of individual Athenian phratries. These are an invaluable source, particularly regarding the character and internal structure of the phratries and the nature of their preoccupations and activities during this period.[18] In addition there are inscriptions of other Athenian citizen groups, notably the demes and the phratry subgroups, that have a bearing on issues such as the relationship of the phratries to those groups; a few produced by central organs of the Athenian state are also relevant.

Second, the works of the late fifth- and fourth-century Attic orators are a source of great importance, particularly the legal speeches from the early to mid-fourth century of Isaeus (ca. 420–350) and Demosthenes (384–322). These typically concern disputed citizenship, inheritance, or adoption, in which context the protagonists' phratry membership, or their lack of it, is referred to or discussed. This evidence tells us much about the significance of phratry membership in Athenian society and about the details of admissions procedures.

These two categories form the larger part of our source material. There is, however, much else in ancient literature that is relevant, most of it broadly contemporaneous with the epigraphical record and the orators, but including a range of writers from Homer to the scholars of late antiquity. The Attic dramatists, particularly Aristophanes (ca. 450–

---

18. For texts, translations, and notes on these inscriptions see appendix 1.

385) and other comic poets, occasionally referred to phratries or matters connected with them,[19] as did the philosophers Plato (ca. 429–347) and Aristotle (384–322). In these authors, mention of the phratry is for the most part incidental; only occasionally is it a subject of treatment in its own right.

There is a little relevant material in the three major Greek historians, Herodotus, Thucydides, and Xenophon, writing in the later fifth and early fourth centuries, and in the works of the Atthidographers, the local historians of Attica, from Hellanikos at the end of the fifth century to Philochoros in the early third. It is likely that the late fourth-century author of the work of the Aristotelian school on the Athenian constitution, the *Ath. Pol.,* a crucial source for our purposes, made use of these local historians, though only fragments of their works, quoted by later authors, survive.[20]

Finally, there is an abundance of material written after 450–250, valuable mostly for what it preserves of earlier works now lost. It is especially informative on points of detail but is sometimes also of wider significance. Mostly it is in the form of commentaries and *scholia* (notes) on earlier works and entries from various lexica, but it also includes more substantial sources, such as the essays of Plutarch (A.D. ca. 40s–120s), the *Greek Guide Book* by Pausanias (fl. ca. A.D. 150), and the fictional description of a scholarly discussion over dinner by Athenaeus (fl. ca. A.D. 200). This last contains an especially large number of references to earlier literature now lost.

There are many problems in working with this evidence. Its quantity is such that there are many basic questions to which the answers are uncertain, a situation exacerbated by the intrinsic biases and other inadequacies of the material: the methods of historians and other writers in antiquity, particularly when dealing with the relatively distant past, do not conform to modern critical standards; orators had cases to make

---

19. There was a comic play entitled *The Phrateres* by Aristophanes' contemporary Leukon. According to *Arg. Ar. Peace,* it won third prize at the City Dionysia in the year Aristophanes came second with the *Peace* (421). Unfortunately almost nothing of it survives. See further, however, p. 34, n. 40 and p. 160, n. 100.

20. Unfortunately, discussion of the nature and role of the phratry in the *Ath. Pol.* is very thin. There may have been more detail in the Peripatetic works by Demetrios of Phalerum (see, e.g., *FGH* 228 Demetrios fr.6 = Harp. s.v. ἕρκειος Ζεύς, cf. p. 213, n. 49. Jacoby ad loc. speculates that D. began his work "On Legislation" with a more juridically precise analysis of citizenship than Aristotle's) and Dikaiarchos in the βίος Ἑλλάδος (Wehrli 1944–59 I fr.52 = Steph. Byz. s.v. πάτρα).

and were freer in ancient courts than they are today to distort the facts to suit their arguments; comic playwrights wrote for the entertainment of their audiences, not for the enlightenment of later historians; the factual and especially the interpretative statements of philosophers cannot be divorced from the theories they wished to propound. Inscriptions are in many ways the most honest items of evidence, but even here care is required. A full understanding of the content depends on an appreciation of historical context and circumstances, and these must usually be a matter of conjecture; also we need always to bear in mind all that may have been done but not written on stone. Finally, texts themselves often present difficulties. Inscriptions are more often than not worn or fragmentary; literary texts have become corrupted over centuries of transmission. These problems mean that there will be little in what follows that is certain and much where new evidence is likely to alter the picture.

I would to make two final points relating to evidence. First, this is a documentary study, addressing problems raised by and answerable on the basis of the written historical record. Where archaeological evidence is relevant to those problems, I have referred to it, but this is rarely the case. Archaeology can make contributions to our knowledge of Athenian society in general; it cannot, at least in the current state of our knowledge, help us to answer questions such as whether every Athenian belonged to a phratry, whether gene exercised any sort of power over phratries, how the Demotionidai were related to the Dekeleieis, how phratries were related to other citizen groups, or what the extent and nature of phratry activities were.

Second, it may be thought that, since there was a tradition that the phratry was common to the Ionian world as a whole, evidence from other Ionian states would usefully complement that from Athens. In fact, in what follows very few references to phratries outside Attica will be found. There are two reasons for this. First, the non-Attic evidence is very limited indeed: one or two incidental references in literature, a few largely late and uninformative citizenship decrees, and a small handful of more substantial inscriptions.[21] There is little it can tell us about phratries in the states which it directly concerns, let alone about phratries in another state. Second, insofar as phratries in the Ionian world shared a common past, that past was, by the most optimistic account, very

---

21. For the phratry in the Ionian world outside Attica, see Roussel 1976, Piérart 1985 and p. 18 with n. 57, below.

distant from the fifth and fourth centuries. During the intervening period we would expect institutions and the societies in which they existed to have evolved; in fact, in nearly every case where we have evidence for the phratry outside Athens, they had been demonstrably affected, directly or indirectly, by reorganizations imposed from the center. On most of the matters discussed in this work, therefore, it would not be reasonable or helpful to make inferences about the Athenian system from what little we know of phratries elsewhere. As we shall see, the very basic question of the relationship of the phratry to the Ionian phyle is a case in point.[22]

In the rest of this Introduction I shall discuss three aspects of the phratry which demonstrate these problems of evidence very clearly. First, there is the issue of its principle of organization. This has been described as personal in contrast to the local or territorial character of the demes.[23] There tends, however, to be a lack of clarity about exactly what is meant by these terms; and an attempt to achieve clarity does no more than expose the inappropriateness of the distinction.

We cannot be certain exactly how the Athenians were organized into demes in 508, but the system seems to have had both personal and territorial characteristics: territorial in that the original deme members were probably registered in the deme center closest to their abode and that this local link was maintained to a greater or lesser extent, in subsequent generations; personal in that, at least to start with, it seems unlikely that there were any lines drawn on a map.[24] In other words, the deme was originally a group of persons, not a tract of territory. It was also personal in that it was to an extent based on kinship: inevitably in a relatively immobile agriculturally based society such as Athens in the archaic and classical periods, persons living in a particular locality

---

22. See below p. 18.

23. See most recently Jones 1987, 4–10, who begins to perceive, however, that the distinction is not entirely satisfactory.

24. On this point I agree with the account of Whitehead 1986a, 27–30, following in large part Thompson 1971. It is unlikely that Cleisthenes would (or could in the probably short time available) have undertaken the bureaucratically complex task of determining from scratch the physical borders of 139 or 140 demes. The existence of deme boundary markers from the fourth century or later and some other indications (see, e.g., p. 227, n. 121) suggest that they may have acquired more exactly defined territories later, with respect to which they had certain responsibilities (though these boundary markers may be of property of the demes, not of the demes themselves, cf. n. 40, below), but there can be no doubt that the demes functioned primarily as groups of persons rather than as tracts of territory and, except at the moment of their foundation, the determination of those groups depended not on where citizens lived, but on who their parents were.

tend to be interrelated. In addition, subsequent to the initial founding of the demes, transmission of deme membership was hereditary, as it was in the phratries.

To try to define phratries as characteristically personal or territorial is even less satisfactory. In contrast to the deme, we do not know exactly when the phratries came into existence;[25] there is no direct evidence for any original principle of organization. It is tempting to try to infer such a principle from features of the phratry known from the period for which we do have relevant evidence, but the approach is futile.

The phratry certainly had strong personal features. Membership was hereditary in the male line. As already mentioned, the cognates of the word phrater, meaning "phratry member" in Greek, signify "brother" in other Indo-European languages.[26] Modern philologists believe that the name of the phratry festival, the Apatouria, derives from *homopatoria,* meaning "the festival of those with the same father."[27] For the Aristotelian school in the fourth century the phratry was seen as originally having been an aggregate of *gene,* groups defined as consisting of persons descended from a common ancestor, *homogalaktes,* literally, "those who share the same milk."[28] In practice, hereditary phratry membership must inevitably have resulted in a degree of interrelationship among members; we do not have the evidence to determine how far this was magnified by a tendency toward phratric endogamy, but it would be surprising if it was not.[29] Finally, as will become clear from the following chapters, kinship was central to the character of the activities of the phratries in the classical period. These activities were concerned, for the most part, directly or indirectly, with the maintenance and control of the principle of descent on which not only membership in the phratries but also Athenian citizenship itself was based.

These features in themselves, however, will not support the conclusion that the original character of the phratry was exclusively personal. First,

---

25. Cf. pp. 267–71.

26. Cf. pp. 268–69.

27. See further p. 144 with n. 17.

28. See p. 60.

29. See R. Osborne 1985, 127–53, who draws attention to the extent to which both kinship and to a lesser degree locality were factors in determining marriage. The absence of an equivalent to the demotic for the phratry means we are in the dark on the question, which would be difficult to determine in any event, of how far phratry membership as distinct from kinship influenced marriage. Interrelation between members of a single phratry or phratric group is most apparent in the list T 18 (see appendix 1).

there is again the problem of definition: in what sense was it personal? Should we envisage some moment at which there existed a certain number of individuals, each of whom was selected by some means to be the ancestor of a phratry? Or was the ancestor identified at some later stage, and, if so, was he identified actually or mythically? Or did one of these two processes create not a phratry but another group that was combined with others like itself to form a phratry? If so, what was the personal means by which the groups were combined? None of the personal features we have identified would enable us to determine the answers to these questions.

Second, it cannot be demonstrated, as is often thought, that Athenians in the fourth century viewed the members of a phratry as descended from a common ancestor; phrater may have meant brother in other Indo-European languages, but there is no evidence that it ever had such a connotation for an Athenian. Apatouria, as has been seen, may in fact derive from *homopatoria,* the festival of those of the same father, but the Athenians knew nothing of this. For most of them it derived from the *apate* (trick) played by Melanthos in the Apatouria foundation myth. There was an alternative tradition that seems to have hit on the correct derivation, from *homopatoria,* but significantly this does not seem to have been interpreted as implying that those participating were descended from a single father. It was rather taken as meaning "the coming together of fathers";[30] if a phrater was perceived as a "brother" we might expect the obvious etymological link to have been made between *homopatoria* and common ancestry.

Most of the phratry names bear the ending -*idai,* which would originally have signified a patronymic,[31] i.e., that the Alkmeonidai were descended from Alkmeon, the Demotionidai from Demotion and so on; but by our period it no longer necessarily seems to have connoted this. The ending was used in the names of demes, for example, the members of which were demonstrably not descended from a single ancestor, just as the Homeridai were not literally descended from Homer; they were followers of his art.[32] For the phratries, evidence of how members of phratries with names of this type related to their eponyms is extremely thin,[33] but there is no indication that phratry members thought of themselves as joint descendants of a common ancestor. Moreover, not all

30. For more on this see p. 146.
31. See Buck and Petersen 1945, 441–42.
32. Cf. Kearns 1989, 72.
33. Cf. pp. 220–22.

phratries used names of this type; two are adjectival in form, Thymaitis and Gleontis.[34] There seems to be no good reason for supposing that the members of a phratry called the Thymaitian or the Geleontian regarded themselves as descended from their respective eponyms, Geleon and Thymoites.

In the case of both deme and formal genos it would seem most likely that the eponym was generally regarded as *archegetes* or founder-hero, not ancestor.[35] There is no reason to posit a stronger relationship between phratries and their eponyms in our period, and we cannot demonstrate that the names in -idai originated in a period when they did have a literally patronymic connotation. Aristotle certainly went further in the case of the genos; he saw its members at least in theory as descended from a common ancestor.[36] As has been seen, his School thought that phratries were aggregates of gene, but there is no sign that anyone thought that members of different gene in the same phratry were related to one another. We cannot, therefore, say that, in the period to which our evidence relates, a phratry was thought of as personal in the sense that all its members were descended from a common ancestor.

Third, there may be a temptation to argue that, whatever the Athenians thought in the fourth century, the actual etymologies of "phrater" and "Apatouria" imply that the members of a phratry must either have actually been, or at some stage come to be regarded as, related to each other. This conclusion would be insecure if for no other reason than that we do not know what the relationship was of the classical phratry to the original entities that these words described. It is possible, for example, that an original use of "phrater" to mean brother was extended to cover members of a group among whom there existed ties that were similar to but were not actually ties of blood; or a set of groups among which at some level there existed ties of blood. And Apatouria might have been the festival of those with the same father in no stronger sense than that it was a festival of families.

Fourth, we know nothing about the extent to which members of a phratry from different families were united by ties of blood in the fourth century. Even if we knew more, little could be deduced: common descent from an ancestor, who lived, say, five hundred years previously could not be detected unless we had perfect or near-perfect genealogical records

---

34. See T 6 and T 13 with notes. Cf. also the Dyaleis, T 5, with notes to lines 5–8.
35. See Kearns 1989.
36. Cf. p. 60.

for every phratry member throughout that period, and any interrelationship could derive from intermarriage at some point subsequent to foundation.

Fifth, I argue in the following chapters that phratries could split and fuse in response to pressures which may have been connected in part to the increasing weakness of ties of kinship over the generations, in part to other factors.[37] Whatever the situation was at an earlier period, those processes may have created institutions in which all members were not related by ties of blood. Furthermore, they cast doubt on whether we should think in terms of original principles of organization that were perpetually preserved.

Sixth, the phratry in the classical period has local as well as personal characteristics, so we cannot infer from its classical nature that it must originally have been exclusively personal. These local characteristics could be seen simply as the logical consequence of hereditary membership combined with a physically relatively static society, for, as we have observed in reverse, so to speak, in the case of the demes, any group of persons who share an ancestor in such a society will naturally tend to live in the same area. This was appreciated well enough by Aristotle, for whom the interrelated homogalaktes, whose groups, the gene, were the phratry building-blocks, formed a community based on a single locality.[38] But in view of the preceding discussion, it is not necessary to see the phratry's local characteristics as solely a consequence of this. Perhaps locality played a role in determining phratry membership in the first place, either originally or, particularly plausibly, at the time of fission or fusion.[39] It could have done so in at least two ways: members could have become associated with one another in the same phratry in part because they lived in the same place, whether or not they were related or thought themselves to be related; or groups of persons, Aristotle's gene, could themselves have all been related, actually or theoretically, but they may have been combined with one another on a local basis, the most obvious being contiguity. Neither of these possibilities would be inconsistent with the personal features of the phratry already identified.

Whatever the explanation, there is evidence that phratries had a local

---

37. See esp. pp. 107–12.

38. Cf. p. 60. The mixture of kinship and locality in the Aristotelian concept of the homogalaktes is well brought out in the discussion of Bourriot 1976, 669–76.

39. Cf. pp. 107–12.

aspect in the classical period, short of actually having definable territories.[40] Our evidence is not sufficient to produce a clear general pattern, but we know phratries had meeting places and might own other property such as shrines and agricultural land.[41] In the few cases where we know the demotics of members and know where such meeting places and/or property were located there is a degree of correspondence, implying that, at least in 508, there were members who lived at or near what we might legitimately call a phratry center.[42] We can be fairly certain that in some cases at least there was more than one such center. It seems that a phratry could contain more than one genos.[43] We know that a genos could be divided into two sections, based on different localities.[44] Therefore we should expect that a phratry could itself contain groups based on different

40. T 1, a boundary marker of the phratry Achniadai, should not be interpreted as marking the boundary of the phratry, but of property belonging to it (see pp. 280–81).

41. On phratry properties see further chapter 5. The site of one phratry altar, found in situ with a temenos wall, has been excavated. See figs. 1 and 2, pp. 354–55. The associations of phratries with specific locations are discussed in the notes in appendix 1 under "Location." Cf. now also Hedrick 1991.

42. The following examples are attested (see further appendix 1): the Achniadai had a shrine and other landed property at Kephale, which was probably close to Leukonoion, the deme of the probable phratry member Apollodoros in Isaeus 7; the Demotionidai/ Dekeleieis set up decrees in front of the altar, celebrated the Apatouria, and posted names of prospective candidates for membership in a shrine of Leto (for the cult at which they seem to have been responsible), at Dekeleia (but see also pp. 112–13, n. 64), the probable deme of the proposer of a motion, Nikodemos and the priest Theodoros, while the phratriarch, Pantakles, was from the neighbouring Oion Dekeleikon; the Dyaleis owned an agricultural estate, including a house, and set up an inscription on the estate at Myrrhinous, the deme of the two phratriarchs and the lessee of the estate, who was also a phratry member; the Medontidai may have had something to do with property near the Acropolis and had an interest in other property in the city deme Melite, which was also the deme of the leader of a group of orgeones that probably belonged to the phratry (but see also n. 46); an unknown phratry probably set up an honorific decree at Paiania, which was also the deme of the two phratry members being honoured (T 17). Another phratric group also set up a list of members at Paiania (T 18). They may or may not have belonged to the same phratry that produced T 17. See now also Hedrick 1991. I would not, however, claim as strongly as he does that the omission of demotics in names on phratry inscriptions suggests strong ties between phratries and demes (Hedrick 1991, 264–65, cf. De Sanctis 1898, 66). These omissions can be interpreted in a number of other ways, e.g., demotics may simply have been irrelevant to a phratry's, as opposed to a deme's, purposes. T 35, cited in support of the interpretation, may not be a phratry inscription and in fact contains examples where it is known that names without demotics did not come from the local deme, Alopeke (pace Humphreys 1990, cf. p. 370).

43. See n. 65 below.

44. The clearest case of this is the genos Salaminioi, divided into one section at Sounium and another whose members are described as "of the seven phylai." See further pp. 64–65, 108.

locations. There may be evidence for this in the so-called Demotionidai decrees. The interpretation of these, our single most important phratry document, is difficult and controversial, but if the view put forward in chapter 3 is correct, the Demotionidai was a phratry in which a group of members, the House of the Dekeleieis, lived at Dekeleia, but in which there were also one or more other phratry centers.[45]

The existence of phratry members with demotics far from a known phratry center can therefore be explained in at least two ways consistent with the local aspect of the phratry system. The members may have been persons whose ancestors had once lived at a phratry center but had moved away before 508, or they may have lived in a second phratry center whose existence is otherwise unattested.[46] The two possibilities are not mutually exclusive.

A final point in this connection. We know that there were phratries that, in the fourth century, had connections both with the city of Athens and with places elsewhere in Attica. Some of these double connections may be explained by positing an original city base, from which persons moved out over time. In other such cases, it is possible that the phratry had traditional centers both in the city and elsewhere. In still others, however, no doubt as a consequence of the cumulative effect of persons moving away from phratry centers in general and the enforced mass migration of Athenians into the city during the Peloponnesian War in particular, it may well have become convenient for the phratries based outside Athens to hold meetings and possibly carry out other activities in the city, making the city in essence a new phratry center.[47] A similar phenomenon is detectable in the case of the deme.[48]

---

45. See p. 106 and pp. 112–13, n. 64.

46. The clearest case of a phratry with scattered demotics is the Medontidai. On the interpretation of this as possibly a consequence of population movement from an original base in the city of Athens, see pp. 316–17, and for a similar pattern in the possible phratry T 35, p. 359. We have no case where the quantity of evidence is sufficient to support a reasonable inference from demotics and property locations that there was more than one phratry center, though the Medontidai may in fact have been like this.

47. The clearest case is the Demotionidai/Dekeleieis who used a barber's shop by the Hermae in the city as an informal meeting place and even posted notices about prospective phratry candidates there (see p. 139). See also sections on location in appendix 1 at T 6 (Gleontis), T 10 (Medontidai), T 12 (Therrikleidai), T 13 (Thymaitis), T 16, T 22, T 25. For the migration of Athenians into the city in the Peloponnesian War see Thuc. 2.14. Cf. now Hedrick 1991, 260–61.

48. De Ste. Croix 1972, 400–401; Whitehead 1986a, 86–90; cf. p. 390, n. 5. Manville 1990, 63, (cf. Hedrick 1989) stresses the local character of the phratry, though on 65–66

I suggest, therefore, that it is not appropriate or possible to describe the phratry as personal in contrast to local or vice versa—appropriate in respect of its character in 450–250, appropriate or possible in respect of any original principle of organization. Insofar as the combination of local and personal elements suggests a single principle or characteristic, it may perhaps be described as that of natural community, the community that arises when groups of people related to each other live and work in the same place as others with whom they become involved. The extent to which phratries themselves were natural communities and the extent to which they were aggregates of such communities, however, is unclear. Moreover, we lack grounds for claiming that when members of the same phratry lived at a distance from each other they must have been related. Factors other than contiguity and kinship may have played a role, either originally or at the possible stage of fusion or fission, in determining the membership of a phratry. We shall glimpse what some of these may have been in chapter 3.

The formal relationship of the phratry to other citizen groups must also be discussed at this stage. According to *Ath. Pol.* fr. 3, under the dispensation of Ion the phratry was identical to the old pre-Cleisthenic trittys and was a subdivision of the old phyle. I argue in appendix 2 that these two assertions, involving two institutions, the phyle and trittys, that were for all practical purposes obsolete by the fourth century, are part of a speculative schematization typical of the way the *Ath. Pol.* and the Atthidographic tradition dealt with the very distant past and are of no worth as historical evidence. In addition, I argue that a good case can be made against the identity of phratry and trittys, and that the supposition that the phratry was a subgroup of the phyle may simply have been a consequence of that false identification.

That *Ath. Pol.* fr. 3 is of no authority on the matter does not in itself demonstrate that the phratry was not a phyle subdivision. Unfortunately, however, the question cannot otherwise be settled on the basis of current evidence. It is clear from the foregoing that the question could not be resolved on the basis of the phratry's having a personal or local character; to demonstrate that the phyle had a principle of organization such that it either could or could not have been an aggregate of phratries is quite

---

goes some way toward recognizing the mix of personal and territorial characteristics. Hedrick 1991 discusses in detail the territorial associations of phratries; but the evidence for these is insufficient to support his claim that they were originally territorial, any more than the evidence for personal characteristics implies the contrary.

impossible. We may reasonably suppose that, as in the phratry, membership in the phyle was hereditary,[49] but that in itself is scarcely informative.[50] Nor is it of any help that phyle and phratry were conceived of by some in the classical period as having been coeval. The only other indications of the principle by which the old phylai were organized are their names and those of their subgroups. Some interpretations of phyle names indicate local associations, others do not; the evidence for the naukrary and trittys names is in part suggestive of locality, in part not.[51] Nothing can be concluded from this line of inquiry about whether or not the old phylai were aggregates of phratries.

There is one concrete piece of evidence that can be taken to suggest that the phratry was a phyle subgroup. In Nikomachos' revision of the sacred calendar of the state, carried out between 403/2 and 400/399, provision was made for a sacrifice to Zeus Phratrios and Athena Phratria on 16 Hekatombaion, the festival of Synoikia. The sacrifice was "on the authority of the *phylobasileis,*" or possibly "from the fund of the *phylobasileis,*" for the old phyle Geleontes, and a *phylobasileus* partic-

---

49. There is no direct evidence for this, but it may be inferred from the fact that membership in Cleisthenes' phylai was hereditary. It was also the general pattern for groups of this sort in the Greek world. See Jones 1987, 10–11.

50. We could not have told, for example, on the basis that membership in the Cleisthenic phyle and in the phratry was hereditary whether one was, or was not, a subgroup of the other.

51. One naukrary was called Kolias, also the name of a place in Attica and the basis of the name of a genos, Kolieis (cf. p. 252 with n. 35 for other indications of the local character of the groups). One trittys was called Leukotainioi, "the white-ribboned," a name with no obvious topographical association (cf. pp. 256–57). The four old phylai were called Geleontes, Hopletes, Argadeis, and Aigikoreis, which can be explained in a variety of ways, some of which would have local implications: (a) as deriving from the cult titles of deities (Geleon = "the Splendid," Argos = "the Bright," and so on, first suggested by Maass 1889, 805–8, followed, e.g., by Rhodes 1981, 67–68; but none of the titles is attested before the fifth century and they may themselves therefore derive from the phyle names); (b) from occupational classes (Geleontes = "farmers" or "nobles," Hopletes = "warriors" or "artisans," Argadeis = "workers," Aigikoreis = "goat-herds" or "goat-priests," see Plut. *Sol.* 23.5, Strabo 8.7.1, 383, with Nilsson 1972, 146–48) or possibly from the typical occupations of members of particular localities (see Owen 1939, 144–46); (c) as having connotations of particular areas of Attica on which they were based (Kienast 1965, based in part on the dubious series of earlier phyle names given by Pollux 8.109, some of which apparently have local connotations, and in part on other alleged, and unconvincing, local associations of the names). This is the sort of issue on which the character of phylai in other states cannot be taken as evidence. Centuries after the institutions may, on the most optimistic view, have had common ancestors (see further pp. 267–71), there is no reason to suppose a phyle in one state would have been similar in this regard to a phyle in another.

ipated.[52] Apart from this, all our evidence for the cult of these deities has to do with phratries or phratry subgroups.[53] There is therefore some attraction to the suggestion that the phyle was participating in the sacrifice as an aggregate of which the phratries were component parts.[54] The case is attractive, but not conclusive. Our evidence is not sufficient to support an argument from silence that the cult of Zeus Phratrios and Athena Phratria was invariably restricted to phratries, their aggregates or subgroups. Moreover, Nikomachos is alleged to have made substantial alterations to the laws he was responsible for republishing; a change may have resulted in a link between phyle and phratry cult which was not there before.[55]

On the other hand, it is not easy to find strong arguments that the phratry was not a subgroup of the phyle. Arguments based on differences in principle of organization get us nowhere, as has been seen. The lack of indication of a relationship between phyle and phratry in the rest of our evidence may seem to be an argument, but we must bear in mind that all the epigraphical and nearly all the literary evidence comes from or deals with a time when the old phylai were for most practical purposes obsolete.[56]

The point is so fundamental and the absence of other arguments so marked that it would be legitimate to adduce evidence from other Ionian states. This is of no help. There is no Ionian state in which old phylai and phratries are known to have existed where it can be demonstrated that a phratry either was or was not a subgroup of a phyle; this is mainly because the old phylai had been reorganized or abolished before the period to which any evidence for phratries pertains.[57] On the basis of

---

52. See p. 257 with n. 57.

53. See pp. 208–10.

54. Ferguson 1936, 156. On the synoecism, cf. p. 268.

55. Nikomachos was prosecuted for his conduct of this work. The prosecution case alleged that he had cut out three talents worth of ancestral sacrifices and put in a lot of new ones, see Lysias 30.21. Insofar as there is likely to be any truth in the allegation, this would be precisely the sort of sacrifice on which Nikomachos might have economized. One could imagine, for example, that he might have replaced (potentially expensive?) arrangements in which the phratries had been directly involved with a (cheaper?) sacrifice in which they were merely represented by their patron deities.

56. Cf. p. 245. Note that there is also little indication on the inscriptions of phratries and their subgroups, all far from obsolete at this period, that the latter were in fact subgroups of the former.

57. We know phylai were divided into phratrai at Argos (see Jones 1987, 112–18) and into phratries at Syracuse (Jones 1987, 173–76), but even if we were prepared to posit a

current evidence, therefore, the question of the relationship of old phyle to phratry must be left unanswered.

It has been mentioned that the genos was a subgroup of the phratry. Our evidence for this is better than that concerning the relationship between the phratry and phyle, though even here it must be admitted that the arguments are not conclusive. The crucial difference here is that, while the old phylai were effectively obsolete by the fourth century, gene still existed. The implication of *Ath. Pol.* fr. 3[58] that the genos was a subgroup of a phratry therefore has greater weight; it would be unexpected for the *Ath. Pol.* to assert that one set of groups had been a subdivision of another if those groups did not also bear that relationship in contemporary Athens. As far as we know, the *Ath. Pol.* did not believe the phratries and gene had been directly involved in any reorganizations that may have affected the relationship of the groups subsequent to Ion's dispensation.[59] Moreover, other contemporary evidence

---

similarity between these Dorian states and the Ionian world in this respect, in both cases the equivalents of phylai and/or phratries had been subject to some sort of reorganization in the historical period (cf., for the Spartan case, Forrest 1968, 44–45) and it is possible this may have created the phratry-phyle link. On Thasos the indentification of a group described on a late fifth-/early-fourth-century inscription as Γελέοντες οἷς μέτεστιν ("the Geleontes who share," i.e., in the cult of Artemis Orthosia, Rolley 1965, 449, no. 8) as a "patra" forming a subgroup of the phyle Geleontes is no more than hypothetical (Rolley 1965, 460, cf. Jones 1987, 184–86), and the unusual description of the group suggests that it may have been formed following some relatively recent reorganization. On Chios we know that phratries were aggregated into larger units in the fourth century (one of which was the Klytidai, see Forrest 1960), but we do not know whether these larger groups were "phylai." Again, even if they were, the known names of the aggregates, including one apparently called after the early tyrant Polyteknos, and other features suggest that they may have been of relatively recent origin (see Forrest 1960; Jones 1987, 191–95; there is no trace of the normal Ionian phyle names). In no other case where both old phylai and phratries are attested is there any evidence for how they were related to each other. On Miletos at least two of the old phylai, the Argadeis and the Hoplethes (*sic*), were divided into at least two subsections in the fifth century, but there is no indication of how, if at all, phylai or subsections were related to phratries, which are not attested firmly before the first century (see Piérart 1983, 4, n. 25; Ehrhardt 1983, esp. 305; Jones 1987, 320–27). The cases of Andros (Jones 1987, 206–7), Tenos (Jones 1987, 207–11), Delos (Jones 1987, 211–12; firm evidence for old phylai divided into trittyes, but no indication how the phratries, attested on *IG* 11.547, fit in) and Teos (Piérart 1985, 160–90) are also uninformative. Arguments either way based on alleged territorial or personal characteristics of the groups (as used by Jones, e.g., in the case of Tenos) carry no weight in any of these cases. Hom. *Il.* 2.362–63 (see p. 270) could, but need not, be interpreted to imply that phratries were, for Homer, subdivisions of phylai.

58. See p. 61 with appendix 2.

59. We also lack positive grounds in this case for suspecting an error by the *Ath. Pol.* like his mistaken identification of phratry and trittys.

supports the *Ath. Pol.* on the point. On two occasions in the orators, the apparently simultaneous introduction of a person to genos and phratry is described, the probable implication in one, possibly both, being that a genos meeting took place in the context of a phratry meeting.[60] We hear of one phratry that shared its altars with a genos,[61] and Philochoros fr. 35 tells us that gennetai were admitted automatically to phratries.[62] None of these items taken individually proves that gene were phratry subgroups, but taken together that is the natural implication.

There may have been exceptions. I shall be arguing in the following that it is possible that gene might on occasion have formed their own phratric groups independent of any phratry.[63] I shall also be arguing that both gene and phratries had the capacity to split and fuse.[64] We have no evidence for it, but it is conceivable that this may sometimes have happened in such a way that members of the same genos belonged to different phratries. We do not know for certain whether there were phratries which contained more than one genos, but it seems likely that they could.[65] It was not the case, however, in the period for which we have evidence that every citizen belonged to a genos.[66]

There were phratry subgroups other than gene: groups of orgeones that were similar to gene in their relationship to phratries;[67] at least one group, I shall be arguing, known as an *oikos* (house);[68] and other groups.[69] The phratry stood in no formal relationship to the deme or to any other part of Cleisthenes' phyle system.[70]

The third, and final, basic question we must consider at this stage is that of the number and size of the phratries. Little can be said with certainty. According to the *Ath. Pol.* fr. 3, there were twelve phratries in the dispensation of Ion. I argue in appendix 2, however, that no weight can be placed on this statement; the figure is probably simply a con-

---

60. Isae. 7.15–17 (see pp. 66–68); Dem. 59.59–61 (see p. 68).

61. Aeschin. 2.147 (see p. 55).

62. See p. 46. For the epigraphical evidence see p. 61.

63. See pp. 65–66, 68.

64. See pp. 107–12.

65. *Ath. Pol.* fr. 3 is probably reliable on this point. There is probable evidence for a phratry with two gene in it in T 21. See pp. 78–79. See also p. 357.

66. See p. 61.

67. See pp. 74–77.

68. See p. 78.

69. The so-called thiasoi. See pp. 78–93.

70. There are hints, however, that there were phratric groups based on demes. See further p. 109, n. 52.

sequence of the false identification of phratries and trittyes, of which there were twelve. There are no explicit statements on the matter in any ancient evidence that is independent of this source.[71]

Nine certain or probable phratries are known by name, of which seven are epigraphically attested.[72] In addition, we have the names of thirteen groups for which a case can be, or has been, made that they are phratries, and thirteen items of epigraphical evidence that pertain, or may pertain, to phratries whose names are not known.[73] This, taken with a comparison of the quantities of surviving epigraphical evidence for demes and phratries, suggests there were probably at least about thirty phratries in the fourth century.[74]

As for the maximum of the possible range, it is perhaps unlikely that there were as many phratries as there were demes, of which there were 140. Phratries typically contained subgroups whereas demes did not; and it is reasonable to suppose that this was in part a function of their relative size.

We are equally in the dark about the size of the average phratry. There were about 20,000, or possibly 30,000, adult male citizens in the fourth century.[75] If there were as many phratries as demes, the minimum

---

71. The list of twenty phrateres, T 18, is of no help, since it is unclear whether it is a whole phratry or a subgroup; nor is the longer, only partially preserved list, T 35, which may not be of phrateres.

72. Epigraphically attested: Achniadai, Demotionidai/Dekeleieis (counted as one phratry for this purpose), Dyaleis, Gleontis, Medontidai, Therrikleidai, Thymaitis. Attested in literary source: Thyrgonidai and Titakidai. See appendix 1. According to Hedrick 1991, 259, there were certainly at least thirteen phratries. But this is based on the doubtful assumption that all the documents he attributes to anonymous phratries pertain to phratries different from those whose names are known.

73. Appendix 1 C; appendix 1 B, plus T 35 and T 36.

74. A comparison of the quantity of surviving evidence for demes and phratries tells us nothing firm, because pure accidence of survival plays a role, and because of the many differences between the two institutions. However, from what we know of those differences, demes appear to have been more active than phratries in the kinds of activities that produced inscriptions during this period (see further pp. 201–3, 223–25). We would therefore expect the average deme to have produced more inscriptions than the average phratry. Forty-four of the 139 or 140 demes are attested in the epigraphical documents listed in Whitehead 1986a, appendix 3. It is unlikely, therefore, that our surviving epigraphical evidence represents more than one third of the total actual number of phratries. Given that there are at least about ten phratries epigraphically attested, there were probably therefore at least twenty more that are not.

75. The question of the size of the citizen population of Athens in the fourth century is much disputed. There are two main schools of thought, one favoring twenty thousand, the other thirty thousand. For the latter, see most recently Hansen 1991, 90–94 (cf., e.g.,

possible average size would have been about 140 adult males per phratry. If there were as few as thirty phratries, we arrive at a maximum average size of 1,000. The range is so wide that it tells us almost nothing. To put this in perspective, however, the small deme, Halimous, with a Bouleutic quota of three, had about eighty to eighty-five adult male members in 346/45.[76]

That we can say so little on the basic questions considered in this Introduction is indicative of the severe problems of evidence that we shall encounter throughout this work. Our inquiries have not, however, been altogether fruitless.

The principle of organization of the phratry in the period for which we have relevant evidence was neither exclusively personal nor exclusively territorial. Membership was hereditary in the male line; matters of kinship and descent were a central preoccupation; there was a certain degree of interrelationship of members. On the other hand it cannot be demonstrated that phratry members were, or conceived of themselves as being, descended from a common ancestor. Also, there are indications that a phratry might typically be associated with one or more particular localities in Attica, where there was phratry property, where phratry meetings took place, and where, at least in 508, a proportion of phratry members lived. Insofar as this mixture of personal and local characteristics can be expressed as a single principle, it may perhaps be described as that of natural community. The attempt to discover an original principle of organization is, on the basis of present evidence, futile, and, given that phratries apparently could split and fuse, probably inappropriate.

We do not know whether the phratry was, or had been, a subgroup of the old Ionian phyle. The phratry itself, however, did or might contain subgroups: gene, orgeones groups, and others.

In the fifth and fourth centuries there may have been as few as about thirty or as many as about 140 phratries in Attica. Their average size is likely to have been somewhere between 140 and 1,000.

A final point. Full phratry membership was exercised, generally speaking, only by adult male citizens.[77] It has been assumed in the foregoing that all adult male citizens belonged to a phratry in the fifth and fourth

Rhodes 1980). Contrast Ruschenbusch 1984 (cf. 1988). The only full study of the question is Gomme 1933, now in serious need of updating.

76. See appendix 5.

77. On women and the phratry see pp. 178–88.

centuries. This has been doubted by many, and will be the subject of the next chapter. But we should bear in mind that, in addition to sixty thousand or so women and children, there also lived in Attica in the fourth century a substantial number of metics (resident foreigners— possibly about forty thousand) and possibly about one hundred and fifty thousand slaves. In relation to the total human population of Attica, phratry membership was indeed an exclusive privilege.[78]

---

78. An exact estimate of the number of metics and slaves in fourth-century Attica is even more impossible than of citizens. For the figures given, see Hansen 1991, 93–94. They should be taken as an indication of order of magnitude only.

Part 1
After Cleisthenes

Chapter 1

Phratry Membership
and Athenian Citizenship

At the start of book 9 of the *Iliad* there is dissension in the Greek camp. Achilles has quarrelled with Agamemnon and is taking no part in the fighting against the Trojans. The war is going badly. Fear descends upon the Greeks. Agamemnon calls an assembly and proposes that they abandon the struggle and return home. Diomedes rebukes him: the gods may have granted Agamemnon supreme authority, but they have not given him courage, the greatest power. He and his companion Sthenelos, at any rate, will stay and fight. Nestor rises to his feet to try to calm the disputes. "The man who loves the horror of war among his own people," he remarks, "is an outlaw, without phrateres and without a home."[1] For Nestor, a man without phrateres would have been simply beyond the pale of civilized society.

We cannot, of course, place Nestor's concept in a precise historical context; Homer was not a historian. But the implication that all the citizens of his mythical world would have had phrateres also applied at Athens in the seventh century. Under Draco's law of homicide, passed probably in the 620s,[2] the father, brother, and sons of a victim of unintentional homicide might, if they all wished, pardon the killer, who would otherwise be required to go into exile. If the victim had no father, brother, or sons, the decision rested with his relatives to the degree of his cousins and his cousins' sons. If he had no relatives even of that degree, the responsibility fell to ten members of the victim's phratry,

---

1. ἀφρήτωρ ἀθέμιστος ἀνέστιός ἐστιν ἐκεῖνος/ ὅς πολέμου ἔραται Ἐπιδημίου ὀκρυόεντος. Homer *Il.* 9.63–64.

2. *IG* I³.104 (= *ML* 86). The canonical date was 621/0. See Rhodes 1981, 109. The law was republished in 409/8. Cf. p. 48, below.

25

chosen by the Fifty-One according to rank.[3] No further possibility is provided for; everyone, it is assumed, at least had phrateres.

There is no reason to suppose this situation changed during the period of a little more than a century from the passing of Draco's law to Cleisthenes' decision in 508 to take the people into his faction in his power struggle with Isagoras.[4] One of the consequences of this action, as we have seen, was the creation of a new organizational structure for the citizen body: 10 new phylai divided into a total of 30 trittyes and about 140 demes.[5]

The question of whether the phratry was in any sense an objective of Cleisthenes' reforms is an important one, but we shall not be in a position to address it until chapter 8. I wish to start with a more restricted issue bearing on that question, that of the extent and nature of the link between phratry membership and citizenship after Cleisthenes.[6] I shall address this on the basis not of any preconceptions about Cleisthenes' intended purpose, on which our direct evidence is opaque, but of the evidence for the situation in the classical period, which, at least on the fundamentals, is clear.

Citizenship: Some Preliminaries

What do we mean by citizenship? A full theoretical analysis is unnecessary for our purposes, but if we are to avoid confusion in describing

---

3. Cf. p. 248–50.

4. οὗτοι οἱ ἄνδρες (sc. Cleisthenes and Isagoras) ἐστασίασαν περὶ δυνάμιος, ἑσσού-μενος δὲ ὁ Κλεισθένης τὸν δῆμον προσεταιρίζεται. Hdt. 5.66.2. Solon may have legislated to allow certain classes of immigrants to become citizens, but they would also have needed to become phratry members. See below, p. 53 and appendix 3.

5. Cf. p. 54.

6. The issue has been much disputed. Those who have thought that the introduction of the Cleisthenic deme system entailed the end of an essential connection between phratry membership and citizenship include Wilamowitz 1893, 1: 189 (cf. 2: 276); Ferguson 1910, 264; Wade-Gery 1933 (= 1958, 151, n. 2); Gomme 1937, 81; Latte 1941, 749; Andrewes 1961a, 13; Forrest 1966, 142; Harrison 1968–71, 1.64 with n. 1; Rhodes 1981, 70 (but contrast 258); M. Osborne 1981–83, 3/4:171; implicitly R. Osborne 1985, chapter 4, esp. 72–74; Whitehead 1986a, 97, n.55; Manville 1990, 24, n. 79 and 63. Some of these (e.g., Wade-Gery, Whitehead, Manville) have contended that it continued to be normal to belong to a phratry, but not essential. Others (e.g., Wilamowitz) have denied even that. For the opposite view, see, e.g., Kahrstedt 1934, 231; Guarducci 1937, 19; Hignett 1952, 143–45; Roussel 1976, 145; Patterson 1981, esp. 10–11, 26–27; Ito 1983; Kearns 1985, 404; Sealey 1987, 4. Cf. also Bleicken 1985, 64–65. Davies 1978, 105, n. 2, expressly avoided the question. See also next note.

the relationship between it and phratry membership we need to be aware that it is a complex concept and to be clear about what we have in mind when we make use of the term in any particular instance.[7] To that end I introduce a simple conceptual distinction between what one needs to be or to have in order to qualify for citizenship—typically a particular place of birth or abode or parents with particular attributes—and what one possesses as a result—typically rights and responsibilities, whether potential or actual. Put another way, if we think of citizens as members of a group, it is the distinction between the passport to membership in that group and the privileges that members enjoy. I shall call the passport the qualification for citizenship and the privileges and responsibilities the criteria of citizenship.[8] A qualification may itself also be a criterion.

The qualifications for citizenship in classical Athens are easily summarized. Place of birth or abode were of no account; Athenian parentage was the crucial factor.[9] For most practical purposes it was also necessary to be of the male sex and there were in addition age limits governing the exercise of most of the citizenship criteria.

It is the major qualification itself that is most significant for our purposes, and it is demonstrated very clearly in our evidence when an individual's right to citizenship is the subject of legal dispute. In 346/5 there

---

7. Failure to recognize the complexity of the concept of Athenian citizenship is at the root of much of the disagreement over its relationship to phratry membership. Those who would minimize the connection tend simply to equate citizenship with the exercise of the central political and judicial functions of the polis, and see it therefore as connected exclusively with deme membership. For a thoroughgoing discussion of Athenian citizenship and its development, see now Manville 1990.

8. This distinction corresponds broadly to that between Aristotle's theoretical definition in terms of participation in *krisis* and *arche* (the criteria) and what he describes as a practical definition in terms of descent (the qualification) in the *Politics*. See further below, p. 30 and p. 42. Cf. the distinction drawn by Manville 1990, 4–7 (cf. n. 130 below) between legal/passive and social/active citizenship.

9. The clearest explicit statement of this is at *Ath. Pol.* 42.1: μετέχουσιν μὲν τῆς πολιτείας οἱ ἐξ ἀμφοτέρων γεγονότες ἀστῶν, ἐγγράφονται δ' εἰς τοὺς δημότας ὀκτωκαίδεκα ἔτη γεγονότες. Cf. n. 36 below; *Ath. Pol.* 26.4, quoted at n. 21 below; and Aristotle's "practical definition" of citizenship in the *Politics*, n. 23 below. See also Davies 1978, 105. Whether the parents of a citizen had to be married as well as citizens is unclear and controversial. I incline to the view of Rhodes 1978, 89–92, that they did, and against that of MacDowell 1976, 88–91, that they did not, in part because in cases where we have evidence the parents of a candidate for phratry membership had to be married as well as citizens (see T 3, 109–11; Dem. 57.54; Isae. 7.16, a case of adoption), and since being a member of a phratry and being a citizen overlapped conceptually so closely, we can probably conclude that the parents of every citizen had to be married. See also other works cited in Rhodes and MacDowell and Patterson 1981, 31–32, n. 20.

was a *diapsephisis,* a scrutiny by demes, of the whole citizen body.[10] Appeal from the decision of a deme to the courts was permitted, and we have two speeches, Demosthenes 57 (complete) and Isaeus 12 (surviving only in part), written for appellants in such cases.

In Demosthenes 57 the speaker is one Euxitheos, who had been ejected from the deme Halimous. Euxitheos and the demarch, Euboulides, were on bad terms. According to Euxitheos, Euboulides had rigged proceedings in the deme, ensuring, for example, that the vote on Euxitheos' membership was taken late in the day, when most of the demesmen had set off for home. Only his enemies stayed for the vote, Euxitheos alleges, and were given two or three ballots each by Euboulides, so that although no more than thirty took part in the vote, more than sixty votes were apparently cast.[11] Euxitheos' citizenship was under threat. The main thrust of his defense was to demonstrate his qualification, to prove the validity of his father's and his mother's claims to citizenship. Having done so, he could confidently claim to have shown that he was a citizen.[12]

We do not possess Euboulides' opposing speech, delivered before Euxitheos spoke, but it is clear from Euxitheos' response that Euboulides' major concern had been to demonstrate the noncitizen status of Euxitheos' parents.[13] His father had spoken with a foreign accent, while his

---

10. Aeschin. 1.77 and Σ, 86, 114, 2.182; Isae. 12; Harp. and Suid. s. v. διαψήφισις; Dem. 57.

11. Dem. 57.7–14.

12. λοιπὸν δέ μοι περὶ ἐμαυτοῦ πρὸς ὑμᾶς εἰπεῖν . . . ἐξ ἀμφοτέρων ἀστῶν ὄντα με, κεκληρονομηκότα καὶ τῆς οὐσίας καὶ τοῦ γένους, εἶναι πολίτην–οὐ μὴν ἀλλὰ καὶ τὰ προσήκοντα πάντ' ἐπιδείξω μάρτυρας παρεχόμενος ὡς εἰσήχθην εἰς τοὺς φράτερας, ὡς ἐνεγράφην εἰς τοὺς δημότας, κτλ. Dem. 57.46.

13. R. Osborne 1985, 146–151, has suggested unconvincingly that this case represents a clash of principles between whether a citizen is someone born of two citizen parents (Euxitheos' case) or someone recognized as a demesman by other members of his deme (Euboulides' case). As far as we can tell from Euxitheos' speech (and we have no other evidence), this is wrong. Euboulides seems to have concentrated on questioning the citizenship of Euxitheos' father and mother; i.e., it was taken for granted that the qualification for citizenship was two citizen parents, and the argument centered on whether Euxitheos possessed that qualification. Euxitheos sees it as his task τὰς δὲ λοιδορίας καὶ τὰς αἰτίας ἀνελεῖν (17). He attacks the points made against him in turn: διαβεβλήκασι γάρ μου τὸν πατέρα, ὡς ἐξενιζεν . . . (18) περὶ δὲ τῆς μητρὸς (καὶ γὰρ ταύτην διαβεβλήκασί μου) λέξω, καὶ μάρτυρας ὧν ἂν λέγω καλῶ . . . (30) . . . ἣν γάρ φησι ταινιόπωλιν εἶναι (34) . . . ἐπεὶ κἀκεῖνο περὶ τῆς μητρὸς εἴρηκεν, ὅτι ἐτίτθευσεν (35) . . . καὶ ἅμα μὲν κατ' ἐμοῦ λέγουσιν τὰς ἐκ τῆς πενίας ἀδοξίας καὶ περὶ τὸ γένος διαβάλλουσιν . . . (52) etc. All of these points concern his parentage. When he deals with the principle of the qualification (e.g., at 46) there is no suggestion that he is arguing against some other principle which had been asserted by his opponent. Given the clarity of Pericles' citizenship law

mother had sold ribbons in the Agora and had worked as a nurse; not the occupations of a citizen. Euxitheos vigorously rebuts these arguments: the reason for his father's foreign accent was that he had been taken prisoner during the Dekeleian war, had subsequently been sold into slavery, and had spent a long period abroad before obtaining his freedom and returning to Athens.[14] He calls witnesses to attest his father's citizenship[15] directly and does the same for his mother.[16] He admits his parents were poor, but argues that that should not have any implication for whether or not they were citizens. He can even explain his mother's ribbon selling, citing a law to the effect that such an activity was not permitted in the Agora for noncitizens.[17]

We have only twelve chapters of Isaeus' speech written in support of one Euphiletos for delivery by his half-brother.[18] Euphiletos had been ejected from the deme Erchia. The thrust of the argument was clearly similar to Euxitheos' in Demosthenes 57: how else, the speaker asks, would his opponents demonstrate that they were Athenians other than by showing that both their mother and father were citizens?[19] We may infer that that is exactly what he tried to do for Euphiletos in the earlier part of the speech, now lost.

Athenian descent remained immutable and unchallenged as the major qualification for citizenship throughout the classical period, as no doubt

---

on the nature of the principle (below, n. 21), it would have been surprising if Euboulides had set out to question it; he would not have gotten very far. Nor is it clear, as O. suggests, that Euboulides put a greater emphasis than Euxitheos on the evidence of demesmen as opposed to kinsmen and phrateres. Taking the evidence as a whole, there seems certainly to have been a strong body of opinion against Euxitheos in the deme, and Euxitheos has difficulty in getting demesmen to speak for him—e.g., at 14; and at 21–23 he calls no demesmen qua demesmen to witness to his father's citizenship. On the other hand, there clearly were alleged relatives of Euxitheos among Euboulides' witnesses (52); and note that, strikingly, it was not Euxitheos' phrateres but his demesmen that he called to witness his election as phratriarch (23, cf. p. 109 n. 52).

14. Dem. 57.18.

15. Dem. 57.20–23. Since he was born before the archonship of Euboulides (403/2), when Pericles' citizenship law was re-enacted (cf. n. 104), Euxitheos claims that, strictly speaking, his father would have been entitled to citizenship even if he had only had one citizen parent (30).

16. Dem. 57.37–40.

17. Dem. 57.31.

18. Preserved by D.H. *Isaeus* 17.

19. ... εἰ ἄλλοθέν ποθεν ἔχοι ἂν ἐπιδεῖξαι αὐτὸν Ἀθηναῖον ἢ ἐκ τούτων ὧν καὶ ἡμεῖς Εὐφίλητον ἐπιδείκνυμεν. ἐγὼ μὲν γὰρ οὐκ οἶμαι ἄλλο τι ἂν αὐτὸν <εἰπεῖν> ἢ ὅτι ἡ μήτηρ ἀστή τέ ἐστι καὶ <γαμετὴ καὶ ἀστὸς> ὁ πατὴρ, καὶ ὡς ταῦτ' ἀληθῆ λέγει, παρέχοιτ' ἂν αὐτῷ τοὺς συγγενεῖς μάρτυρας. Isae. 12.7.

it had been as far back as it is meaningful to talk of citizenship. It was to remain so until the Roman period when the term had lost most of its meaning.[20] There was change, however, in what we might call the fine print of qualification, that is in whether Athenian descent meant one citizen parent or two. In the two speeches composed by Isaeus and Demosthenes following the 346/5 diapsephisis, two citizen parents were required, reflecting the situation under the terms of Pericles' citizenship law, originally passed in 451/0.[21] This is the version of the principle of descent apparent in the *Ath. Pol.*'s brief account of citizenship in contemporary late fourth-century Athens.[22] It is also the version behind what Aristotle in the *Politics* called a practical definition of citizenship, in contrast to his theoretical definition, to which we shall return: "They define a citizen for practical purposes as one who has two citizen parents, not just one, i.e., father or mother." Aristotle does not mention Athens specifically, but it is clear enough that he has the Athenian concept in mind—probably among others, for a similar principle applied elsewhere in the Greek world.[23] This restrictive version of the principle remained definitive after 451/0 (in practice it may have applied to some extent), though the law was relaxed during the Peloponnesian War and re-enacted in 403/2.[24]

In 411 as part of the oligarchic program and again in 403 following the restoration of democracy, there were short-lived moves to introduce further qualifications for citizenship—in 411, "being able to be of service with their persons and resources," and in 403, the possession of land.[25] For a brief period from 322 to 318, following the Macedonian occupation of Athens, the possession of more than two thousand drachmas' worth

---

20. Cf. Davies 1978, Patterson 1981, esp. 129–36. For its demise, see Davies 1978, 119. Davies argues that the principle of descent was under siege in the classical period; I do not accept this (see appendix 3).

21. καὶ τρίτῳ μετὰ τοῦτον ἐπὶ ᾽Αντιδότου διὰ τὸ πλῆθος τῶν πολιτῶν Περικλέους εἰπόντος ἔγνωσαν μὴ μετέχειν τῆς πόλεως ὃς ἂν μὴ ἐξ ἀμφοῖν ἀστοῖν ᾖ γεγονώς. *Ath. Pol.* 26.4.

22. See n. 9 above.

23. ὁρίζονται δὲ πρὸς τὴν χρῆσιν πολίτην τὸν ἐξ ἀμφοτέρων πολιτῶν καὶ μὴ θατέρου μόνον, οἷον πατρὸς ἢ μητρός. Arist. *Pol.* 3.1275b22–23. Some, he goes on to say, went even further and required two, three or more generations of citizen ancestors. He also points out that the principle was inevitably inapplicable to the founders of cities. Cf. Newman 1902, 3 ad loc.

24. For more on this, see pp. 48–49.

25. 411: Thuc. 8.65.3 and *Ath. Pol.* 29.5. 403: Lysias 34 with the introduction of D.H. Cf. Davies 1978.

of property became an additional qualification.[26] In 317 it was reintroduced at the level of one thousand drachmas and appears to have remained in force until the restoration of the democracy in 307/6.[27] It is clear, however, that these were all intended to be additional qualifications, supplementary to the principle of descent, not designed in any way to challenge or replace it.[28]

Detailed discussion of the numerous criteria of citizenship is unnecessary for our purposes. Among the major criteria were included economic privileges, e.g., ownership of landed property, and responsibilities, e.g., liability for certain sorts of taxation and for the performance of liturgies, liability for military duties, access to religious rites and ceremonies, and the right to plead in court and to sit on a jury, as well as political privileges and responsibilities, including voting in elections, holding office, and participating in the Assembly.[29]

Citizenship and the Membership of Deme and Phratry

Bearing in mind this distinction between the qualifications for and the criteria of citizenship, we can proceed to investigate the role of one particular set of criteria, membership of hereditary groups and subgroups within the citizen body. As indicated, there has been a lack of consensus about whether there was one such set of groups to which all citizens had to belong in the classical period, the Cleisthenic deme, trittys, and phyle; or whether they also had to be phratry members, as in the Homeric and Draconian contexts mentioned at the beginning of this chapter.[30] I suggest on the basis of the contemporary evidence, first, that both deme and phratry were conceived of as intimately associated with citizenship and, second, that the character of the link, subtly different in each case, can be explained in terms of the nature and functions of each institution with respect to the qualifications and to the other criteria for citizenship in the fifth and fourth centuries. Though different in kind, the link between phratry membership and citizenship was no less strong than that between deme membership and citizenship.

---

26. Diod. 18.18.4–5; Plut. *Phoc.* 27. Abolition: Diod. 18.56.

27. Diod. 18.74.3. Abolition: no explicit evidence but justifiably assumed by Ferguson 1911, 95.

28. See appendix 3.

29. Cf. Davies 1978, 106; Manville 1990, 8–10.

30. See n. 6.

Perhaps the clearest evidence for the dual link is the series of special grants of Athenian citizenship that, from the late fifth century, were made to foreigners who had performed some outstanding service to Athens. There are some exceptions, which we shall consider below, but the general pattern was for the new citizen to be made a member of both a deme and a phratry.[31] Membership in both groups seems normally to have been considered a necessary element in the conferral of Athenian citizenship. If this evidence stood alone, we might be tempted to take the inclusion of phratry membership as evidence of legal conservatism. But it does not. The dual concept is commonplace. To take as another example a speech already mentioned, Euxitheos, defending his claim to citizenship in Demosthenes 57 and having demonstrated that he is a citizen on the basis of his parentage, proceeds to "show that I have all the appropriate attributes, providing evidence that I was introduced to the phrateres and enrolled among the demesmen."[32]

Nor is this dual link restricted to legal contexts. I give three examples from contemporary literature. In Aeschylus' *Eumenides,* produced in 458, Orestes has murdered his mother. The Furies speculate on the social ostracism that results from such a crime: "To what deme altars will he have access? To what phratry's holy waters will he be admitted?"[33] Being rejected from society is envisaged in terms of being refused access to the rites and privileges of deme and phratry.

Two or three generations later the younger Kratinos wrote a comic play, entitled *Cheiron.* In fr. 9 we find the same concept: citizenship is linked with both phratry and deme membership. Returning home after many years in a hostile country, the speaker tells us he has discovered that he scarcely has any relations, phrateres, or demesmen left, so "I've been enrolled . . . in the drinks cupboard . . ."—a comic surprise for the registers of deme and phratry in which citizens were normally enrolled.[34]

The same concept is apparent at Isocrates 8.88, where he complains

---

31. For texts and discussion of these grants, see M. Osborne 1981–83. For the exceptions, see pp. 49–54. For the origin of these grants in Pericles' citizenship law and the involvement of that law directly with the phratries, see pp. 53–54 and 43–49.

32. See n. 12.

33. ποίοισι βωμοῖς χρώμενος τοῖς δημίοις; / ποία δὲ χέρνιψ φρατέρων προσδέξεται; Aesch. *Eum.* 655–66. Aeschylus is clearly imposing Attic demes and phratries on mythical Argos.

34. πολλοστῶι δ᾽ ἔτει/ ἐκ τῶν πολεμίων οἴκαδ᾽ ἥκω, συγγενεῖς/ καὶ φράτερας καὶ δημότας εὑρὼν μόλις/ εἰς τὸ κυλικεῖον ενεγράφην· Ζεὺς ἔστι μοι/ ἑρκεῖος, ἔστι φράτριος, τὰ τέλη τελῶ. Krat. jun. fr.9 K-A and Edm. *Cheiron* (Athen. 11.460f).

about the laxity of citizenship controls during the Peloponnesian War: "They (i.e., the Athenians) ended up filling the public graves with citizens and the phratries and the deme registers with those who had no right to citizenship."[35]

This double link then was a common feature of the contemporary concept of Athenian citizenship. However, our evidence sometimes ties deme or phratry membership alone to citizenship. In the brief comments of the *Ath. Pol.* on citizenship he only mentions deme membership,[36] and in a passage in Isaeus 3, for example, citizenship is associated specifically with phratry membership. The speech concerns one of a series of cases arising from a disputed inheritance. In the passage in question, the speaker wants to show that it is unlikely that his uncle would have married the sister of the speaker's opponent, Nikodemos, for, he argues, Nikodemos "had himself been prosecuted for usurping citizen rights by one of the phrateres whom he claimed to be his own, and maintained his share in the city by four votes." The case against Nikodemos' citizenship was not only initiated by one of his phrateres, it also clearly involved questioning his right to be a phrater.[37]

Aristophanes is particularly liable to associate citizenship with phratry membership without mentioning the deme. In the *Frogs,* for example, the chorus taunts the demagogue Archedemos: "At the age of seven he had no phrateres, but now he's a demagogue among the dead on earth."[38]

---

35. τελευτῶντες δ' ἔλαθον σφᾶς αὐτοὺς τοὺς μὲν τάφους τοὺς δημοσίους τῶν πολιτῶν ἐμπλήσαντες, τὰς δὲ φρατρίας καὶ τὰ γραμματεῖα τὰ ληξιαρχικὰ τῶν οὐδὲν τῇ πόλει προσηκόντων. Isoc. 8.88.

36. *Ath. Pol.* 42.1, see n. 9 above. Some (see, e.g., Harrison 1968–71, 1:64 with n. 1) have seen the failure of the *Ath. Pol.* to mention phratry membership here as evidence that it was no longer in the classical period "an indispensable condition for citizenship." Such an inference is unjustified. The *Ath. Pol.* does not say "they have a share in the polis who are enrolled in the demes," but "they have a share in the polis whose parents are both citizens, and (δὲ) they are enrolled in the demes at the age of 18." Deme membership was certainly more closely connected than phratry membership to the exercise of the central political criteria of citizenship (cf. p. 40) with which the *Ath. Pol.* is primarily concerned in this passage, but failure to mention other qualifications does not demonstrate that there were none. There are many omissions in the second part of the *Ath. Pol.* (see Rhodes 1981, 496, with whom I agree that, although the *Ath. Pol.* does not mention it, it was probably necessary for the parents of citizens to be married as well as citizens. Cf. n. 9 above).

37. εἶτα παρὰ τούτου ὁ ἡμέτερος θεῖος ἠξίωσεν ἂν ἐγγυήσασθαι τὴν ἀδελφήν, ὃς αὐτὸς ξενίας φεύγων ὑπὸ ἑνὸς τῶν φρατέρων ὧν φησιν αὐτοῦ εἶναι, παρὰ τέτταρας ψήφους μετέσχε τῆς πόλεως; Isae. 3.37.

38. (the Chorus speaking)...βούλεσθε δῆτα κοινῇ/ σχώψωμεν Ἀρχέδημον;/ ὃς

Archedemos' right as a citizen to speak in the Assembly, it is suggested, is highly dubious, since, at the age of seven, he still had not entered a phratry. Similarly in the *Acharnians* the son of the Thracian king Sitalces is depicted as longing to exercise the privilege of "eating sausages at the Apatouria," obtained through having been made an Athenian citizen, and he urges his father to send help to his new homeland in the war against Sparta.[39] In the *Birds,* Aristophanes uses "phrater" almost as a synonym for "citizen." At 764–5 the Birds are advertising the dubious attractions of their city in the sky, in many respects a satire of contemporary Athens: "What is normally shameful", they boast, "is creditable with us. . . . Anyone who's a slave and a Carian like Exekestides, let him grow wings with us, and he'll become a phrater."[40]

There is an important question here: why were there two sets of hereditary groups, not one, linked to citizenship in this way? The answer is bound up with answers to questions about the origins of the deme

---

ἑπτέτης ὢν οὐκ ἔφυσε φράτερας,/ νυνὶ δὲ δημαγωγεῖ/ ἐν τοῖς ἄνω νεκροῖσι. Ar. *Frogs* 420–24. Many of the protagonists of the *Frogs* are dead in Hades and it is a running joke in the play that they are given the attributes of live persons while those actually alive are seen as dead from their point of view. φράτερας in 422 is a pun on φραστῆρας, "age-teeth." Cf. n. 79 and n. 114.

39. . . . ὁ δ' υἱός, ὃν Ἀθηναῖον ἐπεποιήμεθα,/ ἦρα φαγεῖν ἀλλᾶντας ἐξ Ἀπατουρίων. Ar. *Ach.,* 145–46. Cf. 158.

40. (The Birds speaking) . . . εἰ δὲ δοῦλός ἐστι καὶ Κὰρ ὥσπερ Ἐξηκεστίδης,/ φυσάτω πάππους παρ' ἡμῖν, καὶ φανοῦνται φράτερες. πάππους means both "grandfathers" (i.e., the legitimate ancestry normally a prerequisite of citizenship) and "wings." All three of these passages demonstrate concern for the pollution of the citizen body with unworthy foreign blood. The complaint seems to have become a commonplace at this time (cf. Isoc. 8.88, quoted in n. 35 above). Just how commonplace is reflected in the use by Lysias at 30.2 of the rhetorical device praeteritio to suggest that Nikomachos, like Archedemos in the *Frogs*, had entered his phratry suspiciously late: ὅτι μὲν τοίνυν ὁ πατὴρ ὁ Νικομάχου δημόσιος ἦν, καὶ οἷα νέος ὢν οὗτος ἐπετήδευσε, καὶ ὅσα ἔτη γεγονὼς εἰς τοὺς φράτερας εἰσήχθη, πολὺ ἂν ἔργον εἴη λέγειν. We may guess that this was also a theme of Leukon's *Phrateres* (cf. p. 7, n. 19), produced in 421. In the one substantial fragment of the play (fr. 1 K-A and Edm. = Hesych. s.v. Παάπης) a certain Megacles is addressed by an unknown character who seems to be suggesting that a man named Hyperbolos, presumably the notorious demagogue of that name, had misappropriated cups sent as a gift to the Athenians by a certain Paapis (whose name shows him to be an Egyptian): ἀτάρ ὦ Μεγάκλεες, οἶσθά που Παάπιδος/ Ὑπέρβολος τἀκπώμαθ' ἃ κατεδήδοκε (for textual difficulties see K-A). That Megacles, who from the name is probably an Alkmeonid (cf. Ar. *Clouds* 46), was a phrater would not have been in doubt. That Hyperbolos was may well have been. His doubtful parentage and citizen status were often the butt of the comic poets; see Connor 1971, 169 with n. 57. Other foreigners seem also to have featured in the play, including Cretans (fr. 5 K-A = Phot. ε 24, see Tsantsanoglou 1984, 127), the fictional (?) Tibians (fr. 4 K-A = fr. 3 Edm. = Phot. s.v. Τίβιοι) and a foreign born slave (fr. 2 K-A P Oxy. 8.1087, 55: δμ[ω]ὸν ἀλλ' οὐκ οἰκέτην).

and the extent to which it was intended to replace the phratry that we shall not be in a position to consider until chapter 8.[41] At this point I wish to tackle a conceptual and legal issue that is perhaps more fundamental: the actual nature of the link between these two groups and citizenship in the classical period. I suggest that a satisfactory explanation must take account of three factors.

The first has to do with the major qualification for citizenship, Athenian descent, for this was also the major qualification for both deme and phratry membership. In normal circumstances, i.e., other than when new citizens were created by decree of the Assembly, the control exercised by the deme and, we shall see, particularly the phratry over their own admissions functioned at the same time as the control over access to citizenship. The fact that in both cases there was provision for appeal to a central organ of the polis was in a sense a recognition of this wider significance.[42] There is, however, a subtle but important difference between the role of the phratry and of the deme in this respect. The deme may certainly be described as a group defined by descent: its membership was hereditary and it therefore concerned itself with the descent qualifications of candidates.[43] But there are a number of indications that the phratry was of particular significance where matters of descent were concerned.

Though it was the major qualification for membership, matters of descent did not otherwise play a major role in the deme's purposes and activities.[44] For the phratry they were much more fundamental to the institution's raison d'être. As we shall see in later chapters, a large proportion of our evidence for the activities of the phratries demonstrates a concern with the affirmation, maintenance and control of kinship ties and the principle of descent.[45] It was the phratry, not the deme, that bore the onus of controlling the implementation of that principle.

A child was presented first not to his deme, but to his phratry. In

---

41. See, however, also p. 40–41 below.

42. For appeal on the admissions decision of a deme see *Ath. Pol.* 42.1–2. Cf. Whitehead 1986a, 101–4, for discussion of related issues. That such an appeal was also possible in the case of phratry and genos admissions is clear from Dem. 59.60, where the speaker tells us that Phrastor had set about appealing against the refusal of his genos (and thereby automatically his phratry, see p. 46) to admit his child, but had not pressed the case. Cf. Harrison 1968–71 2:191, with 20 n. 1.

43. *Ath. Pol.* 42.1–2.

44. This is clear both from Whitehead 1986a and R. Osborne 1985.

45. See especially chapter 4.

fact it would seem that he would normally have undergone a two-stage process of phratry admission, first in infancy at a ceremony known as the *meion,* and second during adolescence at the *koureion,*[46] before he was introduced to his deme at the age of eighteen. Both the *meion* and the *koureion* involved presentation to the phratry of the candidate and at least implicit acceptance of his qualification by descent. Though the precise arrangements probably varied from phratry to phratry, there might also be a process of scrutiny, *diadikasia,* either associated with the meion or koureion or separate from them, at which the candidate's qualification by descent was explicitly affirmed by the introducer and voted on by the phratry.[47] Our longest single phratry inscription consists of provisions for admissions procedures and demonstrates the thoroughness with which a phratry might exercise control over its membership.[48] I suggest that this is not, as often alleged, so much the thoroughness of an exclusive institution obsessed with the need to keep out undesirable members[49] as the thoroughness of an inclusive institution whose essential role in the constitution of the polis was the control of qualification by descent and thereby of access to the citizen body. It is quite clear that the deme was typically much less preoccupied with matters of membership control: in the entire corpus of deme inscriptions there is not one that makes provisions on the subject.[50]

Another important indicator of the strength of the link between the phratry and citizenship is the account taken by the phratries of women, again in contrast to the deme. As we have seen, under the terms of Pericles' citizenship law the citizenship qualification required citizen parents on both sides.[51] It does not seem to have been uniform practice, but there is evidence that women might sometimes be introduced to their fathers' phratries as children[52] and it was normal, probably necessary, that a new wife be presented to and received by her husband's phratry at a ceremony known as *gamelia.*[53] This seems not to have amounted

---

46. For the details, see p. 161–78.

47. See pp. 172–74.

48. See T 3 with chapter 3.

49. The view is so widespread that a list of adherents would include most who have written on the phratry. See especially the first group of authors listed in n. 6.

50. Based on the 143 deme documents listed in Whitehead 1986a, appendix 3. The closest to a deme document concerned with membership is *IG* 2².2394, apparently some sort of list of members of the deme Melite. See Whitehead 1986a, 384, no. 78.

51. Cf. p. 28.

52. The crucial evidence is Isaeus 3.73 and 76. Cf. p. 178–88.

53. Cf. p. 181–85.

to the same sort of tight control that the phratries exercised over the admission of their male members—women do not as a rule seem to have been regarded actually as members of phratries; but there was oversight of a sort exercised by the phratry, whereas there is no evidence for demes having taken any interest in overseeing women's descent qualification.[54]

The special legal link between phratry and matters of descent is also apparent in other quarters. For Euphiletos in Isaeus 12, the evidence of his phrateres is presented as particularly significant with respect to his qualification by descent, together with that of his relations.[55] Euxitheos in Demosthenes 57 adduces the evidence of the phrateres present at his mother's gamelia in favor of her citizenship, and hence his own qualification.[56] To an extent, of course, these two were special cases; evidence regarding their demes was inevitably going to be less important in circumstances where the litigants had recently been ejected from them, but the specific link between phratry membership and qualification by descent is also apparent in other legal contexts where such qualifications are in dispute. Rights of inheritance depended on a similar qualification,[57] and phratry membership was regarded as the crucial factor with respect to them as well.

Aristophanes' *Birds* again provides a good example. In the play, Herakles' relationship with his natural father Zeus is portrayed, with humorous effect, as equivalent to that of an illegitimate son to his father in Athenian law. At 1660-70 Peisthetairos reads out to Herakles Solon's law on inheritance, which makes clear that an illegitimate son may not inherit any of his father's estate. "Does that mean then that I have no

---

54. The argument from silence is strong enough, given the wealth of our evidence on deme membership, but Sealey 1987, 18-19, has correctly pointed out that there is also positive evidence that women were not deme members in the wording of the question at the archontic scrutiny: τίς σοι πατὴρ καὶ πόθεν τῶν δήμων, καὶ τίς πατρὸς πατήρ, καὶ τίς μήτηρ, καὶ τίς μητρὸς πατὴρ καὶ πόθεν τῶν δήμων; *Ath. Pol.* 55.3. Women did take part in some deme activities (see Whitehead 1986a, 77-81), but there is no evidence that they underwent any sort of admissions process.

55. The speaker claims that, had his opponents been on trial, they would have thought it right that the evidence of relations (οἰκείοις) be believed rather than that of accusers:... νυνὶ δὲ ἡμῶν πάντα ταῦτα παρεχομένων ἀξιώσουσιν ὑμᾶς τοῖς αὑτῶν πείθεσθαι λόγοις μᾶλλον ἢ τῷ πατρὶ τῷ Εὐφιλήτου καὶ ἐμοὶ καὶ τῷ ἀδελφῷ καὶ τοῖς φράτερσι καὶ πάσῃ τῇ ἡμετέρᾳ συγγενείᾳ; Isae. 12.8.

56. ὡς οὖν ταῦτ' ἀληθῆ λέγω, κάλει μοι πρῶτον μὲν τοὺς τοῦ Πρωτομάχου υἱεῖς, ἔπειτα τοὺς ἐγγυωμένῳ παρόντας τῷ πατρὶ καὶ τῶν φρατέρων τοὺς οἰκείους, οἷς τὴν γαμηλίαν εἰσήνεγκεν ὑπὲρ τῆς μητρὸς ὁ πατήρ... Dem. 57.43, cf. 69.

57. If children of citizen parents born outside marriage were not citizens, the qualification may have been exactly the same. Cf. n. 9.

rights to my father's estate?" asks Herakles. "You certainly don't," replies Peisthetairos. "But tell me, did your father ever introduce you to his phrateres?" "No he didn't," answers Herakles. "I've often wondered why that was."[58] Phratry membership and inheritance rights are clearly seen as closely linked: lack of phratry membership confirms Herakles' illegitimacy and his lack of right to inherit.

The picture that emerges from actual fourth-century inheritance cases is similar. The significance in this regard of the phratry's concern with women is apparent in Isaeus 3, a speech concerning the rights of the alleged heiress Phile. There the speaker adduces as an argument against Phile's right to inherit the fact that, if she had been legitimate, her father could have introduced her to his phratry. His not having done so, he argues, therefore suggests that she was not legitimate.[59] As in the *Birds*, the deme is not mentioned.

It is not only in the case of heiresses that phratry membership is stressed. In Isaeus 6, for example, the speaker argues against the qualification by descent of the two sons of Alke, the woman with whom Euktemon lived in the later years of his life. He focuses on the irregularity of the way in which the boys were introduced to Euktemon's phratry. Alke, he alleges, persuaded Euktemon to try to introduce the two boys to his phrateres, but Euktemon's adult son Philoktemon blocked the introduction because, it is implied, allowing them in would have involved sharing his inheritance with them. Euktemon then puts pressure on Philoktemon by threatening to marry someone else and have more children. Philoktemon's relatives mediate and a compromise is reached whereby Philoktemon ceases objecting to the introduction of Euktemon's two sons by Alke on condition that their inheritance be limited to one property.[60] It is implicit throughout that the right to inherit is effectively dependent on phratry membership.

Phratry introduction is also stressed in cases of adoption, which was in effect the artificial creation of a legitimate relationship of descent, and is usually referred to in the orators in connection with inheritance

---

58. Ηρ. ἐμοὶ δ' ἄρ' οὐδὲν τῶν πατρῴων χρημάτων/ μέτεστιν; Πι. οὐ μέντοι μὰ Δία. λέξον δέ μοι,/ ἤδη σ' ὁ πατὴρ εἰσήγαγ' ἐς τοὺς φράτερας;/ Ηρ. οὐ δῆτ' ἐμέ γε. καὶ δῆτ' ἐθαύμαζον πάλαι. Ar. *Birds* 1667–70.

59. ...ἐξόν, εἴπερ ἦν ἠγγυημένος τὴν ἀδελφὴν τὴν Νικοδήμου, τὴν θυγατέρα τὴν ἐκ ταύτης ἀποφανθεῖσαν εἶναι εἰς τοὺς φράτερας εἰσαγαγόντι ὡς οὖσαν γνησίαν ἑαυτῷ. Isae. 3.73, cf. 76. Cf. p. 178–81.

60. See esp. Isae. 6.10 and 21–23. Cf. Isae. 8.18; Dem. 43.11.

rights.[61] It is clear that an adoption normally involved presentation to deme and phratry, and to gennetai or orgeones if they existed. The main emphasis, however, tends to be on introduction to the phratry. Sometimes there is a special reason for this. In Demosthenes 39, for example, the speaker attacks the defendant for having usurped his name. The defendant was adopted and enrolled in the phratry under the name Boiotos, but subsequently registered in the deme under the speaker's own name, Mantitheos. It therefore suits the speaker's case to stress the significance of the introduction to the phratry.[62] Similarly, in Isaeus 7 the speaker is anxious to play down the difficulty caused by the fact that an adoption was only recognized by the deme after the adoptor's death.[63] There is no such special reason apparent in Demosthenes 43, however, where Sositheos relates the introduction of his son Euboulides to the phratry of Euboulides' maternal grandfather, also called Euboulides, as the latter's posthumously adopted son; the introduction to the phratry is presented as decisive and the deme is not mentioned.[64] In Demosthenes 44 the adopted son in question, Leochares, is registered in the deme, but that this takes place before his registration in the phratry, subsequently achieved, the speaker implies, by underhand means, is presented as highly irregular.[65] Again in Demosthenes 59 Theomnestos accuses Stephanos of having married a foreigner, Neaira, and of having "introduced the children of others to the phrateres and the demesmen."[66] It may be that

61. For further discussion of the phratry's role in adoption, see pp. 176–78.

62. See esp. Dem. 39.30–31. Sect. 30 contains our most explicit statement of the importance of the phratry in matters of adoption: τί τεκμήριον, εἴ τίς σ' ἔροιτο, ἢ μαρτύριόν ἐστί σοι τούτου (i.e., his adoption by Mantias); εἰς τοὺς φράτεράς μ' εἰσήγαγε, φήσειας ἄν. τί οὖν σ' ἐνέγραψεν ὄνομα, εἴ τις ἔροιτο, Βοιωτὸν ἂν εἴποις· τοῦτο γὰρ εἰσήχθης. It was certainly in the speaker's interest to play down the importance of the deme in this case; but, especially given the evidence elsewhere for the importance of the phratry in matters of adoption, it does not appear that this claim would have unduly strained the jurors' credibility. For an anecdotal case involving Sophocles and his children, in which a phratry considers a matter of naming and inheritance rights, see *Vita Sophocl.*, p. 4.

63. Cf. p. 66–68.

64. Dem. 43.11, 13–15, 81.

65. ... εἰσποιεῖ Λεωχάρην (i.e., Leochares' father Leostratos) τὸν αὑτοῦ υἱὸν Ἀρχιάδῃ παρὰ πάντας τοὺς νόμους πρὶν τοῦ δήμου τὴν δοκιμασίαν γενέσθαι· οὐκ εἰσηγμένου δ' εἰς τοὺς φράτεράς πω τοὺς Ἀρχιάδου, ἀλλ' ἐπειδὴ ἐνεγράφη, τηνικαῦτα πείσας ἕνα τινὰ τῶν φρατέρων ἐνέγραψεν εἰς τὸ φρατερικὸν γραμματεῖον. Dem. 44.41. Leostratos had previously attempted, without success, to have himself registered in Archiades' deme (38ff.). It is not clear exactly why he was unsuccessful on the first occasion or why he was successful on the second.

66. ... ἀλλοτρίους δὲ παῖδας εἰσαγαγόντα εἴς τε τοὺς φράτερας καὶ εἰς τοὺς δημότας ... Dem. 59.13.

adoption was involved here, though it suits Theomnestos' case to leave the point unclear. But again it is introduction to the phratry that is stressed when the matter is referred to later in the speech,[67] and failure on the part of Phrastor, husband of one of Neaira's children, Phano, to introduce a child of Phano successfully to his phratry is adduced as further evidence that Neaira was a foreigner.[68]

Where matters of descent were concerned, therefore, whether with respect to citizenship, inheritance, or adoption, phratry membershp was of particular significance: phratry membership was the criterion of citizenship which played the major role in controlling and maintaining the most important qualification for citizenship.

The second factor in our explanation of the link between membership in deme and phratry and citizenship, important though it is, need not detain us long. It is that most of the criteria of citizenship were acquired through membership in deme and phratry. Here it is the deme's role that is the more significant. Membership in a phratry and participation in a phratry's activities should certainly be regarded as criteria of citizenship, but the mass of political, financial, and military privileges and responsibilities associated with citizenship was connected, conceptually and legally, with membership in a deme and was organized in practice on the basis of the deme/trittys/phyle structure.[69] Membership in a deme was, we might say, a criterion of citizenship which functioned in practice as a secondary qualification for most of the other criteria.

There is a tension, almost a paradox here: the phratry played the fundamental role in controlling qualification for citizenship, but the deme controlled most of the criteria, access to which was dependent on possession of that qualification. This might be resolved if we could demonstrate that deme membership was itself formally dependent on prior phratry membership, if phratry membership functioned as a qualification for deme membership; but this does not seem to have been the case. It is clear enough that the deme made its own examination of candidates,[70]

---

67. At 38 the speaker (at this point Apollodoros) represents Stephanos as having boasted to Neaira, τούς τε παῖδας τοὺς ὄντας αὐτῇ τότε εἰσάξων εἰς τοὺς φράτερας ὡς αὑτοῦ ὄντας καὶ πολίτας ποιήσων. Cf. sects. 55, 118.

68. Sect. 59, see below, p. 68.

69. For the details of this, see especially Whitehead 1986a.

70. Clear from *Ath. Pol.* 42.1 (see above, n. 9) and implicit in a number of cases in the orators (e.g., Dem. 44, above, n. 65). The deme could also eject members at a diapsephisis on the basis of the descent qualification without reference to the phratry, as is demonstrated by Dem. 57 and Isae. 12.

and while, as already observed, it would seem to have been at least normal for admission to a phratry to precede entry into a deme,[71] and while evidence of rejection by his phratry of a candidate for deme membership would no doubt have been considered relevant in case of a disputed application for deme membership, there is no indication that demes were systematically obliged to examine the phratry credentials of candidates before admission. The system would have been tidier if it had worked in this way. That it did not do so is in part to be explained in terms of the circumstances of the origin of the duality, which I shall consider further in chapter 8; but it is also explicable in contemporary post-Cleisthenic terms. Members of the same phratry were not necessarily members of the same deme;[72] the fact that a candidate for deme membership had been refused or granted access to a phratry might be of interest to a deme, but the fact that he had been admitted to phratry X would not necessarily imply that he should be admitted to deme Y rather than deme Z. Moreover, whether or not this was deliberate, involving two separate institutions in the process of controlling qualifications and criteria for citizenship would have acted as insurance against corrupt, lax, or unduly harsh admissions procedures,[73] by no means unknown, on the part of one institution or the other, and would have provided an alternative source of evidence in cases of appeal to the center on questions of citizenship rights. It buttressed qualification by descent and, albeit indirectly, supported the deme's control of it. The other side of this coin, of course, was that the system also provided scope for legal disputes of the sort apparent, for example, in Isaeus 7 and Demosthenes 44 between rights claimed on the basis of deme membership on the one hand and phratry membership on the other.

There is, however, a third factor we need to take into account in explaining the link between citizenship and membership in deme and phratry. It is the conceptual overlap that existed between being an Athenian and both being a demesman and being a phrater. A candidate for

---

71. Above, p. 36. Dem. 44.41 (above, n. 65) cannot quite be understood to demonstrate that it was illegal for an adopted son to be introduced to a deme before he had been introduced to a phratry (the allegation of illegality could be taken to apply only to adoption in advance of deme scrutiny); but it seems to be implied that it was highly irregular. For the normal order, see esp. Isae. 7, where the adoption process was complete in the phratry but had not yet taken place in the deme when the adopter died.

72. The clearest case of this in our evidence is the phratry Medontidai. See pp. 316–17.

73. Cf. p. 173–74.

citizenship did not, so to speak, present his credentials of membership in a deme or phratry to a central organ of the state in order to be admitted to citizenship. Rather, by entering a phratry and entering a deme he became a citizen. These were citizenship criteria of a very special sort: if you did not have them you were in some sense no Athenian at all.

This conceptual overlap has come to be well recognized with respect to the deme,[74] but it applies perhaps more strongly in the case of the phratry. It is of a piece with other well known aspects of the Athenian concept of citizenship: with the absence, more or less, of the abstract concept of the state as distinct from the individual citizens who were its members, apparent most obviously in the absence of a state prosecution system;[75] with Aristotle's analysis of citizenship in book 3 of the *Politics* and in his comments in book 7 of the *Eudemian Ethics,* where he emphasizes the importance of the network of relationships among individual members of the polis and defines the polis essentially as a complex of communities (*koinoniai*).[76]

Where relationships among individuals play such an important role in defining what it meant to an Athenian, the structures in which they are formed and maintained will inevitably be conceptually linked closely to citizenship. The deme was a particularly important koinonia because of its close links with the exercise of the central political criteria of citizenship—participation in the central political and legal processes. The significance of these central criteria should certainly not be underestimated; "participation in *krisis* (judgment) and *arche* (power)" are for Aristotle the most essential characteristics of a citizen.[77] But an analysis of citizenship which overemphasizes those criteria is also inadequate. As will become apparent in later chapters, the phratry was a structure *par excellence* for the formation and maintenance of the natural relations that existed among persons connected to each other by kinship or prox-

---

74. See, e.g., R. Osborne 1985, esp. chapters 1 and 9.

75. R. Osborne 1985, 6–10; Manville 1990, 6.

76. See especially Arist. *Pol.* 3.1280b29–81a1 (cf. 2.1262a6–13). At *Pol.* 1280b40–41 Aristotle defines a polis as ἡ γενῶν καὶ κωμῶν κοινωνία ζωῆς τελείας καὶ αὐτάρκους. At *E.E.* 7.1241b24–26 he talks of the koinoniai τῶν φρατέρων ἢ τῶν ὀργίων, ἢ αἱ χρηματιστικαί (ἔτι πολιτεῖαι). For Aristotle's practical definition of citizenship in terms of the qualification by descent, see n. 23. Although Athens is not explicitly mentioned, it is clear Aristotle has the Athenian case in mind in these passages.

77. πολίτης δ' ἁπλῶς οὐδενὶ τῶν ἄλλων ὁρίζεται μᾶλλον ἢ τῷ μετέχειν κρίσεως καὶ ἀρχῆς. Arist. *Pol.* 3. 1275a22–23.

imity of abode, the relations among citizens. This was basic to its purpose to a greater extent than it was to the demes. Certainly the deme functioned as a local community, but central to its purpose was the fact that it was the structure by and through which the functions of the state were organized. To that extent it had a focus outside itself. To the extent that the phratry did not, it can almost be seen as more purely embodying the concept of the polis as a complex of natural communities, reflected in its capacity to split and fuse in response to demographic and other pressures, a capacity the deme did not possess.[78] It is this sort of factor, I suggest, that may explain why Aristotle mentions the phratry but not the deme as an example of the koinoniai that make up the polis, and why "phrater" comes much closer than "demesman" to being a synonym for "citizen."[79]

The Phratries and Pericles' Citizenship Law

I have already mentioned Pericles' citizenship law as evidence for the nature of the citizenship qualification in classical Athens: the law stipulated that citizenship should be restricted to those of citizen descent on both sides.[80] The detailed interpretation of its purpose and effect is difficult and controversial.[81] We need enter this controversy on one point only: the role played by the phratries in the law.[82]

---

78. For this important difference between the two institutions, see p. 105–10.

79. Particularly in Aristophanes (cf. above, pp. 33–34). Commenting on Aristophanes' satire of Archedemos at *Frogs* 422 (quoted, n. 38), the scholiast makes explicit Aristophanes' implicit identification of Archedemos' dubious status as a phrater with his dubious status as a citizen: λέγει οὖν ὅτι χρονίσας ἐν ταῖς Ἀθήναις οὐκ ἠδυνήθη ἀναγραφῆναι εἰς τοὺς πολίτας. There is a similarly close identification at *Birds* 765 (see above, n. 40); and at *Knights* 255: ὦ γέροντες ἡλιασταί, φράτερες Τριωβόλου ("Old men of the jury, phrateres of the Three Obols"). The reference is to the three obols that were the daily salary of citizen jurymen. I am not aware of any passage where δημότης comes as close to being interchangeable with πολίτης in this way. Cf. Plut. *Per.* 37.5 (quoted, n. 84) and Isae. 3.37 (above, n. 37). Perhaps another contributory factor was that the link between phratry and citizenship was more deeply embedded in Athenian consciousness than the relatively recent link between deme and citizenship.

80. See p. 30 with n. 21. For the fact of the law, cf. Plut. *Per.* 37.3; Ael. *V.H.* 6.10, 13.24, fr. 68 = Suid. s.v. δημοποίητος.

81. The internal value of citizenship would have been enhanced politically by the successes of Ephialtes and Pericles in strengthening the powers of the popular organs of government in the late sixties and fifties of the fifth century, and perhaps financially too by the introduction of jury pay (*Ath. Pol.* 27.3. A date for this measure in the late sixties or fifties seems likely; see Rhodes 1981, 338–40). Its external value would have increased

We should expect, on the basis of the conclusions we have reached about the close link between phratry membership and citizenship, that the phratries were affected by this legislation, particularly since the law concerned the detail of the principle of descent, the phratry's specific concern. Not only that, but the law's new requirement effectively meant that the mother as well as the father of a candidate for citizenship must be of citizen descent, and, as already observed, it was only the phratries that seem to have exercised any oversight in this regard of the daughters and wives of their members.[83] There is a little explicit evidence that confirms this expectation. According to Plutarch, sometime after the passing of his law Pericles asked that it be suspended so that his son by his mistress Aspasia could legitimately succeed him. "The Athenians," says Plutarch, "agreed that he might register his illegitimate son in his phratry, giving him his own name." We cannot be wholly confident about the reliability of such a late source, but there is no positive reason for

---

with the growth of the Athenian Empire, and foreigners would no doubt have found Athens an increasingly attractive place to work and settle (metic status seems to have been developing greater definition at about the same time, see Patterson 1981, 134–35; Whitehead 1977). Whether or not it was also the case that the population of Athens had been rising sharply since the defeat of Xerxes (argued by Patterson 1981, chapter 3; the *Ath. Pol.* attributes the law specifically to "the large number of citizens"), these circumstances would clearly have provided incentive enough to define Athenian citizenship more precisely and/ or more restrictively than before. We do not know whether there was any previous legislation defining citizenship; Patterson 1981 argues that there was not; Whitehead 1986a, 98, doubts this. There seem no strong arguments either way; but the existence of μητρόξενοι before the passage of the law (Cleisthenes, Themistocles, and Cimon are notable examples) makes clear that practice had been at least inconsistent (i.e., from phratry and deme to deme) regarding whether those with only one Athenian parent were admitted to citizenship; at most, one Athenian parent may always have been enough. Some may have viewed the measure as an anti-aristocratic device in general—foreign wives were clearly not uncommon among the aristocracy; we may guess, though we do not know, that they were less so among ordinary Athenians—or as directed against particular aristocrats (notably Cimon, μητρόξενος and opponent of Ephialtes and Pericles). Whether the latter was likely depends on another uncertainty, namely, whether the law took effect retrospectively or applied to those, e.g., entering the citizen body after 451/0; or to those born after that date; or whether, as Plutarch believed (*Per.* 37.3), it was somehow connected with the diapsephisis associated with Psammetichos' gift of corn to the Athenian people in 445/ 4. This cannot be settled on present evidence. For more on this and related issues, see Rhodes 1981, 331–35; Patterson 1981.

82. Whether previous writers have been prepared to acknowledge involvement of phratries in the law has tended to depend on whether they have thought there was a continuing link between phratry membership and citizenship after Cleisthenes. Thus, e.g., Patterson 1981 acknowledges the link. See n. 90 for the argument against it.

83. Cf. p. 36–37.

doubt; and the clear implication is that Pericles' own law had prevented him from introducing his son by Aspasia to his phratry.[84]

There are two further pieces of evidence, both fragmentary, that seem to pertain to legislation on phratry membership, and that should probably be associated with Pericles' law. Indeed, a plausible case can be made for their being extracts from the law itself.

Krateros, in fr. 4 of his collection of Athenian decrees, preserves the following extract from his fourth book: "But if someone of foreign parents on both sides acts as a phratry member, he may be prosecuted by anyone who wishes of the Athenians (who have the right) and the case is to be brought before the *nautodikai* on the last day of the month."[85] Krateros' work was arranged chronologically; it seems that the year 454 was covered in book 3[86] and 410/9 in book 9.[87] It would be consistent with this if book 4 included 451/0. Moreover, it would seem that the preserved clause of Krateros, introduced by "but" and dealing with cases of fraudulent citizens with two citizen parents, was preceded by a clause, or clauses, dealing with those who had only one citizen parent.[88] This suggests very strongly a connection with Pericles'

---

84. συνεχώρησαν ἀπογράψασθαι τὸν νόθον εἰς τοὺς φράτορας, ὄνομα θέμενον τὸ αὑτοῦ. Plut. *Per.* 37.5. This passage again raises the question of the extent to which a *xenos* in Athenian law differed from a *nothos* (n. 9 above). But the fact that the child was specifically excluded by Pericles' own law implies that he was so as a *metroxenos,* for that law was about citizenship, not marriage; Aspasia can with greater certainty be asserted to have been a foreigner than unmarried. Cf. M. Osborne 1981–83, 3.T 5, pp. 27–29; Patterson 1981, 29, n. 3 and ch. 4.

85. ἐὰν δέ τις ἐξ ἀμφοῖν ξένοιν γεγονὼς φρατρίζῃ, διώκειν εἶναι τῷ βουλομένῳ Ἀθηναίων, οἷς δίκαι εἰσί· λαγχάνειν δὲ τῇ ἕνῃ καί νέᾳ πρὸς τοὺς ναυτοδίκας. *FGH* 342 Krateros fr. 4 (= Harp., Suid s.v. ναυτοδίκαι). Kratinos *cheirones* fr. 251 K-A (= fr. 233 Edm.) confirms that the nautodikai dealt with cases of fradulent citizenship. Otherwise they are somewhat obscure (cf. Patterson 1981, 110–11; Cohen 1973, 162–84). We may guess that οἷς δίκαι εἰσί would have included those in the same phratry as the alleged false citizen (cf. n. 37), possibly also other alleged relatives who might wish to disown him, and alleged fellow demesmen.

86. Fr. 1 from book 3 should probably be assigned to the Athenian tribute list of 454, as argued by Meritt, Wade-Gery, and McGregor 1950, 3.9–11. The date was defended cogently by Meiggs 1972, endnote 7 (pp. 420–21), against Jacoby 1923–57 (Introduction to 342 Krateros, 97 with n. 42), who assigned it tentatively to 443/2.

87. Fr. 5, attested as from book 9, dates from this year. See Jacoby 1923–57, ad loc.

88. We can only guess what this clause would have specified. Busolt-Swoboda 1920–26, 1095, n. 1, suggested that the polemarch, Patterson 1981, 111, that the thesmothetai, would have been responsible for such cases.

law.[89] It is not impossible that it belongs to supplementary legislation passed soon afterward, but, in the absence of any other evidence for such legislation, it is economical to take the Krateros fragment as a clause of Pericles' law itself.[90]

Our second fragment, which again concerns the regulation of phratry entry, is fr. 35 of Philochoros, from the fourth book of his *Atthis*. This states, "But the phrateres were obliged to accept both the orgeones and the homogalaktes, whom we call gennetai."[91] Philochoros' work was also arranged chronologically, and we know that the year 464 was covered in book 3 and 395/4 in book 5.[92] Book 4 may well have covered the period from Ephialtes' reform in 462/1 to the end of the Peloponnesian War in 403.[93] It has been suggested that fr. 35 refers to an archaic measure narrated out of context by Philochoros:[94] the term homogalaktes was not in common use in the classical period—Philochoros himself tells us that they were known as gennetai in his time.[95] Apparently such digres-

---

89. Recognized by Andrewes 1961a, 61. Meiggs 1972, 423, disposes satisfactorily of the curious view of Jacoby, ad loc. with n. 73, that Pericles' law contained no more provisions than recorded by the *Ath. Pol.* and that the law's brevity and unclarity were deliberately devised more effectively to threaten the metroxenos Cimon, cf. n. 81. Isae. 3.37 mentions a case of prosecution by a phrater for usurping citizen rights (above, n. 37); this may have been a case under the section of the law from which Krateros fr. 4 derives.

90. Andrewes 1961a, 13, and Jacoby 1923–57 ad 342 Krateros fr. 4 both denied association of this fragment with Pericles' law on the grounds that phratry membership was no longer essential for citizenship and therefore should not have appeared in citizenship legislation after Cleisthenes. Andrewes suggested a mid-thirties date, supposing that there would have been some disputed cases when those allegedly born just before 451/0 attempted to enter the demes using the evidence of their phratry membership; these cases would have given rise to legislation on phratry admission supplementary to Pericles' law, which would have included Krateros fr. 4 as an appendix. The hypothesis is tenuous even if we accept the mistaken (in my view) premise that Pericles' law did not involve phratries. It is not clear, for example, that Pericles' law applied only to those born after its passage (cf. n. 81 above), nor is there any other evidence for a mass of court cases in the thirties or legislation arising from them. The 430s are also perhaps a little late for an event in book 4, bearing in mind that book 9 covered 410/9 and book 3 probably 454.

91. τοὺς δὲ φράτορας ἐπάναγκες δέχεσθαι καὶ τοὺς ὀργεῶνας, καὶ τοὺς ὁμογά-λακτας, οὓς γεννήτας καλοῦμεν. Phot., Suid. s.v. ὀργεῶνες = *FGH* 328 Philochoros fr. 35a. The book number is given by fr. 35b (= Harp., Suid. s.v. γεννῆται): Φιλόχορος δ' ἐν τῇ δ̄ 'Ατθίδος φησὶ πρότερον ὁμογάλακτας ὀνομάζεσθαι οὓς νῦν γεννήτας καλοῦσιν. ἐπάναγκες δέχεσθαι should be taken to imply a legal requirement (pace Glu-skina 1983).

92. Fr. 32 from book 3 can be dated to 464 and fr. 40 from book 5 to 395/4. See Jacoby 1923–57 ad loc.

93. As suggested by Jacoby 1923–57, Intro. to 328 Philochoros, 252–54.

94. Jacoby 1923–57, ad loc.

95. The term occurs before Philochoros only in Ar. *Pol.* 1252b18, cf. p. 60. See especially the discussion of Bourriot 1976, 663–76.

sions were not infrequent in Philochoros;[96] for scholars who have believed that phratries had nothing to do with citizenship after Cleisthenes, legislation on access to them has seemed to belong more appropriately to the archaic period.[97] This last consideration we can discount. That the term homogalaktes was archaic for Philochoros in the late fourth to early third century does not exclude its possible appearance in legislation in the mid-fifth century. Further, there may not have been any thoroughgoing citizenship legislation before Pericles' law.[98] It would be the simpler hypothesis to place this measure within the period covered by book 4 and preferable if a suitable context can be found.[99] Pericles' law again suggests itself. We have already seen that the law not only affected phratries but, if Krateros fr. 4 was indeed a clause of it, that it may well have dealt in some detail with admission to them. Philochoros fr. 35 also deals with admission to phratries and provides that they must accept both gennetai/homogalaktes and orgeones.

There is much that is obscure about orgeones and gennetai/homogalaktes,[100] but it is clear that the groups they formed were normally phratry subgroups. Membership in these groups was restricted to citizens, and there was a process of scrutiny which candidates had to undergo similar to that for phratry membership. The principle of descent functioned similarly as the major qualification for membership, and belonging to a genos or orgeones group is used, like phratry membership, as evidence for possession of that qualification in fourth-century inheritance cases and the like. Unlike phratries, however, not every citizen was a member, and in that sense at least they were exclusive institutions.

Given this link with phratries, with the qualification by descent, and

---

96. Jacoby ad loc., 321 with n. 4.

97. Cf. n. 90.

98. See Patterson 1981. Measures taken by Solon (see n. 53) and Cleisthenes (see p. 262) would have affected citizenship, but it is not clear that they were about citizenship. If there was no previous legislation, I would agree with Patterson 1981, ch. 2, that the phratries would have exercised de facto control over entry to the citizen body before Pericles, though the naukraries may also have had a role (cf. p. 261).

99. I accept the arguments of Andrewes, 1961a, 1, that Philochoros fr. 35 implies that while some potential phrateres were orgeones and gennetai, others were neither. This is also the implication of the orators. It is not, however, the implication of *Ath. Pol.* fr. 3 where everyone is envisaged as a gennete (in the time of Ion probably, see p. 372). I argue in appendix 2 that the authority of this fragment is highly dubious; but it is perhaps an argument slightly in favor of dating Philochoros fr. 35 to the classical period that if it were dated to the distant past it would, by implication, contradict *Ath. Pol.* fr. 3. Contradictions within the Atthidographic tradition are not infrequent, but it is perhaps better to avoid hypotheses which imply them when there are alternatives which do not.

100. For details, see ch. 2.

with citizenship, it is likely that Pericles' law concerned itself with gene and groups of orgeones as well as with phratries and demes. It would certainly have been inconsistent for the law to have provided that phratry members needed two citizen parents while gennetai and orgeones might still have just one. For example, would a gennete with one citizen parent, disqualified from phratry membership, be entitled to inherit property? It seems unlikely that the law would have created anomalies of this sort.

Given, therefore, the association of gene and orgeones groups with phratry membership and citizenship, and given that Pericles' law may well have dealt in some detail with phratry membership, it seems likely that the law also regulated the position of orgeones and gennetai vis-à-vis phratry membership. Pericles' law surely placed the same restrictions on membership in gene and orgeones groups as applied to phratries. Given this, and since gene and orgeones groups were phratry subgroups, it may have seemed sensible to rationalize the situation and grant gennetai and orgeones automatic entry into phratries, the effect of Philochoros fr. 35.[101]

Is there any other plausible context for the fragment within the period of book 4? As with Krateros fr. 4, the suggestion that the fragment belongs to a tidying-up measure in the immediate wake of Pericles' law rather than to the law itself has little to recommend it. Moreover, the potential anomaly of genos members who were not phratry members was, one might think, obvious enough, and it is difficult to believe that it was not dealt with in the first place.[102]

Another possible context, it has been suggested,[103] is the period immediately following the Peloponnesian War; we know there was a tightening up of control of the qualification for citizenship after the laxities of the war period. Pericles' citizenship law was re-enacted with a clause exempting those born before 403/2, and at least one phratry tightened up its own membership regulations.[104] The strongest objection to this is again

---

101. Contrast the position of phratry membership itself vis-a-vis deme membership. Members of the same genos belonged to the same phratry; members of the same phratry did not necessarily belong to the same deme, cf. 40–42. Appeal against ejection from a phratry to a central court was permitted in the fourth century (cf. n. 42), and there seems to have been something of a general prejudice against allowing multilayered appeal processes at Athens (cf. p. 137).

102. Cf. Patterson 1981, 108–9. Andrewes 1961a associated the measure with his suppositious phratry admission legislation of the 430s.

103. Bourriot 1976, 656–62.

104. We do not know whether the law was formally annulled during the Peloponnesian

that we should have to suppose that the law was left in an obviously confused state, in this case for fifty years. Moreover, the impression given by the evidence is that the re-enactment of Pericles' law with the pre-403/2 exemption constituted the entire action taken by the polis on that occasion. At least the exemption implies that there will have been no diapsephisis, and phratries seem to have been left to take their own measures with respect to their own membership. Also, while the use of the archaic "homogalaktes" cannot be ruled out for legislation in 403/2, it is perhaps more plausible in 451/0. If we are right in associating Krateros fr. 4 with Pericles' law as passed in 451/0, it seems more likely that Philochoros fr. 35 also belongs in that context.

Having established and explained the close connection between phratry membership and citizenship, I suggested that in practice the phratry played the major role in controlling the major qualification for citizenship, Athenian descent; and that it was at least normal for procedures governing entry into a phratry to be completed before entry into a deme was granted. We would, therefore, expect the phratries to be involved in the major piece of citizenship legislation of the period, Pericles' citizenship law. If I am correct in arguing that Krateros fr. 4 and Philochoros fr. 35 are closely associated with that law and may be extracts from it, then Pericles' law not only directly affected phratries, but also made detailed provisions concerning access to them, including specifying the form of action to be taken against unqualified members and providing for automatic entry into phratries for gennetai and orgeones.

The Exceptions

There was, therefore, a strong link between phratry membership and citizenship in the classical period. But was there room for any exceptions?

War, or merely ignored. D.L. 2.26 informs us, on the authority of Aristotle, that Socrates took advantage of a measure under which, because of the shortage of men, Athenians were "allowed to marry one citizen woman (aste) and have children from another," but this measure seems only to have applied to astai, and would therefore not have had the effect of annulling Pericles' law. (Cf. Patterson 1981, 142–43; Rhodes 1981, 331). The evidence for laxities consists not only in the nature of the measures taken after the end of the war to tighten up the situation (in particular the exemption from the law for those born before 403/2), but also in the complaints and satires of the comic poets and orators during it, cf. n. 40. For the re-enactment of the law, see Σ Aeschin. 1.39 = FGH 77 Eumelos fr. 2; Dem. 57.30; Caryst. fr. 11 Müller ap. Ath. 13.577 b–c. For the measure taken by the Demotionidai/Dekeleieis, see T 3 with ch. 3. Cf. also T 18 with commentary.

Put another way, were there citizens who were not members of phratries after Cleisthenes? First, there is evidence that might be taken to demonstrate conclusively that there were not, namely Draco's law of homicide. We have already seen that this can be taken to imply that, at the time of its original publication in the late seventh century, all Athenians were in a phratry; it assumes that, even if a person lacked all relations to the degree of cousins' sons, he would still have phrateres.[105] The law was republished in 409/8.[106] It may be thought that we could infer that every Athenian at that time still had phrateres. Such an inference would not, however, be justified. The text of the law may or may not have been revised since the time of Draco,[107] but in its republished form it preserved anachronisms; it mentions frontier markets, for example, which appear to have been obsolete by the classical period.[108] The implication that all Athenians were in a phratry could, it might be argued, be another such anachronism. If the law had undergone revision, the possibility that a murderer might have no male relations whatsoever could have been regarded as so remote that revision of the relevant clauses was thought unnecessary.[109]

In fact, there are some Athenians who indisputably did not belong to phratries, namely some of those foreigners who were granted Athenian citizenship by special decree.[110] As we have seen, the norm was for a grant of citizenship to include membership in deme and phratry. The standard formulation was, "X is to be an Athenian and is to become a member of a phyle, deme, and phratry."[111] Of individual grants of

---

105. See p. 25–26.

106. Archonship of Diokles, see *IG* 1³.104, 2, cf. Stroud 1968, 19.

107. Stroud 1968 thought there was no revision. Contra Ruschenbusch 1974, 815–17, cf. Rhodes 1981, 109–12.

108. Dem. 23.39; Stroud 1968, 53.

109. The view taken by Harrison 1968–71, 1.64, n. 1.

110. On these decrees, see especially M. Osborne 1981–83.

111. Citizenship granted in this way extended to the descendants of an honorand (at least from ca. 369/8, after which this is specified automatically and explicitly in the grants; previously it was a haphazard feature; see Whitehead 1986b, 110; M. Osborne 1981–83, 4.150–54), but it is unclear whether it also extended to the wife. M. Osborne 1981–83, 4.150–54 argued attractively that it did not; Whitehead 1986b persuasively, though not decisively, that the wife's status became ambiguous on the basis of the case of Archippe (the wife first of the banker Pasion and, after his death, of the metic Phormio. Both were granted citizenship by special decree, but the latter only some time after his marriage to Archippe). Whether or not Whitehead is correct, it is not surprising that it was thought necessary to specify explicitly that citizenship would extend to the descendants of honorands, given the normal importance of the status of the mother as well as the father in

citizenship, this applies to all but two attested cases. In the grant for Thrasyboulos of Kalydon in 410/9, deme membership is omitted,[112] and in that of Sthorys of Thasos, phratry membership is omitted.[113] There is nothing special in the content of these grants or in their recipients that might explain these unusual omissions. They seem to arise from a combination of two factors. First, the Thrasyboulos decree is the earliest text of an individual grant of citizenship we possess. The standard formula of entry to deme, phyle, and phratry may simply not yet have been established. The variation from later practice is not very great; Thrasyboulos still has membership in the two key citizenship groups, the phyle and phratry. The absence of an established formula may lie behind the case of Sthorys also; but this decree is poorly drafted.[114] It may well be that omission of phratry membership in this case was simply due to error.[115]

It does not seem that we can read much significance into these two cases. There is, however, another group of citizenship grants where omission of membership in one of the vital institutions is a more regular feature, namely those involving groups rather than individuals. We have three cases of such enfranchisements, all dating to the period of the Peloponnesian War or its aftermath, where the relevant clause survives or can be restored with some confidence. These are the grants to the Plataeans in 427, to the Samians in 405/4 and 403/2, and to the Heroes of Phyle in 401/0.[116] In none of these cases are the groups assigned to

---

passing citizenship on to their children (see p. 30). We may guess that the legislation (dating to the 380s?) that resulted in the explicit extension of citizenship to descendants arose from cases where phratries had objected to accepting such persons where the decree had failed to make such a provision explicit.

112. M. Osborne 1981–83, D2, 1:28–30, 2:16–21. The relevant clause is at lines 15–17: εἶναι δὲ Θρασύ/[βολον 'Αθεναῖον, καὶ φυλὲς τε κ]αὶ φρατρίας hὸ/[ν ἂν βόλεται γράφ-σασθαι αὐτό]ν·

113. M. Osborne 1981–83, D8, 1:43–45, 2:45–48. The relevant clause is at lines 30–31: κα[ὶ ἔναι αὐ]τὸν 'Αθ[ην]αῖο[ν· γρά] < ψ > ασθαι δ[ὲ]/ αὐτὸν εἰς φυ[λὴν κα]ὶ δῆμον ἵ[ν' ἂ]ν βόλ[ηται·]

114. The stele actually consists of two decrees, one of the Demos and one of the Boule. The original grant of citizenship appears to have been badly formulated; in particular it was not clear how many stelai should be set up, or where. This had to be clarified by a supplementary decree of the Boule. See the comments of M. Osborne 1981–83, 2:46 and n. 130; cf. Billheimer 1938, 456.

115. Cf. M. Osborne 1981–82, 4:160; "Almost certainly these omissions are insignificant and they are likely to be examples of defective formulation...."

116. Plataeans: κατανεῖμαι δὲ τοὺς Πλαταιέας εἰς τοὺς δήμους καὶ τὰς φυλάς. Dem. 59.104, 7–8 (Osborne D1). The authenticity of this decree is controversial (accepted by M.

phratries; while the Plataeans are assigned to demes as well as phylai, the Samians and Heroes of Phyle are assigned only to phylai. The regularity of the omissions in these cases suggests that they were not accidental. They are best explained as a definite limitation on the citizenship granted these people, not merely because they are foreigners but because they are enrolled as groups rather than as individuals.

Foreign citizens were, by definition, in an exceptional, paradoxical position. They did not have the legitimate Athenian descent which was normally the major qualification for citizenship, and yet they were citizens, by special decree. In the case of individual enfranchisements, this proved no barrier to the exercise of citizenship in deme and phratry. In the case of group enfranchisements, however, the tension caused by such a paradox would have been more apparent. To have whole groups of foreigners entering demes and phratries would threaten the very principle of descent on which they were based and could overwhelm the existing members of the group. Moreover, Plataeans and Samians, if not the Heroes of Phyle, would have formed their own ethnic units. They would have had their own citizen subgroups and, as it has been put, "would have been as reluctant to enter Athenian phratries as any Athenian phratry would have been to accept them."[117] As we have seen, it was the phratry that was especially associated with the qualification by descent that these specially enfranchised citizens lacked—hence, perhaps, if it is not accidental, the omission of phratry membership in all three of these cases and of deme membership in only two of the three.

These are not the only rights of a citizen denied to enfranchised foreigners. The Plataean decree also stipulates that they are forbidden access to priesthoods and to the archonship, and the speaker in Demosthenes 59 claims that this was the general rule.[118] Further, during

---

Osborne 1981–83, 2:11; MacDowell 1985, 319–20 is skeptical), but the similarity with the other two cases suggests that, in this respect at least, the wording of the decree is typical, whether or not the decree itself is authentic. Samians: καὶ νἐμαι/ [αὐτὸς αὐτίκα μάλα τὸς ἄρχοντας ἐς τ]ὰς φυλὰς δέκαχα· *IG* I³.127, 33–34 (= Osborne D4/5). Heroes of Phyle: ἐψηφίσθαι Ἀθηναίοις ἐναι αὐτοῖς καὶ ἐκγόν[οις πολιτεί]/[αν καὶ νἐμαι αὐτὸς αὐτίκα μάλα ἐς τὰς φυλὰς δέκαχα], *IG* II².10 + additions, 5–6 (= Osborne D6).

117. M. Osborne 1981–83, 4:182–83, pointing out also that neither among the Samians nor the Plataeans would there have been an intention to utilize the grant in the longer term. I do not, however, agree with the other part of Osborne's explanation, that "the phratries were individualistic and private organizations. . . . In such circumstances there would be no necessity upon them to accept new citizens into their ranks, if they did not wish to do so."

118. ὅσους γὰρ ἂν ποιήσηται ὁ δῆμος ὁ Ἀθηναίων πολίτας, ὁ νόμος ἀπαγορεύει

the period 334/3 to ca. 229 there was a restriction on the phratries to which naturalized citizens could be admitted. We know no details, but it has attractively been suggested that the restriction prevented access to phratries with particularly sensitive religious functions.[119] The grant of citizenship to a foreigner can be seen as a sort of fictional award of qualification by descent. But the fiction was a limited one: there were certain criteria of citizenship from which these fictional citizens remained excluded.[120]

In what context should we place the origin of decrees of this sort? The first attested law on naturalization was ascribed, probably genuinely, to Solon and provided that citizenship could only be granted to those "who were in permanent exile from their home or who came to Athens with their whole household to practice a craft."[121] By the 340s, however, a very different law was in force, the details of which are given in Demosthenes 59. 88–93: it provided that only those who had performed a notable service to the Athenian people could be enfranchised.[122] We have no direct evidence as to when this new law came into effect, other than that it should predate the series of grants for notable service that began with Thrasyboulos in 410/9 or possibly with the Plataean grant of 427.[123] It can plausibly be argued, however, that it was part of Pericles' citizenship law, perhaps with later modifications.[124] We have already seen

---

διαρρήδην μὴ ἐξεῖναι αὐτοῖς τῶν ἐννέα ἀρχόντων γενέσθαι, μηδὲ ἱερωσύνης μηδεμιᾶς μετασχεῖν· Dem. 59.92, cf. 104, 106; M. Osborne 1981–83, D1 and 4:173–76.

119. M. Osborne 1981–8 , 4:176–81. Phratries themselves, however, seem to have had distinctive religious function only to a limited extent (see pp. 205–25); it may have been the priestly gene within the n that were more significant here. See also T 13 with commentary. The introduction of the restriction can be dated by D17/23 and D21 to 334/3, very probably a Lykourgan measure in the context of his other religious and phratric interests (see index 2, s.v. Lykourgos). It seems only to have been successful in the short term. A new citizen in ca. 304/3 is granted unrestricted access to phratries; thereafter the restriction only appears sporadically, and not at all after ca. 229.

120. Another case of group enfranchisement is that of the Gephyraioi; Ἀθηναῖοι δέ σφεας ἐπὶ ῥητοῖσι ἐδέξαντο σφέων αὐτῶν εἶναι πολιήτας, <οὐ> πολλῶν τεων καὶ οὐκ ἀξιαπηγήτων ἐπιτάξαντες ἔργεσθαι. Hdt. 5.57.2. Though this grant would have preceded Cleisthenes' reforms, it is notable that the same principle of limited exclusion from certain citizen rights (including presumably priesthoods; possibly also the archonship and phratry membership, though these were hardly οὐκ ἀξιαπηγήτων) applied.

121. Plut. Sol. 24.4, cf. p. 381.

122. Dem. 59.89. Cf. M. Osborne 1981–83, 2:12; 4:141–45.

123. For the dubious authenticity of the Plataean grant see n. 116. The Gephyraioi (see n. 120) were presumably enfranchised under the Solonian arrangements.

124. The view taken by M. Osborne 1981–83, 4:141–45. Subsequent modifications would have included the provision recorded at Dem. 59.89 whereby acts of naturalization have

that the scope of that law was wide. As the Athenian Empire developed, the significance of citizenship grants to foreigners would have increased. The year 451/0 seems to have followed a period of unrest in the Empire and to have marked the start of a period of peace with Persia, an important stage in the transition to more overtly imperialistic Athenian rule. In this context, Pericles may well have perceived special grants of Athenian citizenship as a significant weapon in the imperial armory, encouraging loyalty and good service to Athens on the part of citizens of allied states. Moreover, the wording of the law as reported in Demosthenes 59 is reminiscent of the formulation of the rest of the Periclean law.[125]

The way in which foreigners granted Athenian citizenship were not necessarily given phratry or deme membership can be explained, therefore, in terms of the exceptional position they were in as citizens who did not possess what was normally the major qualification for citizenship: Athenian descent. These cases are of limited help in determining whether or not there were Athenians, other than beneficiaries of special decrees of the sovereign Assembly, who were not phratry members, though they do usefully illustrate that citizenship was in some respects conceptually and legally distinguishable from membership in any citizen subgroup.

Is there any evidence that there were citizens other than those in this special category who did not belong to a phratry? Two passages must be mentioned. First, Isaeus at 12.3 speaks of "nurturing and bringing up a child and introducing it to a phratry" as "a considerable expense."[126]

---

to be ratified at a subsequent Assembly of at least six thousand Athenians. The epigraphical evidence is that this did not become part of the procedure until the early fourth century, M. Osborne 1981–83, 2.12. MacDowell 1985, 320, seems to me unduly skeptical about the proposition that Pericles was responsible for the essentials of the law.

125. Dem. 59.89: μὴ ἐξεῖναι ποιήσασθαι ᾿Αθηναῖον ὃν ἂν μὴ δι᾿ ἀνδραγαθίαν εἰς τὸν δῆμον τὸν ᾿Αθηναίων ἄξιον ᾖ γενέσθαι πολίτην. Cf. *Ath. Pol.* 26.4: μὴ μετέχειν τῆς πόλεως κτλ. See M. Osborne 1981–83, 4:143, emphasizing the negative form of both, which is consistent with Pericles' overall restrictive purpose.

126. καὶ...μεμαρτύρηται ὑμῖν τοῦτον ἐκ παιδίου τρέφων καὶ ἀσκῶν καὶ εἰς <τοὺς> φράτερας εἰσαγαγών, καὶ ταῦτα οὐ μικρὰ δαπανήματά ἐστιν, Isaeus 12.3. That "poor people ceased to register their sons in the phratry" because of the expense of phratry introduction was claimed by Ferguson 1910, 264 (cf. 1911, 216, following Körte 1902, 587, cf. Hignett 1952, 60). His claim that these expenses "were considerable, being in the case of the Demotionidai about 50 drachmas per person" seems unjustified. The only expenses, as far as we know, would have been the single sheep or goat required for the meion and the koureion (the size of the meion may have been regulated, see p. 169) and the insignificant priestly dues payable at those ceremonies (in the case of the Demotionidai/Dekeleieis three obols for the meion, a single drachma for the koureion, in addition

Was the expense of phratry introduction one that some citizens may have foregone? I suggest that the contrary inference can be drawn from the passage, namely that introducing a child to a phratry was as normal and necessary a part of a parent's role as nurturing it and bringing it up. Second, Aeschines at 2.147 expresses pride that his father "belonged by descent to a phratry which shared its altars with the Eteoboutadai."[127] Does this imply that phratry membership was an extensive privilege? It seems clear that it does not. It implies that it was an honor to be in the same phratry with the Eteoboutadai, not that it was an honor to be in a phratry at all.

There is in fact no evidence that any nonnaturalized individual Athenian citizens or category of Athenian citizens were not phratry members. There is a great deal of evidence for Athenians who were. Moreover, from the nature of the link between phratry membership and citizenship, it is clear that phratry membership was much more than simply a social norm; it was part of being an Athenian, and that was the case not only in a theoretical conceptual sense, but practically and legally as well. All the evidence we have discussed would be consistent with there having

---

to some minor items from the sacrifice, see p. 170). There is no reason to suppose that there would have been necessary expenses other than these. These costs are essentially of no different order from the fees for, e.g., registration of birth or coming-of-age celebrations in the modern world. Of course, there may normally have been other hidden costs (new clothes, food, drink; Isaeus may have such things in mind here), but there is no reason to suppose they would necessarily have been great for the poorer citizen. In any case, it is not credible that they would have been a significant disincentive to phratry membership. Even ignoring questions about whether or not opting out of phratry membership would have been socially and legally acceptable for the poorer citizen, it was especially this type of citizen for whom the minor costs of entry would have been outweighed by the benefits not only of phratry membership itself but also of the other citizenship rights of which membership was a guarantee, albeit a partial one (e.g., jury pay, assembly pay).

127. ἐστί μοι πατήρ Ἀτρόμητος . . . εἶναι δ' ἐκ φατρίας τὸ γένος ἢ τῶν αὐτῶν βωμῶν Ἐτεοβουτάδαις μετέχει, ὅθεν ἡ τῆς Ἀθηνᾶς τῆς Πολιάδος ἐστὶν ἱέρεια. Aeschin. 2.147. This passage provides no support for any view that phratry membership is ubiquitous in the orators because it was the preserve of the members of the higher, litigating classes that comprised their clients. I shall not enter into a discussion of the proposition that only the wealthy at Athens engaged in litigation, though it seems to be highly doubtful. That only the wealthy might have been able to afford the services of a Demosthenes or an Isaeus is a different matter, though some of the clients in speeches in the corpus, e.g., Euxitheos in Dem. 57 seem not to have been very well off. In any case, such a view is based on a misunderstanding of the nature of the legal and conceptual connection between phratry membership and citizenship, a connection which would have applied to the poor citizen no less than to the wealthy one. Phratry membership was not an optional extra; if you did not have it, you had lost the major means of defending your inheritance and citizenship rights.

been a law which explicitly required Athenians to be phratry members. There may indeed have been such a law; Pericles' law might have contained such a provision. But there is no direct evidence for one, and it cannot be said that there is anything in our evidence relating to citizenship that clearly implies that there was one. It is no clearer that there was a law which explicitly required Athenians to be deme members. We can, however, be confident that the requirement to be in a phratry, and to be in a deme, was at least implicit in the law. In regulating access to citizenship, Pericles also regulated access to phratry. The significance of phratry membership for the polis is reflected in the likely provision of that law for prosecution of false phrateres in a central court, and in that attested elsewhere whereby appeal to a central court was permitted if admission to a phratry was refused. In practice, the law implied that, if you were not in a phratry, your possession of the major qualification for citizenship, Athenian descent, was liable to successful legal challenge, since whether or not you actually possessed that qualification, you could not demonstrate it. So was your enjoyment of other rights, such as that of inheritance, that also derived from the possession of it. It was invariably crucial to the clients of Isaeus and Demosthenes, whenever they were fighting for rights dependent on the qualification by descent, that they were in a phratry. Had they not been, there can be no doubt that their cases would in practice have been fatally weakened.

On the other hand, it cannot be denied that, given that the demes did not formally depend on candidates for membership already being members of phratries, it may theoretically have been possible for a person with two citizen parents to join a deme and exercise the citizen criteria associated with deme membership, in particular the central political/judicial criteria, while not being a phratry member. There is no evidence for the existence of such an individual, but if he did exist, how would we characterize his position? If there was indeed a law which explicitly required Athenians to be phratry members, such a person would simply not have been an Athenian and would have been exercising citizen criteria illegally. If there was no such law, he might, if he possessed two Athenian parents, claim that he was an Athenian and that he was therefore entitled to exercise citizenship rights. He would be right in the sense that he possessed the major qualification of citizenship, but he would not be an Athenian in the full sense outlined above, of which being in a phratry was an integral part.[128] Moreover, his position would be implicitly anom-

---

128. Note now Manville 1990, 7, stressing that in the concept of Athenian citizenship

alous, in that the law assumed he was a phratry member, and in practice he would therefore be unable, if challenged, to defend it.

We may conclude that, for all practical purposes, even if there was no law that explicitly required Athenians to be phratry members, a point on which we cannot be certain, as a matter not only of social normality but also of legal implication and contemporary concept, every Athenian citizen was a phratry member. The only exceptions were certain naturalized citizens.

---

the legal status and the exercise of that status are intimately connected. A person who possessed the legal status but did not exercise it would not have been understood to be an Athenian citizen.

Chapter 2

Phratries and Their Subgroups

Genos

A full discussion of the genos, on which our evidence, though often intractable, is relatively abundant, would take us beyond the scope of this work.[1] I intend in this chapter to consider in detail only those texts which bear directly on its relationship to the phratry. Nevertheless a little must first be said about what a genos was.

The prevailing view used to be that gene were exclusive groups of persons of high birth that dominated phratries in the archaic period, with relics of that dominance still detectable in a measure of control exercised over phratry admissions procedures in the fifth and fourth centuries.[2] This view was undermined, however, in the 1970s by two French scholars, Roussel and Bourriot,[3] though neither considered the relationship between genos and phratry in any depth.[4]

They broadly agree in outlining three uses of the word genos. In the majority of cases the word has no technical sense; it simply means family, line, race, sort, category. It can also refer to a specifically royal, priestly, or aristocratic line. Third, it can designate an organized, village-type community with hereditary membership, a *genos/kome*. It is this third

---

1. The most recent full treatment, that of Bourriot 1976, runs to 1,421 pages.

2. See, e.g., Andrewes 1961a, b; Wade-Gery 1931.

3. Bourriot 1976; Roussel 1976. The following is similar in outline, if not detail, on the basic concept of the genos, but see n. 5.

4. Bourriot at 1976, 637–39 is rightly skeptical of Andrewes' view that the gene dominated the phratries, but except for discussion of the decrees T 3 (see p. 101 n. 22) does not treat the issue of the relationship between genos and phratry in any detail. Roussel's treatment (1976) is broad-brush.

type of genos that was the subgroup of a phratry and with which we therefore are concerned.[5]

Two crucial texts form the basis of this view of the genos. First, a passage in the *Politics* of Aristotle: "the village (*kome*) seems in its nature particularly like a colony of a household (*apoikia oikias*); some call its members homogalaktes—children and children's children."[6] Aristotle's lecture notes make for clumsy Greek, but he seems to be giving us a theoretical model of a village as a colony, a set of households descended from those of earlier generations, reaching back ultimately to the household of a common ancestor.[7] Then, most importantly for our purpose, Aristotle tells us that the members of such a village[8] were called by some homogalaktes.[9] This is followed by a note, "children and children's children," which may be a later gloss to explain the term homogalaktes, or, perhaps more likely, something inserted by Aristotle himself on which he would have expanded when lecturing, to the effect that a village (kome) could be seen in terms of interrelated groups with a common ancestor.

Second, there is the statement of Philochoros fr. 35. I argued in chapter 1 that this fragment should probably be seen as an extract from Pericles' citizenship law. In it the crucial connection is made between Aristotle's village populated by homogalaktes and the genos: "But the phrateres were obliged to accept both the orgeones and the homogalaktes, whom we call gennetai."[10] The sort of gennetai who were granted automatic entry into phratries were those that could also be described as homo-

---

5. It will be clear in what follows that I differ from Bourriot in seeing the priestly gene as examples of the third type rather than the second. Cf. p. 70 below.

6. μάλιστα δὲ κατὰ φύσιν ἔοικεν ἡ κώμη ἀποικία οἰκίας εἶναι, οὓς καλοῦσί τινες ὁμογάλακτας, παῖδάς τε καὶ παίδων παῖδας. Arist. *Pol.* 1.1252b16–18.

7. Aristotle clearly has the literal meaning of the word ἀποικία (ἀπο-, "from"; οικία, "house") in mind; also Plato *Laws* 6.776a-b (cf. Newman 1887–1902 ad loc.), which illuminates Aristotle's comparison of a κώμη with an ἀποικία οἰκίας: the married couple must leave home...ὧν δὴ χάριν μητρὶ καὶ πατρὶ καὶ τοῖς τῆς γυναικὸς οἰκείοις παρέντας χρὴ τὰς αὐτῶν οἰκήσεις, οἷον εἰς ἀποικίαν ἀφικομένους, αὐτοὺς ἐπισκοποῦντάς τε ἅμα καὶ ἐπισκοπουμένους οἰκεῖν, ...

8. Grammatically it would be possible to take οὓς (above, n. 6) as the members of an οἰκία, but from the context it is clear that this is not intended. Aristotle has just discussed the household and used other technical words with the prefix ὁμο- to describe its members, ὁμοσίπυοι and ὁμοκάποι, to which ὁμογάλακτες is clearly intended to be parallel as a term for the members of a κώμη.

9. For discussion of the implications of this term, see Bourriot 1976, 663–94.

10. See p. 46 n. 91.

galaktes, conceived of as members of a village-type community consisting of households linked by real and/or theoretical ties of common ancestry.

Now, this does not sound like a group of aristocrats: villages are not typically made up solely of persons of high birth. It sounds much more like a group of the same type as the deme and the phratry themselves, with hereditary membership and local associations, but not consisting of persons of any particular status.

This nonaristocratic concept of the genos is supported by two further considerations. First, it suits well the interpretation of Philochoros fr. 35 that we gave in chapter 1: a measure designed to preclude anomalous situations in which there was a disagreement between a genos and a phratry over the admission of a member. There is no reason to suppose it was the expression or institutionalization of aristocratic privilege within the phratries.[11]

Second, it is certainly clear, both from the orators and from Philochoros fr. 35, that not every citizen was in a genos and that genos membership, like phratry and deme membership, could be used in inheritance and citizenship cases as evidence of possession of qualification by descent.[12] Whether it ever had been the case that everyone was in a genos we do not know. *Ath. Pol.* fr. 3 implies they had been, stating that at the time of Ion all the citizens were divided into 360 gene of 60 men each, but this evidence is dubious to the point of worthlessness.[13] In any

---

11. See pp. 46-49.

12. I agree with Andrewes 1961a, 1, that Philochoros fr. 35 is most naturally read to imply that, at the time of reference, while some Athenians were gennetai or orgeones, others were neither. It is difficult to see what the purpose could have been of a measure under which every Athenian was granted automatic access to a phratry. This is borne out by the orators. Among the private speeches of Demosthenes and Isaeus, phratry and genos membershp are mentioned as evidence of legitimacy and citizenship at Dem. 57.23-25, 46, 53-54, 67-69; 59.55, 59 (Phrastor); Isae. 7.13-17, 26-27, 43; phratry and orgeones group membership at Isae. 2.14-17, 44-45; phratry membership only, however, at Dem. 39.4, 20-21, 29-30; 40.11; 43.11-15, 36, 81-83; 44.41, 44; 59.13, 38, 118, 122 ? (Stephanos); Isae. 3.73-76, 79-80; 6.10-11, 21-26, 64; 8.18-20; 9.8; 10.8-9, 15, 21; 12.3, 8. It is clear enough that if a person whose legitimacy was in question was a gennete or an orgeon, it would normally be mentioned; it clearly provided a case with valuable extra support. We may infer, therefore, that where it is not mentioned, the person probably did not belong to a genos or group of orgeones. For further details of the cases where membership of genos or group of orgeones is mentioned see pp. 66-75.

13. See appendix 2. Very little can be said with any confidence about the early history of the genos as phratry subgroup. Our only pre-Cleisthenic evidence which has to be taken as relating to a genos of this sort is *Dig.* 47.22.4, a law which seems at best only partially

case, it is not reasonable to infer from the facts that not everyone belonged to a genos and that gennetai entered phratries automatically that they were necessarily aristocratic or powerful persons at any period. Moreover, it is not clear, in the period for which we do have evidence, that belonging to a genos of this sort was in itself particularly prestigious or that gennetai were particularly aristocratic persons.

Demosthenes and Isaeus make nothing special of gennete status as such when arguing on behalf of those clients who had it. It is evidence for legitimacy, like deme and phratry membership, but is never presented as evidence for a special quality of legitimacy or for aristocratic status. Euxitheos in Demosthenes 57, for example, was, I argue,[14] a gennete; he uses the fact as additional evidence of his legitimacy and claims separately to be among those of best birth in his deme;[15] but the court is nowhere invited to believe that his claim to legitimacy was especially strong simply because he was in a genos. As a matter of fact, the citizen status of both his father and his mother was sufficiently doubtful to cause him to have been ejected from his deme; he also admits that his family was poor and that his mother had served in lowly positions.[16] The flavor is not that of an aristocratic family fallen on hard times; there is no reference, for example, to distinguished ancestors. It is much more that of the local busybody with a shady background.[17] Some individual gene were prestigious, e.g., the Eteoboutadai,[18] but that prestige does not seem to stem from the fact that they were a genos, but from the distinction of former members or, in the case of the priestly gene, e.g., Kerykes and Eumolpidai, from the special role they played in the life of the polis.[19]

The claim of *Ath. Pol.* fr. 3 that everyone had been in a genos in the distant past is not in itself indicative of whether or not the gene were groups of aristocrats in the fourth century, but it is at least consistent

Solonian and the text of which has only been restored to give a reference to gennetai. Bourriot (see 1976, 1376–81) took the view that, while the communities called gene in the fourth century may have existed since the archaic period, they may only have become formal gene at the end of the fifth century. The matter is better left open. Whether or not they had existed for long as gene, the groups in the late fifth and fourth centuries have a well-established appearance.

14. See pp. 71–73.
15. Dem. 57.46.
16. Cf. pp. 28–29.
17. Cf. p. 232.
18. See Aeschines 2.147, below, p. 74.
19. Cf. Andocides 1.125–27, below, pp. 68–71.

with the view that they were not. For the *Ath. Pol.* and its sources, although everyone did not belong to a genos in their day, the contemporary, nonaristocratic character of gene may have been such that it was reasonable to suppose that every citizen may once have been a genos member.

None of this can be taken to demonstrate that one genos was never more powerful than another or that gene themselves might not at some time have been dominated by their aristocratic members. But it does suggest that we lack grounds for supposing that gene as a general rule were likely to have dominated the nongennete members of phratries in the fifth, fourth, or any other century. In fact, once such a presupposition is removed, the supporting evidence taken as suggestive that gene exercised a measure of control over access to phratries in the classical period collapses altogether. While we can observe the operation of the law of Philochoros fr. 35 by which gennetai automatically became phrateres, there is no reason to suppose in any case for which we have evidence that any genos exercised any power over nonmembers. It is that evidence that we must now consider.

First, a further general point. We have seen that the genos was normally a subgroup of a phratry.[20] It is remarkable, however, that in the surviving epigraphical evidence, abundant enough for this purpose, a genos is never mentioned on a phratry inscription nor a phratry on a genos inscription.[21] In fact, there are few epigraphical hints that any genos was a subgroup of a phratry. There is the fact that the genos Salaminioi held a sacrifice at the phratry festival, the Apatouria,[22] though I argue below that it is possible that this genos was not in fact a phratry subgroup; and the appearance on the marker of a *prasis epi lysei* of two groups that may be gene, the Glaukidai and the Epikleidai, together with two groups of phrateres, suggesting that all the groups belonged to the same phratry.[23] Gene have their own names and appear in the orators as groups in their own right, associated with phratries clearly enough, but with a separate institutional identity. They have the appearance of groups which were well established by the late fifth and fourth centuries.[24]

---

20. See pp. 19–20.
21. T 3 has generally been taken as an exception, in my view mistakenly. See next chapter.
22. Ferguson 1938, 3–5, no. 1, line 92.
23. T 21, discussed further pp. 78–79.
24. Cf. above, n. 13.

As we shall see, this feature distinguishes them from some of the other phratry subgroups for which we have evidence.

There are seven pieces of evidence,[25] two inscriptions and five passages from the orators, that have been or can be taken to provide direct evidence of the relationship between phratry and genos. All date from the late fifth and fourth centuries.

The Demotionidai Decrees

A series of three phratry decrees inscribed between 396/5 and about 370–50 that deals with admissions procedures is the longest and single most informative document of the Attic phratries.[26] I devote the next chapter to a discussion of the central problem in the decrees, which is the nature and relationship to each other of the two groups they mention, the Demotionidai and the House (*oikos*) of the Dekeleieis. The general view has been that one of these two goups was a genos exercising some sort of control over the admissions procedure of the other, a phratry. I argue that neither is a genos and that the subgroup, the House of the Dekeleieis, was not exercising any power over the admissions procedure of the phratry as a whole.

The Salaminioi Inscriptions

The two inscriptions of the Salaminioi published by Ferguson in 1938 are our most copious evidence for an individual Attic genos.[27] The first, dating to 363, records the settlement of a dispute on matters of cult between two branches of the genos, the Salaminioi "of the seven phylai" and the Salaminioi "from Sounium." The second, dated by Ferguson to the mid-third century, is shorter, but again records the settlement of a cult dispute. In it the two branches are referred to as separate gene.

---

25. T 21 might have been included in the list, if, as is not unlikely, all the creditors listed on it were from the same phratry (cf. pp. 78–79), but other than being probable evidence of a phratry containing two gene (cf. p. 367), it is not informative about the nature of the relationship between phratry and genos; though it is perhaps worth observing that of the two groups of phrateres named for their leader one put up more money, and one put up less than either of the two likely gene—which does not suggest that these gene were more wealthy than other groups within the phratry.

26. T 3 with chapter 3 below.

27. Original publication and fundamental discussion by Ferguson 1938, 1–74. For more recent work see Bourriot 1976, 574–99; also now Humphreys 1990 with p. 370 below.

I have already remarked on the apparent independence of the Salaminioi from any phratry; the only link is suggested by the sacrifice at the phratry festival Apatouria provided for in the first inscription.[28] Another notable feature is that two of the seven men who swore to the agreement of the first Salaminioi inscription also appear on a fragmentary inscription, T 35, containing a list of names—divided into thiasoi—generally taken to be members of a single phratry. The curiosity here is that the other fourteen attested Salaminioi do not appear, as we might have expected, in this thiasos or elsewhere on T 35.[29]

I argue below that the case for identifying T 35 as a list of phrateres is by no means secure. If it is a phratry document, we may suppose that the other Salaminioi were grouped in another part of the list, now lost, or, bearing in mind that it seems to have been a list of contributors to a fund and therefore did not necessarily contain every member, that they did not appear at all.[30] The implication would be that we have a phratry divided into thiasoi, but containing also a genos. If T 35 is not a phratry there is no problem; the Salaminioi could simply be a subgroup of some unknown phratry. They all attended the same Apatouria along with other phrateres who were not Salaminioi, but in the course of the festival they had their own sacrifices. This would not be unexpected.

There is, however, another possibility. T 35 may not be a phratry inscription. In this case, it is possible that the Salaminioi were not in a phratry at all, but an entirely autonomous group which was not a phratry subdivision. This would apparently be exceptional, but not perhaps unexpected. As I argue in the next chapter, fusions and fissions of phratries in response to social and demographic pressures were probably not unusual; this may be a case of a subgroup that has split off from its parent institution. It would have status as a phratry as well as a genos. Alternatively, an explanation may lie in the name of the genos. We cannot tell what the exact nature of the relationship was between the Salaminioi and Salamis,[31] but if they were indeed originally inhabitants of that island who had at some stage been integrated into the citizen body, this integration may have been similar to the mass enfranchisements of

---

28. See p. 63 with n. 22.

29. See p. 82. The common sacrifice at the Apatouria, the festival at which citizens congregated in their phratries, seems to rule out Ferguson's suggestion at 1938, 28–29 with n. 7 that the Salaminioi were scattered about in different phratries.

30. Cf. Andrewes, 1961a, 10.

31. For the range of possibilities, see Bourriot 1976 and Humphreys 1990, loc. cit.

foreigners discussed in chapter 1. There, it was noted that such mass enfranchisement did not involve access to a phratry.[32] The Salaminioi too would perhaps not have entered a phratry upon integration but would have formed their own independent citizen genos, in effect their own phratry. They certainly look large enough to have done so,[33] and there are some possible parallels.[34]

Isaeus 7.15–17

In this passage,[35] the speaker Thrasyllos claims that he was adopted by one Apollodoros in a hurry after the death of Apollodoros' own son: "And at the time of the Thargelia[36] he presented me at the altars, to the gennetai and the phrateres. Their law is the same, whether a real or an adopted son is being introduced." The introducer, he continues, has to swear to the legitimacy of the child he is introducing, then the others have to vote. If the vote is favorable, the candidate is inscribed in the common register (koinon grammateion), but not before. "Such is the care they take to ensure justice is done. This being their law, the phrateres and gennetai believed him, recognized me as his sister's child, and inscribed me in the common register, all of them having voted."[37]

---

32. Cf. p. 51–52.

33. We do not know how many Salaminioi there were. But the fact that seven men are merely the representatives of one of the branches suggests a considerable size. For size and numbers of phratries in the classical period see p. 20–21; cf. p. 80.

34. Note in particular the Titakidai and Thyrgonidai (T 15) and conceivably the Medontidai (T 7–10), though in neither case is it clear that they were gene in the sense of being formal phratry subgroups, rather than family lines. See also the discussion of Isaeus 7. 15–17 below and the case of the Dekeleieis, discussed in the next chapter.

35. Bourriot 1976, 679, suggested that the genos concerned in this speech was of the priestly type on the basis of the religious connections mentioned by Thrasyllos at sections 9, 27, 36 and 40. If correct, while this would make no difference to its status as a phratry subgroup (cf. p. 70), it is perhaps surprising that the fact does not emerge more directly in the speech. For the identity of the phratry, see next note.

36. This is odd; we would have expected the Apatouria. But it is perhaps explicable as an emergency measure given Apollodoros' fear, justified in the event, that he would not live to the next Apatouria. Moreover Apollodoros' phratry may have been Achniadai, which had a cult of Apollo Hebdomeios, god of the Thargelia. Cf. p. 216 and T 1–2.

37. καὶ ἐπειδὴ Θαργήλια ἦν, ἤγαγέ με ἐπὶ τοὺς βωμοὺς εἰς τοὺς γεννήτας τε καὶ φράτερας. ἔστι δ᾽ αὐτοῖς νόμος ὁ αὐτός, ἐάν τέ τινα φύσει γεγονότα εἰσάγῃ τις ἐάν τε ποιητόν... (description of procedure)... τοιαύτας ἀκριβείας ἔχει τὰ δίκαια τὰ παρ᾽ αὐτοῖς. τοῦ νόμου δὴ οὕτως ἔχοντος, καὶ τῶν φρατέρων τε καὶ γεννητῶν ἐκείνῳ οὐκ ἀπιστούντων ἐμέ τε οὐκ ἀγνοούντων, ὅτι ἦν ἐξ ἀδελφῆς αὐτῷ γεγονώς, ἐγγράφουσί με εἰς τὸ κοινὸν γραμματεῖον ψηφισάμενοι πάντες.... I agree with Wyse 1904, ad loc.,

It is noteworthy that while the child is apparently presented to two groups, gennetai and phrateres, only one proceeding is described, for all Thrasyllos' insistence on the thoroughness of the procedure. The law of Philochoros fr. 35 may provide an explanation. Thrasyllos was introduced, as he claims, to both Apollodorus' genos and to the phratry of which that genos was a subgroup. Under the law of Philochoros fr. 35, however, the actual procedure of swearing and voting only needed to take place in the genos, entry to the phratry then being automatic. Entry into the genos may in fact have taken place at a phratry meeting.[38] Isaeus does not need to explain all this to his Athenian audience. The only point he wishes to get across is that Thrasyllos was accepted into genos and phratry by a thorough procedure.[39]

This interpretation puts some strain on the text, however. It is possible that genos and phratry had a joint register, or that when Isaeus talks about the "common register"[40] he is referring elliptically to the registers of genos and phratry respectively, but there would be no parallels for either usage.[41] It may be more natural to take "the common register" as the register of a single institution, i.e., of a genos that was also a whole phratry.

Such an interpretation may also suit better the statement that "the phrateres and gennetai . . . inscribed me in the common register, all of them having voted," i.e., that all did indeed vote, because the genos was identical with the phratry in this case. If it is not taken in this way, we must suppose either that Isaeus was being a little disingenuous, or that when he said phrateres and gennetai here he meant not two separate groups of people, but one; gennetai were, after all, also phrateres.[42]

---

and Andrewes 1961a, 5, that ἔστι δ᾽ αὐτοῖς νόμος ὁ αὐτός should mean that the law was the same whether the son introduced was natural or adopted (cf. pp. 176–78). Andrewes suggests it might also be taken to mean that the law was the same for genos and phratry, but this seems a little forced.

38. Cf. p. 68 and 176.

39. Cf. Andrewes 1961a, 5–6, whose interpretation differs from this essentially only in that he sees the genos here controlling phratry entry of non-gennetai in the manner of a dominant aristocratic institution. The logical interpretation of this speech (not questioned by Wyse 1904) must be that Thrasyllos became a member of Apollodoros' genos, not simply that he was examined by it in order to gain admission to Apollodoros' phratry (see 7.43, "καὶ εἰς τοὺς γεννήτας καὶ φράτερας ἐγγραφείς . . .": he was inscribed in genos no less than in phratry).

40. τὸ κοινὸν γραμματεῖον, Isae. 7.16.

41. For phratry registration, see pp. 174–75.

42. Another possibility on the basis of this text alone would be that this phratry retained

There is nothing conclusive here, but it is possible that this is another case where a genos had become completely independent of its phratry. It is a phenomenon to which we shall return in the next chapter.

Demosthenes 59.59-61

Here the speaker, another Apollodoros, is describing the introduction by Phrastor of his son by the daughter of Neaira to his phratry: "For when Phrastor, being in ill health, introduced his child by the daughter of Neaira to his phratry, and to the genos Brytidai of which Phrastor was a member . . . ,"[43] the gennetai refused to accept the child. Phrastor brought a suit against the genos[44] but refused, when challenged, to swear to the child's legitimacy. The matter seems to have been taken no further.

There are three points of note here. First, after two uncertain cases, there seems no reason here to doubt that this is a case where the normal relationship between phratry and genos held good: the Brytidai were a subgroup of a phratry. Second, this seems to be a clear example of the law of Philochoros in action, but in reverse: just as acceptance by the genos implies automatic acceptance by the phratry, rejection by the genos implies rejection by the phratry. Third, it is somewhat curious that what is first described as introduction to the phratry should actually turn out to be introduction to a genos. If the law of Philochoros fr. 35 in itself is not sufficient explanation, it may be that introduction to the genos took place in the context of a phratry meeting.[45]

Andocides 1.125-27

Andocides is attacking his accuser Kallias. He claims Kallias married a daughter of Ischomachos and soon after made her mother, Chrysilla, his mistress. The daughter, he alleges, eventually ran away; Kallias tired of the mother, too, and threw her out. "She, however, claimed that she

---

some sort of procedure whereby all the phrateres voted on a candidate together with the gennetai, but that is unlikely given the law of Philochoros fr. 35.

43. ὡς γὰρ εἰσῆγεν ὁ Φράστωρ εἰς τοὺς φράτερας τὸν παῖδα ἐν τῇ ἀσθενείᾳ ὢν τὸν ἐκ τῆς θυγατρὸς τῆς Νεαίρας, καὶ εἰς τοὺς Βρυτίδας ὢν καὶ αὐτός ἐστιν ὁ Φράστωρ γεννήτης. . . . Dem. 59.59.

44. On this procedure, cf. p. 35.

45. Cf. p. 176. I agree with Andrewes 1961a, 6, n. 20, against Guarducci 1937, 25, that there is no implication that the child was registered with the phratry before application was made to the genos.

was pregnant by him; when the child was born he denied this (126). Taking the child, the woman's relatives went to the altar at Apatouria with the sacrificial offering and requested Kallias to begin the ceremony. He asked whose the child was and they replied 'Kallias' the son of 'Hipponikos.' 'I am he,' he said. And they replied, 'And the child is yours.' Taking hold of the altar he then swore that there never was or had been any son of his except Hipponikos, whose mother was Glaukon's daughter; otherwise ruin might fall on him and his house—as it surely will. (127) Some time after this, gentlemen, consumed again with desire for this most reckless old woman, he took her into his house and introduced the now grown child to the Kerykes, claiming that he was his son. Kallikles opposed admission, but the Kerykes voted according to the law they have whereby the father may introduce a child when he swears that the child he is introducing is his. Taking hold of the altar, he swore that the child was his legitimate son, the daughter of Chrysilla: the same child he had previously disowned on oath. Please call me the witnesses to all this."[46]

We must be on our guard against distortions of the truth here; Andocides' intention is clearly to portray Kallias in the worst possible light. But the course of events as described is consistent with other evidence for introduction to the phratry and genos. If there is invention here, it is plausible invention.

There were allegedly two presentations, one at which the father disowned the child, and a subsequent one at which he acknowledged it. The latter procedure was in Kallias' genos: despite objections, the Kerykes accepted Kallias' acknowledgment and so accepted the child. Was the first presentation, as portrayed by Andocides, to genos or phratry? It must, I think, have been to phratry. The mention of Apatouria, although indicative, is not conclusive, since the case of the Salaminioi shows us that gene could undertake activities in the context of the Apatouria.[47] More significant is that, when the genos is introduced in

---

46. ... (126) λαβόντες δὲ οἱ προσήκοντες τῇ γυναικὶ τὸ παιδίον ἧκον ἐπὶ τὸν βωμὸν Ἀπατουρίοις ἔχοντες ἱερεῖον, καὶ ἐκέλευον κατάρξασθαι τὸν Καλλίαν. ὁ δ᾽ ἠρώτα τίνος εἴη τὸ παιδίον· ἔλεγον ''Καλλίου τοῦ Ἱππονίκου.'' '''Εγώ εἰμι οὗτος.'' ''Καὶ ἔστι γε σὸν τὸ παιδίον.'' λαβόμενος τοῦ βωμοῦ ὤμοσεν ἦ μὴν μὴ εἶναί <οἱ> υἱὸν ... (127) ... καὶ τὸν παῖδα ἤδη μέγαν ὄντα εἰσάγει εἰς Κήρυκας, φάσκων εἶναι υἱὸν αὐτοῦ. ἀντεῖπε μὲν Καλλικλῆς μὴ εἰσδέξασθαι, ἐψηφίσαντο δὲ οἱ Κήρυκες κατὰ τὸν νόμον ὅς ἐστιν αὐτοῖς, τὸν πατέρα ὀμόσαντα εἰσάγειν ἦ μὴν υἱὸν ὄντα ἑαυτοῦ εἰσάγειν. λαβόμενος τοῦ βωμοῦ ὤμοσεν ἦ μὴν τὸν παῖδα ἑαυτοῦ εἶναι γνήσιον....

47. Above, p. 61.

section 127, it is clearly intended to be a different body from that involved in the proceedings of section 126: "Some time after this . . . he introduced the child to the Kerykes. . . ." There is clearly no implication that the same body examined the same child twice.

Next, an incidental point. Bourriot does not see the priestly *gene* as belonging to the type that were phratry subgroups. This case casts doubt on this distinction. Membership of the genos Kerykes obviously implied legitimacy and citizenship; it therefore conferred automatic membership in the phratry under Philochoros' law. Acceptance by the genos as recounted in section 127 was, it is implied, a back door to automatic acceptance into the phratry that had, at Kallias' own instigation, earlier rejected the child. There is no difference here from the non-priestly gene. Given the law of Philochoros fr. 35, however, why was the child not introduced first to the genos and then subsequently to the phratry? The normal order seems to have been reversed. Two possible explanations suggest themselves.

First, as we shall see in chapter 4, there appear to have been two stages of introduction to the phratry: the koureion in adolescence, and the earlier meion at which children were first presented to their phratry, normally in infancy. The first presentation described here sounds as if it took place at the meion stage.[48] We do not know whether or not gene had a ceremony like the meion. If the Kerykes did not have the equivalent of the meion, this would explain why the child was presented to the phratry first rather than to the genos.[49]

Another explanation may lie in the possibility that the relatives of Chrysilla, who introduced the child on the first occasion, were not members of the genos Kerykes, but did have access to the phratry.[50] In that case, introduction by them of the child to the genos Kerykes may not have been feasible. Furthermore, if Kallias was phratry priest or phratriarch, as he would appear to have been,[51] those introducing the child may have expected to catch him off guard and embarrass him into recognizing the child to save scandal. But Kallias, Andocides suggests, was unashamed.

---

48. Cf. pp. 163, 165–66.

49. Even if this genos had the equivalent of a meion, it is not clear whether the law of Philochoros would necessarily have applied to the order of presentation to genos and phratry at this stage. Cf. p. 176.

50. Cf. Andrewes 1961a, 6.

51. MacDowell 1968, ad loc. supposed that Kallias was the phratry priest. He might have been phratriarch, cf. p. 234.

There seems no good reason in this case to doubt that the relationship between Kallias' genos, the Kerykes, and his phratry was standard and that the phratry contained the Kerykes as a subgroup.[52]

Demosthenes 57

As we saw in chapter 1, this speech contains Euxitheos' appeal against ejection from the deme Halimous. Euxitheos' concern is to demonstrate his father's and his mother's citizenship, and hence his own. At section 23, the subject is the citizenship of his father Thoukritos, to which he calls as witnesses "the phrateres and then the gennetai."[53] There is no reason to suppose that the genos here was anything other than a subgroup of the phratry, as we would normally expect; but this is another case in which it is apparent that the genos possessed a fair degree of institutional independence of the phratry: the phrateres and the gennetai are called to witness separately as distinct groups.[54]

Were Thoukritos and his son Euxitheos gennetai? It seems clear that they were.[55] When Euxitheos calls "the phrateres and then the gennetai" as witnesses to his father's citizenship in section 23, we naturally suppose that these are fellow members of Thoukritos' own genos, as they are fellow members of his phratry. We can draw a similar inference at section 24, where Euxitheos, summing up this passage, claims that the jury had heard the evidence, as was appropriate, "of relations and phrateres and demesmen and gennetai"; and also later in the same section, where he implies that his father, and he himself "had been scrutinized in as many groups as each of you, I mean by phrateres, relations, demesmen, gennetai. . . ."[56] Explicit confirmation of Thoukritos' genos membership,

---

52. It is conceivable (no more) that this phratry was Thymaitis. See p. 327.

53. κάλει δή μοι καὶ τοὺς φράτερας, ἔπειτα τοὺς γεννήτας.

54. The notable fact that Euxitheos calls his demesmen rather than his phrateres to bear witness to his phratriarchy suggests that this phratry may have overlapped closely with the deme Halimous in the same way as the phratric group Dekeleieis did with the deme Dekeleia, cf. p. 109 with n. 52.

55. If one of them was, we can safely assume that the other was also. In fact the evidence is clear enough for both of them individually.

56. εἰ δ᾽ ἐν ἅπασιν, ὅσοισπερ ἕκαστος ὑμῶν, ἐξητασμένος φαίνεται καὶ ζῶν ὁ πατὴρ καὶ νῦν ἐγώ, λέγω φράτερσι, συγγενέσι, δημόταις, γεννήταις, πῶς ἔνεστιν ἢ πῶς δυνατὸν τούτους ἅπαντας μὴ μετ᾽ ἀληθείας ὑπάρχοντας κατεσκευάσθαι; Andrewes 1961a, 7, is tempted by the view of Wilamowitz 1893, 272, that, since not all the jury would have been gennetai (cf. n. 12), the inclusion of the genos in this list is another indication that the genos could examine nonmembers on entry to the phratry.

if it were needed, comes in section 25, where Euxitheos is arguing that Thoukritos must indeed have been related to those he claims are his relatives: "if he were not related to any of them, they would surely not have given him money and allowed him to be a member of (have a share in) the genos."[57] And then, in section 28, we learn that when Euxitheos' brothers died they were buried at the ancestral burial place, which "belongs in common to such as are members of the genos."[58]

It has, however, been suggested that neither Thoukritos nor Euxitheos was a genos member.[59] Euxitheos refers to gennetai of his own and his father's phratry because they would both have been presented to the genos and in some sense scrutinized by it, though they never actually joined it.[60] It is possible, though forced, to take the references to the genos in sections 23 and 24 in this sense, but sections 25 and 28 seem to rule out the interpretation.[61]

The argument in favor of this view is also unconvincing. It is said to be significant that when Euxitheos deals with his own qualifications for citizenship there is no explicit mention of gennetai, merely of phra-

---

That hypothesis, even if it had more to recommend it, is of little help with respect to this passage, however, for, as Andrewes recognizes, there are a large number of cases where entry to a phratry demonstrably depends on a vote by that body with no genos involvement (most clearly Isae. 8.19; Dem. 43.14; cf. other passages listed at n. 12), so not every juryman would have had even this sort of relationship with a genos. It seems best to understand that Euxitheos is speaking in broad terms. In fact, he does not quite imply that every member of the jury was examined in every group he mentions; he says he was examined "in as many groups as each of you"; all he need mean is that the number of different groups was broadly the same; that some of the jury would not have been in gene does not matter.

57. οὐ γὰρ ἂν δήπου, εἴ γε μηδενὶ ἦν οἰκεῖος, χρήματ' αὐτῷ προστιθέντες οὗτοι τοῦ γένους μετεδίδοσαν. Given the mention of genos in the sense of phratry subdivision in chapters 23 and 24, it must also bear the same sense here. To take "τοῦ γένους μετεδίδοσαν" as "gave him a share of family life" would be odd, both conceptually and in its expression in Greek. To take it as "giving a share in the genos" in the sense that this was the genos that had in some way scrutinized him and in whose rites of Apollo Patroos he in some way shared but to which he did not belong (see further below for this interpretation), would be very forced Greek and intolerable in context. If the relatives he is talking about here were in a position to "give him a share in" the genos they can only have been members of it, and if these relations were members, Thoukritos would have been also. This crucial passage is not mentioned by Andrewes at 1961a, 6–8.

58. ἔθαψε τούτους (sc. his four brothers) εἰς τὰ πατρῷα μνήματα, ὧν ὅσοιπέρ εἰσιν τοῦ γένους κοινωνοῦσιν. For the same reason as that given in the previous note the genos here must be the genos/kome.

59. Andrewes 1961a, 6–8.

60. Andrewes 1961a, 7.

61. See above, notes 57, 58.

teres and demotai. In fact, at section 54, Euxitheos claims that he had been introduced "to the phrateres, to the sacred things of Apollo Patroos and to the other sacred things."[62] Now, by introduction "to the sacred things of Apollo Patroos" Euxitheos probably means to imply introduction to the genos; in section 67, the witnesses to Thoukritos' citizenship include gennetai who are described as "gennetai of Apollo Patroos and Zeus Herkeios."[63] Moreover, Euxitheos had implied earlier in the speech, at section 24, that he as well as his father had been scrutinized in the genos, as they had been in deme and phratry.[64]

Even if Euxitheos were not referring again to entry into the genos at section 54, however, his failure to mention it would be readily explicable. As we saw in chapter 1, membership in phratry and deme was especially connected with citizenship, and it is his citizenship that Euxitheos is trying to demonstrate. Genos membership might indicate citizenship; all members were citizens. But it was not essential; not all citizens were members. Moreover, Euxitheos says he was introduced to the phrateres, and this almost certainly involved, under the law of Philochoros fr. 35, initial introduction to the genos followed by automatic introduction to the phratry. Of this process, introduction to the phratry, though rendered automatic by the law of Philochoros fr. 35, was the more significant regarding qualification as a citizen.

There is, therefore, nothing in the text of Demosthenes to support the view that Euxitheos and Thoukritos were not genos members, but were only scrutinized by a genos on entry to a phratry. In fact, this view seems ruled out by explicit evidence to the contrary.[65]

---

62. ἀλλὰ παιδίον ὄντα μ' εὐθέως ἦγον, εἰς τοὺς φράτερας, εἰς Ἀπόλλωνος πατρῴου [ἦγον], εἰς τἄλλ' ἱερά. Cf. 46: τὰ προσήκοντα πάντ' ἐπιδείξω μάρτυρας παρεχόμενος, ὡς εἰσήχθην εἰς τοὺς φράτερας, ὡς ἐνεγράφην εἰς τοὺς δημότας. On the text at 54 (it is possible, though unlikely, that it read γεννήτας rather than ἦγον) see p. 214, n. 50.

63. ... φράτερες, εἶτ' Ἀπόλλωνος πατρῴου καὶ Διὸς ἑρκείου γεννῆται. Cf. previous note. For more on these passages and the cults of Apollo Patroos and Zeus Herkeios, see pp. 211–16.

64. In the passage cited in n. 56.

65. The view is also based on a conception of the genos as an essentially aristocratic institution, which I believe to be mistaken. Andrewes also cites Lex. Patm. (Sakellion 1877, 152) s.v. γεννῆται· Φιλόχορος δὲ ἐν τῇ τετάρτῃ Ἀτθίδος γεννητὰς καὶ ὁμογά-λακτας καλεῖ. οὗτοι δὲ τοὺς ἐγγραφομένους εἰς τοὺς φράτορας διακρίνοντες καὶ δοκιμάζοντες εἰ πολῖταί εἰσιν καὶ ξένοι ἐδέχοντο ἢ ἐπέβαλλον [ἀπέβαλλον Wil.], ὡς Δημοσθένης ἐν τῷ πρὸς Εὐβουλίδην.... It is easy to see how an ancient scholar might draw this conclusion from Philochoros fr. 35, Demosthenes 57, and possibly other speeches (e.g., Dem. 59, Isae. 7) where entry into a phratry is dependent on prior entry into a genos: "those entering a phratry" are indeed frequently portrayed as first being scrutinized

Aeschines 2.147

Aeschines proudly claims that his father Atrometos "belongs by descent to the phratry which shares the same altars as the Eteoboutadai from whom the priestess of Athena Polias comes...."[66] There is no reason to doubt the straightforward interpretation of this passage: the Eteoboutadai were a genos forming a subgroup of Atrometos' phratry.[67] As such, the two groups shared common altars.[68] Aeschines is proud not of the mere fact that the Eteoboutadai were a genos, for many phratries had gene in them, but that the Eteoboutadai were a prestigious genos.

To summarize, gene were normally subgroups of phratries. However, they seem in the fifth and fourth centuries to have been well established groups with independent identities. They may occasionally have been, or may have become, genos/phratries, gene wholly independent of any phratry, although the evidence for this is not conclusive. Not all Athenians were gennetai. There is good evidence for the effects of the law recorded by Philochoros fr. 35, which I argued in chapter 1 should be seen as Periclean, whereby genos members were admitted automatically to their phratry. There is no evidence that a genos exercised control of any sort over the admissions procedure of any phratry or exercised any other power within a phratry.

Orgeones

As with the gene, a full study of the Attic orgeones in their own right would take us beyond the scope of this work.[69] The following brief

---

by gennetai. While it is possible to take τοὺς ἐγγραφομένους εἰς τοὺς φράτορας as all such persons, i.e., including nongennetai, this is not necessary; and it is certainly not necessary to suppose the source of Lex. Patm. had this implication. One might doubt that the author of this entry, or his source, would be aware of whether or not all phrateres were gennetai in the fourth century. If he had read *Ath. Pol.* fr. 3 he might at least be confused on the question.

66. See p. 55.

67. I side with Andrewes 1961a on this point, against Ferguson 1910, 281, and Guarducci 1937, 24–25, who thought the Eteoboutadai were not a phratry subgroup.

68. Cf. the sacrifice of the Salaminioi at Apatouria, above, p. 63 with n. 22 and hints of joint sessions of phratry and genos, above, pp. 67 and 68. That gene may sometimes also have had their own specific altars outside the phratry is likely enough.

69. The fine studies, Ferguson 1944 and 1949, remain fundamental. See also especially Andrewes 1961a, 1–2; Dow and Gill 1965, 103–14; Kearns 1989, 73–77.

characterization will suffice for our purposes. The major perceptible difference between gene and groups of orgeones[70] seems to lie in the role played by religious activities within them. In the gene, while some had important public religious functions, private cults and sacrifices, insofar as they existed at all, were of secondary importance. The role of private religious cult seems to have been much more central to the orgeones, which were essentially groups formed for the purpose of private cultic activity to do with heroes or minor deities.[71]

There are only two pieces of evidence in which these groups are linked directly to phratries: Philochoros fr. 35 tells us that the phratries were obliged to accept orgeones as well as gennetai as members;[72] and the speaker in Isaeus 2, seeking to demonstrate legitimate adoption, claims that he was enrolled in his adoptive father's group of orgeones as he was in his adoptive father's phratry and deme.[73] The role of the orgeones here seems precisely that normally played by the gennetai.[74]

This evidence suggests that, like the gene, groups of orgeones were subgroups of phratries, and that membership in them was hereditary. Status as an orgeon was itself sufficient guarantee of qualification by descent, and phratries therefore did not need to carry out a second examination.[75] Being a member was evidence of legitimate adoption, which, as we have seen, was in a sense a substitute for possession of that qualification.[76] They differed from gene in that they did not have

---

70. There is no collective noun for a group of orgeones, an extreme example of the tendency for corporate groups of this sort to think of themselves as a collection of individuals rather than an abstract entity (cf. the uniform practice of the orators in speaking of introduction to the phrateres rather than to the phratry). For the orgeones, when use of a collective noun could not be avoided, thiasos was used, and orgeones were occasionally referred to as thiasotai (see *IG* 2².1316; Dow and Gill 1965, 111–2, Texts I and II; cf. p. 87–88) or as a koinon (society, e.g., T 10, 30). See also Ferguson 1944, 61–64; and for the probable etymological connection between ὀργεῶνες and ὄργια (religious acts) 1944, 131–32.

71. Cf. Kearns 1989, 73–74, who seems justified in her claim that cult "essentially defined membership" and "was the most important . . . activity which members pursued together as members," but not in her claim that it was the only such activity. The existence of orgeonic decrees, some honorific (see, e.g., Ferguson 1944, A no. 10 [= Dow and Gill 1965]) and financial transactions including *praseis epi lysei* (see T 10, discussed further at p. 194; *IG* 12(8).19 [both = Ferguson 1944 A no. 9]; IG 2².1294 [Ferguson 1944 A no.11]) makes it clear enough that orgeones engaged as such in nonreligious activities.

72. Cf. p. 46.

73. εἰσάγει με εἰς τοὺς φράτερας παρόντων τούτων, καὶ εἰς τοὺς δημότας με ἐγγράφει καὶ εἰς τοὺς ὀργεῶνας. . . . Isae. 2.14, cf. 15–17: . . . τῆς μὲν ποιήσεως ὑμῖν τοὺς φράτερας καὶ τοὺς ὀργεῶνας καὶ τοὺς δημότας παρέξομαι μάρτυρας . . . ; also 44–45.

74. Cf. pp. 61–62.

75. For this interpretation of Philochoros fr. 35, see pp. 46–49.

76. Cf. pp. 38–39. For the hereditary character of an orgeones group see *IG* 2².2355,

their own proper names: they were either called orgeones of the relevant deity or were named after their leaders.[77] They shared with gene, however, a strong identity independent of the phratries; there is nothing in the decree of a group of orgeones to suggest it was a phratry subgroup, nor anything in the decree of a phratry to suggest it contained orgeones within it. Like gene, too, they seem to have been well established by the fourth century.[78]

To judge from the sparsity of our evidence for them as compared with gene, and in particular from the fact that, while several of Demosthenes' and Isaeus' clients were gennetai, only one in the surviving speeches was an orgeon,[79] it seems likely that in the classical period being an orgeon was less common than being a gennete. But the state of our knowledge is not such that we can tell, any more than with gene, whether any particular type or class of person tended to be an orgeon more than any other.[80]

---

a list of sixteen members belonging probably to no more than four families. Kearns 1989, 73, seems wrong in suggesting that membership was not exclusively hereditary, but might simply have been formed "around a core of family membership." If membership were not hereditary, the orgeones would not have been granted the privilege of automatic entry into a phratry, nor would membership be relevant in an adoption case. See also the implication of *IG* 2^2.1361 for the novelty of admission of those other than descendants of members to the orgeones of Bendis; cf. Ferguson 1949, 153–54.

77. For the latter, see T 10, 30.

78. The early evidence for the orgeones, if anything slightly better than that for the gene, is Philochoros fr. 35; Meritt 1942, no. 55, cf. Ferguson 1944 and 1949 (both demonstrating their existence in the mid-fifth century); *Dig.* 47.22.4 (see p. 250). Cf. also Athen. 5.185c–86a, p. 84; Andrewes 1961a, 2, n.7.

79. Cf. n. 12 above.

80. In earlier literature much energy was devoted to discussing to what class of society orgeones belonged. In particular there was an ill-founded theory that orgeones were at one time the commoners, who, in contrast to the privileged gennetai, were granted access to phratries only at some relatively late date (e.g., by Solon or Cleisthenes. For this see Andrewes 1961a, 1, with nn. 1–3) and whose rights were protected by the law of Philochoros fr. 35. Andrewes punctured this flimsy balloon with his persuasive argument that Philochoros fr. 35 does not imply that orgeones were in a different position or status from gennetai at the time of the law to which it pertains was passed, that it implies rather that at that time there were phrateres who were neither orgeones nor gennetai, and that our other evidence for orgeones groups does not suggest that the mass of the people ever belonged to them, cf. p. 47 n. 99. He might have added that *Ath. Pol.* fr. 3, in which all citizens are portrayed as gennetai at the time of Ion, is worthless as evidence on the matter, cf. appendix 2. Unfortunately, however, he replaced this concept of the orgeones, albeit tentatively, with another, equally ill-supported: that they were a "fairly small and relatively obscure upper class minority." Even if analysis of the few known citizen orgeones (not yet carried out to my knowledge) showed this to be the case, it would be impossible to demonstrate that there were not other, less well-off orgeones who, say, could not afford

There is one item of epigraphical evidence in which we may be able to detect a relationship between a particular orgeones group and a particular phratry. From T 10 we learn that, in 367/6, a certain Aeschines of Melite and his group of orgeones made a successful claim against the property of a certain Theosebes on the basis of a *prasis epi lysei*[81] taken out with them by Theosebes' father. The phratry Mendontidai are recorded as having made a similar claim. I argue in appendix 1 that it would be surprising if Theosebes and his father had taken out a loan with a phratry of which they were not members, and with an orgeones group which was not in the same phratry as themselves. It would seem, therefore, that Aeschines' orgeones were members of the phratry Medontidai. Whether Theosebes and his father were also orgeones we do not know.[82]

Finally it should be mentioned that in the later classical period there were also noncitizen orgeones. The earliest of these seem to have been the orgeones of Bendis, which had a Thracian connection and from the inaugural festivities of which Socrates is portrayed as returning at the beginning of the *Republic*.[83]

Phratry Subgroups Other than Gene and Groups of Orgeones

In addition to the gene and groups of orgeones, well established institutions with a formal, centrally recognized status, a number of other phratry subgroups is attested. They are by and large more elusive; they

---

the considerable expense of stone inscriptions or of a Demosthenes or an Isaeus and are therefore not known to us; and it would certainly be perilous to draw any conclusions about the status of orgeones in the archaic period on the basis of classical evidence, which is all that we have.

81. For the nature of the transaction, see pp. 196–97.

82. See p. 319 and cf. pp. 196–97.

83. On these see especially Ferguson 1944 and 1949. For the difficult question of the date of introduction of the first noncitizen orgeones connected with this cult, see especially Ferguson 1949, 152–57. Ferguson 1944 identified 12 epigraphically attested groups of citizen orgeones (his class A) and 16 including noncitizens (his class B). Cf. also Dow and Gill 1965. The deities of the noncitizen groups tend to be imported and, as Ferguson recognized, it is unlikely to be coincidental that all the evidence pertaining to them comes from the Peiraeus. Ferguson's attribution of evidence to the two categories is not, however, completely secure in every case, as he himself admits (e.g., his class A no. 12, *IG* 2².2947. Meritt 1942, no. 55 (to be read with Ferguson 1949, 130–31) is notable as evidence for the participation of women in the cultic activities of citizen orgeones groups. Cf. p. 186.

are never mentioned in the orators[84] and apparently lack an identity independent of the phratry. It has been suggested that they were a short-lived attempt at democratization of phratry structure, the work possibly of Pericles, and that the term thiasos was given a technical sense to describe them.[85] Lacking evidence for the exercise of power in a phratry by a genos, we may already be suspicious of this hypothesis; we do not need to posit the existence of democratizing groups if we have no evidence for the prior existence of undemocratic ones. A consideration of the corpus of evidence for phratry subgroups other than gene and groups of oregones confirms these doubts.

Oikos

We have just one piece of evidence for a phratric oikos, the House of the Dekeleieis of T 3.[86] The nature of the group is controversial. In the next chapter I argue that it was a phratry subgroup of a type that, as the uniqueness of the term used to describe it suggests, has no parallel in our evidence, but that shows some similarity to the genos.

Unnamed Phratry Subdivisions

We have two inscriptions attesting groups of phrateres where the groups are designated by no collective noun.

The first, T 21, from the earlier fourth century, is a boundary marker of a property subject to a *prasis epi lysei* listing five creditors, namely an individual, Kephisodoros of Leukonoion, and four groups: the Glaukidai, the Epikleidai, the "phrateres with Eratostratos of Anaphlystos," and the "phrateres with Nikon of Anaphlystos." Because, though not impossible, it would be unexpected for loans to be taken out by a borrower with groups of phrateres who belonged to a phratry other than his own,[87] a good case can be made for considering that all these groups, and probably Kephisodoros too, were members of the same phratry. The Glaukidai and Epikleidai would therefore be gene, the other two groups of phrateres of another sort, all within the same phratry.

---

84. Isae. 9.30 is a possible but unlikely exception. See pp. 89–90 below.

85. See Andrewes 1961a, 9–15. Ferguson 1944, 67, posited rather a Cleisthenic origin. Most subsequent writers have followed Andrewes, see, e.g., Hedrick 1990, 57–58.

86. T 3, 32–33 and 41–42. For texts, translations and further discussion of this and the other phratry inscriptions mentioned below, see appendix 1.

87. Argued more fully at pp. 197–98.

Might these two groups have been whole phratries? The common demotic of Nikon and Eratostratos hints not,[88] and furthermore such a reference to a whole phratry would be unparalleled.[89] We would expect them to be referred to by the name of the group, as would be the case if these phrateres were gennetai or orgeones.[90] It seems most likely, therefore, that these are groups within a single phratry, not gene or groups of orgeones, named by reference to their leader.[91] It is impossible to say whether they were formed ad hoc for the purpose of the *prasis* or whether they had a more permanent existence.

The second inscription, T 18[92], also from the early fourth century, is a list of twenty names introduced by a superscription to Zeus Phratrios and Athena Phratria followed by the heading "these are the phrateres" (*Hoide phrateres*). The text is complete, and vertically down the right-hand side runs the statement that Sosippos son of Sosipolis had the list inscribed. Sosippos also appears in the list itself.

It is impossible to determine whether the names on the list represent a full phratry or a subgroup.[93] It would help if we knew the purpose of the inscription, but that is obscure. Perhaps it should be seen in the context of the measures to tighten up citizenship controls following the Peloponnesian War. In that case, this may be intended as an authoritative list of genuine phratry members, possibly following a scrutiny of some sort. Such a scrutiny may have been carried out, however, by a subgroup or a whole phratry.[94] There are also other possible explanations of the list's purpose. This might, for example, be a newly formed subgroup listing its original members.[95]

88. This is not a decisive point. For demes containing members of more than one phratry, see map on p. 352.

89. The use of the name of the leader in the description of a group of this sort is common enough, but a phratry tends to be named, or at least described as such, cf. p. 101. The contrast with two named groups on the stone strengthens the point.

90. And we might in that case have expected them to be referred to as "gennetai with . . ." or "orgeones with . . . ," rather than "phrateres with. . . ."

91. Recognized first by von Premerstein 1910, 113–17 and Ferguson 1910, 267, and generally accepted subsequently. Cf. the case of the Totteidai on Chios, subdivided into Δημογενίδαι, Θρακίδαι, οἱ Τηλάγρου, οἱ Ἕρμιος and οἱ Διονυσοδώρου καὶ Ποσειδίππου. Forrest 1960, 172–89.

92. Discussed most recently by Flower 1985 and Hedrick 1989.

93. Flower 1985 revived the view of Körte 1902 that this is a whole phratry. Hedrick 1989 argued the more usual view that it is a subgroup, for which see also von Premerstein 1910, 113; Ferguson 1910, 266–67 and 284; Hignett 1952, 60; Andrewes 1961a, 11.

94. I believe that T 3 is the record of a subgroup taking action of a similar kind in the same circumstances; see next chapter. On the purpose of T 18 see further p. 336.

95. It is unlikely that the list was simply a phratry register. Such registers would probably

The small number of members may at first suggest a subgroup. We saw in the Introduction that little can be said with confidence about the average size of a phratry, but we can say that a twenty-man phratry would be surprisingly small. It would not, however, be an impossibility, particularly in the wake of the loss of manpower in the Peloponnesian War. Loss of men in the war may also explain the odd fact that only two generations are represented on the list. It is also noteworthy that the list takes up less than half the stone. Perhaps it was intended to be continued, or a generation may be absent because it was listed on a previous stone, of which this is a continuation. The size of the list is not therefore of help in determining whether the list constitutes a whole phratry or a subgroup.[96]

Other features of the inscription are equally uninformative on the point. If this were a whole phratry, we might normally have expected it to have been named. But if the list was set up in the phratry sanctuary, and especially if its purpose was essentially internal, e.g., following a scrutiny of members, this may have been thought unnecessary.[97] For the same reason, there is also no ground to suppose that a subgroup would necessarily have identified itself explicitly as such; especially in view of the use of the description, "the phrateres with X," attested in T 21. T 18 may be "the phrateres with Sosippos." The introductory clause, "these are (the) phrateres," is also not indicative one way or the other;[98]

---

not have been kept on stone, which would have been expensive and inconvenient when it came to erasing deceased members. It is more likely that, on this point, the state described in Plato's *Laws* followed current Athenian practice, and that the register was kept on a whitened board (6.785a). Cf. p. 175; Hedrick 1989, 133. Körte 1902, 582–89 suggested the link with the postwar citizenship measures, followed by Hedrick 1989, 133. For other evidence for this, see pp. 48–49 with n. 104.

96. The size and number of phratries in classical Athens is discussed at pp. 18–20.

97. Cf. Körte 1902, 583; Flower 1985, 233. Hedrick 1989, 129, agrees with Flower and Körte that the inscription would have been set up in a phratry sanctuary dedicated to Zeus Phratrios and Athena Phratria. This is probable but not necessary. In T 3 there is a superscription to Zeus Phratrios; the decrees themselves were set up "before the altar at Dekeleia" (66–67), but the phrateres passing the decrees, the Dekeleieis, seem also to have made use of a temple of Leto as a place for posting notices (125). T 5 (of the Dyaleis) appears to have been set up on the land the rental arrangements for which are contained in the decree (55–57). The two decrees T 19 and T 20 were apparently set up "in front of the phratrion"; see notes thereto in appendix 1 and p. 194.

98. Flower 1985 thought οἴδε + nominative plural could only introduce "the entire category of what it refers to," i.e., in this case the whole phratry. Hedrick in 1989, 130, is rightly skeptical. The force may simply be, "these are the true phrateres as opposed to those whom we have just rejected in a scrutiny," with no implication as to whether it was a whole phratry or a subgroup that had carried out the scrutiny.

neither is the fact that many of the persons on the stone were closely related,[99] nor the superscription to Zeus Phratios and Athena Phratria.[100] All of these features would be consistent with the lists being a whole phratry or a subgroup.

T 18 was found in Attica at a place called Kapsospiti, between Liopesi, site of the ancient deme Paiania, and the foothills of Hymettos. There is a second phratry inscription associated with Paiania, T 17, a decree honoring two related persons, Arrheneides (son of Callikles?) and Eu[ktemon?] son of Arrheneides, for their services in relation to a temple, including, it seems, the fulfillment of some office and the contribution of 200 drachmas. The inscription probably dates to about 305–280, but the family of Arrheneides can be traced back to the fifth century, and no member of it appears on T 18.[101] This does not help us, however, on the question of whether or not T 18 is a whole phratry. If it is a subgroup, the absence of Arrheneides' ancestors presents no problem; if a whole phratry, there is no difficulty in explaining their absence on the grounds that there was more than one phratry in the Paiania area.[102]

So far, then, we have one probable and one possible case of subgroups that are not described in our evidence by a name or collective noun. What of thiasoi?

Thiasoi?

The word "thiasos"[103] can be used to refer to a band or group of revellers, impromptu or otherwise; a more organized cultic association of citizens or noncitizens; or, more generally, to any sort of group or association.[104]

---

99. The twenty names belonged to at most eight families. For stemmata, see Hedrick 1989, 132.

100. Hedrick 1989 rightly pointed out, against Flower 1985, that there is no evidence that groups within phratries, other than gene and orgeones groups, worshipped gods apart from those of the whole phratry. The superscription is therefore consistent with the list's being of such a group, or of a whole phratry.

101. See Davies 1971 no. 2254; Hedrick 1989, 133–35; and the notes to T 17.

102. It would not be surprising if there were more than one phratry associated with Paiania, which had the relatively large Bouleutic quota of twelve, split between Upper Paiania (1) and Lower Paiania (11).

103. See especially Poland 1909; 16–22; Ferguson 1910, 257–84; Busolt-Swoboda 1920–26, 252–53; Guarducci 1937, 44–46; Ferguson 1944, 66–68, 70 n. 12, ap.2; Hignett 1952, 47, 56, 61–67, 114; Andrewes 1961a, 9–12; Dow and Gill 1965, 103–14.

104. Harp., Suid. s.v. θίασος· θίασός ἐστι τὸ ἀθροιζόμενον πλῆθος ἐπὶ τελετῇ καὶ

There are eight possible attestations of thiasoi within phratries, all of them in some way problematic.

T 3, Decrees of Demotionidai/Dekeleieis, First Half Fourth Century

On the basis of the first of the decrees of T 3, passed in 396/5, we can determine that they were passed by a group of phrateres known as the House of the Dekeleieis, which I argue in chapter 3 was a subgroup of the phratry Demotionidai. From the second decree, passed some time later, it is apparent that the Dekeleieis were subdivided into groups called thiasoi, membership in which, as we should expect, appears to have been hereditary (lines 76–78, 105). We do not know how many thiasoi there were, but it was envisaged that a thiasos could have had fewer than three members, possibly suggesting depletion during the Peloponnesian War. In any case, there is an apparent implication that these subgroups had existed for some time before 396/5. This is certainly a case where thiasoi are subgroups within a phratry, but subgroups of what may itself be a phratry subgroup.

T 35, First Half Fourth Century

This inscription, which is not complete, consists of a list of names, after some of which are figures possibly representing monetary contributions to a fund. The list is divided into thiasoi. There are remains of six groups on the stone, of which three are complete including the headings "thiasos of Hagnotheos," "thiasos of Antiphanes," and "thiasos of Diogenes." It has been generally agreed that this is a phratry list.[105] The argument is broadly as follows. The only other case where a group of thiasoi is attested is in the phratry of T 3. There is thus a *prima facie* case that

---

τιμῇ θεῶν. Cf. Hesych. s. v. θίασος· χόρου σύστασις. θιασῶται· χορευταί. For revellers see, e.g., Aristophanes *Frogs* 156; Euripides *Bacchae* 680; Demosthenes reproaches Aeschines for this sort of activity in thiasoi at 18.260. For more organized cultic thiasoi see most of *IG* 2².2343–61—attested mostly from the end of the fourth century and mostly open to foreigners and women (see also n. 142). For use to refer to a group or association more generally: Euripides *Iph. A.* 1059 (centaurs); Aristophanes *Thesm.* 41 (muses); Euripides *Phoen.* 796 (warriors); *Digest* 47.22.4 (see p. 87, pirates or traders). The word could also be used to refer to a group of orgeones (see n. 70).

105. First suggested by de Sanctis 1912, 69; followed by, e.g., Poland 1909, 18; Ferguson 1910, 271; von Premerstein 1910, 110; Andrewes 1961a, 9–10; Hedrick 1990, 57.

these thiasoi are also phratry subdivisions. It is unlikely that any institution other than a phratry would have been subdivided in this way. Moreover, there is a good deal of interrelation between members, as we should expect in phratry subdivisions, and the identification of the thiasoi by a member's name is paralleled in the references to groups of phrateres in T 21 (see, pp. 78–79).

The case, however, is not secure. The *prima facie* argument on the basis of T 3 is severely weakened if we take the thiasoi in that inscription as subdivisions of the subgroup, the House of the Dekeleieis, not of the whole phratry. There are, in fact, other references to thiasoi in the plural in literary and epigraphic texts that suggest that aggregates of thiasoi may not have been unusual.[106] There may well, for example, have been an association of thiasoi of Herakles scattered about Attica.[107] Interrelation of members may occur in subdivisions within other sorts of groups, such as a genos or a group of orgeones, a deme, an oikos, or a cult group of some sort, either formal or informal. T 21 need not imply that any group referred to by the name of one of its members must be a phratry subdivision.[108]

Doubts are perhaps strengthened by two further curiosities. First, there is on the list someone referred to as the *pais* (boy or child) of Euphronios (col. 2. 131). The form of nomenclature on this inscription is irregular: patronymic and demotic are added only inconsistently, and this precludes firm conclusions about such a stray form of reference. The stone has not been cut with great care. Nevertheless, this form is unique on the inscription and is strongly suggestive that the pais of Euphronios was of a different status from the rest. There are three possibilities: a child of Euphronios that was a minor and/or an unmarried female; or a slave.[109] We would not expect any of these three to be listed in a phratric thiasos, and there is no parallel. One thinks rather of the women and foreigners that appear in nonphratric thiasoi.[110] On

---

106. See Ferguson 1910, 258 and n. 1; 1944, 70–71, n. 12. The clearest case of thiasos in the plural implying an association of thiasoi is Isae. 9.30, though the MSS text giving this sense has been unnecessarily doubted (see below, p. 89). Other possible cases: Dem. 18.260; *IG* 2².1177; Euthias, *Phryn.* (Sauppe *Fr. Or. Gr.* 2.320); Harp., Suid. s. v. θίασος.

107. See p. 89.

108. Note for example the reference to a group of orgeones by their leader at T 10, 30.

109. Euphronios himself does not appear, but two sons do (col. 2.11, 30 and 40). The Εὐφρονίο παῖς is clearly in a different category from these. For the range of possible meanings of παῖς, which can signify descent (son or daughter), age (young person) or condition (slave), see *LSJ*.

110. See n. 142. I cannot agree with Ferguson 1910, 272, that "the appearance of a

the other hand, it is not impossible. Both women and minors came within the purview of a phratry,[111] even if they could not strictly be described as members. Although the same could not be said of slaves, it is in any case not clear, even if these thiasoi are phratry subdivisions, that this need be a full list of phratry members. It seems rather to be a list of contributors. In a case where the pais of Euphronios made a contribution on his or her own behalf, whether he or she was a slave of Euphronios or a young son or daughter, and where this family belonged to a thiasos within a phratry, it is possible that he or she may have been entered on the list in this manner.

The second curiosity concerns two of the members of Diogenes' thiasos, Stratophon and Demon of Agryle, who, as already remarked, are also attested as members of the genos Salaminioi.[112] We saw in section two that we cannot be certain that the Salaminioi were a phratry subgroup; they may have been wholly independent of any phratry. In the latter case, T 35 cannot be a phratry list. In the former, we can accept T 35 as a phratry list and the Salaminioi as a subgroup on the hypothesis that the other attested Salaminioi—three Acharnians, two Boutadai, one Epikephisios, eight from Sounium—were bunched together, as those from Agryle are, on another part of the list, now lost.[113] Or perhaps they simply did not contribute to whatever fund (if it was such) T 35 was set up to record.

Neither of these curiosities constitutes decisive evidence that these were not phratric thiasoi, but they do confirm that the question is better left open.[114]

Hesperia 1947, 63 No. 1, 250s

This fragmentary inscription,[115] consisting of a three-line introductory formula followed by a list of names, is from a dedicatory base. Though

---

παῖς, which is unexampled in the case of the foreign *thiasotae* is sufficient almost of itself to prove that the *thiasi* are the same as those which entered into the phratry of the Demotionidae." It is unexampled in the case of phratric thiasoi and more likely in the nonphratric thiasoi with their more widely drawn membership.

111. See 161–88 for details.

112. T 35, 77, 79. Cf. Ferguson 1938, 3–5, lines 76, 79 with Ferguson's comments 14, 28, n. 7, and Andrewes, 1961a, 10. Cf. pp. 65–66 for further discussion.

113. As suggested by Andrewes 1961a, 10.

114. In the most recent treatment of T 35, Humphreys 1990, it is accepted without discussion as a phratry list. Cf. p. 370.

115. The publication was by M. and E. Levensohn, with assistance from Ferguson. The

it is relatively certain that it involved thiasoi, it is not clear whether or not they were phratric.[116] It can be restored as a dedication to Zeus Phratrios and Athena Phratria by the thiasotai with Epikrates; the form of name would be the same as in T 21 and T 35, above. The thiasos also seems to contain a relatively small number of interrelated men,[117] as we would expect in a phratry subdivision. A group of this size and nature, however, could easily be non-phratric. In alternative restorations suggested by the original editors, the dedicators may be "thiasotai of the Mother of the Gods" and the word above the list of four names on the left side restored as "Athena" may instead be the heading "treasurers."[118] Four treasurers may seem an unduly large number, but there is a tempting parallel in *IG* 2².2941, where there are three; and the Mother of the Gods is simply the most suitable of a number of cult deities beginning with *m*.[119] Moreover, a certain Agathon son of Agathokles is praised in a contemporary decree of non-phratric orgeones.[120] These orgeones call themselves thiasotai in the crowns of the decree, and since both Agathon (twice) and Agathokles appear on this inscription it is attractive to connect them.[121] So again we can identify these thiasotai as only possibly phratric.

---

inscription is dated to the archonship of Antimachos (3), which was probably in the 250s (Habicht 1979, 128–33 and 144–45).

116. The first three lines as restored by the editors read [τὸ ἄγαλμα ? Ἐπι]κράτη[ς ἀνέθηκεν ὑπὲρ]/ [τῶν θια]σωτῶν τῶν μ[εθ᾽ ἑαυτοῦ Διὶ καὶ]/ [᾽Αθην?]ᾶι ν ἐπ᾽ ᾽Αντιμάχο[υ ἄρχοντος]/... list of names, probably in three columns, of which the third is missing, follows. θια]σωτῶν seems secure enough; τῶν μ[εθ᾽ ἑαυτοῦ Διὶ καὶ]/ [᾽Αθην?]ᾶι is less so.

117. Probably, as the editors suggested, about 13, though it is not certain how many names were in the assumed third, right-hand column of the list. The interrelation is inferred from the similarity of the names, in particular two Agathons (7 and 8) and one Agathokles (11).

118. Lines 2–3 would then read, θια]σωτῶν τῶν Μ[ητρὸς θεῶν]/ [ταμί]αι.

119. See further M. and E. Levensohn 1947.

120. *IG* 2².1316. Cf. also τὴν θεόν in 17 of that inscription and M. and E. Levensohn's alternative restoration of their inscription to involve thiasotai of the Mother of the Gods. It is also tempting to connect it with *IG* 2².2348, a short list, plausibly reconstructed by Kirchner (first ed. E. Pottier 1878, 417) as of thiasotai, with mention in the heading of a γραμματεύς and possibly also of a ταμίας. The γραμματεύς is an Agathon, and both he and an Agathokles also appear on the list. Kirchner dated this list, however, by letter forms, to the end of the fourth century. If this pertains to the same group as our dedicatory base, whether or not at an earlier stage in its history, it would be another argument that the thiasos on that base was not phratric, since the list contains a woman (Σωτηρίς, 7).

121. Cf. n. 70.

IG 2².2720 (= Finley 1952 No. 43),
Fifth–Early Fourth Century

This is a marker of land subject to a *prasis epi lysei* in which the creditors are named as thiasotai but the interpretation of the text following that word in the dative is uncertain. It is possible that the thiasotai are described as "of Is..." (the name of a man), though the reading is very insecure.[122] Even if it is correct, there would be no sure implication that the thiasos was phratric; there is no reason why a nonphratric thiasos might not also have called itself after its leader.[123]

Athenaeus *Deip.* 5.185c–186a, Date of Reference Uncertain
(Late Fourth Century ?)

The lawgivers, making provision for the dinners we have today, established the phyle and deme dinners, and moreover for the thiasoi the phratric dinners, and again those known as the orgeonic.[124]

Thiasoi provided with phratric and possibly orgeonic[125] dinners by the lawgivers (*nomothetai*) in the same context as dinners provided for phylai and demes may certainly be phratry subdivisions;[126] but the sense may

---

122. Poland 1909, 19, n. 2, building on a suggestion of Hiller, read ὅρος χωρίο πεπραμένο ἐπὶ λύσει θιασώταις Ἰσ<ο>δήμο το<ῦ> Ἡ[-. But with Ἰσ<ο>δήμο we should expect τὸ rather than τοῦ (cf. χωρίο πεπραμένο earlier in the text), and it is difficult not to think that the final H, which would therefore be standing on its own, represents the amount of the *prasis,* which is generally specified at the end of a marker of this sort (cf. the other examples at Finley 1952, 122–46). Further reconstruction must be uncertain without re-examination of the stone, but a possibility may be to take ΔΗΜΟΤΟ as the genitive of δημότης and ΙΣ as the start of a name in the genitive, possibly of a deity (i.e., "the thiasotai of the deme deity Is...," or perhaps rather "of the Cult of Is... as practiced in this deme?" For the cult of Isis at Athens, see most recently Simms 1989. Whether it was established this early is controversial, but *IG* 2².1927, 148–50 and Ar. *Birds* 1296 with Σ suggest this is possible) or of a man (i.e., "the thiasotai of Is... of this deme").

123. E.g., T 35 above, p. 82. Cf. Andrewes 1961a, 11.

124. τῶν δὲ νῦν δείπνων προνοοῦντες οἱ νομοθέται τά τε φυλετικὰ δεῖπνα καὶ τὰ δημοτικὰ προσέταξαν, ἔτι δὲ τοὺς θιάσους καὶ τὰ φρατρικὰ καὶ πάλιν <τὰ> ὀργεωνικὰ λεγόμενα. It is not clear whether the sense is that the orgeonic dinners are also for the thiasoi along with the phratric, or whether they are a separate item in the list, like τὰ φυλετικὰ and τὰ δημοτικά.

125. See previous note.

126. Cf. Andrewes 1961a, 10. The mix of institutions mentioned makes it clear that Athenaeus has Attica in mind.

also simply be "and (even) for the cultic associations they provided for phratry dinners...," i.e., the phratry, and perhaps the orgeones, may simply be an example of a thiasos in the general sense of a group that has some religious purpose.[127] So again this can only be classed as a possible reference to thiasoi within a phratry.

Digest 47.22.4 (= Ruschenbusch 1966, f. 76a), Uncertain Date

> But if a deme or phrateres or orgeones of heroes or "sailors" [on alternative readings, "gennetai" or "naukraries"] or members of dining clubs or burial associations or thiasotai whose purpose is trade or piracy regulate their own affairs, those regulations are to be valid so long as they are not overridden by decrees of the People.[128]

Whenever we date the reference to thiasotai in this law,[129] they probably have nothing to do with phratries; they are best understood simply as members of companies of pirates or traders.

Dow and Gill 1965, Text I, Probably Fourth Century after 316/5[130]

> ... The decree shall be inscribed and set up in the thiasos so that all the other orgeones may see it....

---

127. Cf. pp. 81–82 for the senses of "thiasos." A classical Athenian perhaps would not have been likely to characterize a phratry as a thiasos (with one conceivable exception, see n. 88, there is no parallel; apart from a certain inappropriateness, there might have been confusion with such thiasoi as there were within phratries) but it is quite possible that Athenaeus, in the third century A.D., might have done so. It is, of course, not clear how far A. was quoting directly here, or the extent to which his source was reliable. Nor, if reliably reported, can the action of the nomothetai be dated with any confidence, though the mention of demes suggests it should be post-Cleisthenic, and if the Athenian officers known technically by that term are intended, a date after 400/399 is more likely than one before. (See Hansen 1987, 98 with n. 623, and other bibliography on the nomothetai cited there, to which should be added Hignett 1952, 299–305). This may have been a piece of Lykourgan revivalism (cf. p. 53, n. 119; p. 154, n. 75).

128. For the text, see p. 250, n. 27.

129. This part at least of the text may be genuinely Solonian, cf. p. 251, n. 27.

130. This is Dow and Gill's publication of the earlier text, an honorific decree, to be found on the palimpsest on which the later text is *IG* 2².1246. For the date see their 104. At lines 3–4 their restored text, from the inscription formula, reads ... ἀναγράψαι δὲ τὸ δόγμα τόδε καὶ στῆσαι]/ ἐν τῶι θιάσωι ὅπω[ς ἄν καὶ πάντες οἱ ἄλλοι ὀργεῶνες ὁρῶσιν τοῦτο κτλ. ἐν τῶι θιάσωι clearly means "in the group" (cf. Dow and Gill 1965, 112), an unusual, but not problematic, usage.

Here we have a group of orgeones describing themselves as a thiasos. Unfortunately, it is not clear whether they were citizen or noncitizen orgeones.[131] If noncitizen, the case is uninformative for our purposes. If citizen orgeones, it is possible that they also formed a subgroup known as a thiasos within a phratry, but it is perhaps more natural to take thiasos here in the simple sense: the decree is to be set up "in the group"; the orgeones would have formed a phratry subgroup as orgeones, but not otherwise.

The Etionidai and Heraklean Thiasoi

(α) *SEG* 10.330, a dedicatory base, early to mid-fifth century.

... kle ... the thiasos of the Etionidai set it up.[132]

Who are the Etionidai? The name in *-idai* implies they should be a phratry, a genos, or a family organization of a looser type.[133] We can only guess what sort of thiasos they formed. If they were a loose family-type organization, they may have been a thiasos of any type. If they were a genos in the sense of phratry subgroup, we would normally expect them to be described as such; but, as we have seen, it was possible for both citizen and noncitizen orgeones to describe themselves as thiasoi.[134] It would make sense for a citizen genos to do the same. Alternatively, the Etionidai, like possibly the citizen orgeones/thiasotai, as well as being a genos may also have been one of a number of subgroups of a phratry, all known as thiasoi.[135] We have no classical example of a phratry described as a thiasos; but given the range of groups that could be described by the term, that possibility cannot be ruled out.[136]

There is, however, also the possibility that, whether phratry or genos of any type, the Etionidai were a Heraklean thiasos. We have two other firm references[137] to Heraklean thiasoi:

---

131. It was placed tentatively in Class A (citizen orgeones) by Ferguson 1944, 93 (no. 10).

132. -]ε[--]μ[--]ο[--]κλεο[ς]/ [--h]ίδρυε ὁ θίασος ['E]τιονιδôν.

133. For the different types of gene, see pp. 59–60.

134. See previous item and n. 70.

135. As suggested by Guarducci 1935, 337, (cf. 1937, 45, 52, 90).

136. Cf. n. 127 above for another possible case.

137. Aristophanes' *Daitaleis* also seems to have been set in a temple of Herakles and to have involved thiasotai. See e.g. Suid. s.v. δαιταλεῖς. Cf. also Harp., Suid. s.v. Ἡράκλεια; Athen. 6.260b; 14.614d.

(β) Isaeus 9.30

My father took Astyphilos as a child with him to religious ceremonies everywhere, as he did me; and he introduced him to the Heraklean thiasoi so that he might take part in their activities. The thiasotai themselves will bear witness to this for you.[138]

(γ) *IG* 2².2343, early fourth century. A dedication by a priest and thiasotai of Herakles with fifteen names.

As Ferguson suggested,[139] Heraklean thiasoi were probably associations connected with the various shrines of Herakles scattered about Attica. The use of the plural thiasoi in the Isaeus passage suggests that there were a number of them associated with one another, possibly with some sort of collective membership.

The basis for supposing the Etionidai to be a thiasos of Herakles is the restoration of "... kle-..." in line 1 of *SEG* 10.330 to give a reference to Herakles or a Herakleion, a sanctuary of Herakles. The restoration is very insecure, however, and others are possible.[140] If the Etionidai did form a Heraklean thiasos, it is very unlikely that it was also a phratry subgroup; it is clear enough that Astyphilos was not introduced to these thiasoi as a stage of introduction to a phratry.[141] If the Etionidai did

138. Εἰς τοίνυν τὰ ἱερὰ ὁ πατὴρ ὁ ἐμὸς τὸν Ἀστύφιλον παῖδα ἦγε μεθ᾽ ἑαυτοῦ ὥσπερ καὶ ἐμὲ πανταχῇ· καὶ εἰς τοὺς θιάσους τοὺς Ἡρακλέους ἐκεῖνον [αὐτὸν] εἰσήγαγεν ἵνα μετέχοι τῆς κοινωνίας. αὐτοὶ δ᾽ ὑμῖν οἱ θιασῶται μαρτυρήσουσιν. Ferguson 1944, 70–71, n. 12, defended the MS reading τοὺς θιάσους against editorial emendations, θιασώτας or θίασον (cf. Wyse 1904 ad loc.), rightly in my view (pace Andrewes, 1961a, 11, n. 36). "He introduced him to the Heraklean thiasoi" is perfectly acceptable in English, as in Greek, implying introduction to one of a group of thiasoi. It does look as though there may have been several Heraklean thiasoi (in addition to these three possible references see also previous note) and there are other contexts where θίασος in the plural may imply associations of θίασοι (cf. n. 106).

139. 1944, 71, n. 12.

140. Palaios 1929 restored κλεο in line 1 as [Ἑρα]κλέος, Meritt ap. Ferguson 1944, 134, as [Ἑρα]κλείο[?ι]. Ferguson 1944, ap. 2, 133–34, restored the whole to read, [τὸν βομὸν ἐν τ]ô[ι hερα]κλείο[ι]/ [καθ]ίδρυε ὁ θίασος [Ἐ]τιονιδôν. κλεο or κλείο could of course, however, derive from some name other than Herakles, and in fact Dow quoted at Ferguson, loc. cit. read κλετο.

141. The purpose of the introduction is described simply as ἵνα μετέχοι τῆς κοινωνίας. It is not mentioned as evidence of legitimacy, as membership of gene and orgeones groups is elsewhere in the orators, but of the way the speaker's father treated Astyphilos as his own son, and as the speaker's brother, by involving them together in religious activities. (Cf. Andrewes 1961a, 11). These Heraklean thiasoi sound much more like the thiasoi of other cults which were clearly not phratry subdivisions in that foreigners and women were members (see next note). Earlier scholars (see Kirchner ad loc.) seem therefore to have been wrong to see the thiasos of *IG* 2².2343 as phratric.

not form a Heraklean thiasos, it is possible that they were a genos of some sort that also formed a thiasos within a phratry, but it is by no means the only possibility.

There are many other references to thiasoi on inscriptions and in literary texts, but we have now discussed all those that may be phratry subdivisions.[142] Were there, then, phratry subdivisions, thiasoi in a special sense, short-lived innovations of the late fifth century designed as a means of democratizing the phratries? I doubt it.

First, it is at least possible that we have a genos in the fifth century (in *SEG* 10.330) and a group of citizen orgeones in the late fourth (in Dow and Gill 1965 I) that describe themselves as thiasoi, but using the term in its general sense. Given that these groups were, as genos and group of orgeones, phratry subgroups, such usage would, I suggest, be inconsistent with the existence of a technical meaning of the term thiasos that referred to a particular sort of phratry subgroup.

Second, on the basis of this evidence it is not clear that the term thiasos was used in any special sense at all. We have only one certain case in which groups are explicitly termed thiasoi within a phratry, but they are designated thiasoi as subdivisions of the House of the Dekeleieis. Of the seven other possible cases, excluding the *Digest* passage, where the term may be used in this sense, not one is secure. In contrast, it is remarkable that in T 21, the most securely attested case of a phratry subgroup other than genos or orgeones group after the thiasoi of T 3, and in the two others where such groups may very possibly be attested— T 3, the House of the Dekeleieis, and T 18—the term thiasos is not

---

142. The decisive factor that rules out the cultic thiasoi, attested mostly from the end of the fourth century, as phratry subdivisions is that they included foreigners (e.g., *IG* 2².1263, 1271, 1273, 2346) and women (e.g., *IG* 2².2347, 2348). The status of women in phratries is discussed at pp. 178–88. Though there seems to have been some variation in the extent to which they were taken account of in the phratries, it is clear enough that they were not as a rule regarded as full phratry members and would not therefore be mentioned in a list of phratric thiasos members passing a decree, as in *IG* 2².2347. Other thiasos inscriptions which do not mention foreign or female members tend to fit the pattern of those that do, both in the characteristics of the groups (e.g., their cultic nature, their tendency to have officers such as epimeletai whom they reward with honorific inscriptions and small sums of money at the conclusion of terms of office) and/or in incidental detail (e.g., a number of examples of this type of thiasos seem to have flourished in the Peiraeus at the end of the fourth and in the early third centuries; see e.g., *IG* 2².1261, 1262, 1263, 1271, 1273, 1275). Golden 1979, 38, n. 41, is probably therefore mistaken in his implication that *IG* 2².2343 (see also previous note), 2347, and perhaps 2346 and 2348, are phratric thiasoi.

used. Moreover, such a special sense is not noted by the lexicographers[143] or by any other historical source. Given the wide range of groups to which the term could be applied, all this suggests that, where thiasos may have been used to describe a group of phrateres, these may have been instances of the normal, general use of the word in the sense of group or association, without special connotations or meaning.

Third, there is the question of dating. Again, apart from T 3, of the six possible cases of the term thiasos being used to refer to phratry subgroups, only T 35 certainly fits the hypothesis of the late-fifth-century invention of a sense that peters out in the mid-fourth century.[144] The two cases of unnamed groups of phrateres, T 21 and T 18, also fit, as may *IG* 2².2720, though it could be earlier, as could *SEG* 10.330. Dow and Gill 1965 I, from the late fourth century, looks too late, as does *Athen.* 5.185c, which, insofar as it can be dated at all, may come from the same period. *Hesp.* 1947, 63 is certainly too late.

There is a concentration of evidence in the late fifth and fourth centuries, but that would be expected in any case; the same chronological pattern would emerge from the evidence for almost any institution of classical Athens. Insofar as we are justified in saying anything at all about the life span of phratric thiasoi, we would not on this evidence be justified in restricting it to a brief period in the late fifth and early fourth centuries.

Fourth, even if we suspend our doubts about this evidence and accept it all as attesting phratric thiasoi—we lack grounds to pick and choose among it except that we can exclude the *Digest* passage—there are still features of it that sit uneasily with the view that thiasoi were centrally imposed institutions with a democratizing intent. In particular, we might have expected some regularity in the relationship between thiasoi and gene/groups of orgeones; in particular that thiasoi would have invariably cut across the older groups. In fact, there is notable inconsistency in this respect. In the Dekeleieis everyone was in a thiasos; there is no sign of any genos. In T 35 some, but not all, the members of the genos Salaminioi may have been in one thiasos. In T 21 some members of a phratry may be in gene and some in groups named after their leaders, while in Dow and Gill 1965 I and *SEG* 10.330 we may have respectively a group of orgeones and a genos actually forming a thiasos. This inconsistency, I

---

143. Admitted by Andrewes 1961a, 10.
144. Cf. p. 78.

suggest, is what might be expected from phratries generating subgroups at different times, each in its own way and for different purposes.

Maintaining our suspension of doubt about the evidence, another feature of it is that, in contrast to the gene and orgeones groups, thiasoi lack independent identity. They do not have their own proper names, tending, it seems, to be called after their leader.[145] Their members tend to be attested explicitly as phrateres or in the context of their phratry,[146] and they do not seem to have their own cults.[147] These features do not suggest that the institutions were centrally imposed but short-lived so much as that such of them as were phratry subdivisions were created by the phratries themselves for their own purposes. Subdivisions of this sort did not need a separate identity, with separate names, eponyms, and cults. Membership in a phratry subdivision of this sort signified nothing with respect to legitimacy over and above phratry membership, and there was therefore no reason for them to appear in contemporary literature or history or in the orators.

If we reintroduce our doubts about the evidence and consider the overall picture, the impression of a variety of subdivisions produced by phratries for their own purposes is strengthened. We have one case of a phratric house that was divided into thiasoi. We have one certain case of groups of phrateres named after their leader, possibly as regular and official subdivisions of the phratry, possibly as simply ad hoc groupings for the purpose of a *prasis epi lysei*. We have one possible subdivision that is undescribed, and we have a number of other groups called thiasoi. None of them is certainly a phratry subgroup, but some or all of them may be. In any case, they have the appearance of groups spontaneously created by the phratries for their own reasons rather than of centrally imposed groupings.[148]

What, then, is the explanation of the existence of subgroups within phratries other than gene and groups of orgeones? I suggest there are two features of gene and groups of orgeones which may have been

---

145. T 21, T 18?, T 35, *Hesp.* 1947, 63?, *IG* 2².2720?; the Etionidai of *SEG* 10.330 are probably not called such qua thiasos.

146. T 21, T 18?, T 3.

147. At T 18 and *Hesp.* 1947, 63, there is an association with phratry deities. *SEG* 10.330 and Dow and Gill 1965 I might be exceptions.

148. To this list of different sorts of phratry subgroup should perhaps be added for completeness τῶν φρατέρων τοὺς οἰκείους, among whom gamelia was celebrated at Dem. 57.43 (cf. p. 183). Gamelia had some formal legal status (see p. 184), so it is possible that this group was more than simply an ad hoc collection of phrateres.

relevant. Neither of them has anything to do with those groups having contained a historically dominant class. First, not everyone was a gennete or orgeon. Second, gene and groups of orgeones were old institutions. The first meant that if an individual phratry wished for whatever purpose to include all its members in a system of subdivision, it would have had to create subgroups that were not gene or orgeones groups. The second meant that, with the passage of time, the older groups, subject to social and demographic pressures, the effects of which we shall consider further in the next chapter, may in some cases have ceased to constitute usable phratry subgroups.

When, therefore, a phratry wished, for example, to ensure that all its members went through a preliminary process of scrutiny before being voted on by the whole phratry, it would have had to create new subdivisions that perhaps incorporated, perhaps cut across, gene and orgeones groups. When a group of phrateres got together for some financial or cultic purpose, whether they were gennetai, orgeones, or neither, they may have formed new groups, either ad hoc or with a more permanent existence. In either case the term thiasos may, but need not, have been used to describe the resulting group as it was used to describe all sorts of other groups outside phratries. The thiasoi lack independent identity no doubt not only because at the period for which we have evidence they were relatively recent creations, but also because they were created either by the phratry as a whole for its own purposes or by groups of citizens associated in their capacity as phrateres.

Conclusion

Two themes that have emerged from this chapter are of particular importance for the next. First, the absence of traces of aristocratic domination in phratry structure in the classical period in general, and of any degree of control by gene over the admission of nongennetai to phratries in particular. Second, what might be described as the untidy picture of phratry subgroups: some people in gene, others in groups of orgeones, still others in neither; some gene possibly wholly independent of any phratry; and scraps of evidence for other subgroups, some possibly known as thiasoi, but not formed according to any clear pattern. Behind all this lie the forces which cause groups of people to come into being, to stay in existence, to split, to join with each other, or to pass away. They are forces that play an important role in explaining the background to our single most important piece of evidence for the internal organization of a phratry. In it is found a phratric group, described uniquely in our evidence as an oikos, (house). It comprises the three so-called Demotionidai decrees.

Chapter 3

Demotionidai and Dekeleieis

I have argued in the previous chapter that, while there is good evidence for the operation in the classical period of the principle of Philochoros fr. 35, whereby gennetai and orgeones entered phratries automatically, there is no evidence of a genos controlling the access to a phratry of other than genos members, or in any other way dominating a phratry. I also argued that this supports the view, for which there is also other evidence, of the genos as a group that was not essentially, as genos, a group of aristocrats, but of persons with ties of common locality and linked, at least in Aristotelian theory, by bonds of kinship. So far, however, I have said little about the document most informative about the internal constitution and admissions procedure of a phratry, *IG* $2^2.1237$ (T 3), the so-called Demotionidai decrees.[1]

The central problem in these decrees concerns the nature and identity of the two groups they mention, the Demotionidai and the House of the Dekeleieis. The common view has been that one of these was a privileged group, usually seen as a genos, which exercised a measure of control over the admissions procedure of the phratry as a whole.[2] The

---

1. See also appendix 1, T 3.

2. The bibliography is very large. The major contributions—those which have significantly advanced the argument on the identity of Demotionidai and Dekeleieis—have been: Wilamowitz 1893, 2.259–79; Wade-Gery 1931 (= 1958, 116–34); Andrewes 1961a. For the main bibliography before Wade-Gery, see his 118, n. 2, and Diller 1932. For the pre-Wilamowitz view of Schaefer 1888, see n. 42. Writers since Wade-Gery have tended either to follow his hypothesis or to defend that of Wilamowitz. Wade-Geryites: Guarducci 1937, 41–50; Andrewes 1961a; Thompson 1968, 51–68 (cf. n. 97); Ito 1988. Wilamowitzians: Kahrstedt 1934, 234, n. 1; Hignett 1952, Ap. ii c. Bourriot 1976, 641, develops from a Wilamowitzian starting point a view not far from my own about the identity of the groups; he sees the Demotionidai as the phratry and the Dekeleieis as a group of phrateres within it, not a genos. His interpretation of the roles played by these groups in the decrees,

95

last chapter argued that there was no evidence that gene performed such a role within phratries. I shall offer another plausible explanation of the relationship between Demotionidai and Dekeleieis, based in part on the internal evidence of the decrees and in part on external considerations, and fully consistent both with the picture of the genos/phratry relationship that emerged in the last chapter and with that of the classical phratry that emerged in the last two.

I shall first summarize the content of the decrees, then identify unsatisfactory aspects of existing hypotheses concerning the identity of the Demotionidai and Dekeleieis, and present a new hypothesis. Finally, I shall offer a brief interpretation of the decrees as a whole.[3]

Summary of Decrees

The inscription consists of a preamble and three motions. The preamble and first motion date to the archonship of Phormio (396/5). The third motion is in a different hand from the rest and uses a later orthography. It seems to date to ca. 370-50. The second motion is in the same hand as the first, but a different priest was apparently responsible for its inscription.[4] It probably followed the first after an interval. The content of the inscription may be summarized as follows.

Preamble (1-12)

Superscription to Zeus Phratrios; statement that the inscription was set up by the priest; assignment to him of his portions of the meion and the koureion; introduction of the proposals passed by the phrateres in

---

however, is not convincing. See n. 22. Roussel 1976, 147 with n. 54, in a very brief treatment, reaches a conclusion with which I agree:

> On n'y discerne rien qui puisse vraiment étayer une telle idée, aucun indice suggérant l'existence d'une stratification ou d'une hiérarchie entre phratères selon la qualité sociale ou la naissance,

though this conclusion is not consistent with Wilamowitz' interpretation of T 3, which he supports in n. 54. For the interpretation of Hedrick 1984 and 1990 (which includes, at 75-77, summary of earlier views), see notes to this chapter, passim.

3. I shall not discuss in any detail in this chapter matters arising from the decrees which are not relevant to the central question of the identity and relationship to each other of the Demotionidai and the Dekeleieis. These are discussed in their appropriate place elsewhere (e.g., the nature of the thiasos in chapter 2, meion and koureion in chapter 4. Cf. now also Hedrick 1990).

4. For more detail on the dating of the three decrees, see p. 290.

the archonship of Phormio (396/5)[5] and the phratriarchy of Pantakles of Oion.

Motion of Hierokles (13–68)

There is to be an immediate scrutiny[6] of all who have not been scrutinized "according to the law of the Demotionidai." The phrateres are to vote on them; those rejected are to have their names removed by the priest and the phratriarch from both the register "in the keeping of the Demotionidai"[7] and the copy. A fine of one hundred drachmas is to be paid by the introducer of a rejected candidate, to be collected by the priest and the phratriarch (13–26). Arrangements for the regular annual scrutiny:[8] it should take place on Koureotis[9] a year after the candidate's koureion. A rejected candidate may appeal to the Demotionidai; for the appeal, the House of the Dekeleieis[10] is to appoint five *synegoroi*,[11] who are to be sworn to keep false phrateres out of the phratry. The penalty for an unsuccessful appeal is to be one thousand drachmas, to be collected by the priest of the House of the Dekeleieis (26–45). This is to take effect from the archonship of Phormio [396/5]. The phratriarch is to carry out the vote annually and is to be fined five hundred drachmas should he fail to do so. In future, meia and koureia are to be brought to the altar at Dekeleia and the phratriarch is to sacrifice them; he is to be fined (fifty drachmas?)[12] should he fail to do so. Provision is made, should it be impossible to carry out the ceremony at Dekeleia, for the priest to give notification of an alternative location on the fifth day before Dorpia[13] at the resort of the Dekeleieis in the city (45–64). The decree and the priestly dues are to be inscribed in front of the altar at Dekeleia by the priest at his own expense (64–68).

---

5. Diodoros 14.54.1.

6. I refer to this as "the extraordinary scrutiny."

7. ἐν Δημοτιωνιδῶν.

8. I refer to this as "the regular scrutiny."

9. Third day of the phratry festival Apatouria (see chapter 4).

10. τὸν Δεκελεῖων οἶκον.

11. "Assessors," "advocates," or "accusers." The precise meaning in this context is open to question (see p. 127).

12. Epigraphically eighty or ninety are also possible restorations, since the requirement is for a ten-letter number ending in α. The rounder figure is preferable.

13. First day of the Apatouria (see p. 158, n. 89).

Motion of Nikodemos (68–113)

Concurrence with previous decrees; but the three witnesses required for the preliminary scrutiny, the *anakrisis,* [apparently provided for in an earlier decree not now extant] are to come from (the candidate's) own thiasos; if the thiasos does not have that many members, the witnesses may come from the other phrateres (68–78). Before all the phrateres vote on a candidate, the thiasotai are to vote secretly. Their votes are to be counted before all the phrateres and announced by the phratriarch. Should the phratry as a whole reject a candidate accepted by the thiasos, the thiasotai are to be fined one hundred drachmas, except for those who have made plain their opposition during the scrutiny. If the candidate is rejected by the thiasotai but accepted by the phrateres, his name is to be entered on the registers. If he is rejected by both thiasos and phratry, the introducer is to pay a fine of one hundred drachmas. On rejection by the thiasos there is no obligation to appeal to the whole body of the phrateres; the rejection in that case is to stand. In the vote by the whole phratry, thiasotai are not to vote on candidates from their own thiasos (78–106). This decree is also to be inscribed by the priest. The words of the oath for the witnesses are specified.

Motion of Menexenos (114–26)

Concurrence with previous decrees; but so that the phrateres may know who is to be introduced, their names and details of their parentage are to be published in advance in the resort of the Dekeleieis in the city and in the temple of Leto.

Difficulties with Earlier Hypotheses

Who are the Demotionidai and the Dekeleieis and what is their relationship to each other? We learn the following about their respective roles from the decrees. In Hierokles' decree, it is those who have not been scrutinized "according to the law of the Demotionidai" (14–15) who are now to be voted on in the extraordinary scrutiny. Those who are rejected are to have their names erased from the register in the keeping of the Demotionidai and from the copy (20–21). A candidate rejected at the regular scrutiny is permitted to appeal to the Demotionidai (30–31). On the other hand, it is the House of the Dekeleieis (32–33) who are to choose the synegoroi for this appeal. It is the priest of the House of the Dekeleieis (41–42) who is to exact the fine from a failed appellant. If there is to be an alternative location for the sacrifice of meia and koureia, it is to be notified at the place in the city which the Dekeleieis frequent (63–64), as are the names of candidates in Menexenos' decree (122–23). Further, it is to Dekeleia (53) that meia and koureia are to be brought and it is before the altar at Dekeleia that the decrees are to be posted (67).

There have been two main schools of thought, headed respectively by Wilamowitz and Wade-Gery,[14] regarding the identity of these two groups. In both a smaller, privileged group is envisaged as exercising some sort of control over the admissions procedures of the phratry as a whole. Wilamowitz thought the Demotionidai were the phratry, the Dekeleieis a privileged gentilitial subsection of it. Wade-Gery took the Dekeleieis as the phratry and the Demotionidai as a small aristocratic committee of experts who oversaw it. None of Wilamowitz' disciples has significantly improved his hypothesis, and, like Wade-Gery, we are justified in directing criticism in the main at Wilamowitz' version.[15] Wade-Gery's hypothesis has undergone one significant modification, that of Andrewes, who replaced Wade-Gery's unsatisfactory and otherwise unattested committee with a genos and adduced other evidence which he took to indicate that gene exercised some such power over phratries in the classical period. In this case, criticisms are best directed at Andrewes' version.

To take Wilamowitz first,[16] the strongest argument against him is

---

14. Cf n. 2.

15. Wade-Gery 1931 = 1958, 124, n. 3. For Bourriot's version of the Wilamowitz view, see nn. 2 and 22. Hedrick 1984 and 1990 followed Wilamowitz in seeing the Demotionidai as the phratry and suggested that the Dekeleieis were the demesmen of Dekeleia. This simple solution has attractions. However, it is not tenable because: (a) the House of the Dekeleieis should have been a group distinct from the deme; it seems to have pre-existed it (see p. 113); (b) if it were a deme there is no apparent reason why it should not have been called one in these decrees, rather than being described by the unique term "house" (cf. pp. 101–2); (c) we would have here a phratry giving instructions to a deme (to appoint synegoroi) and to its priest. I know of no parallel for one citizen group instructing another where the group being instructed is not a subgroup; I find it intrinsically implausible, especially as some deme members would not have been phratry members. Hedrick is also required to posit that the body passing the decrees is the Demotionidai. This falls foul of Wade-Gery's major argument against Wilamowitz, to the effect that the body passing the decrees must be that from which appeal is permitted to the Demotionidai (see further below).

16. The arguments adduced against Wilamowitz here are slightly developed versions of some of those used by Wade-Gery and Andrewes.

derived from lines 26–32, where Hierokles turns from the extraordinary scrutiny to the regular one: "In future the scrutiny is to be in the year following that in which the koureion is sacrificed, on Koureotis in Apatouria, carrying the vote from the altar.[17] If anyone who has been rejected in the vote should wish to appeal to the Demotionidai, he may do so. . . ." The essence of the argument is that those who are to carry the votes from the altar[18] here must be understood as the phrateres whose decree this is, and that since appeal is to be from their vote to the Demotionidai, the Demotionidai cannot themselves be identical with those phrateres.

First, at 15–18 it is stated explicitly that it is to be the phrateres who are to carry out the extraordinary scrutiny: ". . . the phrateres are to hold a scrutiny of them immediately . . . carrying the vote from the altar."[19] The phrase "carrying the vote from the altar" used there is also used in relation to the regular scrutiny eleven lines later, clearly as a sort of shorthand for a well-known procedure. There has been no hint of a change of subject in the intervening text. The implication is that the procedure is to be the same in both cases, and that the phrateres are to be responsible for the regular scrutiny, as they are for the extraordinary. Second, it is clear that the effect of Nikodemos' motion is to supplement the existing procedure with an initial vote by thiasotai, and that the existing procedure involved a vote by the phrateres.[20] Finally, since this is a decree of the phrateres (9), the unexpressed subject of a verb in the decree ought to be the body voting the decree unless there is some definite implication to the contrary. Here there is not.[21] On any logical reading of the text, therefore, those carrying the votes from the altar in the regular scrutiny must be the phrateres whose decree this is.

---

17. I have left this in the active without a subject to preserve the Greek construction, since the determination of the understood subject is crucial to the argument against Wilamowitz. It would be more normal to translate with a passive in English (cf. n. 21).

18. φέρεν δὲ τὴν ψῆφον ἀπὸ τὸ βωμῶ (29).

19. . . . φέροντας τὴν ψῆφον ἀπ/ὸ τὸ βωμῶ (17–18).

20. It is clear throughout Nikodemos' motion that the existing established scrutiny procedure involved the phrateres (e.g., lines 81, 89–90, 96–97). The obvious implication of this, that it is the phrateres who are to vote in the regular scrutiny as provided for by Hierokles, can only be escaped if we take (intolerably—see below) Nikodemos' motion as replacing Hierokles' altogether, not merely supplementing it.

21. Active verbs without subject in Greek, normally best translated by a passive in English, can produce uncertainty as to the subject intended (e.g., in the Spartan Great Rhetra, Plut. *Lyc.* 6), perhaps particularly where the subject would have been obvious to the original audience, but not to us. But there is no good reason in this case to take the subject as other than that most naturally implied by our text, i.e., the body passing the decree.

Appeal is to be allowed from them to the Demotionidai, so the Demotionidai cannot themselves be identical with those phrateres.[22] All other interpretations put an intolerable strain on the text. It has been suggested, for instance, that it may have been implicit in earlier decrees or practice such as the "law of the Demotionidai," that the Dekeleieis carried out the regular scrutiny.[23] This would not, however, get around the problem that the text as it stands implies that both the procedures for the regular and extraordinary scrutinies and the bodies carrying them out were the same. Moreover, it is not only stated explicitly (14-16) that the extraordinary scrutiny is to be carried out by the phrateres, it is also implied that it is to be according to the law of the Demotionidai.[24] The implication of this in turn is naturally taken to be that scrutinies carried out according to the law of the Demotionidai were carried out in general by the phrateres. It could not therefore be the case that the law of the Demotionidai implied, for the regular scrutiny, that it should be carried out by some other group. We cannot satisfactorily get around this by claiming that the procedure at an extraordinary scrutiny was carried out by the whole phratry, the Demotionidai, and that a regular scrutiny was conducted by the subgroup, the Dekeleieis.[25] Such a distinction would have to have been more clearly explicit in the text; and it is not credible that there

---

22. Busolt-Swoboda 1920-26, 962, n. 2, indeed argued that the appeal was from the Demotionidai to the Demotionidai. Bourriot 1976, 639-48, esp. n. 446, has effectively revived this position with his view that the Demotionidai first take a vote in which they effectively judge between two opposing parties, the introducer and his opponents, but for the appeal make use of the better informed opinion of the synegoroi, which he takes to be a five-man Commission appointed by the Dekeleian House at the request of the Demotionidai to investigate the case. Wade-Gery's objection (1931 = 1958, 127, n. 1; cf. Andrewes 1961a, 4) to Busolt-Swoboda here is also decisive against Bourriot: "Improbable in itself such an appeal could not be called simply appeal 'to Demotionidai'." Bourriot argues against this (n. 446) that there would be point in an appeal of this sort because, at the appeal stage, the phratry would have had the extra benefit of the expertise of the five man commission. But this fails to get round the main thrust of Wade-Gery's argument, that the text as it stands in 30 definitely implies that the body that carried out the first stage of the process was different from that to which the appeal was intended to be made. B's account contains other implausibilities, of which I mention two: (a) since the Dekeleieis could not be expected to know about non-Dekeleieis members of the Demotionidai, it seems inexplicable that the Demotionidai should require them to appoint the "Commissioners" (this understanding of synegoroi is not in itself impossible, see p. 127) in every case, even when non-Dekeleieis are involved; (b) Nikodemos' motion has to be taken implausibly as totally replacing Hierokles', cf. below.

23. Cf. Hignett 1952, 314.

24. ... κατὰ τὸν νόμον τὸν Δημοτιωνιδ/ῶν (14-15).

25. As Wilamowitz is forced to do, 1893, 260.

was a special law of the Demotionidai dealing with extraordinary scrutinies.[26]

The second argument against Wilamowitz' view derives from its implication that Nikodemos' motion does not merely modify and supplement that of Hierokles, but completely replaces and nullifies it. Under Hierokles' motion, a procedure is set up for the regular scrutiny whereby there is a preliminary vote by the subgroup, the Dekeleieis, followed by optional appeal to the Demotionidai. In Wilamowitz' view, Nikodemos replaces the Dekeleieis with the thiasoi for this purpose.

This is intolerable. When Nikodemos turns to deal with the regular scrutiny procedure in 78, he says, "The phratriarch shall not put the vote about the children to the whole phratry before the candidate's own thiasotai have voted in secret. . . . " There is no hint that this preliminary vote by thiasos is replacing a preliminary vote by some other body. The clear implication is that the thiasos vote is a new procedure, supplementing the regular scrutiny arrangement already in place (i.e., the vote by phrateres in Hierokles' decree, here "all the phrateres"[27]) and to take place before it. It is those arrangements that were the subject of Hierokles' decree, and the appeal to the Demotionidai provided for by him in 30, with its heavy fine for failure, is clearly intended to be an appeal after the vote by phrateres. The supplementary nature of Nikodemos' decree is confirmed by the wording used to introduce it, indicating a degree of concurrence with previous decrees on the introduction of children; he specifies that his motion is to be set up alongside previous ones.[28] This sounds more like a supplementary measure than one which completely overrides previous decrees.[29] On no natural reading, therefore,

---

26. Hedrick 1990, 78–80, impressed (as am I) by Wilamowitz' argument that the Demotionidai have the characteristics of a phratry (see n. 30), and by the parallel between the scrutinies in Hierokles' decree and Nikodemos', argues that the phrateres in Hierokles' decree are members of subgroups (which he takes to be identical with N's thiasoi), not the whole phratry. He is right to think of the phrateres in H's decree as a subgroup, but to be referred to in this way they must also, pace Hedrick, be the body passing the decree (cf. above). In other words, it seems to put intolerable strain on the text to suppose that the phratry Demotionidai would, in their own decree, use "the phrateres," unqualified, to refer not, as one would naturally take it, to themselves, but as shorthand for their subgroups. In seeing the Demotionidai as passers of the decrees, Hedrick also falls foul of the main thrust of Wade-Gery's argument against Wilamowitz, see above.

27. Cf. pp. 137–38.

28. See lines 68–71 and 106–7.

29. Even if we accept that Nikodemos' decree was passed at a later date than Hierokles' (see p. 292) and that there may have been other relevant legislation in the intervening

can these be decrees of a phratry Demotionidai in which the Dekeleieis are a privileged subgroup.

The view of Wade-Gery and Andrewes that the Dekeleieis are the phratry, the Demotionidai the privileged subgroup is equally implausible. First, the Demotionidai performed functions we would expect of the phratry itself: it is their law that governs procedure; the master copy of the phratry register is in their keeping. We should expect the law governing phratry procedure to be the phratry's law, and the master copy of the phratry register to be kept by the phratry.[30] This not only makes good sense, but there are also no attested cases where the arrangement was otherwise.

Second, there is a difficulty with the term used to describe the body which, by this view, is the phratry passing the decree, the House of the Dekeleieis. In all other cases we know of, a phratry is either referred to simply as "the phrateres" or, where a name is used, as, e.g., the Achniadai or the phratry of the Achniadai or the society (*koinon*) of the Achniadai.[31] We know of phratries (and demes and gene) which owned houses,[32] and we know of two groups of probable seafarers, who described themselves corporately as houses, apparently from the buildings in which they met,[33] but these cases are not good parallels. There was no special term like phratry or deme that would have been appro-

---

period (see p. 131), there would seem to be an implication that N's motion was in some way supplementary to H's. The intervening legislation may have abolished Hierokles' provisions for appeal to the Demotionidai (see p. 136) but would not have affected the basic element in the scrutiny, the vote by Dekeleieis, which is the essential thread of continuity between Hierokles' decree and Nikodemos'.

30. Cf. Wilamowitz 1893, 2.261: "Die Bruderschaft sind die Demotioniden: Niemand anders als das Plenum kann über die Appellation richten, und die Liste der Brüder ἐν Δημοτιωνιδῶν kann nur im Hause der Bruderschaft liegen. Jede andere Auffassung ist in sich verkehrt."

31. See appendix 1 passim. On the term koinon with respect to a phratry, see further pp. 315–16.

32. T 5, 18, 40–41 (Dyaleis); T 23 (name unknown); and on Chios the Klytidai, = Sokolowski 1969, 118, 1–6. Cf. also *IG* 2².1672, 24 (oikos of the genos Kerykes); Zenob. 2.27 and Hesych. s.v. Μελιτέων οἶκος (oikos of the demesmen of Melite, cf. Hedrick 1990, 50–51)

33. Meritt 1961a, no.s 28 and 29, 229–30 (dating to 112/1 and 111/0); L. Robert 1936, no. 8 (late fourth–early third cent.) and 1969, 7–14. Cf., for the term used of seafarers in the Black Sea, Poland 1909, 459–64. Hedrick 1990, 48–52, observing the parallel with the house of the Meliteans (see previous note) suggests the House of the Dekeleieis were also a deme, called a house because they met in one. But there is no evidence that the term House of the Meliteans was ever used to refer to the deme as opposed to the deme's literal, bricks and mortar, house.

priate for such groups. There is certainly nothing inappropriate in principle in the description of a group of phrateres (or gennetai or demesmen) as a house. Aristotle described the genos/kome as a colony—the Greek word for which, *apoikia,* is a derivative of the word for house—of a household.[34] But there is no analogous case in which a whole group which can be described by a specific term, i.e., phratry, genos, deme, is described as a house, nor is there anything in the context that would explain why it should have been. In short, if a group was an ordinary whole phratry, why was it not described as such? Society (*koinon*) is a general term used to describe groups of this sort; house, as far as we know, is not. A unique reference of this sort requires explanation, and the Wade-Gery/Andrewes view does not provide a satisfactory one.[35]

Third, doubts raised by these internal implausibilities are confirmed when we take broader considerations into account, considerations that, incidentally, also count against Wilamowitz' view. In the view of Wade-Gery/Andrewes, a genos, functioning as a court of appeal, exercises a degree of power over phratry admissions procedures. Andrewes sees parallels for the apparent exercise of power by a genos over nongennete phratry members—parallels which might justify oddities such as a law other than the phratry's law governing phratry practice—in other texts attesting the relationship of phratry and genos. But in chapter 2 we saw that those texts are best interpreted otherwise. There is certainly evidence of gene effectively determining whether their own members can enter phratries, but not of their doing so for nonmembers.

Fourth, there is, so to speak, the other side of the same coin. A supposed genos is here alleged to be exercising unparalleled power with respect to other phratry members, but remarkably, in view of that alleged power, it does not seem to be exercising the absolute control over the access of its own members to the phratry that, on the basis of Philochoros fr. 35, we would expect and for which there are parallels. Whatever the supposed privileges of the Demotionidai, they are, in Andrewes' view, phratry members; yet there is no indication in the decrees that they are exempt from the extraordinary and regular scrutinies to be carried out by the phratry as a whole in Hierokles' motion, nor, particularly sur-

---

34. See p. 60 above.
35. The obvious and, I submit, correct explanation is that this house was not in fact an ordinary whole phratry.

prisingly, from Nikodemos' provisions for scrutiny arrangements at the subgroup level.[36]

Fifth, an argument perhaps more persuasive than decisive. That institutionalized power was exercised in the phratry by a privileged subgroup is inconsistent with evidence within this decree and elsewhere as to how phratries were run in the classical period. Phratriarchs were elected; they did not acquire their positions by hereditary right or by appointment.[37] Both in this phratry and others, all phrateres voted on candidates for membership in a secret ballot unless the candidates had already passed scrutiny in a genos or a group of orgeones.[38] Phratriarchs who failed to carry out their duties properly could be fined, and any phrater could take it into his own hands to collect fines if a phratriarch or priest failed to do so.[39] There is no evidence that decisions on business affecting the phratry as a whole were made by any subgroups. There is plenty of evidence, including these three decrees, that phratries made decisions about their own affairs by the standard contemporary democratic model: motions were introduced by individuals at an Assembly, were discussed, and were voted on by all present.[40] The format of the decrees is identical

---

36. The adherents of the Andrewes view might respond that it would have been well understood—perhaps under the law of the Demotionidai—that the provision of the decree did not apply to the Demotionidai. But it would have been easy enough to refer to this in a text which, as it stands, implies there was no such privilege. Wilamowitz faces a similar problem: if the Dekeleieis have the right of automatic entry into a phratry accorded by the law of Philochoros fr. 35, they should not be providing for appeal from their own decisions to the phratry as a whole. I cannot agree with the view of Thompson 1968 that "those who have not been scrutinized according to the law of the Demotionidai" means those who were not gennetai. Cf. n. 97.

37. The priesthood of the Dekeleieis may have been hereditary or restricted to certain families (cf. p. 291), but that was a common enough feature of democratic Athens, seen at one level in the state priesthoods of the Kerykes and Eumolpidai and the religious duties of the hereditary phylobasileis (cf. pp. 257-58), at another in the nomination by a deme (Halimous) of a short-list of best-born (εὐγενέστατοι) candidates for a priesthood of Herakles (Dem. 57.46-48 and 62). For the uncertain significance of the use of election rather than lot (the former at least clearly not undemocratic) see pp. 230-31. There are some other minor features of the role of the phratriarch which may be somewhat old-fashioned, but nothing to suggest they dominated their phratries any more than demarchs did their demes. See pp. 225-33. Hedrick 1990, 31 with n. 50, draws attention to the apparent archaism τάδε in the introductory formula at 9.

38. Cf. p. 173.

39. Cf. pp. 229 and 235.

40. For this, cf. T 4, T 5, T 16, T 17 (proposals made by individuals); T 5 (1), T 16 (1), T 17 (11) (decisions taken by all phrateres).

to those of other democratic bodies in the polis: introductory formula ("it was decided by the phrateres in the archonship of X and the phratriarchy of Y") followed by motions passed under the name of the proposer ("X proposed . . ."). The classical phratry, as far as our evidence suggests, was not dominated in its procedures by any subgroup within it.

Such are the objections to the view of Wade-Gery and Andrewes: the body doing the things we expect of a phratry should be a phratry; the body called something other than a phratry should not be a phratry. The body supposed to be a genos should exercise the privileges of automatic entry to phratry attested elsewhere; it should not exercise powers over the admission of nonmembers which it is not seen exercising elsewhere. The body whose procedures and constitution are otherwise democratic should not be institutionally dominated by a privileged subgroup within it.[41]

A New Hypothesis

I offer in the following a new proposal as to the identity of Demotionidai and Dekeleieis. In the present state of our evidence, as with all previous interpretations, it can be no more than a hypothesis, but it is one for which the case can be made much more strongly that it both provides a basis for explaining the texts of our three decrees and is more consistent with the external evidence. To summarize, it is that the Demotionidai were a phratry, the House of the Dekeleieis a group within that phratry which was broadly similar to a genos. It was a well-established group and for a long time prior to these decrees had had the sort of semi-independent status observed among gene in chapter 2. In these decrees, which are decrees of the Dekeleieis, it is developing that independence further. I suggest it may be doing so in response in part to social and demographic pressures generated by the Peloponnesian War in general, and by the unique experience of the Dekeleieis in that war in particular. It is possible by the time of Nikodemos' decree, that the split was complete.[42]

---

41. A further oddity, recognized by Wade-Gery (cf. also Thompson 1968, 53), is that a subgroup rather than the plenum should be the court of last instance; but this is consistent enough with the Andrewes view that gene in general exercised controls over the admission of nongennetai to phratries.

42. Schaefer 1888, writing before the publication of face B of T 3, also thought the

I adduce four arguments in favor of this view:

(i) Fission and fusion of phratries and gene was a natural way for those groups to react to demographic and other social pressures and is well attested. The hypothesis that such a process was at work in the Demotionidai therefore is plausible in principle and has the support of relevant parallels;

(ii) the hypothesis fits what is known or can reasonably be inferred from T 3 and other evidence about the nature of the group, the House of Dekeleieis, and its previous history;

(iii) the hypothesis disposes satisfactorily of the difficulties raised by those of Wilamowitz and Wade-Gery/Andrewes;

(iv) it makes possible a satisfactory interpretation of the content of T 3.

Fission/Fusion

We have seen in chapter 2 that the structural pattern of phratry subgroups was by no means neat, uniform, or systematic; that there were some

---

Dekeleieis were a subphratry of the Demotionidai, but saw this as a systematic feature of classical phratry structure and a consequence of central action rather than natural evolution. He reconciled Arist. *Pol.* 6.1319b19–27, which he took to imply that Cleisthenes created new phratries, with *Ath. Pol.* 21.6, which he took to imply that the phratries remained as they were (on which see p. 246) by supposing that Cleisthenes, intent on securing the entry of new men into the phratries, did indeed retain the old phratries but for most purposes split them into a number of smaller entities. The old names were retained for the parent bodies, which still had some functions of overseeing the subdivisions, but the sub-phratries, although they did not usually have their own names, were nevertheless the bodies which performed most of the phratry functions: hence the absence of phratry names from literary evidence. I do not believe that Arist. *Pol.* loc. cit., should be taken to imply that Cleisthenes tampered with the phratries. There is no sign in our other evidence for the Attic phratries, which is now considerably more than when Schaefer wrote, of the existence of systematic sub-phratries of the sort he posited. Phratries did contain subgroups, but not, as we saw in chapter 2, according to any systematic pattern. They might also split and fuse, but this was not so far as we know the result of central action, but of social and demographic pressures. (In the case of the double phratry, the Dyaleis, Schaefer accepted that a more natural, demographic process had taken place and he actually raised the possibility that the Demotionidai may have been similar, but dropped it without argument, see his pp. 32–33.) That phratries are never named in the literary evidence is not quite true (see appendix 1, T 15 and T 32). That they are not named in the orators, which form the bulk of our literary evidence, I suggest is because it was the fact that a person had phrateres at all that was normally important, not what phratry he belonged to. Demes also tend not to be named in these contexts. The tendency to regard all Athenians as in some sense fellow phrateres (cf. p. 43) and the ease with which phratries split or fused may have been contributory factors.

groups with and some without strong independent identity; some long-standing by the fourth century, some probably relatively new; some phratries with one sort of subgroup, some with another, some possibly crisscrossed with subgroups of different types. The phenomena of fission and fusion, well attested in both phratries and their subgroups, are part of the same fluid picture.

The inscriptions of the Salaminioi (Ferguson 1938) are our most copious evidence for an Attic genos. They clearly document a developing split in the organization between the mid-fourth century, when it had two branches, the Salaminioi "of the seven phylai" and the Salaminioi "from Sounium," and the mid-third century, when those two branches had become separate gene.[43] Another genos with Salaminian associations, the Eikadeis, had multiple archons and, in the late fourth century, some members on Salamis and others elsewhere.[44] Again a process of fission seems to have taken place; or it may in this case conceivably have been fusion.

It certainly seems to have been fusion in another case, that of the citizen orgeones of the Heroines based "near the property of Kalliphanes" and the orgeones of Echelos, attested in an early-third-century decree that re-enacts fifth-century regulations. In the mid-fifth century the two groups appear to have become associated for purposes of common sacrifices, and in the early third century they took steps to secure the continuation of the link "for all time."[45]

There is evidence of similar processes of fusion or fission at the level of the phratry. Indeed in the phratry's semi-independent subgroups there were units ready-made, so to speak, for the purpose. We have already

---

43. For the two separate branches, described as οἱ ἐκ τῶν Ἑπταφυλῶν and οἱ ἀπὸ Σουνίου, in the first inscription from 363/2, see, e.g., 3-4; for these described as separate gene in the second inscription, from ca. 250, 3-5 of that inscription: ἐπί τοῖσδε διελύσαντο τὰ γένη π/ρὸς ἄλληλα, τό τε Σουνιέων καὶ τὸ/ ἀπὸ τῶν ἐξ Ἑπταφυλῶν. . . . See also the comments of Ferguson 1938, 12. Both these inscriptions concerned the settlement of disputes between the two groups over the property, offices, distribution of sacrifices and religious privileges assigned to each.

44. See notes to T 27.

45. Meritt 1942, 282-287, no. 55. See esp. Ferguson 1944, 76, 79. (Cf. also Ferguson 1949, 130-31). At 2-5 the inscription reads: ὅπως ἂν δι[ατηρῆται των]/[θυσιῶν ἡ κοινω]νία εἰς τὸν ἅπαντα χρό[νον τῶι κοι]/[ν]ῶι τῶι πρὸς τοῖς Καλλιφάνους καὶ τῶ[ι τοῦ ἥρωος Ἐ]/χέλου. . . . Note also *IG* 2².1289, an early-third-century record of arbitration between two groups of orgeones of the Goddess, apparently branches of the same group, settling a dispute over sacred property. Again an earlier gemination of the group may be implied. See Ferguson 1944, 79 and A no. 6.

seen that it is possible, but no more than that, that in the Salaminioi themselves we have to do with a genos that had come to form its own phratry.[46]

We know that the phratry Dyaleis had two phratriarchs in 300/299;[47] their name, whatever its true etymology, is also suggestive of duality.[48] It looks as though they were, or had been, a phratry in two independent parts;[49] that either two separate phratries had fused to form one, or that a single phratry had split into two parts, though retaining some common identity and, as this inscription shows, common property.[50]

For the Therrikleidai, it is clear from T 12 that in the first quarter of the third century it also had more than one phratriarch; and there are other hints in the document indicating that the phratry was composed of quasi-independent parts.[51] Again, the hypothesis that this phratry was undergoing or had undergone a process of fusion or fission is attractive.[52]

The details of the process and the causal factors involved, except to a limited extent for the Salaminioi,[53] are obscure. It is not difficult,

46. Cf. pp. 65–66. The genos/phratry of Isae. 7 may also be of this type, see p. 67.

47. T 5, 5–7.

48. See notes on T 5.

49. This has been the generally accepted explanation of the dual phratriarchy (see, e.g., Wilamowitz 1893 2.267–68; Ferguson 1910, 270; Guarducci 1937, 51–52). The connotation of duality in the name seems to reinforce that view.

50. We cannot decide between fusion or fission in this case. If the origin of the name of the phratry is related to its dual character, it would perhaps be better explained as a result of fusion (e.g., as a way out of any dispute about which of the two original names should be retained) than fission (why in that case was the original name not retained when the two parts act in concert, as here). The common demotic of the two phratriarchs perhaps weighs slightly in favor of the same conclusion.

51. See T 11–12 with commentary. We do not know how many phratriarchs there were in this case, nor their identity at the time of this decree.

52. For further details, including the suggestion that one of the subgroups in this case was the Miltieis, a group in a position vis-à-vis the deme Melite and the phratry Therrikleidai analogous to that of the Dekeleieis vis-à-vis Dekeleia and the Demotionidai, see pp. 364–65. There are other possible but uncertain parallels or near-parallels in the Ikarieis (T 31, deme Ikarion, phratry unknown? But see notes, app. 1); the Aigilieis (T 33; deme Aigilia, phratry Pyrrhakidai? But again see notes, app. 1); and conceivably the Medontidai (T 7–10), certainly a phratry and also a genos, though it is not clear that this genos was ever of the type that was a formal subdivision of a phratry, see app. 1. Note also the case of the gene/phratries Thyrgonidai and Titakidai (T 15). It would be natural enough for such genos/phratry breakaway groups to be centered on demes. It is just possible that in the phratry of Dem. 57, we have another case: Euxitheos remarkably calls fellow demesmen of Halimous rather than his fellow phrateres to attest to his phratriarchy (cf. p. 230) and the plural "common registers" of SEG 2.7, 20–21, could be joint registers of deme and phratry (cf. pp. 175–76). Cf. also p. 368 on the Philieis.

53. See below, n. 56.

however, to formulate a general explanation in terms of natural changes in the characteristics of the groups over a more or less lengthy period of time giving rise to changes in their structure. There are four obvious relevant factors; there were doubtless others. First, changes in population size, either in Attica as a whole or at the level of an individual phratry or genos, will have had an effect. There was certainly no standard size for these groups,[54] but increase in size beyond a certain point would inevitably have threatened coherence, decrease viability. Second, there is the effect of persons and groups of persons moving their homes, for whatever reason, from one place in Attica to another. Third, there is the process whereby, over a few generations, the descendants of persons once closely linked by kinship would, other things being equal, no longer be as closely related to one another.[55] Fourth, there is the whole range of potential fluctuations in the factors holding groups of persons together, such as increasing or decreasing commonality of interest or experience,[56] among which will probably have been changes in cult practices.

There are three features of phratries and their subgroups that meant they were likely to respond structurally to processes of this sort. First they were very old: by the fourth century a phratry might already have existed for centuries.[57] Even if the processes identified above were rare, slow, and gradual, the chances were considerable that their effect would be significant over time.

---

54. Cf. pp. 18–20.

55. That is, e.g., unless further intermarriage took place, as in practice it often would have done.

56. It is not necessary, for the purposes of this argument (and it might be foolhardy to try in the current state of evidence) to assign absolute or relative significance to these four factors as they actually applied in Athens, in the fifth and fourth centuries. But it is a matter of common sense that each of them would have operated to some extent and that at the very least over a long period of time there was the potential for significant cumulative effects. In the case of the Salaminioi I agree with Ferguson 1938, 13, that the name of one of the subgroups, Heptaphyloi, is most naturally taken to refer to seven Cleisthenic phylai and that these were probably the seven phylai in which the non-Sounian members happened to be under the Cleisthenic dispensation. As for the factors determining the split, separateness of physical location is the most obvious. We cannot say how that came about, but it is noteworthy that names for the branches based on the Cleisthenic system should have been chosen, and it is possible that their origin was somehow linked to changes in group identity caused by the Cleisthenic reforms themselves. An increase in population may also have played a role—that each branch furnished seven men to act as mediators in the first inscription at least suggests a fairly big organization—as may the weakening of kinship ties—there are none apparent between the two branches.

57. Exactly how old they were is controversial (see pp. 267–71), but does not matter here.

Second, regardless of the extent to which phratries and gene were originally natural institutions, in that they came into being through the initiative of any or all of their members, or were artificial, in that they were created by external action such as imposition, by a central authority, what one might term the principle of natural community, in particular community of kinship and shared home location, was of fundamental importance.[58] We would expect alterations in the pattern of natural communities resulting from the processes of change outlined above to have had a significant impact on such groups.

Third, unlike the Cleisthenic phylai and their subdivisions, in particular the demes, there were no significant restrictions on the extent to which phratries and gene could change structurally in response to changes in natural community. The deme was locked with other demes into a structure of trittyes and phylai; it had to provide a certain fixed number of members of the Boule, the phylai and probably the trittyes,[59] had to provide a certain number of soldiers, and so on. These groups had roles in the central organization of the state such that, once established by Cleisthenes, any change had to come from the center;[60] a deme could not decide at will to split itself up or merge with another deme without disturbing the whole system. The phratry was subject to no such restrictions. The role it played in the central organization of the state by controlling access to citizenship did not require structural immutability. Whatever its relation had been to the Ionian phyle,[61] it effectively ceased to be a subdivision of any other group at least from the time of Cleisthenes; it was not locked into a particular relationship with other phratries, as were the demes in their trittyes, and it did not have to provide a certain unchanging number of members for any function of the state as a whole. Phratry subgroups would have differed only in that they were such, but if the case of the Salaminioi is at all typical, that will have had little effect on their scope for structural adaptation.

It is no surprise, therefore, to find phratries undergoing structural changes in response to changes in patterns of community over time. Fusion or fission was one means of response, though not of course the

---

58. Cf. p. 14.

59. Cf. pp. 2–3.

60. As happened in 307/6 with the creation of the new phylai Antigonis and Demetrias, and again in 224/3 (Ptolemais) and 200 (Attalis) and during the reign of Hadrian (Hadrianis) (see Traill 1975, 25–31).

61. See pp. 14–17.

only one. The development of new subgroups was another and, at a rather different level, so was the adoption by phratries of special meeting places in the city in addition to their traditional locations elsewhere in Attica.[62] It is significant for the importance of the principle of descent that one means, obvious enough to us, of responding to these pressures, that of allowing individuals to change phratry, for example when they moved home, was not adopted. There is no reason to suppose that the principle of descent would have stood in the way of fusion or fission of phratries, except perhaps insofar as there may have been anxiety that a new phratry formed by fission might not be recognized as legitimate for the purpose of enrolling citizens; but that would perhaps argue for a gradual process and the maintenance of ties with the parent or co-phratry, for a period at least.[63] Fusion and/or fission was therefore in a sense a natural way for phratries to respond to forces for structural change, and it is attested in a large proportion of those phratries and their subgroups for which our evidence is sufficient for such processes to be detectable at all.

Of course, that it happened or may have happened in these cases does not of itself demonstrate that we must be dealing with the same phenomenon in the case of the Demotionidai/Dekeleieis, but we shall have better support for this than for a hypothesis involving dominance of one of the two groups over the other. In fact, there are other factors that seem to point in the same direction.

The Dekeleieis and the Demotionidai

The Demotionidai have left no trace in the historical record apart from the decrees T 3.[64] The Dekeleieis seem to have had a much higher profile.

---

62. Including the Dekeleieis with their meeting place in the barber's shop by the Hermae (see further below). Cf. p. 13.

63. This may be a factor behind the commonality maintained in Salaminioi, Dyaleis and Therrikleidai; and also Demotionidai/Dekeleieis.

64. We do not even know anything about the eponym, Demotion, except for one uncertain reference in a Vergilian scholium. Wilamowitz 1893, 2.278–79, restored Σ Verg. *Aen.* 6.21, a garbled list of names of children rescued from the Minotaur by Theseus, to include Δημοτίων Κύδαντος (MSS demolion cydani), following Μενεσθεύς Σουνίου, Ἀμφίδοκος Ῥαμνοῦντος (MSS mnesteus sumiani phidocus ramuntis). The names of the three fathers are all those of demes in the eastern coastal area, as opposed to the female names in the list, which have West Attic associations. This suits also the association of

Herodotus, discussing those who had fought with distinction at the battle of Plataea in 479, mentions the exploits of one Sophanes, son of Eutychides, of the deme Dekeleia, and this provides him with the occasion for a story about the Dekeleieis of old: the Tyndaridai had come to Attica to recover Helen from her abductor Theseus. They ravaged the land in their search for her. The Dekeleieis, or, according to Herodotus, in some versions of the story Dekelos himself, angered by the pride of Theseus and fearing for Attica, revealed all to the Tyndaridai, as a result of which they were awarded honors at Sparta, freedom from taxes (*ateleia*), and seating precedence on public occasions (*proedria*). The special relationship still existed in his own time, Herodotus tells us, for when the Spartans invaded Attica in the Peloponnesian War, they left the lands of the Dekeleieis unharmed.[65]

We may infer from this story that, as a matter of fact, the Dekeleieis enjoyed privileges of Sparta in the mid-fifth century. This has two important implications for the historical Dekeleieis. First, at the time of Herodotus I suggest it is likely they had enjoyed these privileges longer than anyone could remember; and at the time of Herodotus the reforms of Cleisthenes were within living memory. It would be surprising if the privileges of the Dekeleieis did not predate those reforms. Second, if a group is to enjoy specific privileges of this sort, it should have some institutional identity. It is difficult to imagine that such privileges were enjoyed by people who merely lived at Dekeleia. Indeed, the Dekeleieis' role in the myth of the Tyndaridai surely presupposes the existence of a well-defined association already enjoying these privileges; the myth is

---

Demotion with Dekeleia via the Demotionidai. If there were phratries called Menestheidai and Amphidokidai, however, we have no record of them. We can, of course, base nothing firm on such doubtful evidence but it is plausible that the main center of the Demotionidai may have been elsewhere than at Dekeleia, and it is at least not implausible that the center may have been at Kydantidai (tentatively located northeast of Athens, just south of Pentelikon, see Traill, 1986; it has no other known associated phratry). There were several persons of prominence called Demotion at Athens: an archon in 470/69 (Diod. 11.60.1); an apparently well-known speaker in the Assembly in 366/5 (Xen. Hell 7.4.4) who might possibly be identical with a member of the Boule in 367/6 (*Agora* 15.14, 39, Demotion son of Dem- of Lamptrai); and two others, one son of Demon of Phrearrhoi, the other from Acharnai, mentioned in Davies 1971 (See nos. 3738 and 10037). But there is nothing beside the name to connect any of these persons with the Demotionidai (or with Kydantidai).

65. ... Ἀθηναίων δὲ λέγεται εὐδοκιμῆσαι Σωφάνης ὁ Εὐτυχίδεω, ἐκ δήμου Δεκελεῆθεν, Δεκελέων δὲ τῶν κοτε ἐργασαμένων ἔργον χρήσιμον ἐς τὸν πάντα χρόνον, ὡς αὐτοὶ Ἀθηναῖοι λέγουσι κτλ. Hdt. 9.73.

itself part of its institutional identity. This group cannot be identified with the Cleisthenic deme Dekeleia, for the group pre-existed the deme. We need have no hesitation in identifying it with the House of the Dekeleieis of T 3.[66]

Thus far, then, we have a group that was well established, with an institutional identity dating to before Cleisthenes,[67] with its own legends and with special privileges at Sparta. From the decrees T 3 we can add that the group had something to do with a phratry, hereditary membership, and had its own priest. Both Herodotus and T 3 confirm the natural implication of the name, that the group was based in the village of Dekeleia. Given the pre-existence of a well-defined group of Dekeleieis, it is not surprising that Cleisthenes chose to make Dekeleia one of his demes—a fairly small one providing four bouleutai, with nearby Oion Dekeleikon providing a further three.[68] What degree of overlap was there between the demes of Cleisthenes and the older institution?

We know of one member of the House of the Dekeleieis, the phratriarch Pantakles, whose deme was Oion Dekeleikon, but we otherwise have no idea to what extent the House contained members of that deme.[69] Apart from this, there must have been residents of Dekeleia in 508 who became members of the deme, but who were not members of the old Dekeleieis because they were more or less newly settled there and therefore did not belong to the old hereditary grouping. There must also have

---

66. As did Wade-Gery 1931 (= 1958, 123, n. 1, 133–34). Hedrick 1990, 44–48, argues that neither Hdt. 9.73 nor Lysias 23.2-3 (see below, n. 76) shows there was a group called Dekeleieis other than the demesmen. But Herodotus implies an institution that would have existed before Cleisthenes' reforms, and hints, if he does not definitely imply, awareness of a distinction between deme and house. In any case the house in T 3 cannot be taken as identical with the deme (see n. 15).

67. It should also be noted in this connection that Dekeleia was one of the towns of Philochoros' ancient Athenian Dodecapolis (Strabo 9.1.20, 397 = *FGH* Philochoros fr. 94). If nothing else, this would tend to confirm the antiquity of the place and its institutions. Cf. Jacoby's comments ad loc. and p. 379.

68. Traill 1986, 137.

69. I pass over here the big question of whether it was any part of Cleisthenes' intention to cut across or undermine pre-existing kinship institutions (cf. Lewis 1963, esp. 26–27; *contra* Siewert 1982, 118–20. This would seem to be a case where he did not do so, unless we wish to interpret the existence of Oion Dekeleikon in this way. We know the demotics of three House members, Pantakles the phratriarch (ἐξ Οἴο—must be Oion Dekeleikon, cf. Hedrick 1990, 32), the priest Theodoros (Dekeleia, cf. p. 291) and Nikodemos, the proposer of the second motion (Dekeleia, cf. p. 291). These are the only two demes that are clearly members of this trittys (possibly called Epakria) of Hippothontis, though Traill 1986, 137, suggests possible association with Anakaia, to the east of Oion Dekeleikon, and tentatively with Oinoe and Azenia at the other end of Mt. Parnes. See map, p. 352.

been members of the old Dekeleieis who, by 508, were not resident in the area of the deme Dekeleia and were therefore assigned to different demes. Beyond this, the extent of overlap would have depended on the extent to which the old Dekeleieis were an exclusive institution, either socially or in any other way. There is no conclusive evidence on this point, and since we know of no other House of this sort in Attica we cannot argue from parallels; but there are hints that it was not exclusive and that the overlap of house and deme was considerable.[70]

After Cleisthenes, Dekeleieis could be used to refer both to members of the House, as in T 3, and to members of the deme.[71] The old group clearly did not think it necessary to change its name as the Eteoboutadai, "the true Boutadai," seem to have done in the face of the creation of a deme Boutadai.[72] But in the classical period a distinction could be made between the two institutions, where necessary, by use of the terms House for the older and deme for the newer. If the older institution had not always referred to itself as a House, there is a good chance that it started to do so after the Cleisthenic reforms precisely in order to make itself distinct from the deme.[73] The impression of a slight rather than a marked distinction between the two groups is certainly consistent with Herodotus' account of Sophanes and the Dekeleieis. The exploits of a deme member lead directly into a tale about those of the House, implying some common identity. Sophanes' demotic, however, is not simply *Dekeleieus,* as it might legitimately have been, but more deliberately "from the deme Dekeleia." Herodotus then starts his story about the older group; in the Greek the very next word, juxtaposed to "from the deme Dekeleia," is Dekeleieis.[74]

There is another reference to the Dekeleieis in speech 23 of Lysias, roughly contemporary with our decrees. The speaker has attempted to summon a certain Pankleon to court and, assuming he was a metic, has tried to begin proceedings before the polemarch. Pankleon, however, claimed to be an Athenian citizen: he was a Plataean and the Plataeans had all been granted enfranchisement as Athenian citizens during the Peloponnesian War.[75] Moreover, he claimed to belong to the deme Deke-

70. As recognized by Wade-Gery 1931 (= 1958, 133–34).
71. Cf. Wade-Gery 1931 (= 1958, 123, n. 1).
72. Cf. Lewis 1963, 26.
73. For the connotations of the term house, see pp. 103–4.
74. It is unclear whether we should be justified with Wade-Gery 1931 (= 1958, 123, n. 1) in supposing that Sophanes was a member of both institutions.
75. Cf. p. 51.

leia. "So I went," continues the speaker, "to the barber's shop by the Hermae, which the Dekeleieis frequent, and asked such of the Dekeleieis as I could find if any of them knew a Pankleon of the deme Dekeleia. . . ."[76] Now, this barber's shop by the Hermae is clearly to be identified with the "place in the city which the Dekeleieis frequent" mentioned in Hierokles' decree (63–64).[77] The speaker in Lysias 23, however, goes there to find out specifically about a member of the deme Dekeleia. It sounds as if this place was used by Dekeleieis in both senses and that one might go there to find out about House business and about deme members.[78] Again there is the suggestion of two broadly overlapping institutions.[79]

There is one further factor that is of crucial importance in understanding the background of the decrees. The detail is by and large irrecoverable, but it is clear enough that a war of the importance and duration of that between Athens and Sparta in the last third of the fifth century would have functioned as a powerful catalyst for the sort of demographic and social changes that we saw in the last section were likely to have an effect on phratry structures. The decimation of the population caused by the war itself and the devastating plague that struck Athens in its early years, together with the effects of great numbers of Athenians moving into the city for protection against the invading Spartans, a process which Thucydides tells us many Athenians found disturbing, are perhaps the two most obvious phenomena associated with the war that would have had an impact on phratry structures.[80] A third must have been the notorious laxity of citizenship controls.[81] T 3 itself provides abundant evidence of the dislocation and disturbance phenomena such as these would have caused: the implication of the provision for the extraordinary scrutiny; the fact that it is envisaged by Nikodemos that there may be fewer than three men in a thiasos; the need for a

76. . . . ἐλθὼν ἐπὶ τὸ κουρεῖον τὸ παρὰ τοὺς Ἑρμᾶς, ἵνα οἱ Δεκελειεῖς προσφοιτῶσιν, ἠρώτων, οὕς τε ἐξευρίσκοιμι Δεκελειῶν ἐπυνθανόμην εἴ τινα γιγνώσκοιεν Δεκελειόθεν δημοτευόμενον Παγκλέωνα. Lysias 23.2-3.

77. On the precise location of this place, see Hedrick 1990, 54–55. Cf. n. 144.

78. As noted by Wade-Gery 1931 (= 1958, 123, n. 1).

79. There is nothing to suggest great disimilarity of size between the two groups. The division of the house into thiasoi suggests a fair-sized group (over about fifty?). The deme had a Bouleutic quota of four; compare Halimous, with a quota of three, which had about 80 to 85 members in 346 (see appendix 5).

80. Thuc. 2.14–16.

81. See p. 34 n. 40.

meeting place in the city to be used for the publication of names of candidates and the like; Hierokles' provisions obliging the phratriarch to conduct meia and koureia at Dekeleia; and in general the measures taken by Nikodemos and Menexenos to ensure that the reliability of admission controls was not jeopardized by ignorance of the candidate within the phratry. In the case of the Dekeleieis, however, there would have been an additional factor at work in all this, for their collective experience in the Peloponnesian War was unique. As we have seen, according to Herodotus their special relationship with Sparta induced the Spartans to leave Dekeleian lands unharmed whenever they invaded Attica. A strong parallel comes to mind. In 431 Pericles feared that he might enjoy a similar privilege and was wary of the resentment it would cause among the Athenians. In advance of the Spartan invasion, he therefore proposed that his land be made public.[82] How much resentment the favorable treatment of Dekeleian land actually caused we do not know, but it must at least have had the effect of setting Dekeleieis somewhat apart from other Athenians. Later, in 413, the Spartans occupied and fortified Dekeleia and used it as a base for effective and damaging operations against Athens for the rest of the war. Thucydides does not tell us why Alcibiades recommended this course of action to the Spartans in 415/4,[83] but we may guess that the traditional Spartan ties with the Dekeleieis were a factor in the choice of site. We do not know what happened to the Dekeleieis during the period of the fortification, but in the context of the general dislocation caused by the War and the previous special treatment by the Spartans, we can imagine that it may have resulted in a further reinforcement of their group identity over against other Athenians and, I suggest, other Demotionidai also.

What sort of a group, then, were the Dekeleieis of T 3? The description "house," unique in our surviving evidence, is suggestive of a unique status and we need not be surprized to discover no exact parallel; but even ignoring the phratry association, the similarities with a genos of the type outlined in the last chapter are striking.[84] The house has a local base and hereditary membership. It appears to be an inclusive group rather than an exclusive one, probably overlapping to a large extent with the deme Dekeleia and possibly also Oion Dekeleikon. It has a long history, a priest, and a strong independent identity. Even the term house

---

82. Thuc. 2.13.
83. Thuc. 6.91, 6–7. Advice executed in 413: Thuc. 7.19.
84. Cf. Bourriot 1976, 639–48.

itself is more nearly suggestive of a genos than of any other sort of group.[85] Its position as a phratry subgroup would be wholly consistent with this and strengthens the parallel further; but it is here that the difference also seems to lie. It is difficult to be confident or precise, especially since, in my view, the relationship between Demotionidai and Dekeleieis was changing in the early fourth century, but it looks as though in some respects the House of the Dekeleieis had been less independent of its phratry than might be expected of the typical genos, if there was such a thing. Its members are called phrateres. Moreover, it does not have full control over its own membership, for the process of admission does not seem to have been quite that observed in the last chapter, in which gennetai automatically became phrateres, and rejection by a genos prevented access to phratry. Instead, a candidate becomes a phrater upon joining the Dekeleieis, but if he is rejected by them he may appeal to the Demotionidai. It looks as though, despite the long-standing strength of its independent identity, the House of the Dekeleieis had always been institutionally more highly integrated into its phratry than most gene.

There are two points in particular here, then, of significance. First, the similarity in certain respects between this House and another phratry subgroup, the genos; but also a certain dissimilarity from any other known group. To draw parallels with the groups mentioned in the last section, I suggest that before the Peloponnesian War the House was in a position something like the Salaminioi in respect to their phratry, if the Salaminioi belonged to a phratry at all,[86] like the Salaminioi of Sounium or of the Seven Phylai in respect to the Salaminioi as a whole in 363,[87] and possibly also like the constituent parts of the Dyaleis and Therrikleidai.[88]

Second, against the background of what was said about fission and fusion in the last section, it would be reasonable to see the unique experience of the Dekeleieis in the Peloponnesian War as the sort of factor that would have had a powerful effect on their institutional identity such as to cause them to break further away from the phratry of which they were a subgroup. Just as the Salaminioi from Sounium developed

---

85. Note in particular Aristotle's use of the idea of the house in his concept of the genos/kome. Cf. p. 60.

86. Cf. p. 65.

87. Cf. pp. 64–65.

88. Cf. p. 109.

from a branch of a genos in the mid-fourth century to a separate genos in the mid-third century, so the Peloponnesian War would have helped push the Dekeleieis, already with a well-established independent identity, in the same direction. That is reflected, I suggest, in our decrees, passed in the War's aftermath.

Disposal of Difficulties Faced by Hypotheses of Wilamowitz and Wade-Gery/Andrewes

Earlier in this chapter I identified a number of difficulties with the hypotheses of Wilamowitz, that T 3 were decrees of the Demotionidai and that the Dekeleieis were a privileged subgroup, and of Wade-Gery and Andrewes, that the reverse was the case. It is an argument in favor of my hypothesis that it disposes satisfactorily of both sets of difficulties.

To take those faced by Wilamowitz first, in my view the decrees are decrees of the Dekeleieis, and the Dekeleieis are the understood subject of "carrying the votes from the altar" in 29, as argued by Wade-Gery. At both extraordinary and regular scrutiny it is the Dekeleieis, the body passing the decrees, that votes on the candidates; there is no need to draw Wilamowitz' implausible distinction between the two scrutinies. But the vote is according to the procedure laid down in the law of the phratry as a whole, the Demotionidai. There is also no need to follow Wilamowitz in taking Nikodemos' motion as wholly replacing Hierokles'. Hierokles establishes that the Dekeleieis are to vote on candidates; Nikodemos' preliminary vote by the Dekeleian thiasoi supplements this.

I identified five difficulties with the view of Wade-Gery and Andrewes. First, that the functions performed by the Demotionidai in Hierokles' decree are, as was recognized by Wilamowitz, functions we would expect the phratry to perform. This presents no difficulty. At the time of Hierokles' decree the Demotionidai kept the master copy of the register, were a forum for appeal by candidates rejected by the Dekeleieis, and the law of the Demotionidai governed the practice of the Dekeleieis, because the Demotionidai were the whole phratry, the mother phratry, and the Dekeleieis were a subgroup. Subject to this, the Dekeleieis have a fair degree of independence, including control in the first instance over membership and possession of their own copy of the register. One could envisage a similar arrangement operating with respect to the two branches of the Salaminioi and the Salaminioi as a whole in 363.

Second, the use of the term House was odd if the Dekeleieis were a straightforward phratry. I have already shown that the term is wholly appropriate for an institution whose precise characteristics are unique in our evidence, though similar to those of a genos.

Third and fourth, it is implausible that a genos would have a measure of control over the admission of nongennetai to the phratry that is otherwise unattested, and that it should fail to have the absolute control over the admission of its own members to the phratry that is attested elsewhere. According to my hypothesis, no power is being exercised by any group over the admission to the phratry of nonmembers of that group; and there is no automatic entry for anyone because neither the Dekeleieis nor the Demotionidai were a genos.

Fifth, our other evidence for the structure and procedures of the phratry in the classical period, which suggests that they operated on the democratic model, is inconsistent with the systematic exercise of power over the phratry as a whole by a privileged subgroup. I suggest there is no such power.

Interpretation of T 3

The fourth argument in favor of this view of the relationship between Demotionidai and Dekeleieis is that it makes possible a satisfactory interpretation of the decrees T 3. That is its most crucial test. It does so on issues where the interpretations of Wilamowitz and Wade-Gery faced particular difficulties, but we must also show that it does so with respect to the decrees as a whole.

Preamble: The Priest and the Phratriarch

Two phratry officials are mentioned in the preamble, a priest and a phratriarch. The priest is named in 2 as Theodoros son of Euphantides. As already noted, there was probably a different name inscribed here when each decree was passed.[89] Of the other references to a priest in the decrees, only one carries any further description: at 41–42 the "priest of the House of the Dekeleieis" is required to collect a fine from a failed appellant to the Demotionidai. Were the priests inscribed in 2 also priests of the House of the Dekeleieis? And are other references to a priest in the decrees to the holder of the same office? The answer is almost

---

89. Cf. p. 291.

certainly yes to both questions.[90] At 35–36 it is "the priest," along with the phratriarch, who administers the oath to the synegoroi appointed by the Dekeleian House for an appeal to the Demotionidai; we would indeed expect him to be priest of the Dekeleian House. The fine-collecting activity of the "priest of the House of the Dekeleieis" in 41–42 is carried out elsewhere in the document by "the priest" (see below). The uniqueness of the form of reference at 41–42 need not trouble us. It was probably meant, as Wade-Gery saw, to stress that although the fine results from a vote of the Demotionidai, it is the priest of the Dekeleieis who is to be responsible for collecting it.[91] That the priest is "priest of the Dekeleian House" throughout suits my hypothesis well, since on that hypothesis it is the Dekeleieis who are the body passing the decree and therefore an unspecified priest in the decrees should be the priest of the Dekeleieis.

The phratriarch is identified at 11–12 as Pantakles of Oion[92] and thereafter simply as the phratriarch. What is his position vis-à-vis the priest, the Demotionidai, and the Dekeleieis? It may be useful first to list the functions of the phratriarch and priest mentioned in these decrees. They were as follows:

(A) The priest
    (a) Receives priestly dues from the meion and koureion (preamble).
    (b) Collects one thousand-drachma fine from a failed appellant to the Demotionidai (Hierokles, 41–42).
    (c) Collects five hundred-drachma fine from the phratriarch should he fail to hold the regular scrutiny (Hierokles, 50).
    (d) Collects fifty-drachma fine from the phratriarch if he fails to sacrifice meion and koureion at the altar at Dekeleia (Hierokles 56–57).

---

90. As recognized by Wade-Gery 1931 (= 1958, 122–23) against Töpffer 1889, 291, who left the identity of the priest in 60 open.

91. Wade-Gery 1931 (= 1958, 128). We do not know whether the Demotionidai contained other priests, but 41–42 suggests they might have done. Hedrick 1990, 83, doubts Wade-Gery's case and argues that on this basis we would also have expected the priest to be described as "of the Dekeleian House" at 35 and 20, where priest and phratriarch together administer an oath and erase names from the register in the keeping of the Demotionidai. But in both cases it is clear from the mention of the phratriarch that representatives of both groups are intended. If separate priests were intended at different points in this text, we would expect that to have been made clearer.

92. Cf. n. 69.

(e) Is charged with the inscription of the decrees (all three decrees, 2–3; 66; 107).

(f) Is to decide on an alternative venue for the meion and koureion, should this prove necessary, and give notice of this at the resort of the Dekeleieis in the city (Hierokles, 59–60).

(g) Is charged in Menexenos' decree with the posting of candidates' names in the temple of Leto (Menexenos, 123).

(B) The phratriarch

(a) Conducts the scrutinies (Hierokles and Nikodemos, passim) and sacrifices the meion and the koureion (56).

(b) Is charged in Menexenos' decree with the posting of candidates' names at the resort of the Dekeleieis in the city (Menexenos, 121).

(C) The priest and the phratriarch together

(a) Expunge the names of those expelled at the extraordinary scrutiny from the register in the keeping of the Demotionidai and the copy (Hierokles, 19–20).

(b) Collect one hundred-drachma fine from the introducer of anyone expelled at the extraordinary scrutiny (Hierokles, 25).

(c) Administer the oath to the synegoroi of the House of the Dekeleieis for appeal to the Demotionidai (Hierokles, 35–36).

There are three possible explanations of the position of the phratriarch consistent both with my hypothesis and this allocation of functions: that he was phratriarch only of the Dekeleieis, that he was sole phratriarch of the Demotionidai, or that he was one of two or more phratriarchs of the Demotionidai with specific responsibility for the Dekeleian branch. Of these I would suggest the last two are more likely than the first: if a subgroup were sufficiently independent to call its leader a phratriarch, one might wonder why it doesn't call itself a phratry and do away altogether with the links to the Demotionidai.

Moreover, there are hints that, while the priest was exclusively priest of the Dekeleieis, the phratriarch represented a body that was to some extent external. We are very badly informed about priests in Attic phratries other than in this decree: none of the other references in our evidence to such persons is informative as to function. It is not even clear that phratries normally had priests distinct from those of their subgroups.[93]

---

93. See pp. 233–35.

But the extent of the priest's administrative rather than purely religious activities in T 3 is perhaps remarkable. He certainly performs at least one function which in every other attested case was performed by the phratriarch, namely inscribing the decree,[94] and one suspects the same may have been true of other functions such as posting names of candidates, collecting fines, and so on. Most notably, the priest is empowered to collect a fine from the phratriarch should the latter fail to hold the regular scrutiny and to sacrifice the meion and the koureion at Dekeleia. The impression is that the Dekeleieis are using their own dedicated official, the priest, as a check on a power that is to some extent external. This impression of externality is strengthened by the provisions of Menexenos' decree, under which the priest posts information at Dekeleia, and the phratriarch at the resort of the Dekeleieis in the city.[95] It may also be significant that, while the phratriarch is empowered with the priest to collect the one hundred-drachma fine from the introducer of someone rejected at the extraordinary scrutiny, it is the priest alone who is to collect the large one thousand-drachma fine from an unsuccessful appellant from Dekeleieis to Demotionidai. Both House and phratry have an interest in getting rid of illegitimate members, but it is essentially the House rather than the phratry that has the interest in dissuading appeals to Demotionidai from its decision.

There are no decisive arguments as to whether Pantakles was sole phratriarch of the Demotionidai or whether there was more than one, with Pantakles responsible for the Dekeleian branch, but an attractive case can be made for the latter. We would have parallels for multiple phratriarchs in the Dyaleis and Therrikleidai, and in spite of the impression of the phratriarch's externality in some respects, other features suggest specific association with the Dekeleieis: the three joint functions with the priest, for example, and Pantakles' local demotic. Moreover, the phratriarch is required to conduct meion and koureion ceremonies and the scrutiny of new members each year for the Dekeleieis at Dekeleia;

---

94. T 5, 55–56; T 19, 24–26; ?T 20, 10–11.

95. There is a notable contrast here with Hierokles' provision that notice of alternative location of the meion and the koureion, if it is not possible to conduct them at Dekeleia, should be given in the city meeting place of the Dekeleieis by the priest. The explanation may be that this was a matter in which the Dekeleieis were asserting control to some extent over against the phratriarch. They have just obliged him in normal circumstances to sacrifice the meion and the koureion at Dekeleia, and they do not wish to give the phratriarch an opportunity to make excuses and move the ceremony somewhere else (? to the Demotionidai center). The priest is therefore given control.

it might have been difficult for him during the same festival to carry out the same functions for the rest of the Demotionidai elsewhere. In either case, however, it is attractive to see the priest as essentially an officer of the House, and the phratriarch as an officer of the phratry.

Viewing the respective roles of priest and phratriarch in this way is, I suggest, more satisfactory than viewing both phratriarch and priest as officers of the Dekeleieis, as is necessary on the hypothesis of Wade-Gery and Andrewes. Such a view provides no fully satisfactory explanation of why two persons are required to carry out essentially similar administrative functions, or of why those functions are distributed between them in the way they are.[96]

Motion of Hierokles

Lines 13–26 contain Hierokles' proposals for a once-and-for-all, extraordinary scrutiny. It is not a diapsephismos of all the phrateres; it is stated explicitly that the procedure is to apply to "such as have not yet been scrutinized according to the Law of the Demotionidai": the implication is that this does not include everyone.[97] The procedure of the scrutiny is not described in detail, for it is to follow the law of the mother phratry; suffice it to say that the phrateres are to swear to Zeus Phratrios and carry their votes from the altar.

There is no difficulty in identifying the probable background to this proposal. As already noted, the laxity of citizenship controls during the

96. One might make some sense with the explanation that one officer is acting as a back-up for and a democratic check on the other. But this does not explain why it is always the priest who seems to be performing this function with respect to the phratriarch. Indeed, one might, by this view, have expected the opposite: the elected phratriarch should surely be acting as a check on the hereditary priest.

97. Thompson 1968 held that the extraordinary scrutiny was a diapsephismos, representing a conservative reaction to the loosening of admissions regulations, and from which only the Demotionidai, as gennetai, were exempt as having already been scrutinized according to the law of the Demotionidai. In that case, however, it is not clear why Hierokles did not simply specify that the Demotionidai should be exempt, rather than those who had not been scrutinized according to their law. μήπω, "not yet," here also seems inconsistent with this view. Thompson's premise was that it was not plausible that the law of a body other than itself could control the phratry's proceedings; but there is no difficulty with this if we accept the Dekeleieis as a subgroup of the Demotionidai. It is much more natural to take the exclusion as applying to those Dekeleieis who had been properly scrutinized despite, or before, the recent period of laxity in the application of the rules. His view is also subject to the other objections raised against the Wade-Gery/Andrewes view above. Cf. now also Hedrick 1990, 33–36.

Peloponnesian War is well attested.[98] It seems likely that this action by the Dekeleieis a few years later was intended to weed out those who had managed to get in under false pretenses during conditions of war, exacerbated in this case perhaps by the Spartan occupation of Dekeleia during the latter part of the war.

Those discovered at the extraordinary scrutiny not to be qualified as members are to have their names erased by the phratriarch and the priest from the register in the keeping of the Demotionidai and from the copy. The main copy of the phratry register will have been kept by the Demotionidai; the Dekeleieis will have had a copy containing only Dekeleieis. I imagine that the phratriarch would have erased names from the Demotionidai copy, the priest from the Dekeleieis version. Finally Hierokles details the arrangements for fining the introducer of a "rejected" phrater.[99]

At 26, Hierokles turns to deal with the regular scrutiny. The procedure itself is summarized even more briefly than the extraordinary: "carrying the votes from the altar." As already remarked, we may suppose that, as with the extraordinary scrutiny, the details of the procedure followed the familiar Law of the Demotionidai, and there is therefore no need for detail. It goes without saying that the voting is to be carried out by the Dekeleieis, the body passing the decrees and so naturally understood as the subject. There is, however, one point of detail specified for the regular scrutiny, we must suppose because it is an innovation, namely that in future it is to take place the year after a candidate's koureion. The scrutiny itself was nothing new; this procedure had been provided for under the law of the Demotionidai, albeit that it had fallen into disuse. The innovation is in the timing; we shall guess that it had previously taken place at the same time as the koureion, as it may have

---

98. Cf. p. 34 n. 40.

99. Ἀποδικάζω normally means "acquit" or "dismiss a case from court" (cf. Hedrick 1990, 39–40). Usually when cases are dismissed from court, it implies acquittal, but here τὸν ἀποδικασθέντα must be the one whose case to remain in the phratry has been dismissed at the diadikasia (note the verbal echo). Hedrick takes it to refer to someone who, by some legal decision (possibly the amnesty of 403 from the requirements of Pericles' citizenship law), had bypassed scrutiny. There is no parallel for such a meaning, and in context it cannot be right. The reference must be to a case decided at a legal or quasi-legal process, not to a situation in which there was no process at all. That process in this context must be the diadikasia. In other words, you do not merely need to have sponsored someone who had bypassed scrutiny to be fined (surely harsh if such bypassing had been legal); you need to have had your case rejected at the scrutiny.

done in some other phratries.[100] The purpose of the innovation is not immediately obvious, but perhaps it is best seen as another means of tightening up on controls, the importance of the scrutiny emphasized by its being set apart from the ceremonial of the koureion, with a year allowed between the two for the qualifications of the candidate to be confirmed or doubts to be voiced and resolved.

Hierokles now turns to deal with the procedure for appeal to the Demotionidai (29–44).[101] There are two points of particular significance here. First, as with the procedures described above, where detail is specified we shall assume there is innovation: the fact of the extraordinary scrutiny is an innovation and is provided for explicitly, but not the procedure, which is familiar and can be referred to in shorthand. There already existed a regular scrutiny procedure, though it may not have

---

100. Cf. p. 173.

101. Hedrick 1990, 61–68 (cf. 1984) argues that lines 29–52 do not, as had previously been thought and as I think, apply to the regular scrutiny, but to a separate scrutiny, involving a vote on all members, which is to take place annually. This is unconvincing, not least because there would logically be no person to whom the scrutiny could apply. It is clearly Hierokles' intention that all non-scrutinized existing members are to be covered by the once-and-for-all extraordinary scrutiny, to take place immediately, and all new members by his tightened provisions for the regular scrutiny, to take place annually. An annual extraordinary scrutiny of all members would be redundant. He supports the interpretation with four main arguments from the text (for more detailed discussion of these see Lambert 1986b, 346–52). First, he takes the dual occurrence of τὸ λοιπὸν, "in the future," at 27 and 52 to imply that, somewhere between the two, Hierokles had reverted to the subject of the extraordinary scrutiny. But on his own view the annual extraordinary, as well as the regular scrutiny will occur in the future, so the occurrence of τὸ λοιπὸν anywhere could not be a guide as to which Hierokles has in mind. I take τὸ λοιπὸν in 27 as marking off discussion of the extraordinary from that of the regular scrutiny, and at 52 as implying that the meion and the koureion had previously been conducted elsewhere than at Dekeleia, and that this should not happen in the future. Second, Hedrick argues that, in 31 and 38, it is the candidate who may be rejected and may appeal. In the regular scrutiny as described by Nikodemos, however, the candidate is rejected, but the introducer appeals. Therefore the appeal at 29–44 must relate to the extraordinary, not the regular, scrutiny. This distinction is not present in the text. In the description of the regular scrutiny at 88–91, 94–96, 97–100, and 100–102, the object of ἀποψηφίζομαι (reject) is ambiguous as between introducer/thiasotai and candidate. It is the candidate who is "rejected" or "disfranchised" and the introducer or thiasotai whose case, or view, is thrown out or "rejected" (ἀποψηφίζομαι has both senses, see *LSJ*). There is the same ambiguity at 31 and 38. At 31 those who are rejected (i.e., the introducers, whose cases have been rejected, or the candidates who have been voted out) may appeal. Line 38 parallels 100–102 very closely; in both cases there is ambiguity, but the introducer is primarily intended: "an appellant whose case is rejected by the Demotionidai shall pay one thousand drachmas." (38); "if someone rejected by the thiasotai does not appeal to all the phrateres . . ." (100–102). For Hedrick's other arguments in support of this interpretation, see nn. 102 and 111.

been properly applied in recent years. Again, it can be referred to in shorthand; the innovation is the timing, the year after koureion. The very fact of appeal to the Demotionidai is provided for explicitly by Hierokles and must in some way be new; hence, too, the need for detailed specification of procedure. It would not just be new in the sense that it was being re-established after the disorder of the War, because in that case a shorthand reference would have sufficed, as earlier in the decree.

Second, the nature of the procedure provided for by Hierokles makes it clear that the Dekeleieis are anxious to protect the validity of their decision against possible reversal by the Demotionidai. Although appeal is to be allowed, the fine for failure, one thousand drachmas, is twice the largest fine stipulated elsewhere in the decrees and is intended, it would seem, to discourage appeal. If the appellant nevertheless goes ahead, five synegoroi are to be elected by the House of the Dekeleieis and are to be sworn not to allow anyone "not being a phrater" to be a member of the phratry.[102] These synegoroi are speakers of some sort. The term does not in itself imply which side they are to speak on; but it is clear in this context that they are to argue the case of the Dekeleieis before the Demotionidai. They are to be advocates for the Dekeleieis, accusers of the rejected candidate.[103] By the same principle that thiasos members in Nikodemos' decree are not to vote on their own members

---

102. I agree with Hedrick 1990, 52, that φρατρίζεν does not mean "join a phratry," but "be a member of a phratry," or perhaps rather "take part in the phratry" (cf. Krateros fr. 4, p. 45 above). However, it is not necessary to translate it, with Hedrick, in this context as "continue to be a phrater" (cf. previous note).

103. Wade-Gery 1931 (= 1958, 128–29) recognized that synegoroi can be assessors, advocates, or accusers and argued that they should be assessors in this case, because it would be "improper for accusers to take an oath as to what verdict they will permit (lines 36/37)." The argument is weak. οὐκ ἐᾶν can mean "to advise or persuade not to" (*LSJ* cites Thuc. 1.133 for this sense); it does not necessarily imply that the persuader has power of decision. I take the force of συν- here to be primarily that they are to speak with or on behalf of those who have appointed them (i.e., in this case the Dekeleieis), as is usual with this term (cf. Dem. 21.112, discussing the advantages enjoyed by the wealthy in legal proceedings: καὶ μάρτυρές εἰσιν ἕτοιμοι τούτοις καὶ συνήγοροι πάντες καθ' ἡμῶν εὐτρεπεῖς. The synegoroi are set up by rich Athenians to speak with them, against us, i.e., in this case ordinary Athenians. Cf. MacDowell 1978, 61–62; 170–71 and 1971, 198–99; Hedrick 1984, 56–58). Where there are multiple synegoroi as here, however, there may be a secondary force of speaking with each other. ἐπ' αὐτοῖς in 32 in ambiguous. It may refer to the Demotionidai (as understood by Wade-Gery), in which case I take the sense to be that the Dekeleian House is to elect five synegoroi for them, but with the undertone that their role is to speak in the face of, almost against, the Demotionidai. Alternatively, it may refer back to ὧν ἂν ἀποψηφίσωνται in 31, i.e., "on the subject of," but effectively "against." See now also Hedrick 1990, 43–44.

when the whole phratry decides to accept or reject a candidate, it seems that the Dekeleieis under Hierokles' arrangements are to be excluded from the vote of the Demotionidai.[104]

By my hypothesis both these features of the appeal are readily explicable. We cannot know the details, but whatever the scrutiny procedure had been in the past, it would not have involved a process of appeal to the Demotionidai as described by Hierokles. I suggest this will have been because the Dekeleieis had previously had less control over the admission of fellow phrateres: perhaps there was an automatic vote by the Demotionidai on each candidate, perhaps some other procedure involving the Dekeleieis less exclusively. Now, however, the Dekeleieis are establishing a procedure which is more independent: the Demotionidai are still to be involved, but only as a court of appeal. The claim to that new independence is fortified by a heavy fine for a failed appeal and supported by the procedure whereby the synegoroi are to make their case before the Demotionidai and ensure that no false phrateres are admitted.[105]

After providing for the fining of a failed appellant to the Demotionidai, Hierokles stipulates that "these things shall come into effect from the archonship of Phormio." This straightforward little provision in fact has some significant implications. First by "these things" Hierokles must mean the whole of the regular scrutiny procedure, including the appeal, just described, i.e., lines 26–44.[106] The extraordinary scrutiny was a once-and-for-all event and might have been described as intended to take place in the archonship of Phormio, but not from it. In any case, the timing of the extraordinary scrutiny has already been specified in line 16: it is to happen "immediately." This chronological distinction between the two procedures seems to have the further implication that, since the appeal procedure is described as part of the regular scrutiny, it will not also have applied to the extraordinary scrutiny. That would otherwise have

---

104. T 3, 103–6.

105. Why did the Dekeleieis not break away altogether from the Demotionidai at this stage? We do not know, but a semi-independent status of this sort is not in itself surprising. The Dekeleieis would have enjoyed some form of semi-independence for a long time, as typically did many gene (cf. pp. 63–74). One of the most important reasons for maintaining links, however, apart from natural conservatism, must have been the implied legitimacy of the group to confer phrater and hence citizen status on its members. This consideration may have been particularly strong at this time, when the Dekeleieis clearly were generally concerned to secure the legitimacy of their admissions procedures after the disturbances of the War.

106. Cf. Hedrick 1990, 53, for ταῦτα as referring normally to what has gone before in the text.

been a natural way to understand lines 29–30, "the regular scrutiny is to take place, the votes being carried from the altar. If anyone wishes to appeal . . . ," but not the only way; "If anyone wishes to appeal . . ." might have been taken to refer to both scrutinies previously described, extraordinary and regular. We can probably conclude from this that the Demotionidai were not intended by Hierokles to be involved in the extraordinary scrutiny at all.[107] Why should he involve them in the regular scrutiny and not the extraordinary one? The difference may be that all those not yet scrutinized according to the law of the Demotionidai must already have gone through some process of admission to House and phratry, however unrigorous, unlike those affected by the regular scrutiny. The smaller body may see itself as fully competent to exercise what is effectively a revisionary function, but may not feel it has full competence to deal alone with the primary process of decision on conferral of the status of phrater, and hence of citizen.[108]

Second, an incidental point. When Hierokles says, "these things are to take effect from the archonship of Phormio," he should mean that the new regular scrutiny arrangements are to apply for the first time at the Apatouria which fell in the archonship of Phormio. Since the decree was also passed in that archonship (396/5), this implies that the decree was either passed at a phratry meeting at the same Apatouria at which the new arrangements were to come into effect, i.e., at the Apatouria in Pyanepsion 396,[109] or at a separate meeting of the phratry in the late summer of 396 after the start of Phormio's archonship (1st Hekatombaion) but before the Apatouria.[110]

Next, Hierokles makes a provision obliging the phratriarch to conduct the regular scrutiny every year and imposing a fine of five hundred drachmas should he fail to do so (45–52).[111] Similarly, the phratriarch

---

107. I say only probably because we do not know enough about the law of the Demotionidai to be able to rule out Hierokles' reference to it implying that the extraordinary scrutiny involved the Demotionidai plenum in some way. If this were the case, however, we would expect Hierokles to be more explicit; since there are specific provisions on the extent of Demotionidai involvement in the regular scrutiny, the decree as it stands would be very unclear on the point, whatever the content of the law of the Demotionidai. It is easier to take it that, by referring to the law of the Demotionidai, Hierokles meant and would have been understood as meaning simply the details of the procedure to be followed by the Dekeleieis described in abbreviated form as "carrying the votes from the altar."

108. Cf. n. 105.

109. For the date of the Apatouria, see p. 157.

110. For phratry meetings other than at the Apatouria, see p. 202.

111. Hedrick 1990, 62–63, takes 45–48 as requiring the phratriarch to take a vote each

is to conduct the meion and the koureion annually and is to be fined fifty drachmas if he does not (52–58). Hierokles has already stipulated that the scrutiny should take place a year after the koureion in any individual case: the two procedures are now separate, their relative importance indicated by the size of the fines imposed for failure to carry them out: five hundred drachmas for the scrutiny, the decisive process of admittance to full phratry membership, but only fifty drachmas for the meion and koureion, the significance of which now presumably becomes more ceremonial.[112]

On the subject of the meion and koureion, Hierokles provides explicitly that they are in the future to be brought to the altar at Dekeleia, the obvious implication being that they had previously been conducted elsewhere. The War is certainly one possible explanation of what lies behind this:[113] the occupation of Dekeleia may have made it necessary for the meion and the koureion to be celebrated elsewhere, if they were celebrated at all. But there is also another possibility: if the phratry center of the Demotionidai was elsewhere than at Dekeleia, it may be that the meion and the koureion had been conducted there. This provision would in that case be another manifestation of the Dekeleieis' efforts to increase their independence. Should the phratriarch of the Demotionidai show reluctance to observe the provision, he is to be encouraged by the prospect of a fine, to be exacted by the priest, the protector of the interests of the Dekeleieis. In case of emergency, it is to be the priest, not the phratriarch, who decides on and gives notice of an alternative location. This notice is to be posted at "the place in the city which the Dekeleieis frequent." Menexenos also stipulates that this place should be one of the two locations where names of prospective candidates are to be posted. As we have seen, it can be identified more exactly from Lysias 23 as a barber's shop by the Hermae.[114] It is notable that although the Dekeleieis clearly had a strong sense of their institutional identity, it was

---

year on who should be subjected to the extraordinary scrutiny. I do not believe Hierokles meant to provide for a regular extraordinary scrutiny of this sort (cf. n. 101) and, with other previous writers, take the sense to be that he is to put to the vote each year those who have to be scrutinized, i.e., he is to hold the regular scrutiny. The necessity of δέηι here is not a necessity determined by a new vote of the phratry every year, but is that which arises from the provision in 26–28 that the scrutiny is to take place one year after the koureion.

112. Cf. n. 125–26.
113. Cf. Hedrick 1990, 54.
114. Cf. p. 115–16.

not at Dekeleia but in the city that many of them could be found. Some no doubt would have now lived there, and those who did not could presumably be expected to travel to Athens regularly for business, festivals, Assembly meetings, and so on.[115] The stele itself on which the decrees are recorded, however, is to be posted not in Athens nor at the phratry-center of the Demotionidai, if indeed that was elsewhere than at Dekeleia or Athens,[116] but at Dekeleia.

Motion of Nikodemos

As already noted, this decree was probably passed at some interval of time after the passage of Hierokles' decree.[117] The decree contains two main proposals. The first concerns the preliminary scrutiny (*anakrisis*). From line 71, which talks of the three witnesses specified for the preliminary scrutiny, it is apparent that there was previous legislation on this subject, now lost. It sounds as if it may have been recent, and possibly supplementary to Hierokles' motion.[118] At Athens "anakrisis" was usually a preliminary inquiry into a case conducted by an archon before the case came to court.[119] Something similar must be envisaged here: a procedure preliminary to the main scrutiny and involving three witnesses supporting the candidate's claim to membership. We might naturally suppose this would have taken place immediately before the regular scrutiny, but there are hints that it may have been associated instead with koureion, which took place a year later.

At the start of his motion Nikodemos speaks of the decrees about the introduction of children and the scrutiny.[120] Rather than taking these terms as tautological it seems better to take "the introduction of children" as including the meion and the koureion as well as the subsequent scrutiny. Since his second proposal certainly concerns the scrutiny proper,

---

115. Cf. p. 13.

116. Cf. n. 64.

117. Cf. p. 292.

118. It would be economical to suppose that the anakrisis procedure was established by this apparently recent legislation for the first time. However, we cannot rule out the possibility that it existed before Hierokles and that Hierokles did not mention it because he was not changing it.

119. See Harrison 1968–71, 2. 94–105. Cf. Hedrick 1990, 56–57.

120. Hedrick 1990, 56, notes that while both Nikodemos and Menexenos mention children, Hierokles does not. But that will not bear Hedrick's inference that Hierokles' proposals had nothing to do with children and that Nikodemos' decree cannot therefore be modifying Hierokles'.

it would then make sense if Nikodemos' first proposal, about the pre-liminary scrutiny, concerned meion and koureion, part of the introduction of children.

The impression is confirmed by Nikodemos' wording when he turns to deal with his second proposal at line 78: "...but when the scrutiny takes place...." It sounds as though this was at a different time from the anakrisis he has just been dealing with.

There is a further measure of confirmation in Nikodemos' last pro-vision. After dealing with his proposals for the thiasoi and the scrutiny, Nikodemos rounds off the decree in the usual way (cf. 64–68, 126) by providing for its inscription (106–8). But then, almost as an afterthought, he specifies the wording of the "oath of the witnesses at the introduction of the children." It is natural to take this as a reference to the witnesses at the preliminary scrutiny which were dealt with at the beginning of the decree, where it was simply stated that they "are to swear by Zeus Phratrios." What exactly they are to swear by Zeus Phratrios is now specified, namely that the child being introduced is the legitimate son of the introducer. The implication seems to be that the preliminary scrutiny is part of the introduction of children, specifically of the kour-eion rather than the main scrutiny. We know from elsewhere that it was normal for the introducer in a phratry to swear as to the legitimacy of his candidate, usually at the start of the meion or the koureion proce-dure.[121] It seems best to associate the three witnesses for the preliminary scrutiny with this.[122] The reason for having the preliminary scrutiny a year before the main scrutiny is clear enough. Not only would it easily fit in with the ceremonial introduction of the candidate at the koureion, but it would also establish credentials at this stage and allow a year for them to be proven and for any possible difficulties to emerge before the scrutiny proper.[123]

Nikodemos' proposal on the preliminary scrutiny is that the three witnesses for it should come from the candidate's own thiasos.[124] If there

---

121. Cf. p. 171

122. While the anakrisis is part of the eisagoge, I do not agree with Hedrick 1990, 71, that they may be "alternative names for the identical procedure." There was more to introduction than just the anakrisis; namely, the meion and the koureion and the main scrutiny.

123. Cf. the provision of Menexenos' decree, that details of candidates be published during this year (p. 139–40).

124. It is perhaps better to take εἰσαγομένο in 82 as passive rather than, with Wade-Gery, as deponent, i.e., as implying that the thiasotai are the candidate's rather than the

are not as many as three in that thiasos, Nikodemos allows the witnesses to come from the other phrateres. Insofar as a thiasos with fewer than three members was a real possibility at the time of this decree, not simply a logical possibility for which Nikodemos felt he should make provision, it should probably be explained as a consequence of loss of members during the Peloponnesian War.[125] In any case, it is difficult to envisage circumstances in which thiasoi were created with less than three members; we may perhaps infer that the House of the Dekeleieis had been divided into thiasoi for some time.[126]

Nikodemos' second main proposal (78-106) also concerned thiasoi, this time in relation to the main scrutiny. Under Hierokles' decree the regular scrutiny was to involve a vote by all the Dekeleieis, from which appeal was to be allowed to the Demotionidai. It is Nikodemos' proposal that this vote be preceded by a secret vote of the candidate's thiasos, to be publicly counted and declared by the phratriarch at the phratry meeting. The thiasotai are to be fined one hundred drachmas if the phratry as a whole rejects a candidate accepted by them, though any thiasos member that opposed the candidate is to be exempt.[127] On the other hand, if the introducer is rejected by his thiasos but appeals successfully to the phratry as a whole, his candidate is to be accepted. If the appeal fails he is fined one hundred drachmas. He is not obliged to appeal. If he does not, the vote of the thiasos stands. Finally, the thiasotai are not

---

introducer's; though the thiasos would normally have been the same, there were circumstances (e.g., lack of surviving father or close male relatives) in which the introducer was not the father of the candidate and may have belonged to a different thiasos or even to a different phratry (cf. p. 170 n. 155). However, in specifying the words of the witnesses' oath at the introduction of candidates (109-11) Nikodemos does not take account of unusual circumstances of this sort; the wording assumes that the introducer would always be father of the candidate. So it is possible he would also have discounted such circumstances in 82.

125. In appendix 1, I translate 76-77, "If, however, there are not as many as this in the thiasos." The Greek, as the English, is naturally taken as referring to the total number of persons in the thiasos, not to the number of witnesses. The latter, however, is perhaps possible. The implication of a very small thiasos, however, would remain.

126. It is possible, however, as suggested by Hedrick 1990, 58, that the thiasoi did not exist at the time of Hierokles' decree, in which they are not mentioned. If the Dekeleieis had made a further break with the Demotionidai after Hierokles' decree (see p. 136), the thiasoi may have been created then.

127. Wade-Gery 1931 (= 1958, 125, n. 3) may be right that this means one hundred drachmas in all, not one hundred per thiasos member, but the clause as drafted seems ambiguous on the point. The provision for an individual exemption perhaps weighs slightly in the other direction.

to vote with the other phrateres when a candidate from their own thiasos is put to the vote in the plenum.[128]

How are we to explain Nikodemos' purpose in these two proposals? The intention seems to be to ensure that decisions on membership of the phratry are properly informed by the knowledge of those who are likely to know the candidate and his introducer best, the members of his own thiasos. Their initial vote is to form the basis for the decision of the phrateres as a whole one way or the other. The phrateres are not bound by the thiasos vote, but they are to be informed by it, and in the normal course of events would be expected to follow its lead.

It should be clear enough by now that this is not the action of an exclusive, aristocratic institution obsessed with ensuring that only the "right people" get in. It is the action of a body on whose decision rested the enjoyment of the citizenship and other rights dependent on demonstrable possession of qualification by descent; and it is an action taken against the background of lax citizen controls during the War. But why this particular change now? The War had probably been over for more than a decade by the time of Nikodemos' motion,[129] and though they had apparently existed for some time, it seems that the Dekeleian thiasoi had not been used in admissions procedures before. Again I suggest that the crucial explanatory factor should be seen not simply as the laxity of citizenship controls during the War, but more widely as the social and demographic disruption of natural community caused by it, which, over a period of years, is giving rise to changes in phratry structure. It may be that one effect of this disruption has been that the thiasoi of the Dekeleieis have become separated from each other, physically or otherwise, to the extent that the Dekeleieis as a whole can no nonger make informed decisions on the admission of members. Particularly if we take into account the additional passage of time between the War's end and Nikodemos' decree, this would be consistent with the War's having also created pressures that separated the Dekeleieis as a whole from the Demotionidai. If the Dekeleieis are finding themselves growing apart from one another a decade or so after the War, it is not difficult to imagine that they would have felt even more distant from the Demotionidai. But it is that increasing independence from the Demotionidai that I suggest may be the essential point in all this. Before Hierokles the regular scru-

---

128. For the procedural parallel to the appeal from Dekeleieis to Demotionidai, see p. 127.

129. Cf. p. 292.

tiny, according to the law of the Demotionidai, did not involve anything that could be termed an appeal to the Demotionidai. I have suggested that this may have been because the Demotionidai were previously more directly and automatically involved.[130] Under Hierokles' measures it is established that the Dekeleieis are to run their own procedure. Appeal to the Demotionidai is permitted, but discouraged. Nikodemos' decree, passed somewhat later, takes the process a stage further: an already existing subgroup of the Dekeleieis is given the task of conducting the vote at first instance. The subgroup is effectively taking on the role of the Dekeleieis as a whole in Hierokles' decree; the vote of the Dekeleieis now in a sense performs the role of the vote of the Demotionidai under Hierokles' dispensation, in that it is the vote of second instance. Nikodemos talks of appeal to the Dekeleieis as Hierokles had of appeal to the Demotionidai,[131] and both are optional. The crucial difference is that the appeal process now takes place within the Dekeleieis; they are assuming more of the competence over decisions on admissions to themselves. In Hierokles' decree we have the impression that the Demotionidai are in some sense an external power; there is a heavy fine for a failed appeal and synegoroi are appointed to argue the Dekeleieis' case apparently in some external forum. In Nikodemos' decree the court of second instance has become the Dekeleieis themselves. A fine for a failed appeal is unnecessary.

What has happened to the Demotionidai in Nikodemos' decree? They are not mentioned in it and we cannot be certain, but there are two possibilities consistent with my interpretation. First, it may be that appeal to the Demotionidai remains possible, the difference from Hierokles' decree being that they become a court of third instance, so to speak, rather than second. Though this change may reflect Nikodemos' intention to bring more of the admissions process within the competence of the Dekeleieis, he is concerned in practice with setting up a new first stage, not with abolishing the old third stage; the major element in the process, the vote by the Dekeleieis, remains. Nikodemos does not mention the third stage appeal; it may be his intention, by means of inserting a new first stage, to insure even more effectively than Hierokles had with his synegoroi and heavy fine, that it should not be used in practice, but it remains as a possible last resort for the introducer thwarted at the two

---

130. See p. 128.
131. Compare 29–31 of Hierokles' decree with 94–95 of Nikodemos'.

previous stages. This explanation would suit the internal indications in Nikodemos' decrees which, as we have already seen, suggest that his motion was in some sense intended to supplement rather than replace entirely Hierokles' measure; Nikodemos' overall intention can be explained readily enough by the wish of the Dekeleieis to maximize their independence while continuing perhaps to feel that their phratric legitimacy depended on their continued identity as Demotionidai.[132]

The likelihood that Nikodemos' motion was passed at some interval of time after Hierokles',[133] however, together with the implied existence of other decrees, now lost, that may have been passed subsequent to Hierokles' decree, suggests another possibility: between Hierokles' decree and Nikodemos' the Dekeleieis had broken more completely with the Demotionidai, possibly in the same legislation that provided for the preliminary scrutiny procedure which Nikodemos modifies. At the split, we may suppose, the possibility of appeal to Demotionidai, provided for by Hierokles, was abolished, and, perhaps, to ensure the continued effectiveness of the scrutiny, the preliminary scrutiny procedure was introduced. Nikodemos modifies this by making use of thiasoi at the preliminary scrutiny and introducing in addition an initial vote by thiasos at the main scrutiny, so that there was a first instance and appeal procedure mirroring those that had existed previously when the Dekeleieis were also Demotionidai.

There are a number of arguments in favor of such an interpretation. First, it would explain why Nikodemos does not mention the possibility of appeal to the Demotionidai. As it stands, his motion begs the question as to whether or not the appeal provision is to remain, as the opposing views of Wilamowitz and Wade-Gery on the matter tend to suggest. It sounds as if the vote of the Dekeleieis in Nikodemos' motion is intended to be final; we would never have guessed anything about an appeal to any other body if we did not also have Hierokles' decree. But if he meant it to continue, a short sentence could have clarified the point; as indeed it could if he had intended it not to continue. The impression is that there is something missing; something has happened to the relationship between the Demotionidai and the Dekeleieis since Hierokles' motion about which Nikodemos and the rest of the Dekeleieis knew, but about which we do not, something specified in those other decrees that dealt with the preliminary scrutiny.

132. Cf. p. 112.
133. Cf. p. 292.

A second difficulty with the view that appeal to Demotionidai is implicitly maintained in Nikodemos' decree is that we should then have a double appeal provision at the local level: if appeal from thiasos to Dekeleieis failed, a further appeal could be made to Demotionidai. In fact yet a further appeal would be possible, for the failed appellant to the Demotionidai could bring a suit in a public court if he still wished to press his case.[134]

This is not impossible, but it is improbable. Hierarchies of courts with the possibility of multiple appeal are familiar to us, but the concept is essentially foreign to classical Athens. Indeed it seems to have been expressly resisted; that a case once decided was then closed seems to have been recognized as something of a legal principle.[135] There were exceptions: as we have seen, admissions decisions of subgroups of the citizen population, whether demes, phratries, or gene, were subject to appeal to a central court,[136] but this was not a multilayered process. A decision of a deme on admissions was not subject to appeal to trittys or phyle, it went straight to the People. Moreover, if the interpretation of Philochoros fr. 35 in chapter 1 was correct, that fragment reflects resistance to multilayered processes of precisely this sort: that decisions of subgroups of subgroups should not be subject to appeal to the larger subgroup was the principle on which the measure was based. That law applied only to gene and orgeones groups. We are dealing with neither here, and there can be no doubt that this decree must reflect something of an exception to this principle, for in any case there is the possibility of appeal from smaller subgroup to larger in addition to subsequent appeal to the center. But I submit that adding yet another layer at the local level would at least have gone against the grain; at most it may have been unacceptable. It is perhaps easier to believe it was never Nikodemos' intention.

The possibility that the Dekeleieis had completed the break is supported finally by another feature of Nikodemos' decree: the description of the Dekeleieis as "all the phrateres." Nikodemos uses the term several

---

134. Cf. p. 35 n. 42.

135. The principle is enunciated by Demosthenes at 20.147: οἱ νόμοι δ᾽ οὐκ ἐῶσι δὶς πρὸς τὸν αὐτὸν περὶ τῶν αὐτῶν οὔτε δίκας οὔτ᾽ εὐθύνας οὔτε διαδικασίαν οὔτ᾽ ἄλλο τοιοῦτ᾽ οὐδὲν εἶναι. The text of a law on the matter is given by him at 24.54; cf. Harrison 1968–71, 27.190.

136. Cf. p. 35. The Athenian concept of ephesis was not exactly that of appeal; often "retrial" would be a better translation (see Harrison 1968–71, 2.190–91), but appeal is close enough in our case. For other examples of it, see Harrison 1968–71, 2.190–99.

times when he is talking about the Dekeleieis as a whole in contrast to the thiasoi.[137] Now, it is possible to explain this in a way consistent with the Dekeleieis' continuation as a subgroup of the Demotionidai: it would be clear both from the implied contrast here with the thiasos, and from the fact that this is a decree of the Dekeleieis that "all the phrateres" meant the Dekeleieis, not the Demotionidai. Perhaps by describing his House in this way Nikodemos was implicitly asserting independence from the Demotionidai, just as he was in the substantial provisions of his decree, though formal ties remained. However, it would perhaps be more straightforward to take the phrase as implying that the Dekeleieis were indeed now fully independent of the Demotionidai.

This alternative view, if adopted, would have two noteworthy consequences. First, Nikodemos' motion would not in every respect be supplementary to Hierokles'. That need not disturb us. Enough remains—the vote of the Dekeleieis remains fundamental—to be consistent with Nikodemos' concurrence, both stated and implied, with previous decrees, especially since those previous decrees included more than just Hierokles' decree.[138] Second, we would need to suppose that the phratriarch would have broken away from the Demotionidai with

---

137. Lines 81, 85, 96, 96–97, 99, 102. Cf. Hedrick 1990, 58.

138. As far as the inscription of the decrees is concerned, we can, with a little imagination, guess at the sequence: priest A, perhaps not a poor man (cf. p. 291) is charged with having Hierokles' decree inscribed at his own expense (67–68). He commissions a stone cutter to do the work on the new stele (it was the first decree, at least on this subject, to be passed by the Dekeleieis for some time, perhaps even the first ever, so a new stele was obviously required). It might as well be a large one: more decrees on this subject could be expected and investment in a large stele now would prevent the need for expenditure on a new one next time. If he did not himself survive to benefit, his successor as priest (probably his heir) would. Hierokles' decree was therefore inscribed on this stone, covering fifty-eight lines on one face and nine and a half on the other; I do not accept the supposition of Wade-Gery 1931 (= 1958, 125, n. 1) that this distribution of the text between the two sides implies that both decrees were inscribed together. Priest A proved right in his expectation that there would be further decrees, but unfortunately the next one, the one about the anakrisis and possibly making the final break with the Demotionidai, was too long to fit in the remaining space on the stele. It was inscribed on another one and is lost to us. However, a little later Nikodemos' motion was passed. It stood in the same series as Hierokles' and did not expressly contradict it. It was also short enough to fit on the same stele, so that was where the stonecutter was instructed to inscribe it. Priest B blessed the memory of his predecessor for his prudence, but preferred nevertheless to advertise his own name at the head of the stone. Some years later another short decree (Menexenos') was passed on this subject and the third priest, Theodoros, found he could squeeze it onto the bottom of the same stele. Perhaps he also found a cheaper stonecutter. But like his predecessor, he replaced his predecessor's name at the head of the stone with his own.

the Dekeleieis: his somewhat ambiguous position in Hierokles' decree would now be resolved.[139]

By my hypothesis about the identity of Demotionidai and Dekeleieis, we may therefore either see Nikodemos' decree as increasing the self-sufficiency of the Dekeleieis' admissions' procedures over against the Demotionidai, or as developing the consequences of a more complete break with them that would have been brought about by one or more decrees passed since Hierokles' decree. There are no decisive arguments, though on balance perhaps the second interpretation is preferable.

A final point: to which treasury are the fines provided for by Hierokles and Nikodemos payable? They both specify that they should be sacred to Zeus Phratrios; but Hierokles twice says they are for the common (benefit or treasury).[140] Again both Hierokles and Nikodemos talk of the common registers (*ta koina grammateia*), of which, for Hierokles at least, there were two copies.[141] In Hierokles' decree it seems likely that the treasury, like the register, was common. In Nikodemos' the situation is less clear. In neither case does the use of the term koinon bear the necessary implication that the fund, or the registers, were held jointly by the Demotionidai and the Dekeleieis. "Koinon" can, and often does, mean common to the members of a single institution. Nor, in the case of the registers, can we read much into the use of the plural.[142] If there were still links between Demotionidai and Dekeleieis in Nikodemos' time, registers and treasury may have remained joint; but if the split had been completed, they may both now have been the Dekeleieis' alone.

Motion of Menexenos

This decree seems to have been passed some years or more after that of Nikodemos, in ca. 370-50. It was inscribed in a different and later hand, in a sloppy manner, and probably under a different priest.[143] Menexenos starts, as did Nikodemos, by concurring with "previous decrees about the introduction of children." He proceeds with his own amendment,

---

139. Cf. pp. 122-24. References to the phratriarch in Nikodemos' decree: 79 and 86.

140. Sacred to Zeus Phratrios: for Hierokles 23-24, 40, etc., and for Nikodemos 91-92, etc. For the common fund: 44, 52.

141. T 3, 20-22. Cf. p. 125. Wade-Gery 1931 (= 1958, 124) is, I think, overly categorical in claiming that the language of 44 implies that the treasury was "of the whole."

142. Cf. pp. 175-76 with n. 182.

143. Cf. p. 292.

which is that the names of candidates, together with details of their fathers and mothers, should be posted by the phratriarch at the place the Dekeleieis frequent,[144] and by the priest on a white board "in the temple of Leto" (which, since no location is given, can be taken to have been at Dekeleia[145]), "during the first year after the koureion."[146]

This is not a major change in procedure. Clearly there were Dekeleieis who did not live at Dekeleia[147] and it is an assumption throughout these decrees, as in the orators, that the effectiveness of the control exercised over membership of a group depended on knowledge of the candidate by those voting on whether or not to accept him. This is part of the reason, I have suggested, why the Dekeleieis would have sought to acquire increasing independence of the Demotionidai in the first place, and why Nikodemos sees the need at the scrutiny for a vote by thiasotai prelim-

---

144. He does not specify that this is in the city, but the intention must be the same as Hierokles' in providing for the publication of details of alternative locations for the meion and the koureion. Whether this meeting place was still the barber's shop by the Hermae, however, we do not know. Cf. p. 116.

145. For the significance of this temple for the interpretation of T 4, a very fragmentary inscription of religious content, probably also of the House of Dekeleieis, see p. 294.

146. This is my understanding of the meaning of τῶι πρώτωι ἔτει ἢ ὧι ἂν τὸ κούρεο/ν ἄγει (118–19), which makes good sense given the year's gap between koureion and scrutiny in the Dekeleieis (cf. p. 125). The use of ἢ in precisely this sense with πρῶτος does not seem to be found elsewhere, but it is not problematic. It is very close to the well attested temporal use, e.g., at Plato, *Krito* 44a, Socrates speaking: τῇ γάρ που ὑστεραίᾳ δεῖ με ἀποθνῄσκειν ἢ ᾗ ἂν ἔλθῃ τὸ πλοῖον, and can be taken as (? colloquial) shorthand (i.e., ἢ ὧι = "after that in which"). Compare T 3, 27. Guarducci 1937, 49, cf. Schöll 1889, part 2, 10 took the sense to be "in the year before koureion," but this sense of πρώτωι is apparently not attested before the Christian period (see Hedrick 1990, 59), and the purpose of such timing would be obscure given that the scrutiny, at which such information would be necessary, took place a year after the koureion. To take ἢ as "or," with the sense "in the first year" (i.e., presumably of the child's life) "or in that in which koureion is celebrated" (Lipsius 1894, 163, followed by Hedrick 1990, 60) will not work. Koureion did not take place in a child's first year, so we can not take ἢ as joining two equivalents (for the timing of koureion in adolescence see pp. 163–66), and if "the first year" and "that in which koureion is celebrated" are meant to be alternatives, it is very difficult to see the sense of the provision. There could be no purpose in publishing names of candidates sixteen years or so before the scrutiny took place; and I find it difficult to think that Menexenos has the meion in mind here (on which see p. 159–64). Unless a lot had changed since the decrees of Hierokles and Nikodemos, the main processes of scrutiny in the Dekeleieis were associated with the koureion. Even if the meion were intended, the provision would still be very odd: we can hardly envisage a scrutiny process in which there were two stages, meion and koureion, and it was optional at which stage information about candidates was published. What would happen if the candidate were challenged at the stage at which no information had been provided?

147. Cf. p. 114–15.

inary to the vote by phratry. Menexenos' proposal is a small practical measure with precisely the same purpose.

Conclusion

I suggest, therefore, that the House of the Dekeleieis were a subgroup of the phratry Demotionidai. In our decrees they are developing greater independence as a phratry in the years following the Peloponnesian War, a war that would in general have had general social and demographic effects which we would expect to be detectable in changes in phratry structures; a war in which, in particular, the experience of the Dekeleieis is known to have been such as might have set them apart from other Athenians and other Demotionidai. I do not believe I have demonstrated this conclusively to be true; that could not be claimed of any interpretation on current evidence. I hope, however, that I have demonstrated that it is a hypothesis that is superior to those previously advanced. It disposes of the serious objections that can be raised against earlier interpretations. It is consistent with our evidence outside these decrees with regard to historical context, with regard to the Dekeleieis, and with regard to the internal structure and constitution of phratries; and it provides a satisfactory interpretation of the provisions contained in the decrees.

Chapter 4

Apatouria, Admission, and Membership

The focus of attention in the last two chapters has been the phratry's internal structure. In this and the following two chapters, the aim will be to give an account of the phratry's activities. I shall start with the central event in the phratry calendar, the festival of the Apatouria, and with the processes of phratry admission normally associated with it; in this context I shall also consider the meager evidence for women in the phratry. In chapter 5 I shall consider those phratry activities not related to admission processes and in chapter 6 phratry religion and officers. Throughout our evidence is weak; new material may change the picture, possibly significantly.

Apatouria

Preliminaries

Nearly all the literary evidence and the largest single piece of epigraphical evidence for the phratry's activities pertain directly or indirectly to the phratry festival, the Apatouria,[1] and to the processes of phratry admission and reception[2] normally associated with it.[3] The interpretation of

---

1. On the festival in general, see S. Mommsen 1864, 302–17; 1898, 323–49; Töpffer 1894, cols. 2762–80; Deubner 1932, 232–34; Guarducci 1937, 33–41; Labarbe 1953; Nilsson 1972, 165–70; Mikalson 1975, 79; Parke 1977, 88–92; Hedrick 1991, 251–53. For the festival myth, see notes to next section.

2. I use the term reception to refer to the processes by which the phratry recognized women, which did not normally amount to admission (cf. pp. 178–88).

3. That phratry admission processes took place on Koureotis, the third day of the Apatouria, is reported as a general fact by ancient scholars, including our best evidence for the detail of Apatouria, Σ Ar. *Ach.* 146 (see below, n. 59). There is contemporary evidence for the timing at Apatouria at Andoc. 1.126 (meion ?, see p. 69); Dem. 39.4

this fact is itself a matter of some importance to which we shall return.[4] There can be no doubt, however, that the festival of the Apatouria, in which phratry membership itself was the central theme, was the focal point of the phratry year, and it is with an account of that festival that I begin.[5]

The Apatouria was also celebrated in other Ionian cities; indeed Herodotus identifies it as one of two criteria of Ionian identity: "Those who are descended from the Athenians and who celebrate the festival of the Apatouria are all Ionians." He qualifies this somewhat by noting that there were two Ionian peoples without the Apatouria, the Ephesians and the Colophonians.[6]

When seen in conjunction with other evidence for the origins of the phratry before the Ionian migration from Attica to the Ionian coast, it is likely that the widespread occurrence of the festival in the Ionian world betokens its having predated that migration in some form; and this contention is perhaps bolstered by the timeless character of its themes. But this is a point to which I shall return later.[7] For the moment it must be said that we know nothing for certain about the content of the festival at an early period; all our evidence for it comes from the late fifth century or later.

The Myth

Writers in antiquity seem to have been more interested in the festival's foundation myth than in the details of the festival's events.[8] The myth

---

(adoptive introduction, see n. 178) and T 3, 28–29 (regular scrutiny of the Demotionidai/ Dekeleieis. The specification that the scrutiny should take place on Koureotis "a year after the koureion is sacrificed" suggests that the koureion also took place on that day in this phratry. The obvious connection between the names of the day and of the sacrifice confirms that this would generally have been the case). Admission to a phratry took place on an occasion other than the Apatouria, however, certainly in one case (Isae. 7.15, adoptive introduction, at Thargelia, cf. p. 66) though it is probable that there were special reasons for this (see pp. 216–17). For the timing of the introduction of girls insofar as it took place, see n. 205 and for that of gamelia, p. 185.

4. See further pp. 188–89.

5. With two exceptions, we have evidence for the activity of no groups other than phratries at the festival: under arrangements established in 363/2 the genos Salaminioi sacrificed a pig at the Apatouria (Ferguson 1938, 3–5, no. 1, 92), but they were either a phratry subgroup or conceivably formed a separate independent group like a phratry (see p. 65); and in the third century there was a sacrifice during the Apatouria at Panakton, which in some way involved soldiers stationed there. See below, n. 10.

6. Hdt. 1.147.2. On the festival in other Ionian states see p. 267–68 n. 105.

7. See further pp. 267–71.

8. For a list of the numerous sources see Vidal-Naquet 1986 (= 1981), 123, n. 15. To his list should be added Ibn al-kifti, see Lippert 1894, 486–89.

has also received considerable attention from modern scholars. My account will be brief.

Though the outline of the story is the same in all accounts, the details vary. According to the oldest version, that of Hellanikos,[9] there was a dispute between Athens and Boeotia over borderland, "some say over Oinoe and Panakton, others over Melainai."[10] The Boeotians proposed a duel between the rival kings, but while Xanthios, or Xanthos, of Boeotia accepted, Thymoites of Athens[11] declined and promised his kingdom to whoever would fight in his stead. The challenge was taken up by Melanthos, or Melanthios, The Dark One,[12] who, having armed himself, approached to do single combat with Xanthios, The Fair One.[13] "You do me wrong, Xanthios," said Melanthos, "in coming against me with another and not alone as we agreed." Xanthios, hearing this, turned around, wishing to see if anyone had followed him, and while he was turned Melanthos struck and killed him and became king of Attica.[14] Thus the Athenians, who had gained control of the land, decided to celebrate a festival, which they called originally Apatenoria, later Apatouria, after the trick (*apate*) which had taken place.

This explanation of the origin of the festival's name, from the apate of Melanthos, is the one generally given by our Greek sources, except

---

9. *FGH* 323a Hellanikos fr. 23 (= Σ Plato *Symp.* 208d). The only other pre-Hellenistic source is *FGH* 70 Ephoros fr. 22 (= Harp. s.v. 'Απατούρια), which is very close to Hellanikos' version. I do not fully share the despair of Vidal-Naquet 1986, 156, about distinguishing older and newer versions of the myth. There may never have been a single accepted version and it may be that in some cases later sources preserve genuine alternative traditions, but this later material is just as likely to be the result of unreliable scholarly speculation and reconstruction.

10. For Oinoe, cf. *FGH* 26 Konon fr. 1(39); *Lexica Segueriana* (= Bekker, *Anecdota Graeca*) 1.416–17; for Melainai cf. Apostolios 3.31; *L.S.* 1.416–17; Ephoros fr. 22; also Suid. s.v. 'Απατούρια and Σ Ar. *Ach.* 146 (both "Kelainai"). For Panakton cf. *IG* 2².1299, 29–30, a third-century decree from Eleusis, probably of Athenian soldiers stationed there, at Panakton and Phyle, in which honors for a general are to be announced among other occasions ἐμ Πανάκτω[ι 'Απα/το]υρίων τῆι θυσίαι. It sounds as if this sacrifice was a regular event, presumably associated in some way with the Apatouria myth, though we cannot tell for how long before the third century it had taken place. If the festival and myth were not linked until the later fifth century (cf. p. 152), it would have started later than that.

11. Cf. the phratry named Thymaitis, T 13 and T 14, and p. 222.

12. An Arcadian immigrant, or according to Polyainos, an Athenian general, cf. next note. Again there is a related phratry, the Medontidai, T 7–10, esp. pp. 312–14.

13. We also hear of an oracle, τῷ ξάνθῳ τεύξας ὁ μέλας φόνον ἔσχε Μελαίνας (Polyain. 1.19) and a vow to Dionysos (E.M. s.v. 'Απατούρια, s.v. Κουρεῶτις; *L.S.* 1 416–17) or Zeus Apatenor (*L.S.* 1.416–17).

14. According to Paus. 9.5.16, Xanthios was killed by Andropompos, who in other traditions, e.g. Paus. 2.18.8, is the father of Melanthos. See further n. 32.

for the scholiast on Aristophanes *Acharnians* 146,[15] who preserves a variant tradition that it derives from homopatoria, from the coming together of fathers at the registration of their children.[16] Modern philologists have agreed with the latter etymology, but take the sense to be rather that the festival was for those of the same father, i.e., phrateres.[17]

In some versions of the legend, Dionysus, in particular Dionysus Melanaigis, plays a role. We hear that Melanthos made a vow to him before the battle,[18] and that when Melanthos distracted Xanthios he had seen Dionysus Melanaigis standing behind him.[19] Moreover, the events of the legend are said to be the cause of the establishment of this god's cult in Attica;[20] one source even claims that the Apatouria was a festival of Dionysus.[21] It is remarkable, however, that Dionysus does not appear in either of our two pre-Hellenistic sources, Hellanikos and Ephoros, and it has thus long been suspected that he was a late intruder into the legend and the festival[22]—probably the festival before the legend.[23] His presence in the legend tends to undermine the trick around which it is centered. The Apatouria clearly, as we shall see, had a Dionysiac character in the classical period, and was celebrated just after the wine harvest in the same month as the wine festival Oschophoria.[24] The cult of Dionysus as a wine god, however, did not apparently become prevalent in Attica until the mid-sixth century,[25] so it would not have been until at least after that that he intruded into the festival; the silence of our classical sources suggests that it may well not have been until the Hellenistic period that he was incorporated into the legend. I doubt, however, whether the Apatouria was ever a festival specifically of Dionysus; this is probably an ancient scholar's mistake, albeit an understandable one.

---

15. Cf. also Ibn al-kifti loc. cit. at n. 8.

16. The connection between Ἀπατούρια and πατέρες appears to be made by Xen. *Hell.* 1.7.8 (cf. n. 47), which may have been the origin of the ὁμοπατόρια etymology in antiquity.

17. See Boisacq 1907; Chantraine 1968–80; Frisk 1960–70; cf. p. 10.

18. Cf. n. 13.

19. Nonnos *Dion.* 27.301–8; E.M. loc. cit.; Σ Aristid, *Panath.* 118.20; Σ Ar. *Peace* 890; *FGH* 26 Konon fr. 1 (39) says Melanthos saw a beardless young man; Apostolios, L.S., Σ Ar. *Ach.* and Suid. loc. cit. that it was someone wearing black goatskins.

20. L.S. loc. cit.; Suidas s.v. Ἀπατούρια; Σ Ar. *Ach.* 146.

21. E.M. loc. cit.

22. First suggested by Halliday 1926, 179–81.

23. As suggested by Parke 1977, 88–92.

24. See Parke 1977, 77–80; Deubner 1944.

25. Parke 1977, index s.v. Dionysus.

Insofar as the festival did have particular patrons, these will always have been Zeus Phratrios and Athena Phratria.[26]

There have been numerous attempts at interpreting this myth, none of them entirely satisfactory. As far as its quasi-historical features are concerned, Melanthos was traditionally the founder of the second royal dynasty at Athens; his son was Kodros and his grandson Medon, who was reputedly the first archon for life (if that was not his son Akastos).[27] Whether a person with some or all of the attributes of Melanthos ever existed is impossible to say. Conflicts between the neighboring inhabitants of Attica and Boeotia were probably frequent in the archaic period and perhaps earlier, and it is possible that this myth relates in some way to such an encounter.[28]

It has seemed more appropriate to look for symbolic interpretations. There must at least be some symbolism in the fact that the two combatants are named The Fair One and The Dark One, though it is not clear how far we are justified in attributing to fairness and darkness their modern symbolic significance.[29] It looks as though fairness is straightforward and darkness tricky. It is possible that fairness is also summer and darkness winter; this has some attraction, given the timing of the Apatouria in early autumn.[30] But it may be going too far to see in the not particularly blameworthy founder of an Athenian royal house a symbol of Bad, achieving victory over Good.[31]

It has also been suggested that the contest represents an early form of tragedy[32] or a means of establishing a royal claim to territory by ritual combat.[33] Apart from the possible summer/winter symbolism, the

---

26. In the case of Athena Phratria perhaps not quite always, see below p. 211. Another deity associated with the legend by L.S. is Zeus Apatenor. It says it was either to him or to Dionysus that Melanthos made his vow before the battle and that Melanthos also bade the Athenians sacrifice to Zeus Apatenor. There is apparently no further evidence for this cult in Athens or elsewhere, however, though elsewhere in Greece the epithet is associated with Athena and Aphrodite. See, e.g., Paus. 2.33.1 ("Athena Apatouria").

27. See pp. 315-19.

28. See Töpffer 1889, 225-41; Wilamowitz 1886, 112, n. 2; Jacoby ad *FGH* 323a fr. 23.

29. Cf. p. 149.

30. Cf. Maass 1889, 805, n. 13; Usener 1898, 329-79 (= 1913, 259-306. Cf. 1904, 301-13). See also Farnell, 1909a, 130-31 and 134-36; 1909b; Rose 1951, 131-33; Cook 1941-40, 1.689. On the timing of Apatouria between summer and winter, see p. 157.

31. Cf. however pp. 220-22 on the generally undistinguished character of Athenian phratry eponyms.

32. Nilsson 1911, 674 (cf. 1951-60 1:61-110, 111-16). The connection with Dionysus is crucial here, but that seems to have been a late development. See p. 146.

33. Jeanmaire 1939, 382-83. He thought the ritual joust might have been followed by

relevance of any of this to the content of the festival is not clear. Vidal-Naquet, however, in an ingenious interpretation, has suggested that the ephebia provides the crucial link between festival and myth.[34] He noted that the battle in the myth takes place in border territory and that the victory is won by unorthodox means. In reality, young Athenians introduced to their phratries at the Apatouria were about to embark on their period of military service, the ephebia, in border territory, in circumstances in which they needed to employ unorthodox, i.e., non-hoplite, tactics to be successful. Similarities to the Spartan *krypteia*,[35] the system whereby young Spartan men were expelled from society for a period and obliged to live in the wild without the normal weapons of a hoplite, can be detected; the ephebe is also a hunter, a lone fighter in the wild. A profound reversal of the norm is at work: the example presented to the new ephebe in Melanthos is of a lone fighter using unorthodox and dishonest tactics; yet the ephebe is to become precisely the opposite of this—a member of a closely knit, honorable and orthodox hoplite phalanx. Hence the unexpected prevalence of blackness in the myth.[36] Similar examples of role reversal are adduced elsewhere;[37] a "law of symmetrical inversion"[38] is seen to be at work in general in the rites and myths surrounding passage from childhood to adulthood:

In historical terms, the ephebe in archaic and classical Greece was a pre-hoplite. By virtue of this, in the symbolic enactments that are the rites of passage, he was an anti-hoplite: sometimes a girl, sometimes a cunning hunter, sometimes black. It is not in the least surprising that a mythical figure like Melanthos should have been considered a model for the ephebe.[39]

---

a procession (cf. the alternative tradition replacing Melanthos with Andropompos, n. 14) and compared the similar duels at Plut *QG* 13.294b–c and the sources cited by Will 1955, 381–83. Cf. Garlan 1972, 15–17.

34. Vidal-Naquet 1986, 106–28, acknowledging a debt to Brelich 1961, 56–59.

35. Vidal-Naquet 1986, 112–14 cf. Jeanmaire 1913.

36. Melanthos, Melainai, Dionysus Melanaigis, all from μέλας = "black." Cf. also n. 19 and, more doubtfully, the black cloaks associated with the Apatouria, p. 150. Also the hunter Melanion at Ar. *Lys.* 781–96.

37. E.g., girls taking on the attributes of men in marriage related ceremonies at Argos (Plut. *de Mul. Virt.* 4.245f) and Sparta (Plut. *Lyc.* 15.5) and at Athens boys taking on the attributes of girls at the Oschophoria (Plut. *Thes.* 23) and in capturing Salamis (Plut. *Sol.* 8–9).

38. Vidal-Naquet 1986, 114, based on the thesis of Lloyd 1966 that polarity played a fundamental role in archaic Greek thought.

39. Vidal-Naquet 1986, 120.

The interpretation may seem at first sight attractive, but there is, as often, a danger that an imaginative, theoretical construction of this sort may go beyond what the evidence will support. Four crucial doubts or uncertainties cannot be overlooked.

First, it is not clear that the ephebia at Athens was conceived of as in any way a preparation for hoplite warfare through experience of the opposite; it seems to have been simply a period of all-around military training.[40] The ephebe was not alone, nor was he characteristically a hunter. Nor is it clear that the sort of guile shown by Melanthos would have been regarded by any Greek, hoplite or otherwise, as the opposite of what would normally be expected of him; fair play is not a Greek concept. One doubts, in short, whether the perceived polarity of myth and reality was really there.

Second, there is considerable doubt about what form the ephebia took in Athens before 335/4.[41] Some have seen the institution as established at that time as entirely new;[42] in any case it seems that before this citizens were not necessarily removed from normal life for two years to do border service.[43] Moreover, it has been thought that even after 335/4 the thetes would not have participated;[44] it may be that the cavalry did not either. One wonders how far it is appropriate to interpret a myth of this sort, concerning a festival in which all citizens were participants, such that its central significance lies in an institution the character and possibly even the existence of which are uncertain before the late fourth century, and in which a significant proportion of participants in the festival seem likely even then to have played no part.

The third uncertainty is connected with the second. It concerns the relationship between the alleged age of the myth and the chronological position of the reality to which it is supposed to correspond. On the basis of Vidal-Naquet's theory, the myth originated at an early date in the archaic period; yet the reality which supposedly lies behind it, hoplite warfare and the ephebia, is securely attested only after 335/4 in the case of the ephebia and about 650 in the case of hoplite warfare.[45]

The fourth uncertainty concerns how and at what stage the myth

40. On the ephebia, see especially *Ath. Pol.* 42 with Rhodes 1981.
41. Before, that is, the law of Epicrates of that date mentioned by Lykourgos fr. 5.3 (= Harp. s.v. Ἐπικράτης). See Rhodes 1981, 494.
42. E.g., Wilamowitz 1893, 1.193–94.
43. See Antiphon fr. 69, cf. Rhodes 1981, 494, and Bryant 1907, 74–88.
44. Rhodes 1981, 503.
45. See especially Salmon 1977 and Cartledge 1977.

became associated with the festival. Vidal-Naquet's theory seems to presuppose that the association was longstanding, but this is far from demonstrable. Indeed there are indications which suggest the opposite.

First, what we know about the Apatouria aside from the myth does not indicate that it was a festival concerned characteristically with the ephebia. The only apparent connection between what we know of the details of the festival and the ephebia, apart from the obvious fact that at least some of those introduced to phratries at the Apatouria would have gone on to become ephebes,[46] is the black cloaks allegedly worn by both ephebes and participants at the Apatouria. This link, however, is dubious. The crucial passage is from Xenophon's account of the machinations of the party of Theramenes following the battle of Arginousae in 406:

> After this the Apatouria took place, at which the fathers and the kinsmen come together. The party of Theramenes therefore arranged for a large number of men to wear black cloaks and have their heads shaven at the festival in order that they should come to the Assembly as being relations of those who had died . . . [47]

As has been pointed out by Maxwell-Stuart,[48] the black cloaks here do not, as initially supposed by Vidal-Naquet,[49] seem to be connected directly with the festival itself; they seem rather to be intended as a sign of mourning by those who had lost relatives at Arginousae, and are part of Theramenes' party's ruse designed to create ill feeling in the Assembly against the Athenian generals.[50]

It is, however, curious that several centuries later there is evidence

---

46. There is also the link between the ephebia and oinisteria, p. 164.

47. μετὰ δὲ ταῦτα ἐγίγνετο Ἀπατούρια, ἐν οἷς οἵ τε πατέρες καὶ οἱ συγγενεῖς σύνεισι σφίσιν αὐτοῖς. οἱ οὖν περὶ τὸν Θηραμένη παρεσκεύασαν ἀνθρώπους μέλανα ἱμάτια ἔχοντας καὶ ἐν χρῷ κεκαρμένους πολλοὺς ἐν ταύτῃ τῇ ἑορτῇ ἵνα πρὸς τὴν ἐκκλησίαν ἥκοιεν, ὡς δὴ συγγενεῖς ὄντες τῶν ἀπολωλότων. Xen. *Hell.* 1.7.8

48. Maxwell-Stuart 1970.

49. At 1986, 124, n. 31, in response to Maxwell-Stuart, Vidal-Naquet withdrew his earlier interpretation of this passage and his claim that ephebes are regularly portrayed wearing black cloaks on Greek vases (see Maxwell-Stuart 1970, 113–14).

50. Apart from this being the sense of the passage in context, note also that Istros reports that participants at the Apatouria would, at least for the torch ceremony he is describing, normally wear the finest clothes (cf. p. 154) and that Xenophon speaks of ἄνθρωποι in general, not ephebes (or future ephebes), as wearing the black cloaks.

that Herodes Atticus made a donation to enable the ephebes to wear white cloaks for the procession to Eleusis.[51] Philostratos reports:

Before that, they [the ephebes] used to wear black cloaks whenever they sat together at public assemblies or walked in public processions, as a sign of the mourning of the Athenian people for the herald Kopreos whom they themselves had killed when he was trying to drag the sons of Herakles from the altar.[52]

I find it difficult to follow Maxwell-Stuart in associating the wearing of black cloaks before Herodes Atticus specifically with the Eleusis procession and the mourning of Demeter for her daughter Persephone;[53] Philostratos suggests that it was a more general feature of ephebic dress and, however we might wish to interpret the mythical explanation, it does at least suggest the authenticity of the real fact with which it is associated. The coincidence with the black worn by the mourners in Xenophon's account of the Apatouria of 406 remains striking. It may, of course, be no more than a coincidence; but it is possible that the events of 406, or perhaps simply Xenophon's account of them, easily enough misinterpreted, combined no doubt with the central role played in the Apatouria myth by The Dark One, Melanthos, led to the adoption of black cloaks for ephebes sometime during the five and a half centuries between Arginousae and the benefaction of Herodes Atticus.[54] The introduction/reform of the ephebia in 335/4[55] suggests itself as a possible occasion; it was a period characterized by its archaising innovations, probably not least with respect to the Apatouria.[56]

The connection between the ephebia and the Apatouria, either in its broad themes or its detailed features, at any pre-Hellenistic date seems weak. As we shall see, the festival was more about the control, maintenance, and affirmation of kinship and of membership in society at every level. Similarly, the apparent main themes of the myth, whatever

---

51. Philostratos *Vit. Soph.* 2.550; *IG* 3.1132; *IG* 2².3606 (c. 176 A.D.).

52. Philostratos loc. cit.

53. Maxwell-Stuart 1970, 115–16.

54. When Kopreos and Herakles' sons became involved we cannot tell; nor is it easy to discern the relationship between this development and the traditions about black goatskins or Dionysus of the black aegis in the Apatouria myth, though it may be significant that they are not a feature of earlier accounts of it.

55. Cf. above p. 149.

56. Cf. the probable measures relevant to the Apatouria introduced by Lykourgos, n. 75.

the symbolic significance of the battle between The Fair One and The Dark One, seem to have very little to do with the main themes of the Apatouria.

Second, we have no evidence that anyone in antiquity perceived any thematic connection between festival and myth. The one connection that was made, that between the apate of Melanthos and the name of the festival, the Apatouria, is quite artificial.

The lack of apparent thematic connection and the existence of an obviously artificial one suggests that festival and myth may have been linked by no more than etymological speculation. Such speculation could easily have been the work of Hellanikos himself, a well-known rationalizer of myths.[57] The sequence of events may have been somewhat as follows. Hellanikos knew about the festival Apatouria and wanted to explain its origin. He also knew a good deal of mythical material from Homer[58] and elsewhere about tricky persons called Melanthos and about Athenian kings, one of whom bore that name. Combining these, he came up with a composite aetiological myth designed, rationally enough, to explain the origin of the Apatouria in terms of the festival's obscure name, though the myth's subject matter was unrelated in theme to the festival. The connection between myth and festival proposed by Hellanikos came to be generally, if not universally, accepted and perhaps gradually came to influence the details of the festival itself.

If an interpretation of this sort is correct—I claim for it only plausibility and consistency with the evidence—we would not be justified in seeing in the myth connections with the themes of the Apatouria based on the alleged polarity of early Greek thought. Insofar as the mythical material existed before Hellanikos, its interpretation may be argued about, but it would have no thematic relevance to the festival.

The Festival

We are on somewhat firmer ground in dealing with the events of the festival itself, though here again we have to beware of chronological uncertainties. Much of our evidence on matters of detail is of late-fourth-century origin or later, and we cannot be certain how far it reflects the festival as celebrated in the fifth and earlier fourth centuries, let alone in any earlier period.

---

57. See Jacoby's commentary on *FGH* 323a Hellanikos, passim. Cf. pp. 316–17.
58. Hom. *Od.* 17.212; 18.321–22; 22.159, 161, 182, etc.

A scholium on Aristophanes provides a clear and concise outline of the festival. We do not know its origin, but on most points it is consistent with our best evidence from elsewhere.[59] The gloss relates to the passage in the *Acharnians,* discussed in chapter 1, where the son of the Thracian Sitalces is portrayed as "longing to eat sausages at the Apatouria."[60] The scholiast comments:

> he is referring now to the Apatouria, a notable festival at public expense (*demoteles*),[61] celebrated by the Athenians in the month of Pyanepsion over three days. The first day is called Dorpia, when the phrateres, coming together in the evening have a feast; the second, Anarrhysis, from *anarrhyein,* to sacrifice; they sacrificed to Zeus Phatrios and Athena; the third Koureotis, from the registration of boys and girls (*kouoi* and *korai*) in the phratries.

The gloss continues with a version of the foundation myth, and also gives the etymology for Apatouria from homopatoria, a version of which, as we have seen, is close to that favored by modern philologists.[62]

Whether the festival had always been at public expense or whether this was a late development, an innovation perhaps of Lykourgos, it is impossible to say. But it was appropriate that it should be. Phratry membership was a fundamental aspect of citizenship.[63] Partaking in the festival of the phrateres was hence an exercise and affirmation of an Athenian's status as citizen and of the principle of kinship on which that status was based, expressed and guaranteed by his membership in a phratry.

This nationalistic aspect of the festival is reflected in the involvement

---

59. λέγει δὲ νῦν περὶ 'Απατουρίων, ἑορτῆς ἐπισήμου δημοτελοῦς, ἀγομένης παρὰ τοῖς 'Αθηναίοις κατὰ τὸν Πυανεψιῶνα μῆνα ἐπὶ τρεῖς ἡμέρας. καλοῦσι δὲ τὴν μὲν πρώτην δόρπειαν, ἐπειδὴ φράτορες ὀψίας συνελθόντες εὐωχοῦντο· τὴν δὲ δευτέραν ἀνάρρυσιν, ἀπὸ τοῦ ἀναρρύειν, τοῦ θύειν· ἔθυον δὲ Διὶ φρατρίῳ καὶ 'Αθηνᾷ· τὴν δὲ τρίτην κουρεῶτιν, ἀπὸ τοῦ τοὺς κούρους καὶ τὰς κόρας ἐγγράφειν εἰς τὰς φρατρίας. Σ Ar. *Ach.* 146. The only significant point of doubt concerns the implication that girls as well as boys were normally registered on Koureotis. See pp. 161–62, 185.

60. Cf. p. 34.

61. Cf. Hedrick 1991, 252. *L.S.* 1.240.28 is valuable on the contrast between δημοτελῆ and δημοτικὰ ἱερεῖα: τὰ μὲν δημοτελῆ θύματα ἡ πόλις δίδωσιν, εἰς δὲ τὰ δημοτικὰ οἱ δημόται κτλ. Cf. Harp. (Suid.) s.v. δημοτελῆ καὶ δημοτικὰ ἱερά and Hesych. s.v. δημοτελῆ ἱερά, with Mikalson 1977, 424–35.

62. See above, p. 146.

63. Cf. chapter 1.

of Athena Phratria with Zeus Phratrios in the religion of the festival, in particular in the sacrifices on Anarrhysis.[64] It is also apparent in the festival's torch ceremony. Istros informs us that at the Apatouria the Athenians, dressed in fine robes, took burning torches from the hearth and sang to Hephaistos in memory of his gift of fire. It seems that Istros recorded a tradition that the use of fire originated at Athens and that this ceremony—he may have thought it was the first such torch ceremony—commemorated this.[65] It is not clear from his account whether this was a single central ceremony or whether it took place in individual phratries. The latter is perhaps more likely; citizens would have gathered for the Apatouria in their own phratries, many of them based outside Athens, and would therefore not have been able to attend events based in the city as well.[66]

We cannot be certain, but the public, national significance of the festival may also have been reflected in the organizing functions of two sets of minor officials, possibly officials of the polis. One of these was the *oinoptai,* the wine-overseers,[67] of whom there were three. It is not clear whether this meant three per phratry or three altogether, but the

---

64. In addition to Σ Ar. *Ach.* 146 (above, n. 59), see Suid. s.v. ᾿Απατούρια and s.v. φράτορες. In T 3, however, oaths were sworn to Zeus Phratrios alone at the scrutiny and this may have been generally the case. See further pp. 207–11.

65. *FGH* 334 Istros fr. 2: ... ῎Ιστρος δὲ ἐν ᾶ τῶν ᾿Ατθίδων * * * (lacuna) εἰπὼν ὡς ἐν τῆι τῶν ᾿Απατουρίων ἑορτῆι ᾿Αθηναῖοι + (text corrupt) οἱ καλλίστας στολὰς ἐνδεδυκότες, λαβόντες ἡμμένας λαμπάδας ἀπὸ τῆς ἑστίας, ὑμνοῦσι τὸν ῞Ηφαιστον θύοντες, ὑπόμνημα τοῦ + κατανοήσαντος τὴν χρείαν τοῦ πυρὸς διδάξαι τοὺς ἄλλους. (= Harp. s.v. λαμπάς). ῎Ιστρος δέ φησιν λαμπάδα νομίσαι ποιεῖν πρῶτον ᾿Αθηναίους ῾Ηφαίστωι θύοντας, ὑπόμνημα κτλ. (= Epit. Harp. [cf. Suid.] s.v. λαμπάδος). The text of Harp. is corrupt, but it would seem from it that Istros said the use of fire started at Athens, and Epit. Harp., unless it represents some confusion between first use and first ceremony, states explicitly that this was the first λαμπάς. Cf. Jacoby ad loc. Philochoros (see *FGH* 328 frs. 93–98) had also tended to ascribe the origin of civilizing discoveries to Athens.

66. See, however, pp. 158–59.

67. There are two sources for the oinoptai (*IG* 2.²1357 should probably not be read to include a reference to them, see Oliver 1935, 23, line 22 with p. 29): a) Athen. 10.425a–b, who cites Eupolis *Poleis* fr. 219 K–A (= fr. 205 Edm.), where the speaker complains "men whom you would not have chosen as oinoptai before, we now have as generals," and reports that these officials ensured that the company at dinners drank equal quantities. He goes on to report Philinos' claim in the case of the Krokonidai that the office was εὐτελής (cheap) and that the oinoptai were three in number and provided lamps and wicks for the diners. (On this speech, cf. p. 368.); b) Photios s.v. οἰνόπται, who says they were ἐπιμεληταὶ τοῦ τοὺς φράτορας ἡδὺν οἶνον ἔχειν· Δίδυμος οὕτως ἀποδίδωσιν. On a possible connection with oinisteria, see n. 124. One wonders whether they (or the protenthai) might also have had responsibilities with respect to the regulation of the weight of the meion, on which see pp. 168–69.

latter seems more likely.[68] They were well-established by the later fifth century[69] and seem to have been concerned in some way with the organization of this and perhaps other festivals.[70] Their precise functions are obscure, but they were apparently publicly elected;[71] perhaps they were, or became, responsible for overseeing the expenditure of public money on the festival.

A second group of officials, the *protenthai* ("foretasters") were also associated with the Apatouria.[72] Again we have late-fifth-century evidence for them and again the nature and function of the group is unclear, but it seems that they were most notable as "anticipators." They apparently ate the dinners most people enjoyed on Dorpia, the first day of Apatouria, on the day before, which could be referred to in official documents as "the day the protenthai celebrate."[73] The explanation of this is obscure; perhaps they were responsible in some way for the organization of phratry dinners on Dorpia and in consequence had their own a day early.[74]

---

68. See n. 71.

69. The clear implication of the quotation (above, n. 67) from the later fifth-century comic poet Eupolis.

70. The connection with other festivals is suggested by the fact that they were mentioned by Philinos/Lykourgos (cf. p. 368) in a speech which concerned a dispute between two gene, the Krokonidai and the Koironidai, and in which the festival Theoinia was also mentioned (cf. p. 217 n. 69). On the other hand, the Philieis, which may have been the phratry to which these two gene belonged (see p. 368), were also mentioned in the speech, and while Athenaeus does not mention phratries in connection with them, Photios does.

71. The apparent implication of Eupolis' parallel with the generals (above, n. 67). This parallel, together with the nature of their apparent function, the silence of the sources on them in relation to any individual phratry, the possibility that their activities extended beyond phratries (see n. 70), and the fact that Athenaeus does not say that there were three in each phratry are what suggest that they may have been a board of three centrally-elected minor officials rather than three appointed in each phratry. There were very large numbers of central officials at Athens, some of them with similarly minor functions (cf. Hansen 1980, who reckons there were ca. 700 "home" officials in total, though he does not include oinoptai or protenthai in his list).

72. In his collection of evidence on the protenthai Athenaeus at 4.171c-e includes: (a) Ar. *Clouds* 1196-1200, where magistrates taking deposits in legal cases on the last day of the month rather than the first are compared to the protenthai: ὅπερ οἱ προτένθαι γὰρ δοκοῦσί μοι παθεῖν / ὅπως τάχιστα τὰ πρυτανεῖ᾿ ὑφελοίατο, / διὰ τοῦτο προυτένθευσαν ἡμέρᾳ μιᾷ (1198-1200); (b) Pherecrates (late fifth cent.) *Agrioi* fr. 7 K-A (= fr. 7 Edm.): μὴ θαυμάσῃς· / τῶν γὰρ προτενθῶν ἐσμεν, ἀλλ᾿ οὐκ οἶσθα σύ; (c) Philyllios (early fourth cent.) *Herakles* fr. 7 K-A (= fr. 8 Edm.), in which a character describes herself as ἡ τῶν προτενθῶν Δορπία καλουμένη; (d) the decree of Phokos (cf. n. 76). On the basis of this evidence Athenaeus claims that the protenthai were ὥσπερ τι σύστημα . . . καθάπερ καὶ οἱ παράσιτοι (officials assisting at religious dinners) ὀνομαζόμενοι.

73. The apparent implication of (c) and (d), above, n. 72.

74. This is little more than a guess. Like the oinoptai they sound like minor central rather than local officials, but we cannot be certain.

Another mark, perhaps, of the national significance of the festival was the Boule's decision, probably in 323/2,[75] to give itself five days holiday for the festival "like other Boulai," so that it could "celebrate the Apatouria with the other Athenians in the traditional way."[76] We need not necessarily suppose that they had no holiday at all before this;[77] the Boule regularly seems to have taken days off during festivals. But including not only the three days of the festival proper but two extra days as well would perhaps have been unusual, and may have been the innovation.[78] The proposer of the decree was a man named Phokos. This may be the same Phokos who was the infamously dissolute son of the austere general Phokion. As we shall see, the Apatouria seems to have been a notably orgiastic festival; such a proposal from the son of Phokion would, it seems, have been in character.[79]

---

75. Dated by Athenaeus to the archonship of Kephisodoros, i.e., 366/5 or 323/2 (see Develin 1989). The latter, as a measure of the Lykourgan type (cf. p. 53 n. 119) is more likely, and would also suit the identifications suggested in n. 79.

76. Φῶκος εἶπεν· ὅπως ἂν ἡ βουλὴ ἄγῃ τὰ Ἀπατούρια μετὰ τῶν ἄλλων Ἀθηναίων κατὰ τὰ πάτρια, ἐψηφίσθαι τῇ βουλῇ ἀφεῖσθαι τοὺς βουλευτὰς τὰς ἡμέρας ἅσπερ καὶ αἱ ἄλλαι βουλαὶ αἱ ἀφεταὶ ἀπὸ τῆς ἡμέρας ἧς οἱ προτένθαι ἄγουσι πέντε ἡμέρας. Athen. 4. 171e. I see no reason to accept Wilamowitz' suggestion of ἀρχαι for MSS Βουλαί. This is the Athenian Boule giving itself a holiday as long as that enjoyed by Boulai in other Ionian states (an example of daughter institutions influencing the parent ?) and, possibly, the Areopagos at Athens, which was also a "Boule."

77. At Xen. *Hell.* 1.7.8 (cf. above p. 150) sessions of both Boule and Assembly appear to take place during the Apatouria. These may, however, have been extraordinary meetings in the wake of Arginousae; or any Bouleutic holiday at the Apatouria before 323/2 may not have covered all three days of the festival (cf. the Thesmophoria, n. 78).

78. For holidays of the Boule see esp. *Ath. Pol.* 43.3; Lucian *Pseudol.* 12; Ar. *Wasps* 660–63, 663 (giving number of holidays for the courts as sixty days a year, which should probably be taken to apply to the Boule also) with Rhodes 1981, 520–21 and other discussions cited there. At Ar. *Thesm.* 78–80 it is mentioned that the courts and Boule will not be sitting specifically because it is the third day of the Thesmophoria. This might suggest that in the late fifth century there was not normally a public business holiday on every day even of a major festival. (There were certainly more than sixty festival days a year. Mikalson 1975 suggested there were Bouleutic holidays on annual [about sixty], but not monthly festival days, but cf. also Xen. *Hell.* 1.7.8, n. 47.)

79. καὶ γὰρ ἦν ἄλλως φιλοπότης καὶ ἄτακτος ὁ νεανίσκος. Plut. *Phoc.* 20.1, cf. 30, 38; Athen. 4.168e–f. The name Phokos is rare (seven instances in Kirchner 1903, of which at least two and up to five are related to Phokion) and the son of Phokion (married, twice, from ca. 370s, see Davies 1971, n. 15076; Davies' suggestion that Phokos was the son of Phokion's second wife is possible, but not necessary, especially given Phokion's longevity, 402–318) would have been the right age for service on the Boule in 323/2 (thirty to sixty; the latter not perhaps fixed, but Bouleutai of over sixty must have been rare, see Rhodes 1972, 1–2 with n. 8). It is also attractive to identify both these with Φῶκος Φαληρεύς, attested as βουλευτής on *Agora* 15.46.41, dated by Lewis 1955, 27 to 330s–

The three days occupied by the Apatouria proper, Dorpia, Anarrhysis, and Koureotis, seem to have fallen sometime between 15 and 29 Pyanepsion, possibly 19–21 or 26–28.[80] The day after Koureotis was called *Epibda,* the regular name for the day after a festival, a day for cleaning up and recovering from the celebrations.[81] The Boule's five-day holiday seems to have included the day before Dorpia as well, "the day the protenthai celebrate."[82] We do not know what significance there was, if any, in the timing of the festival. Depending on our interpretation of the Apatouria myth, we might adduce the festival's concern with the battle between summer and winter,[83] or its celebration of the return home of trained soldiers from summer campaigns and the start of the trainees' ephebia.[84] As we have seen, however, attempts to connect the themes of the myth with those of the festival may be misguided.[85] It has also been suggested that the festival fell at the time when the "Month of Weddings," Gamelion, would have produced children for presentation to the phratries ten months later, in Pyanepsion.[86] This is not impossible, though it would

323, excluding 335/4, 334/3 and 327/6. 336/5 (*Agora* 15.42), 333/2 (*IG* 2².340) and 329/8 (*IG* 7.4254) can also now probably be ruled out. If correct, that would imply that Phokion was also Φαληρεύς, pace Tritle 1981, 1988, who suggested Ποτάμιος on the basis of *Agora* 15.206.

80. The month attested by Σ Ar. *Ach.* 146; Theophr. *Char.* 3.5; Harp. s.v. ᾿Απατούρια; Ferguson 1938, no. 1, 92–93. The decree of Phokos (above, n. 76) and Xen. *Hell.* 1.7.8 (above p. 47) confirm what we would expect, that all phratries celebrated on the same day. The Apatouria would also have been very unusual if it was not celebrated on the same days each year. However, the exact dates have not come down to us. Ferguson 1938 no. 1, 92–93, implies a date later than 6 Pyanepsion, when the Salaminioi sacrificed to Theseus and after which they sacrificed at the Apatouria. If, with Mikalson 1975, 79, we exclude all days on which other festivals took place or on which the Boule and/or Assembly are attested as meeting, there remain two possible periods of three consecutive days: 19–21 (but note that the restorations of *IG* 2².367 suggested by Kirchner [18th] and Meritt 1961 [19th] fall in this period, though that of Dinsmoor 1931 [25th] does not) or 26–28. However, the decree of Phokos (see n. 76), Xen. *Meu.* 1.7.8 (see n. 47) and n. 78 above cast some doubt on M's exclusion of dates on the grounds that meetings of Boule or Assembly are attested on them. If we exclude only days after 6 Pyanepsion on which other festivals are attested, the three main days of the Apatouria could have fallen anywhere between 15 and 29 Pyanepsion.

81. Cf. Pind. *Pyth.* 4.140 with Σ4.249. Inclusive of Epibda, the festival could be thought of as lasting four days: Hesych. s.v. ᾿Απατούρια; Harp. s.v. ᾿Απατούρια; Simplic. on Aristotle *Phys.* 4.11, 708.17 Diels.

82. Cf. p. 155.

83. See p. 147.

84. See p. 148. Vidal-Naquet 1986, following Jeanmaire 1939, sees all the festivals of Pyanepsion as concerned with the return of young men from the summer campaigns.

85. See pp. 149–52.

86. Parke 1977, 92.

seem to imply confidence in a remarkable level of fertility. Moreover, in the classical period at least, children were not necessarily presented to their phratries at birth.[87] The orgiastic character of the festival and the apparently well-established association with it of wine-overseers and fore-tasters suggests another possibility: that it was a harvest celebration of some sort. The Dionysiac character of the festival may have been deep-rooted, even if Dionysus himself was not. Again, however, as with the mythical explanation, a connection to the main themes of the festival is not immediately apparent. If, however, the festival's origins were very ancient,[88] we should not be surprised if clear explanations of the timing are not immediately obvious.

The Aristophanic scholium tells us that on the first day of the festival proper, Dorpia,[89] the phrateres congregated as a phratry for a communal evening meal.[90] We shall suppose that this would typically have taken place at the traditional phratry center;[91] the evening starting time would have given those families who had moved away time to make the journey "home" across Attica. They may not invariably have done so, however. During the Peloponnesian War we know that many Athenians moved into the city,[92] and in 406, at least, there seem to have been a good number on hand during the Apatouria to attend a meeting, possibly specially summoned, of the Assembly.[93] In addition, after the War we

---

87. See next section. It is possible that the situation was different at some earlier period.

88. Cf. p. 144.

89. δόρπον was the Homeric word for an evening meal. That Dorpia was the first day, Anarrhysis the second, is attested by Σ Ar. *Ach.* 146; Hesych. and Suid. s.v. Ἀπατούρια; Pollux 6.102 and Simplicius on Aristotle *Phys.* 4.11, 708.17 Diels; and confirmed by T 3, 61–64, where notice of an alternative location for the meion and koureion in the Demotionidai/Dekeleieis is to be given five days before Dorpia, best understood as five days before the beginning of the festival. Some ancient scholars, however, thought Anarrhysis came first (Σ Plat. Tim. 21b; Proclus on *Tim.* 21b; E. M. s.v. Κουρεῶτις). This is probably the result of a too literal interpretation of Ar. *Peace* 887–99, cf. n. 101, though the story of Eudemos in Simplic. (see below) is another possible source of the confusion; it implies that feasting took place on the day before Koureotis, and Dorpia was clearly the usual feast-day of the festival. In fact it is clear that feasting might take place on any of the days.

90. The sausages of Ar. *Ach.* 146 would presumably have been on the menu.

91. This seems to be the implication of Σ Ar. *Ach.* 146, above, p. 59, and the decree of Phokos, above, n. 76. Cf. Simplic. on Arist. *Phys.* 4.11, 708 Diels (below) where it is necessary to the point of the story about the Apatouria told there that the celebrations take place in a group set apart from other citizens (in fact in a cave) and T 3, 52–54, where it is explicitly provided that meion and koureion should take place at Dekeleia.

92. Thuc. 2.16.

93. Xen. *Hell.* 1.7.8. See p. 150.

find phratries with a rural base that now have a meeting place of some sort in the city.[94] It may be that some of them would have found it more convenient to continue to celebrate the Apatouria there.[95]

The name of the second day, Anarrhysis, implies sacrificing,[96] and we are indeed told that there were sacrifices on this day to the patron deities of the phratries, Zeus Phratrios and Athena Phratria.[97] Two other references to Anarrhysis in ancient literature give us a flavor of the activities on this and the following day.

First, there is the story of Eudemos, a pupil of Aristotle, related by Simplicius in his commentary on Aristotle's *Physics*[98] in the context of a discussion of the nature of time. A group of people, he says, was feasting in an underground cave. They eventually went to sleep in a drunken state in the early hours and slept through the whole of the following day and into the following night. When they woke up, they did not realize that they had missed a day until they noticed that they were celebrating Koureotis a day late.

Second, Aristophanes, personifying the delights of a festival in the character of Theoria in the *Peace*, alludes principally, it seems, to the Apatouria. He uses anarrhysis as a synonym for sexual intercourse and, following that, promises an athletic festival involving boxing and wrestling for "tomorrow," and, "on the third day," horse racing.[99] All are described in such a way as to maximize sexual double entendre and make Theoria seem particularly attractive to the Bouleutai who would have been in the front rows of the audience when the play was first performed.

We must, of course, allow for parody and exaggeration here; but it is not clear why Aristophanes would have chosen to allude in this way to the Apatouria rather than to any other festival unless it had a

94. Cf. p. 13.

95. It is possible that before 396/5 the Demotionidai/Dekeleieis had met in the city. Cf. pp. 130-31.

96. See *LSJ* s.v. ἀναρρύω, "draw back the head" of a sacrificial victim.

97. See n. 59.

98. Simplic. on Arist. *Phys.* 4.11, 708.17 Diels.

99. Trygaios is presenting Theoria to the Bouleutai: βουλή, πρυτάνεις, ὁρᾶτε τὴν Θεωρίαν./ σκέψασθ᾽ ὅσ᾽ ὑμῖν ἀγαθὰ παραδώσω φέρων,/ ὥστ᾽ εὐθέως ἄραντας ὑμᾶς τὼ σκέλει/ ταύτης μετεώρω κᾆτ᾽ ἀγαγεῖν ἀνάρρυσιν./ τουτὶ δ᾽ ὁρᾶτε τοὐπτάνιον... (887-91). The slave interjects that "before the War" the Council did a good deal of "cooking" in Theoria's "oven" (cf. Sommerstein 1985 ad loc.). Trygaios continues, ... (894) κἄπειτ᾽ ἀγῶνά γ᾽ εὐθὺς ἐξέσται ποποιεῖν/ ταύτην ἔχουσιν αὔριον καλὸν πάνυ, (1896a) ἐπὶ γῆς παλαίειν... (899) τρίτῃ δὲ μετὰ ταῦθ᾽ ἱπποδρομίαν ἄξετε.... Ar. *Peace* 887-99.

reputation for being particularly riotous and orgiastic, as its effects in Eudemos' story would also suggest. No doubt it was this sort of liveliness that led to the use of the word *phratriazein* (to phratryize) to mean to have a feast or to have a good time in a phratry.[100]

When it comes to using this passage of Aristophanes as a source for detailed factual information about the Apatouria, however, caution is necessary. Aristophanes' allusions must be clear enough to be recognizable, but it is not necessary that the details be authentic. The order he gives of the days of the festival is certainly wrong: he makes Anarrhysis (890) first, followed by the day with boxing and wrestling ("tomorrow," 895), with the horse racing "on the third day" (899). In fact, Anarrhysis was the second day of the Apatouria, not the first.[101]

A scholiast, however, tells us explicitly that there was horse racing on the third day of the Apatouria,[102] and though we may have suspected that wrestling and boxing were included for the purposes of sexual allusion, Plato provides us with more sober evidence for competitive activities at the festival. In the *Timaeus* he has old Kritias relate a conversation between his grandfather Kritias and a certain Amynander on Koureotis when he was about ten and his grandfather nearly ninety. Kritias the grandson remarks that "our fathers set us the recitation contests then as they usually do for the children every time at the festival."[103] It is

---

100. Steph. Byz. s.v. φρατρία says φρατριάζειν meant ἐν τῷ φρατρίῳ εὐωχεῖσθαι, the term used for feasting following a sacrifice. It may also not be coincidental that it was in a play entitled the *Phrateres* (produced in 421, see p. 5 with n. 19) that the comic poet Leukon ridiculed the tragic poet Melanthos for gluttony (Athen. 8. 343c = Leukon *Phrat.* fr. 3 K-A [= fr. 2 Edm.]).

101. As often, some ancient scholars seem to have interpreted Aristophanes too literally. This passage was probably the origin of the mistaken view that Anarrhysis preceded Dorpia (cf. n. 89). Similarly a scholiast on 893a saw in πρὸ τοῦ πολέμου a reference to the mythical war between Athens and Boeotia in the Apatouria foundation myth. It is of course a reference to the Peloponnesian War.

102. On line 899b: τῇ τρίτῃ τῶν Ἀπατουρίων ἱπποδρομία ἤγετο. Whether any more than this passage of Aristophanes itself lies behind this scholium, however, is impossible to say.

103. ... ἡ δὲ Κουρεῶτις ἡμῖν οὖσα ἐτύγχανεν Ἀπατουρίων. τὸ δὴ τῆς ἑορτῆς σύνηθες ἑκάστοτε καὶ τότε συνέβη τοῖς παισίν· ἆθλα γὰρ ἡμῖν οἱ πατέρες ἔθεσαν ῥαψῳδίας. Plat. *Tim.* 21a–b. Plato's reason for setting this scene at the Apatouria seems to have been primarily to introduce plausibly discussion of a supposedly unfinished poem of Solon. A number of the children at the festival are said to have recited Solon's poems because, says Kritias, they were "new at the time" (in fact Plato's fictional chronology is impossible) and were overheard by Kritias. It is notable, however, how Plato uses the timelessness of what he can portray as an unchanging festival to enhance the literary effect: τὸ ... σύνηθες ἑκάστοτε καὶ τότε συνέβη.... Proclus and Σ on Plat. *Tim.* 21b state that

appropriate perhaps that Aristophanes should provide us with evidence for physical activities and Plato for intellectual; but we may infer that the children of phrateres, probably including those being admitted to the phratry at the festival,[104] were put through their paces in a range of pursuits, athletic and intellectual, over the three days.

Admission of Men and Boys

The central feature of the Apatouria, however, was the processes of phratry admission which normally took place on Koureotis.[105] There were probably two such processes involving male candidates, the meion and the koureion, and in addition there might be a scrutiny (*diadikasia*), which could take place separately under either. Unfortunately, though the quantity of evidence relating to these processes is relatively abundant, it is often either uninformative, intractable, or suspect. We must proceed with caution.

It is clear enough that there were two sacrifices associated with phratry admission, the meion and the koureion, but it is less clear exactly what the distinction between the two was.[106] Those ancient scholars who had an opinion on the matter seem to have thought that these were two names for the same sacrifice.[107] But this cannot be right, for the preamble to T 3 provides that the phratry priest should receive dues for each of the two sacrifices individually.[108] Aside from this, few of the more obvious possibilities can be ruled out, and several have their modern adherents.

It has been thought, for example, that the meion was the female equivalent of the koureion.[109] We know that girls could occasionally be

---

there were recitation contests at the Apatouria as a matter of fact, but again (cf. previous note) this may be based ultimately on no more than an inference from this passage.

104. There is no indication that Plato intended it to be understood that Kritias himself was introduced on this occasion. Cf. n. 128.

105. Cf. n. 3.

106. See, e.g., Harp. s.v. μεῖον καὶ μειαγωγός· θῦμά ἐστιν ὃ τοῖς φράτορσι παρεῖχον οἱ τοὺς παῖδας εἰσάγοντες εἰς τούτους. Cf. the similar description of the koureion at *L.S.* 1.273.2.

107. E.M. 533.37 s.v. κουρεῖον; Σ Ar. *Frogs* 798 (see n. 144).

108. T 3, 5–8.

109. See Gilbert 1893, 213, with n. 3; Lipsius 1894, 165; Ledl 1907/8, 223. Another view is that boys were presented just once to a phratry and that, depending on the age at which this took place, either the meion or the koureion would be sacrificed (see Hermann-Thumser 1892, 329–31). Needless to say, there is no positive evidence for this and the implication of T 3, which provides for scrutiny of candidates after the koureion, must be

introduced to their fathers' phratries,[110] and the apparent connection between koureion and kouros (boy) has suggested to some that that sacrifice would not have included girls. We cannot rule this out, but there is no evidence for it, and there is a little against it, in that our only source for the details of the meion ceremony talks explicitly of the introduction of sons.[111] Moreover, the impression given by the evidence is that the introduction of a girl to her father's phratry was an occasional event, while the meion was a regular one; and if we wish to make a link between koureion and kouros we can scarcely exclude a link with the related word for girl, *kore*.[112]

The weight of more recent modern opinion has favored the view that there were two admissions ceremonies for boys: the meion in infancy or young childhood and the koureion in adolescence.[113] With some hesitation I agree that this is most likely to be correct, on the basis of current evidence.

It is apparent that in the normal course of events a male child would be presented to his father's phratry within the first few years of its life. The clearest general evidence for this is a passage of Aristophanes where the demagogue Archedemos is made fun of for not having "grown phrateres at the age of seven";[114] but there are also specific cases in the orators where there is talk of introduction soon after birth[115] and in one papyrus

that all candidates underwent that process. A logically possible view that does not appear to have attracted modern support but which would be contradicted by no evidence, is that the meion and the koureion were two sacrifices associated with the same ceremony of introduction, the meion being a preliminary sacrifice offered perhaps on an earlier day of the Apatouria. It cannot, however, be said that this has much intrinsic plausibility; and it leaves the apparent fact that there were introductions both in infancy and in adolescence unexplained—if it was not simply a matter of variation between phratries.

110. See below, p. 178–81.

111. μεῖον λέγουσι τοὺς ὑπὲρ τῶν υἱῶν εἰς τὰ ᾿Απατούρια ὅϊς (om. RV) ὑπὸ τῶν πατέρων εἰσφερομένους... (see n. 144) Σ Ar. *Frogs* 798, cf. Suid. s.v. μειαγωγήσουσι τὴν τραγῳδίαν. Again we would be left with the need to find an explanation of the evidence for introduction of male children in both infancy and adolescence.

112. Note especially Σ Ar. *Ach.* 146, discussing the days of the Apatouria... τὴν δὲ τρίτην κουρεῶτιν, ἀπὸ τοῦ τοὺς κούρους καὶ τὰς κόρας ἐγγράφειν εἰς τὰς φρατρίας. This etymology, however, is generally rejected today in favor of a direct link between koureion and κείρειν. See n. 117 below.

113. For this view see in particular Labarbe 1953 and the earlier writers cited by him at 364, n. 2. Also Cole 1984, 233, and Hedrick 1990, 26–30.

114. Ar. *Frogs* 420–24, see p. 33 n. 38. There is a pun on φράτερας and φραστῆρας, "age-teeth" (or possibly "milk-teeth," see Labarbe 1953, 370–72). Since the age of seven is not obviously significant in the teeth-growing processes, the point must be that it would be abnormal not to have been presented to a phratry by that age.

115. ἐπειδὴ δ᾿ οὑτοσὶ ὁ παῖς ἐγένετο καὶ ἐδόκει καιρὸς εἶναι... ἐγὼ... εἰσήγαγον

fragment of a late-fifth- or early-fourth-century orator the speaker claims to have been introduced to his phratry "when three or four years old."[116]

On the other hand, there are also indications that an introduction occurred during adolescence and that this was the koureion. This is suggested by the etymological link between koureion and the verb *keirein* (to cut),[117] apparently implying an association with haircutting ceremonies of a type associated with puberty and passage into manhood, not infancy.[118] It is confirmed by the evidence of Hesychios, who tells us in his note on Koureotis that it was "the day on which the hair is cut from the head of children and dedicated to Artemis,"[119] and, in his note on the *oinisteria,* that "those going to come of age (*ephebeuein*) at Athens, before having their hair cut, brought as a dedication to Herakles a measure of wine," the *oinisteria.*[120]

How exactly haircutting and the oinisteria were fit into procedures for entry into phratry and deme is impossible to say. Haircutting looks to

---

εἰς τοὺς φράτερας (in this case, involving posthumous adoption, these were not the speaker's own phrateres, cf. n. 155), Dem. 43.11; ἀλλὰ παιδίον ὄντα μ' εὐθέως ἦγον εἰς τοὺς φράτερας, Dem. 57.54 (this does not certainly imply introduction); ὅ τε πατὴρ ἡμῶν, ἐπειδὴ ἐγενόμεθα, εἰς τοὺς φράτερας ἡμᾶς εἰσήγαγεν, Isae. 8.19; . . . καὶ ἐπειδὴ ἔτεκεν υἱόν, ἔξαρνος ἦν μὴ εἶναι ἐξ αὐτοῦ τὸ παιδίον, (126) λαβόντες δὲ οἱ προσήκοντες τῇ γυναικὶ τὸ παιδίον ἧκον ἐπὶ τὸν βωμὸν Ἀπατουρίοις, Andoc. 1.125–26 (cf. p. 69). Dem. 39.20 and 59.56–61 (adoptive) may also be cases of early introduction; see n. 178.

116. πρῶ]τον μὲν οὖν ὡς εἰσήγαγέ με εἰς τοὺς φράτερας ἔ[τ]η γεγονότα τρ[ία] ἢ τέτταρα μάρτυρας μ μῖν παρέξομαι. POxy 31.2538, fr. 1, col. 2.23–28. The editors of POxy were inclined to attribute this speech to Lysias. If the reading of the numbers on the papyrus is correct (it appears not entirely secure), it may be this passage that lies behind the statement of Proclus on Plat. *Tim.* 21 that boys were registered in phratries when three or four years old. Generalization from this case is clearly unjustified, however, as is the claim of E.M. s.v. Ἀπατούρια that children born in the course of the immediately preceding year were enrolled at the Apatouria. The precise timing could vary, cf. p. 167.

117. See Boisacq 1923, s.v. κουρεῖον; Frisk 1960, s.v. κουρά; Chantraine 1970, s.v. κουρά; Labarbe 1953, 359, n. 1; Hedrick 1990, 28–29. Σ Ar. *Ach.* 146 (see n. 59); Σ Ar. *Frogs* 798 (see n. 144) and Proclus on Plato *Tim.* 21b imply a link between κουρεῖον and κοῦρος. See also next note.

118. For haircutting as a rite of passage, see Plut. *Thes.* 5.1; Sommer 1912, col. 2106; Jeanmaire 1939, 380, n. 1; Labarbe 1953, 366–69 (cf. Latte 1941, col. 752), who compares the earlier fourth-century inscription from Thebes on Mykale (Sokolowski 1955, no. 39), where he sees the κουρεῖον sacrifice specified in 12–15 as a victim "immolée à l'occasion de la tonte"; cf. Hedrick 1990, 29, with n. 41.

119. Hesych. s.v. Κουρεῶτις· μηνὸς τοῦ Πυανεψιῶνος ἡμέρα, ἐν ᾗ τὰς ἀπὸ τῆς κεφαλῆς τῶν παίδων ἀποκείροντες τρίχας Ἀρτέμιδι θύουσιν.

120. Hesych. s.v. οἰνιστήρια· Ἀθήνησιν οἱ μέλλοντες ἐφηβεύειν, πρὶν ἀποκείρασθαι τὸν μαλλόν, εἰσέφερον Ἡρακλεῖ μέτρον οἴνου καὶ σπείσαντες τοῖς συνελθοῦσιν ἐπεδίδουν πίνειν. ἡ δὲ σπονδὴ ἐκαλεῖτο οἰνιστήρια. Cf. Phot. s.v. οἰνιστήρια; Eust. 907.18; Athen. 11.494f (= Eupolis fr. 146 K–A [= fr. 102 Edm.]); Pollux 3.51–53; 6.22.

have been definitely linked to Koureotis and entry into the phratry. For the oinisteria, on the one hand Hesychios' use of the term ephebeuein[121] and the fact that the ceremony was apparently mentioned in Eupolis' comic play, the *Demes*, suggest it may have been a part of deme admission procedures;[122] on the other hand, Pollux associates it explicitly with entry into the phratry,[123] and Hesychios makes the connection with haircutting.[124] The picture is further confused by other evidence for dedications of hair to the river god Kephisos, also seemingly associated with entry into the phratry.[125] It may be that practice varied in different demes and phratries and/or at different times. But the association of these ceremonies, directly or indirectly, with a procedure of entry into the phratry at a boy's coming of age seems clear and is confirmed by the explicit statement of Pollux that the koureion was sacrificed for those "coming to maturity."[126]

Unfortunately, the one certain case of a koureion in the orators, that of the elder son of Euktemon's mistress Alke in Isaeus 6, which was blocked by Euktemon's son Philoktemon, cannot be dated to a specific time in the child's life with any confidence. He was "not yet over 20

121. Becoming an ephebe in the technical sense at Athens took place with entry to the deme at 18, cf. *Ath. Pol.* 42. The term could also, however, be used more generally to mean "come of age." Compare the archaic expression ἐπὶ διετὲς ἡβῆσαι, whose precise significance is unclear. It seems to have been used to refer to the completion of two years after reaching puberty in the law at Dem. 46.20 (cf. the two years of the classical ephebia, *Ath. Pol.* 42), the two years before coming of age in Hyp. fr. 192, cf. *L.S.* 1.255.15, and the period between 14 and 16 years of age by Didymos reported by Harp. s.v. ἐπὶ διετὲς ἡβῆσαι; Σ Aeschin. 3. 122. Cf. n. 139. If, as is possible, Eupolis' *Demes* ultimately lies behind Hesychios' gloss (cf. next note), he is probably using ephebeuein in the technical sense, but we cannot be certain.

122. Phot. s.v. οἰνιστήρια explicitly derives the association with ephebes about to have their hair cut from Eupolis.

123. ἡ δ' ὑπὲρ τῶν εἰς τούς φράτορας εἰσαγομένων παίδων οἴνου ἐπίδοσις οἰνιστήρια ἐκαλεῖτο. τὸ δ' ἱερὸν τὸ ὑπὲρ αὐτῶν μεῖον, καὶ μειαγωγεῖν τὸ εἰσάγειν ἱερεῖον. Pollux 3.52, though it looks as if his implied link with the meion must be wrong. See also next note.

124. Deubner 1932, 233, Ziehen 1937 col. 2229–30 and Hedrick 1990, 30, all accept a link between oinisteria and koureion. Ziehen and Hedrick also draw attention to the inclusion of wine in the priestly perquisites for the koureion (but not the meion) at T 3, 4–9. It is also tempting to see some link between the oinoptai and oinisteria. The former were associated with phratries, but we do not know if they were exclusively so. Cf. pp. 154–55.

125. See further p. 309.

126. καὶ εἰς ἡλικίαν προελθόντων ἐν τῇ καλουμένῃ κουρεώτιδι ἡμέρᾳ ὑπὲρ μὲν τῶν ἀρρένων τὸ κούρειον ἔθυον, ὑπὲρ δὲ τῶν θηλειῶν τὴν γαμηλίαν. Pollux 8.107. (On gamelia as the female equivalent of koureion, see p. 184.)

years old"[127] at the time Isaeus 6 was delivered, but, though there are a number of other chronological indications in the speech, they are insufficient to enable us to determine how long it was before that that Euktemon had tried, unsuccessfully in the first instance, to introduce the boy.[128] The speech is not inconsistent, however, with a koureion in the child's late teens.[129]

Given the two sacrifices[130] and the indications of procedures of intro-

---

127. Isae. 6.14.

128. Labarbe 1953 attempted with ingenuity, though unsuccessfully, to demonstrate that the koureion took place at the age of sixteen in this case. There are simply too many uncertainties in his complex argument, including, crucially, the dating of *IG* 2^2.1609 (see Labarbe 1953, 378–79), the chronological relationship of this speech to events surrounding the Samian cleruchy (Labarbe 1953, 378–86), the precise meaning of the statement that it was fifty-two years since the sailing of the Sicilian expedition (sect. 14, Labarbe 1953, 377) and, more simply but of fundamental importance, the time lapse between the eventually successful introduction of the child at section 23 and the trierarchy of Philoktemon περὶ Χίον at 27, which is introduced with no more chronological specification than μετὰ ταῦτα τοίνυν. Labarbe's attempts to pin down these points do not wholly convince; e.g., he is required to posit that Euktemon's eventual successful introduction of Alke's son took place at the Thargelia of 366. Phratry introduction at the Thargelia is attested in only one case (cf. p. 66) and seems to have been ad hoc or at least specific to the phratry in question (probably the Achniadai, see p. 282) of which there is no indication that Euktemon's family were members. In any case Euktemon may have presented this child as adopted, in which case the timing of introduction may have been abnormal (cf. Wyse 1904 ad loc.; εἰσαγαγεῖν εἰς τοὺς φράτερας ἐπὶ τῷ αὐτοῦ ὀνόματι [21] would be consistent with adoption). In my view Labarbe's premise that the koureion took place at a specific uniform age is mistaken (see p. 167), so even if he were right that sixteen was the age of introduction here it would be of no general significance. The only other mention of an age over seven (cf. p. 163) in connection with phratry entry is Plat. *Tim.* 21, where Kritias portrays himself as ten years old when participating in recitation contests at the Apatouria. But, as correctly noted by Labarbe 1953, 372–73, there is no indication that Kritias was supposed to have been introduced to his phratry on this occasion.

129. Of other cases of phratry admission mentioned in the orators, several imply an introduction in the first few years of life (see nn. 115 and 116 above; but note that in Andoc. 1.125–27 a failed introduction after birth is followed by a successful one when the child was grown, albeit explicitly to the genos, not the phratry, cf. n. 133); two are unclear on the age of the candidate (Lysias 30.2: ὅσα ἔτη γεγονὼς εἰς τοὺς φράτερας εἰσήχθη, πολὺ ἂν ἔργον εἴη λέγειν [cf. p. 34]; Isae 12.3 [see p. 54]); and the rest, in addition possibly to Isaeus 6, involve presentation to the phratry following adoption, which could take place in childhood (e.g. Dem. 43.11) or adulthood (e.g. Isae. 7.13–17; note the stress on the procedure's being the same in this phratry whether a child was adopted or not; cf. Dem. 44.41). See further pp. 176–78. Only in Isae. 6 is the meion or the koureion specifically mentioned.

130. Deubner 1932, 234, followed by Guarducci 1937, 37, thought there was a third presentation between the meion and the koureion at Choes, the feast on 12 Anthesterion at which children were given miniature wine jugs (see Parke 1977, 108–9). This conclusion was drawn from a supposed connection between the implication of Philostratos *Heroic.*

duction both in infancy and during adolescence, of which the latter was the koureion, it seems reasonable to suppose that the meion was the sacrifice associated with earlier introduction. This conforms with our other evidence well enough. It was thought in antiquity, rightly or not, that the term meion was, or was related to, the word meion meaning "the less";[131] the priestly dues from the meion provided for in the preamble to T 3 are indeed less than those from the koureion, suggesting it was a smaller sacrifice, appropriate for a younger child.[132]

It is somewhat disturbing that there is no explicit mention in the relatively abundant evidence, particularly in the orators, that there were these two ceremonies for the male child.[133] Perhaps this can be explained by the fact that the precise admission arrangements, in particular the arrangements for scrutiny procedures and their relationship to meion and koureion will have varied from phratry to phratry. Though there were two sacrifices, there would not have been more than one full-blown scrutiny; it is the scrutiny that must have been the most important admissions procedure.[134] The orator would not have wished to distract the jury with unnecessary details of the procedures of the particular phratry in question. In some cases to go into too much detail may have caused difficulties; some phratries were clearly more rigorous in their admissions procedures than others,[135] and it could well have been convenient to gloss over detail.[136] The orator would merely stress the fact

---

35.9, 187, that Choes took place in the third year, with that of Proclus on Plat. *Tim.* 21 that boys were registered in phratries at three or four years old. The latter, however, should be taken as no more than a somewhat overprecise reference to the age of the meion, see n. 116.

131. See Σ Ar. *Frogs* 798, see n. 144.

132. T 3, 4–9, cf. p. 172.

133. Andoc. 1.125–27 is perhaps an exception, though it is an odd case in that the initial introduction failed and the second introduction was to the genos Kerykes, not explicitly to a phratry (cf. p. 68–71). The only other possible exception is POxy 31.2538 where, after reference to the speaker's introduction by his father at the age of three or four (see n. 116), we read, ὡς ..[.......ε]ἰσ/ήχθη[ν εἰς τοὺς φ]ράτερας [ὑπὸ τοῦ πα]/τρὸς μ[εμαρτύρη]/ται ἔτι κ[αὶ ὑπὸ τῶν συγγεν]ῶν (fr. 1, col. 3, cf. fr. 2, col. 4.27). Hedrick 1984, 422, suggested that this may imply that the father had died before the koureion and that his relatives were therefore responsible for it. The Greek, however, is also consistent with the συγγενεῖς of fr. 1 col. 3 having been witnesses to the introduction by the father, not agents of a second introduction.

134. Cf., e.g., p. 172–74.

135. Cf. n. 169.

136. The vagueness at Isae. 6.21 on whether Euktemon had adopted the elder son of Alke when he presented him to his phratry (cf. n. 128) is a case in point. There is a similar lack of clarity, e.g., in Demosthenes 59, cf. pp. 176–77.

of introduction, implying that the procedures had been gone through without delay and that they had been thorough.[137]

Another respect in which there was clearly variation in practice was in the age at which the meion and the koureion took place. For the earlier procedure there can be no doubt about this; there is not even any evidence that individual phratries regulated the age: it seems to have been at the discretion of the parent.[138] There has been a tendency to suppose that the age of the koureion was more closely regulated,[139] but there is no justification for this. If there had been a fixed age we would expect it to have been preserved in our evidence. In particular, it is difficult to believe that ancient scholars, normally so assiduous about technicalities of this sort, would have overlooked the point; it would surely have been mentioned somewhere by an orator. Is is much more likely that the silence of the evidence implies that, as with the meion, there was no fixed age. That would be appropriate enough given the implicit link with physical maturity in the haircutting ceremony and the different ages at which physical maturity occurs. Hierokles in the first decree of T 3 does not specify at what age the scrutiny of a new member is to take place. It is to be "in the year following the koureion."[140] The implication is not certain, but it is natural to understand that the exact age of the candidate at that point may have varied. If there were a fixed point, we would expect it to be the scrutiny which, as T 3 shows, did not need to take place at the same time as the koureion. T 3 also implies, however, that all phratries would not have set the scrutiny at the same age.

It is instructive to contrast this with the deme, where the age of admission was fixed at eighteen.[141] The reason for the fixed date here is clear enough: deme entry was linked to arrangements for the exercise of age-limited political rights and military service that were administered

---

137. On this variability of practice see further below, p. 173.

138. See pp. 162–63.

139. Note in particular the attempt of Labarbe 1953 to show that the age of the koureion was sixteen (see n. 120). At 392 he also adduced the phrase ἐπὶ δίετες ἡβῆσαι, but it is not clear that this referred to a specific age in the archaic period, and if it did so in the classical period, that age seems to have been a matter of uncertainty even in antiquity (see n. 121). This uncertainty may have been caused by the imposition of a classical two-year ephebia that was linked to specific ages (eighteen to twenty) onto a world in which there may already have been a two year ephebia, but one that, like the age of phratry entry to which it may have been tied, was not linked to any specific age.

140. T 3, 27–28.

141. *Ath. Pol.* 42.1, and for other texts see Rhodes 1981, 497–98.

through the deme/trittys/phyle structure and organized on the basis of age. On the other hand, no particular purpose would have been served by fixing the age of entry into the phratry, except perhaps to connect it to that of the deme.[142] But this was clearly not thought necessary. In normal practice phratry membership would have preceded deme entry, but it is not clear that this was an absolute rule. The deme, as has been observed in chapter 1,[143] was responsible for deciding its own admissions, subject to supervision by the Boule.

There was a reference to the meion in a lost play of Aristophanes, the *Dramata,* which apparently contained a parody of the ceremony, exploiting the fact that meion could also mean "less" or "too little." The accounts of ancient scholars are confused, but as far as we can tell there was supposed to be a minimum permissible weight of the meion offering, a sheep. The phrateres, looking forward to a good dinner, all gathered round the scales, shouting out as the sheep was weighed, "Meion, meion," meaning that it was not big enough.[144] In the two lines we possess[145] from the scene, the provider of the meion addresses the sheep, hoping that it will weigh enough, lest the phrateres make further exactions.[146]

---

142. It is not impossible that the age had been fixed at some time in the distant past (before Cleisthenes introduced the deme structure), but it seems unlikely. The natural progression would surely have been toward rather than away from greater precision and standardization in such areas.

143. See p. 41.

144. μεῖον λέγουσι τοὺς ὑπὲρ τῶν υἱῶν εἰς τὰ ᾿Απατούρια ὅις (om. RV) ὑπὸ τῶν πατέρων εἰσφερομένους διὰ τὸ ἐπιφωνεῖν τοὺς φράτορας ἐπὶ τοῦ σταθμοῦ τοῦ ἱερείου "μεῖον, μεῖον". ὅτι δὲ ἵστατο, ᾿Αριστοφάνης ἐν Δράμασι δεδήλωκε. τοῦτο δὲ κέκληται κουρεῖον ἀπὸ τῶν κούρων ὑπὲρ ὧν ἐθύετο, μεῖον δὲ διὰ τὴν προειρημένην αἰτίαν. καὶ ἐπιζήμιόν τι τοῖς ἧττον εἰσάγουσιν ἀπεδέδοτο, καθάπερ αὐτός φησιν ᾿Αριστοφάνης κτλ. Σ Ar. *Frogs* 798; cf. Harp. s.v. μεῖον καὶ μειαγωγός (containing Eratosthenes fr. 91 Str. and *FGH* 244 Apollodoros fr. 108, which clearly derive from the *Dramata*); Photios s.v. μεῖον; Suidas s.v. μειαγωγήσουσι τὴν τραγῳδίαν and μειαγωγία; Pollux 3.53. There was confusion as to whether the limit was a maximum or minimum. The latter seems to suit our verbatim fragment better and should therefore be preferred (see next note), but it is clear how the shouting of "μεῖον, μεῖον" could be taken to imply the former. For more detail see Labarbe 1953, 360, n. 1.

145. ἀλλ᾿ εὔχομαι ᾿γωγ᾿ ἑλκύσαι σε τὸν σταθμόν,/ ἵνα μή με προσπράττωσι γραῦν οἱ φράτερες. Preserved by Σ Ar. *Frogs* 798 = Ar. *Dramata* fr. 299 K-A (= fr. 286 Edm.). Some MSS read προστάττωσι, some omit με, and some omit γραῦν.

146. It is not clear what they will exact. γραῦν could have its common meaning "the old woman" (his wife? the sense perhaps being "or else the phrateres will demand the old woman from me as well") or the more unusual one, "the cream" (so Edmonds' translation; γραῦς in this sense could be used for the scum or froth on top of any liquid,

It is difficult to know how far this has a basis in reality and how far it is parody or invention. There was a verb *meiagogeo* meaning, it would seem, "bring the meion to be weighed," and in the *Frogs* Aristophanes uses it by extension to refer to the weighing of a tragedy.[147] This suggests at first sight that ancient scholars may have been right in their assertion that the weight of the meion was regulated in some way,[148] though whether the limit would have been an upper or a lower one,[149] and whether it was set by the state or by one or more individual phratries, we could not tell. It is also possible, however, that the association of the verb meiagogeo with the meion sacrifice was looser, or more distant than this. There is a word in Sanskrit, possibly related, that means simply "sheep";[150] meiagogeo could originally have meant "lead a sheep (to be weighed?)" more generally than in the context of the meion, and the specific link with the meion could have been part of Aristophanes' joke. There may in reality never have been any weight limits for the meion. Whatever the case, the shouting of "meion" by the assembled phrateres looks more like a piece of Aristophanic humor than authentic ritual; in which case the claim that it explains the real etymology of the word will be wrong.[151] It may be that the significance of the term lay in its being the lesser, in which case we may reasonably suppose that it was so in comparison with the koureion which, as the preamble to T 3 shows us, was a larger offering and was probably for an older child.[152] Alternatively the meion, like its possible Sanskrit cognate, may have originally meant simply "sheep."[153]

see *LSJ* Supplement s.v.), but without the context it is impossible to say which was intended here. The emendations of Kaibel, γλαύχ', comparing Hesych. s.v. γλαύξ· νόμισμα Ἀθήνησιν τετράδραχμον and of Blaydes, οἶν, seem unnecessary.

147. (Xanthios speaking) τί δέ; μειαγωγήσουσι τὴν τραγῳδίαν; Ar. *Frogs* 798; cf. the use of μειαγωγὸς at Eupolis *Demes* fr. 130 K-A and Edm. at Harp. loc. cit.

148. Most clearly Eratosthenes fr. 91 Str. at Harp. loc. cit., but cf. also Σ Ar. *Frogs* 798. Cf. n. 144.

149. Cf. n. 144 with Labarbe 1953, 359, n. 5. A maximum limit (less likely, see n. 144) would presumably be intended to curb excess (Σ Ar. *Frogs* says σταθμοῦ ... ὡρισμένου διὰ τοὺς φιλοδοξοῦντας; compare the Solonian sumptuary legislation, Ruschenbusch 1966 frs. 71–73) a minimum to ensure phrateres did not benefit from the generosity of others while skimping on their own contributions. There could, of course, have been both.

150. See n. 153 below.

151. So, with slight variations of detail, the ancient scholars at n. 144.

152. Cf. p. 166.

153. Frisk 1970 supports an etymological link with μείων, "less" (pace Hedrick 1990, 26–27, the fact that μεῖον, the sacrifice, could be used as a second declension noun does not rule this out); Labarbe 1953, 359, n. 5 supports the relationship with skr. mēṣá-h zd maēša-, "sheep," preferred by some earlier philologists (see Boisacq 1923).

Apart from this evidence, we are wholly reliant on the orators and T 3 for the details of what actually happened at the meion and the koureion. As already noted, in every case in the orators only one presentation to the phratry is certainly mentioned,[154] and except for Isaeus 6, where the koureion is named, it is never made explicit whether meion or koureion is involved. We can only distinguish between them by fastening on indications in the speeches of the age of the candidate, relying on the hypothesis that the meion was for young children and the koureion for adolescents. The impression given by this evidence is that the procedures of the two ceremonies were similar, or at least that any differences would not have concerned an Athenian jury, and unless and until we obtain contradictory evidence from other sources, it must be our working hypothesis that this was indeed so.

In the presence of the phrateres, the introducer, who would usually but not always be the father of the candidate and a phratry member,[155] would approach the phratry altar with the sacrificial victim,[156] a sheep or goat.[157] There he would be received by the phratry priest or the phratriarch, who would ask the introducer the identity of the candidate.[158] In several instances an oath of the introducer is mentioned at this stage, to the effect that the candidate was born of a legally married citizen mother, and, where appropriate, that he was the introducer's own son.[159]

---

154. See p. 166.

155. If the father had died, relatives would perform the task. There may be hints of this at Dem 57.54 (see below n. 159) and POxy. 2538 (n. 133). In cases of posthumous adoption the introducer was necessarily not the father. At Dem. 43.11–15 (cf. 81–83) it is the candidate's natural father, who was not even a phratry member (cf. Dem. 44.41, 44). At Andoc. 1.125–26 the relatives of the child's mother introduce the child and Kallias, the alleged father, denies paternity. It is not clear whether the mother's relatives were phratry members.

156. E.g., Andoc. 1.125–26 (see p. 69).

157. Sheep: Σ Ar. *Frogs* 798 and other evidence relating to the parody of the meion in the *Dramata*, above, n. 144. Cf. Pollux 3.52: καὶ δὶς φρατήρ (sic, cf. n. 145 ?); καὶ φράτριος αἴξ ἡ θυομένη τοῖς φράτορσιν.

158. Reception and questioning by priest/phratriarch (it is unclear which, see p. 234): Andoc. 1.126. In T 3 both priest and phratriarch are involved, but exactly what roles each plays in the ceremony is unclear.

159. Cf. the wording of the oath of the witnesses "at the introduction of children," specified for the Dekeleieis by Nikodemos at T 3, 109–13 (i.e., at the preliminary scrutiny, which I suggest at p. 131 took place in this phratric group at the koureion, a year before the main scrutiny). The fact that N. specifies it suggests that the wording was not prescribed by a central authority; though the sense effectively would have been determined by Pericles' citizenship law. Dem. 57.54 (? meion) may similarly imply a variation in wording from phratry to phratry: (the subject is the speaker's father) ὀμόσας τὸν νόμιμον τοῖς φράτερσιν

In Andocides 1, Kallias, the alleged father of the child, at this point grasps the altar and denies paternity on oath.[160] Whether an oath was always necessary at both the meion and the koureion, however, is unclear. It is possible that, depending on the individual phratry, it was only required at one or the other, or at the separate scrutiny procedure, if there was one. At this point, whether before or after the oath is not clear, there was an opportunity for phrateres to object to the candidate. To do this, the person making the objection took hold of the sacrificial victim and led it away from the altar, thus in effect putting a halt to the proceedings while the matter was resolved, presumably by recourse to a vote if necessary.[161] If there were no objections, the victim would be slaughtered and relevant parts of it burnt on the altar;[162] the rest of the meat was distributed to the phrateres, who, in the one case where the point is attested, would apparently take it home rather than eat it on the spot.[163] From the preamble to the decrees of the Demotionidai/Dekeleieis[164] it is clear that, as was usual with such sacrifices, the priest would be allotted a portion of the meat, in this case a thigh, a rib, and an ear from both the meion and the koureion, and for the koureion only, a cake weighing one choinix and half a chous of wine.[165] In addition there was a small fee, paid presumably by the introducer:[166] three obols

---

ὅρκον εἰσήγαγέν με, ἀστὸν ἐξ ἀστῆς ἐγγυητῆς αὐτῷ γεγενημένον εἰδώς, though it is perhaps more likely that τὸν νόμιμον here is a reference to Pericles' citizenship law, which provided that citizen descent was necessary in the female line (cf. p. 30). The form of oath implied here is essentially the same as that given elsewhere in the orators: ἐπιτιθέναι πίστιν κατὰ τῶν ἱερῶν . . . whether own son or adopted . . . ἦ μὴν ἐξ ἀστῆς εἰσάγειν καὶ γεγονότα ὀρθῶς (Isae. 7.16, adult adoption); ὀμόσας κατὰ τοὺς νόμους τοὺς κειμένους ἦ μὴν ἐξ ἀστῆς καὶ ἐγγυητῆς γυναικὸς εἰσάγειν (Isae. 8.19, meion).

160. Andoc. 1.126.

161. At Isae. 6.22 (koureion) the consequence was negotiation between the introducer and the objector (his son), which resolved the issue; the introduction was subsequently completed successfully. At Dem 43.82 (cf. 11–15, adoption soon after birth, ? meion) the speaker claims that Makartatos, by not seizing the victim and leading it from the altar when he had the opportunity to do so, effectively voted openly that the younger Euboulides was being properly introduced as the posthumously adopted son of the elder Euboulides. He did this, the speaker alleges, to avoid making himself ὑπεύθυνος, i.e., obliged to justify himself in whatever proceedings followed an objection in this phratry; but there is no indication of exactly what those proceedings were. Cf. Isae. 8.19.

162. Dem. 43.14 (adoption, ? meion).

163. ἀλλὰ καὶ τὴν μερίδα τῶν κρεῶν ᾤχετο λαβὼν παρὰ τοῦ παιδὸς τουτουί, ὥσπερ καὶ οἱ ἄλλοι φράτερες. Dem. 43.82.

164. T 3, 5–9.

165. The wine may have been from the oinisteria, see n. 124.

166. Cf. p. 54 n. 126 and p. 200.

for the meion, a drachma for the koureion. Again the fact that this was specified probably implies that there would have been different arrangements in other phratries.

In the Demotionidai/Dekeleieis there was, in addition to the meion and the koureion a separate process, the scrutiny (diadikasia).[167] All three decrees are mainly concerned with this scrutiny and specify the procedures in some detail. Their content has been discussed at some length in chapter 3; it is not necessary to repeat the details here. After the passage of the third decree the main features were, first, that there was an anakrisis, a preliminary scrutiny that, I argue in chapter 3, probably took place at the same time as the koureion, and that seems to have involved the swearing of the oath by the introducer verifying the qualifications of his candidate, supported by three witnesses from his thiasos. Second, during the following year details of the candidate's qualification for membership had to be published. Third, one year after the koureion, there was the scrutiny proper, at which the candidate's acceptability was voted on by his thiasos prior to a vote by all the phrateres with, at least under the terms of the first decree, the possibility of appeal to the Demotionidai if the candidate was rejected. The nature and identity of the groups involved in these decrees are controversial—I suggested in chapter 3 that "all the phrateres," the body passing the decree, was a subgroup of the phratry Demotionidai in the process of establishing itself as an independent phratry. But for the purposes of this chapter, the issue is not significant. All that need concern us is that in relevant respects the body passing the decree had the essential characteristics of a phratry. This body was clearly free to make its own decisions about how best to ensure that unqualified phrateres were not admitted and chose to do so by developing a particular scrutiny procedure. The implication is clearly that other phratries were equally free to arrange matters as they wished.

This variability is borne out by the orators, where, despite a general vagueness on the details of procedures, there are several indications that provision in the law of the phratry in question was made for a specific procedure, the implication being that other phratries were different. In the case of phratry admissions,[168] Isaeus on two occasions stresses the

---

167. T 3, 26. There was also to be a once-and-for-all special scrutiny immediately after the decrees were passed (T 3, 13–26).

168. For a similar implied variability (though of fact rather than detail) in admissions of girls, cf. pp. 178–81.

thoroughness of the procedure. At 8.19, which, since the introduction is portrayed as taking place soon after birth, should be a case of meion, the speaker claims that none of the phrateres disputed his father's oath regarding his legitimacy, "although there were many of them and they examined such things exactly";[169] and at 7.13-17, a case of adoption, though it is stressed that the procedure in the phratry was the same for adopted and nonadopted children, the speaker emphasizes the fact that he was not registered in the phratry until a vote had been taken "such is their exactitude in seeing justice is done."[170] At Demosthenes 43.11-15, where the adoptive introduction took place soon after birth and sounds like meion, the phrateres are described as collecting a voting pebble from the altar while the offering was still burning and then using it to cast their vote on the candidate.[171] In this case, as in the scrutiny of the Demotionidai/Dekeleieis, it is specified that the ballot was secret.[172]

It seems unlikely that a candidate would have undergone more than one voting procedure in his lifetime in the same phratry. We only ever hear of one in the orators. In the Demotionidai/Dekeleieis there was clearly only one. To go through such a process more than once would have been otiose; but it seems from our evidence that it was up to the individual phratry whether this took place at the meion or the koureion or at a separate procedure altogether. Indeed it was up to the phratry whether they held a scrutiny procedure at all: Isaeus 7 would scarcely stress that a vote had taken place in addition to the introducer's oath unless there were some phratries in which there was no such vote,[173] and I take it that the Demotionidai/Dekeleieis were free to decide not only on the detail but also the fact of their scrutiny procedure.[174]

---

169. There was apparently less exactitude in this respect in the phratry of Dem. 44 (posthumous adoption, cf. p. 39) and the kerykes (Andoc. 1.127, see p. 67).

170. Cf. p. 66-68.

171. λαβόντες τὴν ψῆφον καομένων τῶν ἱερείων ἀπὸ τοῦ βωμοῦ φέροντες . . . ἐψηφίσαντο τὰ δίκαια. Dem. 43.14. Carrying votes from an altar was also a common procedure in other contexts, cf. Plut. Per. 32.3; Dem. 18.134.

172. οἱ μὲν ἄλλοι φράτερες κρύβδην ἔφερον τὴν ψῆφον, οὑτοσὶ δὲ Μακάρτατος φανερᾷ ψήφῳ . . . (cf. n. 188). Dem. 43.82. Cf. T 3, 82. Note the possibility of appeal from an admissions decision of a phratry to the center, p. 35 n. 42.

173. ποιήσαντος δὲ τοῦ εἰσάγοντος ταῦτα (i.e., the oath) μηδὲν ἧττον διαψηφίζεσθαι καὶ τοὺς ἄλλους. . . . Isae. 7.16. Cf. also Andoc. 1.127 (p. 67).

174. Previous to our decrees there would appear to have been a scrutiny procedure (apparently in disuse) "according to the law of the Demotionidai" (T 3, 13-14). I take this in chapter three to be the law of the phratry from which the body passing the decrees,

In the Demotionidai/Dekeleieis entry of the candidate in the phratry registers takes place following successful completion of the scrutiny,[175] as it does in Isaeus 7.[176] In Demosthenes 44 we seem to have a phratry with less rigorous procedures, or at least the speaker portrays it as such. There Leostratos is described as having his son Leochares dubiously adopted as a son of the deceased Archiades and enrolling him in Archiades' phratry—irregularly, and only after introducing him to the deme—"having persuaded one of the phrateres."[177] Some underhand method is implied, though if there was a vote it would have been in the speaker's interest to conceal the fact. Registration is also explicitly mentioned at Demosthenes 39, both that of the speaker Mantitheos by his father and that of his opponent Boiotos, his father's adopted son, who was allegedly trying to usurp Mantitheos' name.

The age of registration in the cases in Demosthenes 39 is unclear, though the speaker's may have been connected with the meion.[178] With apparently no registration in the deme until eighteen, and bearing in mind the importance of accurate recording of age for determining eligibility for military service and political rights, it would have made sense for phratries to register members at the meion.[179] Moreover, in the the-

---

the Dekeleieis, is in the process of establishing its independence. The existence of that law itself implies the power of the phratry to arrange these matters as it wished, subject to any overriding requirements of the state. Cf. the law of Solon at *Dig.* 47.22.4, providing that phratries, among other institutions, should be free to make their own regulations ἐὰν μὴ ἀπαγορεύσῃ δημόσια γράμματα (see p. 250). In light of this law, the situation in the classical phratry seems exactly as we would expect.

175. T 3, 97–98.

176. Isae. 7.16 (adult adoption, but procedure claimed to be same as for nonadopted candidate, cf. p. 66 n. 37).

177. Cf. p. 39 n. 65.

178. The subject is the speaker's father, the persons enrolled his adopted sons: εἰσή-γαγεν, ἐποιήσατο, ἵνα τἀν μέσῳ συντέμω, ἐγγράφει τοῖς Ἀπατουρίοις τουτονὶ μὲν Βοιωτὸν εἰς τοὺς φράτερας, τὸν δ' ἕτερον Πάμφιλον. Dem. 39.4. At Dem. 39.20 (cf. 29–30) the speaker deals with his own enrollment; the reference to the tenth-day naming ceremony in the same context suggests that it took place at an early age, presumably in connection with the meion: ἵνα τοίνυν εἰδῆτε ὅτι οὐ μόνον εἰς τοὺς φράτερας οὕτως, ὡς μεμαρτύρηται, ὁ πατὴρ τὴν ἐγγραφὴν ἐποιήσατο, ἀλλὰ καὶ τὴν δεκάτην ἐμοὶ ποιῶν τοὔνομα τοῦτ' ἔθετο, λαβέ μοι καὶ ταύτην τὴν μαρτυρίαν. In Dem. 59 the adopted son whom the genos Brytidai refused to register when Phrastor introduced him "to the phrateres ... and to the Brytidai" (cf. p. 68) seems also to have been an infant (Dem. 59.56–61). The speaker in Isaeus 2, however, was already an adult when adoptively enrolled in the orgeones (Isae. 2.14, cf. 12. See p. 75).

179. The demes were fully responsible for deciding on their own authority on the admission of candidates, subject to the scrutiny of the Boule, particularly on the question

oretical State of Plato's *Laws* the phratry register is to record the ages of children from birth onward, the names being erased at death.[180] It is tempting to suppose that this is to some extent based on contempoarary Athenian practice. On the other hand, in the Demotionidai/Dekeleieis, registration seems to have taken place a year after the koureion;[181] and in Isaeus 7, which records an adoption procedure alleged to have been similar to that for nonadopted candidates, and Demosthenes 44, also dealing with adoption, the candidate was adult. Again we get the impression of variations in practice from one phratry to another; and we cannot rule out the possibility that an entry may have been made in the register in some phratries at each stage of the introduction/admission process; we know that the register (*grammateion*) could also function more widely as the minutes of an organization. It was not necessarily simply a list of members whose names were entered on it once and for all.[182]

---

of age (*Ath. Pol.* 42, cf. p. 27). It is difficult to believe that the only method of investigation available to the Boule on this point was the examination of a candidate's genitals mentioned in this context by Philokleon at Ar. *Wasps* 578. Sometimes the evidence of the phratry registers would surely have been adduced. For more detail on deme admission procedures see Whitehead 1986a, 97–109. Note that Isaeus at 2.14 (εἰσάγει με εἰς τοὺς φράτερας . . . καὶ εἰς τοὺς δημότας με εγγράφει) and Demosthenes at 57.46 (ὡς εἰσήχθην εἰς τοὺς φράτερας, ὡς ἐνεγράφην εἰς τοὺς δημότας) both talk of introduction to the phratry and registration in the deme (and orgeones group in the Isaeus case). If this is not merely a rhetorical variation of terms, it may be that in these two cases the more general term is used for the phratry process because, under the law of Philochoros fr. 35, registration may only have taken place in the genos or orgeones group since entry to the phratry followed automatically.

180. κόρῳ καὶ κόρῃ παραγεγράφθω δ' ἐν τοίχῳ λελευκωμένῳ ἐν πάσῃ φρατρίᾳ τὸν ἀριθμὸν τῶν ἀρχόντων τῶν ἐπὶ τοῖς ἔτεσιν ἀριθμουμένων· τῆς δὲ φρατρίας ἀεὶ τοὺς ζῶντας μὲν γεγράφθαι πλησίον, τοὺς δ' ὑπεκχωροῦντας τοῦ βίου ἐξαλείφειν. Plato *Laws* 6.785a–b. The inclusion of girls here is a consequence of Platonic theory, not contemporary practice. Using a whitened board for this purpose, however, is likely enough to reflect contemporary reality (cf. T 3, 124).

181. T 3, 97–98.

182. In *SEG* 2.7. 20–21 (ca. 330–25), for example, an honorific decree is to be written up in the koina grammateia of the deme Halimous and in *IG* 2².2501 (late fourth century) the terms of a lease in the koinon grammateion of a group of orgeones. Apart from the passage of Plato quoted in n. 180, we have three references to phratry registers. In Dem. 44.41, where a sharp distinction is being made, with the deme register, it is referred to as the *phraterikon grammateion*. In the Demotionidai/Dekeleieis there were two copies of the register, one in the keeping of the Demotionidai, the other presumably in that of the Dekeleieis (T 3 passim). The common term for the register of any group, koinon grammateion (see instances cited above), is used in the plural to refer to these registers, though we cannot be certain that both are referred to in the second decree of T 3, by which time the Dekeleieis may have become more independent of the Demotionidai (see p. 139). Hedrick 1990, 60, notes that 125 of T 3 [τὸ δὲ φρ-...] could be restored to give a reference to

The same variability must have applied to the arrangements made by individual phratries, gene, and orgeones groups to comply with the requirement, mentioned in Philochoros fr. 35, that gennetai and orgeones were to have automatic access to phratries.[183] In the two cases where the orators describe combined entry to both groups in sufficient detail to be informative, Isaeus 7 and Demosthenes 59,[184] there seems to be only one admissions process described. In the first case there is a slight possibility that we are dealing with a genos which formed an independent phratry of its own; but otherwise it looks as though in these two phratries genos admission took place in the context of a phratry meeting. The procedure presumably would have worked in a way similar to that provided for in the second decree of the Demotionidai regarding thiasoi, whereby at the scrutiny there was to be a preliminary vote in the candidate's thiasos before the vote of the phratry as a whole.[185] In Isaeus 7 and Demosthenes 59, however, as a consequence of the law of Philochoros fr. 35, there would have been no subsequent vote in the phratry. On the other hand, in Andocides 1, following the disowning of his alleged child by Kallias in the phratry at the meion, there is a subsequent admission of the child to his genos, the Kerykes, some years later, with no mention of the phratry.[186] It appears that gene and orgeones groups may sometimes have admitted members at their own private meetings and that phratry enrollment would then have followed automatically.

In the majority of cases of introduction to a phratry described in the orators the candidate was adopted.[187] If already in a phratry and/or deme, the adoptee would have to be transferred to that of his adopted parent, if it was different from his own.[188] As discussed in chapter 1,

---

the phraterikon grammateion). Koinon grammateion is also used in the plural at Isae. 7.1 and in the singular at Isae. 7.16–17 to refer to the register of a phratry which may, but need not, be taken as a joint register with a genos (cf. pp. 66–68). The use of the plural (cf. English "register[s]") should probably not necessarily be taken to imply joint registers or multiple copies. On the case of Halimous, however (Dem. 57), see also p. 109 n. 52.

183. Cf. p. 46.

184. Isae. 7.13–17; Dem. 59.59. Cf. Isaeus 2.14, Dem. 57.54.

185. T 3, 71.

186. See p. 68–71.

187. Isae. 2.14–17, cf. 44–45; 6.21–26?; 7.13–17, cf. 26–27; 9.33; 10.8–9, cf. 15, 21; Dem. 39.4 cf. 20–21, 29–30, 40.11; 43.11–15, cf. 81–83; 44.41 cf. 44; 59.55–59 and ? 13, 38 and 118. In Dem. 43 and 44 and Isae. 10 the adoption was posthumous (for this procedure in Attic law see Harrison 1968–71 1) and in Isae. 7 partially so in that the adoptive parent had died before deme registration.

188. The case of Dem. 43 is noteworthy in this respect. At 11–15 Makartatos is portrayed

proper introduction to a phratry was an important criterion of a legitimate adoption; it was the means by which the adoptee's qualification by descent, in this case created artificially, was publicly recognized. Isaeus 7 mentions that in Apollodoros' phratry the procedure was the same whether the candidate was adopted or not: the introducer had to swear that the candidate's mother was a legally married Athenian citizen, and the phrateres had to vote;[189] in other accounts in the orators there is also no apparent distinction between procedures for adopted and nonadopted candidates. It would appear that in Demosthenes 43, where the adoption is described as taking place soon after birth, the standard meion procedures were followed, and a vote on the candidate took place during the ceremony.[190] It may be that, if adopted at a sufficiently young age, a child would simply have undergone the meion and/or the koureion along with nonadopted children, though phratries must also have had separate arrangements for those adopted in adulthood, however similar they were to those for nonadopted members. But in stressing the similarity of procedures for adopted and nonadopted candidates in the phratry of Isaeus 7, the speaker again alerts us to the fact that procedures would have been different in other phratries. For all the detailed provisions of the scrutiny process established in the Demotionidai/Dekeleieis in T 3, there is no mention of adopted candidates, for whom the exact wording of the oath specified in the second decree would have been inappropriate;[191] but we have no idea whether the scrutiny would in fact

---

as still a member of the phratry of his natural father Theopompos and of the elder Euboulides (both of Oion Kerameikon) although he had been adopted into the house of his maternal uncle, Makartatos of Prospalta (Dem. 43. 77–78). It cannot be ruled out that Sositheos, the speaker, is being dishonest and that the younger Makartatos was not in fact any longer in this phratry when Sositheos had the younger Euboulides adopted into it; Sositheos' point was to show that, by raising no objections at the phratry introduction, Makartatos had implicitly accepted the legitimacy of Euboulides' adoption. But it is simpler to suppose that the elder Makartatos of Prospalta belonged to the same phratry as the younger Makartatos' natural father, and that the younger Makartatos therefore did not need to change phratries when he was adopted. It is possible, however, that Davies 1971, 78, is right that the younger Makartatos had had himself adopted back into the house of his natural father to secure his natural inheritance, leaving a son to take his place in the Prospaltian line perhaps by the posthumous adoption process (at Dem. 43.77–78 Makartatos is criticized for introducing his own son into the Prospaltian house rather than that of Hagnias, Euboulides, etc.).

189. Isae. 7.16, see pp. 66–68.

190. Dem. 43.11–15.

191. T 3, 109–13. Note, however, that the wording would also have been inappropriate for introduction by someone other than the father of the candidate, and yet the procedure in such a case would presumably have been essentially the same.

have applied to them and, if not, what other arrangements would have been made.

Women and Girls

I argued in chapter 1 that the account taken of women by the phratry, in contrast to the deme, is significant in explaining the continued importance of phratry membership in a state where the exercise of citizenship rights depended on legitimate citizenship descent through the female line as well as the male.[192] The details of what this meant in terms of the nature and extent of a woman's practical involvement in phratry life are to a large extent obscure, but some of the broader outlines are clear enough; again there seems to have been a good measure of variation from one phratry to another.[193]

First, it is important to distinguish the reception of a woman into her husband's phratry at the gamelia, where there was some uniformity in the fact if not the details of procedure, from the introduction of a girl to her father's phratry, where the extent of the practice is difficult to determine and the detail wholly obscure.[194]

To start with the latter, there is in fact just one firm piece of evidence. In Isaeus 3 the speaker is concerned to demonstrate that a certain Phile was not the legitimate issue of a marriage between Pyrrhos, whose estate had been in dispute, and a sister of Nikodemos, the defendant in the case, " . . . he (i.e., Pyrrhos) had the option," the speaker says at 3.73, "if he had really married the sister of Nikodemos, of introducing the daughter who is allegedly hers to his phrateres as his own legitimate child, and of leaving her as heiress of his whole estate."[195]

---

192. See pp. 36–37.

193. Other recent discussions of women in phratries are Le Gall 1970, Gould 1980, Cole 1984, and Golden 1985. Of these, only Golden gives full weight to the importance of variation in practice from one phratry to another (see also next note). For earlier work, see the bibliographies of those authors, esp. Golden 1985, 9, n. 1. Discussion has tended to take the form of dispute between those who would maximize the woman's role (Le Gall, less emphatically Golden) and those who would minimize it (Gould, less emphatically Cole), the main point of contention being whether the single known case of female introduction in Isae. 3 (on which see further below) is typical or exceptional.

194. Not all earlier accounts (see e.g., Gould, op. cit.) fully recognize this distinction, which also confused ancient scholars (see n. 219 below).

195. ἐξόν, εἴπερ ἦν ἠγγυημένος τὴν ἀδελφὴν τὴν Νικοδήμου, τὴν θυγατέρα τὴν ἐκ ταύτης ἀποφανθεῖσαν εἶναι εἰς τοὺς φράτερας εἰσαγαγόντι ὡς οὖσαν γνησίαν ἑαυτῷ, ἐπὶ ἄπαντι τῷ κλήρῳ ἐπίδικον καταλιπεῖν αὐτήν, . . . Isae. 3.73.

This passage shows that a girl could be introduced to her father's phratry,[196] but it certainly cannot be taken to demonstrate that this was the rule. It stands remarkably alone in the evidence. Elsewhere in the orators when the legitimacy of a woman is being established, there is never any mention of her having been introduced to her father's phratry; when phrateres associated with her are mentioned they are described as phrateres of her male relations, the implication being that she was not herself a member of, and therefore had not ever been introduced to, any phratry.[197]

There are two passages in the ancient scholars that seem to imply that girls were more generally introduced to phratries, but in one case it is made explicit that the gamelia is being referred to. It may be that gamelia was also the basis for the other; at most we need suppose no more than awareness of Isaeus 3 at some point in the tradition.[198]

---

196. This passage and the evidence for gamelia show Gould's unqualified statement at 1980, 42, that "girls were not introduced to, still less registered as members of the phratry" to be erroneous. The extent to which Isaeus may have been "throwing sand in the eyes" of the jury in this particular case is irrelevant here, for it must have at least been credible to them that a daughter could have been introduced to her father's phratry, from which one may infer that there were some phratries where this did take place (whether or not this was one; I doubt that Isaeus would in fact make such a false statement on such an easily controvertible point).

197. There is no case in the orators apart from Isae. 3 where the legitimacy of an unmarried woman is directly at issue, and for a married woman it is, as we might expect, acceptance in her husband's phratry at gamelia that tends to be mentioned (see n. 215). In Dem. 57, however, Euxitheos, clearly anxious to list as many proofs as possible of his mother's legitimacy, extends his evidence back to before her marriage to his father (40–43) to include evidence relating to a previous marriage; he calls relatives specifically to witness that she was the daughter of Damostratos of Melite (68): ἐμοὶ γάρ ἐστι μήτηρ Νικαρέτη Δαμοστράτου θυγάτηρ Μελιτέως. ταύτης τίνες οἰκεῖοι μαρτυροῦσν; πρῶτον μὲν ἀδελφιδοῦς κτλ. Nowhere is there any suggestion, however, that she had been introduced to Damostratos' phratry; phrateres are called as witnesses to her parentage, but they are described as phrateres of her (male) relatives, not her own: ἀλλὰ μὴν καὶ φράτερες τῶν οἰκείων αὐτῆς καὶ δημόται ταῦτα μεμαρτυρήκασι (69, cf. 40). Isae. 8 carries a similar implication. The speaker's opponent had apparently alleged that his mother had not been the legitimate daughter of Kiron, whose estate was at issue. In response the speaker makes no mention of any introduction of his mother to her father's phratry; we hear only of witnesses to her wedding, to the gamelia, and to the facts that she had been chosen by the wives of the demesmen to hold office at the Thesmophoria and that her son was accepted into his father's phratry. It is conceivable that the speaker's opponent had alleged that she should have been introduced to her father's phratry; but in that case we would have expected some response to the charge. Note also that she had two stepbrothers; cf. pp. 185–86 below; for other evidence of women not being actual members of phratries either before or after the gamelia, see below, n. 215.

198. ἐν τῇ καλουμένῃ κουρεώτιδι ἡμέρᾳ ὑπὲρ μὲν τῶν ἀρρένων τὸ κούρειον ἔθυον,

On the other hand, considering the importance accorded to descent in the female line by Pericles' citizenship law,[199] the sense of introducing girls as well as boys to phratries is clear enough; even more so where, as in the case of Isaeus 3, the child was, or could have been, an *epikleros:* the heiress of an estate, who would normally be claimed with her property by her husband's closest male relative.[200] The significance of phratry membership in matters of inheritance was considerable. To infer, however, that all epikleroi, and only epikleroi, were introduced to their fathers' phratries would not be justified. We can perhaps overcome the apparent logical and legal difficulties implied by the fact that an epikleros would not strictly speaking become one until after her father's death by supposing that a daughter intended by her father to be an epikleros would be introduced before his death.[201] More crucially, however, Isaeus 3 itself makes clear that this was another area in which practice varied from one phratry to another.[202] When the speaker introduces the written evidence of the phrateres, he says that it will demonstrate "that neither did our uncle celebrate the gamelia, nor did he think it fit to introduce the daughter whom these men claim to be his legitimate child to the phrateres, even though this was their law."[203] Clearly in this particular

---

ὑπὲρ δὲ τῶν θηλειῶν τὴν γαμηλίαν. Pollux 8.107. τὴν δὲ τρίτην κουρεῶτιν, ἀπὸ τοῦ τοὺς κούρους καὶ τὰς κόρας ἐγγράφειν εἰς τὰς φρατρίας. Σ Ar. *Ach.* 146 (cf. n. 59). The parallel in language and thought suggests a common source; and if Σ Ar. *Ach.* did not mean by τὰς κόρας ἐγγράφειν to refer to the gamelia, the inclusion of κόραι with κοῦροι may simply be due to the apparent etymological link of both with Koureotis; at most we need suppose no more than an awareness somewhere in the tradition of Isae. 3. E. M. s.v. γαμήλια and *L.S.* 1.228.6 are of no independent worth and can safely be ignored. See also the authorities cited by Harp. s.v. γαμηλία (below, n. 219), where there are also signs of confusion on this point.

199. See p. 43.

200. See Harrison 1968-71 1.9-12 and 132-38 for the detailed rules of this procedure.

201. Golden 1985, 10-11, somewhat exaggerates this difficulty. I agree with him that a father might be induced to introduce rather than not introduce a daughter by uncertainty about whether she might turn out to be an epikleros; but there was probably flexibility and variability of practice. The matter may have been regulated by the individual phratry to a greater extent than he allows. The signs are that it was primarily at the phratry level (see Isae. 3.76, below, n. 203), not at the state or the individual level, that decisions in this area were made.

202. This has now been recognized by Golden 1985, 10; see also the earlier authors cited at his n. 7.

203. ἀλλὰ μὴν ὥς γε οὔτε γαμηλίαν εἰσήνεγκεν ὁ θεῖος ἡμῶν, οὔτε τὴν θυγατέρα, ἥν φασι γνησίαν αὐτοῦ εἶναι οὗτοι, εἰσαγαγεῖν εἰς τοὺς φράτερας ἠξίωσε, καὶ ταῦτα νόμου ὄντος αὐτοῖς, ἀναγνώσεται [δέ] ὑμῖν τὴν τῶν φρατέρων τῶν ἐκείνου μαρτυρίαν. Isae. 3.76.

phratry it was customary to introduce daughters, possibly only those whose fathers intended them to be epikleroi. But the implication is that other phratries would have arranged things differently.

The situation, therefore, is clear enough within certain parameters, and may be summarized as follows:

(a) in some phratries daughters intended by their fathers to be epikleroi were introduced to their fathers' phratries (Isaeus 3.73, 76);

(b) it is possible that, in some phratries daughters other than intended epikleroi were introduced to their fathers' phratries (possible implication of Isaeus 3.73, 76, taking into account the logic of Pericles' citizenship law);[204]

(c) in some phratries daughters, at least those who were not epikleroi, were not introduced to their fathers' phratries (Isaeus 3.76, and the weight of negative evidence in other cases).[205]

The reception of a woman into her husband's phratry at the gamelia is more firmly attested, though much of the detail is obscure. To understand its precise significance, an important legal and conceptual distinction between two aspects of legitimacy must be grasped, determined respectively by the marital and descent, or citizen status of the parents.[206]

---

204. Golden 1985, with much of whose account on this point I agree, nevertheless takes the view that introduction of girls to paternal phratries was more customary than I would allow on the basis of current evidence. This stems essentially from his opinion, mistaken in my view (cf. chapter 1), that citizens may not have had to belong to phratries in the classical period and a consequent tendency to exaggerate the extent to which the decision about which children, male or female, to introduce would have been at the father's discretion (cf. also n. 201 above). He also rather underestimates the weight of negative evidence (cf. n. 197).

205. We can only speculate on the age at which girls may have been introduced. Isae. 3 seems to envisage a fairly early introduction, which is also implied by the fact that the gamelia would normally have taken place at roughly the same time as the koureion for boys. It is difficult to imagine that girls would have been introduced to their fathers' phratries only just before being transferred to their husbands'. It is conceivable therefore that the meion involved girls, where appropriate, as well as boys (see, e.g., Deubner 1932, 232-3), though the idea favored by some scholars that the meion was actually the female equivalent of the koureion seems, on balance, unlikely (see pp. 161-62 above).

206. The issues surrounding the concept of legitimacy (γνησιότης) at Athens are complex and controversial and I cannot fully do them justice here. Phratry membership is an important element in the picture and perceptions of its role and significance affect other aspects of the overall view. The otherwise useful account of Harrison 1968-71, 1 (esp. 61-70), for example, is, in my view, vitiated by his underestimation of the significance of phratry membership with respect to citizenship.

The first was bestowed by the betrothal or marriage contract (*engye*) between, usually, the husband and the wife's father;[207] the second aspect, under Pericles' citizenship law, by the citizen descent of both father and mother.[208] For many purposes the concepts overlapped, and after the passage of Pericles' law and the law prohibiting a citizen from marrying a noncitizen,[209] the two groups of persons legitimate on the basis of either criterion were in fact probably identical.[210] For this reason the distinction is generally blurred in sources such as the fourth century orators. But at the time, probably the archaic period, when the marriage process achieved its classical form, the two groups did not precisely coincide, and the earlier distinction continued to be reflected in that process as performed in the classical period.

Essentially marriage consisted of three stages.[211] First there was the betrothal, engye, crucial in determining the legitimacy by marital status of the issue of the marriage. Second there was the physical union of man and wife, the start of their life together.[212] Although this was a crucial stage in the marriage process, it was in fact of little significance with regard to the legitimacy of the children of the marriage, the major legal point of concern; and though it might be accompanied by private celebrations,[213] it was not marked by any legal ceremony, albeit that in practice it may often have followed immediately upon the engye.[214]

The third stage was the gamelia. From the three cases recorded in the orators,[215] it appears that a conventional phrase was used to refer

---

207. Demonstrated indisputably by the law quoted by Dem. 46.18: ἢν ἂν ἐγγυῦσῃ ἐπὶ δικαίοις δάμαρτα εἶναι ἢ πατὴρ ἢ ἀδελφὸς ὁμοπάτωρ ἢ πάππος ὁ πρὸς πατρός, ἐκ ταύτης εἶναι παῖδας γνησίους. Cf. Dem. 44.49; Hyp. 3.16.

208. Cf. p. 43.

209. We do not know when this was passed other than that it predated Dem. 59 (ca. 340). See sect. 16 of that speech with Harrison 1968–71, 1.26.

210. Assuming, that is (see p. 27 n. 9), that those born to citizen parents outside wedlock were excluded from citizenship.

211. For this see Harrison 1968–71, 1.3–9, though he underrates the significance of the gamelia. Cole's account of the gamelia at 1984, 236–37, based on a more satisfactory view of the significance of phratry membership, comes close to my own. See also Wyse 1904, esp. on Isae. 3.73 and 76 and Jacoby on *FGH* 325 Phanodemos fr. 17.

212. See Harrison 1968–71, 1.6–7.

213. See, e.g., Isae. 8.18–20.

214. But not always. See Dem. 28.15–16 and 29.43.

215. The three cases are: (a) Isae. 3. The point at issue is the legitimacy of an alleged daughter of the speaker's uncle, Pyrrhos. See sects. 76 (quoted n. 203; the qualification καὶ ταῦτα νόμου ὄντος αὐτοῖς should be understood to refer only to the [demonstrably variable] practice of introducing the daughter); and 79: καὶ περὶ τῆς τοῖς φράτερσι

to it: "bring in the gamelia on behalf of the woman for the phrateres."[216] From ancient scholars we learn that a sacrifice was involved,[217] followed by a meal;[218] and though this seems to have been a matter of some confusion, the details of which are lost, it was also characterized by at least one ancient scholar, Didymos, as "the introduction of women to the phrateres."[219] From the accounts in the orators we gather that the process was that whereby a man presented his new wife to his phrateres and they effectively accepted her as capable of bearing children whom they could subsequently receive as phratry members and citizens.[220] Under

γαμηλίας μὴ ἀμνημονεῖτε· οὐ γὰρ τῶν ἐλαχίστων πρὸς τὴν τούτου μαρτυρίαν τεκμήριόν ἐστι τοῦτο. δῆλον γὰρ ὅτι, εἰ ἐπείσθη ἐγγυήσασθαι, ἐπείσθη ἂν καὶ γαμηλίαν ὑπὲρ αὐτῆς τοῖς φράτερσιν εἰσενεγκεῖν καὶ εἰσαγαγεῖν τὴν ἐκ ταύτης ἀποφανθεῖσαν ⟨εἶναι⟩ θυγατέρα ὡς γνησίαν οὖσαν αὐτῷ; (b) Isae. 8. The speaker lists the acts of his grandfather, Kiron, which demonstrate that his mother was his grandfather's legitimate daughter (θυγάτηρ γνησία), ὅτε γὰρ ὁ πατὴρ αὐτὴν ἐλάμβανε, γάμους εἱστίασε . . . τοῖς τε φράτερσι γαμηλίαν εἰσήνεγκε κατὰ τοὺς ἐκείνων νόμους (18) . . . if she had not been legitimate μήτ' ἂν τὸν πατέρα ἡμῶν γάμους ἑστιᾶν καὶ γαμηλίαν εἰσενεγκεῖν (20); (c) Dem. 57. Among the witnesses to his mother's citizenship Euxitheos includes τῶν φρατέρων τοὺς οἰκείους οἷς τὴν γαμηλίαν εἰσήνεγκεν ὑπὲρ τῆς μητρὸς ὁ πατήρ (43). In the list of evidence for his own citizenship at 69, which he compares to the statements of quali- fication for office provided by the thesmothetai, he includes, καὶ γὰρ ὅτι κατὰ τοὺς νόμους ὁ πατὴρ ἔγημεν καὶ γαμηλίαν τοῖς φράτερσιν εἰσήνεγκεν μεμαρτύρηται. It is notable that the gamelia is not mentioned by Theomnestos and Apollodoros in their prosecution of Stephanos for having married an alleged non-Athenian, Neaira in Dem. 59. We should probably assume that Stephanos had celebrated the gamelia for Neaira, but that it suited his accusers not to mention the fact.

216. γαμηλίαν ὑπὲρ τῆς γυναικὸς τοῖς φράτερσιν εἰσφέρειν. See previous note.

217. Pollux 8.107 (see n. 198).

218. Hesych. s.v. γαμήλια describes the gamelia as a δεῖπνον.

219. The source is the puzzling and unsatisfactory gloss of Harpocration s.v. γαμηλία (= FGH 325 Phanodemos fr. 17): Δημοσθένης ἐν τῇ πρὸς Εὐβουλίδην ἐφέσει καὶ Ἰσαῖος. καὶ Δίδυμος ὁ γραμματικὸς ἐν μὲν τοῖς Ἰσαίου ὑπομνήμασί φησιν εἶναι γαμηλίαν τὴν τοῖς φράτορσιν ἐπὶ γάμοις διδομένην, παρατιθέμενος λέξιν Φανοδήμου, ἐν ᾗ οὐδὲν τοιοῦτον γέγραπται. ἐν δὲ τοῖς εἰς Δημοσθένην ὁ αὐτὸς πάλιν γαμηλίαν φησὶν εἶναι τὴν εἰς τοὺς φράτορας εἰσαγωγὴν τῶν γυναικῶν, οὐδεμίαν ἀπόδειξιν τῆς ἐξηγήσεως παραθέμενος. Confusion with introduction of girls to their fathers' phratries may be surmized, but whether or not Didymos had the evidence, which Harpocration or his source found him not to have provided, for his claim that the gamelia was "the introduction of women to the phrateres," he seems to have been right up to a point (as recognized by Jacoby on 325 Phanodemos fr. 17). It is doubtful whether, with Gould 1980, 41, n. 25, we can assert that this passage demonstrates that Phanodemos did not explain the γαμηλία as "the introduction of women to the phrateres." What H. says is merely that P. provided no evidence for D.'s assertion that it was "something given to the phrateres at marriage."

220. See above, n. 215. In only one of the three attested cases of gamelia, that of Dem. 57, is it referred to specifically as evidence for what we might term citizenship legitimacy alone; in the others it is legitimacy with respect to inheritance that is at issue, and that

Pericles' law that meant in effect accepting the wife as of citizen descent. The gamelia therefore did not strictly speaking itself bestow legitimacy by descent—that derived from the citizenship status of the parents—but it was a guarantee of it with respect to the woman. Though not demonstrable with any certainty on the basis of current evidence, it may be that, like the equivalent guarantee for the male, it was not only a desirable, but a necessary guarantee. We do not know that there was a law that explicitly required the gamelia, but there is no case known to me where it can be demonstrated that legitimate citizen children were born of a mother for whom the gamelia had not been "brought in for the phrateres."[221] Moreover, in Isaeus 3 the fact that Pyrrhos had not brought in the gamelia for the mother is used as evidence against the legitimacy of Pyrrhos' daughter: "it is obvious," says the speaker, "that if he had been persuaded to be betrothed, he would have been persuaded to bring in the gamelia on her behalf for the phrateres and to introduce her alleged daughter as his own legitimate child."[222] He has stated previously that the introduction of the daughter was this phratry's custom;[223] but the betrothal and the gamelia are, the implication seems to be, generally required elements of the marriage process. The gamelia was in a sense, as one ancient scholar characterizes it, the female equivalent of the koureion;[224] the satisfactory completion of the phratry admissions processes in both cases seems to have guaranteed the capacity of those involved to bear citizen children.

In keeping with her legally insubstantial status, a woman did not, generally speaking, exercise citizen rights in her own person, and this is reflected in the fact that the gamelia did not bestow actual phratry membership on her. A woman is never spoken of in the orators as having been introduced to her phratry at gamelia in the same way as a man after koureion and scrutiny.[225] The process of acceptance of a woman by the phratry at the gamelia would therefore probably have been less involved; we hear nothing of any scrutiny. However, there may have been

---

probably depended on both marital and citizenship legitimacy, though as usual in the fourth century, it was not necessary to draw an explicit distinction between the two.

221. The closest to an exception seems to be Dem. 59; but that can be explained readily enough, see n. 215. Dem. 57.69 (see n. 215) could, but need not, be taken to imply gamelia was a legal necessity.

222. Isae. 3.79, see n. 215.

223. Isae. 3.76, see n. 203.

224. Pollux 8.107, above, n. 198.

225. See n. 197, cf. n. 219.

an opportunity for phrateres to object,[226] and it is possible that some phratries would have made an entry on the phratry register. Again, however, we should expect that there was variation from one phratry to another in the details and probably the rigor of the procedure; and again this is implied by a passage of the orators where we are told, "he brought in gamelia for the phrateres according to their laws."[227] Each phratry's laws (*nomoi*) for the gamelia would have been different. This variety may also have affected matters such as whether the gamelia was celebrated by the whole phratry, or, as explicitly mentioned in one case,[228] by a smaller group within it, and possibly even matters such as when it was celebrated. Ancient scholars attest it on Koureotis,[229] but this may be an unjustified inference on their part drawn from its equivalence to the koureion. The information that it was celebrated by a group smaller than the whole phratry in one case is perhaps suggestive that its timing may sometimes have been linked to the other marriage events.

Apart from the evidence of the actual processes of the gamelia and juvenile introduction, we have very little idea exactly what a woman's association with her father's and/or her husband's phratry would have meant in practice. There is no evidence that women partook in any decision-making activities in their fathers' or their husbands' phratries, and there is some evidence that they did not do so. There is no woman on our one certain list of phrateres,[230] nor is one mentioned in any source as a participant in phratry meetings or other business. We would hardly expect this to be otherwise, given the woman's almost nonexistent role in any other social or political decision-making processes at Athens.[231] Moreover the gamelia, as we have seen, does not seem to have bestowed actual phratry membership; and for such girls as may have been introduced to their fathers' phratries, age, as for boys before koureion and scrutiny, as well as sex would have precluded participation to any significant extent. The

---

226. As at the koureion cf. p. 171. It may be, however, that effectively the introduction of any future child of the woman was the opportunity to raise objections to her legitimacy.

227. Isae. 8.18, see n. 215. Harrison 1968–71, 1.7, n. 2, appears to interpret this, wrongly in my view, as suggesting that it was only in some phratries that the gamelia was "laid down by their law." It was the details not the fact of the procedure that would have varied.

228. Dem. 57.43, see above, n. 215.

229. E.g., Pollux 8.107 (see n. 198). The name of the month Gamelion may, but need not, imply that the gamelia at one time took place during it. Cf. Deubner 1932, 177, and above, pp. 157–58.

230. T 18.

231. For their highly restricted legal and political status in general, see Just 1989.

only groups of women who might conceivably have played a fuller role in this respect were adult epikleroi who had not married, at best very rare,[232] and widowed, unremarried epikleroi who, as we shall see, Menander hints may have enjoyed a position in the phratry in their own right, or rather in the right of their deceased husbands.

We know, however, that women played much fuller roles in the religious life both of the polis as a whole and of the demes.[233] It would be surprising, given the greater degree of their quasi-membership in the phratries than in the demes, if women did not enjoy a similar level of participation in phratry cult activities. I argue in chapter 6 that, strictly speaking, the extent of such activities was probably very limited in the classical period, at least in part because they were carried on by the phratry subgroups. But there is certainly evidence for the participation of women at that level, perhaps most strikingly in the inscription of a citizen orgeones group in which the wives and daughters of members seem to have participated at sacrifices and received their own specifically allocated portions.[234] We also have an extremely fragmentary fourth-century inscription, possibly of a phratry subgroup, possibly of a whole phratry, in which a woman is mentioned.[235] No context survives, but the subject matter of the exiguous part of the text remaining seems to have been religious. If it is the inscription of a whole phratry, it was one of very few with a specifically religious content. In any case there is nothing particularly to recommend the original editor's suggestion that a woman was here being prevented from participation in some phratry religious activity.[236] Moreover, there is some indication that women as mothers were associated with the haircutting ceremonies that played a role in the koureion process linked with the passage to adulthood of thier sons. At least we have evidence of monuments erected by mothers to the river god Kephisos commemorating dedications of hair by their sons, and we know that one phratry, Gleontis, had a shrine to this deity.[237]

Two further pieces of possible evidence of women in the phratry

---

232. The pressures of law, tradition, and family interest all conspired to ensure that an epikleros or potential epikleros was quickly married. Cf. Harrison 1968–71, 1.10 and 132–38.

233. See Whitehead 1986a, 77–81.

234. Meritt 1942, 283 no. 55, with Ferguson 1944 and 1949.

235. T 20, 5. See commentary, pp. 346–47.

236. Wilhelm 1905, on the basis that the surviving letter μ immediately following the word γυνὴ was the initial letter of μή. Cf. p. 347.

237. See T 6, with commentary.

cannot be passed over, though they tell us little of substance. First, in a fourth-century inscription that may or may not be a list of phratry members, recording contributions for some unknown purpose, one of the names is "child of Euphronios," a unique description in the list. It could be an illegitimate or underage son or even a slave, but it is not inconceivable that the daughter of a phratry member might make a contribution on her own behalf to some common purpose and be listed in this way.[238]

Second, it has recently been suggested[239] that the character Sostrata in Terence's *Adelphoe* may have been described as the phrater of the character Hegio in the lost version of the play by Menander produced toward the end of the fourth century on which Terence's is based. In Terence's version, Sostrata sends for help to Hegio when she learns that her future son-in-law has abducted a slave-girl;[240] Hegio is described as a relation of Sostrata's and a great friend of her dead husband Simulus. In Donatus' Latin commentary on Terence's play, however, we read that "Hegio is introduced in Menander as a brother (*frater*) of Sostrata."[241] From Hegio's appearances elsewhere in Terence's play and from a surviving fragment of Menander's it seems unlikely that this is literally true. For Sostrata to have had a brother would have undermined the situation in the play at this point, relying as it does on her lonely widowed status; and this appears to have been her position in Menander's version, too.[242] Our version of Donatus' commentary, in fact an abridgement of Donatus' own work, is unreliable; the statement may simply be a mistake or the result of a muddle. There is, however, some attraction in Golden's suggestion that, in Menander, Hegio was in fact a fellow phrater of Sostrata (i.e., of her deceased husband?) and that Donatus simply transliterated the term into Latin as frater, apparently in line with his common practice with Greek technical terms.

---

238. T 35, 30. See pp. 83–84. It could not be an epikleros; two brothers appear at 30 and 40.

239. Golden 1985, 11–13.

240. Sostrata addressing her slave Geta: "tu, quantum potes, / abi atque Hegioni cognato huius rem enarrato omnem ordine; / nam is nostro Simulo fuit summus et nos coluit maxume." Ter. *Ad*. 350–52.

241. Apud Menandrum Sostratae frater inducitur. Donatus on Ter. *Ad*. 351 (3.2.53.1 Wessner).

242. As argued by Gaiser in Rieth 1964, 72–77, associating Menander *Ad*. fr. 4 Edm. (= Stob. *FL*. 10.24), which refers to the difficulty faced by a poor relation in getting help, with Sostrata's isolated and therefore, by implication, brotherless state. Gaiser took Hegio to be Simulus' brother in Menander and Donatus to be describing him loosely as Sostrata's. See Golden 1985, 12, who also discusses other attempts to sort out this puzzle.

We can scarcely give weight to such uncertain evidence, but though a woman is never described elsewhere as a phrater in her own right, in view of the conclusions we have already reached, this would not be particularly surprising in the unusual case, apparently exactly that of Sostrata, of a widowed, unremarried epikleros, anxious to obtain a proper heir by marrying off her daughter, with no close male relatives on either her own or her husband's side. That she might, in the absence of relatives, turn next to phrateres for help is credible enough.[243]

Conclusion

All the evidence for the phratry's activities discussed in this chapter, for the most part connected with the Apatouria, has related directly or indirectly to admission and membership. In the first place this was membership in the phratry itself. The Apatouria was celebrated in phratries; the admissions processes that were the central feature of that central event in the phratry calendar were, in the first place, processes of admission to the phratry; the religious and competitive activities and the eating and drinking that surrounded those processes in a sense underpinned and supported that membership; the Apatouria was not simply about membership control, it was also about the maintenance and affirmation of the community of the phratry. But because of the close link between phratry membership, legitimacy, and citizenship, the Apatouria and the admissions processes were not simply about phratry membership, but about membership in society both more narrowly and more broadly. It was his possession of the qualification by descent, his membership in a particular family, sometimes more broadly of a particular genos, that qualified a person to enter his father's phratry and to inherit a share of his property. It was the possession of that qualification, and the phratry membership that guaranteed it, that in turn in a sense made that person an Athenian citizen. Admission to a phratry was therefore also admission to the wider community of phrateres that was the Athenian polis; and this is reflected in the various national or nationalistic aspects of the Apatouria we have noted. The community extended in fact even beyond the Athenian level to the shared Ionian heritage of which phratry membership and the celebration of the Apatouria were conceived to be vital elements.

---

243. Cf. the similar "back-stop" role of the phratry in Draco's homicide law, pp. 248–49.

It is the connection between phratry membership and legitimacy and citizenship that explains the large proportion of our evidence for the phratry that pertains to admissions and membership matters. It is because of that connection that phratry membership is mentioned so frequently in our major literary source, the speeches of the Attic orators about inheritance and citizenship rights, and therefore by scholars later in antiquity commenting on those speeches. It is because of that connection that phratry membership was of sufficient general and public interest that matters related to it were referred to, for example, in Attic comedy. And it was no doubt in part because of that connection that the Demotionidai/Dekeleieis made and published such detailed admissions regulations. But we must be wary of concluding from this apparent preoccupation of the evidence with membership matters that a phratry was something to which one belonged and no more. As we shall see in the next chapter, this preoccupation is not reflected in the epigraphic evidence as a whole; the phratry also had other features characteristic of a functioning social group in this period.

Chapter 5

Property and Finances

At the end of the last chapter, I observed that it would be wrong to suppose on the basis of the large quantity of evidence for activities to do with phratry admissions and membership that the phratry was an institution to which it may have been important to belong, but which did not otherwise function as a social group in its own right.[1] This preoccupation with membership is certainly a feature both of most of the literary evidence and of the longest single phratry inscription (T 3); it is explained by the important role played by phratry admission and membership in controlling and guaranteeing membership in the wider community of the Athenian polis and the rights associated with that membership. Taken as a whole, however, the epigraphical evidence presents a rather different picture. Of the twenty-five items of such evidence that certainly or probably pertain to individual phratries,[2] T 3 is the only one that unquestionably has to do with phratry admissions, though the early-fourth-century list of members of an unknown phratry,

---

1. There has been no previous synoptic discussion of phratry property and finances. The accounts of property and finances in the demes by Osborne 1985 and particularly Whitehead 1986a are useful in suggesting parallels and points of contrast between deme and phratry. The treatment in this chapter does not claim to be a full picture of phratry activities in this area; that would have to take account of the activities of the phratry subgroups, which lie beyond the scope of this work.

2. I.e., the documents in appendix 1, T 1–T 26, less T 15 (literary evidence for the Thyrgonidai and Titakidai; it is uninformative on phratry activities). For the texts of these documents and those mentioned below, with further discussion of detail, see appendix 1. In a rather different category, since it pertains to phratries in general rather than to the activities of any one phratry in particular, are the surviving special grants of Athenian citizenship (see pp. 50–54) and Draco's homicide law as republished in 409/8 (see pp. 248–50).

T 18, may have been set up following a membership scrutiny,[3] and it is possible that the very fragmentary earlier-third-century (?) decree of the Therrikleidai or a group connected with the Therrikleidai, T 12, also concerned phratry admissions.[4] Most of the rest of our epigraphical material, some twenty-two mostly fragmentary items, has to do directly or indirectly with phratry property and finances.

There are seven markers (*horoi*) of landed properties owned by phratries,[5] dating from the late fifth century to the end of the fourth and probably a little later: four of sanctuaries,[6] one of a house (*oikia*),[7] two of property of uncertain nature.[8] In addition, there is a fourth-century marker of a property that a phratry had "bought subject to redemption";[9] another fourth-century marker of which so little is preserved that its purpose is obscure, but may either have had a similar function or have belonged to a phratry sanctuary;[10] and what is apparently the base of a dedication from the late fifth century or possibly later, described as "sacred of the Medontidai." We do not know whether this is a reference to the phratry of that name or to the mythical royal house, but in either case there is a good chance that the sanctuary in which it was placed belonged to the phratry.[11] An earlier-fourth-century marker pertaining apparently to sacred objects of Zeus Phratrios and Athena Phratria seems to fall into a similar category.[12]

We have more substantial evidence of phratry property interests in the text of a lease of land owned by the phratry Dyaleis in 300/299,[13] and in the accounts of the *poletai* for 367/6, attesting a claim made by the Medontidai on a confiscated property resulting from a purchase

---

3. See p. 336.

4. See p. 318. Among the documents of possible phratries there is another list of uncertain purpose from a period similar to that of T 18, T 35, though the appearance of figures against some of the names suggests that it may have been a record of financial contributions not of a membership scrutiny.

5. In addition there are four such markers among the documents of possible phratries: T 28, T 29, T 30 and T 34, and two inscriptions on monuments from Delos which may have belonged to an Attic phratry (T 33).

6. T 2 (Achniadai); T 6 (Gleontis); T 11 (Therrikleidai); T 13 (Thymaitis).

7. T 23 (phratry unknown).

8. T 1 (Achniadai); T 7 (Medontidai).

9. T 21 (phratry unknown). On the nature of this transaction, the *prasis epi lysei*, see p. 197.

10. T 14 (Thymaitis).

11. T 8.

12. T 25.

13. T 5.

subject to redemption.[14] There are also one certain and five possible cases in the Rationes Centesimarum, the accounts of the 1 percent tax or deposit on property sales from the later fourth century, of phratries selling landed property.[15]

Enough of two honorific phratry decrees survives to give us some idea of the specific benefits that had been bestowed on the phratry by the honorands. In one, from the earlier fourth century,[16] a legal case had been decided by default. We do not know what it was about, but it is a good guess that it involved property. In the other, from ca. 305–280,[17] two members of a distinguished phratry family had apparently donated two hundred drachmas toward a phratry building project.

Of the remaining six inscriptions, two are on altars of Zeus Phratrios and Athena Phratria and do no more than name those deities.[18] One very fragmentary text[19] and possibly a second even more so[20] appear to have contained regulations regarding religious cult; we shall consider these further in the next chapter. Finally, there is one certain[21] and one possible[22] honorific decree, both too fragmentary to allow the nature of the service rendered by the honorand to be determined.[23]

It is well known that the right to own landed property at Athens was normally restricted to citizens, and that it extended to citizens in aggregate. It is not remarkable, therefore, that phratries are attested as having owned land and buildings for the purposes of their own meetings and cults.[24] The focal point of the phratry was its altar, situated at the local phratry center, where the members met to celebrate the Apatouria and

---

14. T 10.

15. T 26 for the certain case. No details are known other than that the property in question was an ἐσχατιά and that the phratriarch -]ς 'Αρ[ι]στω[ν- acted as the phratry's agent (cf. p. 228). The possible cases are detailed at T 27.

16. T 16 (phratry unknown).

17. T 17 (phratry unknown).

18. T 22 (late fourth century), T 24 (fourth century).

19. T 4 (late fourth to early third centuries).

20. T 20 (mid- to late fourth century).

21. T 9 (fourth century or later).

22. T 19 (late fourth century).

23. Of the three documents of possible phratries not mentioned so far, T 32 (Philieis) (not epigraphical) is uninformative as to phratry activities; T 31 (Ikarieis, earlier fourth century), if it does pertain to a phratry (or, more plausibly, to a phratric group such as the Dekeleieis) shows that it passed an honorific decree jointly with the deme that shared its name; and T 36 (name unknown, could be -antidai) of the mid-fifth century appears to have regulated some matter of inheritance.

24. Cf. Harrison 1968–71, 1.235, 241–42.

conduct other business.[25] Phratry meetings were held around the altar, which, in the fifth and fourth centuries, seems normally to have been situated in a bounded area in the open air, sometimes known as a *phratrion*.[26] At least this seems to have been the arrangement at the one phratry precinct that has been excavated.[27] Dating from the late fourth century and situated in the northern part of the city of Athens, probably in the deme Skambonidai, the site consists of an altar of Zeus Phratrios and Athena Phratria and a corner section of a temenos wall. We also know of two *oikiai* (houses) owned by phratries; we cannot tell whether they were used for purposes other than phratry meetings.[28] In addition, we have evidence for a number of phratry sanctuaries (*hiera*)[29] and one shrine (*naos*);[30] and phratries could also make use of and possibly own additional meeting places in the city.[31]

It is of considerable interest that, in addition to owning property for their own use, phratries, like demes and other citizen groups, also sold

---

25. Cf. Hedrick 1991, 255–56. The prominence of the altar in T 3 is typical. It is "from the altar" that votes are carried at scrutinies (T 3, 17–18, 29, 83); the meion and the koureion are brought "to the altar at Dekeleia" (53–54); if he does not sacrifice "at the altar" the phratriarch is to be fined (54); the decrees are to be set up "in front of the altar at Dekeleia" (66–67); oaths of witnesses at the preliminary scrutiny are to be sworn "holding the altar" (76). Elsewhere (Isae. 6.22; Dem. 43.82) we learn that it was possible to express objections to a candidate for membership by removing the sacrificial victim from the altar. See also Isae. 7.13–17; Dem. 43.11–15; Andoc. 1.126; Aeschin. 2.147. The two surviving altars, T 22 and T 24, are both inscribed to Zeus Phratrios and Athena Phratria. At Dem. 43.14 the altar is described as of Zeus Phratrios only. Cf. p. 211.

26. Steph. Byz. s.v. φρατρία (cf. Eust. 239, 31–32; 735, 51) describes a phratrion as a place (τόπος), Pollux 3.52 as a sanctuary (ἱερόν). There is no instance of the term, however, in surviving contemporary literature and only two, neither wholly secure, in Attic epigraphy: T 19, 27 (end of the fourth century) and T 20, 11 (mid- to late fourth century); in both cases from a provision to set up the inscription "in front of the phratrion". (Hedrick 1990, 60, notes that 1. 125 of T 3, τὸ δὲ φρ[-, could also be restored to give a reference to a phratrion. Cf. however also p. 176 n. 182). This wording, if correctly restored, together with the rarity of the word and the relative lateness of these two inscriptions, suggests the possibility that it did not come into use until the later fourth century, or perhaps that it was used to refer to a phratry structure of a particular sort (a roofed meeting place? Cf. further on *oikiai* below).

27. Kyparissis and Thompson 1938. See now also Hedrick 1991, 256–59. See T 22 and diagrams, pp. 346–47.

28. See T 5, 18, and T 23 with notes thereto.

29. See above, n. 6.

30. T 17, 6.

31. See p. 13 with n. 47. There may also have been buildings belonging to central state cults of the major phratry deities, see pp. 209–10, 212, 213 n. 47.

and leased out landed property[32] and acted as creditors in *praseis epi lysei.*[33]

We have only one case of a phratry lease, that of a piece of agricultural land with a house, by the Dyaleis to a certain Diodoros, son of Kantharos of Myrrhinous, a phratry member,[34] in 300/299. The leasing of property by a group to one of its members was normal enough; indeed, leasing outside the group was unusual.[35] But there are features of this lease, discussed in greater detail in appendix 1, which seem particularly to reflect the internal nature of the transaction. First, the lease takes the form not of a contract between two independent parties, but of a phratry decree; this is essentially a private affair between the phratry and one of its members, a phratry regulating its own business. Then there are the financial arrangements. Uniquely in our evidence for Attic leases, the lessee, Diodoros, not only pays an annual rent, six hundred drachmas, in the normal way over the ten-year period of the lease, but he also has the option to purchase the property outright at any time during the ten years for a lump sum, five thousand drachmas. The effective total price Diodoros has to pay for the property is therefore much greater if he waits than if he exercises his option to buy immediately. The arrangement is reasonable enough in its own way, but is perhaps not what might be expected in an ordinary commercial transaction. It is also notable that the size of the rent, six hundred drachmas a year, payable in two install-

---

32. It is remarkable that neither phratries nor groups of any other sort are clearly attested buying land before the Roman period (Finley 1952, 104; Millett 1982, 228). For the possible explanation of this, see p. 198.

33. Note the mode of description of the group in the three cases of financial transactions involving phratries: "the phratriarchs and the society (*koinon*) of the Dyaleis" (T 5); "Kichonides and the society (*koinon* again) of the Medontidai" (T 10) and "the phrateres with Eratostratos"/ "the phrateres with Nikon" (T 21). It may be that this usage represents something like the phratry's legal personality, though it would remain to be explained why the term is not used for demes (though it is sometimes for orgeones groups. Cf. T 10, 30). Note, however, the skepticism (perhaps exaggerated) of Finley 1952, 89, and index s.v. "person, juristic" about the existence of abstract legal personalities at Athens. There is certainly no reason to suppose (as argued by Ferguson 1910, 270) that the term is used in these cases in the sense of an association of two or more groups. The Dyaleis probably were divided into two subphratries (cf. p. 109), but there is no reason to suppose this for the Medontidai and certainly not for the orgeones of T 10, 30. For other uses of koinon in relation to phratries see pp. 295 and 330. For another possible implication of this form of nomenclature see p. 228.

34. T 5. On Diodoros' membership of the phratry see p. 302.

35. Cf. R. Osborne 1985, 54–56.

ments, is higher than that attested for any single property or for the totality of properties let by an individual deme in a year;[36] and the rate of return on capital for the Dyaleis, at 12 percent, is also unusually high.[37] These high values may simply be a reflection of the size and/or quality of this particular estate; or they may have been distorted as a consequence of the unique lease-purchase arrangement. But it would be characteristic enough of the relationship between wealthy citizens and fellow members of citizen groups if Diodoros, clearly a man of some substance, was paying an amount above the going rate for his property, effectively subsidizing his fellow phrateres. A similar lack of disinterestedness needs to be borne in mind in considering other phratry property transactions.

We know nothing about the one certain case of a sale of phratry property, an "outlying estate," other than the fact of it;[38] but we know more about the two certain cases[39] in which phratries acted as creditors in *praseis epi lysei,* both from the fourth century.

In T 10, Kichonides, son of Diogeiton of Gargettos and "the society of the phrateres of the Medontidai" are recorded in the accounts of the poletai for 367/6 as making a one-hundred-drachma claim against a confiscated property arising from a *prasis epi lysei*[40] held by them on the property. It had belonged to a certain Theosebes son of Theophilos of Xypete, who had been prosecuted for sacrilege and had fled Attica without awaiting the verdict. The claim was allowed, as were two others: a similar one involving a group of orgeones, very probably from the same phratry,[41] and another by a certain Isarchos, who claimed the expenses of burying Theosebes' father, Theophilos, and his wife.

In the second case, from about the same period, T 21, two groups of phrateres, "the phrateres with Eratostratos of Anaphlystos" and "the phrateres with Nikon of Anaphlystos" are named as creditors on a marker of another *prasis epi lysei* together with an individual, Kephisodoros of Leukonoion, "the Glaukidai" and "the Epikleidai." As has

---

36. See p. 303.
37. See p. 303.
38. See further T 26.
39. T 10 (Medontidai); T 21 (phratry unknown). The one possible case, T 14 (Thymaitis) is too fragmentary to be informative.
40. Recorded on the inscription as a sale, which in this case must in fact have been a fictional sale, i.e., a *prasis epi lysei,* see p. 319.
41. See p. 319.

already been argued, it is likely that Kephisodoros and the four groups all belonged to the same phratry.[42]

The detailed legalities of a *prasis epi lysei,* "sale subject to redemption," are uncertain,[43] but the principle involved is clear enough. The property concerned was fictionally sold in return for an actual sum of money. If the money was repaid according to the terms of the agreement, including any interest, the property was released from this sale, i.e., it reverted to the original owner. If not, the person or group who had "bought" it owned it in the sense that they had a claim on it to the extent of the sum owed.[44] In other words, the property was in effect security for a loan.[45] In cases attested in the orators, the purpose of the loan was usually some commercial enterprise,[46] but we have no idea of the range of possible or actual uses to which the money borrowed could be put; there is nothing in the nature of the transaction itself to suggest any particular limitations.[47] We do not know what the use was in these two cases.

It is unfortunate that we also cannot be certain about the relationship between borrower and creditors in either of these cases. It is, however, reasonable to suppose that in both cases the borrower was a member of the phratry to which the creditor phrateres also belonged. The mutuality of interest and benefit would be characteristic of the relationship between a phrater and his phratry; we have already observed it in the case of the Dyaleis lease. On the other hand, it would be unexpected for a phratry to become involved in a transaction of this sort with a nonmember. In effect the phratry would be acting as a public bank, a role that is not otherwise attested, and that would be uncharacteristic for a phratry or any other group of this sort. It cannot be ruled out that nonmember loans may have been made occasionally in individual

---

42. See p. 78.

43. See Finley 1952, updated usefully by Millett 1982.

44. Cf. Finley 1952, 31–37.

45. There are obvious similarities to the concept of a mortgage in English law, but there are also differences; in particular the positions of the "buyer" and the "seller" are reversed. See Finley 1952, 8–9, 37; Millett 1982, 246, n. 4.

46. Finley 1952, 31–37.

47. Finley 1952 seems to overstate the case against the money being used for the purchase (i.e., by the fictional seller) of the property to which the *prasis* related, as with the English law mortgage. Finley 1952, no. 3, and Millett 1982, no. 12A, seem almost certainly to be transactions of this sort (see Millett 1982, 227–30), though in the latter case and possibly in the former, the creditor seems also to have been the vendor (i.e., actual vendor and fictional purchaser). The fact that the wording is less explicit in other horoi should not be taken to demonstrate that the nature of the transaction was necessarily different.

cases; indeed, while we may suppose the borrower of T 21 belonged to the same phratry as the creditors, he can scarcely have belonged to all four of the phratry subgroups listed. It seems that here we have a loan by one or more phratry subgroups to a person who was not a member of the same subgroup. But it is difficult to believe loans outside the phratry were common.

The mutuality of interest that is perceptible in these individual property transactions also plays a role in explaining their general purpose.[48] There is no reason to suppose that phratries, or any other corporate body of this sort, tended to own agricultural estates as a straightforward commercial undertaking for the benefit of the group. If they did, we would expect to find them buying land occasionally, and there seems to be no clearly attested instance of this for a phratry, or for any other corporate group, before the Roman period.[49] But if they did not buy the property, how did they acquire it for the leasing and selling for which there is evidence? That they had once been massive landowners and were gradually disposing of their land over the course of the classical period is logically possible, but surely implausible.[50] It is more likely that the land was acquired from time to time by means other than regular purchase. Of these the most obvious is as a consequence of debtors defaulting on loans taken out with the phratry on the security of their property. This may have been the typical way such property was acquired, though I would guess that benefactions may have been another source.

If this is right, the lending of money will normally have been the logically and chronologically prior activity and the owning of agricultural land an occasional consequence of it. The explanation for a phratry's money-lending activities can be found easily enough in general terms in a principle of mutual social and economic benefit that is quite consistent

48. I would say that this applies to other groups as well, including demes, where the pattern seems broadly similar.

49. The silence of the evidence should not be taken to rule out the possibility that corporate bodies ever bought property. They may have done so occasionally for such things as meeting places, but the negative evidence is sufficient to suggest that it was at best a rare occurrence.

50. Some indeed (see Manville 1990, 110–12) have thought that there was a greater degree of common ownership of land in the pre-Solonian period, systematically controlled by the powerful. There is no good argument for this. Our evidence for Solon's work suggests rather that it was the ownership of land by a few individuals, not corporate entities (*Ath. Pol.* 2.2), that was the background for Solon's reforms, and that even common lands were not exempt from their rapacity (Solon *Poems* fr. 4, 12–14).

with a phratry's general character, and which was present also in the property transactions that might follow from those activities.

The specific benefit to the phratry member of borrowing from his phratry clearly lay in the private purpose to which he would have applied the funds. Presumably he may also have felt reassured by the knowledge that, if he defaulted, his creditors would be persons with whom he was associated. What, then, was the specific benefit to the phratry as a whole; or in other words, on what did a phratry spend its money?

Apart from interest on loans and income from leases, the only other sources of phratry income for which there is firm evidence are individual donations by wealthy members (T 17) and fines resulting from misdemeanors of officers and members (T 3); but it is also likely that financial contributions from members were organized for particular purposes (T 35?), and possibly more generally.[51] The pattern is similar to that in the demes,[52] and it may be that, as in the demes, there were also phratry liturgies. We have no evidence, however, that phratries raised property taxes from resident nonmembers, as demes could, and it seems unlikely that they did so if for no other reason than that a phratry's territory would have been too ill-defined for it to be feasible.[53]

The direct evidence for phratry expenditure is very thin, but some is obvious enough, and the parallel with demes and other groups is suggestive in other areas. There is no reason to suppose that there were any salaried officials in phratries any more than there were in other corporate bodies,[54] but as in other bodies, benefactions might be expected to be honored with an inscription and an award of some sort. In only one of our three certain phratry honorific inscriptions[55] is the passage specifying the award sufficiently preserved, but in that case, as typically in the demes, it was a golden crown.[56] In demes such a crown would typically be worth five hundred drachmas.[57] In addition, there was the cost of inscriptions, whether for honorific or other purposes. In demes there is record that this was between ten and thirty drachmas,[58] though in a

51. See T 5, 13–17, with notes thereto. For this in the demes cf. Whitehead 1986a, 150–52.

52. Cf. Whitehead 1986a, 150–60.

53. Cf. pp. 12–13.

54. For the demes, cf. Whitehead 1986a, 161. For phratry officers in general, see pp. 225–36.

55. T 9 (Medontidai), T 16 and T 17 (names of phratry unknown).

56. T 16, 14–15.

57. Whitehead 1986a, 163.

58. Whitehead 1986a, 162.

phratry the official responsible for having a decree inscribed would sometimes be required to pay for this out of his own pocket.[59]

As with demes, however, it seems likely that religious or quasi-religious activities were the main object of expenditure and were therefore the major driving force behind the phratry's financial and landed property related activities.[60] We are told that the festival of the Apatouria itself was at public expense, *demoteles,*[61] which must mean that it was funded by the state; but the activities undertaken by individual phratries at this festival must have varied,[62] and it is difficult to believe that they were invariably fully funded by the state. In any event, phratry activity at other festivals, such as the Thargelia,[63] would presumably have been paid for from phratry funds, as would activities associated with the phratry cults attested by the markers of sanctuaries and by two very fragmentary regulatory decrees.[64] Apart from expenditure on the sacrifices themselves, the most significant cost seems likely to have been the upkeep of phratry buildings, whether meeting places or cult structures or other property.[65] The honorific decree, T 17, seems to have been the consequence of a donation made toward the building or repair of a shrine of Zeus Phratrios and Athena Phratria. It seems, however, that the expenses of sacrifices relative to phratry admission, the meion and the koureion, and with marriage, the gamelia, and presumably any celebrations associated with them, were the responsibility of the introducer and the husband respectively.[66]

I argue in chapter 6 that the extent of the average classical phratry's

---

59. This is specified explicitly for the first of the three decrees of the Demotionidai/ Dekeleieis T 3 (67–68, priest), and should probably be understood to have applied to the other two as well (106—unspecified; Menexenos' decree—relevant passage not preserved). In the only other case where enough of the relevant passage has been preserved, it seems that the phratriarch, who had the decree inscribed, was also required to contribute a certain amount to the cost (T 19). For the contrast here with the demarch see p. 228.

60. For the demes see the useful synoptic discussion of Whitehead 1986a, 163–75. The much richer evidence we have for demes, in particular the surviving fifth-century "source and application of funds" statement of the deme Plotheia, *IG* I³.258, leads him to the conclusion that the deme's religious activities were "the fundamental raison d'être of the budget as a whole."

61. Cf. p. 153.

62. Cf. pp. 152–61.

63. Cf. pp. 216–17.

64. Cf. pp. 219–20.

65. Cf. pp. 193–94.

66. See p. 54 with n. 126, pp. 171–72 and p. 183 with n. 219. In addition to the expenditure described here phratries were also liable for property taxes, see pp. 304–5.

cult activity, at least that which was specific to the individual phratry and distinct from that of its subgroups, was probably less than that of the average deme. This may have meant that phratries were generally better off than demes or that their income was also generally somewhat lower. The fact that the single phratry lease for which we have evidence brought in more rental income for the Dyaleis in a year than any lease or the totality of leases attested for any single deme may suggest a higher level of wealth, but I have suggested there may be particular reasons for this,[67] and it would in any case be unreasonable to generalize on a matter of this sort from just one case. There is nothing in the other financial documents of phratries to suggest extraordinary wealth;[68] the old idea that the phratries were especially wealthy institutions is no better founded than the idea that they were socially exclusive.

On the other side of the books, the possibly lower level of expenditure on cult activities compared with the demes may have been balanced by lower income, the major obvious difference here being the lack of an equivalent to the deme's taxes on property. Until we have enough evidence of phratry finances to support generalized conclusions, however, we must keep an open mind in this area.[69]

The theme of mutual interest and benefit of group and members apparent in phratry property transactions is nowhere more obvious than in the two honorific inscriptions of which enough survives to give us an idea of their context. In T 17, dated to about 305–280, two members of a distinguished local family from Paiania, one named Arrheneides, the other probably called Euktemon, appear to have been chosen to fulfill some office or function in the phratry, of which they were clearly members, with respect to a shrine, probably having to do with its construction or repair, and to have contributed two hundred drachmas for the purpose

---

67. See p. 196.

68. The sums involved in the two certain *praseis epi lysei,* 100 drachmas in the Medontidai claim (T 10) and a total of 2,550 or 3,550 for the phratric creditors of T 21, are in the normal range.

69. We can, however, suggest an answer to the question posed by Lewis 1973, 198, as to what the Dyaleis would have done with the five thousand drachmas they would have gained if Diodoros opted to buy under the terms of the lease, T 5. To judge from what we know from elsewhere, if they wanted to invest it they would most likely have sought to lend it, preferably to a member. Purchase of another property seems unlikely, though cannot be ruled out (cf. p. 198). Alternatively, if income from other sources was sufficient to meet regular expenditures, as was presumably the case here, the money might have been spent on capital works, such as a temple or other building, or on increases in religious or quasi-religious activities (cf. p. 200).

from their own pockets. The phratry honored them with a public inscription and, though the relevant part of the text is missing, no doubt with golden crowns or some such reward. Rewarding the expenditure of wealth for the public good with honor is a commonplace of classical Athenian life, and it is no surprise to find it within a phratry.

In T 16, the honorand is a certain Eugeiton. We are not told explicitly that he is a phratry member, but it can be inferred with a high degree of probability from the surviving text. Eugeiton's services to the phratry clearly extended back a long way; he is described as having "furthered the phratry's interests both now and in times past." Recently, however, he had rendered some special service in a legal case which had been decided by default in the phratry's interest. He is rewarded with a golden crown of a specified, but unknown, value; by setting up the honorific inscription on the Acropolis the phratry seems to have intended to give him special prominence.[70]

Such, then, is the evidence for the phratry's financial and landed property activities in the classical period: lending money to members; owning, leasing out, and selling landed property; honoring benefactors; seeing to the administration of its own affairs, the upkeep of its buildings, and the balancing of its budget. Behind it all was the religious activity that will be the subject of the next chapter. We know about these matters for the most part because property, money, and transactions pertaining to them by their nature are materially important and require relatively permanent written records. They may be taken as representative of a range of other more mundane activities that were not felt to justify the expense of an inscription.

How often a phratry met to conduct its business is impossible to say with any confidence or accuracy. We have firm evidence for phratry meetings only at the Apatouria and in one, probably exceptional, case at the Thargelia.[71] But it is possible that our two major phratry decrees were passed at meetings that did not take place at the Apatouria;[72] and in the most recently published decree of a phratry or phratric group, T 12 (Therrikleidai), there may be reference to a *kyria agora,* a term generally used to refer to a principal, regular, or general meeting of a

---

70. On these points, see further appendix 1.

71. On the Apatouria, see chapter 4; for the Thargelia, pp. 216–17. It is also possible that phratries were involved with the celebration of the Theoinia and the Synoikia, see p. 217.

72. See p. 219 and p. 305.

group, and implying the potential or actual existence of other, irregular, or extraordinary meetings, at which the phratry may not have been fully empowered to deal with the full range of business.[73]

These property and financial inscriptions, essentially similar in type to those attested for demes, show clearly enough that a phratry might function as a social group in its own right, that it might meet to conduct business other than that pertaining to admissions, and on occasions other than the Apatouria. How common these other activities were in the average phratry and how far one phratry might vary from another is impossible to say in absolute terms. We have no way of knowing what proportion of total phratry activity is represented by the few items of evidence we possess. In relative terms, however, the overall quantity of our epigraphical evidence is in striking contrast to that of the demes. In 1986, Whitehead listed a total of 143 epigraphical documents from all periods recording activity by demes, of which about 95 are from deme decrees.[74] In 1985, R. Osborne listed 75 deme decrees to the end of the fourth century.[75] In contrast, we have about 30 epigraphical documents recording activity by phratries,[76] of which about 10 are phratry decrees.[77] In other words the total number of our phratry documents is between a fifth and a quarter of the number of deme documents;[78] and the total number of phratry decrees is less than a seventh of the total number of deme decrees to the end of the fourth century. The difference is too large for it to be likely that accidence of survival is the major determining factor. What, then, are the reasons for the disparity? If the major determinant of the level of activity of the sort that produced inscriptions was the nature and level of a group's religious activities, it is important to investigate these before we attempt an explanation.

---

73. T 12, 11 (-]/ἐν τῆι κυρία[ι-]). For a discussion of the kyria agora in the deme (attested in *IG* 2².1202, 1–2) see Whitehead 1986a, 90–92.

74. Whitehead 1986a, appendix 3. He lists only those which he mentions in his text, but that must be nearly all in existence. I say about 95 decrees, because there are a few whose identification as deme decrees is uncertain (e.g., no. 136).

75. R. Osborne 1985, 206, table 6.

76. Calculated as total number of items in appendix 1, T 1–T 26, i.e., those certainly or probably pertaining to phratries (=26), minus the one literary item (T 15), plus half the total number of epigraphic items in appendix 1, T 27–T 36, i.e., the possible phratry documents (=4½), which gives a total of 26 − 1 + 4½ = 29½.

77. T 3, T 4, T 5, T 9, T 12, T 16, T 17, T 19, T 20, ?T 31, ?T 36.

78. The period covered by both sets of evidence is roughly the same, though there are a few deme documents and no phratry documents that postdate 250.

Chapter 6

Religion and Officers

Religion

The nature and extent of religious activity in the classical phratries is a matter of considerable interest, not only in its own right, but also because of its implications for other questions.[1] For Wade-Gery, the phratry in the fifth and fourth centuries not only displayed signs of aristocratic domination, it was also an essentially religious institution, the ancient equivalent of the ecclesiastical parish, in contrast to the deme, seen as the equivalent of the English secular parish.[2] This view, as we shall see, is no longer tenable.

In fact, all groupings of persons at Athens, as elsewhere in the Greek world, tended to have a religious aspect.[3] This applies at the macro-level of the polis itself, Aeschylus' "city-holding gods,"[4] and at the micro-level of the great variety of citizen subgroups of which Athenian society consisted. If religion is a means of ordering, explaining, and interacting with the world, this was so for the communally-minded Athenians typically in a social context rather than at the level of the individual. Accordingly, religious activity at Athens typically took place in, and was

---

1. While much has been written on individual aspects of phratry religion, there is no overview of the sort now available for the demes, particularly in the works of Mikalson 1977, R. Osborne 1985 and 1987, Whitehead 1986a, and Kearns 1985 and 1989. Kearns' reflections on phratry religion, however (1985, 204–5; 1989, 75–77), provide a useful starting point.

2. See Wade-Gery 1933 (= 1958). Note especially the ecclesiastical flavor imparted to the institution by his translation of the decrees of the Demotionidai/Dekeleieis.

3. Cf. Kearns 1985, 190–92.

4. Aesch. *Seven Against Thebes,* 312, 822; cf. Hdt. 8.41.

often an expression of the concerns of, the groups to which the citizen belonged.[5]

In recent years, in particular as a result of the discovery of new epigraphical material, the extent and variety of religious activity in the demes has come to be recognized.[6] Some of it, as would be expected of groups to which all citizens belonged and which played an important role in the political organization of the state, reflected and expressed interests held in common with other citizens and other demes;[7] but there was also a great variety of localized activity, and cultivation of what seem to us obscure, in many cases apparently ancient, local heroes and minor deities, that in some sense clearly served to express and maintain the particular identity of individual demes.[8]

The picture in the deme in this respect was perhaps not very different from that in the phratry subgroups, gene, orgeones groups, and others, though a full and up-to-date study of the religious activities of these is lacking and would no doubt produce some interesting comparisons and distinctions.[9] But at the level of the phratry itself the picture in the classical period is at once strikingly similar and strikingly different. The commonality of cult was very strong, apparent, interestingly, in the worship of the same deities, though in different aspects, that played a unifying role in deme religion: Zeus, Apollo, and Athena;[10] but the local particularism characteristic of deme religion was almost entirely absent.

Phratry religion was almost entirely a matter of the expression or

5. For a recent vivid general discussion of the role of religion in local Athenian life, see R. Osborne 1987, 165–97.

6. See n. 1.

7. E.g., the local celebrations of state festivals (on which see esp. Mikalson 1977) and the ubiquity of cult of certain of the Olympian deities (n. 10 below; cf. Whitehead 1986a, 206–8).

8. See Whitehead 1986a, 207; Mikalson 1977, 432, on the cult of, e.g., Ares in Acharnai, Hebe in Aixone, Poseidon in coastal demes, etc. It is also difficult to believe, for example, that cults such as that of the Sican hero Leukaspis or Epops the hoopoe were widespread outside the deme in which there is evidence for them (Erchia in this case: SEG 21.541 Γ, 48–53; Δ, 18–23; E, 9–15. Cf. Whitehead 1986a, 203), though some obscure deme cults do seem to have had external links (Whitehead 1986a, 203–5). See also the evidence for cult of deme eponyms, conveniently collected by Whitehead 1986a, 210–11.

9. On these subgroups in general, see chapter 2. Building on the basis established by Bourriot 1976, Kearns 1989 has advanced our understanding of hero cult in gene, orgeones groups, demes, and phratries, and notes (75) its apparent absence from the phratries in contrast to the other groups.

10. For the ubiquity of these three deities in deme religion, in contrast, according to Mikalson, to their "somewhat limited" importance in state cult, see Mikalson 1977, 432–33; Whitehead 1986a, 206, with n. 179.

symbolization on the religious plane of the ideas and forces of community
that were fundamental to the phratry's raison d'être;[11] but this was
essentially the community that linked members of one Attic phratry with
members of another, and with phrateres in Ionia and the Greek world
as a whole, not the community of one local group as opposed to other
local groups within Attica or outside it. I have already noted this emphasis
on community transcending the individual phratry with respect to the
Apatouria, but it is also a feature of phratry religion in general.[12]

The three major deities associated with the phratries at Athens were
Zeus Phratrios, Athena Phratria, and Apollo Patroos. Zeus, the greatest
of the Greek gods, can probably be taken to represent the panhellenic
aspect of phratry membership, though it would appear that the worship
of him as Phratrios was specifically Ionian. The sense of Ionian identity
bound up in phratry membership and activities was further reinforced
by the cult of Apollo Patroos, Apollo in his aspect as father of Ion,
and of Athena Phratria, also common to the Ionian world, but for an
Athenian also clearly a reflection of the intimate association of phratry
membership and Athenian citizenship.

The commonality of interests and attributes represented by these deities is explicit in one of our most important pieces of evidence, a fictional,
but nonetheless informative, scene in Plato's *Euthydemos*.[13] Euthydemos
and his brother Dionysodoros are portrayed in the dialogue as Chians
by descent, who had moved as exiles to the colony of Thurii in Italy
many years previously, apparently as children.[14] Although an Athenian
colony (444/3), there were contingents from other Greek cities at Thurii
and the Peloponnesian influence appears soon to have become dominant.[15] In any case, Dionysodoros is not aware that, in the Ionian world

11. Cf. Kearns 1985, 204–5: "...they are very neatly Durkheimian gods, who appear
to be simply the correlative on the religious plane of the social group involved in their
worship."

12. It is also reflected very clearly in the contemporary literary evidence, which contains
not one name of an individual phratry and in which being a phrater often comes close
to meaning being an Athenian and hardly ever has the connotation of being a member
of one phratry rather than another. Cf. p. 43.

13. Plato *Euthydemos* 302b–d.

14. 217c. It is not clear (pace Ehrenberg 1948, 169) that they were supposed to be
founding members of the colony. Plato does not state that they were children when they
moved to Thurii, but their ignorance of Ionian religion would suggest it.

15. Diodoros 12.10.4. On the extent and nature of Athenian leadership and Peloponnesian influence, see the contrasting accounts of Wade-Gery 1932 (= 1958), 255–58, and
Ehrenberg 1948, esp. 157–70. The latter seeks to play up the Athenian influence on the

in general and for Socrates in particular, Zeus is not Patroos, ancestral, as he was outside the Ionian world. "What a wretched man you are and no Athenian if you have neither ancestral gods (*theoi patrooi*) nor cults (*hiera*) nor anything else fine and good (*kalon kai agathon*)." Socrates replies that he does indeed possess all these things: "I do have altars and household and ancestral cults and all the other things of this sort that other Athenians have." Zeus, he explains, is not ancestral (*patroos*) for any Ionian, at Athens or elsewhere, "but Apollo is Patroos through his fatherhood of Ion, and Zeus is not called Patroos, but Herkeios and Phratrios and Athena Phratria."[16]

Zeus Phratrios and Athena Phratria were, as their epithets suggest, the primary deities of the phratries[17] and the evidence for them at Athens is fairly abundant, particularly in our epigraphical sources. Phratry inscriptions tend to be headed with the name of Zeus Phratrios, sometimes together with Athena Phratria, in the genitive, suggesting that the phratry's activities and decisions were conceived of as in some way under their tutelage.[18] Phratry altars were either "of Zeus Phratrios" or "of Zeus Phratrios and Athena Phratria,"[19] who were doubtless intended to be the recipients of the sacrifices performed on them.[20] In the Demotionidai/Dekeleieis it was to Zeus Phratrios that oaths were sworn at scrutinies[21] and to whom fines paid for failure to comply with phratry

---

colony's institutions, but does not note the apparent implication of this passage that it did not adopt Athenian institutional cult practices.

16. It is perhaps notable that while Dionysodoros describes these cults in terms implying that their possession was a matter not only of Athenian citizenship but also of high social standing (ταλαίπωρος ... ῷ̣ ... μήτε ἄλλο μηδὲν καλὸν καὶ ἀγαθόν), the implication is absent from Socrates' response; he simply states that he is the same in this regard as other Athenians. This may be intended to hint at Dionysodoros' lack of understanding of democratic Athenian society (cf. previous notes). It is credible that there were distinctions in the manner in which θεοὶ πατρῷοί were cultivated by Athenians of different qualities of lineage, but not, Socrates implies, in the fact of it.

17. Cf. Pollux 1.24; 3.51. Earlier discussions to be found, e.g., in Guarducci 1937; Latte 1941, 756–58.

18. Zeus Phratrios: T 3, T 19. Zeus Phratrios and Athena Phratria: T 18. T 17 has the common [θε]οί. For texts, translations, and further discussion of epigraphical documents mentioned in this and following notes, see appendix 1. On the implication of tutelage, cf. Hedrick 1989, 129, and other works cited there.

19. Cf. pp. 193–94.

20. Nowhere stated explicitly for the meion and the koureion, but attested in general for the sacrifices on Anarrhysis by Σ Ar. *Ach.* 146 (above, p. 153 n. 59), cf. Suid. s.v. Ἀπατούρια and s.v. φράτορες.

21. T 3, 16–17 (oath of phrateres at extraordinary scrutiny); 74 and 111 (oath of witnesses at anakrisis in regular scrutiny).

regulations were described as sacred.[22] It may be that a phratry's financial resources in general were conceived of as in the possession or safe-keeping of the two deities, at least those resources with a religious origin or purpose, which would have been the majority.[23] In a phratry that had a base at Paiania, a contribution of two hundred drachmas made by two individuals seems to be described as "to Zeus Phratrios and Athena Phratria"; its purpose may have been to fund building work on their local temple.[24]

There is no indication that the Zeus Phratrios and Athena Phratria of an individual phratry would have been regarded by members as deities that were particularly their own, as distinct in any way from those of other phratries in Attica or indeed in Ionia as a whole.[25] Indeed, the significance of the cult lay precisely in the communal bond reinforced and maintained by the fact that it was the same Zeus and Athena that were cultivated by other phratries.

It is possible, in fact, that there was a central, state cult of the two deities. Mid-fourth-century remains of a small temple next to that of the related deity Apollo Patroos were discovered in the Agora before World War II and associated then with an altar of the two deities[26] and a marker referring to them[27] that apparently related to a dedication or sacred objects of some sort found in the vicinity.[28] The identification of the building has recently been questioned, albeit indecisively,[29] and, at the current state of knowledge and debate on the issue, that the altar and marker and/or the temple belonged to an individual phratry cannot be ruled out. Given, however, not only the significance of this cult as the major religious expression of groups that bound Athenian citizens together as such, but also its close association with Athens' status as

22. T 3, 23–24; 40; 49–50; 55–56; 91; 100.

23. Cf. p. 200.

24. T 17, 7–9. For a possible depiction of Athena Phratria (and possibly Zeus Phratrios also), see notes to T 16.

25. I differ here slightly from Kearns 1985, 205, with n. 46 and 1989, 75–76 with n. 53, citing Plat. *Euthyd.* 302c–d (esp. ἔστιν γάρ σοι, ὡς ἔοικεν, Ἀπόλλων τε καὶ Ζεὺς καὶ Ἀθηνᾶ) and *Ath. Pol.* 55.3 (see below, n. 48). I take the distinctiveness among the cults in different phratries etc. implied by these passages to consist not in a conception that the Zeus Phratrios and Athena Phratria worshipped by different phratries were different but simply in that the same cult was practiced in different places by different groups.

26. T 24.

27. T 25.

28. See Thompson 1937.

29. By Hedrick 1988b. See appendix 1, pp. 357–58. Cf. also Wycherley 1957, 52.

the Ionian metropolis, it is highly plausible that there was a central cult of these gods at Athens, whether or not the specific remains have been correctly identified.

That plausibility is increased by one of the two pieces of evidence we have for this cult not directly connected with the phratries. In the sacred calendar of the Athenian State as republished in the second stage of the work of Nikomachos, 403/2–400/399, but which was clearly archaic in origin, provision was made for a small sacrifice by the old Ionian phyle Geleontes to Zeus Phratrios and Athena Phratria at the festival Synoikia.[30] It is perhaps best to envisage this representative act as having taken place in a central temple of the two deities; the Geleontes had for all practical purposes long since ceased to exist,[31] and it is implausible that they still maintained their own temple and cults. It was highly appropriate, given their significance as deities representing communal bonds, that Zeus Phratrios and Athena Phratria should be honored at a festival which commemorated the unification of Attica; and although effectively obsolete by the end of the fifth century, it is easy enough to see how the old phylai would still have been regarded symbolically as the appropriate groups to perform such a sacrifice, not only because they were no doubt conceived of as the phylai into which the inhabitants of Attica had been distributed on unification,[32] but also because they seem to have been thought of by some in the classical period, whether rightly or not, as having been aggregates of the phratries.[33]

This instance of the cult of Zeus Phratrios and Athena Phratria in a group regarded as an aggregate of phratries is balanced by our one secure piece of evidence for it in what was probably a phratry subgroup, the genos Salaminioi. We know that this genos, in the fourth century and no doubt before, sacrificed to Zeus Phratrios at the Apatouria.[34] The two deities may also have been the objects of a mid-third-century dedication from the Acropolis of another phratry subgroup, in this case a thiasos, though the inscription is very fragmentary and its restoration in this sense uncertain.[35]

---

30. Oliver 1935, 21, no. 2, lines 44–59. Cf. p. 256 n. 52.
31. See p. 245.
32. Cf. appendix 2.
33. See p. 4.
34. Ferguson 1938, 3, no. 1, 92–93. Cf. pp. 64–66.
35. M & E Levensohn 1947, 63, no. 1. The crucial point of uncertainty is the restoration of the names of the deities at 2–3, θια]σωτῶν τῶν μ[εθ' ἑαυτοῦ Διὶ καὶ]/['Αθην?]ᾶι. pp.

The origin of these cults is obscure. That of Zeus Phratrios may be very ancient, though we have no way of determining whether it in fact predated the Ionian migration or was a later product of a sense of Ionian solidarity. Athena Phratria looks newer, since she does not always accompany Zeus Phratrios and never apears alone. She may have been introduced alongside Zeus at some time when Athens was seeking to emphasize her hegemony in the Ionian world, perhaps in the sixth century.[36]

The third major cult associated with phratries was that of Apollo Patroos, "ancestral Apollo."[37] As the epithet suggests, the link here was not just with phratries, but with hereditary groups in general, including gene. As Socrates explains to Dionysodoros, Apollo was ancestral for Athenians because he was traditionally the father of Ion;[38] and we know from elsewhere that Ion was regarded not only as the eponym of the Ionian race but also the founder of the Ionian phylai and the groups understood by the *Ath. Pol.* to have been their subdivisions, phratries and gene.[39] We have evidence for the cult in the phratry Therriklei-

---

85–86. For completeness Krat. Jun. *Cheiron* f. 9, 4–5 K-A = Athen. 11.460f (see p. 32) should also be mentioned. The speaker, in a parody of the archontic scrutiny (see n. 213), claims that, following his "enrollment in the drinks cupboard" (he has returned home to find he has no phrateres or demesmen left and has clearly taken refuge "in his cups"), Zeus is Phratrios and Herkeios for him.

36. The sacrifice to Zeus Phratrios and Athena Phratria by the Geleontes ἐκ τῶν φυλοβασιλικῶν in Nikomachos' revision of the sacrificial calendar of the state may suggest both deities were antique. But not everyone believed that Nikomachos had not tampered with his inheritance (see Lysias 30, cf. p. 16), and it is not unlikely that Solon had tampered with his. Cf. below, the theories that Apollo Patroos was also a sixth-century invention for a similar purpose.

37. Hedrick 1988b is a useful, if not wholly convincing, discussion of the archaeology and history of the cult. He does not explore the important question of the nature of its links with phratry and/or genos membership and citizenship. On this, see in particular Andrewes 1961a. See also on this cult De Schutter 1987. The literary and epigraphical testimonia are usefully collected by Wycherley 1957, 50–53.

38. ἀλλὰ Ἀπόλλων πατρῷος διὰ τὴν τοῦ Ἴωνος γένεσιν. Plat. *Euthyd.* 302c.

39. See esp. *Ath. Pol.* fr. 1 and fr. 3 (see app. 2); Eur. *Ion* 1575–88; Hdt. 8.44, 7.94 (for other relevant texts see Rhodes 1981, 66). There is no justification in these passages for the oft-repeated claim (even by the best authorities, see, e.g., Rhodes 1981, 66, 618; Hedrick 1988b, 203–4, 210) that Apollo and Ion were regarded in the classical period as ancestors of all Athenians and other Ionians. In both our fifth-century sources there is a clear implication that the Athenians already existed before Ion became their commander-in-chief (Herodotus) or their phylai were named after his sons (Euripides, cf. *Ath. Pol.* frs. 1 and 3. Xouthus is portrayed as king of Athens in the *Ion,* so Euripides can hardly have intended to imply that all Athenians were descended from his supposed son Ion. Cf. also the strong tradition that the Athenians were autochthonous, Thuc. 1.2, etc. τῶνδε in τῶνδε δ' αὖ/παῖδες γενόμενοι σὺν χρόνῳ πεπρωμένῳ/ Κυκλάδας ἐποικήσουσι

dai,[40] in the phratry or genos Elasidai[41] and in the gene Salaminioi and, at a very late period, Gephyraioi;[42] and for the related cult of Apollo Hebdomeios, Apollo "of the Seventh," in the phratry Achniadai.[43] In this case we can be more confident that there was also a central observation of the cult. Later fourth-century remains discovered in the Agora have been identified as the temple that, according to Pausanias, contained Euphranor's statue of Apollo Patroos.[44] Until recently it has been thought that this temple had a sixth-century predecessor on the same site, but the physical remains of the earlier building are exiguous and their identification has recently been questioned, albeit indecisively, mainly on the grounds that there is a gap of a century and a half between the supposed destruction of the earlier building in 480 and the construction of the later one, during which the supposed temenos was—implausibly, it is suggested—infringed upon by other structures.[45] As with Zeus Phratrios and Athena Phratria, the origin of the cult is obscure. The sixth century has been favored, again in connection with developing claims to Athenian hegemony over Ionia, but there are no decisive or even persuasive arguments on the basis of current evidence, and we cannot exclude the possibility that the cult was much older.[46]

νησαίας πόλεις κτλ. at *Ion* 1581–83 refers back not to Ion's sons mentioned in 1574 before the lacuna in the text, but to the members of the phylai named after them, mentioned in 1580 and the immediately preceding lines, now lost).

40. T 11.

41. T 29.

42. Salaminioi (fourth century): Ferguson 1938, no. 1, 89. Gephyraioi (second century A.D.): *IG* 2².3629–30. Cf. the Apollo cult attested for the Erysichthonidai (second century A.D. *IG* 2².4991; *BCH* 1929, 182–83).

43. T 2. Cf. p. 216 for probable activities of this phratry at the ancient Ionian Apollonian festival, the Thargelia.

44. Paus. 1.3.4. Remains identified by Thompson 1937. Cf. Hedrick 1988b, esp. 191–200, whose suggestion (210) that the building was a consequence of Lykourgan revivalism is attractive.

45. Hedrick 1988b, 189–91. He recognizes (190–91) that his argument against Thompson's identification of the building is indecisive.

46. Jacoby 1944, 72–73 guessed at Solonian institution. Hedrick 1988b argues for a sixth-century origin, part of a Peisistratid policy of asserting Athenian hegemony over Ionia. This is not impossible, though I find his arguments at most indecisive; e.g., he makes much of the link between Apollo Patroos and Apollo Pythios and between the latter and Peisistratos, but his claim that Patroos must have been subsequent and "subordinate" to Pythios is doubtful. It is not implied by Dem. 18.141, which simply asserts that Apollo Pythios is Patroos for the city, and certainly not by second-century evidence (Sokolowski 1962, no. 14, 52) that the priest of Apollo Pythios was responsible for sacrifices to Apollo Patroos. That implies no more than Dem. 18.141—that the cults had become

Socrates in the *Euthydemos* talks not only of Zeus Phratrios and Athena Phratria as cults distinctively associated with Athenian citizenship, but also of those of Apollo Patroos and another related cult, that of the regular Greek household god, Zeus Herkeios, "Zeus of the Hearth."[47] The last two also figured in one of the questions put to an archon at his scrutiny before taking up office: "whether Apollo is Patroos for him and Zeus Herkeios, and where these sacred things are."[48] The formulaic question seems also to have been made rhetorical use of by fourth-century orators, apparently in cases involving citizen rights and the like, and Demetrios of Phaleron in his work on Athenian legislation also mentioned their association with citizenship.[49]

Exactly how it was that the cults of Apollo Patroos and Zeus Herkeios marked a person as a citizen is uncertain. It seems unlikely that it was entirely a matter of tradition and practice, at least not at the level of individual citizens, since that would scarcely prevent a foreigner intent on usurping citizen rights from simply observing the cult at will. The only place in the orators where the two cults are mentioned with context surviving is Demosthenes 57 on the citizenship of Euxitheos of Halimous. Euxitheos claims that as a child his relatives immediately introduced him

---

associated—but that could be due to any number of causes (cf. the implied association of Apollo Pythios and Patroos in Euripides' *Ion*) and cannot be taken to demonstrate prior origin of Pythios four centuries previously. Moreover the appearance of the deity in the archontic scrutiny procedure (see n. 48, though this procedure did admittedly refer to Cleisthenic demes) and the fact that the tradition that Athens was the Ionian metropolis predated Peisistratos (see Solon *Poems* fr. 4a) and was probably historically correct (as Hedrick recognizes, 204) suggest the possibility of a much earlier origin. In any case, however, sixth-century manipulation of the cult is not unlikely.

47. Harp. s.v. ἕρκειος Ζεύς (quoted below, n. 49) seems to imply that altars of Zeus Herkeios were to be found in the courtyards of individual houses. As with Apollo Patroos and, probably, Zeus Phratrios and Athena Phratria, there was also a central cult (*FGH* 328 Philochoros fr. 67; Oliver 1935, 21, no. 2, 1.61). We also have evidence for it in a deme (Thorikos, see Daux 1983, 157–58, 160) and in association with gene (Dem. 57, see below, n. 51).

48. εἰ ἔστιν αὐτῷ Ἀπόλλων πατρῷος καὶ Ζεὺς ἑρκεῖος, καὶ ποῦ ταῦτα τὰ ἱερά ἐστιν. *Ath. Pol.* 55.3.

49. Harp. s.v. ἕρκειος Ζεύς· Δείναρχος ἐν τῷ κατὰ Μοσχίωνος "εἰ φράτορες αὐτῷ καὶ βωμοὶ Διὸς ἑρκείου καὶ Ἀπόλλωνος πατρῷου εἰσίν." ἕρκειος Ζεύς, ᾧ βωμὸς ἐντὸς ἕρκους ἐν τῇ αὐλῇ ἵδρυται· τὸν γὰρ περίβολον ἕρκος ἔλεγον. ὅτι δὲ τούτοις μετῆν τῆς πολιτείας οἷς εἴη Ζεὺς ἕρκειος, δεδήλωκε καὶ Ὑπερείδης ἐν τῷ ὑπὲρ δημοποιήτου, εἰ γνήσιος, καὶ Δημήτριος ἐν τοῖς περὶ τῆς Ἀθήνησι νομοθεσίας. (= Deinarchos fr. 32; Hyperides fr. 94; *FGH* 228 Demetrios of Phaleron fr. 6. Cf. Jacoby ad loc.). For a similar device, cf. Dem. 57.67–69, where Euxitheos rhetorically asks himself questions about his family etc. in the form in which they were put at the scrutiny of the thesmothetai. For a parody of this, see n. 35.

"to the phrateres and to the hiera, those of Apollo Patroos and the others";[50] and he calls as witnesses to his father Thoukritos' citizenship "the gennetai of Apollo Patroos and Zeus Herkeios."[51] On this basis Andrewes developed the hypothesis[52] that the cult of Apollo Patroos was under the control of the gene, that non-members such as Euxitheos might be presented to the gennetai as custodians of the cult, and that they could claim after this to have been "examined by the gennetai."[53] I argued in chapters 2 and 3 that Euxitheos and Thoukritos should be seen as members of the genos in question here and that there is not the supporting evidence Andrewes claimed for his view that gene generally exercised power over nongennete phratry members in phratry admissions and scrutiny procedures.[54] Any hypothesis which restricts the cults to the control of the gene is also not easy to reconcile with the evidence for the Apollo Patroos cult in phratries as well as gene and that of Zeus Herkeios in demes.

For the cult of Apollo Patroos perhaps the best hypothesis on the basis of current evidence is that it was the preserve of phratries and their subgroups such that, whatever precise arrangements existed for its observance in those groups—arrangements which, like so many other aspects of phratry activities, we may take to have varied—generally speaking all citizens, and only citizens, by virtue of phratry and/or phratry subgroup membership, were deemed to have a share in the cult. The question about Apollo Patroos at the scrutiny of archons would in that case therefore have been in effect a shorthand way of asking what phratry and/or phratry subgroup a citizen belonged to.[55] It may be that,

---

50. ἀλλὰ παιδίον ὄντα μ᾽ εὐθέως ἦγον εἰς τοὺς φράτερας, εἰς Ἀπόλλωνος πατρῴου ἦγον, εἰς τἄλλ᾽ ἱερά. Dem. 57.54. I do not much sympathize with the need felt by editors to tamper with the text here. Schaefer, followed by Rennie in *OCT*, bracketed the second ἦγον, Blass added με before it. Another possibility, I suppose, would be γεννήτας for the second ἦγον by analogy with section 67 (see next note), taking the first three letters as having been corrupted into the last three of ἦγον (for the justification for this, see p. 73). But it seems natural enough to take ἱερά μ᾽ as understood before the second ἦγον from the rest of the sentence. Cf. p. 73 with n. 62.

51. εἶτ᾽ Ἀπόλλωνος πατρῴου καὶ Διὸς ἑρκείου γεννῆται. Dem. 57.67.

52. Andrewes 1961a, 7.

53. ἐν γεννήταις ἐξητασμένος. Dem. 57.24.

54. See esp. pp. 71–73.

55. This would also account for the fact, otherwise somewhat curious in a procedure with clearly archaic origins, that the candidate is not explicitly asked to name his phratry as he is his deme. It may be that the letter of the law on qualifications for archonship was no longer enforced in the fourth century (see Rhodes 1981, 145–46). If those who were officially thetes were by then in practice able to stand for the archonship, in addition

because under the provisions of the law of Philochoros fr. 35[56] a gennete was automatically a phratry member, one would expect a prospective archon with a genos to allude to it rather than to his phratry in answering the question, just as in Demosthenes 57 Euxitheos describes specifically his gennetai rather than his phrateres as "of Apollo Patroos."

Zeus Herkeios was not a phratry deity; we can take it that Zeus was always Phratrios in the phratry. But he was cultivated by phratry subgroups and by demes.[57] Again, arrangements were probably such that, in answer to the question at the archonship scrutiny, a citizen could refer to his membership either in a phratry subgroup—for Euxitheos his genos—or in a deme which observed the cult.[58]

In both cases the limitation of the practice of these cults to citizens alone would therefore have consisted simply of the fact that only citizens were admitted to the groups by which the cults were practiced. If these cults were also observed in individual households, as is possible at least in the case of Zeus Herkeios,[59] perhaps these were regarded as extensions

---

to the zeugitai permitted in 457/6 (*Ath. Pol.* 26.2), those whose phratries may not have been strong in these cults would presumably also have been let through (cf. Rhodes 1981, 330–31).

56. Cf. pp. 46–49.

57. See n. 47 above. I agree with Ferguson 1938, 322–23 against Kahrstedt 1934, 231, that there is no reason to suppose Zeus Herkeios and Zeus Phratrios were identical.

58. Why were Zeus Phratrios and Athena Phratria not referred to in the archontic scrutiny? Surely not because the cults did not exist at the time this part of the procedure was formulated, but conceivably because at that time the archonship was restricted to persons of high birth and the cults of Apollo Patroos and Zeus Herkeios may have been more exclusive than those of Zeus Phratrios and Athena Phratria; or perhaps because Zeus Herkeios and Apollo Patroos tended to be cultivated in the smaller, more local groups (cf. next note) and part of the intention behind the question was to pin down exactly where the candidate came from. In the light of Ar. *Pol.* 6.1319b 19–27 (see p. 246 with n. 6) and the actual case of making public private cults in the Klytidai on Chios (see Forrest 1960), it cannot be ruled out that the cults of Apollo Patroos and Zeus Herkeios had once been private in some sense though in what sense and how it may be relevant here is obscure.

59. The apparent implication of Harpocration, see above n. 49. Ferguson 1938, 31–32, argued that both Zeus Herkeios and Apollo Patroos properly belonged to the households on the grounds that Plat. *Euthyd.* 302c talks of ἱερὰ οἰκεῖα and that their absence from the known priesthoods of the gene Kerykes and Salaminioi shows they could not have been invariably under the control of gene; gene and phratries would have observed the cults at will. There is no evidence for Apollo Patroos in a household, however, and it is difficult to reconcile this view with the control necessary to restrict the cults to citizens. Moreover, I suggest it is not significant that there was no specific priest of Apollo Patroos in Salaminioi or Kerykes. It is enough that the cult is attested in the former and that of the closely related Apollo Pythios in the latter (Ferguson loc. cit.).

or offshoots of the cult as practiced in the wider group and therefore in some sense still under its control.

The same pattern of non-phratry-specific cult activity apparent in the cults of Zeus, Athena, and Apollo was also a feature of the cults of the secondary deities with which phratries were associated. As has been observed, Dionysus had come to be associated with the Apatouria at least by the classical period, most clearly through his role in the foundation myth, but also through the orgiastic character of the festival itself; the hair cut from the heads of candidates for the koureion was dedicated at the oinisteria to Artemis; and a measure of wine was offered to Herakles before the haircutting ceremony.[60] This all seems to have been of relevance to phratries generally. We cannot, however, rule out the possibility that there was an element of phratry individuality in relation to the only festival apart from the Apatouria at which there is firm evidence for phratry activity, the Thargelia. Like the Apatouria this was an ancient Ionian festival, celebrating the birthday of Apollo on the seventh day of the seventh month, Thargelion. Its main features seem to have been a primitive scapegoating purification rite on the first day and some sort of agricultural offering, the *thargela,* on the second. There is evidence for the celebration of this festival, however, in only one phratry. In Isaeus 7 the speaker, Thrasyllos, relates that he was introduced by his adoptive father to his genos and his phratry at the Thargelia.[61] A good case can be made that phratry was the Achniadai, in part on the grounds that the Achniadai had a temple of Apollo Hebdomeios, "Apollo of the Seventh."[62]

Whether there was phratry activity at the Thargelia more generally than in this single case is unclear.[63] Apollo Patroos, by his association with kinship groups, was identifiable with Apollo Pythios, the specific deity of the Thargelia;[64] and the antiquity and panionian character of the festival may suggest wider participation. But the rest of our sources are remarkably silent; there is no evidence for it in any other phratry, and indeed there is some indication that in the classical period the festival

---

60. For the cult of Kephisos in the phratry Gleontis, also connected with haircutting rites, see pp. 218–19.

61. Cf. pp. 66–68.

62. For more detail on this, see appendix 1, T 2.

63. Labarbe's suggestion at 1953, 389, that the successful admission of the elder son of Alke to Euktemon's phratry in Isaeus 6 took place at the Thargelia is a hypothesis based on doubtful reasoning concerning the chronology of that speech (cf. p. 165 n. 128).

64. See esp. Dem. 18.141; Hedrick 1988b, 200.

was organized on the basis of the Cleisthenic phylai.[65] Moreover, the introduction of Thrasyllos to the Achniadai at the Thargelia has the appearance of an emergency measure.[66] Thrasyllos says that Apollodoros' own son had died in Maimakterion, the month immediately after that of the Apatouria, Pyanepsion, and it seems that Apollodoros feared, rightly as it turned out, that he would not live to the next Apatouria. On the other hand, it is perhaps not plausible that the phratry would have gathered merely for the admission of one man, and if the identification of Apollodoros' phratry as the Achniadai is correct, we would expect some more regular activity in connection with Apollo of the Seventh. It seems best to suppose that there was a regular meeting of Apollodoros' phratry at the Thargelia,[67] and that there was some arrangement, probably specific to this phratry and possibly ad hoc, whereby admissions could be made in circumstances where delay until the Apatouria was not feasible. We do not know whether Thrasyllos' opponents attacked this admission at the Thargelia as irregular. It is perhaps not unlikely, though Thrasyllos passes over the point with no explanation or excuse.

The two other festivals with which our evidence hints phratries may have been associated in the classical period also seem to have had some generalized significance. We know almost nothing about the Theoinia, but like the Apatouria it seems to have had Dionysian associations.[68] The link with phratries is a tenuous one, however. The gene Krokonidai and/or Koironidai apparently celebrated the festival and the obscure officials, the oinoptai, elsewhere associated with phratries, seem to have been involved.[69] Whether the phratries participated at the Synoikia, as did the old phyle Geleontes with a sacrifice to Zeus Phratrios and Athena Phratria, is unclear. The pan-Attic significance of this festival celebrating the unification of Attica has already been observed.[70]

For cultic activity in the phratries unconnected with particular festivals

---

65. *Ath. Pol.* 56.3.

66. Cf. Wyse 1904, 558.

67. For phratry meetings other than at the Apatouria see p. 202.

68. See Parke 1977, 174.

69. Harp. s.v. θεοίνιον (= Lykourgas fr. 7.3) reports that Lykourgos' speech in the case of the Krokonidai versus the Koironidai attested that gennetai sacrificed at Theoinia. Athen. 10.425a–b (= Lykourgas fr. 7.5) records that Philinos mentioned the oinoptai in connection with dinners in his speech in the same case. For the oinoptai and phratries, see pp. 154–55.

70. Cf. p. 210.

or with the major deities already mentioned, our evidence is very weak. The possibility must be borne in mind that a significant accession of new epigraphical material would alter the picture, but the impression on the basis of current evidence is that there was very little such activity and that what there was contained a considerable element that was of general significance to all phratries. There are three phratries or gene, the Zakyadai, the Pyrrhakidai, and the Euergidai, that cultivated the Tritopatreis.[71] Even by the later fourth century the significance of these deities seems to have been uncertain. Aristotle apparently held the view that they were the third in line of ascent, i.e., great-grandfathers; others took them to be third in line of descent, apparently from the Original Being, i.e., Titans or Winds or the like.[72] Insofar as there was an element of ancestor-worship involved, as some of the specific evidence for the cult also seems to suggest,[73] the cult would have been to a degree individual to the group concerned; insofar as the cult involved primeval beings, it would have generated a bond that transcended the group. In this connection it is noteworthy that the cult is attested in demes as well as in these gene/phratries and, as with Apollo Patroos, that it seems also to have been observed centrally.[74] However, it must be stressed that there is no sure evidence of the cult in a phratry.

With the partial exception of the cult of Apollo Hebdomeios of the phratry Achniadai already mentioned, there are only two phratry cults securely attested that are apparently unique to the phratry concerned: those of Zeus Xenios of Thymaitis and of Kephisos of Gleontis.[75] In the first case there must be some link between the cult and the phratry eponym Thymoites. He was the cowardly king of Athens in the Apatouria legend, in which Eleusinian gifts of guest-friendship (*xenia*) played a crucial role in determining his successor, Melanthos, to settle in Attica. It is surely significant, in connection both with the myth and with the

---

71. There is brief discussion of these deities at Kearns 1989, 76–77, though she overstates somewhat the case for the identification of the Zakyadai and Euergidai as probable phratries. See notes to T 30, T 33, T 34 in appendix 1.

72. For further detail, see notes to T 34 in appendix 1.

73. In particular the naming of a single "Tritopater of the Aigilieis of the Pyrrhakidai" on an inscription of ca. 400 from Delos (T 33) and their grouping with the founder Battos at Cyrene, Sokolowski 1962, 115A, 22–23.

74. *IG* 1².870 (see further at T 34).

75. Thymaitis: T 13. Gleontis: T 6. See also notes in appendix 1 ad loc. Whether any significance should be read into the fact that all three of these cases date from the earlier period of our epigraphical evidence (i.e., late fifth to early fourth century) is unclear.

comparatively recent accession of the foreign Eleusis to Athens, that the base of the phratry Thymaitis was close to the border with Eleusis.[76] In the case of Gleontis, it can at least be said that there is no evidence for the cult of the river god Kephisos in any other phratry.

Even with these two cults, however, there is a strong general significance that is not specific to an individual phratry. The role of xenia in the Apatouria foundation myth was, like the myth itself, the common property of all phratries; the way that this "foreign" aspect of Zeus exactly mirrors the characteristically Athenian Zeus Phratrios and Zeus Herkeios also makes the significance general. In the case of Kephisos, this generalized aspect is even clearer: we know that youths at Athens made dedications of hair to this god in puberty rites that must have been associated in some way with the phratry admission ceremony, the koureion.[77]

This impression of very limited particularized cult activity is confirmed by the evidence, or rather the lack of it, for the regulation of cult in phratries. R. Osborne counted eleven deme decrees with a religious purpose, six of them sacrificial calendars, in his list of seventy-five deme decrees to the end of the fourth century.[78] Among the admittedly much smaller corpus of phratry documents, we have only one that is concerned primarily with the regulation of cult,[79] T 4, which I have identified somewhat tentatively as a fourth- or third-century decree of the House of the Dekeleieis. It seems to make provision for the observance of the cult of Leto (for which there is also evidence in the decrees of the Demotionidai/Dekeleieis) T 3, to be maintained "according to tradition" (kata ta patria). In this connection, it seems that certain persons were appointed to fulfill some function, and there is mention of religious functionaries distributing and/or taking as dues something, possibly honeycomb, associated with Leto's daughter "Artemis the Leader."[80] I argued in chapter 3, however,[81] that the House of the Dekeleieis was not originally an ordinary phratry, but a subgroup of the phratry Demotionidai, though it may have become independent by the mid-fourth century. This unique evidence for cult regulation in a phratry therefore

---

76. See pp. 327–28.

77. See p. 306. It should be admitted, however, that we do not know how general this practice was outside the phratry Gleontis.

78. R. Osborne 1985, 206, table 6.

79. For the significance of the phratry's limited cult activities see pp. 223–25.

80. See further notes to T 4 in appendix 1.

81. See esp. pp. 106–7, 135–39.

may be a reflection of the atypical status of the group involved; particularized cult in phratry subgroups is more usual.[82]

The only other regulation of a phratry that may have regulated cult is the extremely fragmentary mid-to-late-fourth-century T 20. Again, however, we cannot be certain that the group that passed it was a phratry rather than a phratry subgroup. The fact that it was apparently set up in front of the phratrion suggests the former, but scarcely proves it. As for the content, something priestly or sacred is mentioned in lines 3–4 of the inscription—the verb sacrifice is used in 8–9, and a priest is mentioned in 9–10 in the formula for having the decree inscribed. Apart from the tantalizing mention of a woman, however, the subject matter of the decree is otherwise wholly obscure. We do not know how much text is missing at either end of what survives, and it is possible that the main purpose was not religious.[83]

A consonant impression is obtained from consideration of phratry eponyms. It has recently been observed in the case of the demes that there was no uniformity in the manner in which a deme related to its eponym: sometimes there was cult, sometimes not; sometimes there was no eponym. Often there was obscurity in antiquity, and there is greater obscurity today.[84] The picture in the phratries is in some ways similar, but the obscurity is even greater.[85] There is not one secure piece of evidence for the cult of an eponym in a phratry. The closest we come to it is the case of the Medontidai, but the waters are muddied here by uncertainty over whether documents mentioning the group relate to the phratry of that name, Medontidai (P), or the mythical royal house, Medontidai (R). We have a fifth-century marker, found close to the entrance to the Acropolis, of a piece of land or meeting place "of the Medontidai"[86] and a fifth-century dedicatory base from Kephale "sacred of the Medontidai."[87] In neither case is it clear whether the Medontidai (P) or the Medontidai (R) are intended. What the relationship was, or was conceived as being, between the two is also wholly obscure. It would

---

82. For this see esp. Kearns 1989.

83. See further notes to T 20 in appendix 1.

84. See esp. Whitehead 1986a, 208–11; and in more detail Kearns 1989, 92–101. Note that there is no evidence that phratry members were conceived of as descended from their phratry eponym, see pp. 9–10.

85. For some remarks on phratry eponyms in the context of discussion of other cults, see Kearns 1985, 204–5; 1990, 76.

86. T 7.

87. T 8. Cf. also T 9–10.

be perverse to deny any connection at all; presumably some of the tradition about the Medontidai (R), apparently manipulated and to some extent standardized by Hellanikos in the late fifth century, was preserved by the phratry. But to go any further would be mere guesswork on the basis of present evidence. Certainly there is no evidence that can be taken to demonstrate a cult of the royal house in the phratry.[88]

Apart from this, the only hint of a phratry cult of an eponym is the mention in a very fragmentary earlier fifth-century religio-financial decree of something Therrikleian, generally taken as a temple of Therrikles, the eponym of the phratry Therrikleidai.[89] But it is not clear that a temple or cult of Therrikles, a hero otherwise totally unknown,[90] is being referred to rather than something else Therrikleian. And even if a temple or cult is referred to here, this document is on no account a decree of the Therrikleidai. The original editor of the inscription implausibly took it to be a decree of the Areopagos. I argue in appendix 1 that it may instead be a product of the group Miltieis, which I suggest may have been a phratry subgroup, related to the deme Melite as the House of the Dekeleieis was to the deme of the same name, and to the Therrikleidai as the Dekeleieis were to the Demotionidai. Even if there was cult of Therrikles, therefore, there is no evidence that it was practiced in his eponymous phratry; as with the evidence for phratry religious activity discussed earlier in this section, there would, if anything, be a case for associating it rather with a phratry subgroup.

Our ignorance about Therrikles extends also to the eponyms of the phratries Achniadai and Thyrgonidai.[91] Another, Demotion, is almost equally obscure, with one possible mention in a Vergilian scholium in a list, obviously manufactured, of children rescued by Theseus from the Minotaur.[92] Another phratry, Gleontis, shared another artificial eponym with the old phyle Geleontes, Geleon the eldest son of Ion.[93] Another, the Dyaleis, had no eponym at all; the name seems to derive either from a cult title of Dionysus, or from the duality of this phratry which had two phratriarchs and was probably a geminated group.[94]

It is a curious feature of phratry eponyms that, insofar as they are

---

88. For more detail on this, see pp. 316–18.
89. For more detail on this and the following, see pp. 322–25.
90. There was an archaic archon by this name. See p. 321.
91. Cf. p. 283 and p. 333.
92. Cf. pp. 112–13 n. 64.
93. Cf. p. 15 n. 51, p. 308.
94. Cf. p. 109.

known at all, their mythical roles range from the unedifying to the positively nasty. Medon was distinguished only by his weakness as the first king to allow restrictions on his power.[95] His supposed relative in an earlier generation, Thymoites, the eponym of the phratry Thymaitis, not only killed his half-brother Apheidas—another possible phratry eponym[96]—to get the throne, he also played the coward in refusing to fight the Boeotian king Xanthos, and lost his kingdom to his stand-in Melanthos as a result.[97] Dekelos of the Dekeleieis and Titakos of the Titakidai were both traitors to the invading Tyndaridai. Dekelos betrayed Helen to them and Titakos colluded.[98]

It may be tempting to see in this another example of the polarity characteristic of early Greek thought and detected by Vidal-Naquet in the Apatouria myth.[99] I do not wish to rule out some explanation of this sort, but it seems intrinsically implausible that the phratries concerned ever made offerings to such negative figures.[100] Taking into account the obscurity of the other phratry eponyms and the general lack of individuality in phratry religious activities, it seems possible that, while there may have been some preexisting traditions, the eponyms of phratries may in general have been as obscure in the fifth century as they are to us; that there was little, if any, cult of them at that or any later period; and that, when Hellanikos and his colleagues came to rationalize and organize Attic mythology, the eponyms provided a good source of names for negative roles.[101] Whether the eponyms had been livelier figures in phratry life and tradition in the archaic period, we cannot tell.

What is the explanation for this lack of individualized cult among the phratries? The question is important not only in its own right, but also because the answer to it will be an important element in the answer to the question about the relatively low quantity of evidence we have for the activities of phratries as compared with demes. Religious activity, both directly and indirectly through the financial activity which supported

---

95. Cf. p. 316.

96. Cf. pp. 363–64.

97. Cf. pp. 144–45.

98. Hdt. 9.73. Cf. p. 113 and p. 335.

99. See pp. 148–52 above, where I argue that Vidal-Naquet's explanation of the Apatouria myth is not entirely satisfactory. For the supposed polarity of archaic Greek thought, see especially Lloyd 1979.

100. Cf. the remarks of Kearns 1989, 93, with n. 72, and 12–13 in relation to the maleficent deme eponym Anagyros.

101. Cf. Jacoby on *FGH* 323a Hellanikos fr. 23 and below, pp. 316–18.

it, will have been a major determinant of the quantity of epigraphical material a group produced.

It has recently been suggested by Kearns in her study of hero cult in Attic local groups that, in contrast to the gene and orgeones groups, where there is substantial evidence of such cult, phratry religion reflected the commonality and uniformity of phratry membership and activity in Attica. In the gene and orgeones groups, to which not everyone belonged, individualistic cults expressed their distinctiveness.[102]

Up to a point this explanation is attractive; it certainly fits the picture of an institution that bound Athenian citizens together as such. It is a plausible enough partial explanation of the relatively limited quantity of epigraphical material produced by phratries that, generally speaking, the religious activity in which they engaged was not of the local cultic variety that generated a large budget. But this cannot be the whole story, for on this basis we would hardly expect the rich variety of particularized cult activity in demes, to which all citizens also belonged. I suggest there are two other important factors that need to be taken into account.

First, and most importantly, the existence of the phratry subgroups must itself have been a significant factor. Nearly all the inscription-producing activity of the institutional structure of which the deme was a part took place in the deme itself, the Cleisthenic phylai and particularly the trittyes being much less active in this regard.[103] In the phratry structure, on the other hand, the subgroups, which the deme lacked, generated much of this activity. Cultic activity is much more pronounced in the evidence for gene, orgeones groups, and other phratry subgroups than it is in the phratries themselves;[104] for example, orgeones groups appear not infrequently as lessors of property, creditors on *praseis epi lysei,* and so on.[105] It seems that the group-specific aspects of phratric religious activity, and therefore much of the inscription-producing activity may have tended to take place in the subgroups, while religion in the phratries themselves expressed the commonalities of phratry membership at the Attic and super-Attic levels. We can only speculate about why this might have been, but the relative sizes of the groups probably had something

---

102. I paraphrase, I hope not too inaccurately, Kearns 1989, 76.

103. The phyle and trittys documents are conveniently listed by Jones at 1987, 65–67. The almost complete absence of trittys documents is no doubt in part a consequence of the artificiality of these units, made up of groups of demes from different regions, in contrast to the more natural and lively phratries.

104. See n. 9.

105. See p. 75, n. 71.

to do with it; group-specific cultic activity may be more likely in a smaller group as an expression of relatively tight natural community, while a larger group may naturally tend to look outward to the community beyond itself. The demes, generally not subdivided and probably usually smaller than the average phratry, may have been nearer in character to the phratry subgroups in this respect. It is probably also relevant that phratries might consist of more than one particular local group and/or of members more or less spread about Attica.

Second, however, it cannot be ruled out that the average deme, certainly in some senses the more important local political unit, for that reason generated more cultic activity and was generally more active as a social group in its own right than the phratry. It has been observed by recent writers on the subject of deme religion that much of the cultic activity for which there is evidence in the demes in the classical period must have originated before Cleisthenes.[106] Scholars have understandably been reluctant to speculate on the groups in which that activity would have taken place in the archaic period, for we lack any evidence on the matter. Could some of this cult activity have been transferred, deliberately or otherwise, to the demes from the phratries? Aristotle, in a famous and much debated passage of the *Politics,* speaks of the founding of new phylai and phratries and the nationalization or "making common" of private local cults as an important weapon of democratic reformers, mentioning Cleisthenes and the democrats at Cyrene as examples. The *Ath. Pol.,* on the other hand, makes it clear that, in the Athenian case, Cleisthenes did not tamper directly with phratries, gene, or cults.[107] Moreover, I argue in chapter 8 that it was rather the naukraries and the old trittyes and phylai that were the objects of his reforms. It may be, therefore, that those groups, particularly perhaps the naukraries, had practiced cults that were transferred to the demes.[108] But one suspects the picture was more complex than this: there were clearly pre-Cleisthenic quasi-deme units, komai and the like, some actually known as demes, which did not fit into any regular pattern of Attic subdivisions[109] and from which cults may have naturally been transferred to the new structures of community, the demes. And, though we know the phratry sub-

---

106. See esp. Kearns, op. cit. and Whitehead, op. cit.
107. See pp. 246–47.
108. On the naukraries, see further pp. 252–55.
109. See Whitehead 1986a, 5–16, for deme-type groups before Cleisthenes; cf. also above p. 109 n. 52.

groups continued to practice their own cults and that Cleisthenes does not seem to have tampered with them, perhaps Aristotle may be taken to suggest the possibility that some of these cults, and perhaps some phratry cults too, as an indirect consequence of his reforms, may have been transferred to the demes.

Phratry Officers

Phratriarch

The phratriarch is the only phratry officer for whom, strictly speaking, we have evidence in groups which we know are phratries and not phratry subgroups. That evidence, however, is very thin. We now know of fifty demarchs, forty by name; there are only five known phratriarchs.[110] With this quantity of evidence, we can claim to do no more than collect impressions, and may expect that some of them will be shown by new evidence to have been ill-formed.

Having said that, the role of the phratriarch in his phratry and outside it and the type of person he was are matters of considerable interest. The obvious analogy to the demarchs is particularly instructive: there appear to be strong similarities and interesting differences.

The first point of contrast concerns the number of phratriarchs per phratry. There is no evidence for any deme with more than one demarch.[111] There were certainly two phratriarchs in the Dyaleis in 300/299[112] and certainly more than one in the Therrikleidai in the early third century.[113] There is only one mentioned in the earlier fourth-century decrees of the Demotionidai/Dekeleieis, but I argued in chapter 3 that there may have been more than one in the Demotionidai as a whole.[114] As for the rest, there are three or four cases where a single phratriarch is probable or almost certain.[115] The explanation for this difference will

---

110. See below p. 232. Note also p. 234 n. 159.

111. Whitehead 1986a, 59 with n. 85. The plural demarchs of *IG* 2².1174, 3 and 4–5 seem to be a series extending into the future.

112. T 5, 5–7 and passim.

113. T 12, 7.

114. T 3, 11–12 and passim. See pp. 122–23.

115. It is difficult to be certain in any case since the argument tends to be *e silentio*, but a single phratriarch is highly probable in (a) the Medontidai in 367/6 (T 10, 1–2, Kichonides and the society of the phrateres making a claim on the property of Theosebes; cf. p. 316. Had there been two phratriarchs we would expect them both to act for their phra-

have become apparent from the preceding chapters. While demes, apart from occasional centrally imposed reforms, were essentially immutable units, phratries, probably normally larger institutions, could and did adapt structurally, in particular by splitting and fusing, in response to demographic and other pressures. Changes of this sort would occasionally have given rise to phratries with more than one phratriarch. Given that such developments typically would have been gradual and cumulative, it may not be coincidental that the two sure pieces of evidence for multiple phratriarchs are both relatively late, from the early third century.[116]

The internal functions of a phratriarch seem to have been broadly similar to those of a demarch. We have evidence that he administered admissions procedures and acted as bursar, registrar, disciplinary officer, religious functionary, and general administrator.[117] In the case which provides us with the most evidence here, that of the Demotionidai/Dekeleieis, he shares some of these functions with a priest. The extent to which we may regard such a sharing of functions as usual will depend on the view we take of the relationship between the Demotionidai, the phratriarch's group, and the Dekeleieis, the priest's. In my view, the Dekeleieis were a subgroup of the Demotionidai in the process of breaking away from their parent phratry. The relationship between the groups, and therefore the distribution of functions between phratriarch and priest, though possibly not uncommon, would not therefore be typical. On other interpretations, the relationship between phratry and priest in this case might be regarded as more normal.[118] Whatever the structure

---

try in business of this sort, cf. T 5); (b) T 26 in the later fourth century (-]ς ’Αρ[ι]στω[ν-, a phratriarch, representing his phratry in a land sale. There is only room for one name. Again, were there two phratriarchs we would expect joint action in business of this sort, cf. T 5); and probable in (a) T 19 in the late fourth century (for textual doubts about this case, see p. 345; the balance of probability does not incline strongly in favor of a single phratriarch); (b) the phratry of which Euxitheos of Halimous was phratriarch in the 340s (Dem. 57.23, but see n. 137 below).

116. See T 5 and T 12.

117. The phratriarch can be found fulfilling all of these roles in the Demotionidai/Dekeleieis (for greater detail see pp. 120–24 and further below). In the Dyaleis lease, T 5, the role as general administrator and executive officer of the phratry is in evidence, as is the financial function (rent is to be paid to them at 28–29). The phratriarch is responsible for having a decree inscribed in all cases where the relevant clause survives except T 3 (on which see below. Cf. T 5, 54–55; T 19, 24–25; also T 18 and T 20). For the parallel functions of a demarch see Whitehead 1986a, 122–30.

118. Cf. pp. 120–24.

in the Demotionidai, however, there was clearly scope for variation in this regard,[119] as in many others, from phratry to phratry.

Two points of contrast with the deme are notable here. First, by virtue of a deme's much greater political and administrative role in relation to what might be termed central government,[120] the demarch fulfilled a number of functions, particularly in relation to the forfeit of property to the state, the collection of taxes, the administration of naval conscription, and the performance of religious rites, in which he acted effectively as its agent.[121] With the exception of the procedures concerning homicide law, there was only one area of the phratry's activities in which the state as a whole had an interest, namely the procedures of admissions that controlled access to the citizen body.[122] We would expect, therefore, that the phratriarch's responsibilities with regard to admissions would have taken up a larger proportion of his time than in the case of the demarch; and it is clear that in this area the phratriarch would have been subject to control and regulation by the center.[123] But the absolute burden of the work as agent of the state must have been less for the phratriarch than for the demarch.

---

119. See esp. chapter 4 passim.

120. It should be borne in mind, however, that modern concepts of the distinction between central and local government are in many respects inappropriate.

121. See Whitehead 1986a, 130–38. Also included in this category should be the demarch's electoral and registration functions. The demarch's legal obligations with respect to the burial of the dead, though perhaps in a slightly different category, are of particular interest. He was required to act to ensure proper burial of those for whom their relatives had not performed this duty (law at Dem. 43.57–58; cf. pp. 318–19) and was fined if he failed to do so. It is characteristic that the community as a whole felt itself responsible, at both local and state levels, to act as an extension of the immediate family in this matter, and would no doubt have risked pollution had it failed to do so (a recurrent theme of Athenian tragedy, e.g., Sophocles' *Antigone*). The point of interest is that it should have been the deme, rather than the phratry, which in other ways had the more obvious role of backing up the family, that was charged with this responsibility. It is best to suppose that this was because, at least by the time this law was passed (apparently late fifth or early fourth century), the demarch, unlike the phratriarch, was responsible for a tract of territory as well as for a group of persons, and though this is not quite clear in the text, it seems that the intention was that he should attend to any unburied bodies that might be lying in that territory, whether or not they were those of deme members. It would not have been feasible to give this responsibility to a phratriarch. R. Osborne 1985, 74, in my view rather oversimplifies the contrast between the role of the deme in exercising the "general civic responsibility" in contrast to that of the phratry in "looking after its own." The deme's role in this case is very close in character to the phratry's, e.g. in homicide law (cf. pp. 248–50).

122. See chapter 1 and pp. 161–88.

123. For example, by the provisions of Pericles' citizenship law.

Second, a minor detail, but an interesting one: in two cases in a phratry the officer charged with inscribing the decree, in one case the phratriarch, in another the priest, was required to contribute to or meet the cost of the inscription from his own pocket.[124] There seems to be no evidence for this in any deme. It is possible this may have been a relic of a time before Cleisthenes when the phratriarch or priest would automatically have been among the wealthiest persons in a phratry in a way that a demarch would never necessarily have been in his deme.[125]

The external functions of the phratriarch were also for the most part analogous to those of the demarch. The phratriarch acted for or represented his phratry in the sale of land[126] and other landed property transactions,[127] as the demarch did for his deme. Here again, however, there was a minor but intriguing difference. In legal descriptions of the deme in its transactions, particularly those of a financial or property related nature, the deme was typically mentioned by itself.[128] In both the relevant pieces of evidence in the case of the phratry, however, the phratry is named together with its phratriarch.[129] It is possible that there is no very great significance in this; it may be one of those minor legal distinctions which are essentially meaningless. But it is again possible that it may be a relic of a time before Cleisthenes' demes were invented, when a phratriarch had more power to act on behalf of his phratry independently of phratry control than a demarch would ever have possessed.

In general, however, it cannot be said that the balance between the power exercised in his phratry by a phratriarch and that exercised by his phratry over him was significantly different from in the case of the deme. We do not have the evidence to judge how far a phratriarch's influence stemmed from formal powers, for example from control over arrangements for phratry meetings,[130] and how far it arose more informally from

---

124. T 3, 67–68 (priest, whole cost); T 19 (phratriarch, part cost).

125. Cf. p. 199.

126. T 26. Cf. for the demarch, e.g., *IG* 2².1598, 37.

127. T 5 (lease); T 10 (claim on confiscated property). Cf. also T 21 (*prasis epi lysei*, though the groups involved are probably phratry subgroups).

128. In leases this is invariably the case. See Behrend 1970. I have not searched other deme financial documents.

129. T 5; T 10. Cf. T 21.

130. That the phratriarch, like the demarch in the deme (Harp., cf. Suid. s.v. δήμαρχος; Σ Ar. *Clouds* 37) was responsible for summoning phratry meetings is nowhere attested but can safely be assumed. The sort of control a demarch could exercise over his deme by astute arrangement of business is well illustrated in Demosthenes 57, where Euboulides succeeds in having Euxitheos ejected from the deme by taking the vote when most of the demesmen had gone home (cf. appendix 5).

the weight of his position in the phratry and his general standing in the community; but we can see it at work, albeit implicitly, in the provisions of the Dyaleis lease, where the clear impression is given that the phratriarchs were in control of the arrangements.[131]

On the other hand, the phratriarch was also no less accountable and subject to his phratry than the demarch to his deme. There is a strong indication of this side of the relationship in the first decree of the Demotionidai/Dekeleieis, where Hierokles placed firm and possibly unwelcome obligations on the phratriarch, for example, to sacrifice the meion and the koureion in the future at Dekeleia, and indeed provided for him to be fined if he failed to do so.[132] I have suggested, too, that the priest was used in the decree as a check on the phratriarch's actions.[133] We should resist any temptation to see in this the dying embers of a struggle of the People versus the Artistocracy. The priest was much more likely than the phratriarch to have been "aristocratic," as we shall see.[134] The point seems to be rather that the phratriarch represented a power external to the sub-phratry that passed the decree: that of the whole phratry, the Demotionidai. In any case the principle that the phratriarch was ultimately subordinate to the decisions of his phratry is clear enough.

The method of appointment is crucial to the relationship of a group to its leader, and here is another point of subtle contrast with the deme. On the one hand, there was no apparent difference between phratry and deme with regard to conditions of eligibility, a major area of dispute in general in the sixth and fifth centuries. As far as we know, there were no such conditions for the demarch, and while we cannot be certain, it seems from Demosthenes 57 that there were none for the phratriarch either.[135] There appears, however, to have been a slight difference in the

---

131. The impression arises not only from the fact that the phratriarchs are invariably mentioned together with the phratry whenever a course of action for the phratry is provided for (to the extent that the lessor is actually described as "the phratriarchs and the society of the phrateres," T 5, 4–8, cf. above, n. 129) but also from the fact that the phratriarchs are to receive the rent (see above, n. 117) and, though the text is unfortunately incomplete at this point, seem to have some specific interest in the detailed agricultural requirements imposed on the lessee by the lease (20).

132. T 3, 45–56. Cf. p. 123.

133. See p. 123.

134. p. 234.

135. See below, n. 137. If there had been some special qualification for eligibility for the phratriarchy we can be fairly confident that Euxitheos would have mentioned it. He is at pains to adduce every point in his favor; also he was apparently not a wealthy man, so it seems unlikely there was a property qualification. Cf. p. 232.

method of selection. Phratriarchs seem to have been elected. (We can be fairly certain they would also have held office for one year, like the demarch).[136] This is admittedly only attested in one case, that of Euxitheos in Demosthenes 57, where, interestingly, it is Euxitheos' relatives and his demesmen, not his phrateres, who give the evidence.[137] We cannot tell how far there was uniformity of practice in this regard, but although the situation in the demes is unfortunately still not wholly clear, there is no evidence for election of a demarch, and, by the fourth century at least, it seems probable that sortition was the standard practice.[138]

The significance of the distinction between election and sortition, however, is not easy to assess.[139] It may not have been particularly great—certainly not as great as that which obviously existed between election and sortition on the one hand and appointment and hereditary succession on the other. In the fifth and fourth centuries election and sortition were used side by side both in demes and for offices of central government, though there seems to have been a tendency, usually attributed to the immediate post-Ephialtic period, to switch from election to sortition for the selection of general political officers such as Bouleutai and archons, with election reserved for those, such as the generals, where particular

---

136. The probable implication of the identification of the year of the first decree of the Demotionidai/Dekeleieis (T 3, 11–12) by the name of the phratriarch as well as the archon at Athens.

137. λαβὲ δὴ καὶ τὰς τῶν δημοτῶν μαρτυρίας, καὶ τὰς τῶν συγγενῶν περὶ τῶν φρατέρων, ὡς εἵλοντό με φρατρίαρχον. Dem. 57.23. I do not think it would be justified to read into this any more than that the overlap between deme and phratry in this case must have been great, though I would not rule out the possibility that the Halimousians formed a sub-phratric group with their own phratriarch, like the Dekeleieis, cf. p. 109 n. 52.

138. See the somewhat inconclusive discussion of Whitehead 1986a (index, s.v. demarchs, appointment procedure, esp. 114–15, closely following Damsgaard-Madsen 1973). Evidence for appointment by lot is at *Hesp.* 1939, 177–80, 7, cf. *IG* 1³.258, 12–14; Dem. 57.25; *Ath. Pol.* 54.8. For evidence of sortition from prokritoi (a pre-elected pool) followed by election, which we have only for other deme officials, see Whitehead 1986a, n. 147. I agree with Whitehead 1986a, 59, that it is likely that procedures for appointment of officials with such important central state functions would have been centrally standardized. R. Osborne's theory at 1985, 77, that all demarchs were appointed at central meetings of their demes in the city, based on *SEG* 28.103, 27–28 (where rents are to be paid to the deme Eleusis on the occasion of the elections at the meeting in the Theseion) is rightly rejected by Whitehead 1986a, 116 with n. 154, and ch. 9C. (There is little in Osborne's idea that a single deme meeting in the city, which he takes to be the circumstance envisaged in *SEG* 28 despite *Ath. Pol.* 62.1, would somehow be less corruptible than a meeting in its deme.)

139. Cf. Mignett 1952, 221–32. New work in this area is badly needed.

competences were a prerequisite.[140] In Whitehead's view, this switch is likely to have taken place with respect to the demarch in the 450s and 440s, though he does not rule out the possibility that sortition was used from the start.[141]

It is generally assumed, though without indisputable basis either in the comparative logic of the processes or in evidence for contemporary attitudes, that sortition was thought to be more democratic than election.[142] Election is certainly not inferior to sortition in the level of accountability to the electors. It must also be borne in mind that some elective offices were retained in the fourth century demes,[143] and that even for sortitive offices, possibly including the demarchy, some form of pre-election was often retained.[144] It may be, therefore, that we would be justified in regarding the retention of the election of the phratriarch in the mid-fourth century as a little old-fashioned, and possibly as suggesting that a phratriarch in some way needed special qualifications or expertise not required of a demarch, though it is not easy to see what they may have been. But the implied distinction between the two officers is subtle rather than significant; it may belong in the same category as the other slight differences between demarch and phratriarch already noted.

This leads us to the final point of interest: what sort of people became phratriarchs? Were they different from the demarchs? The difficulty here is that while our forty known demarchs provide a reasonable sample on which to base some general conclusions, we cannot extract much of statistical significance from our five known phratriarchs.

For what it is worth as suggestive evidence, however, three of the five—Pantakles of Oion Dekeleikon from the Demotionidai/Dekeleieis,[145] Kallikles son of Aristeides of Myrrhinous from the Dyaleis,[146]

---

140. I state here the current orthodoxy (see most conveniently Rhodes 1981, indexes under relevant offices), though there are many points of uncertainty.

141. Whitehead 1986a, 115–16. The supposition that the method was originally election is taken as the possible implication of the use of the term *archairesiai* ("elections") to describe appointments to deme offices (Isae. 7.28; Dem. 44.39).

142. See, e.g., Rhodes 1972, 6–7 on the Boule. But the implication of Thuc. 8.69.4 and *Ath. Pol.* 32.1 that the Boule expelled by the Four Hundred in 411 was characteristically democratic because εἰληχυῖαν τῷ κυάμῳ was surely in contrast to the immediately successive co-opted body (Thuc. 8.67.3), not to any elected one.

143. See above, n. 138. According to Whitehead 1986a, 115, there tended to be something "special, unusual, temporary or *ad hoc*" about elective offices in demes.

144. Stated without argument by R. Osborne 1985, 77. Whitehead 1986a, 115, is more cautious, but inconclusive.

145. T 3, 11–12.

146. T 5, 6–7.

and Kichonides son of Diogeiton of Gargettos from the Medontidai[147]—
are otherwise unknown. The other Dyaleis phratriarch, Diopeithes son
of Diophantos of Myrrhinous, probably came from a known family of
means and of local prominence, active in naval affairs.[148] We know most
about the fifth, Euxitheos son of Thoukritos of Halimous, the speaker
in Demosthenes 57.[149] There are three points of particular interest: he
claims to have been "among those of best birth" in his deme;[150] he also
claims, however, not to have been well off,[151] and his background was
clearly sufficiently dubious to lend a degree of credibility to the charge
that he was not qualified to be a citizen. Finally, not only had he been
demarch, he was clearly a regular busybody (though the Athenians would
not perhaps have recognized the description), keen to hold any local
office available.[152]

If all five of these phratriarchs had also been demarchs, there would
be no conflict with the pattern that emerges from the larger sample of
demarchs: a majority of unknowns, a good number of local worthies,
and no one of known distinction at the national level.[153] It would not
be surprising if the similarity were to be confirmed by a larger sample
of phratriarchs. On the face of it, we might expect the difference in
methods of appointment to produce fewer unknowns in the ranks of the
phratriarchs than among the demarchs. But the effect here may have
been marginal rather than significant. It does not seem that the three
demarchs mentioned in Demosthenes 57 Antiphilos, his son Euboulides,
and Euxitheos, were mere randomly selected members of their deme.
They enjoyed and seem to have sought out the opportunity provided by
the office for exercising power in their communities and for pursuing

---

147. T 10, 16–17.

148. T 5, 6–7. *PA* 4324, s.v. Davies 1971, No. 4435.

149. Above, n. 137, for his phratriarchy. His family is also known from elsewhere; *PA*
5902, see Davies 1971, s.v. no. 3126 and Lacey 1980.

150. Dem. 57.46 (ἐν τοῖς εὐγενεστάτοις).

151. Dem. 57.25, 34–35, 41, 45; cf. the comments of Davies 1971, 93.

152. Demarchy: Dem. 57.63–64 and passim. Other offices: Dem. 57.46–48. Among these
was a priesthood of Herakles (for which Euxitheos passed the prokrisis stage but got no
further) organized on a deme basis, but for which good birth was apparently a criterion.
Another example of the deme's involvement in the sphere of the hereditary and the familial
(cf. n. 121).

153. See the fifty individuals conveniently collected by Whitehead 1986a, 408–15, and
his remarks on them at 115, n. 153. R. Osborne's discussion at 1985, 83–87, comes to a
similar conclusion. Both reject the older views, based on much less evidence, of Haussoullier
1884 and Sundwall 1906, that the powerful and wealthy predominated.

petty politics and private vendettas. If one wanted to become demarch it looks as though the sortition process was not a barrier, though we can only guess at how this was possible in practice. Prokrisis may be part of the explanation; and we can certainly not rule out tampering with the lots. Moreover, the combined logic of deme size and an annual office, possibly tenable only once in a lifetime, may have helped in smaller demes.[154] We can scarcely guess at the effect of factors such as the generally larger size of phratries and the various differences in the nature and functions of phratry as opposed to deme. But the impression on the basis of current evidence is that the sort of people who served as phratriarchs were probably similar to those who served as demarchs.

The overall picture, then, of the relative characteristics of phratriarchs and demarchs is, on the basis of present limited evidence, one of broad similarities and subtle differences. There are no radical differences of the sort we would expect from an institution whose relationship with its leader was significantly different from that between the deme and its demarch; there are some minor ones suggesting an institution that was perhaps slightly old-fashioned in some details of its arrangements.

Priest

The role of priests in phratries is highly obscure. Our only substantial evidence is for the priest of the House of the Dekeleieis in the decrees T 3. His functions, which overlap considerably with those of the phratriarch, are set out on pp. 121–22. It is difficult, however, to determine whether the office was normal in phratries as opposed to their subgroups, let alone whether we should be justified in generalizing from individual functions performed by this priest in the Dekeleieis to hypothetical priests in other phratries. Much, as often, depends on our view of the nature of the Dekeleian House. If the hypothesis in chapter 3 is correct, it was

---

154. Halimous, the deme of Euxitheos and other protagonists in Dem. 57, was on the small side (Bouleutic quota: three). Fortunately we know almost exactly how many adult males there were in the deme in 346/5: ca. eighty to eighty-five (see appendix 5). Even with no prokrisis or gerrymandering, it is clear that if iteration was indeed disallowed (see Whitehead 1986a, 139), around half of these would have needed to have served a term as demarch (on the reasonable assumption that the demarchy was held between the ages of thirty and sixty-five). It is also difficult to avoid the conclusion that, in the case of the Halimousian phratry, which seems to have been roughly coterminous with the deme (see n. 137), most of the same people who would have been demarchs must also, like Euxitheos, have served as phratriarch.

not originally an ordinary phratry, but a phratry subgroup which obtained a measure of independent status.[155] Priests in phratry subgroups, whether gene, orgeones groups, or others, with their range of religious activities, were common enough;[156] and it may be that in phratries as a whole, which, as we have seen, were notably lacking in cult activity,[157] a separate priest was unnecessary, or that one of the subgroup priests would perform the function. There may be a hint of this at Andocides 1, 125–26,[158] where it is possible that Kallias, as a member of the priestly genos, Kerykes, is performing a priestly—if it is not a phratriarchal—function in the admissions procedure of the phratry to which the Kerykes belonged.[159] But evidence of this sort scarcely does more than blur an already faint picture.

Though of uncertain general significance, two further points should be noted. First, the priesthood of the House of the Dekeleieis may have been hereditary; at least three successive priests of the House appear to have been related.[160] This need cause no surprise; tradition and hereditary right were potent forces in the religious field and were tolerated in the state as a whole as well as in its subgroups. Again we need look no further than the Kerykes for an example of a hereditary office of this sort, and that in a phratry subgroup.[161] If it were clear that we had a typical instance of formal hereditary power exercised in a classical phratry in this priestly role in the Dekeleieis, that might be of some interest. But not only is it not clear that we are dealing here with a phratry rather than with a subgroup, but also the power, though possibly hereditary in its mode of acquisition, does not seem to have been characteristically aristocratic in its manner of exercise. The priest was no more and no

155. See pp. 106–41.
156. Cf. chapter 2.
157. See first section of this chapter.
158. See pp. 68–71.
159. It is clear enough from the fact that Kallias ceremonially poses the question about the child's parentage that he holds some official position in the phratry, but we cannot determine with certainty whether he was priest or phratriarch. Even in T 3 precisely who was responsible for what parts of the admissions ceremony is unclear, and we have no other parallel case that could help. However, since he was a member of a priestly genos, it is perhaps more likely that he was also phratry priest. It would have been a curious coincidence if he had happened to be elected phratriarch for the year in question (and we might have expected Andocides to mention it?). The only possible phratry priest we know by name, other than Theodoros in T 3, is Theosebes in T 10, but his status as such is no more than conjecture (see note to T 10, 24–25).
160. Cf. p. 291.
161. See Kearns 1989, 69; cf. Töpffer 1889, 80–92.

less subject to the phratry's decision and direction than the phratriarch;[162] and, as suggested in chapter 3, he seems to have been used by his phratry as a representative of the local group over against the phratriarch, who may have been elected but seems nevertheless to have been regarded as an agent of a partially external power, the Demotionidai.

Second, the only other apparent evidence for a priest in a phratry is in the highly fragmentary T 20, where there is mention of sacrificing and sacred dues or sacred things, and where the priest may have been charged with setting up the stele on which the decree was inscribed.[163] It is possible, however, that the group that passed the decree was a whole phratry rather than a subgroup.[164]

Others

Hieropoioi, minor religious functionaries, are mentioned as distributing something, probably including honeycomb, in the religious decree T 4, which is likely to be a product of the House of the Dekeleieis.[165]

Epimeletai, usually minor administrative officers, are now attested at T 12, line 6, a decree of the phratry Therrikleidai or a subgroup of that phratry.[166] Their precise functions in this context are unclear, but it seems there were more than two of them and that they were appointed for some special purpose. In the Rationes Centesimarum epimeletai of the possible phratries Oikatai, Dipoliastai, and Apheidantidai are recorded as having acted on behalf of their groups in a property sale.[167]

Two other sets of officials associated with phratries are attested: the oinoptai and the protenthai. It seems more likely, however, that these were officials of the polis rather than of individual phratries.[168]

---

162. T 3 contains a string of impositions on the priest. E.g., he is to collect a fine from the phratriarch if the latter fails to sacrifice at the altar at Dekeleia, but if he fails to collect it is subject to a fine himself (T 3, 54–58).

163. T 20.

164. See pp. 346–47. Apart from the inscriptions already mentioned, the very fragmentary T 4, probably another decree of the House of the Dekeleieis, is religious in content and mentions hieropoioi (see below) but no priest in what little survives; T 12 mentions the taking of priestly dues (ἱερεώσυνα, cf. T 20, 3, 4) but again may be a decree of a phratry subgroup.

165. T 4, 7–8.

166. See pp. 322–27.

167. See T 27.

168. See pp. 154–56.

Chapter 7

After Cleisthenes: Conclusion

In concluding this part of the work, I would like to draw out from the preceding chapters five points of general significance for an understanding of the phratry and its role in Athenian society between 450 and 250. It should be emphasized again that the evidence is of such quantity and quality that new material may alter the picture significantly.

First, and crucially, for all practical purposes every native-born Athenian citizen was and had to be a phratry member. In the contemporary concept of citizenship, reflected in both law and literature, there is an institutional link between citizenship and phratry membership which parallels that between citizenship and deme membership. This is explained by the fundamental association between the phratry and the principle of descent—after Pericles' law the possession of citizen parents on both sides—which functioned as the major qualification for Athenian citizenship. The phratry played the major role in controlling this principle through its entry procedures, and in affirming and maintaining it in the general character of its activities. That role is also reflected in the fact that the phratry, to a greater extent than the deme, took account of women, the citizenship status of whom was crucial under Pericles' law, and also of children. Women were not normally regarded as actually members of phratries, but they might sometimes be introduced to their fathers' phratries as girls and were normally (possibly invariably) presented to their husbands' phratries at the gamelia. Male children probably underwent two processes of introduction: the meion in infancy or early childhood and the koureion in adolescence. In addition, there might be a procedure of scrutiny, associated with or separate from the meion or the koureion. In contrast, a child was not normally presented to a deme until he was eighteen, and a woman not at all.

We do not know whether any law specifically provided that every

237

Athenian had to be in a phratry; but in practice membership was not optional either socially or legally. Properly understood, being a citizen involved membership and participation in the activities of a phratry, and failure to belong could be adduced in a court of law as evidence against legitimate Athenian descent, and therefore against the rights to inherit property and to exercise the privileges of citizenship that Athenian descent conferred. On the basis of current evidence, the only exceptions to the requirement of phratry membership were certain categories of naturalized citizens, in particular those naturalized as members of a large group.

Second, this has important consequences for our picture of Athenian society and the role of phratry membership in it. Aristotle emphasizes the crucial role of *krisis* and *arche,* decision and power, in citizenship. Hence from one point of view the Athenian citizen may be seen most characteristically as such in his right of decision, together with other citizens, in the courts, and his power to determine with other citizens the affairs of the state in the Assembly and the Boule. Hence, too, an emphasis physically and conceptually on the center. It is now recognized, however, that a proper understanding of the role of the Cleisthenic phyle system, and particularly of the deme within it, entails a broadening of the concept of citizenship to encompass the local towns of Attica and their interlocking relationships with each other and with the center that bound the inhabitants into a single whole. A recognition of the importance of the phratry in Athenian citizenship adds a different perspective on Athenian society, at once narrower and broader.

Being in a phratry, being an Athenian citizen, was in the first place about being in a family, about the relationship of children to their parents and wives to their husbands. At Athens these relationships were not solely a private matter within families; on them depended rights to inherit property and other privileges of membership in society. The recognition of parenthood, the accession of adults to full membership in society and associated rights, and the recognition of a woman as capable of bearing children who would subsequently be entitled to exercise those rights, therefore took place in the context of, and under the oversight and control of, what may be characterized as the immediate community beyond the family. In some cases this was, in the first place, the genos or another phratry subgroup, possibly conceived of, at least theoretically, as consisting of persons among whom there existed ties of kinship. Not everyone belonged to such a subgroup, though admissions processes carried out in one did not, during the period in question, invariably have to be repeated at the phratry level. More often the group within which admissions processes took place was the phratry itself. The members of a phratry could be expected to know each other sufficiently well to be able to pass informed judgment on candidates for admission; membership was hereditary, but members were not at this period, as far as we know, conceived of as all related by ties of kinship, theoretical or actual, to the exclusion of other factors, such as place of abode, that determined natural community.

Community at the phratry level, however, was not only a matter of the controls exercised on membership by phratries, but also of the other common activities of the phratry, characteristically but not exclusively those of the phratry festival Apatouria: eating and drinking together; communal celebration, often riotous; competitive activities for the children, both physical and intellectual; communal sacrifices and other religious activities; and communal regulation of the phratry's affairs.

Outside the context of the Apatouria, the phratry's role as a functioning social group can be seen in its obligation to act in the family's stead when a victim of unintentional homicide had no surviving relatives, in the obligations of fellow phrateres to support in court members whose rights of citizenship or inheritance were under threat or, alternatively, to ensure that false claimants to those rights were exposed. A phratry might pursue distinctive communal cultic activities, though it did so apparently to a more limited extent than its subgroups or the demes. This is probably to be explained by a number of factors: in part cultic activity may have been generated more naturally by smaller groups—in the phratry structure by the phratry subgroups; in part, in line with the special character of the phratry's association with Athenian citizenship, the phratry's religious activity may have been oriented more to the Athenian level; in part it may be that, as the more significant groups in terms of krisis and arche, the demes came to acquire some of the cultic activity that would otherwise have been, and possibly had actually been, exercised by the phratries.

A phratry would finance its common activities in the same way as other contemporary citizen groups, including the demes, primarily by means of the ownership, leasing, and selling of land, and the lending of money at interest. Typically these transactions were internal, that is, they involved members, and mutuality of interest between the group and its individual members is a feature of the transactions. That we have less evidence for such transactions in phratries than in demes is probably a reflection in large part of the phratry's more restricted cultic activities, the major driving force for the financial enterprises of a group of this sort. Like other groups, the phratry functioned as a forum within which those with money to spend or particular skills or influence to exercise could be expected to do so in the interests of the group and to receive honors from it in return.

At the next level, precisely because Athenian citizenship was fundamentally a matter of descent, being a member of the group which stood immediately behind the family in controlling and maintaining the principle of descent was also an expression of Athenian citizenship. A powerful indication of this is the bias of our evidence, particularly the literary evidence, toward matters of phratry admission and phratry membership. These were not simply matters for the individual phratry concerned, they were of general, public interest, and that is why we hear more about them than about other phratry activities. Again, the theme is reflected at the Apatouria, not only in the focus of that festival on admissions procedures, but also in the nationalistic torch ceremony celebrating the gods' gift of fire to the Athenians, and generally in the national status of the festival, with public funding, associated official holidays, and public officials possibly involved with its organization. The theme is also reflected very strongly in the character of the phratries' religious activities, in the emphasis on the community of Athenian citizens as phrateres transcending the level of the individual phratry, notably in the cults of Zeus Phratrios and Athena Phratria.

It is remarkable that the phratry enjoyed national significance without being directly linked to the central political and judicial aspects of citizenship. Yet it is clear enough, in patterns of association that to some extent cut across those of the demes, that the phratries served to bind citizens together in a manner which complemented, and may even have reinforced, Cleisthenes' system, designed to "mix up the people." There is no indication that the two systems were perceived then, or should be perceived by us, as in conflict. The principle of descent was no less fundamental to citizenship in the demes than it was to citizenship in the phratries, and in their activities supporting and controlling that principle the phratries in a sense underpinned and supported the demes; and if, as I have argued, phratries enjoyed a certain structural and constitutional flexibility, the patterns of community they represented need not be seen as especially conservative. Indeed, the phratries may have been capable of adapting to change more readily than the structurally inflexible demes.

The community represented by phratry memership, however, unlike that of deme membership, went beyond the level of the Athenian polis. Phratries were held to be institutions common to the Ionian heritage. At the Apatouria an Athenian would have been aware that he was celebrating a festival that was a hallmark of Ionian identity, and would have been reminded of that fact by the major cults his phratry practiced in common with other phratries in the Ionian world.

The aspect of citizenship represented by phratry membership was therefore at once narrower and wider, but also complementary to, that of Cleisthenes' phyle system. It is clear enough that it also in a sense went much deeper: insofar as the deme had an external focus, it was the common activities organized on the basis of the deme, especially the central political and judicial functions of the polis; insofar as the phratry had an external focus, it was the individual's origins in his own family and immediate community, the community's origins in a distant past, and the bonds that that shared past created with other communities in Attica and beyond.

The third general point is that the internal constitution of the phratry in this period does not seem to have been dominated by aristocrats or to have been otherwise notably archaic. There is no reason to suppose that there was a particular class of phratry subgroups, whether gene or orgeones groups or both, that typically controlled the affairs of a phratry, nor is there any trace of any specific subgroup exercising or having exercised any such control, whether over admissions or otherwise. There were no new centrally imposed subgroups, thiasoi, designed to democratize the phratry's structure. The procedures of the phratry mirror those of other democratic groups in Athenian society: proposals for action were made by individual members and voted on by all phrateres; secret ballots were cast on membership issues; decrees were published on stone to insure general awareness and open verification; phratry officers, whose backgrounds as far as we can tell were not of a different sort from deme officers, were fully subject to control by the phratry as a whole. In some details, however, such as the selection of the phratriarch by selection rather than by lot, there may be hints of a slight conservatism, a consequence perhaps of the phratry's tendency to mirror, perhaps sluggishly, the norms of society as a whole.

Fourth, I have suggested that the phratry in this period, in contrast to the deme, had the capacity to split and to fuse in response to social, demographic, and other pressures. This is suggested by the importance of natural community as a basis for the phratry and the natural tendency for that community to be weakened over time. It is confirmed at the level of the phratry subgroups by the complex and shifting pattern of those groups and by some specific instances of fusion and fission. In the case of the phratries themselves, it is suggested in particular by the phenomenon of multiple phratriarchs. I have also argued that it provides a much more satisfactory explanation than those proposed hitherto of the background and circumstances of the so-called Demotionidai decrees. In these decrees, I suggest, a well-established phratry subgroup similar to a genos, the House of the Dekeleieis, was in the process of establishing its status as a phratry independent of its parent group, the Demotionidai, soon after the end of a war in which the special experiences of Dekeleia may have played a role in confirming the separate identity of the group.

Fifth, it cannot, I believe, be maintained that the phratry was an institution which could only have existed in a particular set of political and social circumstances. Its fundamental functions were those of the natural local community beyond the family. It played a wider role in the polis because membership in the polis was based on the same qualification as membership in the phratry and because, in this sense, the polis was an aggregate of phratries. But it could have functioned as a unit of community and regulator of the rights of inheritance in circumstances where the qualification for membership was not also a qualification for membership in a wider polis, with all that that entailed during this period. The phratry was a flexible institution, responding to structural pressures and, I suggest, to norms of procedure established elsewhere. There is no reason in principle why it could not have functioned as a unit of community in wholly different circumstances, in an absolute monarchy, or in a society in which there was a dominant aristocracy, in circumstances in which everyone belonged or in which everyone did not belong, in which the phratries or their members were parts of larger groups, or in which the phratry was a self-sufficient sociopolitical unit. This conclusion will be important as we consider the shadowy world of the phratry before Cleisthenes and its role in Cleisthenes' reforms.

Part 2
Cleisthenes and Before

Chapter 8

The Phratry in Cleisthenes' Reforms and Before

Preliminaries

We have been concerned almost exclusively so far with the phratry in the period 450 to 250. In common with most Athenian institutions, direct evidence for the phratries, both literary and epigraphical, is all but nonexistent for the half century following Cleisthenes' reforms.[1] There may have been evolutionary changes in the character of the institution during that period—in its internal constitution, for example, or in the nature of its religious activities; but there is no reason to suppose that the role of the phratry in Athenian society in 500, in particular as regards the connection between phratry membership and Athenian citizenship, would have differed significantly from that in 450 or 350. In 508, however, Cleisthenes had undertaken a major reform of the groups into which the citizen body had been organized. What effect did these reforms have on the phratry's character and role?

In the view of the *Ath. Pol.*, Cleisthenes, in establishing his ten new phylai, subdivided into trittyes and demes, was replacing a nominally similar set of institutions that had existed previously: the four "Ionian" phylai, also subdivided into trittyes and into groups like demes called naukraries.[2] The gene, phratries, and priesthoods, the *Ath. Pol.* explicitly

---

1. The earliest post-Cleisthenic literary evidence is the reference to phratries in the *Eumenides* of Aeschylus, produced in 458 (see p. 32). Of the three certain phratry inscriptions dateable by letter forms to the fifth century (T 7, ?T 8, T 13; note also T 6), none seems particularly early and all are merely horoi. There are two fifth-century inscriptions of possible phratries, T 28 and T 36; neither is helpful. Note also *IG* 1³.243 (c.480) which may relate indirectly to the phratry Therrikleidai (cf. pp. 322–27).

2. πρῶτον μὲν οὖν συνένειμε πάντας εἰς δέκα φυλὰς ἀντὶ τῶν τεττάρων, ἀναμεῖξαι

states, Cleisthenes left as they were.[3] To a greater or lesser extent, modern writers have found reason to differ from the account of *Ath. Pol.*: in some way or other the phratry tends to be seen as having played a greater, or at least different, role in Attic society in the seventh and sixth centuries from that attested in the classical period, a role that was deliberately altered by Cleisthenes. Cleisthenes is thought at least to have deprived it of exclusive control over access to citizenship.[4] At most the whole political organization of the archaic state is seen in terms of a structure based on the phratry.[5] These views are highly questionable.

First, however, a red herring. Aristotle in the *Politics* asserted that democratic reformers ought to create new and more phylai and phratries on the model of Cleisthenes at Athens and the democrats at Cyrene.[6] A few have taken this to imply, despite the *Ath. Pol.*, that Cleisthenes created new phratries at Athens.[7] As most have seen, however,[8] this inference should not be drawn. Aristotle is talking in the most general terms; it is not necessary to suppose that he means that both new phylai and new phratries were founded both by Cleisthenes and at Cyrene. We do not know anything more about the details of the reforms at Cyrene— perhaps they did involve phratries;[9] but for Cleisthenes it is quite sufficient for consistency with Aristotle's comment that he created ten new phylai. The *Ath. Pol.*, with its specific focus on the Athenian constitution, is in any case more likely to be a reliable guide as to the actual details of

βουλόμενος, ὅπως μετάσχωσι πλείους τῆς πολιτείας· . . . (he avoided division into twelve phylai so as to avoid coincidence with the preexisting twelve trittyes) . . . διένειμε δὲ καὶ τὴν χώραν κατὰ δήμους τριάκοντα μέρη, . . . καὶ ταύτας ἐπονομάσας τριττῦς ἐκλήρω-σεν τρεῖς εἰς τὴν φυλὴν ἑκάστην . . . κατέστησε δὲ καὶ δημάρχους τὴν αὐτὴν ἔχοντας ἐπιμέλειαν τοῖς πρότερον ναυκράροις· καὶ γὰρ τοὺς δήμους ἀντὶ τῶν ναυκραριῶν ἐποίησεν. *Ath. Pol.* 21.2-5.

3. τὰ δὲ γένη καὶ τὰς φρατρίας καὶ τὰς ἱερωσύνας εἴασεν ἔχειν ἑκάστους κατὰ τὰ πάτρια. *Ath. Pol.* 21.6.

4. E.g., Rhodes 1981, 253-54, 258.

5. E.g., Forrest 1966, 195-96: ". . . it can hardly be doubted that in every department the administration was more or less closely married to the phratry system." Cf. Wade-Gery 1933 (= 1958, 150); Andrewes 1961b, 129-40.

6. ἔτι δὲ καὶ τὰ τοιαῦτα κατασκευάσματα χρήσιμα πρὸς τὴν δημοκρατίαν τὴν τοιαύτην, οἷς Κλεισθένης τε Ἀθήνησιν ἐχρήσατο βουλόμενος αὐξῆσαι τὴν δημοκ-ρατίαν, καὶ περὶ Κυρήνην οἱ τὸν δῆμον καθιστάντες. φυλαί τε γὰρ ἕτεραι ποιητέαι πλείους καὶ φατρίαι, καὶ τὰ τῶν ἰδίων ἱερῶν συνακτέον εἰς ὀλίγα καὶ κοινά, καὶ πάντα σοφιστέον ὅπως ἂν ὅτι μάλιστα ἀναμειχθῶσι πάντες ἀλλήλοις, αἱ δὲ συνήθειαι διαζευχθῶσιν αἱ πρότερον. Arist. *Pol.* 6.1319b19-27.

7. E.g., Hammond 1973, 142-44.

8. E.g., Wade-Gery 1933, 26-27 (= 1958, 150-51); Rhodes 1981, 258.

9. The likely date of these reforms seems ca. 440, but the details of them are not recoverable. See Jones 1987, 218.

the reforms; in fact on this point it probably represents the views of the author of the *Politics* as well.[10]

Moreover, it is clear enough from our evidence for the classical phratries that they were not new creations of Cleisthenes. If the conclusions of the previous chapters have been correct, there are not, it is true, the great archaic relics in their constitution that some have perceived;[11] but the signs of pre-Cleisthenic origin remain clear enough in the scattered demotics of the Medontidai;[12] in the probable identity of the House of the Dekeleieis with the institution Herodotus thought had been granted privileges at Sparta for assisting the Tyndaridai;[13] in the fact that gene continued to relate to phratries as subgroups,[14] which we would scarcely have expected if the phratries had been refounded by Cleisthenes; and possibly in some other hints, particularly in the character of the phratriarchy.[15]

That Cleisthenes did not found new phratries, however, does not

---

10. That we are right to look for consistency between *Pol.* and *Ath. Pol.* here is suggested by the fact that both interpret the objective of the exercise as to "mix up the people." It is true that, despite Aristotle's claim at *EN* 10.1180b20–1181b24 that he would use the "collection of *politeiai* (constitutions)" as a basis for the *Politics,* there are some differences between Arist. and the *Ath. Pol.* as we have them in their treatment of the Athenian case (see Rhodes 1981, 60–61); but there is no inconsistency in relation to matter treated in books 4–6 of the *Pol.,* generally considered the latest part of the work (Weil 1960, 179–323; Rhodes 1981, 59) and likely to have post-dated at least early versions of the *Ath. Pol.* (for the dates, see Rhodes 1981, 51–59. The *Pol.* and early versions of the *Ath. Pol.* may both have been written ca. 335–330, but given the statements at the end of *EN* and the points of agreement between the *Pol.* and the *Ath. Pol.,* it would be perverse to suppose that all of the *Pol.* was written before any of the *Ath. Pol.*). Given also that there was probably a Κυρηναίων Πολιτεία probably also written in the 330s (Arist. fr. 529 at Pollux. 9.62; Kraay 1976, 299), which was surely the source of the *Pol.*'s comment with respect to Cyrene, and the emphasis in both the *Pol.* and the *Ath. Pol.* on "mixing up the People," it seems probable that this was a point where, as promised in *EN,* the *Pol.* was indeed based on already existing πολιτείαι, that is the *Kyr. Pol.* and a version of the *Ath. Pol.* that, though earlier than ours (for the likelihood that we possess a later version of the work, see Rhodes 1981, loc. cit.), did not differ from it on this issue.

11. Especially in internal structure, see chapters 2 and 3.

12. Unless, as is unlikely, Cleisthenes invented a second, otherwise wholly unattested, system of subdivision alongside the ten phylai (which apparently formed the basis of organization even of Cleisthenes' new naukraries, cf. n. 45) we would expect phratries to have been reorganized according to the phyle/trittys/deme system; but the demotics of the phratry with the most attested members not obviously related by blood, the Medontidai, bear no relation to that system. See pp. 319–20.

13. Cf. p. 113.

14. Cf. pp. 17–18.

15. On the somewhat old-fashioned characteristics of the phratriarchy, see pp. 228–33. Note also the provision for following "ancestral custom" made in the fourth century by a group which may well have been the phratric House of the Dekeleieis (see T 4).

necessarily imply that, directly or indirectly, he did not change their role or function in Attic society. What does the direct evidence for the phratry before Cleisthenes have to say on the matter?

The Direct Evidence

The answer is very little. Taking the evidence in apparent chronological order, we have just the following four items.

First, *Ath. Pol.* fr. 3,[16] which derives probably from the *Ath. Pol.*'s account of the work of Ion, tells us that, under his dispensation, there were four phylai, divided into twelve parts called trittyes and phratries, each phratry being arranged or marshalled into thirty gene of thirty men each. I argue in appendix 2 that this fragment is of no independent worth as evidence for the realities of the archaic or any earlier period, that in particular the identity of phratry and trittys it claims is false, and that there were never twelve phratries or 360 gene. We need not, therefore, concern ourselves with whether or not the word I have translated "arranged" or "marshalled" has military significance,[17] and whether or not the archaic Athenian army was therefore divided into 360 genos-based regiments.[18] As evidence for the number and functions of the pre-Cleisthenic phratries, the fragment can safely be ignored.

Second, according to Draco's Law of Homicide as republished in 409/8, but originally dating from the 620s, we know that, in a case of unpremeditated homicide the killer could be pardoned by the kin of the victim. In case the victim had no surviving relatives to the degree of sons of male cousins, his phratry was to decide on the matter: "ten members of the phratry are to admit him [i.e., the killer] to the country, if they are willing. The Fifty-One are to choose these men according to their excellence (*aristinden*)." If it is decided to prosecute, the conduct of the case is to be in the hands of the victim's relatives and the members of his phratry.[19]

---

16. For the text of this fragment, see appendix 2.

17. διακεκοσμῆσθαι. Given the strong tradition that Ion was a military leader (*Ath. Pol.* 3.2 with other references cited by Rhodes 1981 ad loc.), an intended military implication is not unlikely (cf. Oliver 1980, 31; for the range of other meanings of διακοσμέω however see *LSJ*), but is historically worthless.

18. As understood, e.g., by Oliver 1980, who accepts the evidence of the fragment at face value Cf. n. 54.

19. ... ἐὰν δὲ τούτον μεδὲ hὲς ἔ̣ι, κτ]έ/νει δὲ ἄκο[ν], γνῶσι δὲ hοι [πε]ντ[έκοντα καὶ hὲς hοι ἐφέται ἄκοντ]α/ κτέναι, ἐσέσθ[ο]ν δὲ h[οι φ]ρ[άτερες, (-ορες, previous

This text cannot be said to demonstrate that the phratry's role in Attic society at the time of Draco was essentially different from its role in the classical period. It implies that every Athenian was in a phratry in the late seventh century; the situation was no different in the fourth.[20] In a sense, of course, this text obviously cannot demonstrate differences in the phratry's function between the archaic and classical periods, for this law continued to regulate cases of homicide in the fourth century. But the character of the activities is also at one with those the phratry performed in the fifth and fourth centuries. Then phrateres acted as representatives of the closer community beyond the family in inheritance and citizenship cases.[21] Their role in Draco's arrangements is precisely similar: supporting the immediate family and, when there was no family, taking on its role.

In the fourth century, functions of this sort were shared with the deme, though the line of demarcation was sometimes unclear, or at least not clearly explicable.[22] But it begs the question to suppose that there was no other institution which performed any functions of this sort in the late seventh century.

The one difference in Attic society which seems clearly implied by this law consists in the word aristinden, "according to rank" or "excellence," which describes the way the Fifty-One are to select the ten phrateres to act in the absence of surviving relatives. This apparently means that the ten most aristocratic members are to be selected,[23] in which case we have to envisage distinctions of rank among phratry members that may well have played a role in seventh-century Attic society more generally,[24] and, other than in conservative areas such as homicide law,

---

eds.; the form in -o occurs only in post-classical texts, lexicographers, etc., and never in fifth- and fourth-century Attic epigraphy) ἐὰν ἐθέλοσι, δέκα· τούτος δ]ὲ ḥο/ι πεντέκο[ν]τ[α καὶ] ḥὲς ἀρ[ι]στ[ίνδεν ḥαιρέσθον.]. . . /[. . . προειπὲν δ]ὲ τὸι κ/τέγαγ[τι ἐν ἀ]γορ[ᾶι μέχρ' ἀνεφσιότετος καὶ ἀνεφσιō̂· συνδιόκ]εν/ δὲ . . . . κ/αὶ φρ[ά]τ[ε]ρ[ας . . . ([ο]ρ[ας previous eds.; see above)]. *IG* 1³.1045 16–23. See especially Stroud 1968.

20. See chapter 1.

21. Cf. pp. 31–40.

22. It is common for demesmen to appear as witnesses alongside phrateres in inheritance cases and the like. It is notable that in the fourth century the deme, not the phratry, acted to back up the family in ensuring proper burial (see esp. Dem. 43.57–58. For a suggested explanation of this, see p. 227, n. 121).

23. So taken by Stroud 1968, 50; cf. Hignett 1952, 55, 67, 117; Andrewes 1961a, 1. It cannot perhaps be ruled out that it means rather the ten closest in rank to the victim, or even conceivably the ten best, in the sense of the ten most competent for the task.

24. A major thrust of Solon's work was to shift the balance of power from birth to

clearly played a lesser role in the fourth century. This would certainly lead us to suppose, though we might have expected it anyway, that in the seventh century phratry procedures, and possibly structures of sub-groups,[25] would have reflected the dominance of the *aristoi*. The internal organization of a phratry in the seventh century will have differed from that in the fourth, when that organization broadly mirrored the democratic norms of the period;[26] but that in itself would not justify any conclusion that the functions of the phratry in seventh-century Attic society were essentially different from those in the fourth century.

The third item is an extract from allegedly Solonian legislation in which provision is made that phrateres, along with "a deme," and—the text is corrupt—probably orgeones, possibly sailors (or gennetai or naukraries), dining clubs, burial associations, and piratical and trading companies are to be allowed to make their own regulations as long as they do not conflict with the law of the polis. Odd features, including obvious corruption of the text, the omission of phylai and trittyes, and the mention of a "deme," cast doubt on whether this law is either complete as we have it or wholly Solonian. Even if it were both, it may be notable for the assertion of the supremacy of the polis as a whole over its constituent groups, but it is scarcely otherwise informative about the role of the pre-Cleisthenic phratry in Attic society.[27]

---

wealth (see *Ath. Pol.* 3.1; 6–8 with Rhodes 1981, 150. Cf. the aristocratic phylobasileis, p. 258 n. 57.

25. According to the old view of gene, they were groups of aristocrats exercising a measure of control over phratries in the classical period, and *a fortiori* therefore a stronger power in the archaic period. Once that view is rejected, however (see chapters 2 and 3), we are left completely in the dark about exactly how aristocratic power was reflected in the structure of the seventh-century phratry.

26. See, e.g., pp. 105–6.

27. ἐὰν δὲ δῆμος ἢ φράτορες ἢ ἡρώων ὀργεῶνες ἢ ναῦται [or γεννῆται or ναυκραρίαι, MSS: ἢ ἱερῶν ὀργίων ἢ ναῦται] ἢ σύσσιτοι ἢ ὁμόταφοι ἢ θιασῶται ἢ ἐπὶ λείαν οἰχόμενοι ἢ εἰς ἐμπορίαν ὅτι ἂν τούτων διαθῶνται πρὸς ἀλλήλους, κύριον εἶναι, ἐὰν μὴ ἀπαγορεύσῃ δημόσια γράμματα. *Dig.* 47.22.4 (= Solon *Laws* fr. 76a Ruschenbusch). The best discussion of the text is at Ferguson 1944, 64, n. 5, who suggested ἢ ἡρώων ὀργεῶνες ἢ γεννῆται for the descriptions of the third and fourth groups, apparently corrupt in the MSS. This may be right. For ἡρώων cf. Solon *Laws* fr. 76b R (= Seleukos fr. 35 Mü = Phot., cf. Suid. s.v. ὀργεῶνες), in which Seleukos, probably commenting on this law, described the orgeones as τοὺς συλλόγους ἔχοντας περί τινας ἥρωας ἢ θεούς. But there is room for doubt about whether gennetai of this sort were called gennetai at an early period (cf. p. 61 with n. 13). Associations of ναῦται cannot be ruled out (cf. L. Robert 1969, 7–14, for admittedly late examples; the thiasotai mentioned later in the text must have been similar); and on the other hand it is possible that some late author or scribe, unaware of the obscure and long-obsolete ναυκραρίαι, which, as proto-demes of

Much the same can be said about another legal fragment. Athenaeus records that law-makers provided for dinners for, among others, phratries. It is possible he had Solon in mind, though a much later date seems more likely.[28] In any case, dining by the phratries at the provision of the polis at any date would suit the fourth-century character of the institution; we are reminded of the fact that the celebrations of the Apatouria as a whole were at public expense.[29] No suggestion of a different role here.

The Political Organization of Attica before Cleisthenes

The direct evidence for the Attic phratry before Cleisthenes, therefore, is extremely weak. But we have found nothing so far to contradict the *Ath. Pol.* or to suggest a fundamental difference of role from the classical period. Let us try a different approach, broaden the issue, and ask more generally into what groups Athens' population was organized for political purposes[30] before Cleisthenes. The answer is much more clearly negative as far as the phratry is concerned. The *Ath. Pol.,* as already observed, thought it was not the phratries, but the four phylai, conceived like the phratries to be a common Ionian inheritance, the trittyes and the naukraries that Cleisthenes replaced with his new phylai, trittyes and demes.[31] The supporting evidence is scant, difficult, and rarely secure on individual

---

a sort, would suit the context well enough (cf. n. 2), corrupted that word to ναῦται. As for the Solonian attribution of the law, the fact that we have δῆμος in our text rather than δημόται, which would have paralleled the form of reference to the rest of the groups listed, arouses suspicion. It could be taken in its pre-Cleisthenic unofficial sense (i.e. = "village"), but Whitehead 1986a, 13–14, may be right in seeing it as a post-Cleisthenic insertion into the text (cf. Wade-Gery and Andrewes at Andrewes 1961a, 12, n. 40). The mode of reference to traders and pirates is odd and seems genuinely archaic; institutional piracy would have been out of place in classical Athens (cf. Ferguson 1944, 66). ἢ φρατόρες may or may not have been another genuine archaic element; Solon would probably have written φράτερες (cf. n. 19). See further Whitehead loc. cit. and other discussions referred to there.

28. Athen. 5.185c–186a. See p. 86.

29. Cf. p. 153.

30. I use "political purposes" as shorthand for financial, central and local political, military, naval, judicial and other administrative purposes—essentially those performed after Cleisthenes by the phyle system. I assume that these functions existed before Cleisthenes, though not that they had the same character or that their organization was necessarily similar.

31. Cf. n. 2.

points, but still sufficient to demonstrate that the *Ath. Pol.* is likely broadly speaking to have been correct.[32]

Outlined briefly below is what I consider a reasonable view of the functions of these institutions, with supporting argument in the footnotes. It should be admitted that we are dealing generally with historical likelihood here, not historical fact.

Before Cleisthenes there were forty-eight naukraries,[33] subdivisions of the phylai,[34] with a local and hereditary character similar to the demes,[35]

---

32. I would not maintain that the parallel in nature and functions was exact, nor do we need to suppose the writer of the *Ath. Pol.* thought it was.

33. The bibliography on the naukraries is very large. See Lambert 1986a, 105, n. 2, to which should be added Jordan 1975, 5–20; Roussel 1976, 201–3; Frost 1984, 286–87; Gabrielson 1985; Haas 1985; Develin 1986; Figueira 1986; Bugh 1988, 4–5. Evidence for the institutions is not as weak as might be gathered from some writers on the subject. In particular there are five relevant fragments of probably genuine Solonian legislation. For text, translation, and discussion of these, see appendix 4.

34. For the number of the naukraries and their relationship to the phylai we rely on *Ath. Pol.* 8.3 (appendix 4, document 1). There is nothing to suggest unreliability on the point. I argue in appendix 4 that the *Ath. Pol.* made use of genuine Solonian legislation on the naukraries. It is possible that these facts were implicit in that legislation or, on a matter as basic as this, that they were simply correctly remembered. On the number, there is also some implicit support in a source apparently independent of the *Ath. Pol.* on this point, *FGH* 323 Kleidemos fr. 8, which states that it was altered to fifty to suit the new ten-phyle system (see below, n. 45). If, as is possible, the new naukraries, like the old, had to provide a ship each for the navy (below, n. 43), it is plausible that there was only a small change in their number. Cleisthenes was not known to have been a naval reformer; that task was left to Themistocles.

35. For the general question of the principle of organization of these groups, see pp. 14–15. In the case of the old phylai and its subdivisions, the details and the original principle are wholly obscure, but as with the demes they appear to have had both local and personal characteristics (cf. p. 15 with nn.). It is unlikely that the naukraries were tracts of territory with precisely defined borders as well as groups of persons; the demes themselves only seem to have acquired this character at a later stage (cf. p. 7). But, like the demes throughout our period, it is clear that they were essentially hereditary groups of persons (cf. pp. 7–8, p. 15 with n. 44) associated with particular localities. In one fragment of a Solonian law the naukraroi are described as collecting (sc. taxes) (appendix 4, document 1); this sounds like exacting money from the inhabitants of a locality. In another, provision may have been made for naukraroi to perform some function in their naukraries (appendix 4, document 3). Most suggestively, *L.S.* 1.275.20 reports Κωλιάς· τόπος Ἀττικός ... ἦν δὲ καὶ ναυκραρία. A link between the "place" and the naukrary is clearly to be inferred. (The argument of Beloch 1922-23 1.2², 323 [accepted by Thomsen 1964, 127] that the naukrary derived its name from the genos Κωλιεῖς is unconvincing; the naukrary name corresponds exactly to the place, not the genos. The argument is also based on a false dichotomy between local and nonlocal organizations, with gene falling into the latter category. The Kolieis were no doubt also based on Kolias. The most likely view is that there was a place, Kolias, which gave its name to a genos, Kolieis, which had its base or center there. It also, probably later [cf. p. 272], gave its name to a naukrary

each under the charge of a naukraros.[36] Monetary taxes[37] were exacted from them by the naukraroi[38] and kept centrally in the naukraric treasury,[39] which seems, in some respects, to have been a precursor of the public treasury of the classical period.[40] Naval functions of some

---

based in the same area. For more on this place [probably modern Hagios Kosmas], naukrary, and genos, see Raubitschek 1974, including the somewhat fanciful suggestion that not only the sanctuary of Aphrodite there but also the genos had existed since the end of the third millenium.) How far Cleisthenes' fifty new naukraries (see n. 45) were organized on a new basis is impossible to say. Kleidemos' comparison of them with the fourth-century symmories, which were not locally based groups in the same sense as the demes, suggests they may have been, as does the correspondence with the post-Cleisthenic phyle system. It is difficult to see how each phyle, made up of physically separated groups of demes, could have been, or indeed needed to be, divided into five local units for the remaining naukraric purposes. It would be a mistake, however, to infer from this that the naukraries had a non-local character before Cleisthenes. It will be apparent from the above that I do not accept the arguments of Hignett 1952, 67–71, and Thomsen 1964, 122–31, that the naukraries did not have local characteristics.

36. *Ath. Pol.* 8.3 (see appendix 4, document 1); 21.5 (see n. 2); Phot. s.v. ναυκραρία (appendix 4, document 3). Many have thought there was more than one naukraros in a naukrary (e.g., Thomsen 1964, 132, claimed this as "indisputable fact." Cf. Hommel 1935, col. 1947; Hignett 1952, 68; Jordan 1975, 14; Velissaropoulos 1981, 15), a view which has tended to exacerbate the confusion and uncertainty about whether the *Ath. Pol.* was right to compare the pre-Cleisthenic naukrary with the deme. This is based, however, on no more than an erroneous reading in Naber's 1864 edition of Photios s.v. ναυκραρία (appendix 4, document 3): τοὺς ναυκράρους τοὺς κατὰ τὴν ναυκραρίαν, "the naukraroi in" or "by the(ir) naukrary," which might indeed be taken to have such an implication. Dr. C. Theodoridis confirms by letter, however, that, according to both the MS Galeanus and the new MS Zavordensis 95, Porson's 1822 edition of Photios gave the correct reading without τὴν (i.e., "the naukraroi in [their respective] naukrary," or "the naukraroi by naukrary"), which has no such implication (see further appendix 4).

37. See appendix 4, document 1. Coinage probably did not exist at Athens before Solon (Rhodes 1981, 167–68 and works there cited) but the economic significance of the development tends to be exaggerated. "Money," that is, uncoined weights of silver (and gold) with specific values, was well established before Solon. Fines, etc., were paid in drachmas (see the Solonian laws quoted at Lysias 10.18 [fr. 68 R]; at Plut. *Sol.* 21.1 [fr. 32a R]; 23.1 [fr. 30a R]; 23.3 [frs. 77, 81, 143a R]); in fr. 24, 1–3 of Solon's poems a rich man has gold and silver among his possessions. There is no difficulty in envisaging "monetary" (in this sense) taxes at this period.

38. A reasonable inference from the Solonian laws in *Ath. Pol.* 8.3 and Phot. s.v. ναυκραρία (appendix 4, documents 1, 3). No doubt each naukraros was responsible for the collection of taxes in his own naukrary, like the demarchs with the eisphora after Cleisthenes (Davies 1984, 143–50, cf. Whitehead 1986a, 132–33). Cf. Hesych. s.v. ναύκλαροι; Pollux 8.108 (neither likely to be independent of the *Ath. Pol.*).

39. See appendix 4 documents 1, 2.

40. Because (a) the *kolakretai,* responsible in appendix 4, document 2, for making payments from the naukraric treasury, had the same function with respect to the public treasury in the fifth century (*IG* 1³.78, 51–52; *IG* 1³.84, 28. From 411 their duties seem to

sort[41] are suggested by the name, which should mean "ship-head,"[42] and are explicitly attested by two late sources;[43] they seem likely to have

have been taken over by an enlarged board of Hellenotamiai. See Rhodes 1972, 99, with n. 4. *FGH* 324 Androtion fr. 5 seems to have thought that the *apodektai* [receivers of public money] were created by Cleisthenes to take the place of the kolakretai. Perhaps before Cleisthenes the kolakretai were receivers as well as paying officers, and the former function was transferred to the apodektai by him. See also Jacoby on Androtion loc. cit.); (b) the fund was used for the general, public purpose of paying for the travel and other expenses of visitors to Delphi (appendix 4, document 2). In the fourth century all citizens seem to have been eligible for such payments (see Rhodes 1972, 105–6, and works cited there), but perhaps only official envoys obtained the money at the time of Solon. In the later fourth century these expenses were met from a special theoric fund, which was also used for other purposes (e.g., public works, Rhodes loc. cit.), the earlier history of which is controversial, but it seems likely that this fund was at some stage separated from the naukraric, or, perhaps more likely, later from the main public treasury. It appears that the treasury of Athena also existed at this time. See *Ath. Pol.* 8.1 and 47.1 with Rhodes 1981, 148, (treasurers appointed under Solonian law by sortition among the pentakosiomedimnoi), cf. Suid. s.v. ταμίαι, where they are said to have been custodians of the statue (*agalma*) of Athena on the Acropolis, apparently that at which the Cylonian conspirators took refuge, Hdt. 5.71. On the basis of the Cylonian link, Jordan 1970, 173–74, ingeniously connected this treasury with the naukraroi through the role of the presidents of the latter in raising the Cylonians from the agalma at Hdt. 5.71, but this is part of a hypothesis about the Cylonian affair which I believe to be mistaken; see Lambert 1986a, 106–7. In any case it is unlikely that the naukraroi were involved with this treasury, first because the naming of the naukraric fund as such suggests that it was the only fund under naukraric control and, second, because the principle of distinction between sacred and secular treasuries, very strong in the classical period, should also have applied in the early sixth century. Cf. Rhodes 1981, 149, 391, 549–50.

41. It would be unreasonable to doubt that there was Athenian naval activity before Cleisthenes. See Hdt. 1.64; 82–88; 94–95; Polyainos 5.14 with Jordan 1975, 6–7; Haas 1985.

42. See Frisk 1960–70; Chantraine 1968–80; cf. Hommel 1938. There was also a word ναύκλαρος, "shipowner," "captain," (and in Athens apparently one who rented houses), with which the ναύκραρος is sometimes confused in the lexicographers (e.g., Pollux 8.108, some MSS; Hesych. s.v. ναύκλαροι). The alternative etymology proposed by Billigmeier and Dusing 1981, 11–16, connecting ναύκραροι with ναός, "temple," rather than ναῦς, "ship," is unconvincing. See Lambert 1986a, 111, n. 26.

43. *L.S.* 1.283.20: ναύκραροι. οἱ τὰς ναῦς παρασκευάζοντες, καὶ τριηραρχοῦντες, καὶ τῷ πολεμάρχῳ ὑποτεταγμένοι. Pollux 8.108: ναυκραρία δ᾽ ἑκάστη δύο ἱππέας παρεῖχε καὶ ναῦν μίαν, ἀφ᾽ ἧς ἴσως ὠνόμαστο. Since neither of these texts mentions financial functions, which for the *Ath. Pol.* were the most notable pre-Cleisthenic feature of this institution, it seems likely that they relate specifically to the post-Cleisthenic naukraries. How reliable they are we do not know, but their specificity and plausibility (but see n. 46) suggest a factual basis. That the naukraroi commanded ships and were subordinate to the polemarch before Cleisthenes as well, however, is likely (see next note), as it is that each naukrary provided one ship (cf. n. 45). On the cavalry function, see below n. 46.

extended beyond the mere raising of money for ships.[44] It appears that some naval functions were retained by the naukraries after Cleisthenes, who apparently did not abolish them altogether, but changed their number to fifty to suit the new ten-phyle system and may have adapted them into groups of taxpayers similar to the later symmories.[45] One late source of uncertain reliability attests that the provision of cavalry was also organized by naukrary.[46] Herodotus describes officers known as the presidents of the naukraroi as having ruled or been in charge at Athens at the time of the Cylonian conspiracy,[47] probably 636 or 632.[48] Given the obvious incompleteness of our evidence, it is plausible that the

44. We should expect a "ship-head" (above, n. 42) to have commanded his naukrary's ship, as explicitly stated by L.S. (see previous note).

45. Ὁ Κλείδημος ἐν τῇ τρίτῃ φησὶν ὅτι Κλεισθένους δέκα φυλὰς ποιήσαντος ἀντὶ τῶν τεσσάρων, συνέβη καὶ εἰς πεντήκοντα μέρη διαταγῆναι αὐτούς, ἃ ἐκάλουν ναυ-κραρία⟨ς⟩, ὥσπερ νῦν εἰς τὰ ἑκατὸν μέρη διαιρεθέντα⟨ς⟩ καλοῦσι συμμορίας. Phot. s.v. ναυκραρία (=FGH 323 Kleidemos fr. 8). I do not believe this is inconsistent with Ath. Pol. 21, which does not actually say that the naukraries (any more than the phylai or trittyes, see below) were absolutely abolished. Its credibility is increased by the likelihood that the post-Cleisthenic navy consisted of fifty ships (see Jacoby ad loc. and esp. Hdt. 6.89). Whether Kleidemos had in mind the trierarchic symmories founded by Periandros in 357/6 or the earlier eisphora symmories is a matter of controversy (see, e.g., Jacoby ad loc.; Thomsen 1964, 86–88). It is generally assumed that the naukraroi were finally abolished by Themistocles (see, e.g., Rhodes 1981, 257, Jacoby loc. cit).

46. See n. 43. Insofar as this has a factual basis, it is likely to be in the post-Cleisthenic naukraries (cf. n. 43). Whether it also applied before Cleisthenes is impossible to say. Bugh 1988, 4–5, is not entirely skeptical.

47. τούτους (the failed Cylonians) ἀνιστᾶσι μὲν οἱ πρυτάνιες τῶν ναυκράρων, οἵ περ ἔνεμον τότε τὰς Ἀθήνας, ὑπεγγύους πλὴν θανάτου· φονεῦσαι δὲ αὐτοὺς αἰτίη ἔχει Ἀλκμεωνίδας. Hdt. 5.71. On the interpretation of this controversial statement, see Lambert 1986a, where I argue the πρυτάνιες τῶν ναυκράρων may have been "in charge" in the absence of the archons at the Olympic Games. Though not demonstrable, I also think it likely that the naukraric prytanies were naukraroi holding office monthly in rotation, like the later Bouleutai in the Bouleutic prytanies (i.e., four each month), the system being designed, I would assume, to enable the naukraroi to combine central and local functions. Figueira 1986 argues that the Xanthippos ostrakon from the 480s (Χσάνθ[ιππον τόδε] φεσὶν ἀλειτερὸν πρυτάνειον/ τὸστρακ[ον Ἀρρί]φρονος παῖδα μά[λ]ιστ' ἀδικεν, ML 21, 42), refers to the πρυτάνιες τῶν ναυκράρων. I doubt, however, if the latter survived Cleisthenes, or if they did, that they would have remained sufficiently prominent to have been referred to as "prytanies" without qualification. If πρ[υτ]άνειον is, as is likely, gen. pl. of πρύτανις rather than nom. or acc. sing. of πρυτανεῖον, "townhall" (see on this ML 21, 42), I would take it either as "leaders" generally (for this sense see Figueira 1986, 266 with n. 38) or conceivably as the Bouleutic prytanies in particular, which, pace Figueira, I believe to have existed at this time. Cf. Lambert 1986a, 112. It is quite plausible that the whole naukraric organization was under the ultimate control of the polemarch (cf. n. 43).

48. There have been attempts to downdate this event. Rhodes 1981, 81–82, with works

naukraroi also performed other local administrative functions, as the analogy drawn by the *Ath. Pol.* with the demarchs would also tend to imply.[49]

The old phylai were also divided into twelve trittyes, three in each phyle;[50] it is not clear whether the naukraries were also trittys subdivisions.[51] Our only specific evidence attests one of them, the trittys Leukotainioi of the phyle Geleontes, performing a sacrifice in the state calendar as revised by Nikomachos in 403/2.[52] It is unlikely that religion was their raison d'être before Cleisthenes;[53] that was probably similar to that of their homonymous successors: military organization[54]—

there cited, convincingly defends the traditional date, which is also consistent with the prominence of naukraroi in Solonian legislation (see appendix 4). On the possible origins of the naukraries, see p. 272.

49. On the method of appointment of naukraroi, see p. 263.

50. *Ath. Pol.* fr. 3 (wrongly identifying them with the phratries, see appendix 2); 8.3 (appendix 4, document 1); 21.3 (n. 2). The τρι- root designates threeness. Eliot 1967 (followed by Rhodes 1971, 400–401; 1981, 68; Humphreys 1974, 351 = 1978, 195) pointed out that it should originally have referred to something itself divided into three parts, by analogy with similar terms found elsewhere, e.g., hekatostys (Samos), chiliastys (Ephesos and Samos, cf. Roussel 1976, 211–12). Eliot compares the loss of the original meaning of the Latin "tribus" ("one of three") at Rome. However, pace Eliot, it seems the connotation of threeness was retained at Athens both before and after Cleisthenes—that there were three trittyes per phyle is unlikely to be coincidental—and was also retained elsewhere (e.g., Delos, Jones 1987, 212; Keos, Lewis 1962, 1, cf. Jones 1987, 202–4. Eliot's suggestion at 81, n. 10, that there might have been four trittyes per phyle on Keos does not convince).

51. Cf. p. 258.

52. Ἑκατομβαιῶνος/ πέμπτηι ἐπὶ δέκα/ ἐκ τῶν φυλο/βασιλικῶν/ Γλεόντων φυλῆι Λευκοταινίων/ τριττύϊ οἰν ⊢⊢⊢ λειπογνώμονα/ ⊢⊢⊢ΙΙ ἱερεώ[σ]υνα/ φυλοβ[α]σιλεῦσι/ ⊢ νώτο/ κήρυκι ὦμο/ ΙΙΙΙ ποδῶν κεφαλῆς. Oliver 1935, 21, no. 2, 31–43. This was obviously a small affair, which could have been little more than symbolic; it is difficult to believe that many Athenians at the end of the fifth century knew which Ionian phyle their ancestors had belonged to. Indeed this may have been the sort of ancestral sacrifice with which Nikomachos was accused in 399/8 of having tampered. See Lysias 30.21.

53. The fact that the sacrifice with which the Leukotainioi were involved (see previous note) was related to the festival Synoikia (see Ferguson 1936, 154–56), a celebration of the coming together politically of the parts of Attica to form a unified whole, confirms that, as with the old phylai which also participated, and as with the post-Cleisthenic phyle system, this religious role arose out of wider functions of the trittyes within the polis. The hero cults of those, less artificial, groups whose function can be seen as primarily religious, such as the orgeones, are religion of a different sort.

54. Trittyes as subdivisions of the classical fleet are firmly attested by Dem. 14.22-23 and fifth-century trittys markers from the Peiraeus. Similar markers have been found in the Agora and are likely to have been used for marshalling the army. Further support at Plat. *Rep.* 475a (trittyarchy as lesser alternative to *strategia*); Hdt. 9.21-23 (which suggests the trittys-based units were known as lochoi on the field) and see Bicknell 1972, 20-21 with nn. 62, 67, and esp. Siewert 1982, 141-45. Also Traill 1986, esp. 112-13. Lewis 1983,

"Leukotainioi" means "the white-ribboned," possibly a reference to distinguishing marks on spears[55]—and, very likely, other purposes of the polis where regular phyle subdivisions were needed.[56]

The old phylai and their leaders, the phylobasileis, also continued to play a role in the religious life of the state in the classical period;[57] and

---

435 is unduly skeptical about the trittyes as military units after Cleisthenes. He points out that "neither the marines nor the citizen sailors of *IG* 2².1951 show any sign of organization by any sort of trittys," but that *naval* forces were organized in trittyes is not in doubt, so perhaps we should take it that the trittys organization was simply not necessarily followed in lists of this sort. The same may apply to ephebic lists, in which, Lewis also points out, no trittys pattern is detectable, though one wonders whether the trittys organization of the full army need have been mirrored at the ephebe level. On the archaic trittyes Hommel 1935 and Wüst 1957, 189, n. 1, guessed military functions; as did Oliver 1980, though in this case based on the highly dubious support of *Ath. Pol.* fr. 3 (see appendix 2) and Aristid. 1.261 Oliver (= 382 Lenz, 313–14 Dindorf; of no worth on the early organization of Attica independent of the *Ath. Pol.* and Hdt.). His supposition on this basis that gene were also military units carries no weight. Greenhalgh 1973, 151–53, suggested that the gene formed the basis of the pre-Cleisthenic army, but his implied assumption that they were the only groups in which (aristocratic) power could be exercised before Cleisthenes is mistaken. Hoplite tactics, in which units of men interlocked to form a continuous phalanx (introduced ca. 650, see Salmon 1977 and Cartledge 1977) would have lent themselves to organization by units of regular size and number, which the gene could not have provided, but for which the regular size and number of the trittyes would have been ideal.

55. At Diod. 15.52.5 such a ribbon is blown off the spear of the secretary bringing instructions from the leaders at Thebes in 371/0—taken as a bad omen for Epameinondas' forthcoming battle with the Spartans. The word could also be used for the identifying pennant of a ship (Dio Chr. 74.8; Pollux. 1.90) or for a headband worn as a sign of victory (Euboulos fr. 3) or generally on festive occasions (e.g., Plato *Symp.* 212e). Ferguson 1936, 157, suggested these were the ribbons worn by participants at sacrifices. But it seems better to associate the name with a key rather than a secondary function of the group. Note also the objection of Wüst 1957, 188, that sacrificial ribbons would be more suitable for the holder of priestly office.

56. That the old trittyes were at least roughly regular in size as well as in number is intrinsically likely and is suggested by the fact that their successors were so (now well established by Traill 1978, cf. 1986, and Siewert 1982). I suggest a role in the organization of the Solonian Boule of four hundred (the case against the existence of this body is weak, see Rhodes 1981, 153–54), because units of one hundred (i.e. the phyle subdivisions) would not, I believe, have been small enough to prepare the Boule's business; that there was probably not much of it is irrelevant. The archons or other officials may have performed the function, but since trittyes existed at the time of Solon, and since their successors probably functioned from the start as prytany subdivisions in the Cleisthenic Boule (the implication of the conclusions of Traill and Siewert, op. cit.), it seems more reasonable to suppose they also functioned as phyle subdivisions in the Solonian Boule.

57. Four sacrifices from the second term of Nikomachos' revision of the sacred calendar of the state (403/2–400/399) are described as ἐκ τῶν φυλοβασιλικῶν, which may mean "from the fund of the phylobasileis" (as thought by writers before Dow 1959, following Oliver 1935), or, as attractively suggested by Dow 1959, 15–21, "on the authority of the phylobasileis" (Oliver 1935, p. 21 [Dow fr. C], 33–34 and 45–46 [n. 52 above]; p. 23 [Dow

in the ceremonial judgment of cases of homicide where the killer was an animal or inanimate object.[58] Again original raison d'être clearly lies elsewhere; and again a role in the military organization may be surmised.[59] Two further functions are attested: they were the basis for the selection of the Solonian Boule of 400[60] and, according to the *Ath. Pol.*, for the pre-election of archons prior to sortition under the Solonian system.[61]

When we have only a few scattered and very worn pieces of a large jigsaw puzzle, it is hard to demonstrate with any degree of certainty what the picture as a whole looked like; but the impression given by the pieces we do possess is that the political affairs[62] of the pre-Cleisthenic polis were organized in terms of phyle, trittys, and naukrary.

It seems that the groups formed an interlocking system—again similar to Cleisthenes'. Both trittyes and naukraries were phyle subdivisions, and while we do not know the institutional relationship between trittys and naukrary, if we were correct in attributing a military role to the former, functional interconnection seems likely: there would have been a natural association between naval organization (naukrary) and military (trittys

---

fr. A = *IG* 2².1357a], 6–7; Dow 1941, p. 34 [Dow fr. E], 44–45). The phyle Geleontes participates at one of these sacrifices and the trittys Leukotainioi of that phyle at another (Oliver 1935 p. 21, 31–43 and 44–59; both connected with the festival Synoikia, see Ferguson 1936). The phylobasileis themselves are involved individually or together in all four cases and also probably appear on a fragment of a sacred calendar from the Eleusinion of ca. 500–480 (Jeffrey 1948, 93, no. 67 II A a 13 = *IG* 1³.232, 43. Jeffrey's alternative restoration φυλοβασι]λεῦσι is preferable to βασι]λεῦσι, since the parallel between this sacred calendar and Nikomachos' is closer than that with the administration of homicide law, the only context in which βασιλεῖς occur in the plural). Note also the statement of Pollux 8.111; οἱ φυλοβασιλεῖς· ἐξ εὐπατριδῶν δὲ ὄντες, μάλιστα τῶν ἱερῶν ἐπεμελοῦντο, συνεδρεύοντες ἐν τῷ βασιλείῳ τῷ παρὰ τὸ βουκολεῖον.

58. In this they were associated with the basileis, whose former residence, the Basileion, or royal palace, was apparently their office (Pollux 8.111, see previous note, cf. *Ath. Pol.* 3.5). See *Ath. Pol.* 57.4 with Rhodes ad loc.; Dem. 23.76, cf. 38; Plut. *Sol.* 19.4; Harrison 1968–71, 2:36–43; MacDowell 1963.

59. For the military role of the post-Cleisthenic phylai, see, e.g., the narrative of the battle of Marathon in Hdt. 6, cf. Siewert 1982, 141–45; and for phylai conceivably as military units at an earlier period, Hom. *Il.* 2.362–63 (below, n. 116). Note also the strong tradition that the founder of the phylai, Ion, had been a military commander (Hdt. 8.44.2; *Ath. Pol.* 3.2, cf. fr. 3; Paus. 1.31.3), and see also Hdt. 5.69.2 with Roussel 1976, 201.

60. *Ath. Pol.* 8.4, cf. n. 56.

61. *Ath. Pol.* 8.1. The reliability of the *Ath. Pol.* has been doubted on grounds of conflict with Arist. *Pol.* 2.1273b35–1274a3; 1274a16–17; 3.1281b25–34, which states that Solon made no change in the method of election, but retained the aristocratic principle. For a cogent defence of the *Ath. Pol.* on the point, however, see Rhodes 1981, 146–48.

62. See n. 30.

and phyle), whether or not we believe the naukrary also played a role in the organization of the cavalry; and it seems unlikely that a citizen army, still less Peisistratos' mercenary forces,[63] could have been organized, equipped, and supported without some involvement of the naukraric financial system.[64] For the functional linkage of phyle and trittys, their implicit association in the Synoikia sacrifices[65] in the state calendar should be suggestive enough to compensate for the inconclusive evidence of joint role in the army or Boule.

The regularity of the numbers and, it may be supposed, the size of the groups confirms the impression of an interdependent system: no more than speculation may lie behind the theory of *Ath. Pol.* fr. 3 that the Attic system of phylai and their subdivisions was designed to reflect the seasons, months, and days of the year.[66] But the idea that groups of this sort were regular in number, the larger divisible into the smaller and the numbers matching the calendar, in order to enable functions and responsibilities to be allotted, subdivided, and, in the case of military roles, organized on the field and rotated in a regular manner, is in itself plausible enough.

Considerations of this sort have the effect, I suggest, of shoring up evidence that may seem inconclusive if regarded in isolation. If, for example, we are inclined to doubt the specific evidence that the cavalry were organized by naukrary,[67] it would still be reasonable, assuming there were cavalry before Cleisthenes,[68] to suppose that they were organized in terms of the phyle/trittys/naukrary system, because of the more or less closely related functions the system performed. And where there are gaps in the evidence altogether, we can reasonably hypothesize a role for the system. It would be surprising, for example, if the naukraries, with their responsibilities for finances and taxation, did not have something to do with the administration of the property classes.[69]

---

63. On these, see Hdt. 1.61; *Ath. Pol.* 15.2, 4–5; Frost 1984, 291–92; Siewert 1982, 155–56 (to be read with Lewis 1983, 435); Rhodes 1981, 210.

64. This should not be taken as implying any argument with the general assumption that men will have been responsible for arming themselves in the archaic period.

65. See above, n. 53, with Ferguson 1936.

66. See appendix 2.

67. See p. 255.

68. On this question, see Bugh 1988, 3–38, who concludes that there were.

69. The pentakosiomedimnoi, hippeis, zeugitai, and thetes. According to our evidence, the function of the classes was to determine eligibility for office; but it is not unlikely that they were also used for other purposes, of which taxation would be the most obvious, at least at an earlier period. See *Ath. Pol.* 7.3 with Rhodes ad loc., and cf. p. 363–64 below.

The phratries and their subdivisions stand in sharp contrast. The evidence for the political functions of the phyle/trittys/naukrary system may be patchy, but for the phratry it is nonexistent. But if we have no reason for supposing the phratry played any of the roles performed by Cleisthenes' phyle system, might it not nevertheless have exercised more subtle influence? Might the phratry not have been more closely integrated into the old phyle system than it was in the new one? Unfortunately, our evidence is not sufficient to determine the matter. If the phratry was a phyle subdivision, this may have been the case; but as we have seen, that is itself at best unclear.[70] It must be said, however, that once we have rejected the authority of the *Ath. Pol.* fr. 3, as we must,[71] on the numbers of phratries and gene, we have no grounds for supposing that there was a regular number or size of phratries or phratry subdivisions in the archaic period any more than in the classical; or that the tendency to fuse and divide, which can be observed in the classical period,[72] did not also operate in the archaic. In that case, the phratries would scarcely have fitted into the regular system of the phyle/trittys/naukrary any better than they did into its Cleisthenic successor; and even if they were phyle subgroups, they could hardly have been so in any more than a notional sense. Certainly Kolias gave its name to a genos as well as a naukrary;[73] but then Boutadai was a genos and a deme.[74] We cannot assert that the extent of overlap between phratry and phyle systems would have been greater, or less, before Cleisthenes than after.

In fact, the assumption behind this question is itself doubtful. Whether it was more or less closely integrated into the phyle system before Cleisthenes than after, it is not clear that we have in the phratry an institution that characteristically influenced the social and political system rather than one that was influenced by it. We saw in Part One that the phratry in the classical period broadly reflected the democratic constitutional norms found in other organs of the polis, both local and central.[75] In this chapter I noted that Draco's law of homicide suggests that the phratry in the seventh century will have been constituted on aristocratic lines.[76] The question arises as to how the change came about. There is no hint

---

70. See pp. 14–17.
71. See appendix 2.
72. See pp. 107–12.
73. Cf. n. 35.
74. Cf. p. 115. In neither case would the institutions have overlapped completely.
75. See pp. 105–6, 241–42.
76. See pp. 248–50.

that there was ever any central legislation on the matter. We may suppose that the phratries adapted themselves to reflect patterns of procedure and structure normal in society at any given time. That may help to explain the slightly old-fashioned features of the phratry we noted in Part One; an institution that follows norms established elsewhere may be expected to do so somewhat sluggishly. Particularly if it did not have a wider political role in the archaic period than it had in the classical, it may be that the phratry was no more a determinant of political power structures before Cleisthenes than after.

Citizenship

This leads us to the point at which the view that Cleisthenes effected a change in the role of the phratry is perhaps most deep-rooted: in its control over citizenship. After Cleisthenes, the deme at least shared control over access to citizenship with the phratry. Before Cleisthenes, it is thought, the phratry held the field. This view might hold some attraction if the phratry were a phyle subdivision and part of a single integrated system for the organization of citizens, but we have seen that that is at least uncertain, at most improbable. In fact, there is no direct evidence that registration with a body other than the phratry was a Cleisthenic innovation.[77] We have seen that political rights and responsibilities seem to have been organized in terms of the phyle/trittys/naukrary system, a system which may have existed independently of the division of the population into phratries and gene and may have cut across it.[78] We might expect that, just as the deme after Cleisthenes operated a system to control access to those rights and responsibilities independently of the phratry, so the phyle/trittys/naukrary system would have had its own means of controlling such access in the archaic state. More specifically, we would expect, as the *Ath. Pol.* perhaps implies,[79] that the naukraries, like the demes, performed this role. It is difficult to see how they could have exercised their financial and other functions without some sort of registration system on a naukraric basis. The origins of the archaic-sounding *lexiarchikon grammateion,* the deme's register in the classical period, have long been in dispute. But it would never

---

77. Indeed, the statement of the *Ath. Pol.* 21.5 that the demarchs took over their responsibilities from the naukraroi is prima facie evidence to the contrary.

78. See previous section.

79. See n. 77.

have been the phratry register; that was the *phraterikon grammateion.*
I suggest it may originally have been the register of the phyle/trittys/
naukrary structure.[80]

We can take the argument further. The Aristotelian School was aware
of a tradition that access to citizenship (*politeia*) was one of the issues
that lay behind Cleisthenes' reforms. First, the *Ath. Pol.* records that
there was a diapsephismos of the citizen body following the expulsion
of the tyrants, presumably designed to exclude persons, such as the
tyrants' mercenaries, who had obtained access to citizen rights by dubious
means under the tyranny.[81] Second, Aristotle in the *Politics* tells us that
after the expulsion of the tyrants Cleisthenes enrolled in the phylai foreign
immigrants and slaves. Presumably he means at least some of the same
people who, according to the *Ath. Pol.,* had been deprived of citizenship
at an earlier stage following the fall of the tyranny.[82] Third, the *Ath.
Pol.* believed that one of Cleisthenes' purposes in instituting the use of
the demotic was to prevent the parentage of newly enfranchised citizens—
presumably those referred to by Aristotle—from being revealed. Finally,
the *Ath. Pol.* also believed that it was part of Cleisthenes' intention in
creating the ten new phylai "to mix people up, so that more might have
a share in the citizenship,"[83] and that this was the origin of the phrase,
"Don't judge by phylai," used against those who sought to inquire into

---

80. I incline to the view of van Effenterre 1976, esp. 7–16 (following Töpffer 1895, 391–
400; accepted in part by Whitehead 1986a, 35–36, n. 130) that the lexiarchikon grammateion
should be associated with the lexiarchoi, six officers who seem to have had central functions
to do with the registers and "keeping order in the Assembly" (Pollux 8.104), and who
seem likely to have been pre-Cleisthenic in origin (in particular because their number fits
the pre-Cleisthenic duodecimal system). Van Effenterre's conclusion that the lexiarchika
grammateia were originally military lists by year-groups, however, seems less well founded
(cf. Whitehead 1986a, 36, n. 30). I doubt that they had to do with the capacity to inherit
(as most lexicographers and modern writers have taken it, from *lexis,* "claim to inheritance," see, e.g., *Ath. Pol.* 43.4) since that was the special sphere of the phratry. Perhaps
they had to do with the processes of "allotment" to office (the more general sense of *lexis,*
see e.g., *Ath. Pol.* 30.3 with Rhodes 1981 ad loc. and Plut. *Sol.* 19.1 [see n. 92]; cf. *Ath.
Pol.* 8.1 with n. 61 above). For the responsibility of the phyle/trittys/naukrary system in
this regard, see p. 258.

81. *Ath. Pol.* 13.5. There are no good grounds for doubting this. Cf. Rhodes 1981 ad
loc. On the diapsephismos see now also Manville 1990, 173–85.

82. ἀλλ᾽ ἴσως ἐκεῖνο μᾶλλον ἔχει ἀπορίαν, ὅσοι μετέσχον μεταβολῆς γενομένης
πολιτείας, οἷον <ἃ> Ἀθήνησιν ἐποίησε Κλεισθένης μετὰ τὴν τῶν τυράννων ἐκβολήν·
πολλοὺς γὰρ ἐφυλέτευσε ξένους καὶ δούλους μετοίκους. Arist. *Pol.* 3.1275b34–37. I
agree with Rhodes' account at 1981, 255–56, of the controversial issues surrounding this
passage.

83. *Ath. Pol.* 21.2 (see n. 2).

people's origins. The phrase was later used to refer more generally to being over-exact in distinguishing between different sorts of people.[84]

It is difficult to determine here where fact ends and speculative and/or politically motivated reconstruction begins; to go into the range of relevant issues would take us far beyond the scope of this work. In my view, the kernel of fact is likely to include a deliberate policy on the part of Cleisthenes to widen access to involvement in political processes. That must be part at least of what Herodotus meant when he described Cleisthenes as having taken the people into his party in his struggle against Isagoras.[85] Whether or not the targets of that policy were in fact to any extent persons who had been deprived of that involvement by a diapsephismos following the fall of the tyranny, it may have suited Cleisthenes' actual opponents at the time, and his ideological opponents subsequently, to allege that such persons were the sole objective of the policy. Whether, however, it was really membership of institutions that was mainly at issue is unclear: to determine that, we would have to know exactly who belonged to phratries and/or naukraries before Cleisthenes and who did not, and of that we are ignorant.[86] But in any case membership without associated powers—at least contributing to decision-making processes, if not eligibility for office—will scarcely have been the point.[87] And there are plenty of hints that the absence of such powers must have been what was fundamentally wrong with the phyle/trittys/naukrary system as far as Cleisthenes and his supporters were concerned. The phylobasileis, we are told, were from the aristocratic eupatridai.[88] There is no indication that there was anything democratic in the process and criteria by which naukraroi were appointed, and, in the tantalizing Solonian legal fragment, "if anyone disputes a naukrary," some hint to the contrary. Some wealth-based criterion seems likely.[89] About the trit-

---

84. See Thuc. 6.18.2; Suid. s.v. φυλοκρινεῖ.

85. ἐσσούμενος (by Isagoras) δὲ ὁ Κλεισθένης τὸν δῆμον προσεταιρίζεται. Hdt. 5.66.2.

86. We do not know whether the parallel between deme and naukrary also meant that the criteria for membership in both were the same.

87. Correctly stressed now also by Manville 1990, 186–87.

88. Pollux 8.111, see n. 57.

89. ἄν τις ναυκραρίας ἀμφισβητῇ (appendix 4, document 3). Hignett's suggestion, 1952, 71, that this "may indicate a dispute between rival claimants to the position of prytanis" must be wrong. If Solon had meant prytany he could have said so. It is the naukrary that is being disputed, not the prytany. But in what sense? It is conceivable that the allocation of a citizen to a particular naukrary or the level of a naukraric tax assessment is intended, but it seems best to take it as dispute of appointment to the office of naukraros,

tyarchs we are told nothing beyond the fact of their existence, but there is certainly no hint of a democratic process or criteria of appointment.[90] Moreover, there is nothing implausible in the apparent view of Plutarch that the members of the Solonian Boule, organized on the basis of the phyle/trittys/naukrary,[91] were also appointed rather than elected.[92] Again wealth, and with it the naukrary's registers, seems likely to have played a role.[93] It is in this area that the Cleisthenic system was designedly so different.

So we have a factual kernel in the Aristotelian account and some traces of distortion. The latter should also include the imputed motive for Cleisthenes' invention of the demotic: to cover up the incorporation of dubious persons into the citizen body. First, the allegation reeks of political bias. Second, the demotic was in use before Cleisthenes.[94] Third, it did not replace the patronymic—the classical style used name, patronymic, and demotic—and it is incredible that it was ever intended to do so. Heredity continued to be the principle by which deme membership was acquired; Cleisthenes cannot have intended otherwise. That implied attention to parentage, which in turn implied retention of the patronymic. Use of a demotic could in any event scarcely have prevented inquiries

---

cf. Hommel 1935, col. 1947. There is an apparent echo here of the classical liturgies (including, notably, the trierarchy), appointment to which was made on the criterion of wealth and could be disputed under the procedure known as antidosis on the grounds that someone else was wealthier (see Thalheim 1894, cols. 2397–98; Rhodes 1981, 624, and further bibliography cited there. Hommel 1947 draws attention to Dem. 42.1, where the law on antidosis is said to be Solonian, but Ruschenbusch assigns it as fr. 107 to the category "Falsches, Zweifelhaftes, Unbrauchbares, Redner"). That wealth was at least a criterion of appointment would also suit both the tendency, still observable in the classical period, for offices with financial responsibilities to be assigned to the wealthy (presumably to reduce incentives for fraud; note especially the treasurers of Athena, *Ath. Pol.* 8.1 with Rhodes ad loc.) and Solon's general practice of making wealth rather than birth the main criterion of political office (cf. n. 24).

90. τῆς τριττύος μέντοι ὁ ἄρχων τριττύαρχος ἐκαλεῖτο, τριττύος δ' ἑκάστης γένη τριάκοντα. Pollux 8.109. From the reference to the subdivision of the trittys into thirty gene it is clear that the pre-Cleisthenic trittyes are intended, as described (wrongly, see appendix 2) by *Ath. Pol.* fr. 3. It is not unlikely that the *Ath. Pol.* mentioned the trittyarchs in that same context (for the *Ath. Pol.*'s tendency to discuss groups and their leaders together, see *Ath. Pol.* 8.3 and 21), but we know nothing about how they were appointed.

91. For this, see nn. 56 and 60.

92. δευτέραν προσκατένειμε βουλήν, ἀπὸ φυλῆς ἑκάστης (τεσσάρων οὐσῶν) ἑκατὸν ἄνδρας ἐπιλεξάμενος. Plut. *Sol.* 19.1.

93. Cf. p. 253 and p. 261 with n. 80.

94. The most famous case is Μύρων Φλυεύς, prosecutor of the Cylonians in Plut. *Sol.* 12.4. Cf. Whitehead 1986a, 11–12.

into background and parentage by those with an interest, official or otherwise.[95]

The main point I wish to make, however, is that insofar as wider access to political rights is at issue here, as I believe it to have been, the phratries may not have had anything to do with it, or at least not directly. For, if our earlier analysis was correct, those political rights would have been organized on the basis of the phylai, trittyes and naukraries. It was not, we might note, specifically the phratries to which Cleisthenes was accused of admitting a lot of slaves and foreigners, it was the phylai.[96] It was not distinguishing among phratries which was regarded as, shall we say, impolite, it was distinguishing among phylai.[97]

Herein may lie the reason why Cleisthenes left the phratries as they were and why they continued to share with the demes control of access to citizenship.[98] I do not believe, as is frequently alleged, that it had much, if anything, to do with religious conservatism; the old phylai were institutions as venerable as any phratry and Cleisthenes did not hesitate to dispose of them for most practical purposes. As Aristotle indicates, the abolition of old phratries and the creation of new ones was an entirely plausible step for democratic reformers to take, if necessary.[99] It is more likely that the reason was simply because the objective of the exercise was not, directly or indirectly, the phratry, but the phyle/trittys/naukrary structure.

I do not mean to imply by this that phratry membership would not have been affected, either by the diapsephismos which followed the tyranny, or by such new enfranchisements as may have been involved in the creation of the demes. But the effect may have been indirect, as it must have been in the subsequent diapsephismoi of the fifth and fourth centuries.[100] We do not know the mechanism by which deme members expelled at a diapsephismos were ejected from their phratries in the classical period. It may be that the phratries could be relied on to see to the matter themselves; if not, there was presumably an appropriate

---

95. Cf. Rhodes 1981, 254–55.

96. πολλοὺς γὰρ ἐφυλέτευσε ξένους καὶ δούλους. See above, n. 82.

97. μὴ φυλοκρινεῖν. See above, nn. 83 and 84.

98. For the aspects of citizenship associated with phratry membership, see ch. 1.

99. Arist. *Pol.* 6.1319b19–27, see n. 6. This appears to have happened at Cyrene, possibly also at Corinth (Jones 1987, 99, cf. 1980, 161–93).

100. We know of two, in 445/4 (associated with Psammetichos' gift of corn and possibly having something to do with Pericles' citizenship law, cf. p. 44 n. 81, and 346/5 (cf. p. 28).

clause in the Assembly's diapsephismos decree. For the diapsephismos following the fall of the tyranny we cannot be certain that the phratry was not used directly, though if there were naukraric registers, the analogy with the later process may suggest that they would have been used, and that therefore whatever procedure was adopted to eject those removed from the lexiarchikon grammateion in the classical period may also have been used on this occasion.[101] For any new enfranchisement involved in the creation of the demes, a clause in Cleisthenes' Reform Bill would have insured consequent, or conceivably prior, admittance to a phratry readily enough.[102]

A final point in this connection. The question arises as to why there were two institutions controlling access to citizenship after Cleisthenes.[103] We may be inclined to answer that, while there was some degree of overlap, the sort of citizenship criteria to which phratry and deme gave access were subtly but significantly different: rights especially connected with legitimacy of descent the province of the phratry, political rights of the deme. But such an answer begs a further question. I suggest that there is no reason or principle for the division of these two roles between two institutions. The phratry functions could have been transferred to the demes had Cleisthenes thought it necessary or desirable. If, as I have argued, however, the phratry was not an objective of Cleisthenes' reforms, the duality will have predated his work and the explanation of it will have nothing to do with him. It will rather go back to the point at which the organization of political rights, responsibilities, and activities was established in terms of a different structure from the clearly more primitive and more fundamental community membership/inheritance regulation of the phratry, to the origins of the naukrary and trittys, if not of the phyle.

Cleisthenes and the Phratry: Conclusion

The direction of the preceding argument will be clear. The internal structure of the phratry in the archaic period will have been different

---

101. Cf. now Manville 1990, 177, 183, who correctly questions the common assumption that the phratry would have been (sole) implementer of this diapsephismos.

102. It was a clear principle that the polis as a whole could direct phratries to accept new citizens, whether individuals (as with the special grants of citizenship from the later fifth century onwards, cf. p. 32) or general categories (such as, under Solonian arrangements, exiles and those moving to Athens to practice a craft. Plut. *Sol.* 24.4 [= Solon *Laws* fr. 75 R], cf. p. 373).

103. Cf. pp. 34–35.

from in the classical, perhaps more because the phratry tended to reflect contemporary constitutional norms rather than determine them. And it can not be ruled out, though it is far from demonstrable, that the phratry was more closely integrated into the pre-Cleisthenic phyle structure than the post-Cleisthenic. But the role of the phratry in Athenian society may, I suggest, have been essentially the same before Cleisthenes as after. As observed in the previous chapter, the functions it performed in the classical period were not necessarily linked to that period's particular social or political circumstances, and there is no reason in theory why those same functions could not have been performed at other times and in other circumstances. The direct evidence for the pre-Cleisthenic phratry does not, in fact, suggest differences. The evidence for wider political functions, performed after Cleisthenes by his phyle system, suggests that before Cleisthenes they were the province of the phyle/trittys/naukrary structure, not of the phratry. It will have been these wider functions that were the objective of his reforms. There are not even good grounds for supposing that Cleisthenes deprived the phratry of exclusive control over access to citizenship. In short, there is no good reason on the basis of current evidence for rejecting the explicit statement of the *Ath. Pol.* that Cleisthenes left the phratries as they were.

Beginnings and Endings

The much disputed question of the origins of the phratry[104] and the neglected question of its demise take us beyond the stated chronological and geographical scope of this work. I give here no more than a few thoughts on these issues; our evidence is in any case too insubstantial to support anything approaching a comprehensive account. I have already discussed, without firm conclusion, the theoretical question of the original character of the phratry and the extent to which it was a personal or a territorial unit, and, with similar inconclusiveness, whether or not the phratry was a subgroup of the phyle. A little may be added.

The question of the date of origin of the phratry is no more easily soluble than that of its original character. Opinion has been divided, broadly speaking, between those who, with the Greeks themselves, see the phratry as an extremely ancient institution, a genuine element of the common Ionian heritage, predating the Ionian migration that followed

---

104. For a good overview of work on this subject, see Roussel 1976.

the end of the Mycenaean kingdoms; and those who would rather see it as a product of later developments, the unsettled social and political circumstances of the earlier Dark Ages, or of the later period during which the polis acquired its historical character.[105] A number of interlocking issues of similar uncertainty and controversy immediately arise, concerning the historicity of the Ionian migration, the character of Greek society in the Dark Ages, and the origins of the polis.[106] In the case of Athens, the picture is complicated further by questions surrounding the synoecism of Attica, the process by which later Athenians believed their city had been formed by political combination of previously independent Attic settlements. It is not even certain that this was a historical event, let alone whether it had any effect on the phratries.[107]

I suggest, however, that the balance of argument currently remains in favor of the view that phratries in some form dated back at least to the later Mycenaean period. As Roussel has argued, the extent of institutional commonality in the Ionian world demonstrable by current evidence is not in itself a decisive argument.[108] Herodotus tells us that there were two Ionian states which did not celebrate the Apatouria,[109] and there remain gaps in our evidence as to whether there had at one time been phratries in every Ionian state.[110] Such commonality as there is might plausibly be interpreted as a relatively late consequence of a sense of, or desire for, Ionian solidarity, and is not necessarily a symptom of common origins.

---

105. According to Hdt.1.147.2, the phratry festival Apatouria was a touchstone of Ionian identity. *Ath. Pol.* fr. 3 held Ion to be the creator of both phylai and phratries (see appendix 2). In the Ionian world there is evidence for the phratry at Chios, Miletos, Phocea, Tenos, and Delos; also at Eretria. The month Apatourion, which probably implies the existence of phratries and/or the phratry festival Apatouria, is attested for Samos, Priene, Iasos, Amorgos, Paros, Thasos, Chalcis, and Eretria in addition to Miletos, Tenos, and Delos. See Roussel 1976, 153–56; Piérart 1985; Jones 1987; Samuel 1972, index s.v. Apatourion. Most have supported the idea that phratries were extremely ancient institutions (see, e.g., Meyer 1913–39 3.270; Busolt-Swoboda 1920–26, 250–52). Andrewes 1961b suggests they were refounded in the Dark Ages. Roussel 1976 is skeptical about whether they had existed at all before the polis.

106. On the Ionian migration and the character of Greek Society in the Dark Ages, see especially Snodgrass 1971 and works referred to in Roussel 1976. On the origins of the polis, see the contrasting accounts of van Effenterre 1985 and de Polignac 1984 (and the review of both, Snodgrass 1986), and now also Manville 1990.

107. It was ascribed to Theseus. See esp. Padgug 1972, 135–50; Coldstream 1977, 70–71; Snodgrass 1980, 34; Diamant 1982, 38–47 and the sensible summaries of Whitehead 1986a, 8–9 and Manville 1990, 55.

108. Roussel 1976, 153–54.

109. Ephesus and Colophon.

110. Cf. n. 105, cf. p. 16 n. 57.

There is, however, one crucial argument in favor of the traditional view that, though not decisive, remains persuasive. I have already remarked on the relationship of the word "phrater" to the Indo-European word, "*bhrater," the descendants of which in other Indo-European languages mean brother.[111] The uniformity with which in all dialects of Greek before the Roman period such a common original meaning was obliterated and a technical meaning acquired by the word is remarkable. Such uniformity would be unexpected if the technical meaning had simply spread by diffusion.[112] It suggests a very early origin of the technical sense, possibly in advance of the differentiation of Greek into dialects around 1200.[113]

An attempt to argue on the basis of the character of the phratry's role in the polis that it cannot have predated the origins of the polis in

---

111. See Boisacq 1907; Frisk 1960–70; Chantraine 1968–80.

112. Even in Homer there is no hint of the original meaning (see further below). Other words had to be found for brother: ἀδελφός, κασίγνητος, γνωτός. The idea that the institutional sense of *bhrater was original and the "literal" sense a later development is unsupportable. If an apparently more basic meaning is prevalent in a family of languages, and an apparently derived, metaphorical, meaning occurs only rarely, the best explanation is that the basic meaning is earlier and that the metaphorical meaning represents a divergence from it (cf. Roussel 1976, 95–97, Perpillou 1984, 205, and earlier works cited by those authors, esp. Benveniste 1973). Perpillou 1984, 205–20 and 221–36 (cf. Gallavotti 1961, 20–39) would reconstruct the Mycenaean words *35-to and au-to-*34-ta-ra as equivalent to φράτηρ and Αὐτοφράτρα (taken as a woman's name, derived from and expressing her relationship to a named man; cf. Φιλοπάτρα, ʼΑλεξάνδρα). I offer no comment on this hypothesis from a linguistic point of view; however, his further argument, that since a man is being described as a phrater of a woman, it must be a blood relationship rather than a common phratry membership that is being described, is not conclusive. There is evidence that women could occasionally be phratry members (or something close to it, see pp. 178–88) in the classical period; we certainly cannot rule out that they may have been in the Mycenaean period (cf. the postscript of Lévêque to Piérart 1985; it is difficult to resist entertaining the possibility that Αὐτο- may bear its normal classical sense, and that the significance of the name therefore may have been that it was used of a woman who was "herself a phrater," or "a phrater in her own right"). The only other instance in Greek of φρήτηρ = "brother" is Hesych. s.v. φρήτηρ· ἀδελφός. Andrewes 1961b saw this as evidence that some Ionic community retained the primitive sense, but the phratries were, by any account, deep-rooted in the Attic/Ionian world, and it is precisely there that we would expect not to find such a sense. I suspect, pace Andrewes and despite the eta, that the gloss betrays the influence of Latin. For the reverse of this, in which φράτηρ in a Greek context may have become frater in a Latin one, see pp. 187–88. Roussel 1976, 95–97, thought the technical sense could have spread by diffusion from a single source, comparing the name "Hellenes," thought to have derived from a single individual, Helles (Th. 1.3.2). But Helles is a transparently mythical figure, invented to explain the name. Even if he were not, the analogy would not be close: "Helles" is allegedly a proper name, not a word with a meaning as common as brother; this would not be a case of an original common meaning being supplanted by a narrow technical one.

113. For the date, see Snodgrass 1971, 303.

its historical form carries no weight, as we saw in the last chapter.[114] The phratry could have played its fundamental role as a unit of community beyond the family in any number of social and political circumstances. Its wider role in the polis derived from the fact that polis and phratry had the same qualification for membership by descent; but it does not follow from this that both institutions must have originated at the same time.

Andrewes adopted a skeptical position on the extreme antiquity of the phratry, at least in its historical form, on rather different grounds.[115] He started from the observation that phylai make only one appearance, phratries two, in the Homeric poems. First, at *Iliad* 2.362–63 Nestor gives Agamemnon advice for the vigorous pursuit of the war: "Divide the men by phylai and by phratries, Agamemnon, so that phratry may support phratry and phyle phyle."[116] Second, in the passage we cited at the start of chapter 1, *Iliad* 9.63–64, it is again Nestor who mentions the phratry in his intervention in a dispute between Diomedes and Agamemnon: "The man who loves the horror of war among his own people is an outlaw, without phrateres and without a home."[117] Despite Nestor's advice in the first passage and Agamemnon's positive reception of it, there is no further mention of military organization by phylai and phratries. Andrewes offered the explanation that in the Mycenaean period itself and in the subsequent centuries in which the epic conventions were being developed, there were no phylai or phratries; hence their absence from most of Homer. In, say, the late ninth and early eighth centuries the institutions came into being as a means for competing groups of aristocrats to organize retainers and dependants. By Homer's own time, understood as around 700, they were taken for granted; hence their insertion into the text.

The interpretation lacks conviction. To identify these two passages as particularly recent layers of the Homeric poems seems arbitrary. On this basis we might have expected references to the institutions in the *Odyssey,* generally agreed to be a later work. The association of the phratries with a character, Nestor, normally a representative of the old order, and

---

114. It is on this point in particular that the thesis of Roussel 1976 fails to convince. Cf. p. 242.

115. Andrewes 1961b. Cf. n. 105.

116. κρῖν' ἄνδρας κατὰ φῦλα, κατὰ φρήτρας, Ἀγάμεμνον,/ ὡς φρήτρη φρήτρηφιν ἀρήγῃ, φῦλα δὲ φύλοις. Hom *Il.* 2.362–63.

117. See p. 25.

with venerable concepts such as *hestia* (hearth) and *themis* (divine right), suggests institutions whose roots run deep. It is not difficult to explain the absence of phylai and phratries from the rest of Homer: he is interested in his characters, not in the institutions in which they lived, about which he is invariably vague—a vagueness exacerbated by the wide temporal and geographical scope of both composition and subject matter. The fact that Nestor's advice is not heeded by Agamemnon in *Iliad* 2 is not surprising in an oral epic: the *Iliad* and the *Odyssey* are full of inconsistencies of this sort. The point is merely that Nestor has been wise; Agamemnon has acknowledged this. The plot can move on.

Arguments against the extreme antiquity of the phratry, therefore, are not convincing; arguments in favor, while not conclusive, appear to carry more weight. It would be reasonable to suppose that, if it did exist at an early period, the phratry would have performed the functions of the unit of community beyond the family, including control of access to that community and regulation of inheritance, attested for it in the historical period. Beyond that, however, its prehistorical character remains obscure.[118]

How far we should, with Andrewes, associate phylai with phratries in arguments about the origins of the institutions is also obscure. If the phratry was a phyle subdivision, the case is clear; but we have seen that this relationship is far from certain.[119] We have nothing more to go on in the case of the phylai than the degree to which phyle names were shared in the Ionian world, which, as in the case of the phratries and Apatouria, cannot be taken necessarily to imply an origin prior to the Ionian migration.[120] For the phylai, there is nothing like the strong linguistic argument that suggests early origins for the phratry; and, insofar as we can determine the early functions of the phylai, they may have been more clearly linked than those of the phratry with the specific organizational requirements of the archaic polis[121]—not that that would preclude the possibility that the polis had adapted preexisting institutions for its own purposes.

We are scarcely in a stronger position with regard to the naukraries

---

118. See also pp. 272–73 below.

119. See pp. 14–17.

120. Hdt. 5.66, 69; Eur. *Ion* 1575–88 (see p. 211, n. 39); *Ath. Pol.* fr. 3 (see appendix 2). There is evidence for one or more of the names, or forms close to them, at Miletos (and colonies Kyzikos, Odessos, Tomoi, and Istros), Ephesos, Teos, Perinthos (colony of Samos), Delos, Colophon, Erythrae, and Thasos. See Piérart 1985.

121. I.e., in the organization of the army and the Solonian Boule, see p. 258.

and trittyes. It looks, however, more clearly than in the case of the phratries and phylai, as if their origins probably lie near the dawn of the historical period: there are no hints of commonality with the Ionian world here, and there is a clearer link between plausible raison d'être and the organizational requirements of the archaic polis. If the trittyes were in the first place military units, designed for the organization of hoplites,[122] we may guess at an origin connected with the introduction of hoplite tactics at Athens, i.e., sometime after 650.[123] If that is correct, the naukraries may be older than the trittyes;[124] at least archaeological evidence suggests ca. 770–730 as the most plausible pre-Cylonian context for the origin of an institution the name of which suggests a naval raison d'être.[125]

Whatever the origins of phyle, trittys, and naukrary, I have suggested that they, not the phratry, will have provided the framework for the

---

122. Cf. pp. 256–57.

123. See p. 149.

124. The *Ath. Pol.* seems to have thought them newer, since they do not appear in the organizational scheme attributed to Ion in fr. 3; but that signifies nothing of historical worth (cf. appendix 2).

125. At this period the circulation of Attic pottery within the Aegean reaches its highest peak before the sixth century, the major recipients being the Cyclades, Aegina, Knossos and Thebes; see Coldstream, 1977, 109 with 137, n. 1. The finds at Al Mina and elsewhere in the Levant suggest a burst of Attic activity in the early eighth century (Coldstream 1977, 93–94). In broader terms, the period also apparently witnessed rapid population expansion, indicated by eight-fold increase in the quantity of graves (Snodgrass 1980, ch. 1); three-fold increase in number of wells in the Agora area (Coldstream, 1968, 360, n. 1. Note, however, the controversey surrounding the interpretation of this evidence, conveniently summarized by Manville 1990, 89–91); increase in coastal settlements (Coldstream 1977, 134, fig. 43); and the rediscovery of writing with the help of the Phoenicians—Attica boasts the earliest datable inscription (Coldstream 1977, 298, fig. 95a with 298–99); all of which seem to imply an increase in overseas contact. For the depiction of ships on contemporary vases, see Coldstream 1977, 135; Morrison and Williams 1968, ch. 2 with plates. The question of whether these are representations of real life or legendary themes is disputed (see, e.g., Boardman 1983, 15–36; Hurwit 1985), but to deny the likelihood that there was intense Athenian maritime activity at this time and that, directly or indirectly, this had some connection with the depiction of ships on contemporary pottery (whether or not the scenes are mythical) would be perverse. For further speculation about the origin of the naukraroi, see Hommel 1935, cols. 1941–43, who recognizes the attraction of placing it during a period of attested maritime activity, but whose view that the seventh century was such a period is now outdated. Beloch 1912–27 *IG* 1².390; 2².123 (cf. Hignett 1952, 67–74) mistakenly takes them to be of Peisistratid origin on the basis of the dubious downdating of Cylon to the sixth century (cf. n. 48) and rejection of Solonian authorship of the naukraric legal extracts (cf. appendix 4). French 1957 (cf. Kahrstedt 1934, 246–49) thought they might have originated from cooperation between owners of merchant ships—not impossible, but undemonstrable by current evidence.

political organization of the archaic state. What of the phratry's role before trittys and naukrary, and possibly phyle, existed? In the absence of evidence, the question must remain open; but while the phratry could have performed at any time essentially the same role as that attested in the historical period, there is also nothing about the nature or functions of the institution in the classical and, I have argued, archaic periods that would have prevented it from fulfilling a wider role at an earlier time; and whatever Agamemnon thought of the idea that phratries be used for the organization of the Greek army, Nestor's suggestion shows that it was at least conceivable to Homer that phratries might perform roles that extended beyond those observed at Athens in the historical period.[126]

The neglected question of the demise of the Attic phratry is, in its way, no less intriguing than that of its origins. The contemporary literary record ceases in the fourth century, the epigraphical record at around 250,[127] except for the allocation of naturalized citizens to phratries, the evidence for which continues for as long as those grants were made by inscribed decree, i.e., until the mid-second century.[128] The ceasing of the literary record is a general phenomenon, which cannot be related directly to the fate of the phratries; that of the epigraphical in ca. 250 looks at

---

126. We cannot, of course, know for how long before Draco everyone at Athens had belonged to a phratry. However, Manville 1990, 69, is overly dismissive of the possibility that phratries "in early times . . . provided a uniform and recognized standard, entitling each Attic phrator to a sort of Athenian passport." For all that they may be mentioned in the same breath by *Dig.* 47.22.4, there is a distinction between groups to which all citizens necessarily belonged and those such as thiasoi, syssitoi, and homogalaktes. The earliest evidence (Draco, and also, of broader significance, Homer) shows the phratry among the former, and it is not impossible that comprehensive membership was an original characteristic, essential to the phratry's raison d'être.

127. The latest precisely datable phratry document in appendix 1 is T 5 (300/299), but there are four that have been dated by letter forms to the first half of the third century, or for which that period lies within the range of possible dates (T 4, T 9, T 12, T 17). Note also M. and E. Levensohn 1947, 63, no. 1 (inscription of possible phratric thiasos from 250s). There are several inscriptions of citizen orgeones which date, or may date, to the third century (Ferguson 1944, Class A, nos. 1, 4, 6, 8, 10, 11) and one which may date to the second century (Ferguson no. 12, though, as Ferguson realized, this may be a noncitizen group; cf. above, p. 77, n. 83). There is evidence for gene into the Roman period (e.g., *IG* 2².2338, 2340; some features, e.g., names, suggest continuity from the classical period; we have no means of telling to what extent this is illusory). There is no evidence, however, as to whether they were aggregated into phratries at this period.

128. The latest mentions of phratries in these decrees, which represent therefore the latest direct evidence for their existence at Athens, are M. Osborne 1981-83, D 118, dated ca. 190-140; D 107-9, all dated 148/7-135/4; D 112-13, dated ca. 150; and D 111, dated 200-150.

first to be more significant, but we should not assume that it betokens demise, or even a radical decline. The citizenship decrees show that phratry membership was bestowed on new citizens for at least another century, and it is difficult to believe that this was no more than a hollow formality. Moreover, the epigraphical record of the demes shows a remarkably similar pattern: a sharp falling-off in the first half of the third century and almost nothing after 250.[129] Whitehead, while recognizing that demes may simply have ceased to publish as many documents as in the fourth century, was inclined to see in this signs of a real decline and to look for explanation to the "accumulated and accumulating effects of political, social and demographic change"; he saw the phyle reorganization of 307/6 and the early third-century struggles against Macedon acting as accelerating factors.[130] The similarity of this pattern to that of the phratries suggests a common cause, however, and the phratries should have been protected at least against demographic changes by their ability to divide or fuse in response.[131] Moreover, their continuous existence through the transition from the aristocratic world of Draco's homicide law to the fully developed democracy of the fourth century suggests an ability to survive and adapt to radical social and political change.

Insofar as demes and phratries did suffer a real decline after 250, the end of Athens' status as an independent power, a protracted process that started in the fourth century but was consolidated in the third, is the most obvious large-scale development that would have affected them both. Associated with it will have been a decline in the relative importance, to Athenians themselves no doubt as well as to outsiders, of the Athenian political process and the control of access to it, which was crucial to both phratry and deme. The phratry's role in that process may not have been its original raison d'être; but it is not difficult to see that, over a period of centuries, this role may eventually have become so central to its existence that the decline of the polis also entailed a decline in the groups of which the polis in a sense consisted. But the citizenship decrees, in which the demes also continue to figure, suggest that, at least initially, this decline may have been more apparent than real. No one would argue that the phratry was not a lively institution in the earlier

---

129. See Whitehead 1986a, 360–62. There are just two second century deme decrees (*IG* 2².949, Eleusis; *Hesp.* 1942, 265–74, no. 51, Melite), both probably somewhat special cases.

130. Whitehead loc. cit.

131. Cf. pp. 107–12.

fifth, sixth, and seventh centuries, though we have scarcely a scrap of contemporary evidence. We should perhaps look more to changes in the factors which caused these groups to publish decrees on stone for an explanation of the decline in evidence, though this may in the end only lead us to a similar destination via another route: to the decline of the democratic idea as an effective force in Athenian society.

How long the phratry survived its last appearance on citizenship decrees in the mid-second century is impossible to say with any certainty. Although inscribed decrees come to an end at that point, naturalization seems to have continued, and indeed increased, in the subsequent period, though we do not know whether it continued to involve bestowal of phratry membership. From the later second century onward, citizenship seems to have been acquired mainly through ephebic service, which was opened to foreigners at this time.[132] We may guess that this ending of the link between citizenship and the principle of descent, which had been so crucial to the phratry's significance in the polis, may well finally have ushered in its demise.

---

132. See M. Osborne 1981–83, 144–45.

Appendices

Phratry Documents

This appendix is divided into three parts: named phratries, unnamed phratries, and possible phratries.

Under "named phratries" evidence certainly or probably pertaining directly to individual Attic phratries whose names are known is given in English alphabetical order of the names. I have not, however, printed extracts from Isaeus 7, which probably relates to the phratry Achniadai; see pp. 66–68, 283. Evidence pertaining to phratry subgroups, on which see chapter 2, is not included. Each item consists of a brief description of the document, with selective bibliography including all works of relevance to the text, and an indication of the basis of the text. Where an earlier text is adopted without amendment, little or no apparatus is given. A text said to be based on another includes my own suggestions, with those of previous editors indicated in the apparatus. For epigraphical conventions used, see pp. ix–x. There follows a translation in which I have also tried to give an indication, inevitably somewhat imprecise, of words or occasionally even parts of words not present on the stone by use of ( ); [ ] contain alternative possible readings or meanings. In the notes I generally discuss only matters of relevance to the texts and to the individual phratries concerned; matters of wider significance are dealt with in the main body of the book. See index 1, T 1–T 36 and index 2 under individual phratry names. After the notes there is, with inscriptions, an indication of the date. Known topographical associations of a phratry are given in the section entitled "Location"; on the extent to which phratries were local units, see pp. 8–14.

Under "unnamed phratries" epigraphical evidence certainly or probably pertaining directly to individual phratries whose names are not known is given. I have not included the literary evidence in this category, which, though reasonably abundant, is mostly from the orators and is generally uninformative about the individual features of the phratries concerned. With the likely exception of the Achniadai and Isaeus 7, there is no case where a phratry mentioned in the literary evidence can be identified with one epigraphically attested. The list of evidence at index 1, however, includes all the literary evidence. Text and commentary are as for named phratries.

Under "possible phratries" there are brief notes on the evidence for groups, named and unnamed, where positive arguments can or have been made that they are phratries, but which may also be other sorts of groups (usually gene). It does not contain those items that may pertain to phratries, but for which no case can be or has been made that they do so and not to other sorts of groups.

Named Phratries

T 1 Achniadai

Marker (of phratry property?), seen by Milchhöfer built into a house at Keratea (ancient Kephale).
Milchhöfer 1887, 287 no. 206; *IG* 2.5, 1074 F; *IG* 2².2621; Guarducci 1937, no. 11. Text from Milchhöfer's illustration.

ὅρος
φρατρίας
Ἀχνιαδῶν
Η⟦ . . . ⟧Ο
5   ⟦ - - - - ⟧
⟦ - - - - ⟧

Translation

Marker of the phratry Achniadai . . .

Notes

This is unique among phratry markers (*horoi*) in that it does not say exactly what it was a marker of (cf. p. 192). It cannot simply be the boundary marker of a phratry; though phratries had local associations, they were not territorial units (see pp. 8–14). Presumably it would have marked landed property of some sort. The text of 1–3 appears complete, however, despite the traces of letters and erasure in 4–6. These should perhaps be taken as remnants of an earlier text, erased when this one was inscribed. It is possible that the Achniadai acquired this property from an earlier owner, e.g., as a result of a default on a debt (cf. p. 198), and the marker was amended accordingly. For analogous cases of amendment and reuse of markers of this sort, see e.g. Finley 1952, nos. 22, 33, 71, and 152, 80–81, 107–8; Millett 1982, 78A, 80A–81A. This marker (and possibly T 7, q.v.) suggests that it may be wrong to interpret some of the similar markers which show deme names (on which see Traill 1986, 116–22; Whitehead 1986a, 28–29) as marking boundaries of territories of demes, rather than properties. *IG* 2².2623 (ὅρος π[ει]/ραέων [χώ/ρ]ας), for example, might be the marker of a deme property.

3. Ἀχνιαδῶν. Given the apparent indentation of the name in Milchhöfer's illustration and the fact that the name occurs at the start of a line in T 2, Hedrick 1984, 247, noted that it is possible that one or more letters are missing at the start. Certainly Achniadai would be a highly obscure name; there are no known deities or persons with a name from the same root. But such obscurity is a not uncommon feature of phratry names (cf. pp. 221–22).

Date

After about 400 (orthography; Guarducci's "lettere del III/II secolo" seems inadequately supported).

Location

See on T 2.

T 2 Achniadai

Sanctuary marker, from Keratea (ancient Kephale).
CIG 463 (Boeckh from notes by Fourmont); Wilamowitz 1893, 2,268
with n. 10; *IG* 2².4974; Guarducci 1937, no. 10. Text, *CIG* 463.

[ἱ]ερὸν
['Α]πόλλωνος
῾Εβδομείο
φρατρίας
5 'Αχνιαδῶν

Translation

Sanctuary of Apollo Hebdomeios of the phratry (5) Achniadai.

Notes

5. 'Αχνιαδῶν. On the name see note on T 1, 3 above. 'Απολλόδωρος
Πρασύλλου of Isaeus 7 introduced his adopted son to his phratry
uniquely in our evidence not at the Apatouria, but at the Apollonian
festival, Thargelia (see p. 66), which was celebrated on the seventh day
of the seventh month. Since this inscription shows that the Achniadai
had a cult of Apollo "of the Seventh" (Hebdomeios), Wilamowitz 1893,
2,268, n. 10, suggested that the Achniadai was Apollodoros' phratry.
Apollo was commonly associated with phratries, but this is the only
known case of a cult of Apollo Hebdomeios. The suggestion gains a
measure of support from Apollodoros' deme, now attested as Leukonoion
(*SEG* 27.13). Achniadai seems to have had a center in southern Attica
at Kephale (findspots of T 1 and T 2; for associations of phratries with
particular localities see p. 12 with n. 42). The location of Leukonoion
is uncertain, but may have been in this area. *IG* 2².1582, 134 concerns
property at Anaphlystos (southwest of Kephale) bounded by a road to
ΛΕΥΚΟΟΙΟΝ. The reading, and its interpretation as a reference to
Leukonoion, is uncertain (see Traill 1986, 130 n. 22), but attractive (cf.
Lewis 1983, 435, who points out the weakness of the traditional location
at Peristeri, northwest of the city).

 It is possible that the phratry of Isaeus 7, and therefore also the
Achniadai, was a genos as well as a phratry (see p. 67).

Date

Earlier fourth century (orthography).

Location

Area of demes of Kephale (from findspots of both inscriptions at Keratea, cf. Traill 1986, 133) and probably Leukonoion (from demotic of Apollodoros in Isaeus 7, see above). See also T 21.

T 3 Demontionidai/Dekeleieis

Three decrees inscribed on both sides of a marble stele from the royal estate at Tatoi (ancient Dekeleia). Stoichedon 25, lines 2–12 (violated by reinscription of 2); stoichedon 30, lines 13–113 with exceptions; non-stoichedon, lines 114–26. I give here only bibliography relevant to the text. For a selection of other works see p. 95, n. 2. Face A: Koumanoudes 1883, 69–76; *IG* 2.2, 841b (Köhler); Milchhöfer 1887, 320 n. 428. Face B: Pantazides in "Εθημερίζ" (a local newspaper), 1–13 September 1888; Lolling 1888, 159–63. Faces A and B: Pantazides 1888, 1–20; Tarbell 1886–90, 170–88 (= 1889, 135–53); Paton 1890, 314–18; Tarbell 1890, 318–20; Sauppe 1890; Paton 1891, 221–23; *IG* 2.5, 841b (Köhler); *IG* 2².1237; Guarducci 1937, no. 1; Arvanitopoulou 1958; 1959; Hedrick 1990 (with photographs, and at pp. 1–3 account of the history of the inscription). Text, Hedrick 1990.

Face A

  Διὸς Φρατρίο
  ἱερεὺς ⟦ ⟦ θεόδωρος ⟧ Εὐφα⟦ντίδ⟧ο ν ν⟧ ἀν
  έγραψε καὶ ἔστησε τὴν στήλην. ν
  ἱερεώσυνα τῶι ἱερεῖ διδόναι τ
5 άδε· ἀπὸ τὸ μείο κωλῆν, πλευρόν, ὀ̂
  ς, ἀργυρίο ΙΙΙ. ν ἀπὸ τὸ κορείο κωλῆ
  ν, πλευρόν, ὀ̂ς, ἐλατῆρα χοινικια
  ῖον, οἴνο ἡμίχον, ἀργυρίο Ι. ν ν ν ν
  τάδε ἔδοξεν τοῖς φράτερσι ἐπὶ
10 Φορμίωνος ἄρχοντος ᾿Αθηναίοι
  ς, φρατριαρχῶντος δὲ Παντακλέ
  ος ἐξ Οἴο. *vacant 18*
  ῾Ιεροκλῆς εἶπε· ὁπόσοι μήπω διεδικάσ
  θησαν κατὰ τὸν νόμον τὸν Δημοτιωνιδ
15 ῶν, διαδικάσαι περὶ αὐτῶν τὸς φράτερ
  ας αὐτίκα μάλα, ὑποσχομένος πρὸς τὸ Δ
  ιὸς τὸ Φρατρίο, φέροντας τὴν ψῆφον ἀπ
  ὸ τὸ βωμὸ. ὃς δ᾿ ἂν δόξηι μὴ ὢν φράτηρ ἐσα
  χθῆναι, ἐξαλειψάτω τὸ ὄνομα αὐτὸ ὁ ἱερ
20 εὺς καὶ ὁ φρατρίαρχος ἐκ τὸ γραμματεί
  ο τὸ ἐν Δημοτιωνιδῶν καὶ τὸ ἀντιγράφ
  ο. ὁ δὲ ἐσαγαγὼν τὸν ἀποδικασθέντα ὀφε

ιλέτο ἑκατὸν δραχμὰς ἱερὰς τῶι Διὶ τ
ῶι Φρατρίωι· ἐσπράττεν δὲ τὸ ἀργύριο
25 ν τοῦτο τὸν ἱερέα καὶ τὸν φρατρίαρχο
ν, ἢ αὐτὸς ὀφείλεν. τὴν δὲ διαδικασίαν
τὸ λοιπὸν ἐ̃ναι τῶι ὑστέρωι ἔτει ἢ ὦι ἂ
ν τὸ κόρεον θύσηι, τῆι Κορεώτιδι Ἀπατ
ορίων· φέρεν δὲ τὴν ψῆφον ἀπὸ τὸ Βωμὸ. ἐ
30 ἂν δέ τις βόληται ἐφεῖναι ἐς Δημοτιων
ίδας ὧν ἂν ἀποψηφίσωνται, ἐξεῖναι αὐ
τῶι· ἑλέσθαι δὲ ἐπ’ αὐτοῖς συνηγόρος τ
ὸν Δεκελειῶν οἶκον πέντε ἄνδρας ὑπὲ
ρ τριάκοντα ἔτη γεγονότας, τούτος δὲ
35 ἐξορκωσάτω ὁ φρατρίαρχος καὶ ὁ ἱερε
ὺς συνηγορήσεν τὰ δικαιότατα καὶ ὁκ
ἐάσεν ὀδένα μὴ ὄντα φράτερα φρατρίζ
εν. ὅτο δ’ ἂν τῶν ἐφέντων ἀποψηφίσωντα
ι Δημοτιωνίδαι, ὀφειλέτω χιλίας δρα
40 χμὰς ἱερὰς τῶι Διὶ τῶι Φρατρίωι, ἐσπρ
αττέτω δὲ τὸ ἀργύριον τοῦτο ὁ ἱερεὺς
τὸ Δεκελειῶν οἴκο, ἢ αὐτὸς ὀφειλέτω. ἐ
ξεῖναι δὲ καὶ ἄλλωι τῶι βολομένωι τῶ
ν φρατέρων ἐσπράττεν τῶι κοινῶι. ταῦ
45 [τ]α δ’ ἐ̃ναι ἀπὸ Φορμίωνος ἄρχοντος. ἐπι
ψηφίζεν δὲ τὸν φρατρίαρχον περὶ ὧν ἂ
ν ⟦διαδικά⟧ζεν δέηι κατὰ τὸν ἐνιαυτὸν
ἕκαστον. ἐὰν δὲ μὴ ἐπιψηφίσηι, ὀφελέτ
ω πεντακοσία[ς] δραχμὰς ἱερὰς τῶι Διὶ
50 [τ]ῶι Φρατρίω[ι. ἐ]σπράττεν δὲ τὸν ἱερέα
[κ]αὶ ἄλλο[ν τὸν βο]λόμενον τὸ ἀργύριον
τọῦτ[ο τῶι κοινῶι.] τὸ δὲ λοιπὸν ἄγεν τὰ
[μεῖα καὶ τὰ κόρει]α̣ ἐς Δεκέλειαν ἐπὶ τ
[ὸν βωμόν. ἐὰν δὲ μὴ θ]ύσηι ἐπὶ τὸ βωμὸ, ὀφ
55 [ειλέτω πεντήκοντ]α δραχμὰς ἱερὰς τῶ
[ι Διὶ τῶι Φρατρίωι, ἐ]σ̣πραττέτω δὲ ὁ ἱερ
[εύς τὸ ἀργύριον τοῦτο ἢ αὐτὸς ὀφειλέ
[τω..............²⁸..............]

‒ ‒ ‒ ‒ ‒ ‒ ‒ ‒ ‒ ‒ ‒ ‒ ‒ ‒ ‒ ‒ ‒ ‒

Face B

ἐὰν δέ τι τούτων διακωλύηι, ὅποι ἂν ὁ ἱ

60 ερεὺς προγράφηι, ἐνθαῦθα ἄγεν τὰ μεῖ
    α καὶ τὰ κόρεια. προγράφεν δὲ προπέμπ
    τα τῆς Δορπίας ἐν πινακίωι λελευκωμ
    ένωι μὴ 'λατον ἢ σπιθαμιαίωι ὅπο ἂν Δ
    εκελειῆς προσφοιτῶσιν ἐν ἄστει. τὸ δ
65 ὲ ψήφισμα τόδε καὶ τὰ ἱερεώσυνα ἀναγ
    ράψαι τὸν ἱερέα ἐν στήληι λιθίνηι πρ
    όσθεν τὸ βωμὸ Δεκελειᾶσιν τέλεσι το
    ῖς ἑαυτῶ. Νικόδημος εἶπε· τὰ μὲν ἄλλα κατ
    ⟦ ὰ τὰ πρότερα ψηφίσματα, ἃ κεῖται περὶ τ ⟧
70 ⟦ ἐς εἰσαγωγῆς τῶν παίδων καὶ τῆς διαδ ⟧
    ⟦ ικασίας. τὸς δὲ μάρτυρας τρες, ὃς εἴρη ⟧
    ⟦ ται ἐπὶ τῆι ἀνακρίσει παρέχεσθαι ἐκ τ ⟧
    ⟦ ῶν ἑαυτῶ θιασωτῶν μαρτυρ̃ντας τὰ ὑπερωτώμε(να) ⟧
    καὶ ἐπομνύντας τὸν Δία τὸν Φράτριον.
75 μαρτυρὲν δὲ τὸς μάρτυρας καὶ ἐπομνύ
    ναι ἐχομένος τὸ βωμ̃. ἐὰν δὲ μὴ ὦσι ἐν τ
    ῶ⟨ι⟩ θιάσωι τότωι τοσοτοι τὸν ἀριθμόν, ἐ
    κ τῶν ἄλλων φρατέρων παρεχέσθω. ὅταν
    δὲ ἦι ἡ διαδικασία, ὁ φρατρίαρχος μὴ π
80 ρότερον διδότω τὴν ψῆφον περὶ τῶν παί
    δων τοῖς ἅπασι φράτερσι, πρὶν ἂν οἱ αὐ
    τὸ τὸ εἰσαγομένο θιασῶται κρύβδην ἀ
    πὸ τὸ βωμὸ φέροντες τὴν ψῆφον διαψηφ
    ίσωνται. καὶ τὰς ψήφος τὰς τότων ἐναν
85 τίον τῶν ἁπάντων φρατέρων τῶν παρόν
    των ἐν τῆι ἀγορᾶι ὁ φρατρίαρχος διαρ
    ιθμησάτω καὶ ἀναγορευέτω ὁπότερ' ἂν
    ψηφίσωνται. ἐὰν δὲ ψηφισαμένων τῶν θ
    ιασωτῶν ἐναι αὐτοῖς φράτερα οἱ ἄλλο
90 ι φράτερες ἀποψηφίσωνται, ὀφειλόντ
    ων ἑκατὸν δραχμὰς ἱερὰς τῶι Διὶ τῶι Φ
    ρατρίωι οἱ θιασῶται, πλὴν ὅσοι ἂν τῶν
    θιασωτῶν κατήγοροι ἢ ἐναντιόμενοι
    φαίνωνται ἐν τῆι διαδικασίαι. ἐὰν δὲ
95 ἀποψηφίσωνται οἱ θιασῶται, ὁ δὲ εἰσά
    γων ἐφῆι εἰς τὸς ἅπαντας, τοῖς δὲ ἅπασ
    ι δόξει ἐναι φράτηρ, ἐνγραφέσθω εἰς τ
    ὰ κοινὰ γραμματεῖα. ἐὰν δὲ ἀποψηφίσω

νται οἱ ἅπαντες, ὀφειλέτω ἑκατὸν δρα
100 χμὰς ἱερὰς τῶι Διὶ τῶι Φρατρίωι. ἐὰν δὲ
ἀποψηφισαμένων τῶν θιασωτῶν μὴ ἐφῆ
ι εἰς τὸς ἅπαντας, κυρία ἔστω ἡ ἀποψήφ
ισις ἡ τῶν θιασωτῶν. οἱ δὲ θιασῶται με
τὰ τῶν ἄλλων φρατέρων μὴ φερόντων τὴν
105 ψῆφον περὶ τῶν παίδων τῶν ἐκ τὸ θιάσο
τὸ ἑαυτῶν. τὸ δὲ ψήφισμα τόδε προσαναγ
ραψάτω ὁ ἱερεὺς εἰς τὴν στήλην τὴν λι
θίνην. ὅρκος μαρτύρων ἐπὶ τῆι εἰσαγω
γεῖ τῶν παίδων· μαρτυρῶ ὃν εἰσάγει ἑα
110 υτῶι ὑὸν ἔναι τὸτον γνήσιον ἐγ γαμετ
ῆς· ἀληθῆ ταῦτα νὴ τὸν Δία τὸν Φράτριο
ν· εὐορκὸ⟨ν⟩τι μέν μοι πολλὰ καὶ ἀγαθά ἐν
⟦αι, εἰ δ᾽⟧ ἐπιορκοίην, τἀναντία. *vac. 7*
Μενέξενος εἶπεν· δεδόχθαι τοῖς φράτερσι περὶ
115 τῆς εἰσαγωγῆς τῶμ παίδων τὰ μὲν ἄλλα κα
τὰ τὰ πρότερα ψηφίσματα, ὅπως δ᾽ ἂν εἰδῶσι οἱ
φράτερες τοὺς μέλλοντας εἰσάγεσθαι, ἀπο
γράφεσθαι τῶι πρώτωι ἔτει ἢ ὧι ἂν τὸ κούρεο
ν ἄγει τὸ ὄνομα πατρόθεγ καὶ τὸ δήμου καὶ τῆ
120 ς μητρὸς πατρόθεν καὶ τοῦ [δ]ήμου πρὸς τὸν
φρατρίαρχον, τὸν δὲ φρατρία[ρχον ἀπογραψ]
αμένων ἀναγράψαντα ἐκ[τιθέναι ὅπου ἂν Δεκ]
ελέες προσφοιτῶσι, ἐκτιθ[έναι δὲ καὶ τὸν ἱερέα]
ἀναγράψαντα ἐν σανιδ[ίωι λευκῶι ἐν τῶι ἱερ]
125 ῶι τῆς Λητοῦς. τὸ δὲ φρ[ατερικὸν ψήφισμα ἀναγρ]
[άψαι εἰς τὴν σ]τήλην [τὴν λιθίνην τὸν ἱερέα- - -]

– –

Translation

Face A

Sacred to Zeus Phratrios. The priest Theodoros son of Euphantides
inscribed and set up the stele. The following priestly dues to be given
to the priest: (5) from the meion a thigh, a rib, an ear, three obols of
money. From the koureion a thigh, a rib, an ear, a cake weighing one
choinix, one-half-chous of wine, one drachma of money. The phrateres

decided as follows (10) in the archonship of Phormio (396/5), in the phratriarchy of Pantakles of Oion.

Hierokles proposed: as many as have not yet been scrutinized according to the law of the Demotionidai (15) the phrateres are to hold a scrutiny of them immediately, having sworn by Zeus Phratrios, carrying the vote from the altar. Whoever should appear to have been introduced, not being a phrater, the priest (20) and the phratriarch shall erase his name from the register in the keeping of the Demotionidai and the copy. And he who introduced the rejected member shall pay one hundred drachmas sacred to Zeus Phratrios; the priest and the phratriarch shall collect this money (26) or pay it themselves.

In future, the scrutiny is to be in the year following that in which the koureion is sacrificed, on Koureotis during the Apatouria; carrying the vote from the altar (30). If anyone who has been rejected in the vote should wish to appeal to the Demotionidai, he may do so; but the Dekeleian House is to elect for them [sc. the Demotionidai; or possibly "against" the appellants] five advocates over thirty years of age. These (35) are to be sworn by the phratriarch and the priest to speak what is most right and to prevent anyone who is not a phrater from taking part in the phratry. If the Demotionidai reject an appellant, he shall pay one thousand drachmas (40) sacred to Zeus Phratrios. The priest of the Dekeleian House shall collect this money, or pay it himself, but anyone else of the phrateres may also collect the money for the common treasury. These (45) things are to come into effect from the archonship of Phormio. The phratriarch is to take the vote on those who have to be scrutinized each year. If he should not take the vote, he shall pay five hundred drachmas sacred to Zeus (50) Phratrios. The priest and anyone else who wishes is to collect this money (for the common treasury). In future (meia and kourei)a are to be taken to Dekeleia to (the altar. If he [i.e., the phratriarch]) should not sacrifice at the altar, (55) he shall pay (fift)y drachmas sacred to (Zeus Phratrios). The priest shall collect (this money) or pay it himself... [probably passage referring to circumstances which might require sacrifices to be held elsewhere than at Dekeleia].

Face B

... but if any of those things should prevent it, wherever the (60) priest gives notice, there meia and koureia are to be taken. He is to give notice five days before Dorpia on a whitened board not less than one span across at whatever place the Dekeleieis frequent in the city. (65) The priest is to inscribe the decree and the priestly dues on a stone stele in front of the altar at Dekeleia at his own expense.

Nikodemos proposed: In other respects to concur with the previous decrees passed about (70) the introduction of children and the scrutiny. But the three witnesses required for the preliminary scrutiny are to be provided from his own thiasotai, to give evidence on the questions asked and to take the oath by Zeus Phratrios. (75) The witnesses are to give evidence and to take the oath holding the altar. If, however, there are not as many as this in the thiasos, they shall be provided from the other phrateres. When the scrutiny takes place, the phratriarch shall not (80) put the vote about the children to the whole phratry before the introducer's own thiasotai have voted secretly, carrying the votes from the altar. (84) And the phratriarch shall count their votes before all the phrateres present and announce which way they have voted. If the thiasotai have voted for admission to the phratry and the other (90) phrateres vote against, the thiasotai shall pay one hundred drachmas sacred to Zeus Phratrios, except those of the thiasotai who have spoken against admission or have been shown in the scrutiny to be opposed to it. If (95) the thiasotai vote against admission, and the introducer appeals to the whole phratry, and it decides in favor of admission to the phratry, the name shall be inscribed in the common registers. But if the whole phratry votes against, the introducer shall pay one hundred drachmas (100) sacred to Zeus Phratrios. If the thiasotai vote against and he does not appeal to the whole phratry, the negative vote of the thiasotai shall stand. The thiasotai shall not vote with the other phrateres (105) about the children from their own thiasos. The priest shall inscribe this decree also on the stone stele. The oath of the witnesses at the introduction of the children shall be, "I give evidence that this child he is introducing (110) is his own legitimate son born of his wedded wife; this is the truth by Zeus Phratrios; may I enjoy many blessings if my oath is true, but the opposite if my oath is false."

Menexenos proposed: the phrateres decided (115) to concur with the previous decrees about the introduction of children, but so that the phrateres may know who are going to be introduced, a note is to be given to the phratriarch in the first year following that in which koureion is sacrificed of the name, patronymic and deme of the candidate and of his mother, her father's name, and deme. The phratriarch is to write the details up and dis(play them at whatever place the Dek)eleieis frequent, and (the priest) is to write them up on a (white) board and display them (in the temp)le (125) of Leto. (The priest is to inscribe the phratry's decree on a stone) stele . . .

Notes

This document is discussed in chapter 3. Of the five phratry members mentioned, three (Pantakles the phratriarch, and Hierokles and Menexenos, proposers of the first and third decrees, respectively) are not otherwise known. Θεόδωρος Εὐφαντίδου in 2, probably priest at the time Menexenos' (not Hierokles') decree was passed, i.e., ca. 370–50 (see further below), seems likely to be the father of ᾽Εκφαν[τί]δης Θεοδώρου Δεκελ[ε(ιεύς)], lessee of a mine in the second half of the fourth century (Crosby 1950, 267–69, no. 21, 11–12. Note also *IG* 2².1604, 81 with Davies 1971, no. 6029; *IG* 2².1927, 93–98; *IG* 2².2725). The proposer of the second decree, Nikodemos, probably belongs to the wealthy Dekeleian family whose burial ground and grave monuments are known (*PA* 10869, 10870; for stemma see *PA* 14017 and *IG* 2².5983). The monument to the probable parents of Nikodemos, Phanias and Philomene, has been dated on stylistic grounds to the fifth century; those of Nikodemos and his wife, daughter of an Aeschines of Phegous, and children, Phanodemos, Anenkletos, and Philoumene, to ca. 380–70 (see Willemsen 1974; cf. Hedrick 1990, 55–56).

Hedrick 1984 (now published at 1990, 11–12, 21–25) was the first to note signs of double erasure in the priest's name in 2. The first name [. . ¹⁷ . .] was apparently completely erased, but some letters of the second [.⁶.]ΕΥΦΑ[. . . .]Oᵛᵛ, or [. .⁶. .]ΕΥΦΑ[. . . .]ᵛᵛᵛ seem to have been reused in the inscription of the third, ΘΕΟΔΩΡΟΣ ΕΥΦΑΝΤΙΔΟ. The third name was in a different hand from the first two. (Hedrick suggests Εὐφά[νους] for the patronymic of the second priest. Possible, but one might have expected the ν to have been retained by the inscriber of the third name.) His interpretation, that the names were of different priests in office when each of the decrees was inscribed, though not certain— it is possible that the hand that inscribed the third name was not that which inscribed Menexenos' decree; see Hedrick 1990, 23–24—is attractive. The reuse of parts of names would be consistent with a hereditary priesthood, and the resulting date for Theodoros (see below) is consistent with that for his probable son, Ekphantides (see above).

Date

Hierokles' decree was passed in the archonship of Phormio, 396/5 (10) (cf. p. 97, n. 5). Nikodemos' decree followed a little later, though we cannot say exactly how much. On the one hand, it was inscribed by the same hand as Hierokles' decree, and the fact that it seems to envisage that there may be less than three in a thiasos (77) suggests that it was passed in the aftermath of the Peloponnesian War (cf. p. 133). On the other hand, Hedrick 1990 has argued persuasively that the priest who had the second decree inscribed was different from the one responsible for the first (see above; at 1990, 55, he also notes a subtle difference in the stoichedon pattern between Hierokles' decree and Nikodemos'). Moreover the general reference to previous decrees about the introduction of children at the start of Nikodemos' motion, rather than specifically to Hierokles' decree, perhaps suggests a significant gap; and I have suggested at p. 136 that the Dekeleieis may have undergone some change in status vis-à-vis the Demotionidai in this period between the two decrees. The stylistic dating of the family's grave monuments (see above) is too imprecise to help us.

Menexenos' decree, inscribed in a later, sloppier hand, uses -ου rather than the -ο of the earlier hand, a form which is not common before 360 (Threatte 1980, 241–58; cf. Hedrick 1990, 59). The probable son of the priest in office at the time the decree was passed was lessee of a mine in the second half of the fourth century (see above). The continuity of sense between this decree and Nikodemos' decree suggests that there is unlikely to have been a very long gap between the two: ca. 370–350 should be about right.

Location

It is apparent from the name of the group, the findspot of the inscription, the probable demotics of three of the members (Nikodemos and Theodoros from Dekeleia, Pantakles from Oion Dekeleikon), and references to Dekeleia in the decrees, that the group passing these decrees, which I have referred to as the Demotionidai/Dekeleieis (for the controversy surrounding the identity of the group see chapter 3) was based at Dekeleia. For the possibility that there was another Demotionidai phratry center elsewhere (? Kydantidai), see p. 113 with n. 64. Note also Themelis 1971, 32 no. 2, an earlier fifth-century marker, from Tatoi, of the Komadai (HOPOΣ/ TON KO/MAΔON/ HIEPON). Whether this was a genos or a phratry and how, if at all, it related to the Demotionidai/ Dekeleieis, we do not know. It is not impossible, however, that the Komadai were a genos within the Demotionidai.

T 4 Dekeleieis

Decree, from royal estate at Tatoi (ancient Dekeleia). All texts based on a transcript by Münter, published by Köhler in *IG* 2. Non-stoichedon. *IG* 2.5, 633b; *IG* 2².1242; Guarducci 1937, no. 1 *bis;* Sokolowski 1962, no. 125 (= *SEG* 21.528). Text based on Münter's transcript as published in *IG* 2.

> Θεόδοτο[ς] εἶπεν· ὅπ[ως ? - - - - -
> Λητοῖ «ὠ»ς κάλλιστ«α» [- - - - - - κ
> ατὰ τὰ «π»ά«τ» ρια ἐπιδ[- - - - - - ἄ
> νδρας οἵ«τ»ινες συν[- - - - - - πέν
> 5   τε Δεκελεᾶσι οἰκο[ῦντας or ὖσι - - -
> «ἠπέ»μ«πτ»η ?. ἐπειδὰν δὲ [- - - - -
> αντ[..]σ«α»ν σφᾶς αὐτὸς [- - - - τοὺς ἱ
> εροπο«ι»οὺς νέμειν τ[- - - - - -
> ν τῆς Ἡγεμόνος σχ«α»[δόνες ? - - -
> 10   ελόντας τὰ γέρα[- - - - - -

1-2. ὅπ[ως ἂν τὰ ἱερὰ - - συντε]λῆτ«α»ι «ὠ»ς κάλλιστ«α» Köhler, followed by Kirchner. [..τὰ ἱερὰ συντε]λῆτ«α»ι κτλ. Sokolowksi. ΛΗΤΟΙΛΣΚΑΛΛΙΣΤΗ Münter. 2-3. κ]ατὰ τὰ «π»ά«τ»ρια ἐπιδ[- (or ἐπὶ Δ [-?) Köhler, followed by Kirchner. [καὶ τἄλλα γίνηται κ]ατὰ τὰ πάτρια, ἐπι«χ»[ειροτονῆσαι Sokolowski. ΑΤΑΤΑΥΑΥΡΙΑΕΠΙΔ Münter. 3-4. ἑλέσθαι ἄ]νδρας οἵ«τ»ινες συν[επιμελήσονται—Köhler, followed by Kirchner. δέκα ἄ]νδρας οἵ«τ»ινες συν[διεξάξουσι πάντα, Sokolowski. ΟΙΡΙΝΕΣ Münter. 4-5. πέν]τε Δεκελεᾶσι οἰκο[ῦντας Köhler, followed by Kirchner. οἰκο[ῦντας, πέντε δὲ ἐν—Sokolowski. 6. ΝΥΓΜΥΡΗ ἐπειδὰν δὲ [—Münter/Köhler, followed by Kirchner. [ἀποδειχθῶσι–Sokolowski. ΔF Ε Münter. 6-7. -ν σφᾶς αὐτούς Köhler. αντ..σ«α»ν σφᾶς αὐτο[ὺς Kirchner. Sokolowski suggested ὁρκωσ]/ άντ[ω]σαν. ΑΝΤ..ΣΛΝΣΦΑΣΑΥΤΟΣ Münter. 7-8. Köhler, followed by Kirchner. τοὺς δὲ ἱ] Sokolowksi. ΕΡΟΠΟΓΟΥΣ Münter. 8-9. τ[ὰ κρέα τοῖς ὀργεῶσι]ν Sokolowski. 9. ν τῆς Ἡγέμονος (?) σχυ[–Münter/ Köhler, followed by Kirchner. «ἄ»χ«ρ»[ι μνᾶς Sokolowski tentatively. 9-10. ελοντας τὰ γέρ[α Köhler, followed by Kirchner. τῆι ἱερείαι ἀφ]ελόντας τὰ γέρα [τὰ νομιζόμενα—Sokolowski. ΓΕΡΑ Münter.

Translation

Theodotos proposed: in order that . . . Leto as finely as possible . . . according to ancestral custom . . . men, who (together) . . . five (5) who live at Dekeleia . . . the fifth?. But whenever . . . one another . . . the hieropoioi distribute . . . (the honeycomb?) of (Artemis) the (Bee-)Leader. . . . (10) taking the perquisites.

Notes

The original text consisted of a transcript by Münter of a stone from the royal villa at Tatoi. It was obtained by Köhler via Postolakkas and published by him, together with his own suggested restorations, in 1895 as *IG* 2.5, 633b. Köhler's version was included by Kirchner in *IG* 2² almost unchanged. Sokolowski published an adventurous reconstruction in 1962. While most of the letters of Münter's transcript appear accurate, errors are frequent enough to make restoration hazardous, particularly at the start of 6 and 7 where the stone was presumably damaged. This, together with the fragmentary state of the text, makes any confident reconstruction of text not on the stone impossible. I have therefore adopted a conservative approach with respect to unrecorded text and concentrated on the preserved passages. 《》 indicates letters restored other than as recorded by Münter.

2-3. Λητοῖ 《ώ》ς κάλλιστ《α》. Since the Dekeleieis (cf. 5) are attested in association with a sanctuary of Leto at T 3, 125 (details of candidates for phratry membership required to be posted there), and given the religious content of the text (in particular the implications of Ἡγεμόνος, see further below), we should take the first five letters of 2 at face value and read the name of that deity in the dative. The cult of Leto was apparently rare in Attica, see note to lines 8-10 below. I would not otherwise question the sense of the restorations of previous editors. Theodotos is making provision for some aspect of the local cult of Leto to be carried out as finely as possible, and probably, if there was no break of sense in the last part of 2, according to ancestral custom (3).

4-5. οἰκο[ῦντας or ῦσι.. Given συν[- in 4, it cannot be certain that we need the accusative rather than the dative. I agree with previous editors that συν[- (as ἐπιδ[- in 3) is likely to be the start of a verb, but the possibilities are numerous. They include Sokolowski's συν[διεξ-άξουσι and Köhler's συν[επιμελήσονται.

6. «ἠπέ»μ«πτ»η ? Sokolowski thought Münter's reading ΝΥΓΜΥΡΗ contained the name of a place. This cannot be ruled out, but other possibilities emerge if one considers possible misreadings of letters elsewhere in Münter's transcription. He has Υ for Π and Τ in 3, and possibly for Α in 9. Γ is Ι in 8. Π or Ε (cf. F for Ε in 6) must also be possible. Μ he appears normally to get right. Ρ is Τ in 4 and Η is probably Α in 2 and 7. Ν could easily be Η. On this basis we might have «ἠ πέ»μ«πτ»η (or «πέ»μ«πτ»α or «πε»μ«πτ»η, sc. ἡμέρᾳ ?), cf. πέντε in 3-4. Alternatively we might plausibly take Γ and Μ for Α and read ν τὰ αὐτα or ν τὰ αὐτα, the sense being perhaps "(come to)... the same (decision). But whenever...(they disagree?) with one another..."

7. αντ[..]σ«α»ν. This should be an aorist third person plural, but whether Sokolowski has picked the right one in ὁρκωσ]άντ[ω]σαν is impossible to say.

8-10. We have in these lines hieropoioi distributing something (the likely sense of νέμειν), mention of a leader, apparently a feminine one (misreading Α for Η in τῆς is a possibility [see note on 6 above], but, since good sense can be made of the feminine singular, not an attractive one here), and persons, very possibly the same hieropoioi, taking perquisites. Who or what is the ἡγεμών in 9? Previous editors have thought in terms of the epithet of a deity. Artemis is most likely (see e.g., *IG* 2².5012 [cf. T 28] for this designation in Attica. Aphrodite could also bear this title, see Plut. *Thes.* 18.3, *IG* 2².2798. Hegemone was also one of the Graces, see Paus. 9.35.2). This should be right, particularly given the close links between the cults of Leto (cf. 2) and her daughter (Wernicke 1895, cols. 1366-67. Note that Leto and Artemis are conjoined in what is apparently the only other evidence for the cult of Leto in Attica, *IG* 2².5156 [cf. Hedrick 1990, 60], which shows that a seat in the theater of Dionysus was reserved for the priestess of the two deities.) I suggest σχ «α»[δόνες for Münter's σχυ[- (for his misreading of letters as Υ see note on 6 above). For σχαδών meaning bee or wasp larva or honey cell in the singular, and honeycomb in the plural, see, e.g., Aristophanes fr. 333K-A (= fr. 324 Edm.), 6, and other texts cited by *LSJ*. Bees and honey were particularly associated with Artemis (see, e.g., Euripides *Hip.* 77; Ar. *Frogs* 1274; cf. also Pindar fr. 123; Pestalozza 1951, esp. 240–41). ἡγεμών, whether masculine or feminine, can also mean queen-bee (e.g., Aristotle *Hist. Anim.* 5.553a25, 629a3; Xen. *Oec.* 7.32, cf. 38) and may have this connotation here. For the bee as symbol of Artemis on Ephesian coins see *Syll. Num. Gr.* 1946, 206ff. In other words what we have here, I suggest, is hieropoioi distributing and/or taking their share in perquisites of "honeycomb of Artemis the (Bee-)Leader." For a close parallel in several respects, cf. *IG* 2².47, 35–37, an early-fourth-century decree of the Demos concerning the cult of Asklepios: νέμεν δὲ τὰ/ [κρέ]α τὸ μὲν ἡγεμόνος βοὸς ("the leader of the herd") τοῖς πρυτάνεσιν/ [καὶ τ]οῖς ἐννέ᾽ ἄρχοσιν κα[ὶ] τ[οῖ]ς ἱ[ε]ροποιοῖς. . . . For honey in a sacrificial context at Athens, cf. *IG* 1³.232, 61; Oliver 1935, 21, 3. Sokolowski's ⟪ἅ⟫χ⟪ρ⟫[ι μνᾶς has less to recommend it (he compares *IG* 1³.137, 8; [cf. also *IG* 1³.244, A 4], and his own no. 93) and involves the supposition that two (rather than one) of Münter's letter are wrong.

Identity of Group

Köhler thought this should be a document of a phratry or a genos, and not of the deme Dekeleia (Kirchner slightly misrepresents him ad *IG* 2².1242: "Koe. haec ad decretum phratriae pertinere arbitratur"), and suggested it would have been set up in the same place as T 3, the decrees of the House/phratry of the Dekeleieis. Sokolowski, without argument, attributed it to a group of orgeones of Artemis Hegemon. On the basis of current evidence, the latter view can be rejected immediately, not because of any intrinsic implausibility, but because we know of no such group of orgeones at Dekeleia or, indeed, anywhere else, while we do know of two Dekeleian groups, either of which could be responsible for the decree: the deme Dekeleia and the House/phratry of the Dekeleieis. Deciding between these two is more tricky.

The extent of the religious activities of the demes was perhaps not fully appreciated in Köhler's time, but that this document may be a deme decree cannot be ruled out today. We now have abundant evidence that demes made religious regulations involving local cults of deities, hieropoioi, distributions of sacrificial food, and so on, as in this decree (see *IG* 1.³ 244, 245, 250, 256; *IG* 2².1195, 1211, 1213; Vanderpool 1970, 48). In contrast, with the possible exception of the very fragmentary

T 20 (q.v.), we have no other secure case of an Attic phratry passing a regulation of this sort (cf. pp. 219–20). This might appear at first a prima facie argument for attributing this document to the deme; but if the hypothesis about the relationship between Demotionidai and Dekeleieis in chapter 3 is correct, the latter will have been, in 400 if not in 350, a subgroup of a phratry rather than an independent phratry; and there is ample evidence for cult activities of phratry subgroups. Moreover, extremely fragmentary though it is, there are hints that this decree was passed by the group that was responsible for T 3. Both inscriptions appear to have been found in the area of the royal palace at Tatoi and both were associated with a local cult/sanctuary of Leto. Then there is the concern of the group of T 4 with ancestral custom, certainly not inconsistent with its being a deme, but particularly appropriate for an organization, such as the House of the Dekeleieis, with a longer and notable history (cf. pp. 112–14). Finally, T 4 mentions five persons who live at Dekeleia. The House of the Dekeleieis in T 3 was very conscious of distinctions between persons and activities connected with Dekeleia and those not and it is attractive to see that same consciousness underlying this provision.

It is unfortunate that we have no documents of the deme Dekeleia that might have counteracted, or confirmed, these apparent connections, but on present evidence I conclude that the balance of probability lies with this document's being a decree of the House/phratry of the Dekeleieis.

The very fragmentary ? mid-third-century (Kirchner) *IG* 2². 1295 (= *IG* 2.5, 633c), | ΘΥΣ-/-ΕΙΛΑ-/-ΟΚΟΙΝ-/-ΕΣΤΕ-/-ΜΜΑ-, also from the royal estate at Tatoi, may also belong to the House/phratry of the Dekeleieis. (For κοινόν used commonly of phratries and their subgroups cf. p. 195 n. 33.)

Date

?Third century (Kirchner), late fourth–early third centuries (Guarducci). N.B. possibly -o- for -ου- in 7. It is likely, though not certain, that this decree is later than the other three decrees of the House of the Dekeleieis, T 3 (396–ca. 370/50).

Location

See on T 3.

T 5 Dyaleis

Decree, on marble stele from Merenda (ancient Myrrhinous). Now E.M.
7841. Stoichedon (except line 42).
Koumanoudes 1873, 484–86; *IG* 2.600; *IG* 2².1241; Schulthess 1932
col. 2102; Wilhelm 1935, 200–203; Guarducci 1937, no. 6; Behrend 1970,
91–95; Harrison 1968–71 2, 244–47; Hedrick 1984, T 5. In advance of
full publication by Hedrick of his new text, based on the first reexamination of the stone since Koumanoudes, the text given here is based on
that in Hedrick 1984. Registered in the Apparatus are only points on
which he indicates that his reading differs from *IG* 2² as amended by
Wilhelm.

[. . . .]αρχος εἶπεν· δεδόχθαι Δυα[λεῦσιν]
μισθῶσαι τὸ χωρίον τὸ Μυρρινο[ῦντι τὸ]
[κ]οινὸν Δυαλέων Διοδώρωι κατὰ συν[θήκ]
[α]ς τάσδε· κατὰ τάδε ἐμίσθωσαν τὸ χωρί[ο]
5 γ τὸ Μυρρινοῦντι ο[ἱ] φρατρίαρχοι Κα[λλ]
ικ⟨λῆ⟩ς ⟨Ἀ⟩ριστείδου Μυρρινούσιος κα[ὶ Δ]
ιοπεί⟨θη⟩ς Διοφ⟨ά⟩ντου Μυρρινούσιος [κα]
ὶ τὸ κοινὸν Δυαλέων τ⟨ὴ⟩ν Σακκνὴν καλ[ου]
μένην ἔτη δέκα, ν ν ὧι γείτων βωρρᾶθεν κ
10 [ῆ]πος, νοτόθεν Ὀλυμπιοδώρου χωρίον, ἠλ
ίου ἀνιόντος ὁδός, δυομένου Ὀλυμπιοδ
ώρου χωρίον, Διοδώρωι Κανθάρ[ο]υ Μυρρι
νουσίωι ⌐Η ν ν τοῦ & ἐνιαυτοῦ ἑκάστου· ἀτ
[ε]λὲς καὶ ἀνεπιτίμητον [τ]ῶν τε ἐγ Διὸ[ς π]
15 [ά]ντων καὶ πολεμίων ε⟨ἰσ⟩βολῆς καὶ φιλί[ο]
υ στρατοπέδου καὶ τελῶν καὶ [ε]ἰσφορᾶς
καὶ τῶν ἄλλων ἁπάντων· ἐπ[ι]σκευάζειν δ
ὲ τὴν οἰκίαν Διόδωρον ΤΛ[..]ΚΜΕΝ[..]Ε[.]Ε
[...] τὰς ἀμπέλους τῶν Δυ[α]λέω[ν] ΚΛΛ[..]ΑΝ
20 [.]εἶναι τοῖς φρατριάρ[χοις] κα[ὶ] σκάψει
[τ]ὰς ἀμπέλους δὶς κατ[ὰ πα]σ[ῶν] τῶν ὡρῶν· σ
[π]έρει δὲ τῆς γῆς σίτωι τ[ὴ]ν ἡμίσειαν, τῆ
ς δὲ ἀργοῦ ὀσπρεύσει ὁπο[σὴν] ἂν βούλητ
αι· ἐργάσεται δὲ καὶ τἄλλ[α] δένδρα τὰ ἥμ
25 ερα. ἀποδιδόναι δὲ τῆς μ[ι]σθώσεως τὴν μ
[ὲ]ν ἡμίσειαν μηνὸς Βοηδρομιῶνος ν ΗΗΗ,

τὴν δ' ἡμίσειαν μηνὸς Ἐλαφηβολιῶνος [ν]
[Η]ΗΗ τοῖς φρατριάρχοι[ς] Δυαλέων τοῖς ἁ
[ε]ὶ φρατριαρχοῦσιν. ἄ[ρ]χει δὲ τῆς μισθώσε
30 ως ὁ ἐπὶ Ἡγεμάχου Μουνιχιών. μὴ ἐξεῖνα
ι δὲ Διοδώρωι κόψαι τῶν δένδρων τῶν ἐκ
τοῦ χωρίου μηθὲν μηδὲ τὴν οἰκίαν καθ[ε]
λεῖν. ἐὰν δὲ μὴ ἀποδιδῶι τὴν μίσθωσιν ἐ
[ν] τοῖς χρόνοις τοῖς γεγραμμένοις ἢ μὴ
35 [ἐ]ργάζηται τὸ χωρίον κατὰ τὰ γεγραμμέ
[ν]α ἐξεῖναι τοῖς φρατριάρχοις καὶ Δυα
[λεῦ]σιν ἐνεχυράζειν πρὸ δίκης καὶ μισ
θῶσαι ἑτέρωι τὸ χωρίον ὧι ἂν βούλ[ω]νται
[ι, κ]αὶ ὑπόδικος ἔστω Διόδωρος ἐάν τι [πρ]
40 [οσ]οφείλει τῆς μισθώσεως ἢ καθέλει τ[ι]
[τ]ῆς οἰκίας ἢ κόψει τι τῶν ἐκ τοῦ χωρίου·
[ἐὰ]ν δὲ βούληται ἐν τοῖς δέκα ἔτεσιν Διόδω
[ρ]ος ἢ οἱ κληρονόμοι αὐτοῦ καταβαλόντ
[ων] Δυαλεῦσιν ⋈ δραχμάς, καὶ ἐάν τιν[α] μί
45 σθωσιν προσοφείλ[ω]σιν ἀποδ[ό]σθ[ω]σα[ν] α
[ὐ]τοῖς οἱ φρατρίαρχοι καὶ Δυαλεῖς τὸ χ
[ωρί]ον κομισάμενοι τὸ ἀργύριον. ἐὰν δ[ὲ]
[μὴ] καταβ[ά]λωσιν τὰς [[⋈]] δραχμάς καὶ ἐάν τι πρ̣οσ[ο]
[φ]είλωσιν τῆς μισθώσεως ἐν τοῖς δέκα ἔ
50 τεσιν, μὴ εἶναι Διοδώρωι μηδὲ τῶν Διοδ
ώρου μηθενὶ συνβόλαι[[ν α]] pròw τὸ χν̣ρ[ίο]
ν τοῦτο μηθέν⟨α⟩ καὶ μισθωσάντωσαν Δυαλ
εῖς ⟨ὧ⟩ι ἂν βούλωνται τοῦ πλείστου. ἀναγ
ράψαι δὲ τὴν μίσθωσιν ταύτην ἐν στήλε
55 ι λιθίνει τοὺς φρατριάρχους καὶ στῆ[σ]
αι [[................²⁹.............]]
[[.............[[ἐπὶ τô χωρίο [[........]]
[[........]]

A sometimes lacks crossbar and Θ the center dot. A, Η, and Ν are sometimes confused. 15. Behrend prefers to retain ἐγβολῆς, as on the stone. 18. ΓΛ[...]⟨ΜΕΝ[..]ΕΜΕ Kirchner. 19. Ι before τὰς, .. ΚΛΛΣΙΜΝ Kirchner. 26. At end ἔνηι eds. before Hedrick. 27–28. [ἔ/ ν]ηι eds. before Hedrick. 51. συνβόλαιον eds. before Hedrick. According to Hedrick -ον- was originally inscribed, but ο erased and α cut over the v. 52. μηθὲν eds. before Hedrick 57. ἐπὶ τὸ χωρίο[ν] eds. before Hedrick.

Translation

-archos proposed: the Dyaleis have decided to let the common property of the Dyaleis at Myrrhinous [or, have decided that the society of the Dyaleis shall let the property at Myrrhinous] to Diodoros on the following terms. In accordance with the following, (5) the phratriarchs, Kallikles son of Aristeides of Myrrhinous and Diopeithes son of Diophantes of Myrrhinous and the society of the Dyaleis have let the property at Myrrhinous called Sakkne, which is bounded to the north by an orchard, (10) to the south by the property of Olympiodoros, to the east by a road and to the west by the property of Olympiodoros, to Diodoros the son of Kantharos of Myrrhinous for ten years at six hundred drachmas a year. The lessee shall not be liable for payments or otherwise with respect to any act of God, (15) or enemy incursion, or the action of allied forces, or for taxes, or dues, or anything else. Diodoros shall keep the house in good repair . . . the vines of the Dyaleis . . . (20) (for the) phratriarchs and will hoe the vines twice each season. He will sow half the land with grain and will plant with pulse as much of the fallow as he wishes. He will also tend the other cultivated trees. (25) He shall pay half the rent, three hundred drachmas, in the month of Boedromion (ca. September), the other half, three hundred drachmas, in the month of Elaphebolion (March/April), to the phratriarchs of the Dyaleis in office at the time. The lease starts (30) in Mounichion (April/May) in the archonship of Hegemachos (300/299). Diodoros shall not be permitted to cut down any tree on the property or to destroy the house. If he does not pay the rent within the specified time or does not (35) tend the property according to the specified terms, the phratriarchs and the Dyaleis shall be permitted to seize securities in advance of legal settlement and lease the property to anyone else they wish; and Diodoros shall be subject to legal action if he is at all (40) in arrears with the rent or destroys any part of the house or cuts down anything on the land. If Diodoros or his heirs so wish within the ten years, let them pay down five thousand drachmas to the Dyaleis, and if they are (45) in arrears with the rent let the phratriarchs and the Dyaleis hand over the property to them, having collected the money. But if they have not paid down the five thousand drachmas and if they are at all in arrears with the rent during the ten years, (50) neither Diodoros nor any of his household may use this property as security, and the Dyaleis shall lease the property to anyone they wish for the maximum price. The phratriarchs shall inscribe this lease on a (55) stone stele and set it up . . . on the property.

Notes

This is not the place for a detailed commentary on the financial, legal, and agricultural technicalities of this lease. However, since I do not follow the most recent substantial interpretation of the lease (Behrend 1970) on some key points, it will be necessary to deal briefly with some of these matters. In my view this document is a rental agreement covering a period of ten years with an option to purchase at any time during that period (as was understood by scholars before Behrend, e.g., Schulthess 1932, cf. Lewis 1973, 197–98) and not, as Behrend suggests, a lease-to-buy arrangement with a lump sum to complete the sale payable only at the end of the term. The document is clearly and economically drafted. It is important not to be misled into any other interpretation by the obvious mistakes of the stonecutter, whom I take to have been at best semiliterate in Greek.

3. Διοδώρωι. It is almost certain that Diodoros, not otherwise known, is a member of the Dyaleis. I give the reasons in ascending order of strength: because his demotic is the same as that of the phratriarchs and squares with the location of the property and the stone (which was set up on it, 57; on the local links of phratries see p. 12); because there is a strong likelihood that a phratry would seek to let property to its own members where possible, with consequent mutual benefit (cf. pp. 195–99); because he is referred to here in the preamble familiarly, without patronymic or demotic; because this lease takes the form of a phratry decree. If Diodoros were not a member, it would have had to have been in the form of an agreement between the phratry and Diodoros. I take this argument to be all but decisive. This inscription is not a copy of the lease; it is the lease (3–4; 54). In leasing to a member the Dyaleis were not unusual; indeed, this was the norm for institutions of this sort (see R. Osborne 1985, 54).

5–8. ο[ἱ] φρατρίαρχοι . . . τὸ κοινὸν Δυαλέων. For the dual phratriar-chy, probably to be explained as a consequence of fusion or fission,

see p. 109. On the name Dyaleis cf. Hesych, s.v. Δύαλος· ὁ
Διόνυσος, παρὰ Παίωσιν (the connection noted by Töpffer 1889, 39–
40; Wilamowitz 1893, 269; Guarducci 1937, 51–52), but also s.v. Αὐαλός·
ὁ Διόνυσος and ὑάλικος κώμη· Διονύσιος. Δύαλος is thought to be
a word of Illyrian origin meaning "clownish" (Krahe 1955–64, 1, 82–
83; Frisk 1960–70; and Chantraine 1968–80, s.v. Δύαλος). A Dionysian
connection would be appropriate enough for a phratry, though it might
suggest the name was not of very early origin (see p. 146). Note also
that this is not a name in -*idai* (see p. 308 and 327 for the other two
known cases of this, in both of which the explanation may be that there
were other groups with similar names). The name may have been acquired
when the phratry underwent the fission or, perhaps more likely, the fusion
(see p. 109, n. 50) that gave it its two phratriarchs. In that case, however,
the connotation of duality seems unlikely to have been coincidental.

On the phratriarchs, one of whom is probably of a known family of
local prominence, see p. 232.

It is noteworthy that the phratriarchs are named together with the
society of the Dyaleis as lessor. There is apparently no parallel for this
in attested Attic leases of other groups of this sort, where the lessor is
always, e.g., "the demesmen" or "the orgeones" (though cf. *SEG* 22.508
for something similar in the case of the Chian Klytidai). On the possible
significance of this see further p. 228.

13. ⌐H *v v* τοῦ ἐνιαυτοῦ ἑκάστου· The property was clearly large,
though it is impossible to say how large. Six hundred drachmas is a
higher rent than that attested for any single property, or for the totality
of properties, leased by an individual deme in a year (*IG* 2².2496 [after
ca. 350], Kytheros [or possibly the island Kythera], 54 drachmas from
buildings in Peiraeus; *SEG* 28.103 [332/1], Eleusis, 50 drachmas from
quarries; *IG* 2².2492 [345/4], Aixone, 152 drachmas from property; *SEG*
24.151 [ca. 350], Teithras, ?200 drachmas from property; *IG* 1³.258 [425–
413], Plotheia, ? total annual rental income 134 drachmas 2½ obols; *IG*
2².2498 [321/0], Peiraeus, rents divided into those below and above 10
drachmas. The statement of Andreyev 1974 that the average annual rent
received by a deme was "in the vicinity of several hundred drachmas"
seems overbold, cf. Whitehead 1986a, 155). However, higher rents are
attested for properties leased by the state (1,270 drachmas for a property
in the mid-third century [*IG* 2².1592] and several over 500 drachmas in
Walbank 1983. Cf. also the properties listed in the "Rationes Centesi-

marum" [see p. 351], several of which were sold for over one talent, Lewis 1973, app. A), and to draw the conclusion that phratries were in general wealthier institutions than demes would be unjustified on such slim evidence (cf. pp. 200–201). The apparent rate of return on capital for the Dyaleis at twelve percent was also relatively high (apparently the highest attested for this sort of contract, Behrend 1970, 118, cf. 92. Walbank's attempt at 1983, 215, to use this rate of return as a basis for calculating actual values of a large number of properties of known rental value seems wrong and causes him difficulties on 216–17; his values could easily be cut by half), but not of a different order from normal. Moreover, five thousand drachmas is the purchase option price, the full capital value would perhaps have been higher. It is also important to recognize that this was not a contract between unconnected persons in an open market. Indeed, strictly speaking, it is not a contract at all; it is an internal arrangement involving a phratry and one of its members. This may have distorted the values that would otherwise have applied (see further p. 196. For the nondisinterested nature of rentals of this sort cf., e.g., *SEG* 24.151, 6–8, where the lease of property to Xanthippos by the Teithrasioi is justified ἐπειδὴ Ξάνθιππός ἐστι ἀνὴρ ἀγαθὸς περὶ τὰ κοινὰ τὰ Τειθρασίων).

13–17. ἀτ[ε]λὲς ... καὶ τῶν ἄλλων ἀπάντων· Diodoros is clearly being exempted from taxes for which he would be liable on the property if he owned it. This raises a number of interesting but, unfortunately, mostly unanswerable questions. We know demes were entitled to levy taxes, apparently for their own purposes, both on their own members and on nonmembers who owned property in the deme (the *enktetikon* tax, see Whitehead 1986a, 150). We do not know whether property owned by a phratry was subject to such taxation, but if so, the Dyaleis must have continued to pay with respect to Sakkne. In addition, or alternatively, it is possible that this phratry also raised a property-based tax from its own members (that it did so from nonmembers is not likely, see p. 199), and it is here releasing Diodoros from any obligation to pay with respect to Sakkne (cf. Behrend 1970, 120 with 18. His comment that only those entitled to raise taxes can grant exemption from them, however, misses the point; the phratry may effectively be reserving to itself a liability to taxation imposed by an external authority. Indeed, in the case of the *eisphora* this is clearly the sense; see further below). This passage is clear evidence that the property of phratries, like that of demes, was liable for state taxes (*eisphorai*), for which, in this case, the phratry would continue to be liable during the term of the lease. In some analogous cases regarding deme property the lessee was liable. See Whitehead 1986a, 155–56.

18. .. ἐπ[ι]σκευάζειν .. οἰκίαν ... I.e., this is a full repairing lease. There is no implication, as some previous editors have taken it, that the house was in a state of disrepair at the start of the lease. Diodoros is also required explicity at 40–41 not to pull down the house. This may simply have been a farmhouse or other farm building, or may be a phratry meeting place such as the οἰκίαι of the Klytidai on Chios (cf. pp. 194, 347); though in the latter case we might have expected some provisions guaranteeing access etc. (cf. *IG* 2².2499, 24–30, a similar contract involving the meeting place of orgeones).

29–30. ἄ[ρ]χει δὲ τῆς μισθώσε/ως ὁ ἐπὶ Ἡγεμάχου Μουνιχιών. Unless this lease was formulated half a year in advance of the date at which it came into effect (in Mounichion), the Dyaleis will have agreed to it at a meeting other than at the Apatouria (in Pyanepsion, cf. p. 157. See further p. 202). Note that Diodoros does not have to pay anything until after the first year's harvest.

37. ἐνεχυράζειν πρὸ δίκης. This gives the Dyaleis the right to seize securities from Diodoros (crops from the land or anything they can lay their hands on, cf. *IG* 2².2492, 7–9) if he fails to pay rent or tend the property as agreed. For this meaning see Harrison 1968–71 2.244–47, and parallels there cited, e.g., Ar. *Clouds,* in which Strepsiades frequently complains of being threatened with *enechyrasia* for his son's debts (e.g., 34–35, 241, 1214–21). Continental scholars have disputed whether πρὸ δίκης means "as though on the ground of a court judgement," "without the need for legal action," or "before judgement" (see Harrison, 1968–71 2.246). The last meaning, which I would translate "in advance of legal settlement," seems clearly preferable because it involves the more common, temporal, sense of πρὸ and because it makes better sense in context. If distraint is taken to replace a legal judgment, it would seem that the Dyaleis are giving themselves the right to seize an unlimited quantity of Diodoros' property simply, say, because he is a month in arrears with his rent, without his having the possibility of legal redress. This is implausible. On the other hand, an arrangement

whereby securities are seized, inevitably a fairly inexact procedure, in advance of a legal process to determine that the value of the damages seized was appropriate, makes sense. Parallels such as Dem. 35.12 (cited by Mitteis 1891, 406) are wide of the mark, since there the right is given to realize agreed security given in advance in case of default, not seized by unilateral action of the creditor. The δίκη here may in practice, but need not, be the same as that to which Diodoros is made formally subject in 39–41.

42. ἐν τοῖς δέκα ἔτεσιν. It is highly implausible, both as a matter of Greek and in terms of the interpretation of this document, that this means "after the ten years," thought more probable than "during the ten years" by Behrend 1970, 93. There appears to be no case, with one doubtful exception in verse, where ἐν in Greek bears the sense, common in English and colloquial German, of "after" a period of time (e.g., "I shall pay in six months") while the sense "within" or "during" is very common (e.g., Hdt. 1.126, Thuc. 1.118.2). The case of "after" cited by Behrend 1970, 93 n. 202, Schwyzer 1938–71, 458, and *LSJ* is Eur. *Phoen.* 304–7, Jocasta greeting Polynices: ἰὼ τέκνον, / χρόνῳ σὸν ὄμμα μυρίαις τ'ἐν ἁμέραις / προσεῖδον· ἀμφίβαλλε μα/στὸν ὠλέναισι ματέρος... I doubt that we need to make an exception here. I understand προσεῖδον to be metaphorical, "I beheld your likeness for myriads of days" (compare English, "you've been on my mind"), rather than literal, "I behold you after such a long time" (compare English, "it's such a long time since I've seen you"); for this we should expect the present or perfect in Greek. The former also seems imaginatively richer. Even if ἐν did mean "after" in this verse chorus in Doric dialect, in Attic legal prose ἐν meaning "after" seems out of the question. Behrend's interpretation here also springs from a doubtful interpretation of lines 48–52 (on which see below), from a view that it is unlikely that the effective price (i.e., lump sum plus rent paid) of the property would be lower the sooner Diodoros paid his five thousand drachmas (which seems explicable; cf. the modern accounting concept of net present value, whereby, independent of any adjustment for inflation, the present value of a given sum of money decreases if its receipt is delayed. Note also that this is not a disinterested commercial transaction, cf. pp. 195–96) and a concern with the unusually high rate of return, 12 percent, enjoyed by the Dyaleis, which is reduced effectively to 5.45 percent on his interpretation (on this see p. 304).

48–53. ἐὰν δ[ὲ]/[μὴ] καταβ[ά]λωσιν τὰς ⟦ ⋈ ⟧ δραχμάς . . . μὴ εἶναι Διοδώρωι . . . ⟨ὦ⟩ι ἂν βούλωνται τοῦ πλείστου. The sense of the first part of this provision must be that Diodoros may not enter into any contractual arrangements which would give a third party a claim on the property (e.g., by using it as security for a loan) until he has both paid the five thousand-drachma lump sum and all rent due. The Dyaleis might otherwise face a situation in which a third party had a claim on the land by virtue of, e.g., Diodoros' defaulting on a debt, and their own claims on Diodoros might consequently be jeopardized. We need therefore to take ἐάν τι πρǫσ[ο]/[φ]είλωσιν τῆς μισθώσεως as an extra, not an alternative, condition and to punctuate with a stop after ἀργύριον in 47 and probably no comma until after ἔ/τεσιν in 50. "Within the ten years" should probably be taken with both conditions; Diodoros might pay or not pay the five thousand drachmas, or be in rent arrears at any time during the ten years. Behrend's view (92–93) that "von Pachtzinsen aus den ganzen 10 Jahren die Rede ist" (and that therefore the five thousand drachmas could only be paid at the end of the ten-year period) seems groundless (cf. above on 42 on the misunderstanding of ἐν as "after" rather than "during" a period of time). ἐάν τι πρǫσ[ǫ]/[φ]είλωσιν κτλ. must also be taken as an extra, rather than an alternative, condition to make sense of the second part of this provision. The Dyaleis will not be able to lease to someone else merely if the five thousand drachmas have not been paid; rent must be owing also.

Date

300/299 (archonship of Hegemachos, Meritt 1961b, 232, cf. note on 29–30 above).

Location

Given the findspot of the inscription (Merenda, ancient Myrrhinous, Traill 1986, 129) the demotics of the two phratriarchs and the lessee (Myrrhinousioi), and the ownership by the phratry of a large piece of land at Myrrhinous, there can be no doubt that this phratry was closely associated with the area of this deme.

T 6 Gleontis

Sanctuary? marker, found in Agora excavations (Section NN. Agora inventory no. I 5910).
Meritt 1948, 35, no. 18 (with photograph, plate 9). Text, Meritt 1948.

> [ἱερὸν]
> Κηφισô
> Γλεων
> τίδος
> 5 [φ]ρατρίας

Translation

(Sanctuary) of Kephisos of the phratry Gleontis.

Notes

1. [ἱερὸν]. Meritt's restoration seems probable, though there are other possibilities (e.g., hόρος + genitive) if there was more than one line before his 2 (not clear from his photograph, plate 9).

3–4. Γλεων/τίδος. The name of this phratry is related to that of the old phyle Geleontes (attested as "Gleontes" on the state calendar of sacrifices of 403/2–400/399, see p. 256 n. 52. For the meaning of the name, see p. 15 n. 51). It may not be coincidental that one of the only other two securely attested Attic phratries with a name in -*is* rather than -*idai*, Thymaitis (see below T 13 and 14), also shared a similar name with another group (the deme Thymaitadai; note, however, also the Dyaleis, on which see p. 303). It is possible that there was, or had been, some organizational link between the two groups, though we can scarcely guess what (for a discussion of whether phratries were subdivisions of the old phylai see pp. 14–17).

Date

Ca. 400, on the basis of letter forms (Meritt).

Location

The probable presence in the Agora of a sanctuary of Kephisos of this phratry cannot be taken as evidence of a more general association of the group with this part of the city (for city links of phratries not located primarily in Athens, cf. p. 13). There was a sanctuary of Kephisos at new Phaleron (see the dedications *IG* 2^2.4547, 4548, with relief; Walter 1937; Guarducci 1974), but it would be rash to posit on such grounds alone a link between Gleontis and that place. Kephisos was generally associated with youth and haircutting rites; an appropriate deity therefore for any phratry to cultivate (cf. the koureion, pp. 163–65. Paus. 1.37.3 mentions an offering on the Sacred Way erected by a certain Mnesimache and showing her son making a dedication of hair to the river; in *IG* 2^2.4547 the deity is mentioned with a number of others associated with birth; and in the relief of *IG* 2^2.4548 a mother and son are depicted in the company of the gods, cf. Walter 1937, who associates the relief with a phratry. See further, pp. 186–87, 218–19). There were demes called Kephisia (inland trittys of Erechtheis, northeast of Athens, Traill 1986, 125) and Epikephisia (city trittys of Oineis, northwest of Athens, Traill 1986, 133). No attempt appears to have been made to associate this sanctuary with any particular location or remains in the Agora (not mentioned in *Agora* 14.168–70).

T 7 Medontidai

Marker of property or meeting place, found in foundations of Turkish cemetery wall, at entrance to Acropolis. E.M. 10071.

Rangabé 1842–55 2.586–87, no. 891; Pittakes 1856, cols. 1400–1401, no. 2819; *IG* 1.497; Töpffer 1889, 225–44; Wilamowitz 1893, 2.131; *IG* 1².871; Nilsson 1951 (= 1972), 151–52. Text based on *IG* 1².

> hόρο[ς χό?]
> ρας Μεδ[ον]
> τ[ι]δôν

1–2. Hiller preferred χό]ρας to ἄγο]ρας (cf. *IG* 1².896)

Translation

Marker of (property? meeting place?) of the Medontidai.

Notes

Given the uncertainty over exactly what this stone marked—ἄγορα (meeting place) or χόρα (property or territory) seem the possibilities—and the findspot of this inscription, at the entrance to the Acropolis, it is not clear whether it relates directly to the phratry Medontidai or to some sanctuary or relic of the Athenian royal house of the same name (see further below on T 10). Cf. also T 1, with notes.

Date

Probably fifth century (orthography).

Location

See on T 10.

T 8 Medontidai

Dedicatory base, seen by Wilhelm in wall of a house at Keratea (ancient Kephale).
Wilhelm 1909, 49–50, no. 37 (with illustration 23); *IG* 1².872. Text from Wilhelm's illustration.

[h?]ιερὸν
Μεδοντιδõν

Translation

Sacred of the Medontidai

Notes

1–2. [h?]ιερὸν/ Μεδοντιδõν. There was a circular depression between the two lines of the inscription which Wilhelm suggested was meant to receive a dedication. The text should refer to this dedication and not to a sanctuary. Whether the Medontidai are the dedicators (i.e., the phratry; Wilhelm thought the dedication should belong to the group, which he thought was a genos) or the dedicatees (i.e., the royal house, Hiller ad *IG* 1².872), or both, it is impossible to say (cf. on T 7, T 9, and 10).

Date

Fifth century by letter forms and orthography (Wilhelm). Such an early date may not be necessary. There appear to be no distinctively early letter forms (MPEN) and it is not certain that an Attic aspirate should be restored at the start. o for ου is the only notable feature, but that would be consistent with an earlier fourth-century date.

Location

See on T 10.

T 9 Medontidai

Decree, built into wall of church at Kypseli (ancient Erikeia?). Non-stoichedon.
CIG 1.133 B (Boeckh, from notes by Köhler), 902; Keil 1866, 249 (from drawing by L. Ross); *IG* 2.5, 603c; Töpffer 1889, 229; *IG* 2².1233 (Kirchner, using a drawing by Velsen in addition to previous eds.). Text based on *IG* 2².1233.

Face A

```
- - - - - - - - - - - - - - - - - -
             τοῦ μ[ - - - - - - - - - - ἔπαι]
(in corona)  νέσαι ᾿Αρε[- - - - - - - - - - κ]
Μεδοντίδαι   αἰ στεφα[νῶσαι αὐτὸν - - στεφάνωι]
ὁ Δῆμο[ς]  5 δ[ικ]α[ιοσύνης ἕνεκεν καὶ - - - - τ]
             ἧς περ[ὶ - - - - - - - - - - - - -]
- - - - - - - - - - - - - - - - - -
```

Face B
(in corona)   (in corona)
[οἱ ἱπ?]πέες   ἡ βουλή

1. τοῦ γένους] Köhler, *IG* 2, followed by Kirchner, *IG* 2.² 2. τοῦ Μ[εδοντιδῶν Köhler, followed by Kirchner. 5–6. δ[ικ]α[ιοσύνης ἕνεκεν καὶ εὐσεβείας τ]/ῆς περ[ὶ τὸ γένος] Kirchner. ἀ[ρετῆς ἕνεκεν καὶ Köhler. Face A, in corona. ΟΔΗΜΟ Velsen, as reported by Kirchner.

Translation

Face A
. . of (the) M(edontidai?) . . to praise Are- . . . (and) crown (him) . . . (because of his) justice (and) . . . towards . . .
(In crowning): Medontidai. The People.

Face B
       (in crowning):   (in crowning):
       The cavalry (?)   The Boule

Notes

All editions of this inscription, which is built into the wall of a church near Kypseli, appear to have been based on drawings by various persons, in no case on autopsy. The text is clearly of the standard honorific type. The names in the crowns are somewhat curious. We should perhaps see this as a decree of the phratry Medontidai (as previous eds., but taken as a genos before the publication of T 10; Are- in 3 should be a member), with which the demos (Velsen's reading is plausible), the cavalry (presumably, rather than the property class, the knights) and the Boule (was Are- a member of all three? For the δοκιμασίαι performed by the Boule in connection with the cavalry see Rhodes 1972, 174) are associating themselves, or at least are portrayed as doing so; one wonders whether this was an afterthought—note the differing forms of the *pi* in the crown [Γ] and in the decree [Π]. It is less attractive to take it the other way round, i.e., as a decree of Boule and demos; we should not in that case expect the Medontidai to appear so prominently or the inscription to have been set up outside the city. We can be fairly certain that this inscription has to do with the phratry (cf. T 10) and not with the royal house (cf. T 7–8).

Date

Fourth century (Köhler, tentatively. The form of the *pi* in the crown may suggest a slightly later date).

Location

See on T 10.

T 10 Medontidai

Accounts of poletai, on marble stele found in Athenian Agora beneath floor of the "Tholos." Agora Inventory no. I 5509. Stoichedon 39. Crosby 1941, 14–27, no. 1 (= *SEG* 12.100); Ferguson 1944 A, no. 5; Finley 1952, esp. 111–13; Jacoby at *FGH* 323a Hellanikos fr. 23 with n. 70. Text, Crosby 1941, lines 16–35.

Κιχωνί

δης Διογείτονος Γαργήτ (τιος) καὶ κοινὸν φρατέρων Με
δοντιδῶν ἐνεπησκήψατο ἐνοφείλεσθαι ἑαυτῶι κ
αἰ τοῖς φράτερσιν ἐν τῆι οἰκίαι τῆι ᾿Αλωπεκῆσι Η δ
20 ραχμάς ἣν ἀπέγραψεν Θεόμνηστος ᾿Ιωνί(δης) Θεοσέβος
εἶναι Ξυπετα(ίονος) ἧι γείτων βορρᾶ(θεν) ἡ ὁδὸς ἡ ἐς τὸ Δαιδά
λεον φέρουσα καὶ τὸ Δαιδάλειον, νοτόθεν Φίλιππ
ος ᾿Αγρυλῆ(θεν), ἀποδομένο ἐμο⟨ὶ⟩ καὶ τοῖς φράτερσιν τὴ
ν οἰκίαν ταύτην Θεοφίλου Ξυπε(Ταίονος): τὸ πατρὸς τοῦ Θεο
25 σέβος. ἔδοξεν ἐνοφείλεσθαι. ᾿Ίσαρχος Φίλωνος Ξυπ
ε{:}ται(ὼν): ἀμφισβητεῖ ἐνοφείλεσθαι ἑαυτῶι ἐν τῆι οἰ
κίαι τῆι ᾿Αλωπεκῆσι ἣν ἀπέγραψεν Θεόμνηστος Δε
ισιθέο ᾿Ιωνίδης, θάψαντος ἐμὸ Θεοφίλον ὃ ἦν ἡ οἰκ
ία καὶ τὴν γυναῖκα τὴν Θεοφίλο ΔΔΔ: δραχμάς. ἔδοξ
30 εν ἐνοφείλεσθαι. Αἰσχίνης Μελιτε⟨ὺ⟩⟨ς⟩ καὶ κοινὸν ὀ
ργεώνων ἐνεπεσκήψαντο ἐν τῆι οἰκίαι ἣν ἀπέγραψ
εν Θεόμνηστος ᾿Ιωνίδης ἐνοφείλεσθαι ἑαυτοῖς:
ΔΔϜϜϜ δραχμάς, πριαμένων ἡμῶν τὴν οἰκίαν ταύτ
ην παρὰ Θεοφίλου τούτου τοῦ ἀργυρίο ἐπὶ λύσει. ἔδ
35 οξεν ἐνοφείλεσθαι.

Translation

(16) Kichonides, son of Diogeiton of Gargettos and the society of the phrateres of the Medontidai claimed that he and the phrateres were owed 100 drachmas on the house at Alopeke which Theomnestos of Ionidai registered as belonging to Theosebes of Xypete, and which borders to the north the road leading to the Daidaleion and the Daidaleion, to the south (the property of) Philippos of Agryle, "Theophilos of Xypete the father of Theosebes, having sold the house to me and the phrateres (subject to redemption)." (25) The claim was allowed.

Isarchos son of Philon of Xypete argued that he was owed 30 drachmas on the house at Alopeke which Theomnestos son of Deisitheos of Ionidai registered, "I having buried Theophilos, whose house this was, and Theophilos' wife." The claim (30) was allowed.

Aeschines of Melite and the society of the orgeones claimed that 24 drachmas were owed them on the house which Theomnestos of Ionidai registered, "we having bought this house subject to redemption from Theophilos for this amount." The claim (35) was allowed.

Notes

As with the inscription of the Dyaleis (T 5, q.v.), I have restricted my comments on the financial, legal, and other technicalities of this text to a minimum. There are no significant textual difficulties. The inscription, eighty-three lines long in all, from which T 10 is an extract, is the public record of the accounts of the poletai for the year 367/6. The second part (40–83) relates to leases of mines; the first, from which our extract comes, deals with the sale of a single confiscated property. In the preceding text, the date has been given (1, archonship of Polyzelos = 367/6, Develin 1989, 256) and the names of the poletai in office and their secretary (2–6). We have learned that the poletai had received the property in question, which was situated at Alopeke, from the Eleven and sold it on 10 Mounichion following registration (or denunciation, cf. Finley 1952, 111 with n. 14; the details of the process are not well understood) by Theomnestos. The property had belonged to a certain Theosebes, who had been convicted of sacrilege (ἱεροσυλία) and had fled before the outcome of his trial (6–14). The "registration" was for whatever the property was worth in excess of a 150-drachma claim held by Smikythos of Teithras by virtue of a *prasis epi lysei* (14–15). Our extract follows, giving details of three claims against the property lodged with the poletai, all of which were allowed. Finally, the sale of the property, to one Lysanias son of Palathion of Lakiadai, for 575 drachmas, is recorded (35–39).

16–17. Κιχωνί/δης Διογείτονος Γαργήτ·(τιος) καὶ κοινὸν φρατέρων Με/δοντιδῶν. Kichonides must be phratriarch of the Medontidai (cf. p. 228 with nn. 136–27). For the possible significance of the mention of the phratriarch together with the phratry in the description of a phratry's legal person, cf. p. 228; and for the phratry as koinon, cf. p. 195

n. 33. Before the discovery of this inscription, it was generally thought that the Medontidai were a genos, i.e., an aristocratic group descended mythically or otherwise from Medon, the third member, after Melanthos and Kodros, of the second royal dynasty at Athens, and, by most accounts, the first of a series of archons for life (for variant traditions see *Ath. Pol.* 3.3.) The discovery that they were a phratry raises a complex of problems, mostly insoluble on the basis of present evidence, about the relationship between this phratry (= Medontidai P) and both the myths surrounding the royal house Medontidai (= Medontidai R) and the historical persons, if there were any, which were the subject of those myths. Jacoby, writing after the discovery of T 10, took the view that the Medontidai (R) were mostly a concoction of Hellanikos, who wanted to fill "an empty space between the Ionian migration and the first annual archon" and did so "with a series of Athenian names of distinguished sound" (on Hellanikos fr. 23). Though this hypothesis has attractive features, it needs handling with care.

Whether or not we connect T 7 directly to the phratry, its fifth-century date and findspot at the entrance to the Acropolis may suggest association, direct or indirect, with a royal house, or something similar, about which some sort of tradition would already have existed at the time Hellanikos was writing in the late fifth century. Moreover, it would be perverse to suppose that the Medontidai (P), for which there is evidence in 367/6 and possibly earlier (T 7–8), did not exist before Hellanikos recorded his stories about the Medontidai (R). It is possible, therefore, that the Medontidai (P) were already associated in some way with stories about their eponym before Hellanikos recorded them. Jacoby can certainly be taken to have demonstrated the strong probability that Hellanikos manipulated preexisting legendary material, fitting Medon and the Medontidai into a framework into which he also had to fit Melanthos, Kodros, Neleus, and Hippomenes; the silence of our sources on (the) Medon(tidai) before Hellanikos and the naming of the house from the third in the line are particularly suspicious. But it seems unlikely that Medon and the Medontidai (R) were wholly his creations on the basis of merely preexisting, high-sounding names.

Since the discovery of T 10, it has been unclear whether the Medontidai should continue to be regarded as a genos as well as a phratry (Crosby, 21 thought not; Jacoby at Hellanikos fr. 23, n. 70, argued the contrary, adducing the analogous case of the Titakidai and the Thyrgonidai, q.v. below, T 15). If we are careful about what sort of genos we mean, however, we can be a little clearer on the point. Given T 10, there is no longer evidence for a genos of the genos/kome type, the type that was a phratry subgroup (= genos P), but there was a tradition concerning a genos that was a legendary royal house (= genos R; on the distinction between different types of gene see pp. 59–60. The mentions of Medontidai in later literature can all be taken to refer to the genos (R): Vell. Pat. 1.2; Paus. 4.5–10, 4.13.7; Hesych. s.v. Μεδοντίδαι). It is impossible to say whether there were families in the historical period who regarded themselves as descended from the genos (R), and whether such families, if they existed, were the Medontidai (P), in whole or in part, and if in part whether they formed a genos (P) or some other subgroup, formal or otherwise. Peisistratos (Hdt. 5.65.3), Solon (Plut. *Sol.* 1.2–3) and Plato (D.L. 3.1) were traditionally related in some way to Neleus, Kodros, and Melanthos—in Hellanikos' system respectively the brother, father, and grandfather of Medon—and in the case of Peisistratos, if not of Solon and Plato (cf. Jacoby at Hellanikos fr. 23, n. 70), probably regarded themselves as such; but Medon and the Medontidai (R) are not mentioned in those traditions and seem to have been artificially connected with Melanthos and the others at some stage, quite possibly by Hellanikos himself.

It is difficult to generalize about the relationship of phratries to their eponyms on the basis of our exiguous evidence, but they seem to be persons who are otherwise either totally unknown (e.g., Achni-?), or who turn up as mere names in the earlier reaches of the archon list (e.g., Therrikles), or who at most play very minor roles in myths concerned essentially with other characters (e.g., Thymoites). Medon fits the pattern, if such it can be called, very well. If it had not been for his association with the likes of Melanthos, Kodros, Neleus, and the others, we would have no more than a name from the archon list, albeit a very early one (1069/8 according to Eratosthenes, Jacoby on *FGH* 250 Castor fr. 4) and one whose precise status, as last of the kings or first of the archons for life, was disputable (see above). It is possible therefore (cf. Jacoby at Hellanikos fr. 23, n. 70), that in the Medontidai (P) in the fifth century there existed a tradition of some sort concerning their eponym. Whether it consisted of any more than that he had been a notable Athenian leader it is impossible to say. This eponym may have been associated with the ἄγορα or χώρα to which T 7 refers, and possibly with the dedication, T 8. Hellanikos (?), collecting and rationalizing the disparate traditions in Attica about mythical leading personages, found an appropriate slot for this one in the second Athenian royal dynasty. Whether the rest of the Medontidai (R) were inserted by Hellanikos, or whether any of them came, so to speak, as a package with Medon from the Medontidai (P), we cannot say. For more on phratry eponyms see pp. 220–22.

20–21. Θεόμνηστος ᾽Ιωνί(δγς). We do not know whether Theomnestos was a member of the Medontidai, or how, if at all, he was otherwise connected with Theosebes. Perhaps he had been Theosebes' prosecutor.

21–22. Θεοσέβος . . . Ξυπετα(ίονος) It is probable that Theosebes and his father Theophilos were members of the Medontidai. It would be unexpected for them to sell their property (subject to redemption, see next note) to a phratry other than their own (cf. pp. 197–98).

23. ἀποδομένο . . . τὴ/ν οἰκίαν. As was noted by Crosby 1941, 23, ἀπο-δομένο here must relate to a fictional sale (probably a *prasis epi lysei,* cf. Finley 1952, 111), rather than a real one (on the procedure see p. 197). The sum paid is clearly too small for an outright sale, which would also probably be inconsistent with the claim on the property by Aeschines and his orgeones.

24–25. Θεοφίλου Ξυπε(ταίονος): τὸ πατρὸς τοῦ Θεο/σέβος. It is clear that Theosebes' father, Theophilos, and his wife had died fairly recently (cf. 28–29, 34). Whether there was any connection between his parents' death and Theosebes' offense, ἰεροσυλία, we do not know. I agree with Osborne 1985, 5, with n. 25, that the family may have had priestly connections; note also the names in Theo- and that the confiscated property neighbors a Deidaleion. Perhaps it held the phratry priesthood (cf. p. 234).

28–29. θάψαντος ἐμὸ Θεοφίλον . . . καὶ τὴν γυναῖκα. Was the man who buried Theophilos, Isarchos son of Philon of Xypete, a member of his, and hence also Theosebes' phratry, i.e., probably the Medontidai (see note on 21–22)? They share a demotic, but there is nothing else to suggest a connection except for the act of burial (Isarchos' family, on which see further below, was fairly prominent, see Whitehead 1986a, 138 with 451–52, nos. 353 and 358, but there is no detectable link with Theosebes or the Medontidai). Had they been συγγενεῖς, who usually saw to the burial of their own (see further below), we might not have expected them to claim, or at least to be successful in claiming, the expenses. According to the burial law quoted by Demosthenes at 43.57–58, if οἱ προσήκοντες of a deceased person do not carry out the duty of burial, it is the responsibility of the demarch to see to the matter at the lowest possible price and to exact double the cost παρὰ τῶν ὀφειλόντων. ὁ ὀφειλών in this case would have been Theosebes, who, following his ἱεροσυλία, would presumably not have been in a position to fulfill his filial responsibilities. This suggests strongly that Isarchos was demarch of Xypete (Whitehead 1986a, 234, took him to be simply a fellow demesman of Theophilos) and was claiming his due for arranging the burial of Theophilos and his wife according to the law at Dem. 43.57–58 (on which see further p. 227, n. 121). His family—his brother was one of the *komastai* for the deme's victory in the festival of the Tetrakomoi in 330/29, *IG* 2².3103—is of exactly the right type. If so, however, it does not help us to determine whether Isarchos was also a Medontidai member (for demes associated with more than one phratry, see map, p. 352).

30–31. Αἰσχίνης Μελιτε⟨ὺ⟩(ς) καὶ κοινὸν ὀ/ργεώνων. Crosby 1941, 22, thought that Aeschines of Melite and his orgeones should also have been Medontidai members, because it would be "inconceivable that in a technical document of this sort" the group "would not be described at least sufficiently for identification." As Ferguson 1944, 83, observed, however, orgeones generally have an "irritating way of being anonymous." Nevertheless, an argument similar to that used for Theosebes' phratry membership can be applied here: it would be unexpected for him to take out a *prasis epi lysei* with a group of orgeones which did not belong to his own phratry. (He need not, however, have been a member of the orgeones group, cf. T 21 with pp. 197–98.) Apart from the case of Isaeus 2, this is the only evidence linking a specific orgeones group with a specific phratry (cf. p. 77).

Date

367/6 (archonship of Polyzelos, see p. 315).

Location

This phratry has known associations with more localities than any other. I first list the associations, taking Diogeiton, Theosebes, and Aeschines to be phratry members, but not Theomnestos, Isarchos, or Philippos, and T 7–8 to be pertinent:

Athens	(Acropolis)	:	T 7
	(Melite)	:	demotic of Aeschines
	(Northeast boundary)	:	location of property at Alopeke to which T 10 relates (for precise location see Crosby 1941, 20–21)
Southeast of Athens	(Kephale)	:	T 8
Southwest of Athens	(Xypete)	:	demotic of Theosebes
Northeast of Athens	(?Erikeia)	:	T 9
	(Gargettos)	:	demotic of Diogeiton

Crosby 1941, 22–23, while admitting the evidence was inadequate for a definitive opinion, suggested that it pointed to one of two regions as the location of the Medontidai home: the southwest part of the city (T 7, royal name, demotics of Aeschines and Theosebes) or the region to the northeast of the city (T 9, Theosebes' property; she might have added Diogeiton's demotic). She conceded, however, that T 8 fits neither suggestion (Solders 1931, 119, 123, took T 8 to prove Keratea was the original home). Neither of these is impossible; in favor of a base outside the city we might adduce the evidence of other rural phratries with city links (cf. p. 13). However, the case for a city base (not necessarily southwest), especially in view of the apparent connection, whatever its nature, with Medontidai (R), is perhaps stronger. The Medontidai could have spread outward in the archaic period in different directions from a city base (Thuc. 2.14 stresses the static character of the Attic population at the start of the Peloponnesian War, but I doubt whether that has any value as evidence for the period before Cleisthenes). It is possible that there was a connection with the probable steep rise in population of the eighth century, which seems to have involved net emigration from Athens into Attica (Snodgrass 1980, 23; Coldstream 1977, 133–35). There is no reason to doubt that the Medontidai (P) might have existed at that time, though we do not know if the net emigration of the archaeological record involved actual emigration. This is no more than a possible explanation; any chance movements of population from any base in Attica could have produced the pattern of our evidence. But it would account for all the attested associations with locality, including Kephale.

T 11 Therrikleidai

Sanctuary marker, unknown provenience. E.M. 10203.
Köhler 1877, 186–87; Wilamowitz 1893, 269, n. 9; *IG* 2.² 4973; Guarducci 1937, no. 9. See also under T 12, below. Text, *IG* 2².

[ἱ]ερὸ[ν]
['Απόλ]λωνο[ς]
[Πατρ]ώιου φρ
[ατρία]ς Θερρικ
5   [λειδ]ῶν.

1–4. Köhler. 5. Wilamowitz.

Translation

Sanctuary of Apollo Patroos of the phratry Therrikleidai.

Notes

4–5. Θερρικ/[λειδ]ῶν. Wilamowitz' suggested restoration has been confirmed by the discovery of T 12 and *IG* 1³.243 (see below on T 12). The
eponym is unknown, though there was an archon Therrikles in the archaic
period (533/2; see Develin 1989).

Date

Fourth-century (letter forms).

T 12 Therrikleidai

Decree, on marble fragment found in southeast corner of Agora (Grid Square V 13, Agora Inventory no. 17500). Non-stoichedon.
Walbank 1982, 48–50, no. 7 (with photograph, pl. 20); Hedrick 1983, 299–302. Text based on Walbank 1982 and Hedrick 1983.

```
- - - - - - - - - - - - - - - - - - - -
     ΑΚ[ - - - - - - - - - - - - - - - -γεγο]
     νότων ἐκ τῶν ι[ - - - - - - - - - - - - ]
     τῶν ὅρκων μεχρὶ [ - - - - - - - - - - - ]
     αι ἀ[λ]λήλοις καίτοι. [[ - - - - - - - - ]
  5  ναι ἐάν τι ἄλλο ψηφίζων[ται - - ἑλέσθαι]
     δὲ καὶ ἐπιμελητὰς, δυὸ μὲ[ν - - - - -]
     κατα[δ]έηται τῶμ φρατριά[ρχων - - - - ]
     τας διδόναι τὴμ ψῆφον [ - - - - τὰ ἱερε]
     ὥσυνα λαμβάνειν τ[- - - - - τοῖς Θερρικ]
 10  λείδαις ἐπιτιμ[ - - - - - ]
     ἐν τῆι κυρίᾳ[ι - - - - - - - - - - - ]
     φρατρια[ - - - - - - - - - - - - - - - ]
- - - - - - - - - - - - - - - - - - - -
```

1. ΑΚΑ[..]ΔΕΙ[- Walbank. Hedrick was only able to detect ΑΚ[-. 4. In the traces of the last preserved letter of the line, Walbank perceived Α, Hedrick Χ. 7. φρατριῶ[ν] Walbank. Hedrick reports that the last preserved letter "is most certainly Α." 9. τ[ὸν ἱερέα? Walbank. 10. ᾽επιτιμ[- See notes below. 12. φρατρια[ρχ Walbank. 13. - -]Ν[- - Walbank.

Translation

... aged, [or, descended] from the ... the oaths until ... one another and yet ... (5) if they vote otherwise ... and epimeletai be chosen (?), two ... entreats the phratriarchs ... put to the vote ... take the priestly perquisites ... the Therrikleidai (10) in the term of office of Tim- [or, censure the Therrikleidai?] ... in the sovereign (assembly?) ... phratry [or phratriarch] ...

Notes

Walbank 1982, 49 noted parallels with T 3 and supposed that this document was also concerned with regulation of admissions. Hedrick 1983, 299 and 300 n. 4 was rightly skeptical about whether we have enough of the text to determine its purpose. Another possibility is that it concerned the regulation of cult (8–9, cf. pp. 219–20; perhaps more consistent with this being a decree of a phratry subgroup, see further below).

5–6. ἑλέσθαι]/ δὲ καὶ ἐπιμελητὰς. I retain Walbank's ἑλέσθαι], retained also by Hedrick (cf. T 3, 32; T 17, 6; T 20, 7), though it is not certain.

9–10. τοῖς Θερρικ]/λείδαις. Given the mention of something Therriklean in the fragments of *IG* 1³.243 (on which see further below), many of which were found in the same area of the Agora as T 12 (see below), and φρ[ατρία]ς Θερρικ[λειδ]ῶν in T 11, Hedrick's restoration of the name is convincing. There is no other known phratry *-leidai*. If Hedrick's suggestion is also correct that ΕΠΙΤΙΜ[– in 10 is from a dating formula (ἐπὶ τοῦ δεῖνος ἄρχοντος, φρατριαρχοῦντος vel. sim. There is, incidentally, no archon Τιμ- in the first half of the third century, see Meritt 1961b, 232–34) we should, with him, take this as a decree of the Therrikleidai. However, if Walbank is correct, as he may be, that it is from ἐπιτιμέω, "censure," and the object of that censure was the Therrikleidai, it seems less likely that the Therrikleidai are voting the decree than that it is a group associated in some way with the Therrikleidai, probably as a subgroup or vice versa (likely to be the Meliteis or Miltieis of *IG* 1³.243, see further below).

The latter interpretation is attractive in view of the multiple phratriarchs, which strongly suggest a multipartite institution, cf. pp. 107–9, of the fact that one group of persons may vote differently from another (5), that there are epimeletai (not otherwise securely attested in an Attic phratry, see p. 236) who appear to be divided into two (?) groups, and that someone (or some group) may "entreat the phratriarchs"; and perhaps also that there is a "sovereign (assembly?)."

With T 11 and 12 should be mentioned *IG* 1³.243, (first published, Meritt 1967), a collection of seventeen fragments, most found in the Agora, of a stele inscribed, apparently on all four sides, a little before, or, as is generally thought without good cause, after 480. Face D is inscribed in a different hand from faces A–C and was taken by Meritt

1967 to be a separate decree. Little can be said about the content, other than that it appears from the exiguous remains to have been religio-financial. At the top of face B (30), Θερ[ι]κλείο is clearly legible (Meritt prints Θερ[ικ]λείο, but traces of the κ are visible on his photograph, plate 24, 5), though neither preceding nor succeeding words are preserved. (Meritt's reconstruction, θεσ[μὸς ἀπὸ τôν πρόσθεν τô] Θερ[ικ]λείο ['Α]τθί[δον στελôν τός τε νῦν ἡ]ερομνέμον/ας ⋮ κ[αὶ τὸν δέμαρχον τὸν Μελι]τέον ⋮ τôι h, is highly speculative. ΘΕΣ- might be any number of words, possibly something to do with Thesmophoroi or the Thesmophoria in view of Broneer 1942, 265–74, no. 51; ⋮ before κ[αὶ with no break in sense would be odd in this document; and the beginnings and ends of the lines belong to different fragments whose conjuncture is conjectural.) This may be an adjective: the Therriklean something; Lewis' tentative thought at *IG* 1³.243 that "Therrikleian pottery" might be in question seems ruled out if Athen. 7.470f is correct and its inventor was a contemporary of Aristophanes; or conceivably a noun: "the Therrikleion," i.e., a shrine of Therrikles (so Meritt, followed by Hedrick 1983, such a building otherwise unattested). In either case, given the rarity of this name and the fact that T 12, which seems also to mention the Therrikleidai, was also found in the Agora (from the same area as some of the fragments of *IG* 1³.243, see Hedrick 1983, 301), it seems reasonable to connect them.

What group or groups were responsible for *IG* 1³.243? Meritt 1967 took faces A–C to be a decree of the Areopagos, face D a decree of the deme Melite, the latter, he guessed, implementing the former. Both suggestions seem doubtful. The case for the first rests essentially on his restoration of 1, -]ΟΛΕΙ ⋮ ΕΠ[- as an introductory formula, ἐδόχσεν τêι β]ολêι, followed by a dating formula, ἐπὶ + genitive. The Boule involved should, he argues, be the Areopagos rather than the Five Hundred, since we would not expect to find the latter passing decrees with no mention of the demos at this early date. There is, however, no other example or record of an Areopagos decree, and one questions whether it was the sort of body that passed decrees, let alone published them, cf. Wallace 1985/9, 81. That a central body should see fit to give instructions to an individual deme or other group, as opposed to demes or other groups in general, for which there is plenty of evidence (see Whitehead 1986a, esp. 130–38) apparently on detailed religio-financial matters, also seems intrinsically odd and, as far as I know, is unparalleled. In fact, there is no need for a formulaic ἔδοξεν + dative at all here, or indeed at 72; for other opening formulations in comparable documents of the period, cf. *IG* 1³.244; 245; probably 247 (= T 36); 248; 258; also *SEG* 21.541. ἐπὶ [name] ἄρχοντος τε̑ι π]ολε̑ι ⫶ ἐπ[ὶ [perhaps a name of official of group whose document this is], for example, would be an attractive alternative (cf. first document of the Salaminioi, Ἐπὶ Χαρ-ικλεί δ ἄρχοντος Ἀθηναίοις· ἐπὶ τοῖσ[δ]/ε διήλλαξαν οἱ διαιτηταὶ, Ferguson 1938, no. 1, 2; and for dating by official at Athens and official in local group, the preamble to the decrees of the Dekeleieis, T 3, 9–11). Faces A–C could then be documents of the same local group as passed D, as we might have expected prima facie (ΤΘΙ in 31 and ΘΕΝ-ΑΙΟΝ in 59 are inadequate grounds for supposing A–C was a decree of a central organ of the polis).

There is no such intrinsic implausibility in Meritt's identification of the group passing D as a deme, the Meliteis; but a case can also be made that it was the Miltieis. The latter group is mentioned in the Rationes Centesimarum, and I suggest at T 27 that it may have been related to the Meliteis as the pre-Cleisthenic House of the Dekeleieis was related to the deme of the same name. First, as far as can be seen from Meritt's photographs (plate 24, 5 face B; plate 25, 10 face D), the remains on the stone at the two points taken by Meritt to be references to Meliteis seem consistent, possibly more consistent, with Miltieis. At 32, the letter before the E of Meritt's -TEON looks as though it could as easily be I, and at 72 Meritt's -ΕΛΙΤΕΥΣ- appears to be ᐧ Ⅴ ⅼⅼ (with possible traces of the cross-bar of T on either of the last two letters). In this case, the first mark on the stone looks more like I than E. Restorations ΜΙΛΤ]ΙΕΟΝ and Μ]ΙΛΤΙΕΥΣ[Ι seem therefore epigraphically possible, and perhaps preferable.

Second, given the likelihood that in T 12 we have evidence for a multipartite phratric organization in which the Therrikleidai are either the parent or the subgroup, and given the association between the group that passed *IG* 1³.243 and something Therrikleian, there is some attrac-tion in the hypothesis that that group was the phratry or one of the subphratries of T 12. If the parallel with the Dekeleieis and the Demo-tionidai holds (cf. p. 109 n. 52) we should take the Therrikleidai as the parent phratry (like the Demotionidai) and the Miltieis as the subgroup (like the Dekeleieis).

To sum up, in about 480 we have something Therrikleian associated in some way with a group, either the demesmen Meliteis or perhaps more likely the phratric group Miltieis, on a document from the Agora.

In the fourth century we have a phratry Therrikleidai with a sanctuary of Apollo Patroos at a place unknown; and we have a decree of the first half of the third century (see below) from the Agora that shows that phratry to have been a multipartite organization, one part of which may have been the Miltieis. In view of the connections with the Agora, it is possible that T 24, an altar of Zeus Phratrios and Athena Phratria from the Agora, should also be associated with the Therrikleidai. There are, however, other possibilities (see p. 357).

Date

First half of third century (Walbank, based on letter forms).

Location

In view of the above (see notes to 9–10), a tentative association between the Therrikleidai on the one hand and the deme Melite and the area of the Agora on the other (for this location for Melite see Traill 1986, 134) may be posited. Whether this association represents to any extent the city arm of a group which also had a rural base, we cannot tell (cf. p. 13).

T 13 Thymaitis

Sanctuary marker, built into a late wall in the Lesche near the Pnyx.
Hiller 1921, 442; Töpffer 1889, 315; *IG* 1².886; Judeich 1931, 299;
Solders 1931, 3, no. 14; Guarducci 1937, no. 8; Hedrick 1988a, no. 2.
Text, *IG* 1².886.

> hιερὸν
> Διὸς Ξενί
> ο Θυμαιτί
> δος φρα
> 5 τρίας

Translation

Sanctuary of Zeus Xenios of the phratry Thymaitis.

Notes

2–3. Διὸς Ξενίο. It is notable that a phratry, with its fundamental
connections with Athenian citizenship, should be associated with the
cult of Zeus Xenios. An explanation has been sought (see Hiller at *IG*
1².886) in the Apatouria foundation myth (cf. pp. 144–45), in which the
phratry eponym Thymaitis played a role, and in one version of which
(*FGH* 327 Demon fr. 1) Melanthos, driven from his home in Messenia,
consulted the Pythia at Delphi on where he should settle. He is told to
choose the place where he is honored with *xenia* consisting of the head
and feet of a sacrificial victim. Receiving such xenia at Eleusis, he settles
there and eventually becomes king of Athens. Hedrick 1988a, 84–85,
has also suggested a link between Zeus Xenios and Zeus Herkeios (so
to speak the reverse aspect of Zeus), who is attested elsewhere in association with phratry religion (see pp. 213–16). Can we conclude from
the location of Thymaitadai (see next note) and the connection with
xenia that this phratry received newly enfranchised citizens, perhaps
especially Eleusinians when Eleusis was incorporated into Attica (cf. pp.
50–53)?

3–4. Θυμαιτί/δος φρα/τρίας. The eponym, Thymaites or Thymoites
(both forms are attested, cf. Threatte 1980, 296), must be the last of the

Theseid dynasty at Athens, the coward in the Apatouria myth who declined to duel with King Xanthos of Boeotia and lost his kingdom to his stand-in Melanthos as a result (cf. p. 145. The name seems otherwise to be attested only for a Trojan in the *Iliad,* Hom. *Il.* 3.146). Phratry eponyms tend to lack distinction (cf. pp. 220–22). Thymoites seems to have been positively nasty; he also killed his half-brother Apheidas to get to the throne (*FGH* 327 Demon fr. 1; *FGH* 90 Nic. Dam. fr. 48). Unless there is some mysterious polarity at work here (cf. p. 222), it is difficult to believe that Thymoites played such a role in the phratry's own tradition about its eponym (if it had a tradition at all) and we must suspect that, like the unremarkable Medon (cf. p. 316) he was a leader without a role and, with the leads already taken, he was assigned an unedifying bit part by Hellanikos. The link to the Apatouria is, of course, appropriate for a phratry eponym.

There was a deme Thymaitadai, on the coast west of Athens (Traill 1986, 136). It was thought to be a very ancient community; Theseus assembles his fleet there for the attack on Crete (*FGH* 323 Kleidemos fr. 17, cf. 328 Philochoros fr. 111), probably because it was a constituent of the Tetrakomoi (see Whitehead 1986a, 185, 224; *FGH* 328 Philochoros fr. 94). We must suppose that this was also the area of the phratry's base (for the similar name, cf. Dekeleieis). What the phratry would have called itself before Cleisthenes we cannot tell; we do not know how long before Cleisthenes phratry and kome/deme had been distinguishable. But Hedrick's suggestion (1988a, 83–84) that, like Gleontis, the adjectival form of the name in *-is* was designed to distinguish the phratry from another group with the same eponym, is attractive (he compares Boutadai and Eteoboutadai. As Hedrick notes at 1988a, 83, the same adjectival form of the name occurs at Ar. *Wasps* 1138, where a σισύρα (cloak) is described as Thymaitian. This seems likely to have meant more than that such garments were manufactured at Thymaitadai (so van Leeuwen 1909 ad loc.) but exactly what eludes us. The Trojan Thymoites may have something to do with it. He is just a name in Homer, but there must have been other legendary material, now lost, about him (cf. later mentions cited by Hedrick 1988a, 83 n. 10).

There must be some significance in the location of this phratry close to Eleusinian territory, which has associations with Melanthos and his xenia, and hence with the Apatouria myth and Thymoites (cf. previous note and further on T 14 below).

Date

Late fifth century (orthography).

Location

Area of deme Thymaitadai (see above), though with property in central Athens (findspots of T 13 and T 14).

T 14 Thymaitis

Marker, from north slope of Areopagos (discovered in Agora excavations at section X, cf. *Hesp.* 1935, 312).

Fine 1951, 11, no. 21 (with photograph, plate 4); Hedrick 1988a, no. 1. Text based on Fine's photograph and Hedrick 1988a.

$$[- - - - -]$$
$$[.]HP[- -]$$
καὶ ʽHρ[-]
Θυμαι[τίδος or τίδι]
5   φρατρ⟨ί⟩α[ς or ι]

1. -]ρ[- Fine. [ἱερὸν] Hedrick (see note at 1988a, 82). 2. -πε]πρ[αμένων - Fine. 3. καὶ ʽHρ[- Fine. καὶ ʽHρ[άκλεος Hedrick. 4. -]Θυμαι[τάδηι- Fine. Θυμαι[τίδος] Hedrick. 5. φρατρα[ι -]/- - Fine, φρατρ⟨ί⟩α[ς] Hedrick.

Translation

. . .-er . . . and Her- . . . the phratry Thymaitis.

Notes

Hedrick and I realized independently that Fine's restoration of this roughly inscribed document (as a horos of a *prasis epi lysei*) to involve someone with the demotic Θυμαιτάδης was mistaken (clear from Fine's own photograph, plate 4) and that it should be associated with T 13 and the phratry Thymaitis. Hedrick has reexamined the stone and now published his text and interpretation at 1988a. He suggests (p. 85) that this and T 13 should belong to the same sanctuary. Though the inscriptions were found on opposite sides of the Areopagos (neither in situ according to Hedrick), he thinks it "unlikely that the phratry kept two separate shrines in such close proximity in the heart of Athens." This appears plausible, but there is something wrong. If line 1 of T 14 is to be restored [ἱερὸν], we should probably with Hedrick also read ʽHρ[άκλεος in 3 (for Herakles as deity of the Tetrakomoi, see Palaios 1929; N]ηρ[είδων is a possibility for 2, cf. T 6 for a link between another watery deity, Kephisos, and a phratry); in any case there is no mention of Zeus Xenios here. That more than one deity might be worshipped in a single ἱερὸν is possible, but it would surely be odd for the same ἱερὸν to be described as "of Zeus Xenios" on one boundary marker, and "of - and Herakles" on another, though the two markers are admittedly not contemporary. If T 14 does mark a sanctuary it should probably be taken to be separate from, though surely near, that of Zeus Xenios. It is also possible, however, that this is some other sort of marker. We do not know how many lines are missing from the top of the stone; Fine's suggestion of a *prasis epi lysei* might after all be right (for other cases involving phratries see pp. 196–97). We would then need to take [.]ηρ[-/καὶ Ἡρ[- as names of persons, not gods (one at least would need to be a group within Thymaitis; with the Eleusinian connection I had thought of the Kerykes for 2, but a reference to a genos "of a phratry" in this way would be unparalleled). Alternatively we might take the phratry in the dative and 2–3 as separate creditors, also in the dative, cf. next note. That a phratry might be involved in the *prasis epi lysei* of a piece of land in the vicinity of its ἱερὸν is not implausible.

5. φράτρ⟨ί⟩ᾳ[ς or ι]. Hedrick 1988a, 82, may be right that we should insert ⟨ί⟩, since the form φράτρα is not attested in Attica. For this form outside Attica cf. p. 16, n. 57. Perhaps there is some significance in the foreign associations of this phratry in this connection. For a parallel dropping of the first rho in the word in the MSS of Arist. *Pol.* (not all) see p. 246 n. 6., and in *Ath. Pol.* fr. 3, p. 361. The slip would perhaps be marginally more consistent with the restoration of the word in the dative (i.e., as a case of haplography) than in the genitive. Cf. previous note.

Date

After ca. 400 (orthography).

Location

See on T 13.

T 15 Thyrgonidai and Titakidai

Photios s.v. Τιτακίδαι καὶ Θυργωνίδαι (cf. E.M. s.v. Τιτακίδαι; *Lexica Segueriana* [= Bekker *Anecdota Graeca*] 1.308, 16).

Τιτακίδαι καὶ θυργωνίδαι· φρατρίαι τινὲς καὶ γένη ἄδοξα καὶ οὐδενὸς ἄξια· εἰς γὰρ εὐτέλειαν ἐκωμῳδεῖτο· οὐχὶ δὲ δῆμοι ὡς οἴονταί τινες

θυργωνίδαί Velesius (ap. Harp. fr. 187). θυργωνδοι MSS.

Translation

Titakidai and Thyrgonidai: certain phratries and gene, unimportant and of no note, for they are made fun of for their insignificance. They are not demes, as some think.

Notes

These "insignificant" places seem to have been the subject of considerable dispute among ancient scholars. Nicander (Harp., s.v. θυργωνίδαι) claimed that they μετετέθησαν ἐξ Αἰαντίδος along with Aphidna and Perrhidai, and Demetrios of Skepsis (Harp., loc. cit.) that Thyrgonidai belonged to Ptolemais (he seems to have been right, see *IG* 2².2362, 49 ca. 200). Titakidai (this form of the name better attested than Titagidai) also appears in late inscriptions, including two ephebic lists of Ptolemais, and was assigned, wrongly it would seem, to Antiochis by Steph. Byz., see Traill 1975, 88. It seems from Photios that others (or perhaps just Photios himself) thought the notion that they were demes at all nonsense. Since neither is attested specifically as a deme before the late period and both appear in contexts together with the large deme Aphidna and the names of, apparently, communities within that deme, Traill's suggestion (1975, 87–88) that they were also "small communities" within Aphidna, which, by at least the late Roman period, acquired a measure of independent deme status, is attractive, and would account nicely for the dispute in antiquity. We can also make a reasonable attempt to get to the bottom of Photios' claim that Titakidai and Thyrgonidai were phratries and gene. We know the old comic poet Magnes wrote a comedy called Τιτακίδης or something similar (Phot., Suid., s.v. νῦν δή = fr. 6 K-A [= fr. 6 Edm] reads ἐν Πυτακίδηι, -δι or -σκι in different manuscripts.

Bernhardy's correction Τιτακίδης, followed by most scholars [though Kassel-Austin retain Πυτακίδης] must be on the right lines. The one surviving fragment of the play is uninformative). εἰς γὰρ εὐτέλειαν ἐκωμῳδεῖτο in our extract suggests that this play was the source of Photios' claim that these groups were phratries and gene. One suspects that some research had been done into these groups' status as demes and a reference in Magnes tracked down (note that the Photios tradition is our only source for this play). That they were indeed phratries connected with the deme Aphidna in the classical period is quite credible; there seems no reason to doubt that they were reliably attested as such by Magnes, and they could easily have developed into pseudo-demes by the later Roman period, by which time the phratry will have been defunct, cf. p. 275. In what sense they were also gene is unclear. It is not impossible that they were so in the genos/kome sense, cf. pp. 59–63, as well as phratries (cf. p. 18); but Photios and/or Magnes may simply have meant gene in the sense of family lines, cf. on Titakos, below.

It is notable that Isaeus seems to have mentioned the two groups together in his lost speech against one Nikokles on a matter of property (presumably an inheritance case; Isaeus fr. 34) in which κλητῆρες (summoners, or witnesses to a summons) and ψευδοκλητεία (falsely witnessing a summons) appear also to have figured (Harp., s.v. κλητῆρες καὶ κλητεύειν and ψευδοκλητεία). All our evidence for this speech comes from Harpocration, who also preserves the details about Titakidai and Thyrgonidai as demes. But if these groups were not demes in the fourth century, they can hardly have appeared as such in Isaeus. Moreover their appearance together in Magnes' *Titakides* should have preceded by some years their mention in Isaeus' speech; Magnes was producing plays in the late 470s, *IG* 2².2318, 7, 17. We may conclude that the Titakidai and Thyrgonidai were probably not protagonists in that speech. They may have been mentioned in passing (without any clarity as to what sort of group they were?) perhaps, as in Magnes, as well-known examples of some sort of εὐτέλεια.

The eponym of the Thyrgonidai is wholly obscure (as with many other phratries, cf. pp. 220–22. The eponym of the Titakidai should have been Titakos, the betrayer of Aphidna to the Tyndaridai in Herodotus (Hdt. 9.73; interestingly, another phratric eponym, Dekelos, plays a similar role in this story, cf. p. 222). This is vigorously denied, however, by Harp., s.v. Τιτακίδαι; it is not clear on what grounds, but one suspects they were weak. Titakos fits the pattern too well (see p. 222. Cf. however

Detienne 1979, 80 and n. 71, and Pohlenz 1916, 581–83, for possible connections between Titakos and the Titans, cf. *FGH* 328 Philochoros fr. 74).

Location

Aphidna (see above).

Unnamed Phratries

T 16

Decree, on two marble fragments, one found in excavations on Acropolis, the other of unknown provenience. E.M. 7698 + 7739. Stoichedon 25. Pittakes 1853, col. 911, no. 1459; Rangabé 1842–55, 533; *IG* 2.204; *IG* 2.598; Wilhelm 1905, col. 228; *IG* 2².1238; Guarducci 1937, no. 2; Hedrick 1988c. Text, Hedrick 1988c.

```
       [ἔδοξεν τοῖς] φράτερσι· N[. . . . εἶ]
       [πεν· ἐπειδὴ Εὐγ]είτων Εὐ[κλέος ε]
       [ὑηργέτησε τὸ κοιν]ὸν [τῶν] φρατ[έ]
       [ρων . . . . . . . .¹⁵ . . . . . . .]των καὶ [π]
    5  [ράττων διατελεῖ ἀεὶ] τὰ συνφ[έ]ρ
       [οντα τοῖς φράτερσι κ[αὶ νῦν καὶ
       [εν τῶι ἔμπροσθεν χρό]νωι καὶ α[.]
       [. . . . . . . . .¹⁷ . . . . . . .]μενος τὴν
       [. . . . . . . .¹⁵ . . . . . .] ἔρημον κατα
   10  [δικασθεῖσαν ἐν τ]ῶι δικαστ[η]ρί
       [ωι . . . . . .¹¹ . . . . . Ε]ὐγείτονος· δ[ε]
       [δόχθαι τοῖς φράτ]ερσι ἐπαινέ[σ]
       [αι Εὐγείτονα Εὐκ]λέος Φαληρέ[α]
       [καὶ στεφανῶσαι αὐ]τὸν χρυσῶ[ι σ]
   15  [τεφάνωι ἀπὸ . δραχμ]ῶν ἀρετ[ῆς ἕ]
       [νεκα καὶ δικαιοσύν]ης τῆς [εἰς τ]
       [οὺς φράτερας - - - - - - - - - - ]
```

Translation

(It was decided by the) phrateres: N- (proposed: since Eug)eiton son of Eu(kles has done well on behalf of the society of the phrateres) . . . and ((5) in his actions has always furthered) the interests (of the phrateres) both now and (in) times (past) and . . . the . . . (the verdict went) against by default (10) in the court . . . (of E)ugeiton, (it has been decided) by the phrateres to praise (Eugeiton son of Euk)les of Phaleron (and crown him with a) golden (15) (crown worth . . . drachm)as (because of) his goodness (and justice towards the phrateres . . .).

Notes

It was realized by Wilhelm that the two fragments of this inscription belonged together, but Hedrick has discovered that Kirchner, in his first edition of the joint text in *IG* 2², misaligned them, and has published a much improved text at 1988c, which I give here. Part of a crowning relief, showing the bottom halves of two (or possibly three, see Hedrick 1988c, 112 n.8) figures (presumably a representation of the coronation of Eugeiton) survives (see Binnebössel 1932, 12 no. 50; Svoronos 1908–11, 667 no. 442 (1) with plate 217). Hedrick suggests the large female figure crowning the honorand may have been Athena Phratria and the third figure, if there was one, Zeus Phratrios. The decree is of a standard honorific type (see further pp. 201–2), the only feature of note to our purposes being the service of some kind that has apparently been rendered the phratry by the honorand, Eugeiton, in the courts (8–11).

1. [ἔδοξεν τοῖς] φράτερσι· Ν[. . . Hedrick 1988c notes φράτερσιν· [. . . is possible, but would leave very little space for the name of the proposer. He also notes Νίκων as a possible restoration of that name.

2. Εὐγ]ϵίτων Εὐ[κλέος Hedrick's new restoration of the honorand's name ([Δ]αίτων, Kirchner), based on remnants in 2, 11, and 13, seems probable.

3–4. τὸ κοιν]ὸν [τῶν] φρατ[έ]/[ρων. For koinon used of phrateres, cf. p. 195 n. 33.

8–11. ἔρημον κατα/[δικασθεῖσαν ἐν τ]ῶι δικαστ[η]ρί/[ωι. However we restore the start of 10 (Lewis' κατα[δικασθεῖσαν, as reported by Hedrick 1988c, is plausible; a noun, with κατὰ in 9 as a preposition must also be possible) it is clear that there has been a legal process in a public court which has been decided by default (for the ἔρημος δίκη see Harrison, 1968–71, 2, 197–9; the defaulter could be plaintiff or defendant), that Eugeiton played some role in this, and that the phratry must have benefited. We can infer that the phratry was a party to the dispute, and may guess that Eugeiton represented it in court (cf. Hedrick 1988c, 116). More than that it is impossible to say, though we may guess the case involved property (cf. p. 193). The fact that this decree was found on the Acropolis and that Eugeiton is not referred to in it as συνήγορος, ἐπιμελητής vel. sim. is taken by Hedrick 1988c, 117, to suggest that he was someone outside the phratry of particular distinction and influence. This is possible, but doubtful. Eugeiton's services stretched back over years (5–7), and the mutually beneficial pattern of long-standing service and reward between a phratry member and his phratry would be entirely normal (cf. pp. 195–202), while such a close relationship with someone outside the phratry would be unexpected (cf. p. 197). As Hedrick recognizes, the name of Eugeiton's office may have been on the lost part of the stone. In any case, a phratry member could plausibly have rendered the phratry a service of this sort without holding a phratry office. If he did indeed represent the phratry in the case, under the familiar Athenian rule that litigants must represent themselves he would have had to be a phratry member. The placing of the decree on the Acropolis (if indeed that was its original location) perhaps suggests more that the phratry wanted to bestow some sort of national prominence on Eugeiton than that he had necessarily already achieved it. He is not otherwise known.

Date

Early to mid-fourth century (letter forms and -o- for -ου-, Hedrick).

Location

Neither the position of this inscription on the Acropolis nor the demotic of the probable member Eugeiton (Φαληρεύς) provide sufficient basis for identification of the phratry base.

T 17

Decree, on marble stele, once in museum at Liopesi (ancient Paiania). Stoichedon 28.

SEG 3.121 (Ziebarth, with suggestions from Wilhelm and Klaffenbach); Guarducci 1937, no. 3; Kyparissis and Peek 1941, 219–21, no. 2 with plate 77.1 (apparently without knowledge of *SEG* 3.121); Davies 1971, 68, no. 2254; Hedrick 1989. Text based on Hedrick 1989.

[θε]οί
[. . . . . . .¹⁴. . . . . . .]του εἶ⟨π⟩εν· ἐπειδὴ
[Εὐκτήμων ᾿Αρρενε]ίδου καὶ ᾿Αρρενεί
[δης Καλλικλέους?] ἄνδρες ἀγαθοί εἰ
5 [σι περὶ τὸ κοινὸν] τῶν φρατέρων καὶ
[. . . . . .¹². . . . . .αἱ]ρεθέντες τοῦ ναο
[ῦ, τῶι Διὶ τῶι Φρατ]ρίωι καὶ τῆι ᾿Αθην
[αίαι τῆι Φρατρία]ι ἐπέδωκαν εἰς τὴ
[ν. . . . .¹⁰. . . . .δρα]χμὰς διακοσίας ν
10 [. . . . . . .¹⁴. . . . . . .]ξαι τοὺς φράτερα
[ς. . . . . . .¹³. . . . . .] δεδόχθαι το[ῖς φρ]
[άτερσιν ἐπαινέσα]ι Εὐ[κτ]ή[μονα ᾿Αρρ]
[ενείδου καὶ ᾿Αρρενείδην Καλλικλέ]
[ους – – – – – – – – – – – – – –
– – – – – – – – – – – – – – – – – –

1. Inscribed on cymation. 3. [Χαρικλῆς? ᾿Αρρενε]ίδου Wilhelm. [Καλ-λικλῆς ᾿Αρρενε]ίδου Davies. [Εὐ. .η. . .᾿Αρρενε]ίδου Hedrick. 4. [Χαρικλείους?] Ziebarth, followed by Hedrick. 5. Ziebarth. 6. [ἐργε-πιστάται?] Wilhelm. [ἀρχιτέκτονες] Klaffenbach. 7–8. Ziebarth. 9. [οἰκοδομίαν] Klaffenbach. [κατασκευήν] Peek. 10. [β/ουλόμενοι κου-φίσ]αι Ziebarth. ν/[ομίσαντες ἀπαλλά]ξαι Peek. 11. [ς τοῦ ἀναλώμα-τος,] Ziebarth, followed by Hedrick. 12–14. [άτερσιν ἐπαινέσα]ι Εὐ[. . .]η[. . .᾿Αρρε]/[νείδου καὶ ᾿Αρρενείδην Χαρικλείο[/[υς-/- - Hedrick, based on Peek.

Translation

The gods. . . [name of person] proposed: since (Euktemon son of Arrhene)ides and Arrhenei(des son of Kallikles?) are benefactors (5) (of the society) of the phrateres and . . . chosen . . . of the shrine, have contributed two hundred drachmas for the . . . (to Zeus Phrat)rios and Athen(a Phratri)a . . . (10) the phrateres . . . (the phrateres) have decided (to praise) Eu(kt)e(mon son of Arrheneides and Arrheneides son of Kallikles . . .

Notes

Hedrick 1989 published a new version of this text based on a collation of the two previous editions of Ziebarth et al. in 1927 and Peek in 1941, the latter having apparently not been aware of the former. My text follows his except at points where his readings are indicated in the Apparatus. As with T 16, this is a standard honorific inscription, the main point of interest being the half-preserved record of a special service, in this case apparently the contribution of money for some religious purpose, rendered by the honorands. There is a minor subsidiary puzzle over the identification of the honorands. For the currently unanswerable question as to whether this decree belongs to the same phratry as the earlier list of phrateres, T 18, also found at Paiania, see p. 81.

3–4. [Εὐκτήμων ᾽Αρρενε]ίδου καὶ ᾽Αρρενεί/[δης Καλλικλέους?] Care is needed over the identification of these two persons, the honorands. Previous editors have latched onto the well-known ᾽Αρρενείδης Χαρικλέους Παιανιεύς, attested in a number of documents from 357 (a trierarchy, *IG* 2².1953, 11) to 325/4 (paying a debt arising from an obligation as guarantor, *IG* 2².1629, 533, cf. *IG* 2².1623, 177; for full details of him and his family see Davies 1971, no. 2254; Walbank 1983, 193, 198), and identified him with ᾽Αρρενεί[- in 3 of T 17. I have no doubt that the two belong to the same family, but do not think they are the same person. First, the genitive singular of the name of the well-known Arrheneides' father should be Χαρικλέους (so Davies, and all other documents where the man's patronymic is attested). This has to be stretched into the unexpected form Χαρικλείους (attested once for this name, *IG* 2².6261, 1, but never for this man; see Threatte 1980, 156–57, whose view at 147 is that ει for ε tends to be characteristic of certain individuals, though it is admittedly unclear how far this applies to names in which the form occurs only in the oblique cases) to fit the available spaces (established securely enough by the restorations of 7, 8, and 12). Second, while the restoration ᾽Αρρενε]ίδου in 3 is highly probable for the first honorand (cf. Hedrick 1989, 135 n. 46), I doubt whether this man is the son of a restored Ἀρρενεί/[δης Χαρικλείους] in 3–4, as suggested originally by Wilhelm (followed by Hedrick). It is unlikely that Arrheneides' son would be placed in the decree before the distinguished Arrheneides himself, and a son of the well-known Arrheneides is attested and his name was Kallikles (Davies, op. cit), which will not fit the available space in 3, let alone the probable restoration [Εὐ..η-] (cf. 12 and further, below). Neither argument is decisive, but there is a neater solution, namely to restore Arrheneides, the second named honorand, as Ἀρρενεί[δης Καλλικλέους]; the name of the father is both attested as the son of the well-known Arrheneides and fits the available space exactly. We may reasonably suppose this person to be the well-known Arrheneides' grandson. If he was the issue of the marriage of Kallikles which, because it had recently taken place, saved his house from being searched in 324 (*FGH* 115 Theopompos fr. 330 = Plut. *Dem.* 25.7–8), we can establish a likely *terminus post* for this inscription of ca. 305 (it is just possible Kallikles had been married before, cf. Davies, loc. cit.). At the age of about sixty he may have been Ἀρρενείδης [(II)? Παιαν-ιεύς?) *PA* 2252, who was archon in or a little before 260 (cf. Davies, loc. cit; for the date Meritt 1961b, esp. 221–26; Habicht 1979, 113 and 1982, 15–16 cf. 21, 70). In any event, he would have been junior to our first honorand, – Ἀρρενε]ίδου. Who was this person? He cannot be the father of Arrheneides, whose name will not fit the space; he would probably have been dead by now. Hedrick and Peek are probably correct that Εὐ[..]η- in 12 is likely to be from his name. The only name in Davies 1971 which has those letters in those positions is Εὐκτήμων; it fits the space exactly. I restore it here and in 12 as a probability. The name is not previously attested in this family, but it is common enough: six, apparently unrelated, in Davies 1971. The simplest hypothesis is that this man was a (younger) brother of Καλλικλῆς Ἀρρενείδου and uncle of the second honorand. He should have been dead by about 280.

6–9. -αἱ]ρεθέντες τοῦ ναο/ῦ ... δρα]χμὰς διακοσίας. Whatever the correct restorations of these lines, the general sense is clear enough from the preserved text. The two honorands had been chosen by the phratry to fulfill some function or office with respect to the phratry ναός. *SEG* 3 took it, probably correctly, to concern the structure of that building. In this connection they made a contribution of two hundred drachmas "to Zeus Phratrios and Athena Phratria," presumably the deities of the ναός (cf. pp. 208–9). For their services they are being honored with this inscription and, probably recorded in the missing lower section, awarded golden crowns or the like (cf. T 16). They are both clearly members of the phratry.

Date

? ca. 305–280 (see note on 3–4 above).

Location

The findspot of this inscription, not known more precisely than that it was at one stage in the Liopesi museum, and the demotics of the honorands strongly suggest an association between this phratry and the area of the two Paiania demes. T 18 was also found roughly in this area and may or may not belong to the same phratry (cf. p. 81).

T 18

List of names, on marble stele from Kapsospiti (between the site of ancient Paiania and foothills of Hymettos, Hedrick 1989, 128 with n. 13). Stoichedon (3–22, with minor exceptions in 13, 18).

Kastriotis 1901, 158–62; Körte 1902, 582–89; von Premerstein 1910, 103–17, esp. 113–15 (with photograph, plate 15); Ferguson 1910, 257–84 esp. 259–60, 264, 268; *IG* 2².2344; Guarducci 1937, no. 14; Flower 1985, 232–35; Hedrick 1989, 126–35. Text, Hedrick 1989.

	Διὸς : Φρατρίο : ᾿Αθηνάας : Φρατ[ρίας]
	οἵδε φράτερες
	Ποσείδιππος : Ξενοτίμο
	Μνήσαρχος : Μνησικλείδο
5	Σώσιππος : Σωσιπόλιδος
	Μνησίθεος : Μνησιφίλο
	᾿Επιχάρης : Μνησικλείδο
	Σώσιππος : Σωσιστράτο
	Μνῆσος : Μνησιφίλο
10	Μενεκλείδης : Ξενοκλείδο
	Μνησικλείδης : Μνησάρχο
	Σωσίπολις : Σωσίππο
	Μνησιγένης : Μνησιγένος
	Ξενότιμος : Ποσειδίππο
15	Σωσίστρατος : Σωσίππο
	Σώστρατος : Σωσίππο
	Λυσίας : Ποσειδίππο
	Φιλόδημος : Φιλοδήμο
	Μνησικλείδης : ᾿Επιχάρος
20	Φίλων : Σωσίππο
	Μνησιθείδης : ᾿Επιχάρος
	Μνησίφιλος : Μνησιθέο
	Vertically down the right side:
	Σώσιππος : Σωσιπόλιδος : ἀνέγρα[ψεν]

Translation

Zeus Phratrios. Athena Phratria
These are the phrateres
[List of 20 names, see text above]

[Vertically down r.h. side:]
Inscribed by Sosippos son of Sosipolis

Notes

For the questions of whether this is the list of a whole phratry or a subgroup, and whether it pertains to the same phratry as T 17, which was found in roughly the same area, both unanswerable questions on the basis of current evidence, see pp. 79–81. The names can be grouped into at most eight families (for stemmata see Hedrick 1989, 132; none are attested elsewhere), belonging to two generations (for the possible significance of the absence of a third, see p. 80), with the older generation listed before the younger. It is reasonable to suppose that, within the generations, the names are listed in order of seniority; thus the son of Mnesarchos (4) is listed at 11, while the sons of his probable younger brother Epichares (7) are listed at 19 and 21. We would expect that Sosippos, third on the list, who set up the inscription, was phratriarch (cf. T 5), priest (cf. T 3) or head of the subgroup, if it is such. I do not agree with Flower 1985 that he must be priest, nor Hedrick 1989 that he should be neither priest nor phratriarch because he would have described himself as such. The purpose of the list is obscure. Given the early-fourth-century date, when we know there was a general concern with reinforcing citizenship qualifications after the laxities of the Peloponnesian War (cf. T 3, p. 34 n. 40, pp. 48–49), the carefully ordered list (surely based on the phratry register, cf. pp. 174–75, in which case the absence of demotic tells us nothing, despite Hedrick and others 1989, 131–32, who were inclined to think they must all have been Παιανιεῖς; we should not expect a phratry register to have included demotics), the assertive οἵδε φράτερες in 2 and the absence of any figures that would suggest some financial purpose, cf. T 35, the most attractive hypothesis is that it is an authoritative list of the phrateres compiled following a phratry scrutiny, cf. Hedrick 1989, 133. If that is the case, however, it does not decide whether this is a whole phratry or a subgroup.

Date

Early fourth century (orthography).

Location

Probably area of Paiania (findspot of inscription).

T 19

Decree, on marble stele in front of shrine of Panagia at Charvati (site of uncertain deme). Stoichedon 23-25?

IG 2.1, 599 (Köhler, from notes by Velsen); Milchhöfer 1887, 85, no. 13; *IG* 2².1239 (Kirchner); Guarducci 1937, no. 4. Text based on *IG* 2².1239 (with reference to *IG* 2 and Milchhöfer 1887).

> [Διὶ Φ]ρατρίωι
> [..]Λ[.]ΣΣ[.]Τ[.]ΡΟ[..]Υ
>
> ---
>
> – – – – –]Ο[– – – – –
>
> [16 lines illegible]

20　[....⁸....]ο[– – – – – –
　　[....⁷...]λ[.]λο[– – – – – –
　　[φράτ]ερες τι[μήσουσιν τοὺς π?]
　　[ρὸς] τοὺς φράτ[ερας φιλοτιμο?]
　　[υμεν?]ους. ἀν[αγ]ρ[άψαι δὲ τόδε τὸ]
25　[ψήφι]σμα τὸν [φ]ρατρ[ίαρχον εἰς σ]
　　[τήλ]ην λιθίνην κα[ὶ] σ[τῆσαι ἔμπρ]
　　[οσθεν] τοῦ φρατρ[ίου, εἰς δὲ τὴν]
　　[ἀν]αγραφὴν τῆ[ς] στ[ήλης δοῦναι]
　　[τὸ]ν φρατρίαρχο«ν» [– – – – – – –]
30　[..]ω[..]ο[.]χων
　　　　vacat

1. ΔΝΟΑΤΡΙΩΝ Velsen. [Διὶ Φ]ρατρίωι Milchhöfer, on reexamination of the stone. 2. Velsen. -λ[η]ς Στ[ρομβ]υ[λιῶνος Köhler, followed by Kirchner. 22-30. Köhler. 29. ΝΦΡΑΤΡΙΑΡΧΟΙ Velsen.

Translation

> Zeus Phratrios
> [20 lines illegible]

(22) (phrat)eres will h(onor those who are zealous on behalf of) the phrateres. The phratr(iarch?) shall inscribe (this (25) decree on) a stone

stele and set (it up in front of) the phratr(ion?) The phratriarch? shall give..(towards the) inscription of the stele.

Notes

The stone was almost completely worn when Milchhöfer saw it over a century ago. There has been no subsequent autopsy. Given this and Velsen's misreadings in the first line, Köhler's restoration of 2 to give the extremely rare name (one second-century case in Kirchner 1903) Στ[ρομβ]υ[λιῶνος as the patronymic of an honorand on the basis of Velsen's jottings is very doubtful. Köhler's attractive restoration of the handful of letters read by Velsen in 22–30 may not be exactly right—it gives a stoichedon varying between 23 and 25—but the sense from 24 onward is clear enough. These are the provisions for having the decree inscribed. His restoration of 22–24 is plausible, but can be no more, and provides an insecure basis for claiming this to be an honorific rather than some other type of decree. If the restoration in 27 is correct, this is one of only two epigraphical occurrences in Attica of a phratrion (cf. p. 194). It is also a valuable, because increasingly unusual, case of a phratry with a single phratriarch. Or is it, cf. Köhler at *IG* 2? It is somewhat disturbing that the only time the ending is preserved (29), Velsen read the last letter as ι not ν; and what of –χων in 30? τὸν in 25 and ν at the start of 29 perhaps maintain the balance in favor of a single phratriarch, but only just.

Date

End of fourth century (Kirchner).

Location

Traill 1975, 41, assigned Kydantidai to the deme site Kato Charvati but in 1986, 128, he preferred the site at Mendeli for that deme. This seems to leave Charvati unassigned. For Kydantidai as a possible center of the Demotionidai see pp. 112–13, n. 64.

T 20

Decree, from the garden of A.R. Rangabé in Kephisia. Original findspot and present whereabouts unknown.

Wilhelm 1905, cols. 227–28, no. 6; *IG* 2².1240; Guarducci 1937, no. 5. Text based on Wilhelm 1905.

```
- - - - - - - - - - - - - - - - -
     [- - - - - - - - - - - - -]α ὅσα [.]
     [- - - - - - - - - - - - -]έους Χο[λ]
     [- - - - - - - - - - - - -]σα ν τὰ ἱε
     [ρ- - - - - - - - - - - - ]ωι καὶ τη
5    [- - - - - - - - - - - - -]ον γυνὴ μ
     [- -- - - - - - - - - - -] ἐπειδὴ ο
     [- - - - - - - - - - - ἐλέ?]σθαι πέν
     [τε - - - - - - - - - - -] ὅσα θύετα
     [ι - - - - - - - - - - - -]ει τὸν ἱερέ
10   [α- -ἀναγράψαι δὲ τόδε τὸ ψήφισ?]μα ἐν στήλ[η]
     [ι λιθίνηι - - καὶ στῆσαι ἔμπροσθεν το?]ῦ φρατ[ρ]ίο
     [υ- - - - - - - - - - - -]ιτες [ . . . ]
- - - - - - - - - - - - - - - - -
```

1. [.] Wilhelm shows the bottom l.h. quarter of a round letter. 7–8. – εὐθύνε]σθαι πεν/[τε or πεντήκοντα δραχμάς Wilhelm. 10.]μ The remains of this letter look more like Λ in W's illustration. 11. [ι λιθίνηι τὸν φρατρίαρχον or τοὺς φρατριάρχους καὶ κτλ. Wilhelm. 12. [. . .] Wilhelm shows part of a downward stroke in the second of these stoichoi.

Translation

[. . . such as are . . . son of . . es of Cho(largos or –lleidai) . . . the priestly . . . and . . . (5) woman . . . since the . . . (choose?) five . . . such as are sacrificed . . . the priest . . ((10) shall inscribe this) decree on a (stone) stele (and set it up in front of) the phratrion (?) . . .

Notes

We cannot be sure what was the purpose of this decree. Nowhere, except possibly for the formula that provides for the decree's inscription at the end, does enough survive to make continuous sense of the text. Wilhelm thought that the document was religious in character on the basis of ἱε̣[ίρ in 3-4, sacrificing in 8-9 and a priest in 9-10. He is probably right with respect to the surviving fragment of the stone, but we do not know how much we are missing from earlier, or possibly later, parts of the text and therefore cannot be sure that we do not merely have remnants of the religious post- or prescript of a text primarily concerned with something else. Inscriptions of whole phratries the main subject of which is the regulation of religious cult are rare, possibly nonexistent (cf. pp. 219-20). It is possible, therefore, that this is the decree of a phratry subgroup rather than of a whole phratry (cf. p. 235). That would not be inconsistent with the fact that it was apparently set up "in front of the phratrion" (11). It is not difficult to imagine that the phratrion might have been used both by a phratry and its subgroups.

2. -]έους Χο[λ]. This seems likely to be the end of a patronymic and the start of a demotic: either Χολαργεύς (Bouleutic quota 4) or Χολλείδης (Bouleutic quota 2) would fit the initial two surviving letters.

5. -]ον γυνὴ μ/[-. This sole obscure reference to a woman in a phratry decree is tantalizing. We have reason to suppose women were more closely involved in the phratries than they were in the demes (cf. pp. 36-37, 178-88) but we are almost entirely ignorant of what this meant in practice. Wilhelm suggested that they were perhaps being excluded from some religious event (taking μ in 5 as μ/[ή]). This has nothing in particular to recommend it (cf. p. 186). Note the participation of women in the orgeones group of Meritt 1942, no. 55 (cf. Ferguson 1949, 130-31) and the possibility that T 20 was also the decree of a phratry subgroup.

7. I prefer ἑλέ]σθαι here (cf. T 17, 6; T 12, 5-6 and especially T 3, 32-33) to Wilhelm's εὐθύνε]σθαι (unprecedented in a phratry decree), but there are of course other possibilities.

10-11. ἀναγράψαι . . . Wilhelm's restoration of an inscription formula here is plausible. The text in 12 and whatever followed must either contain a postscript of some sort, e.g., details of ἱερεώσυνα, or perhaps the start of another motion (cf. T 3). Whether it is the phratriarch(s) who had the decree erected, however, as Wilhelm supposed, or the priest mentioned at 9-10 (cf. T 3) is uncertain. The latter may be preferable.

11. The sole secure epigraphic attestation of a phratrion (cf. T 19) depends on Wilhelm's reading of the last letter of this line correctly as O rather than A (i.e., φρατρίαρχ-). In his illustration the lefthand half of a round character is shown.

See also notes to T 29.

Date

Mid-fourth century (lettering, Wilhelm and Guarducci); end of fourth century? (Kirchner).

Location

The only topographical indication in this document is the likely demotic Cholargos or Cholleidai in 3. We can draw no conclusion as to phratry base.

T 21

Marker of a *prasis epi lysei,* unknown provenience (the story told to Robinson that it came from near the Agora seems unconvincing).
Robinson 1907, 430, no. 4; von Premerstein 1910, 103–17 (photograph, p. 104); Ferguson 1910, 267–68; *IG* 2².2723; Guarducci 1937, no. 16; Robinson 1944, 18, n. 13; Finley 1952, 110 and no. 41; Hedrick 1984, T 27. Text, Hedrick 1984.

ὅρος χωρ[ίο]
πεπραμέν[ο]
ἐπὶ λύσει Κηφ[ι]
σοδώρωι Λευκογ(οιεῖ)
5   Χ⌐ καὶ φράτερ
σι τοῖς μετὰ ᾽Ερα
τοστράτο ᾽Ανα
φλ(υστίο) ΧΗΗ καὶ Γλ[α]
υκίδαις ⌐Η κạ[ι]
10   ᾽Επικλείδαις
Η⌐καὶ φράτερ
σι τοῖς μετὰ Νίκ
ωνος ᾽Αναφλ(υστίο) Η

7-8. Robinson, ᾽Αναφλυ(στίο) ΗΗ von Premerstein. "The letter after the Λ is certainly not a Y, but a Χ," Hedrick, following Robinson.

Translation

Marker of the property sold subject to redemption to Kephisodoros of Leukonoion for 1,500 drachmas, and to the phrateres with Eratostratos of Anaphlystos for 1,200 drachmas and to the Glaukidai for 600 drachmas and to the Epikleidai for 150 drachmas and to the phrateres with Nikon of Anaphlystos for 100 drachmas.

Notes

For the nature and relationship to one another of the buyers subject to redemption on this stone, see p. 78–79. For the nature of the process see p. 197. It is likely, but not certain, that they and the "seller" of the land, whose identity is unknown, were all members of the same phratry (cf. pp. 78–79, 197–98). I agree with Finley 1952, 110, that this is more likely to be the record of a single transaction than of five successive "mortgages" taken out on the same property; why inscribe them all at once? The total value of the *prasis* was either 2,550 or 3,550 drachmas, depending on the reading in 8. The reading of Robinson and Hedrick gives the higher total and seems preferable; the list would then be in descending order of value. We do not know to what percentage of its value this property was "mortgaged," but compare the substantial property of the Dyaleis (T 5), which was leased in 300/299 for 600 drachmas a year for ten years, with an option to buy at any time during that period for 5,000 drachmas. The total sum of the *prasis,* however, does not seem of a different order from most of the others listed in Finley's appendix. Cf. p. 201.

Date

Earlier fourth century (orthography; an Eratostratos is attested at Anaphlystos in 334/3 in the prytany catalogue *IG* 2².1750, 6).

Location

If, as is probable, all the creditors belonged to one phratry, the two demotics Anaphlystos and the one Leukonoieus suggest a phratry base in southwest Attica; for the location of Leukonoion in this area, see p. 281. It is just possible that this phratry was the Achniadai, who probably also had a member from Leukonoion (see p. 281).

T 22

Altar, inscribed on all four sides, found in situ in association with a temenos wall in the northern part of the ancient city of Athens, probably in the deme Skambonidai. Agora Inventory no. I 6709. Kyparissis and Thompson 1938, 612–25 (with diagrams); Travlos 1971, 573–75. Hedrick 1991, 256–57. Text, Hedrick 1991.

Face A:
[Δι]ὸς
Face B:
Φρατρίο
Face Γ:
’Αθήνας
Face Δ:
Φρα[τρίας]

Translation

Zeus Phratrios, Athena Phratria

Notes

This altar, and the temenos wall with which it was associated, were excavated by Kyparissis and Thompson in 1937 (see now also Hedrick 1991, 256–59). They are the only physical remains found in situ that can be ascribed with some degree of certainty to a structure of an individual Attic phratry (cf. T 24 for another possible case). See figures 1 and 2 and map 1.

Date

Late fourth to early third century (letter forms and archaeological context).

Location

The temenos of this phratry was in northern Athens (probably Skambonidai, cf. map in Travlos 1971, fig. 218, no. 241, and Traill 1986, 130). Whether this is a city property of a phratry with a rural base (cf. p. 13), or whether the main base of the phratry was in this area, is impossible to say.

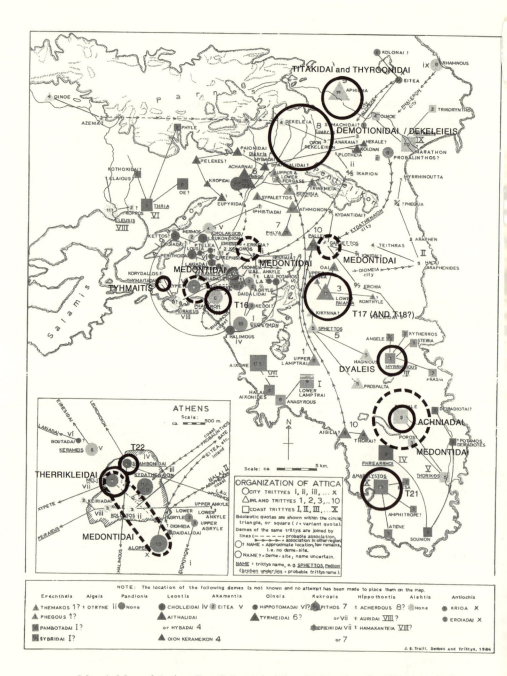

Map 1. Map of Attica. For the associations of phratries with the locations shown see the Introduction, especially n. 42 and notes in appendix 1 under the sections entitled Location. There is no firm evidence for association with specific location for phratry T 6 Gleontis or for unnamed phratries T 19–20 and T 23–26. Possible phratries are not shown. For the probable location of the deme Leukonoion in the area of Kephale, see notes to T 2.

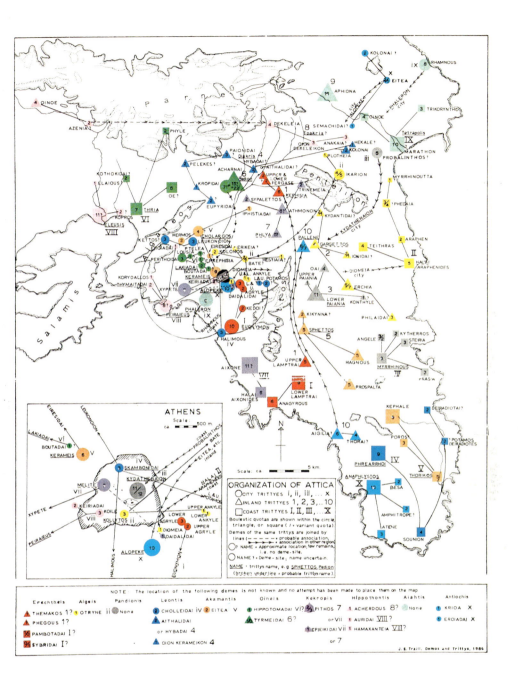

ORGANIZATION OF ATTICA

○ CITY TRITTYES i, ii, iii, ... x
△ INLAND TRITTYES 1, 2, 3, ... 10
□ COAST TRITTYES I, II, III, ... X

Bouleutic quotas are shown within the circle, triangle, or square (/ = variant quota).
Demes of the same trittys are joined by lines (——— = probable association, -------→ = association in other region).
○ NAME? = Approximate location, few remains, i.e. no deme-site.
◯ NAME? = Deme-site; name uncertain.
NAME = trittys name, e.g. SPHETTOS, Pedion (broken underline = probable trittys name).

NOTE: The location of the following demes is not known and no attempt has been made to place them on the map

Erechtheis	Aigeis	Pandionis	Leontis	Akamantis	Oineis	Kekropis	Hippothontis	Aiantis	Antiochis
THEMAKOS 1?	OTRYNE ii	None	CHOLLEIDAI iV	EITEA V	HIPPOTOMADAI VI?	PITHOS 7	ACHERDOUS 8?	None	KRIOA X
PHEGOUS 1?			AITHALIDAI		TYRMEIDAI 6?	or VII	AURIDAI VIII?		EROIADAI X
PAMBOTADAI 1?			or HYBADAI 4			EPIEIKIDAI VII	HAMAXANTEIA VIII?		
SYBRIDAI 1?			DION KERAMEIKON 4			or 7			

J.S. Traill, Demos and Trittys, 1986

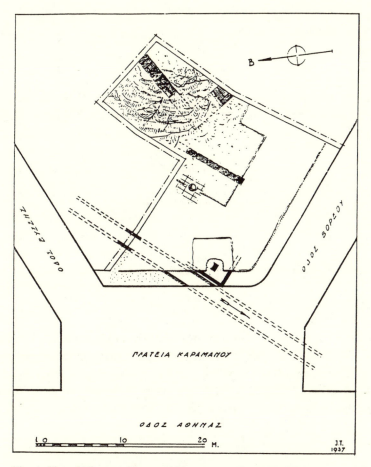

Fig. 1. Site of Phratry Altar and Temenos wall, North Athens.
Karamanos Square and adjacent area as explored in 1937.

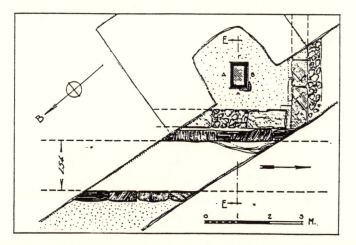

Fig. 2. Site of Phratry Altar and Temenos wall, North Athens.
Sanctuary of Zeus and Athena.

T 23

Marker of a phratry house, unknown provenience. E.M. 10164.

Ziebarth 1898, 791 no. 24; *IG* 2².2622; Guarducci 1937, no. 13. Text, *IG* 2².

ὄρο[ς]
οἰκία[ς]
φρατέρ[ων]

Translation

Marker of the house of the phrateres

Notes

This οἰκία sounds like some sort of phratry meeting place (so Guarducci), but we cannot be certain. The Klytidai on Chios met in οἰκίαι (Soko-lowski 1969, no. 118, cf. p. 103), but it is not clear whether the οἰκία on the property leased by the Dyaleis in 300/299 was used for that purpose, or whether it was simply a farm building (cf. p. 305).

Date

After c. 400 (orthography).

Location

Unknown.

T 24

Altar, found in Agora near Stoa of Attalos. Agora Inventory no. I 3706.
Thompson 1937, 104–7; Hedrick 1988b (with photograph, fig. 6). Text,
from photograph at Hedrick 1988b, 192.

Διὸς Φρατρί[ου]
καὶ ᾿Αθηνᾶς Φρατρίας

Translation

Zeus Phratrios and Athena Phratria

Notes

Thompson 1937 argued that this altar should be associated with a small
building in the Agora of the second half of the fourth century, which
he identified as a central Athenian sanctuary of Zeus Phratrios and
Athena Phratria. His arguments rested essentially on the proximity of
this building to sixth-century remains that in his view were from the
sanctuary of a related cult, that of Apollo Patroos—there was a fourth-
century sanctuary of that cult on the same site—and on his identification
of the bedding block for the altar on the site of the small fourth-century
building. Hedrick 1988b doubts the identification of the sixth-century
remains as a sanctuary of Apollo Patroos (cf. pp. 209–10 and 212) and
the connection between the altar and the bedding block found in the
small fourth-century building. He suggests that the altar may have
belonged to one of the "numerous phratry shrines which were scattered
throughout the Agora," and that it may have come from the same sanctuary as the marker T 25 (see below). The evidence that there were
numerous shrines of individual phratries in the Agora is weak; there is
only one attested with any degree of certainty, that of Thymaitis, T 13
and 14, cf. T 11 and 12 (Therrikleidai). Also, as Hedrick himself recognizes, his case against Thompson's hypothesis is not conclusive. This
may, therefore, be the altar either of an individual phratry or of a state
cult of Zeus Phratrios and Athena Phratria.

Date

Fourth century (letter forms).

Location

Cf. T 25, with which this altar may or may not be associated (see above).

T 25

Marker, from the Agora near Stoa of Attalos.

IG 2².4975; Guarducci 1937, no. 12; Hedrick 1988b. Text, Hedrick 1988b, 193.

ἱερὰ Διὸς
Φρατρίο
καὶ Ἀθηνᾶ[ς]

Translation

Sacred to Zeus Phratrios and Athena.

Notes

The inscription was cut on an already broken marble roof tile. As noted by Hedrick 1988b, 193, it is reasonable to associate it with the altar of Zeus Phratrios and Athena Phratria (T 24), found in the same area of the Agora. Whether the altar belonged to an individual phratry or to a state cult of the two deities is unclear (see above on T 24). In either case it is doubtful whether T 25 should be seen simply as the marker of the sanctuary of that altar; in that case we would expect ἱερὸν, not ἱερὰ in 1. Perhaps it pertains to sacred objects associated with the cult (cf. T 8).

Date

Earlier fourth century (orthography).

Location

It is not clear whether this marker belonged to an individual phratry or to a state cult. If the former, we have no clues to the phratry's location (cf. on T 24).

T 26

Fragment of accounts of one percent deposit or tax on property sale, once in E.M. Non-stoichedon.

IG 2² 1600; Lewis 1973, app. A, stele III, face B, uncertain column, no. 58. Text based on *IG* 2².

> [ὠν.η - -]ππος ⊢ -
> [κεφάλα]ιον : ΧΗΗΗ[Ⴊ]
> [ἑκατο]στή : Δ[⊢] ⊢ ⊢ ΙΙΙ ·
> - - -]ων φρα[τρ]ία[ρχος]
> 5   - - -]ς 'Αρ[ι]στω[ν - -
> [ἀπέδοτο] ἐσχατι[ὰν ἐν - -
> - - καλ]ου[μεν ?

[The description of a new transaction starts at 4]

1. [ὠν. Kirchner. 4. Kirchner. Preferable to his second alternative -ω]ν φρα[τρ]ία[ς φρατρίαρχος.

Translation

> .. (bought by ..-)ppos ? ..
>   (total): 1,350
>   (1 percent): 13½
> (5) .. son of Ariston-, phratriarch of the ... (sold) the outlying property (at ...) called ? ...

Notes

This is one of fifteen fourth-century fragments of accounts, the so-called Rationes Centesimarum, that record the sale of landed property. They include names of buyers and sellers, a brief description of the property, and a record of the full purchase price and of 1 percent of that price. It is not specified to whom the 1 percent was paid, i.e., whether it was a tax or a deposit. Theophrastos fr. 21 (Szegedy-Maszak = fr. 97 Wimmer) tells us that property sales at Athens had to be registered with the authorities (τῆ ἀρχῆ) sixty days in advance and that the purchaser had to put down 1 percent of the price, so that his identity would be clear and opportunity be given for disputing the sale. Lewis 1973 grouped the fragments into three stelai and discussed some of the numerous problems of interpretation; see also Andreyev 1960 and 1967 (in Russian; mentioned with approval by Lewis); Oikonomides 1980 = *SEG* 30.104; R. Osborne 1985, 56–59. Lewis was inclined to play down the connection of these documents with the apparently regular procedure recorded by Theophrastos and, with Andreyev, to see them as records of "something which is happening virtually on only one occasion" (1973 191, cf. 187). This is not the place for a discussion of this point, though some of his arguments against the connection seem unconvincing. For example, at 193–94 he suggests that the texts were set up on the Acropolis, that the 1 percent was paid to Athena, and that "this must mark a final clear distinction between our texts and the procedure recorded by Theophrastos." But Theophrastos does not tell us to whom his 1 percent was paid, so no distinction can be established on these grounds. Moreover, even if it is correct that the surviving fragments belong to stelai set up "virtually on one occasion" that does not demonstrate that the procedure did not occur on other occasions. R. Osborne's suggestion at 1985, 57, building on Lewis' interpretation, that these transactions are leases, not sales, is fanciful and unconvincing.

It is notable that all the sellers in the fragments we possess were corporate bodies, not individuals; we do not know why. This is the only certain instance among the surviving texts of a sale by a phratry. For other possible cases, see T 27. It is no surprise to find a phratry selling landed property; we also have evidence that they leased such property (T 5) and bought it subject to redemption (T 10, T 21, possibly T 14). See further pp. 194–98.

4–5. - -]ων φρα[τρ]ία[ρχος]/ - -]ς ᾽Αρ[ι]στω[ν- -. Comparison with sections of the same stele where the relevant part of the text is preserved (e.g., *IG* 2².1597, 15, 19) suggest ων should be the name of the phratry in the genitive; - -]ς should be the name and ᾽Αρ[ι]στω[ν- the patronymic of the phratriarch. Kirchner's alternative reconstruction (see app. crit. above) is less attractive. For the phratriarch as agent of his phratry in land transactions, see p. 228. For epimeletai performing this function, see T 27.

6. ἐσχατι[ὰν. Lewis 1973, 210–12, attractively suggested that this term,

which designates property in some way on the outskirts, was generally used specifically to designate property in the neighborhood of hills.

Date

Later fourth century (Lewis).

Location

No evidence.

Possible Phratries

T 27 -akinidai, Apheidantidai, Dipoliastai, Eikadeis, Miltieis, and Oikatai

A phratry appears selling land on a fragment (*IG* 2².1600) of the later-fourth-century accounts of the one percent sales deposit or tax, the Rationes Centesimarum, assigned by Lewis 1973 to stele III (see T 26). There are five other wholly or partially preserved names of sellers on fragments assigned by Lewis to this stele; they may be phratries, but may also be other sorts of groups. A sixth was thought to be a phratry, but is almost certainly a genos. Στράτων Μνησιφάνους Κοθωκίδης, epimeletes of the Oikatai (*IG* 2².1597, 15 = Lewis 1973, no. 39) and Λεόντιος Καλλιάδου Ἐπικηφί, epimeletes of the Apheidantidai (*IG* 2².1597, 19 = Lewis 1973, no. 40) sold properties (in both cases a χωρίον) at Kothokidai for one hundred and two hundred and fifty drachmas, respectively; the Oikatai property was bought by the epimeletes. This is the only evidence for these groups, tentatively listed by Töpffer 1889, 169–70, 313, as gene. They could easily be phratries. The office of epimeletes is now attested in the phratry Therrikleidai, or at least in a group associated with that phratry, T 12 and pp. 235–36. It is certainly the phratriarch who acts as agent for the phratry in T 26 and all other attested cases of phratry land transactions; but Apheidas, who was traditionally killed and supplanted as king of Athens by his half-brother Thymoites, eponym of the phratry Thymaitis (*FGH* 327 Demon fr. 1, see p. 323), would be a very suitable phratry eponym: an obscure figure with an unflattering minor role in the Apatouria myth, cf. p. 222.

At Schweigert 1940, no. 38, face B, 7 (= Lewis 1973, no. 43) the seller is -]ακινιδ[-. This must be a name, but whether of an individual, -*akinides*, or a group, -akinidai, is impossible to say. No known phratry name, nor that of any genos listed in Töpffer 1889, nor that of any deme, will fit.

At Schweigert 1940, no. 38, face A, 5 (= Lewis 1973, no. 50) two epimeletai, Ξενότιμος Τιμοθέου Φλ[υεύς] and Σωσιγένης Σωσινόμου [- of the Dipoliastai sold a χωρίον at Phlya. Schweigert took this group to be a thiasos connected with the ancient festival of Zeus, Dipolia. The connection of the festival with the name seems likely enough, but there are no other thiasoi known to have been named in this way. It is possible that they were rather a genos or a phratry. The genos Thaulonidai was also associated with the Dipolia (Töpffer 1889, 149–60). There is no other phratry name connected with a festival, but we possess too few names to rule out the possibility. If it was a phratry, the Thaulonidai were probably a genos within it.

The fifth possible phratry on stele III is a tantalizing case. At *IG* 2².1596 we read the following at the start of face A (= Lewis 1973, no. 51):

> Ⱶ Ι – – –
> Μιλτιέων 'Αλωπ[εκῆσι
> ὠνηταὶ Στράτιππος Στρ[ατ- -
> Λυσίθεος Λυσιθέου Τε[ιθράσιος]·

The record of the next sale follows. (Incidentally, the reconstruction of the text here seems clearly faulty. After each buyer, the total of the sum paid and the 1 percent were noted, even where, as here, there were subsequent listings of grand totals. These could easily be fit onto the end of a line, cf. face B, 24. The use of the plural ὠνηταὶ in 3—the abbreviation ὠνη is usual—suggests Stratippos and Lysitheos were joint purchasers [the property may have been expensive, cf. the large total in 10, 13 talents 3,300 drachmas] and that there would therefore have been a note of the sum paid by them and the 1 percent following Lysitheos' demotic in 4. There is plenty of room for this, cf. 16; the corresponding space in 3 would have contained Stratippos' patronymic and demotic. A similar correction is needed in 9.) With the buyers detailed in 3–4 it is clear from the pattern of these texts that 1–2 are from the description of the property sold (cf. Kirchner ad loc.) That description would probably have started in the line before 1 of the preserved text, since the remnants of the start of that line are not consistent with ἀπέδοτο or ἀπέδοντο, which invariably starts a line in *IG* 2².1596, coming immediately before the description of the property, and immediately after the names of the sellers. The remnants of the start of 1 are, however, consistent with ἐν, which occurs elsewhere in the description of properties (e.g., 14–15). I would reconstruct as follows:

> [Name(s) of seller(s)]
> ἀπέδοτο or ἀπέδοντο χωρίον *vel. sim.* [-
> ἐν?[– – –

Μιλτιέων ᾿Αλωπ[εκῆσι]
5   ὠνηταὶ κτλ.

The sense will be that X sold the property . . . at . . . of the Miltieis at Alopeke. That the Miltieis (or rather their agents) were also the sellers is very possible, but not certain. Who were the Miltieis? Töpffer 1889, 110 n. 1, suggested they were a phratry on the basis of the form of the name (cf. Dyaleis, Philieis). I suspect he was almost right. It sounds as though there should be a connection with the deme Melite, though if they were actually members of that deme we would expect the form Μελιτεῖς and would not expect associations with land in Alopeke. Though apparently not contiguous with Melite (Bouleutic quota 7, situated west of the Agora, Traill 1986, 134), however, the large deme Alopeke (Bouleutic quota 10, situated south of the city, Traill 1986, 139) must have run very close to it; Koile and Kollytos, both quota 3, seem to have interposed. I suggest that they may have been a group that related to the deme Melite as the phratry Thymaitis related to the deme Thymaitadai, or the House of the Dekeleieis to the deme Dekeleia (cf. p. 109, n. 52), i.e., a pre-Cleisthenic association with a local character, either a phratry or a group within a phratry. It may have given its name to the Cleisthenic deme, contained roughly the same members, and continued to exist as a separate entity after Cleisthenes (cf. Whitehead 1986a, 27; also the numerous komai attested in the fourth century, not least in the Rationes Centesimarum, e.g., *IG* 2².1594, 44). I argue further, pp. 323–24, that it is possible that they were responsible for the very fragmentary early fifth-century inscription *IG* 1³.243 and were a subgroup of the phratry Therrikleidai.

Finally, further down on the same face of *IG* 2².1596 (A, 12–15), someone from the Boule of the Eikadeis from Salamis sold some property there. Töpffer 1889, 110 n. 1, suggested that they too were a phratry. *IG* 2².1258, however, a decree of the Eikadeis of 324/3, shows they had at least two archons. Gene had archons; phratries did not. I take it therefore that the Eikadeis were a geminated genos with some members on Salamis, others elsewhere; the parallel to the Salaminioi themselves is striking (cf. p. 108).

T 28 Demokleidai

Möbius 1924, 16, is a fifth-century marker of a sanctuary of Artemis Orthosia of the Demokleidai from northeast of Hymettos. For Möbius (in fact writing in 1925), whether this was a phratry or a genos was "vorläufig nicht zu entscheiden." Sixty-five years later we can scarcely say more. Artemis Hegemon probably appears in the very poorly preserved T 4, which I have argued is probably from a decree of the House/phratry of the Dekeleieis (pp. 297–98); the marker *IG* 2².5012 from the Peiraeus attests Ἡγεμόνη as a specific appellation of Artemis Orthosia. But that appellation was common enough (cf. pp. 296–97) and we should not suppose from Σ Pind. *Ol.* 3.54, which tells us that there was a shrine of Artemis Orthosia in the Kerameikos, that the cult, which seems to have had strong Peloponnesian connections, was restricted to the phratries at Athens.

For the Dipoliastai and the Eikadeis, see T 27.

T 29 Elasidai

IG 2².2602 is a marker (earlier fourth century?) from Kephisia of a temenos of Apollo Patroos of the Elasidai. Töpffer's suggestion that they were a genos (1890, 383–84) has generally been accepted (Hedrick 1991, 244, apparently misreports him as having identified the group as a phratry, and tentatively accepts such an identification). However, the phratry Therrikleidai had a cult of this deity (T 11; for the idea that this cult was the special province of the genos, see p. 214), so there must be a possibility that the Elasidai, too, were a phratry. T 20 came from the garden of Rangabé at Kephisia, but it is unclear whether Kephisia was its original location. Hedrick 1991, 244, is wise, therefore, to be cautious about allocating the two inscriptions to the same group.

For the Epikleidai, see T 21 and pp. 78–79.

For the Etionidai see pp. 88–90.

T 30 Euergidai

Meritt 1961a, 264, no. 80, is an earlier-fourth-century marker of a sanctuary of the Tritopatreis of the Euergidai, found in the wall of a Roman building at the foot of the Areopagos. Meritt gave no opinion on the nature of this group, which is not otherwise attested. Kearns 1985, 205

n. 48, suggested they may have been a phratry rather than a genos because of the Tritopatreis cult. The case either way is thin. See on T 34.

For the Glaukidai see T 21 and pp. 78–79.

T 31 Ikarieis

IG 2².1178 is a decree of the deme Ikarieis (before middle of fourth century, Kirchner) granting honors to its demarch and two choregoi. In it they "praise Nikon the demarch" and crown him, and the herald is required to announce "that the Ikarieis crown Nikon and the deme of the Ikarieis their demarch." Lewis 1963 followed earlier scholars (see note in *IG* 2²) in seeing a distinction here between the deme and another body with the same name, perhaps analogous to the House/phratry of the Dekeleieis, which co-existed with the deme of that name (see pp. 112–19). This may be right (cf. other possible cases, p. 109 n. 52 and p. 323), but the two situations do not look precisely analogous, since the two groups Dekeleieis, though they will have had overlapping membership, were, as far as we know, organizationally independent of each other whereas here both groups are apparently responsible for a single decree. On this hypothesis we would have to posit two groups either with precisely the same membership or at least meeting in joint session. Neither is impossible, but there is a certain implausibility and I know of no parallel. It may be simpler to suppose that we have here just one group, the deme, indulging in grandiose tautology.

For the Miltieis and the Oikatai see T 27.

T 32 Philieis

Harp. s.v. Κοιρωνίδαι (= Lykourgos fr. 7.2, *FGH* 334 Istros fr. 15) relates that there was a speech of Lykourgos, attributed by some to Philinos, in the case of the Krokonidai against the Koironidai; that the Koironidai were a genos mentioned by Istros, who took their name to be from Koiron, said to be an illegitimate brother of Krokon; and that the Krokonidai were therefore held in the greater honor. Whoever the writer of the speech was, Harpocration tells us, he says the Koironidai were addressed by three names: Koironidai, Philieis, and Perithoidai.

Since the Koironidai were a genos and Perithoidai a deme, Töpffer 1889, 109–10, suggested that the Philieis should be the phratry to which the Koironidai—presumably also the Krokonidai—belonged. For the form of the name, he compared the Dyaleis—also Miltieis and Eikadeis, q.v.— and pointed out that the Apatouria seems to have been relevant to this dispute. The argument was accepted by Wilamowitz 1893, 2.269, who suggested they took their name from the epithet of the god they wor- shipped, and Latte 1941 included them in his list of phratries; cf. however Jacoby *ad* Istros, loc. cit., Hedrick 1991, 246, accepts Töpffer's identi- fication (at 1984 he drew attention to Pollux' implication at 3.51 that phratries worshipped in particular θεοὶ φίλιοι). The case seems good, though Töpffer's statement that the Apatouria "played an important role" in this case is scarcely justified by the apparent mention of the oinoptai in Lykourgos'/Philinos' speech (cf. pp. 154–55, 217). It is not, however, conclusive. The tradition on this case was obviously confused. We cannot rule out that the Philieis were some other sort of group, perhaps, as suggested by scholars before Töpffer (see Töpffer loc. cit.), associated with the deme Phlya, or a phratric group like the Dekeleieis and possibly the Miltieis and others (cf. p. 109 n. 52).

T 33 Pyrrhakidai

The Pyrrhakidai are known from two similar round monuments at Delos, with inscriptions dating to about 400, one of which associated them with the Tritopatreis (Τριτοπάτωρ/ Πυρρακιδῶν/ Αἰγιλιῶν, P. Roussel 1929, 171; the second is Νύμφαι/ Πυρρακιδῶν). They were identified by P. Roussel 1929 as an Attic genos. For the putative but undemonstrable link between the cult of the Tritopatreis and phratries, see T 34. With Roussel, 178, we might take Αἰγιλιῶν as a reference to the deme Aigilia (were all the Pyrrhakidai members of this deme?), but the common Τριτοπάτωρ of the two groups suggests the possibility that we have to do with a subgroup of the Pyrrhakidai analogous to the Dekeleieis (i.e., a group with the same name as a deme, but also a phratry subgroup, cf. p. 109 n. 52). In that case the Pyrrhakidai will have been a phratry.

T 34 Zakyadai

IG 2².2615 is an early-fourth-century marker of a sanctuary of the Trito- patreis of the Zakyadai, of unknown provenience (cf. the similar T 30;

also T 33). Köhler 1879, 287, correctly observed that it was not possible to tell whether the Zakyadai were a phratry or a genos, though he inclined to the former. Wilamowitz 1893, 2, 268, n. 11, following the explanation of *FGH* 328 Philochoros fr. 182 and others (= Epit. Harp., cf. Phot., Suid., E.M. s.v. Τριτοπάτορες) that the Tritopatreis were those in the third generation from the Original Being (children of the Earth and the Sun according to Philochoros; of the Earth and Heaven according to the Exegetikon, with the Titanic names Kottos, Briareos, and Gyges; *FGH* 327 Demon fr. 2 says they were Winds) suggested that persons who cultivated such deities would characteristically be "brothers," i.e., "phrateres." He supported this by the observation that the cult was "Athenian" in character (cf. *IG* 1².870 for, it has been thought, a central Athenian cult of the deities), and not that of an individual genos, and that it was customary at Athens to pray to them at marriage for children (*FGH* 325 Phanodemos fr. 6 = Epit. Harp., etc., loc. cit.). This suggested to him a connection with the phratry marriage-related ceremony, the gamelia. He was therefore inclined to take the Zakyadai as a phratry. The argument is obviously thin, even if we ignore Aristotle, who apparently took the view that the Tritopatreis were rather the great-grandfathers (see Pollux 3.17 = Arist. fr. 415 Rose), and doubts about whether "phrater" had the connotation "brother" in the historical period (see pp. 9–10). The question of whether the cult was specific to phratries or gene was properly left open by Jacoby at Phanodemos loc. cit. (suggesting at n. 10 that every family might have had such a cult). Kearns 1985, 205 n. 48, and 1989, 77, however, has again suggested that the Zakyadai may have been a phratry on the basis of the link with the cult. Since the cult is now attested in two demes (Marathon, *IG* 2².1358, col. 2.32, 52–53; Erchia, *SEG* 21.541 Δ, 41–46; see also *IG* 1³.246, 15–16), it seems very unlikely that, outside the demes, it was restricted to either phratries or gene to the exclusion of the other. The question of the identity of the Zakyadai must remain open.

T 35

IG 2².2345 is a list of names from the earlier fourth century, divided into thiasoi. Beside some of the names are figures. For the question as to whether this is a phratry list, see pp. 82–84. The deme affiliations of the members are of interest. Attested on the stone are Agryle (six times), Kedoi, Euonymon, Kephisia. It is just possible that Humphreys 1990,

243 n. 2, is right that the apparent patronymic Παιανίο at 13 and 14 should be taken as a demotic. In addition, it can be deduced from *IG* 2².2407, with Lewis 1955, 14, that those listed at 31–35 were from Alopeke (cf. Lambert 1986b, 357; Humphreys 1990, 243). On that basis, Humphreys 1990 has now argued that all the members listed whose demotics are not given were from Alopeke. This is undermined, however, by the fact that *SEG* 26.302 (fourth century) probably implies that Εὐφράνωρ Εὐφρ[ο]ν (72) comes from Rhamnous; also by the fact that Κηφισόδωρος Κηφισοφῶν(τος) (32) (*PA* 8365) was probably from Aphidna, as understood by Kirchner, and that *IG* 2².1629, 623, shows [Διό]τιμος Ὀλυμπιοδώρο (22) was probably from Euonymon. The rarely named [῎Α]κρυπτος may also be identical with *PA* 482, from Anagyros.

These demotics produce an interesting pattern. There are two groups, those in the area southeast of the city around the south of Hymettos and those on the road running northeast from Athens to Kephisia and Aphidna, branching off to Rhamnous. Guarducci 1937, 54, thought that the Hymettos area was the original site of the "phratry" and saw the members with demotics outside this area as wanderers. If this was an ancient kinship institution and wandering had taken place, it may be preferable to take southeast Athens (the findspot of T 35 is the Phaleron road) as the original base and assume movement out from the city (in the eighth and seventh centuries? cf. T 10) along the main routes from Athens eastward to Kephisia and Euonymon.

T 36

IG 1³.247 is a fragmentary mid-fifth-century text (Lewis) from Spata dealing apparently with matters of inheritance and classified by Lewis in *IG* 1³ as a decree of a genos or a phratry. The name of the group may occur in two places. In 1 we have [. . . . . [10] . . . . .]ΑΝΤ[. . . . [7] . . .] and in 9–10 τὸν κο[ι/νὸν ? . . [8] . .]γτιδὸν. In 1 Mitsos 1965, 137–38 (*SEG* 23.22) suggested hόπος] ἂν τ[ὰ κοινὰ σ/α ἐ̑ι (cf. *IG* 2².1174, 1) or -αντ[ιδ-; Jameson, in notes used by Lewis, Κυδ]αντ[ιδ- (i.e., the deme). In 9–10 Lewis tentatively suggested τὸν κό[μ/αρχον - as an alternative. Among names of phratries and gene there seem to be two that will fit both places, the genos Zeuxantidai (see Hesych. s.v.) and the genos or phratry Apheidantidai (T 27), though neither would suit either κοινόν or κόμαρχον in 9–10, nor leave sufficient space for ἔδοχσεν in 1.

Appendix 2

Ath. Pol. Fr. 3

In the old days, before Cleisthenes' re-organization of the phylai, the Athenian people were divided into *georgoi* and *demiourgoi*.... (summary of division into phylai, etc.)... as Aristotle relates in the *Ath. Pol.*, as follows: "they were distributed into four phylai, in imitation of the seasons of the year, and each phyle was divided into three parts, so that there were twelve parts altogether, like the months of the year, and they were called trittyes and phratries. Thirty gene were marshalled into each phratry, like the days of a month, and each genos consisted of thirty men."[1]

Lex. Patm. s.v. γεννηταί (= Sakellion 1877, 152)

The third fragment of the *Ath. Pol.*[2] purports to be significant evidence for the organization of Attica before Cleisthenes. It should be approached with great caution. That is not because of any doubts about its attribution, context, or content. The Lex. Patm., quoted above, gives us a verbatim passage, the substance of which is accurately reported by a scholiast on Plato[3] and in an abbreviated and garbled manner in our

1. πάλαι τὸ τῶν Ἀθηναίων πλῆθος, πρὶν ἢ Κλεισθένη διοικήσασθαι τὰ περὶ τὰς φυλάς, διῃρεῖτο εἰς γεωργοὺς καὶ δημιουργούς.... (summary of division into phylai, trittyes and gene)... ὡς ἱστορεῖ ἐν τῇ Ἀθηναίων πολιτείᾳ Ἀ., λέγων οὕτως· φυλὰς δὲ αὐτῶν συννενεμῆσθαι δ, ἀπομιμησαμένων τὰς ἐν τοῖς ἐνιαυτοῖς ὥρας, ἑκάστην δὲ διῃρῆσθαι εἰς τρία μέρη τῶν φυλῶν, ὅπως γένηται τὰ πάντα δώδεκα μέρη, καθάπερ οἱ μῆνες εἰς τὸν ἐνιαυτόν, καλεῖσθαι δὲ αὐτὰ τριττῦς καὶ φατρίας· εἰς δὲ τὴν φατρίαν τριάκοντα γένη διακεκοσμῆσθαι, καθάπερ αἱ ἡμέραι εἰς τὸν μῆνα, τὸ δὲ γένος εἶναι τριάκοντα ἀνδρῶν. Cf. Harp., Suid. s.v. γεννῆται.

2. Kenyon also included the Platonic scholium and the passage of Harpocration cited in nn. 3 and 4 in his *OCT* as fr. 3. Much has been written on the fragment. See Bourriot 1976, 460–92, and Rhodes 1981, 67–73. Attitudes have ranged from the highly skeptical (e.g. Hignett 1952, 59, cf. De Sanctis 1912, 58 and Latte 1941, col. 752) to the uncritical (especially Oliver 1980, 30–38; Bourriot 1976, loc. cit., does not address fundamental questions concerning the approach of fourth-century writers to the prehistorical past). More satisfactory are the accounts of those who have sought a middle way (e.g., Rhodes 1981; Ferguson 1936).

3. Σ Plat. *Axioch.* 371e.

text of Harpocration.[4] All three sources attribute the material to the *Ath. Pol.* and also make clear that, though not included in the verbatim passage, there was reference in the same context to a division into georgoi and demiourgoi. The passage is not in our papyrus remains of the *Ath. Pol.* and must therefore come from the lost beginning of the work, i.e., from the account of the period before the conspiracy of Cylon, the first event in the extant text. We know from elsewhere that the foundation of the four phylai was generally attributed to Ion[5] and that the *Ath. Pol.* took the same view.[6] There seems little doubt therefore that this fragment derives from the account in the *Ath. Pol.* of the work of Ion.[7]

While there is room for debate on details, it is well established that the practice of the *Ath. Pol.* and the Atthidographic tradition in dealing with very early Greek history makes them highly unreliable as a guide to the facts. Generally speaking, they had no access to documentary evidence. They had contemporary realities, some of which were thought to be of ancient origin, a limited knowledge of the more recent past, and a quantity of legendary and other traditional, or, as we shall see, allegedly traditional, material. Combined with a measure of speculation and reconstruction and an infusion of political anachronism and superficial rationalizing, the result carries no historical conviction:[8] Theseus becomes a democratic reformer[9] and Draco the sponsor of an oligarchy like that of 411.[10] To Ion, a personification of the common ancestry of the Athenians and other Ionian peoples, is attributed the foundation of the shared, immemorially ancient institutions that were held to be marks of that common ancestry, the four phylai and the phratries.[11]

The process involved can plausibly be traced in some detail in the

---

4. Harp. s.v. τριττύς, which talks of a tripartite division into trittyes, *ethne* (by which he seems to mean the three classes—eupatridai, etc.) and phratries. Busolt 1920–26 2:107–8, n. 3, seems to have based on this an idea that the *Ath. Pol.* actually had the phylai divided in three different ways rather than into three trittyes/phratries. But the verbatim quotation of Lex. Patm. makes it clear enough that this is wrong and that Harp.'s gloss is somewhat garbled.

5. Cf. p. 271.

6. *Ath. Pol.* 41.2.

7. As argued by Wade-Gery 1931 (= 1958, 88–92).

8. Cf. the discussion of the lost opening chapters of the *Ath. Pol.* by Rhodes 1981, 65–79.

9. See *Epit. Herakl.* 1; *Ath. Pol.* 41.2; Plut. *Thes.* 25.3; with Rhodes 1981, 74–76.

10. Rhodes 1981, 84–88.

11. Cf. pp. 267–71 and see Rhodes 1981, 66–73.

case of the division into georgoi and demiourgoi.[12] Unlike the phylai and phratries, there is no indication that the *Ath. Pol.* or its sources had any contemporary reality to go on here. The latest "evidence" for the groups relates to the solution of the crisis of Damasias in about 580.[13] In fact in that context three groups are mentioned, eupatridai, agroikoi, and demiourgoi, and it is in this tripartite form that they appear, in slightly different guise, in Plutarch's claim that Theseus "divided apart the eupatridai and geomoroi and demiourgoi."[14] This would seem to be at odds with *Ath. Pol.* fr. 3 not only in the tripartite nature of the division, but also in its attribution to Theseus rather than to Ion; an unexpected difference, for there is otherwise much in this section of Plutarch which seems to derive from the *Ath. Pol.*; Kenyon indeed included the passage in his text of the *Ath. Pol.* as fr. 2. Wade-Gery proposed a neat solution. The *Ath. Pol.* attributed a two-fold division to Ion and had Theseus divide off the eupatridai from the rest. Plutarch's statement derives ultimately from the account of the *Ath. Pol.*, but with some distortion.[15]

We need not be concerned about the different terms used for the second group by different sources. They all signify agriculturalists of some sort (*georgoi* = farmers; *agroikoi* = rustics more generally; *geomoroi* = land-owners) and would have been subject to distortion in the tradition.[16]

There are, however, other features of these classes that arouse suspicion. We hear nothing of them in any source independent of the *Ath. Pol.*: nothing in Herodotus or Thucydides; no hint of their existence in any law or poem of Solon or in any account of his work. Moreover, we know that the Athenian people were divided in the archaic period not only into the phylai and phratries, but into four property classes: *pentakosiomedimnoi,* literally "those with five hundred measures"; *hippeis,* "horsemen"; *zeugitai,* "those yoked together," i.e., possibly as hoplites, or perhaps "those owning a yoked pair," i.e., of oxen; and *thetes,* the term normally used for landless agricultural laborers. According to the *Ath. Pol.* the property classes already existed before Solon. They continued in some form into the fourth century as a means of determining

---

12. The following is a development of the approach of Gernet 1938, 216–27, esp. 224–27.

13. See below, p. 376.

14. ἀποκρίνας χωρὶς εὐπατρίδας καὶ γεωμόρους καὶ δημιουργούς. Plut. *Thes.* 25.2 = *Ath. Pol.* fr. 2 Kenyon.

15. Wade-Gery 1931 (= 1958, 88–93).

16. Cf. Rhodes 1981, 72.

eligibility for certain political offices.[17] This system of classes is well attested. There does not seem to be room for another system alongside it. What purpose could it have had?

There is, however, talk of similar tripartite classifications of the people in the philosophers. Hippodamos of Miletos, a fellow member with Herodotus of the colony at Thurii founded in 443, was the most famous town-planner of his age, but, as Aristotle makes clear in the *Politics,* he devised a theoretical city as well as real ones. It had ten thousand men divided into three classes: craftsmen (*technitai*), farmers (*georgoi*), and those who fight and bear arms (*to propolemoun kai ta hopla ekhon*).[18] Whether he took the idea directly from Hippodamos we do not know,[19] but Plato also made use of a famous tripartite division in his ideal city as described in the *Republic,* the *Timaeus,* and the *Kritias.* Moreover, in the *Timaeus* and the *Kritias* Plato has Kritias, as often in Plato's dialogues a real person in a fictional setting, tell stories about Athens as it supposedly was nine thousand years before the time of Solon, at the time of the defeat of the kings of Atlantis. It is an Athens divided into three classes: georgoi, demiourgoi, and a military aristocracy set apart, *to makhimon.*[20] Now, it is clear enough to us that the content of the story and the lengthy tradition by which Plato portrays it as having been preserved are a fiction. Plato relates that it had been told to Solon by an Egyptian priest and, recorded by Solon and preserved among his papers, that it was passed down in the family of Kritias, to which, though he does not mention it, Plato himself also belonged.[21] This is a good story-telling device of the sort Plato used frequently to distance himself from his narrative and impart to it a certain mysterious authority. It seems, however, to have misled some writers in antiquity. Plutarch does not express an opinion about the truth of the Atlantis story, but he seems to believe that Solon recorded it.[22] Moreover, traces of Plato creep into later accounts of Egyptian social organization, which in the *Timaeus* and the *Kritias* is said to have been similar to that of

---

17. *Ath. Pol.* 7.3. For the issues surrounding these classes, whose existence, at least from the time of Solon and probably in some form before, is not in doubt, see Rhodes 1981, 137–38. Cf. Smithson 1968, 96; Coldstream 1977, 55.

18. Arist. *Pol.* 2.1267b30–33, with Newman 1887–1902, ad loc.

19. There were other Presocratics who liked things in threes, e.g., Ion of Chios (Isoc. 15.268) and the Pythagoraeans (Arist. *de Caelo* 1.268a10).

20. See esp. Plato *Tim.* 23e; 24a-b; *Krit.* 110c; 112b.

21. Plato *Krit.* 113b2-4. See the comments of Taylor 1929, 103–4.

22. Plut. *Sol.* 31.6.

Athens at the time of the war with Atlantis. Herodotus did not mention georgoi in his account, but Plato does, and they reappear in later authors, including Aristotle.[23]

It looks as though Plato's fiction was, like other legendary material, taken up by an Atthidographer (possibly Kleidemos)[24] or perhaps by the writer of the *Ath. Pol.* himself, as a genuine source for the very ancient history of Athens. We cannot be certain how this worked in detail, but we can imagine that there were certain things a fourth-century writer would have known about early Greek and Athenian society that in general would have lent credence to, but in detail would have had to be reconciled with, Plato's account. It was well known that the eupatridai were a defined group that had formed Athens' ruling class before Solon.[25] They could safely be equated with Plato's military aristocracy, *to makhimon.* Demiourgos was an ancient term, its precise meaning possibly as unclear in the fourth century as it is to us; the demiourgoi appeared as a definite group in Homer.[26] Whatever word was used for them, farmers or rustics would have been a credible class in any Greek society. On the authority of Plato, therefore, we may suppose that a formal division into three groups was introduced into the historical tradition about very early Athens. Ion was well known as the creator of other subdivisions, Theseus as the creator of the eupatridai. The creation of the georgoi and demiourgoi was therefore attributed to Ion, with Theseus dividing off the eupatridai. Hence *Ath. Pol.* fragments 2 and 3.

Two points would remain to be clarified. First, is it not conceivable that Plato and/or the Attihidographic tradition were aware of the genuine existence of this tripartite subdivision in the archaic period? It is conceivable; that there was no genuine awareness is a matter of hypothesis, not fact. But I would suggest that, for Plato, the division is more likely to have been based on philosophical than on historical considerations. It is as a result of his philosophical ideas about the nature of the soul and the ideal organization of a state that a tripartite scheme is introduced

---

23. Arist. *Pol.* 7.1329b1; D.S. 1.73, cf. 1.28, 4–5.

24. Hellanikos' Atthis probably predated the *Timaeus* and the *Kritias.* Of Androtion and Kleidemos the latter seems more likely, cf. Jacoby Intro. to *FGH* 323a Kleidemos, p. 59, and to *FGH* 324 Androtion, pp. 104–5.

25. Even in the classical period eligibility for the post of phylobasileus was apparently restricted to this class, cf. p. 258 n. 57.

26. Hom. *Od.* 17.383–85; 19.135. A demiourgos may be one who worked for the people (demos) or conceivably one who worked the people's land, see Murakawa 1957; Rhodes 1981, 71–72 and other works there cited.

in the *Republic*; in the *Timaeus* and the *Kritias* he elaborates on the concept with a fiction about an impossibly distant heroic Athenian past in which some such tripartite division is portrayed. But the idea is introduced in the first place in a wholly philosophical context. For the Atthidographic tradition, the silence of other sources outside Plato about the division, their known practice with respect to the treatment of the mythical period in other cases, and the fact that we know Plato's account was accepted as historical in some respects in antiquity, suggest strongly that we need look no further than the *Timaeus* and the *Kritias* for its sources.

Second, we are still left with the *Ath. Pol.*'s account of the role of the classes in the Damasias episode. In a crisis that was probably related in some way to the changes Solon had made in the criteria for eligibility for the archonship, Damasias, elected archon probably for 582/1, clung to power illegally for two years and two months before being ejected by force. After this the *Ath. Pol.* tells us that "because of the dispute they decided to choose ten archons, five from the eupatridai, three from the agroikoi, and two from the demiourgoi, and these held office the year after Damasias."[27] These ten archons are a curious phenomenon. If they held office for only one year, it is not clear how the measure could have resolved disputes over the archonship in the long term. But the change does not seem to have been permanent. We hear nothing more of it, and there continue to be eponymous archons as before. On the other hand, it does not seem credible that the compromise is a complete fiction. The *Ath. Pol.* is too specific, we can identify no likely misleading source, and a settlement of the sort described is credible enough in principle. The best solution seems to be Cavaignac's: the ten archons were not in fact archons but the ten pre-elected men (*prokritoi*) from whom, under the Solonian arrangements, the eponymous archon was chosen by lot.[28] The sense of such a measure, a compromise system for ensuring a particular distribution of power, or chances of power, among the classes, is clear enough. But where have the demiourgoi and georgoi come from? It may not be coincidental that the number of the georgoi plus the demiourgoi, five, is equivalent to the number of eupatridai. The fact

---

27. *Ath. Pol.* 13.2. For the date see Rhodes 1981, 180–81.

28. Cavaignac 1924, 144–48. Also found "an attractive guess" by Rhodes 1981, 183. I doubt Gernet 1938 is correct that the whole of the compromise was a later fiction. For the Solonian prokritoi, see *Ath. Pol.* 8.1, convincingly defended against skeptics by Rhodes ad loc.

that this episode concerned the archonship suggests that the official archon list, which we know was made use of by the Atthidographic tradition, was a source. Whether there was information on this list beyond the names of the archons is not known for certain, but it is credible that, when there was a crisis concerning the archonship itself and a change in the election arrangements, there would have been some indication on the list.[29] It would not be surprising if, against the year after Damasias, there was a note: "from five eupatridai, five non-eupatridai." In Greek this would have been ambiguous: the same words would mean "from five" or "five from";[30] hence perhaps the confusion between the archons themselves and the pre-elected group from which they were chosen. The author of the *Ath. Pol.* or his source also thought he knew, however, that the non-eupatridai were divided at this time into georgoi/agroikoi and demiourgoi. It would have been characteristic for him to have reasoned that the non-eupatrid quota must have been divided further between the two groups; and the obvious way would have been to divide it three to two in favor of the georgoi.[31]

All this of course is a hypothetical construct, and on the points of detail will not bear much weight. But on the basis of current evidence it seems reasonable to suppose that, while the eupatridai probably existed as a defined group in archaic Athens, and while there were, of course, people who might be described as georgoi and demiourgoi, the formal tripartite division of ancient Attica found in the *Ath. Pol.* may derive ultimately not from any historical source, but from philosophical theory.[32]

There is good ground for skepticism in general, therefore, about claims made by the *Ath. Pol.* about the very early history of Athens and, as far as the social organization is concerned, specific grounds for doubt

---

29. Cf. Jacoby 1949, 175.

30. I.e., perhaps ἐξ εὐπατρίδων Γ ἐξ οὐκ εὐπατρίδων Γ.

31. This is a development of a suggestion of Rhodes 1981, 183.

32. The hypothesis receives support from two further sources. D.S. 1.28, 4–5 has the Egyptians claim that the Athenians derive from Egypt and that the arrangement of the three classes at Athens (eupatridai, geomoroi and demiorgoi) is similar to the Egyptian. The ultimate source must again be Plato's *Timaeus* and *Kritias,* again erroneously taken as a historical source. Strabo at 383 8.7.1 relates that Ion divided the people into four phylai and also into four occupational classes: georgoi, demiourgoi, hieropoioi (religious functionaries) and phylakes (guardians). This represents a somewhat different compilation of appropriate classes for an ideal/early Athenian city, including not only those of the *Timaeus* and the *Kritias,* but also of the *Republic.* There could be no clearer evidence of the way Plato's philosophical proposals in those works were manipulated by later writers into allegedly historical systems of subdivision of early Athens.

about the alleged tripartite division into eupatridai, georgoi, and demiourgoi. It was in the same context that the *Ath. Pol.* dealt with the old phylai and phratries. In one respect the claims of the *Ath. Pol.* about these institutions are more trustworthy, for phratries and gene still existed in the fourth century, as did successors of the old phylai and trittyes. It would at least be surprising if what the *Ath. Pol.* said about them was inconsistent with the institutions as they actually existed in his own time; indeed, we can probably assume that contemporary reality was up to a point the basis of his statements. Since gene and phratries both existed in the fourth century, for example, it would be surprising if the genos was not normally a subgroup of the phratry, as the *Ath. Pol.* claims. And this is indeed consistent with the relationship between the groups as witnessed by contemporary fourth-century evidence.[33] On other points, even if the institutions themselves were effectively obsolete, there were reliable traditions. There can be no doubt, for example, that there had indeed been four old phylai.[34] On the other hand, where the claims of the *Ath. Pol.* in this fragment go beyond what we have good evidence for from elsewhere, and where they do not seem to have been based on contemporary realities, we should approach them with skepticism.

Crucial is the identification by the *Ath. Pol.* of trittys and phratry.[35] Not only is this attested nowhere else, there are also persuasive arguments against it. First, the *Ath. Pol.* must be correct that there were twelve

---

33. Other points made about the gene in fr. 3, however, would not have been based on contemporary reality, i.e., that there were 360 of them and that every citizen belonged to one. Cf. pp. 17–18 and chapter 2.

34. Cf. p. 15.

35. The best discussion of this point remains Ferguson 1936, 152–58. He adduced as a further argument against the identity of phratry and trittys the supposition that the trittys sacrifice on the eve of Synoikia in Nikomachos' calendar (on which see further below) was a consequence of the later integration of the trittyes into a festival in which the phylai already participated as aggregates of the phratry. This is somewhat speculative, not least because we do not know that the phylai were aggregates of the phratries. Cf. pp. 14–17. Pollux 8.109 draws the inference from *Ath. Pol.* fr. 3 that the genos was a subdivision of the trittys. This of course collapses once the identity of trittys and phratry is rejected. That identity is implicitly accepted by Frost 1976, 67; and Oliver 1980, 30–31, whose view of *Ath. Pol.* fr. 3 appears altogether uncritical. Roussel 1976, 146, suggested that the trittyes may have been regroupings of varying numbers of the phratries for certain purposes, but this is scarcely less vulnerable to the arguments against identity adduced below, and there is in any case no need for a compromise of this sort if, as is likely, the claim of the *Ath. Pol.* is wholly speculative.

trittyes;[36] but it is most unlikely that there were as few as twelve phratries in the fourth century.[37]

Second, when the writer of the *Ath. Pol.* discusses the reforms of Cleisthenes, he deals separately with the old phylai and trittyes, which were reformed, and the phratries and gene, which were not, the apparent implication being that phratry and trittys were not identical.[38]

Third, we have a piece of evidence that seems not to have been used by the Atthidographers, the text of the revision of the sacred calendar of the state carried out by Nikomachos at the end of the fifth century.[39] It provides our only direct evidence for the old trittyes, which continued to play a formal role in state religion. It shows that one of them was called Leukotainioi, "the white-ribboned," a name different in character from all the Attic phratry names we know, which are generally derived from personal or place names and end in *-idai* or *-is*.

Fourth, the actual nature of the relationship between phratry and old phyle may be obscure, but nowhere in any phratry inscription or in any other source independent of the *Ath. Pol.* is it stated or directly implied that the phratry was a subgroup of a phyle, as the *Ath. Pol.* claims here. In contrast, the single piece of evidence for the trittys, Nikomachos' revision of the sacred calendar of the state at the end of the fifth century, attests that the trittys was a phyle subdivision. The contrast suggests that the groups were probably not identical.

It seems very likely that the identification of phratry and trittys was a consequence of the sort of speculative rationalization that lay behind the tripartite division into eupatridai, agroikoi, and demiourgoi. The further division of the phratry/trittys into 360 gene of thirty men each looks impossibly artificial and precise, and again there is no supporting evidence. It is clear that it is part of the same fictional scheme. As with the tripartite division, we can only speculate about the precise sources, the stages of tradition, and the thought processes involved; but one is reminded in this case of another artificial-looking duodecimal system of division of Attica, Philochoros' twelve Attic cities.[40] And for the scheme as a whole there is a likely source of precisely the same sort as that which seems to have lain behind the system of classes. In the *Laws* Plato

---

36. Cf. p. 256.
37. Cf. p. 19.
38. *Ath. Pol.* 21, cf. pp. 245–46 and Rhodes 1981, 68.
39. Cf. pp. 256–57.
40. *FGH* 328 Philochoros fr. 94 with Jacoby ad loc. and Hommel 1939.

advises prospective legislators to ensure a total number of citizens which could easily be subdivided into different sorts and numbers of groups and subgroups for administrative purposes.[41] He himself opts for 5,040, which has no less than 59 divisors. In the *Ath. Pol.* the number is 10,800, which divides nicely, as the *Ath. Pol.* shows, by four and twelve and then twice again by thirty. It appears that the Atthidographic tradition may have drawn the general inference from the *Timaeus* and the *Kritias* that Athens' early social organizers had acted in the way Plato thought ideal legislators ought to act. It also knew that there had been four phylai and twelve trittyes in addition to phratries and gene of uncertain number, though the phylai and trittyes were effectively obsolete by the fourth century and there was therefore plenty of room for speculation about their relationship to the phratries. From what was known of the phratries and the successors of the old phyle system, there was nothing in the nature of any of these groups that would have prevented the smaller ones from being subgroups of the larger.[42] The phyle/trittys system was therefore conflated with the phratry/genos to form a single scheme, neatly in accord with Platonic prescription.

If this is right, not only were there never twelve phratries or 360 gene with thirty men each, but also the fragment becomes worthless as evidence that the phratry was a subdivision of a phyle. That was probably a consequence of the identification of phratry with trittys, which was indeed a phyle subgroup. Whether the phratry actually was a subdivision of a phyle is a different question; I have concluded that we lack the evidence to decide.[43]

Finally, there is one element in the *Ath. Pol.*'s scheme that has generally been seen by skeptics as symptomatic of its artificiality, namely the matching of the subgroups to the seasons, months, and days of the year.[44] For the smaller subdivisions, the objection has some weight, but in principle the idea has sense. In the Cleisthenic system, military and political offices were rotated according to a ten-month system especially designed for the purpose. We can believe that there were twelve trittyes under the old twelve month system for the same sort of reason; and whether or not the four seasons entirely explain the four phylai, it would have been useful to have a system in which duties and offices could rotate on a quarterly basis.

---

41. Plato *Laws* 5.737e1–738b1.

42. For arguments concerning alleged fundamental differences in the principle of organization of phratry and phyle/trittys, see pp. 14–15.

43. See pp. 14–17.

44. See, e.g., Hignett 1952, 49.

The Principle of Descent and Athenian Citizenship

At chapter 1, pp. 29–30, I stated that the principle of descent as the major qualification for citizenship remained immutable in the classical period, indeed throughout the meaningful life of Athenian citizenship. For the period before Pericles' citizenship law, this is not demonstrable with certainty on the basis of current evidence, but given the antiquity of the phratry (see pp. 267–71), its powerful association with heredity and legitimacy (see pp. 35–40), and its deep-rooted links with membership in the community of the polis (to which Draco's law of homicide, pp. 248–51, is sufficient witness), it would require strong evidence to the contrary to demonstrate that this was not so. Davies 1978, on the basis of a definition of citizenship in Aristotle's sense of sharing in krisis and arche (see p. 42; such a definition seems insufficient by itself, particularly for the early sixth century), suggested that Solon made a shift away from the definition of citizens as members of descent groups and toward one that included all free residents. The main basis for this is Plut. *Sol.* 24.4 (Solon, *Laws* fr. 75 R): "His law concerning naturalized citizens is a surprising one, because it granted naturalization only to those who had emigrated with their families to practise a trade. Solon's object here, we are told, was not so much to discourage other types of immigrants as to invite these particular categories to Athens with the assurance that they could become citizens there" (trans. I. Scott-Kilvert). With Davies 1978 I accept the probable genuineness of this Solonian Law. Doubts about laws of Solon that were still current in the classical period are much stronger than about those that would have been obsolete by then. Current laws of whatever origin could wrongly be described by classical authors as laws of Solon, but obsolete laws could not. A good case can be made that the obsolete laws were preserved in the Aristotelian work "On the Axones of Solon" (see appendix 4). I can also accept that enfranchisements were made under this law in the sixth century (Davies 1978, 115, citing Jackson 1976, 80, and M. Lang 1976, no. 18). Given, however, the case in favor of the antiquity and tenacity of the principle of descent, I see these enfranchisements as genuine exceptions to a principle that remained in essence unchallenged, in the same category as the naturalizations of the classical period awarded for special service to the Athenian people (see p. 32, pp. 47–52; in a sense both can be viewed as artificial bestowals of the qualification by descent, as in the case of adoption, see pp. 38–40, 174–76), not as a weakening of the principle itself. I would guess that the Solonian law was in practice an instruction to the phratries, and probably to the naukraries also, see pp. 261–66, to accept persons in these categories (cf. the provision of Solon, *Laws* fr. 76a R that decisions of phratries and other groups should be valid as long as they were not overruled by those of the people as a whole). It was probably only when Athenian citizenship acquired its hugely increased intrinsic value in the fifth century that the classical practice of making citizen grants only by decision of the Assembly became necessary, cf. Patterson 1981, 131–32, whose view on this matter is close to my own. Precisely the same applies to any ad hoc enfranchisements Cleisthenes may have made (see pp. 261–66; cf. Patterson 1981, 131–32). It is a mistake to interpret any of Cleisthenes' measures as an attempt to undermine the principle of descent. Membership in his new demes was no less hereditary than was membership in the phratries.

In the period after the passage of Pericles' Law, Davies 1978 sees the descent principle as having been under siege and in particular sees the additional qualifications proposed in 411 and the following years as attempts to establish alternative principles. Again with Patterson 1981 131–32 and 140–47, I disagree. At no stage is there reason to think that opening the citizenship more widely to include non-Athenians who met the various wealth requirements was what was being proposed. This would have been preposterous, implying that Spartans or presumably even Persians could have become citizens. Instead, I take the intention of these proposals from conservatives to be to restrict citizenship more narrowly by adding financial and other qualifications to the basic, unquestioned, qualification by descent.

It is clear that in all these cases the main purpose was the exclusion of those not possessing the necessary additional qualifications from the central criteria of citizenship (i.e., krisis and arche). It is less clear to what extent they would have been excluded from other criteria. I doubt if property rights were ever in question—Diodoros 18 indicates explicitly that those excluded in 322 retained them—or participation in religious activities, or phratry membership. I would be less surprised if there was exclusion from membership in the demes, which were generally speaking the structures through which access to krisis and arche was organized. The other measures taken to strengthen the principle of descent in the classical period—Pericles' Law, diapsephismoi, and so on—I would see not as indications that that principle was being threatened by alternative principles, but of a concern to ensure, given the high value of Athenian citizenship at this period, that the principle of descent was sufficiently closely defined and properly enforced.

Appendix 4

The Solonian Naukrary Laws

There were four phylai as before and four phylobasileis. Each phyle had been distributed into three trittyes and twelve naukraries. Naukraroi had been set in charge of the naukraries, with responsibility for revenue and expenditure accruing; that is why it is written at many places in the laws of Solon no longer in use, "the naukraroi to collect" and "to pay from the naukraric fund."[1]
Doc. 1 = *Ath. Pol.* 8.3 (from the account of Solon's reforms)

. . . as Androtion says, writing as follows, "the kolakretai are to give money to those on missions to the Pythia from the naukraric funds for travelling and to pay for any other expenses.[2]
Doc. 2 = *FGH* 324 Androtion fr. 36 (= Σ Ar. *Birds* 1541)

A naukraros was something like a demarch. Solon called them this, as Aristotle states, and in the laws, "if anyone disputes a naukrary" and "the naukraroi by naukrary" [or "in their naukraries"].[3]
Doc. 3 = Photios s.v. ναυκραρία

In chapter 8 I made statements about the naukraries that depended on the authenticity of these three extracts as part of the laws of Solon. This is no place for a full discussion of the many and complex issues surrounding the survival of authentic Solonian laws and their use in both

---

1. φυλαὶ δ᾽ ἦσαν δ̄ καθάπερ πρότερον καὶ φυλοβασιλεῖς τέτταρες. ἐκ δὲ τῆς φυλῆς ἑκάστης ἦσαν νενεμημέναι τριττύες μὲν τρεῖς, ναυκραρίαι δὲ δώδεκα καθ᾽ ἑκάστην. ἦν δ᾽ ἐπὶ τῶν ναυκραριῶν ἀρχὴ καθεστηκυῖα ναύκραροι, τεταγμένη πρός τε τὰς εἰσφορὰς καὶ τὰς δαπάνας τὰς γιγνομένας· διὸ καὶ ἐν τοῖς νόμοις τοῖς Σόλωνος οἷς οὐκέτι χρῶνται πολλαχοῦ γέγραπται "τοὺς ναυκράρους εἰσπράττειν" καὶ "ἀναλίσκειν ἐκ τοῦ ναυκραρικοῦ ἀργυρίου."

2. . . . ὡς ᾽Ανδροτίων γράφει οὕτως· "τοῖς δὲ ἰοῦσι Πυθῶδε θεωροῖς τοὺς κωλακρέτας διδόναι ἐκ τῶν ναυκραρικῶν ἐφόδιον ἀργύρια, καὶ εἰς ἄλλο ὅ τι ἂν ἀναλῶσαι."

3. ναύκραρος δὲ ὁποῖον τί ὁ δήμαρχος, Σόλωνος οὕτως ὀνομάσαντος, ὡς καὶ ᾽Αριστοτέλης φησί, καὶ ἐν τοῖς νόμοις δὲ "ἄν τις ναυκραρίας ἀμφισβητῇ" καὶ "τοὺς ναυκράρους τοὺς κατὰ ναυκραρίαν."

legal and historical contexts by later authors. The extreme skeptical case,[4] however, has been well met by the arguments of Ruschenbusch[5] and Andrewes.[6] In summary, objects known as *axones* (axles), thought to contain the original texts of Solon's laws, survived through antiquity at least until the time of Plutarch (later first/early second century A.D.), who saw fragments of them.[7] They were the subject of a fourth-century work of the Aristotelian school, *On the Axones of Solon,* in five books, from which subsequent citations of his laws generally derive; at least, that is, those that do not derive from the orators and are verbatim quotations and/or from specified axones.[8] It is excessively skeptical to suppose that the laws in this category, i.e., those probably deriving from the Aristotelian work, were not what they purported to be; they contained an abundance of archaic features that surprised and intrigued later writers[9] and would have required an improbable degree of historical knowledge and imagination on the part of any forger, official or otherwise. Classical orators tended to refer to the whole corpus of Athenian law loosely, and in some cases inaccurately, as "the laws of Solon." As a consequence there are some laws referred to by them or some sources derived from them that are not what they purport to be; but these cases can be detected readily enough for the most part and can be distinguished from authentic material deriving from the Aristotelian work.[10]

In the particular case of the naukrary laws quoted above, there are good arguments that they derive from that work and should be regarded as authentically Solonian. First, the three sets of quotations share common features. Not only do they all concern the naukraroi, but in the cases of the *Ath. Pol.* and Photios the form of citation is strikingly similar: both consist of abbreviations or paraphrases rather than full quotations. Androtion quotes in full, but there is a strong parallel between his wording, "the kolakretai . . . from the naukraric funds . . . to pay," and that of the second of the *Ath. Pol.*'s paraphrases, "to pay from the naukraric fund." We may draw the conclusion that the extract from the *Ath. Pol.* is a paraphrase of, among others (note that he says

---

4. See, e.g., Hignett 1952.
5. Ruschenbusch 1966, esp. 1–14.
6. Andrewes 1974, 21–28.
7. Plut. *Sol.* 25.1.
8. *Arist. Vita Menag.,* Catalogue of Works no. 140; cf. Ruschenbusch 1966, 40–42.
9. See for example fr. 72a R and fr. 75 R with Ruschenbusch 1966, 8–10, and Andrewes 1974, 25; fr. 70 R; fr. 67 R.
10. See frs. 94–122 R.

"it is written at many places"), the law quoted by Androtion. There may be a similar connection between the first extract cited by the *Ath. Pol.* and Photios' second, which, lacking a verb, does not make clear sense as it stands. Sense could very plausibly be made by supplying the verb from the *Ath. Pol.* ("to collect") and possibly even a participle from the introductory passage of the *Ath. Pol.* extracts ("with responsibility for . . .). A reconstruction would run: "the naukraroi are to be responsible for the collection of taxes in their own naukrary."[11]

In any event, the interconnection of the passages in the three sources is clear enough. It implies that the Solonian authorship of the laws, asserted by the *Ath. Pol.* and implied by Photios, should also apply to the extract from Androtion. It also implies that a common source very probably lies behind all three. That source will not have belonged to the category of those that attested Solonian laws inauthentically. The rhetorical misuse by the orators of the description "laws of Solon" referred to laws in force at Athens at the time, not to obsolete laws dealing with obsolete institutions. Androtion has been suggested,[12] but we know that he differed from the Ath. Pol. in his interpretation of Solon's *Seisachtheia*. There is no hint of this interpretation in the *Ath. Pol.* and we can infer, with Rhodes, that the sources of the Ath. Pol. at this point must therefore be sought elsewhere.[13] Moreover, even if Androtion were the source, we would be left asking where he obtained his quotation from the axones. Ruschenbusch implies autopsy,[14] but if, with Jacoby, we accept Plutarch's assertion that Androtion wrote his work in exile in Megara, this would not have been possible.[15] Consultation of the work of the Aristotelian school on the Solonian axones seems more likely. That work is surely also a more attractive source than Androtion for the *Ath. Pol.,* written in the same school.[16] We have no explicit evidence for the date of the work on the axones, but we know the *Ath. Pol.* was relatively late,[17] so it is quite plausible that the former predated it.

11. τοὺς ναυκράρους τοὺς κατὰ ναυκραρίαν (? τεταγμένους) εἰσπράττειν. There are other possibilities of course, for example τοὺς ναυκράρους τοὺς κατὰ ναυκραρίαν πρυτανεύοντας . . . (details of duties ?), cf. p. 255 with n. 47.

12. By Hignett 1952, 68.

13. Rhodes 1981, 118.

14. Ruschenbusch 1966, 50–51.

15. *FGH* 324 Androtion T 14 = Plut. *De Exil.* 14.605c with Jacoby, Intro. to *FGH* 324 Androtion, p. 103.

16. That there were interconnections between works written by the school (e.g., *Ath. Pol.* and *Pol.,* see Rhodes 1981, 60–61, cf. above, p. 247 with n. 10) scarcely needs stressing.

17. Rhodes 1981, 51–58, cf. above, p. 247 n. 10.

If the extracts from Androtion and the *Ath. Pol.* derive from the Aristotelian work on the axones, the same should apply to the extracts from Photios. The introduction to Photios' quotation may in fact suggest an Aristotelian source. A break is normally understood after "as Aristotle says," which is taken as a reference solely to the *Ath. Pol.;* but this may not be correct. "As Aristotle says" may also apply to what follows, "and in the laws," and may therefore also be a reference to Aristotle's collection of the laws of Solon.

The text of the Solonian laws would have filled at least one of the five books of the Aristotelian work on the axones of Solon.[18] Even if it filled considerably more than that, there would have been plenty of space for exegesis and comment. It seems possible that there was also indexing, cataloging, or summarizing that included abbreviated references to the laws of the type found in the *Ath. Pol.* and Photios.

---

18. Cf. Ruschenbusch 1966, 40–42.

Appendix 5

The Size of the Deme Halimous in 346/5

On p. 20, on p. 116 at n. 79, and on p. 233 at n. 154 I stated that the population of the deme Halimous (Bouleutic quota 3) in 346/5 was about eighty to eighty-five (adult male citizens). I take this to be the implication of Demosthenes 57, the speech in which Euxitheos defends his membership of that deme on appeal following ejection at the 346/5 diapsephisis. But the figure is not given explicitly; it may be arrived at by the following process of reasoning.

Euxitheos does not say that there were seventy-three demesmen in Halimous at the diapsephisis of 346 (Traill 1975, 65, n.23).[1] What he does say is: those who took the oath (clearly an oath preliminary to the voting process, presumably to the effect that votes would be cast honestly) in the deme numbered seventy-three (9); the voting started late in the day (9); he, Euxitheos, was about sixtieth to be voted on and last of all on that day, by which time most of the demesmen had gone home, not more than thirty remaining (10); there were more than twenty demesmen left to be voted on on the following day (15). If we take the seventy-three who took the oath on the first day as the total number of deme members, there is an obvious inconsistency with Euxitheos' subsequent claims that he was last and about sixtieth to be voted on on that day, and that that left more than twenty to be voted on on the following day. The best way of dealing with this is to suppose that, in stating that seventy-three took the oath, Euxitheos is referring only to those who took the oath on the first day and that this was not all the deme members. The Greek at section 9 seems to imply as much: "those of us demesmen who took the oath were seventy-three,"[2] the implication being that there

---

1. Cf. Gomme 1933, 54, who made the figure 85 to 90.
2. καὶ τῶν μὲν δημοτῶν οἱ ὀμόσαντες ἐγενόμεθα τρεῖς καὶ ἑβδομήκοντα.

were some demesmen who did not. There is no need to resort to textual emendation,[3] nor to the hypothesis that Euxitheos is cooking the figures. That he might have done so is not in principle unlikely,[4] but not in such a way as to produce internal inconsistency that would immediately raise the suspicions of any alert member of the jury.

It looks as if Demosthenes/Euxitheos may have been intending a somewhat more subtle deception. Although there were over twenty left to be voted on on the second day, some of those would not have been present on the first day: by Euxitheos' figures about ten, i.e., >20−(73−ca. 60). It would be no surprise if the other ten or so, those who were present at but had not been voted on during the first day's proceedings, were among those who had gone home before the end of the voting, and that Euboulides would therefore have been able to claim in defense of the way he had organized the deme's business, that Euxitheos was voted on on that day because he was the last person present on whom a vote had not yet been taken. But if this was so, it is cleverly obscured, not by any factual inaccuracy in the figures, doubtless easy for the demarch Euboulides to challenge, but in the way the fact that over twenty remained to be voted on is used to give the impression that there was some injustice in Euxitheos' being the last to be voted on on the first day.[5]

To return to the question of the total membership of the deme, we may conclude that, by Euxitheos' figures, it would have been seventy-three (those who took the oath on the first day) plus the difference between "more than twenty" (those who had to be voted on on the second day) and about thirteen (seventy-three minus about sixty who were voted on on the first day). That produces a total of about eighty to eighty-five. The figure is probably reliable. Seventy-three is presented as straight fact and is too precise to be a guess; as already observed, we can assume

---

3. *OCT* records an unconvincing suggestion of Naber: ὑπερεξηκοστός, "more than six-tieth" (which would apparently be a hapax legomenon) for περὶ ἑξηκοστόν in sect. 10.

4. Cf. Gomme 1933, 55, who thought it might be an underestimate.

5. This does not, of course, rule out the possibility that there was some artifice on the part of Euboulides. Perhaps if Euxitheos had been more quick-witted on the day and attended more closely to what was going on in the speech-making and decree-drafting, with which he accuses Euboulides of having frittered the day away (κατέτριψεν τὴν ἡμέραν δημηγορῶν καὶ ψηφίσματα γράφων [9]) he would not have been taken by surprise. (Pace Whitehead 1986a, 92, n. 26, I take it that this business at the start of the first day was in preparation for the diapsephisis, not other routine business, for, as he is otherwise inclined to recognize, the diapsephisis seems likely to have taken place at a special meeting of the deme in Athens dedicated solely to that purpose.)

that it would in any case have been publicly known and documented. The approximations "about 60" and "more than 20" sound more suspicious; but any inaccuracies in these two figures probably cancel each other out.[6]

---

6. I pass over here questions about how far a Bouleutic quota of three was larger than would be expected for a deme of this size. Cf. Gomme 1933, 54–55; Traill 1975, 65, n. 23.

Bibliography

Andrewes, A. 1961a. "Philochoros on Phratries." *JHS* 81:1–15.

———. 1961b. "Phratries in Homer." *Hermes* 89:129–40.

———. 1974. "The Survival of Solon's Axones." In *Phoros: Tribute to B.D. Meritt,* Ed. D.W. Bradeen & M.F. McGregor, 21–28. Locust Valley, N.Y.: Augustin.

Andreyev, V.N. 1960. "The Price of Land in Attica in the 4th Century B.C." *VDI* 72:47–57 (in Russian).

———. 1967. "Attic public landownership from the fifth to the third centuries B.C." *VDI* 100:48–76 (in Russian, summary in English).

Arvanitopoulou, T. 1958. Δεκελεία (῏Πολέμων, παράρτημα῍). Athens.

———, with Sophia and Eirene, Princesses of Greece. 1959. ῍Οστρακα ἐκ Δεκελείας. Athens.

Behrend, D. 1970. *Attische Pachturkunden.* Vestigia, vol. 12. Munich.

Beloch, K.J. 1912–27. *Griechische Geschichte.* 4 vols in 8. Strasburg: Trübner. Berlin and Leipzig: De Gruyter.

Benveniste, E. 1973. *Indo-European language and society* (tables and indices by J. Lallot). Trans. E. Palmer. London: Faber and Faber.

Bicknell, P.J. 1972. *Studies in Athenian Politics and Genealogy. Hist.* Einz. 19.

Billheimer, A. 1938. "Amendments in Athenian decrees." *AJA* 42:456–85.

Billigmeier, J.-C. and Dusing, A.S. 1981. "The Origin and Function of the *Naukraroi* at Athens: An Etymological and Historical Explanation." *TAPA* 111:11–16.

Binnebössel, R. 1932. *Studien zu den attischen Urkundenreliefs des 5 und 4 Jahrhunderts.* Kaldenkirchen.

Bleicken, J. 1985. *Die athenische Demokratie.* Paderborn: Schöningh.

Boardman, J. 1983. 15–36, in *Ancient Greek Art and Iconography,* ed. W.G. Moon. Madison: University of Wisconsin Press.

Boerner, A. 1910. *RE* 7. "Geleontes." Col. 986.

Boisacq, E. 1907. *Dictionnaire étymologique de la langue grecque étudiée dans ses rapports avec les autres langues indo-européennes.* Heidelberg: Winter.

Bourriot, F. 1976. *Recherches sur la nature du genos. Étude d'histoire sociale athénienne- périodes archaique et classique.* Lille.

Brelich, A. 1961. *Guerre agoni e culti nella grecia arcaica.* Bonn: Habelt.

Broneer, O. 1942. "The Thesmophorion in Athens." *Hesp.* 11:250–74.

Bryant, A.A. 1907. "Boyhood and youth in the days of Aristophanes." *HSCP* 18:73–122.

Buck, C.D. and Petersen, W. 1945. *A Reversed Index of Greek Nouns and Adjectives, Arranged by Terminations, With Brief Historical Introductions.* Chicago: The University Press.

Bugh, G.R. 1988. *The horsemen of Athens.* Princeton: Princeton University Press.

Busolt, G. 1893–1904. *Griechische Geschichte bis zur Schlacht bei Chaeroneia.* Gotha: Perthes.

Busolt, G. and Swoboda, H. 1920–26. *Griechische Staatskunde,* (H.d.A. IV i 1), 2 vols. 3d ed., Munich: Beck.

Cadoux, T.J. 1948. "The Athenian Archons from Creon to Hypsichides." *JHS* 68:70–123.

———. 1970. "Phratriai," *Oxford Classical Dictionary.* 2d ed., Oxford: Oxford University Press.

Cartledge, P. 1977. "Hoplites and Heroes: Sparta's Contribution to the Technique of Ancient Warfare." *JHS* 97:11–27.

Cavaignac, E. 1924. "La Designation des Archontes Athéniens jusqu'en 487." *R Ph²* 48:144–48.

Chantraine, P. 1968–80. *Dictionnaire étymologique de la langue grecque, histoire des mots.* 4 vols. Paris: Klincksieck.

Cohen, E.E. 1973. *Ancient Athenian Maritime Courts.* Princeton: Princeton University Press.

Coldstream, J.N. 1968. *Greek Geometric Pottery.* London: Methuen.

———. 1977. *Geometric Greece.* London: Benn.

Cole, S.G. 1984. "The Social Function of Rituals of Maturation: The Koureion and the Arkteia." *ZPE* 55:233–44.

Connor, W.R. 1971. *The New Politicians of Fifth Century Athens.* Princeton: Princeton University Press.

Cook, A.B. 1914–40. *Zeus, A Study in Ancient Religion.* 3 vols. Cambridge: Cambridge University Press.

Crosby, M. 1941. "Greek Inscriptions." *Hesp.* 10:14–27.

———. 1950. "The Leases of the Laureion Mines." *Hesp.* 19:189–312.

Damsgaard-Madsen, A. 1973. "Le mode de désignation des démarques attiques au IVeme siècle avant J.C.," in Blatt Studies, *C & M* diss. 9, Copenhagen, 92–118.

Daux, G. 1983. "Le calendrier de Thorikos." *AC* 52:150–74.

Davies, J.K. 1971. *Athenian Propertied Families.* Oxford: Oxford University Press.

———. 1978. "Athenian Citizenship: The Descent Group and the Alternatives." *CJ* 73:105–21.

———. 1984. *Wealth and the Power of Wealth in Classical Athens.* Salem: The Ayer Company.

De Schutter, X. 1987. "Le culte d' Apollon Patroos à Athènes." *AC* 56:103–29.

Détienne, M. 1979. *Dionysos Slain,* trans. L. and M. Muellner, Baltimore: Johns Hopkins University Press.

Deubner, L. 1932. *Attische Feste.* Berlin: Keller.

———. 1944. *Das Attische Weinlesefest* (Abh. der Preuss. Ak. der Wiss. 1943, Phil-Hist. Kl. nr. 12). Berlin.

Develin, R. 1986. "Prytany systems and eponyms for financial boards in Athens." *Klio* 68:67–83.

———. 1989. *Athenian Officials, 684-321 B.C.,* Cambridge: Cambridge University Press.

Diamant, S. 1982. "Theseus and the unification of Attica," in Vanderpool Studies, *Hesp.* Suppl. 19:38–47.

Diller, A. 1932. "The Decree of Demophilus, 346–5 B.C." *TAPA* 63:193–205.

Dindorf, G., ed. 1853. *Harpocrationis Lexicon in Decem Oratores Atticos,* 2 vols. Oxford.

Dinsmoor, W. 1931. *The Archons of Athens in the Hellenistic Age.* Cambridge, Mass.: Harvard University Press.

Dow, S. 1941. "Greek Inscriptions." *Hesp.* 10:31–37.

———. 1953–57. "The Law Codes of Athens." *Proc. Mass. Hist. Soc.* 71, 2–36.

———. 1960. "The Athenian Calendar of Sacrifices: The Chronology of Nikomachos' Second Term." *Hist.* 9:270–93.

———. 1961. "The Walls Inscribed with Nikomachos' Law Code." *Hesp.* 30:58–73.

———. 1968. "Six Athenian Sacrifical Calendars." *BCH* 92:170–86.

Dow, S. and Gill, D.H. 1965. "The Greek Cult Table." *AJA* 69:103–14.

van Effenterre, H. 1976. "Clisthène et les mesures de mobilisation." *REG* 89:1–17.

———. 1985. *La cité grecque des origines à la défaite de Marathon.* Paris: Hachette.

Ehrenberg, V. 1925. *Neugründer des Staates; Ein Beitrag zur Geschichte Spartas und Athens im VI Jhdt.* Munich: Beck.

———. 1948. "The foundation of Thurii." *AJP* 69:149–70.

Ehrhardt, N. 1983. *Milet und seine Kolonien. Vergleichende Untersuchung der kultischen und politischen Einrichtungen.* Bern: Lang.

Eliot, C.W.J. 1967. "Aristotle *Ath. Pol.* 44.1 and the Meaning of Trittys." *Phoenix* 21:79–84.

Farnell, L.R. 1909a. *Cults of the Greek States, V.* Oxford: Oxford University Press.

———. 1909b. "The Megala Dionysia and the Origins of Tragedy." *JHS* 29:xlvii.

Ferguson, W.S. 1910. "The Athenian Phratries." *CP* 5:257–84.

———. 1911. *Hellenistic Athens: An Historical Essay.* London: Macmillan.

———. 1936. "The Athenian Law Code and the Old Attic Trittyes." *Classical Studies presented to Edward Capps on his seventieth birthday,* Princeton: Princeton University Press, 144–58.

———. 1938. "The Salaminioi of Heptaphyle and Sounion." *Hesp.* 7:1–74.

———. 1944. "The Attic Orgeones." *Harvard Theological Review* 37:61–140.

———. 1949. "Orgeonika." in *Hesp.* Suppl. 8 (Shear Studies), 130–63.

Figueira, T.J. 1986. "Xanthippos, Father of Pericles and the Prytaneis of the Naukraroi." *Hist.* 35:257–79.

Fine, J.V.A. 1951. *"Horoi, Studies in Mortgage, Real Security and Land Tenure in Athens." Hesp.* Sup. 9.

Fingarette, A. 1971. "A New Look at the Wall of Nikomachos." *Hesp.* 40:330–35.

Finley, M.I. 1952. *Studies in Land and Credit in Ancient Athens, 500–200 B.C.* New Brunswick: Rutgers University Press.

Flower, M.A. 1985. *"IG* ii² 2344 and the Size of Phratries in Classical Athens." *CQ* 35:232–35.

Forrest, W.G. 1960. "The Tribal Organization of Chios." *BSA* 55:172–89.

———. 1966. *The Emergence of Greek Democracy: The Character of Greek Politics, 800–400 B.C.* London: Weidenfeld and Nicolson.

———. 1968. *A History of Sparta, 950–192 B.C.* London: Hutchinson University Library.

French, A. 1957. "Solon and the Megarian Question." *JHS* 77(Part II): 238–46.

Frisk, H. 1960–70. *Griechisches etymologisches Wörterbuch,* 2 vols. Heidelberg: Winter.

Frost, F.J. 1976. "Tribal Politics and the Civic State." *AJAH* 1:66–75.

———. 1984. "The Athenian Military Before Cleisthenes." *Hist.* 33:283–94.

Gabrielson, V. 1985. "The naukraroi and the Athenian navy." *C & M* 36:21–51.

Le Gall, J. 1970. *"Un critère de différenciation sociale."* Recherches sur les structures sociales dans l'antiquité classique, Paris.

Gallavotti, C. 1961. "Le origini micenei dell' istituto fraterica." *Parola del Passato* 16:20–39.

Garlan, Y. 1972. *Guerre: la guerre dans l'antiquité.* Paris: Fernand Nathan.

Gernet, L. 1938. "Les Dix Archontes de 581." *R. Ph.³* 12:216–27.

Gilbert, G. 1895. *Greek Constitutional Antiquities (The Constitutional Antiquities of Sparta and Athens).* London: Sonnenschein. (English translation of the 1893 edition of his *Griechische Staatsalterthümer.)*

Gluskina, L.M. 1983. "Phratry and Clan in Fourth Century Athens." *VDI* 165:39–52.

Golden, M. 1979. "Demonsthenes and the Age of Majority in Athens." *Phoenix* 33:25–38.

———. 1985. "Donatus and Athenian phratries." *CQ* 35:9–13

Gomme, A.W. 1933. *The Population of Athens in the Fifth and Fourth Centuries B.C.* Oxford: Blackwell.

———. 1937. *Essays in Greek History and Literature.* Oxford: Blackwell.

Gould, J. 1980. "Law, Custom and Myth: Aspects of the Social Position of Women in Classical Athens." *JHS* 100:38–59.

Greenhalgh, P.A.L. 1973. *Early Greek Warfare. Horsemen and Chariots in the Homeric and Archaic Ages.* Cambridge: Cambridge University Press.

Guarducci, M. 1937–38. *L'istituzione della fratria nella Grecia antica e nelle colonie greche di Italia,* parte prima, *MAL* ser 6, 6, 5–101; parte secunda, *MAL* ser. 6, 8, 65–135.

———. 1935. "Orgeoni e Tiasoti." *Riv. di Fil.* 13:332–40.

———. 1974. "L'offerta di Xenokrateia nel santuario di Cefiso al Falero." In *Phoros,* Tribute to B.D. Meritt, 57–66.

Haas, C.J. 1985. "Athenian naval power before Themistocles." *Hist.* 34:29–46.

Habicht, C. 1979. *Untersuchungen zur politischen Geschichte Athens im 3 Jahrhundert v. Chr.* Munich: Beck.

———. 1982. *Studien zur Geschichte Athens in hellenistischer Zeit.* Göttingen: Vandenhoeck & Ruprecht.

Halliday, W.R. 1926. "Xanthos, Melanthos and the Origins of Tragedy." *CR* 40:179–81.

Hammond, N.G.L. 1961. "Land Tenure in Attica and Solon's *Seisachtheia.*" *JHS* 81:76–98.

———. 1973. *Studies in Greek History.* Oxford: Oxford University Press.

Hansen, M.H. 1980. "Seven Hundred Archai in Classical Athens." *GRBS* 21: 151–73.

———. 1987. *The Athenian Assembly in the Age of Demosthenes.* Oxford: Blackwell.

———. 1991. *The Athenian Democracy in the Age of Demosthenes.* Oxford: Blackwell.

Harrison, A.R.W. 1968–71. *The Law of Athens,* 2 vols. Oxford: Oxford University Press.

Hasebroek, J. 1931. *Griechische Wirtschafts- und Gesellschaftsgeschichte bis zur Perserzeit.* Tübingen.

Haussoulier, B. 1884. *La vie municipale en Attique; essai sur l'organisation des dèmes au quatrième siècle.* Paris: Thorin.

Hedrick, C.W. 1983. "Old and New on the Attic Phratry of the Therrikleidai." *Hesp.* 52:299–302.

———. 1984. *The Attic Phratry.* Dissertation, University of Pennsylvania.

———. 1988a. "The Thymaitian Phratry." *Hesp.* 57:81–85.

———. 1988b. "The Temple and Cult of Apollo Patroos in Athens." *AJA* 92:185–210.

———. 1988c. "An Honorific Phratry Inscription." *AJP* 109:111–17.

———. 1989. "The Phratry from Paiania," *CQ* 39:126–35.

———. 1990. *The Decrees of the Demotionidai,* APhA American Classical Studies 22. Atlanta, Georgia: Scholars Press.

———. 1991. "Phratry Shrines of Attica and Athens." *Hesp.* 60:241–68.

Helbig, M.W. 1898. "Les vases du Dipylon et les naucraries." *Mem. de l'Ac. d'inscr.* 35:1. Paris.

Hermann, K.F. and Thumser, V. 1892. *Lehrbuch der griechischen Staatsalter-tümer*⁶ I 2, Freiburg: Freiburg University Press.

Hignett, C. 1952. *A History of the Athenian Constitution to the End of the Fifth Century B.C.* Oxford: Oxford University Press.

Hiller von Gaertringen, F. 1921. "Attische Inschriften." *Sitz. Preuss. Akad.,* 436–43.

Hommel, H. 1939. *RE* ser. 2, 7:1. "Trittyes." Cols. 330–70.

———. 1935. *RE* 16. "Naukraria." Cols. 1938–52.

How, W.W. and Wells, J. 1912. *A Commentary on Herodotus*. Oxford: Oxford University Press.

Humphreys, S.C. 1978. *Anthropology and the Greeks*. London: Routledge.

———. 1990. "Phrateres in Alopeke, and the Salaminioi." *ZPE* 83:243–48

Hurwit, J.M. 1985. "The Dipylon Shield Once More." *Cl. Ant.* 4:121–26.

Ito, S. 1981. "The enrollment of Athenian phratries." (In Japanese; summary in English), *Legal Hist. Review.*

———. 1983. "Phrateres as Athenian citizens." (In Japanese; summary in English), *JCS* 31:1–18.

———. 1988. "An Interpretation of the So-called Demotionid Inscription." (In Japanese; summary in English), *Journal of History,* 71.

Jackson, D.A. 1976. *East Greek Influence on Attic Vases*. JHS supp. paper 13. London.

Jacoby, F. 1944. "Genesia, a forgotten festival of the dead." *CQ* 38:65–75.

———. 1949. *Atthis, the Local Chronicles of Ancient Athens*. Oxford: Oxford University Press.

———. 1923–30, 1940–58. *Die Fragmente der griechischen Historiker.* 14 vols. Berlin: Weidmann. Leiden: Brill. 1940–58. (Neudruck. 1954–57. 4 vols. Leiden: Brill.)

Jameson, M. 1965. "Notes on the Sacrifical Calendar from Erchia." *BCH* 89: 154–72.

Jeanmaire, H. 1913. "Cryptie: la Cryptie lacédémonienne." *REG* 26:121–50.

———. 1939. *Couroi et Courètes*. Lille: Bibliothèque universitaire.

Jeffrey, L.H. 1948. "The Boustrophedon Sacral Inscriptions from the Agora." *Hesp.* 17:86–111.

———. 1976. *Archaic Greece: The City-States, c. 700–500 B.C.* London: Benn.

Jones, N.F. 1987. *Public Organization in Greece: A Documentary Study.* Philadelphia: American Philosophical Society.

Jordan, B. 1970. "Herodotos 5.71.2 and the Naukraroi of Athens." *CSCA* 3: 153–75.

———. 1975. *The Athenian Navy in the Classical Period.* University of California Publications in Classical Studies 13.

Judeich, W.² 1931. *Topographie von Athen*. (H.d.A. III ii 2.) Munich: Beck.

Just, R. 1989. *Women in Athenian Law and Life.* London and N.Y.: Routledge.

Kahrstedt, U. 1934. *Staatsgebiet und Staatsangehörigkeit in Athen*. Stuttgart: Kohlhammer.

Kastriotis, P. 1901. "Φρατρικὴ ἐπιγραφή." *Arch. Eph.,* 158–62.

Kearns, E. 1985. "Change and Continuity in Religious structures after Cleisthenes," in Cartledge, P.A. and Harvey, F.D., eds., *Crux* (Essays presented to G.E.M. de Ste Croix on his 75th birthday), Exeter: Imprint Academic, 189–207.

———. 1989. *The heroes of Attica.* London: University of London, Institute of Classical Studies, Bulletin, Suppl. 57.

Keil, C. 1866. "Attische Culte aus Inschriften." *Philol.* 23:212–59.

Kienast, D. 1965. "Die Innenpolitische Entwicklung Athens im 6 Jahrhundert und die Reformen von 508." *HZ* 200, 265–83.

Kirchner, J. 1901–3. *Prosopographia attica*. 2 vols. Berlin.

Köhler, U. 1877. "Attische Phratrieninschriften." *Ath. Mitt.* 2:186–87.

———. 1879. "Horosstein der Zakyaden." *Ath. Mitt.* 4:287.

Kolbe, W. 1913. *RE* 8. "Hopleten." Cols. 2294–95.

Körte, A. 1902. "Mitgliederverzeichnis einer attishen Phratrie." *Hermes* 37: 582–89.

Koumanoudes, S. 1873. "'Επιγραφαὶ ἀνέκδοτοι Μεγάριδος καὶ 'Αττικῆς." *Athenian* 2:479–89.

———. 1883. "Ψήφισμα φρατρικόν," *Arch. Eph.*, 69–76.

Kraay, C.M. 1976. *Archaic and Classical Greek Coins*. London: Methuen.

Krahe, H. 1955–64. *Die Sprache der Illyrier*. 2 vols. Weisbaden: Harrassowitz.

Kyparissis, N. and Peek, W. 1941. "Attische Urkunden." *Ath. Mitt.* 66:218–39.

Labarbe, J. 1953. "L'age corréspondant au sacrifice du Koureion et les données historiques du sixième discours d'Isée." *BAB* 39:358–94.

Lacey, W.K. 1968. *The Family in Classical Greece*. Ithaca: Cornell University Press.

———. 1980. "The family of Euxitheos (Demosthenes 57)." *CQ* 30:57–61.

Lambert, S.D. 1986a. "Herodotus, the Cylonian Conspiracy and the *Prytanies ton Naukraron*." *Hist.* 35:105–12.

———. 1986b. *The Ionian Phyle and Phratry in Archaic and Classical Athens*. D. Phil. thesis, Oxford.

Lang, M. 1976. *Graffiti and dipinti*. vol. 21 of *The Athenian Agora: results of excavations conducted by the American School of Classical Studies in Athens*. Princeton University Press.

Latte, K. 1941. *RE* 20. "Phratriarchos," "Phratrie," and "Phratrioi Theoi." Cols. 745–58.

Ledl, A. 1907, 1908. "Das attische Bürgerrecht und die Frauen." *Wiener Studien* 29:173–227; 30:1–46, 173–230.

Levensohn, M. and E. 1947. "Inscriptions on the South Slope of the Acropolis." *Hesp.* 16:63–74.

Lewis, D.M. 1955. "Notes on Attic Inscriptions." *BSA* 50:1–36.

———. 1962. "The Federal Constitution of Chios." *BSA* 57:1–4.

———. 1963. "Cleisthenes and Attica." *Hist.* 12:22–40.

———. 1973. "The Athenian Rationes Centesimarum." In M.I. Finley, ed. *Problèmes de la terre en Grèce anciènne*. Paris: Mouton, 187–99.

———. 1983. Review of Siewert, *Die Trittyen Attikas*. *Gnomon* 55:431–36.

Lippert, J. 1894. "Ibn al-Kifti über den Ursprung der Apaturien." *Zeitschrift der deutschen morgenländischen Gesellschaft* 48:486–89.

Lipsius, J.H. 1894. "Die Phratrie der Demotionidai." *Leipziger Studien* 16:161–71.

Lloyd, G.E.R. 1966. *Polarity and Analogy. Two types of Argumentation in Early Greek Thought*. Cambridge: Cambridge University Press.

Lolling, H. 1888. "Anaskaphai kai heuremata en Dekeleia." *AD* 4:159–63.

Löper, R. 1892. "Die Trittyen und Demen Attikas." *Ath. Mitt.* 17:319–433.

Maass, E. 1889. Review of Toepffer, *Attische Genealogie*. *GGA* 801–32 (esp. 805–8).

Macan, R.W. 1895, 1908. *Herodotus, the 4th to 9th Books*. London: Macmillan.

Macdowell, D.M. 1963. *Athenian Homicide Law in the Age of the Orators.* Manchester: Manchester University Press.

———, ed. 1971. Aristophanes, *Wasps.* Oxford: Oxford University Press.

———. 1976. "Bastards as Athenian Citizens." *CQ* 26:88–91.

———. 1978. *The Law in Classical Athens.* London: Thames and Hudson.

———, ed. 1968. *Andocides, On the Mysteries.* Oxford: Oxford University Press.

———. 1985. Review of M.J. Osborne, *Naturalization. CR* 35:317–20.

Manville, P.B. 1990. *The Origins of Citizenship in Ancient Athens.* Princeton: Princeton University Press.

Maxwell-Stuart, P. 1970. "Black Coats: Remarks on the Black Coats of the Ephebi." *PCPS* 196:113–16.

Meiggs, R. 1972. *The Athenian Empire.* Oxford: Oxford University Press.

Meritt, B.D. 1942. "Greek Inscriptions." *Hesp.* 11:275–303.

———. 1948. "Greek Inscriptions." *Hesp.* 17:1–53 (esp. 35, no. 18).

———. 1961a. "Greek Inscriptions." *Hesp.* 30:205–92.

———. 1961b. *The Athenian Year.* Berkeley and Los Angeles: University of California Press.

———. 1967. "Greek Inscriptions." *Hesp.* 36:57–101, 225–41.

Meyer, E. 1913–39. *Geschichte des Altertums.* Stuttgart and Berlin.

Mikalson, J.D. 1975. *The Sacred and Civil Calendar of the Athenian Year.* Princeton: Princeton University Press.

———. 1977. "Religion in the Attic Demes." *AJP* 98:424–35.

Milchhöfer, A. 1887. "Antikenbericht aus Attika." *Ath. Mitt.* 12:81–104, 227–330.

Millett, P. 1982. "The Attic Horoi Reconsidered in the Light of Recent Discoveries," *Opus* 1:219–30.

Mitsos, M.T. 1965. "'Εκ τοῦ 'Επιγραφικοῦ Μουσείου (VII)." *AE,* 131–38.

Mitteis, L. 1891. *Reichsrecht und Volksrecht in den östlichen Provinzen des Römischen Kaiserreichs.* Leipzig: Teubner.

Möbius, H. 1924. "Neue Inschriften aus Attika und Argos." *Ath. Mitt.* 49:1–16.

Mommsen, A. 1898. *Feste der Stadt Athen.* Leipzig: Teubner.

———. 1864. *Heortologie.* Leipzig: Teubner.

Morris, S.P. 1984. *The Black and White Style. Athens and Aigina in the Orientalizing Period.* New Haven: Yale University Press.

Morrison, J.S. and Williams, R.T. 1968. *Greek Oared Ships, 900–322 B.C.* Cambridge: Cambridge University Press.

Murakawa, K. 1957. "Demiurgos." *Hist.* 6:385–415.

Newman, W.L. 1887–1902. *The Politics of Aristotle.* 4 vols. Oxford: Oxford University Press.

Nilsson, M.P. 1911. "Der Ursprung der Tragödie." *Neue Jahrbücher für das klassische Altertum,* 609–42, 673–96.

———. 1951–60. *Opuscula Selecta.* 3 vols. Gleerup: Lund.

———. 1951, 1972. *Cults, Myths, Oracles and Politics in Ancient Greece.* New York.

Oikonomides, A.N. 1980. *Ancient World* 3:22.

Oliver, J.H. 1935. "Greek Inscriptions." *Hesp.* 4:1–70.

————. 1980. "From Gennetai to Curiales." *Hesp.* 49:30–53.

Osborne, M.J. 1981–83. *Naturalization in Athens (Verhandelingen van der koninklijke Akademie voor Wetenschappen, Letteren en schone Kunsten van Belgie: Klasse der Letteren).* 4 vols. Brussels: Paleis der Academien.

Osborne, R. 1985. *Demos: the Discovery of Classical Attika.* Cambridge: Cambridge University Press.

————. 1987. *Classical landscape with Figures,* London: Philips.

Owen, A.S., ed. 1939. *Euripides, Ion.* Oxford: Oxford University Press.

Padgug, R.A. 1972. "Eleusis and the union of Attica." *GRBS* 13:135–50.

Palaios, A. 1929. "Attikai Epigraphai." *Polemon* 1: passim.

Pantazides, J. 1888. "'Επιγραφὴ ἐκ Δεκελείας." *Arch. Epi.,* 1–20.

Parke, H.W. 1977. *Festivals of the Athenians.* London: Thames and Hudson.

Paton, W.R. 1890. "Comment on Tarbell's Study of the Attic Phratry." *AJA* 6:314–18.

————. 1891. "The Deceleian inscription and Attic phratries." *CR* 5:221–23.

Patterson, C. 1976, 1981. *Pericles' Citizenship Law of 451/0 B.C.* Diss. University of Pennsylvania. Monographs in Classical Studies. Salem: Ayer.

Perpillou, J.-L. 1984. "Frères de Sang ou Frères de Culte," "Les Syllabogrammes *34 et *35." *SMEA* 25:205–20, 221–36.

Pestalozza, U. 1951, 1971. *Religione Meditteranea.* Milan: Bocca. Repr. Milan: Cisalpino-Golliardica.

Piérart, M. 1983. "Athènes et Milet, I: Tribus et dèmes." *MH* 40:1–18.

————. 1985. "Modèles de répartition des citoyens dans les cités ioniennes." *Revue des Études Anciennes* 87:169–90.

Pittakes, K.S. 1853. *AE* no. 1459, col. 911.

————. 1856. *AE* no. 2819, cols. 1400–1401.

Platnauer, M., ed. 1964. Aristophanes. *Peace.* Oxford: Oxford University Press.

Pohlenz, M. 1916. "Kronos und die Titanen." *Neue Jahrbücher für klassische Altertum* 37:549–94.

Poland, F. 1909. *Geschichte des griechischen Vereinswesens.* Leipzig: Teubner.

de Polignac, F. 1984. *La naissance de la cité grecque.* Paris: Éd. La Découverte.

Pottier, E. 1878. "Fouilles au monument de Lysicrate." *BCH* 2:412–18.

Premerstein, A. von. 1910. "Phratern-verbände auf einem attischen Hypothekenstein." *Ath. Mitt.* 35:103–17.

Ramsay, W.M. 1920. "Pisidian Wolf-Priests, Phrygian Goat-Priests and the Old-Ionian Tribes." *JHS* 40:197–202.

Rangabé, A. 1842–55. *Antiquités helléniques.* 2 vols. Athens.

Raubitschek, A.E. 1974. "Kolieis." *Phoros,* Tribute to B.D. Meritt, ed. D.W. Bradeen and M.F. McGregor. Locust Valley: Augustin.

Rhodes, P.J. 1971. "Trittys ton Prytaneon." *Hist.* 20:385–404.

————. 1972, 1985. *The Athenian Boule.* Reissued with additions and corrections. Oxford: Oxford University Press.

————. 1978. "Bastards as Athenian Citizens." *CQ* 28:89–92.

————. 1980. "Ephebi, bouleutae and the population of Athens." *ZPE* 38: 191–201.

————. 1981. *A Commentary on the Aristotelian Athenaion Politeia.* Oxford: Oxford University Press.

————. 1983. Review of Siewert, *Die Trittyen Attikas. JHS* 103:203–4.

Rieth, O. 1964. *Die Kunst Menanders in den Adelphen des Terenz.* Hildesheim: Olms.

Robert, L. ed. 1936. Bibliotheque Nationale, Collection Fröhner, Inscriptions grecques.

————. 1940–65. *Hellenica, recueil d'épigraphie, de numismatique et d'antiquités grecques.* 13 vols. Paris.

————. 1969. "Inscriptions d'Athènes et de la Grèce centrale." *Arch. Eph.,* 1–58.

Robinson, D.M. 1907. "Inscriptions in Athens." *AJP* 28:424–33.

————. "Greek horoi and a new Attic mortgage inscription." *Hesp.* 13:16–21.

Rolley, C. 1965. "Le sanctuaire des dieux patrooi et le Thesmophorion de Thasos." *BCH* 89:441–83.

Rose, H.J. 1951. *Handbook of Greek Literature,* 4th ed. London: Methuen.

Roussel, D. 1976. *Tribu et Cité.* Annales littéraires de l'université de Besançon, v. 193. Paris: Les belles lettres.

Roussel, P. 1929. "Deux familles Athéniennes à Délos." *BCH* 53:166–84.

Ruschenbusch, E. 1966. *"Solonos Nomoi."* Hist. Einz. 9. Wiesbaden: Steiner.

————. 1974. Review of Stroud, *Drakon's Law. Gnomon* 46:815–17.

————. 1979. "Die soziale Herkunft der Epheben um 330." *ZPE* 35:173–76.

————. 1981. "Epheben, Buleuten und die Bürgerzahl von Athen um 330 v. Chr." *ZPE* 41:103–5.

————. 1984. "Zum letzten Mal: die Bürgerzahl Athens im 4 Jh. v. Chr." *ZPE* 54:253–69.

————. 1988. "Doch noch einmal die Bürgerzahl Athens im 4 Jh. v. Chr." *ZPE* 72:139–40.

Sakkelion. 1877. "Ἐκ τῶν ἀνεκδότων τῆς πατμιακῆς βιβλιοθήκης." *BCH* 1:1–16, 137–55.

De Ste Croix, G.E.M. 1972. *The Origins of the Peloponnesian War.* Ithaca: Cornell University Press.

Salmon, J.B. 1977. "Political Hoplites?" *JHS* 97:84–101.

Salviat, F. 1958. "Une nouvelle loi thasiène: institutions judiciaires et fêtes religieux à la fin du iv siècle av. J.C." *BCH* 82:193–267.

Samuel, A. 1972. *Greek and Roman Chronology, Calendars and Years in Classical Antiquity.* H.d.A. i 7. Munich: Beck.

De Sanctis, G. 1912. *Atthis, storia della reppublica ateniense dalle origini alle éta di Pericle,* 2d ed. Torino: Bocca.

Sandys, J. 1912, 1973. *Aristotle's Constitution of the Athenians,* 2d ed. London: Macmillan. Reissued New York: Arno.

Sauppe, H. 1886, 1890. *Commentatio de Phratriis Atticis.* Index scholarum in Academia Georgia Augusta.

Schaefer, C. 1888. *Altes und Neues über die attischen Phratrien zur Erklärung von CIA II 841 b (Beilage zum Jahresbericht der königl. Landesschule Pforta 1888).* Naumburg.

Schlaifer, R. 1944. "The Attic Association of the Mesogeioi." *CP* 39:22–27.

Schoeffer, V. von. 1905. *RE* 5. "Demotionidai." Cols. 194–202.

Schoell, R. 1889. "Die kleisthenischen Phratrien." *Sitzungsb. der Akad. München* 2:1–25.

Schulthess, O. 1932. *RE* 15. "Misthosis." Cols. 2095–2129.

Schweigert, E. 1940. "Greek Inscriptions." *Hesp.* 9:309–57.

Schwyzer, E. 1938–71. *Griechische Grammatik.* Munich: Beck.

Sealey, R. 1987. *The Athenian Republic. Democracy or the Rule of Law?* University Park: Pennsylvania State University Press.

Shear, T.L. 1971. "The Athenian Agora: Excavations of 1970." *Hesp.* 40:241–79.

Siewert, P. 1982. *Die Trittyen Attikas und die Heeresreform des Kleisthenes.* Vestigia 33. Munich: Beck.

Simms, R.S. 1989. "Isis in Classical Athens." *CJ* 84:216–21.

Smithson, E.L. 1968. "The Tomb of a Rich Athenian Lady, ca 850 B.C.," *Hesp.* 37:77–116.

Snodgrass, A.M. 1971. *The Dark Age of Greece.* Edinburgh: Edinburgh University Press.

———. 1980. *Archaic Greece: The Age of Experiment.* London: Dent.

———. 1986. Review of van Effenterre 1985 and de Polignac 1984. *CR* 36:261–65.

Sokolowski, F. 1955. *Lois sacrées de l'Asie mineure.* Paris: L'école française d'Athènes, fasc. 9.

———. 1962. *Lois sacrées des citées grecques, Supplement.* Paris: L'école française d'Athènes, fasc. 11.

———. 1969. *Lois sacrées des cités grecques.* Paris: L'école française d'Athènes, fasc. 18.

Solders, S. 1931. *Die Ausserstädtischen Kulte und die Einigung Attikas.* Lund.

Sommer, L. 1912. *RE* 7. "Haaropfer." Cols. 2105–9.

Sommerstein, A.H. 1985. *The Comedies of Aristophanes V: Peace.* Warminster: Aris and Philips.

Stroud, R.S. 1968. *Drakon's Law on Homicide.* University of California Publications in Classical Studies 3. Berkeley: California University Press.

———. 1979. *The Axones and Kyrbeis of Drakon and Solon.* University of California Publications Classical Studies 19. Berkeley: California University Press.

Sundwall, J. 1906. *Epigraphische Beiträge zur sozial-politischen Geschichte Athens im Zeitalter des Demosthenes. Klio* Beiheft 4.

Svoronos, I. 1908–11. *Das Athener Nationalmuseum.* German ed., W. Barth. Athens: Beck and Barth.

Tarbell, F.B. 1889. "The decrees of the Demotionidai, A Study of the Athenian Phratry." *AJA* 5:135–53.

———. 1890. "Mr. Tarbell's Reply to Mr. Paton's Comment." *AJA* 6:318–20.

Taylor, A.E., trans. 1929. *Plato: Timaeus and Critias.* London.

Thalheim, T. 1894. *RE* 1. "Antidosis." Cols. 2397–98.

Themelis, P. 1971. *AD* 26:31–33.

Thompson, H.A. 1937. "Buildings on the West Side of the Agora." *Hesp.* 6:77–111.

Thompson, H.A. and Kyparissis, N. 1938. "A Sanctuary of Zeus and Athena Phratrios Newly Found in Athens." *Hesp.* 7:612–25.

Thompson, H.A. and Wycherley, R.E. 1972. *The Athenian Agora,* 14. *The Agora of Athens: The History, Shape and Uses of an Ancient City Center.* Princeton: A.S.C.S.A.

Thompson, H.A. et al. 1976. *The Athenian Agora, a Guide to the Excavations and Museum,* 3d ed. Athens: American School of Classical Studies.

Thompson, W.E. 1968. "An Interpretation of the 'Demotionid' Decrees," *Symbolae Osloenses* 42:51–68.

———. 1971. "The Deme in Cleisthenes' Reforms." *Symbolae Osloenses* 46:72–79.

Thomsen, R. 1964. *Eisphora: A Study of Direct Taxation in Ancient Athens.* Copenhagen: Gyldendal.

Threatte, L. 1980. *The Grammar of Attic Inscriptions, 1: Phonology.* Berlin: De Gruyter.

Töpffer, J. 1886. *Quaestiones Pisistrateae.* Dorpati: Laakmann.

———. 1889, 1973. *Attische Genealogie.* Reprint, New York: Arno Press.

———. 1890. "Genealogische Streitfragen und Nachlesen." *RhM* 45: 371–84.

———. 1894. *RE* 1. "Aigikoreis." Cols. 958–62.

———. 1894. *RE* 1. "Apatouria." Cols. 2672–80.

Traill, J.S. 1975. *The Political Organization of Attica. A Study of the Demes, Trittyes and Phylai, and Their Representation in the Athenian Council.* Hesp. Sup. 14. Princeton: Princeton University Press.

———. 1978. "Diakris, The Inland Trittys of Leontis." *Hesp.* 47:89–109.

———. 1986. *Demos and Trittys: Epigraphical and Topographical Studies in the Organisation of Attica.* Toronto: Athenians.

Travlos, J. 1971. *Pictorial Dictionary of Athens.* New York: Praeger.

Tritle, L.A. 1981. "Phokion Phokou Potamios." *AJAH* 6:118–32.

———. 1988. *Phocion the Good.* London: Croom Helm.

Tsantsanoglou, K. 1984. *New Fragments of Greek Literature from the Lexicon of Photios.* Proceedings of Athenian Academy no. 49. Athens: Athenian Academy Press.

Usener, H. 1898. "Göttliche Synonyme." *RhM* 53:365–69.

———. 1904. "Heilige Handlung." *Archiv für Religionswissenschaft* 7:281–339.

———. 1913. *Kleine Schriften IV,* Leipzig-Berlin.

Vanderpool, E. 1970. "Some Attic Inscriptions." *Hesp.* 29:40–46.

———. 1970. "A Lex Sacra of the Attic Deme Phrearrhioi." *Hesp.* 29:47–53.

Velissaropoulos, J. 1980. *Les nauklères grecques: recherches sur les institutions maritimes en Grèce et dans l'Orient hellénisé.* Geneva: Librairie Droz.

Vidal-Naquet, P. 1968. "The Black Hunter and the Origins of the Athenian Ephebia." *PCPS* n.s. 14:49–64. Reprinted 1981 with revisions in *Le chasseur noir,* Paris: Maspero. 151–74, A. Szegedy-Maszak, trans. 1986. *The Black Hunter.* Baltimore and London. Johns Hopkins University Press.

Wade-Gery, H.T. 1931. "Eupatridai, Archons and Areopagos." *CQ* 25:1–11.

———. 1931. "Studies in the Structure of Attic Society: I. Demotionidai." *CQ* 25:129–43.

———. 1932. "Thucydides the son of Melesias." *JHS* 52:205–27.

———. 1933. "Studies in the Structure of Attic Society: II The Laws of Cleisthenes." *CQ* 27:17–29.

———. 1958. *Essays in Greek History.* Oxford: Blackwell.

Walbank, M. 1982. "Greek Inscriptions from the Athenian Agora, Fifth to Third Centuries B.C." *Hesp.* 51:41–56.

———. 1983. "Leases of Sacred Properties in Attica." *Hesp.* 52:100–135; 177–99; 200–206; 207–31.

Wallace, R.W. 1985, 1989. *The Areopagos Council to 307 B.C.* London: Johns Hopkins University Press.

Walter, O. 1937. "Die Reliefs aus dem Heiligtum der Echeliden in Neu-Phaleron." *Arch. Eph.,* 97–119.

Waser, O. 1901. *RE* 4. "Delos." Cols. 2459–2503.

Wehrli, F. 1944–59. *Die Schule des Aristoteles* 10 v. Basel: Benno Schwabe & Co.

Weil, R. 1960. *Aristote et l' histoire. Essai sur la Politique.* Paris: Klincksieck.

Wernicke, K. 1958. *RE* 2. "Artemis." Cols. 1335–1440.

Whitehead, D. 1977. *The ideology of the Athenian metic.* PCPhS suppl. 4. Cambridge: Cambridge University Press.

———. 1986a. *The Demes of Attica, 508/7-ca. 250 B.C.: A Political and Social Study.* Princeton: Princeton University Press.

———. 1986b. *Women and naturalisation in fourth century Athens. The case of Archippe."* CQ 36:109–14.

Wilamowitz-Moellendorf, U. von. 1886. "Oropos und die Graei." *Hermes* 1:91–115.

———. 1893. *Aristoteles und Athen.* 2 vols. Berlin: Weidmann.

——— and Robert, C. 1880. *Aus Kydathen.* Philologische Untersuchungen, 1. Berlin: Weidmann.

Wilhelm, A. 1905. "'Αττικὰ ψηφίσματα," *Arch. Eph.,* 217–81.

———. 1909. *Beiträge zur griechischen Inschriftenkunde.* Vienna: Hölder.

———. 1935. "Attische Pachturkunde." *Archiv für Papyrusforschung* 11:200–203.

Will, E. 1955. *Korinthiaka.* Paris: de Boccard.

Willemsen, F. 1974. "Vom Grabbezirk des Nikodemos in Dekeleia." *Ath. Mitt.* 89:173–91.

Wüst, F.R. 1957. "Zu den *Prytanies ton Naukraron* und zu den alten attischen Trittyen." *Hist.* 6:176–91.

———. 1959. "Gedanken über die attischen Stände. Ein Versuch." *Hist.* 8:1–11.

Wycherley, R.E. 1957. *The Athenian Agora, 3: Literary and Epigraphical Testimonia.* Princeton: A.S.C.S.A.

Wyse, W. 1904. *The Speeches of Isaeus, with Critical and Explanatory Notes.* Cambridge: Cambridge University Press.

Ziebarth, E. 1898. "Neue attische Grenzsteine." *Sitz. Preuss. Akad. der Wiss.* 2:776–84.

Ziehen, L. 1937. *RE* 17: "Oinisteria." Cols. 2229–30.

Index of Texts

Numbers refer to pages, including notes. Bold type indicates textual comments or suggestions. *IG* numbers are given for all inscriptions listed in that work. Other inscriptions are listed only under references used in this book.

Index of Names and Subjects

Numbers refer to pages. An asterisk indicates a known, or possible, Attic phratry (excluding gene that may have functioned also as phratries, on which see chapter 2, and possible phratric groups based on demes, on which see deme).